GLOBAL STU

AFRICA

TWELFTH EDITION

Thomas Krabacher, Ezekiel Kalipeni, and Azzedine Layachi

OTHER BOOKS IN THE GLOBAL STUDIES SERIES

- China
- Europe
- India and South Asia
- Islam and the Muslim World
- Japan and the Pacific Rim
- Latin America
- Russia, the Eurasian Republics, and Central/Eastern Europe
- The Middle East
- The World at a Glance

Articles from the World Press
Selected by William G. Moseley

 Higher Education

Boston   Burr Ridge, IL   Dubuque, IA   New York   San Francisco   St. Louis
Bangkok   Bogotá   Caracas   Kuala Lumpur   Lisbon   London   Madrid   Mexico City
Milan   Montreal   New Delhi   Santiago   Seoul   Singapore   Sydney   Taipei   Toronto

Higher Education

GLOBAL STUDIES: AFRICA, TWELFTH EDITION

Published by McGraw-Hill, a business unit of The McGraw-Hill Companies, Inc., 1221 Avenue of the Americas, New York, NY 10020.
Copyright © 2009 by The McGraw-Hill Companies, Inc. All rights reserved. Previous edition(s) 1985–2008. No part of this publication may be reproduced or distributed in any form or by any means, or stored in a database or retrieval system, without the prior written consent of The McGraw-Hill Companies, Inc., including, but not limited to, in any network or other electronic storage or transmission, or broadcast for distance learning.

Some ancillaries, including electronic and print components, may not be available to customers outside the United States.

Global Studies® is a registered trademark of The McGraw-Hill Companies, Inc.
Global Studies is published by the **Contemporary Learning Series** group within the McGraw-Hill Higher Education division.

1 2 3 4 5 6 7 8 9 0 QPD/QPD 0 9 8

ISBN 978–0–07–337977–7
MHID 0–07–337977–8
ISSN 1098–3880

Managing Editor: *Larry Loeppke*
Production Manager: *Faye Schilling*
Developmental Editor: *Susan Brusch/Jade Benedict*
Editorial Assistant: *Nancy Meissner*
Production Service Assistant: *Rita Hingtgen*
Permissions Coordinator: *Lori Church*
Senior Marketing Manager: *Julie Keck*
Marketing Communications Specialist: *Mary Klein*
Marketing Coordinator: *Alice Link*
Project Manager: *Jane Mohr*
Design Specialist: *Tara McDermott*
Senior Administrative Assistant: *DeAnna Dausener*
Cover Graphics: *Kristine Jubeck*

Compositor: Laserwords Private Limited
Cover Image: Royalty Free/Corbis

Library in Congress Cataloging-in-Publication Data
Main entry under title: Global Studies: Africa, 12th ed.
1. Africa—History—1960–. I. Title: Africa. II. Krabacher, Tom, *comp.*

www.mhhe.com

AFRICA

AUTHOR/EDITORS

Dr. Thomas Krabacher

Dr. Thomas Krabacher, having received his Ph.D. in geography at the University of California, Davis, is currently professor of geography at the California State University, Sacramento. He has conducted extensive fieldwork in Sierra Leone, where he has worked with small-scale village-based marine fisheries, as well as in Mali and South Africa. He has written on economic and ecological change in West African food production systems and historic ecological change in southern Africa.

Dr. Azzedine Layachi

Dr. Azzedine Layachi received his Ph.D. in politics from New York University and is currently an associate professor of politics at St. John's University, New York. He is an expert on political and economic change in North Africa, an area in which he has traveled widely. Among many other books and articles, he is the author of *The United States and North Africa: A Cognitive Approach to Foreign Policy* (Praeger, 1990); *Economic Crisis and Political Change in North Africa* (Praeger, 1998); and *State, Society and Liberalization in Morocco: The Limits of Associative Life* (Center for Contemporary Arab Studies, 1998).

Dr. Ezekiel Kalipeni

Dr. Kalipeni received his Ph.D. from the University of North Carolina at Chapel Hill and is currently associate professor of geography at the University of Illinois at Urbana–Champaign. The author and editor of many books and articles, his research focuses on demographic, health, and environmental issues in sub-Saharan Africa. He is currently working on HIV/AIDS, population, and environmental issues in Malawi. He is the co-editor of *HIV/AIDS in Africa: Beyond Epidemiology* (Blackwell, 2004).

Contents

Global Studies: Africa

Using *Global Studies: Africa* vii
Selected World Wide Web Sites viii
U.S. Statistics and Map x
Canada Statistics and Map xi
World Map xii

Africa Map 1

Africa: Looking for a Renaissance 2

Central Africa Map 10

Central Africa: Possibilities for Cooperation 11

Cameroon (Republic of Cameroon) 16
Central African Republic 20
Chad (Republic of Chad) 23
Congo (Republic of the Congo; Congo-Brazzaville) 27
Democratic Republic of the Congo (Congo-Kinshasa; formerly Zaire) 31
Equatorial Guinea (Republic of Equatorial Guinea) 37
Gabon (Gabonese Republic) 40
São Tomé and Príncipe (Democratic Republic of São Tomé and Príncipe) 43

East Africa Map 46

East Africa: A Mixed Inheritance 47

Burundi (Republic of Burundi) 51
Comoros (Union of Comoros) 55
Djibouti (Republic of Djibouti) 58
Eritrea (State of Eritrea) 61
Ethiopia (Federal Democratic Republic of Ethiopia) 64
Kenya (Republic of Kenya) 69
Madagascar (Republic of Madagascar) 73
Mauritius (Republic of Mauritius) 77
Rwanda (Rwandese Republic) 80
Seychelles (Republic of Seychelles) 84
Somalia 87
Sudan (Republic of the Sudan) 91
Tanzania (United Republic of Tanzania) 95
Uganda (Republic of Uganda) 99

North Africa Map 103

North Africa: The Crossroads of the Continent 104

Algeria 107
Egypt 117
Libya 129
Morocco 138
Tunisia 147
Western Sahara 153

Southern Africa Map 156

**Southern Africa: The Continuing Struggle
for Self-Determination** 157

Angola (Republic of Angola) 162
Botswana (Republic of Botswana) 166

Lesotho (Kingdom of Lesotho) — 170
Malawi (Republic of Malawi) — 173
Mozambique (Republic of Mozambique) — 176
Namibia (Republic of Namibia) — 180
South Africa (Republic of South Africa) — 184
Swaziland (Kingdom of Swaziland) — 191
Zambia (Republic of Zambia) — 194
Zimbabwe (Republic of Zimbabwe) — 197

West Africa Map
202

West Africa: Seeking Unity in Diversity
203

Benin (Republic of Benin) — 206
Burkina Faso — 210
Cape Verde (Republic of Cape Verde) — 214
Côte d'Ivoire (Republic of Côte d'Ivoire) — 217
The Gambia (Republic of The Gambia) — 221
Ghana (Republic of Ghana) — 225
Guinea (Republic of Guinea) — 228
Guinea-Bissau (Republic of Guinea-Bissau) — 231
Liberia (Republic of Liberia) — 234
Mali (Republic of Mali) — 238
Mauritania (Islamic Republic of Mauritania) — 241
Niger (Republic of Niger) — 244
Nigeria (Federal Republic of Nigeria) — 247
Senegal (Republic of Senegal) — 252
Sierra Leone (Republic of Sierra Leone) — 255
Togo (Togolese Republic) — 258

Articles from the World Press

1. **Angola: Plenty of Oil, a Forgotten War and New Hope, That's Cabinda,** Peter Kagwanja, *Africa Insight,* August 4, 2006. The tiny Cabinda enclave accounts for close to 65 percent of Angola's oil, amounting to more than 80 percent of the country's revenues. But the province, which has fought for three decades to secede, remains one of the poorest in Angola. A recently signed peace deal preserves Angola's territorial unity while granting special status to this oil rich northern province. 263

2. **Post-Apartheid Vineyards: Land Redistribution Begins to Transform South Africa's Wine Country,** William Moseley, *Dollars & Sense,* January/February 2006. The African National Congress (ANC) promised to redress the legacy of discriminatory land ownership policies in the farming sector through a land redistribution program that facilitates the transfer of land from whites to blacks. While this program has its problems, South Africa's wine country now has a handful of worker co-owned vineyards. If American and European consumers support a growing market for such wines, this will encourage more white farmers to go into partnership with their workers. 266

3. **ABCs of AIDS Prevention,** Jessica Weisberg, *Dollars & Sense,* January/February 2005. Uganda has been widely recognized for its successes in stemming the AIDS crisis, but its policies fail to address the inequalities that make women vulnerable to the disease. More women than men have become infected with HIV since Uganda's renowned ABC (Abstinence, Be faithful and Condoms) policy was implemented. 271

4. **The Fight to Save Congo's Forests,** Christian Parenti, *The Nation,* October 22, 2007. The rainforests of the Congo Basin are home to an estimated 40 million people who depend upon it for their traditional livelihoods. Ecologically, the rainforests also play a major role in trapping carbon dioxide, a key culprit in global warming. In recent years the future of the rainforest has been threatened by timber companies, often with the support of development bodies such as the World Bank, that seek to harvest the valuable hardwoods the forests contain. The Democratic Republic of the Congo has been unable to regulate the pressure on the forests due to the lack of an effective plan for forest management and widespread corruption. The leaders in the fight to preserve the forests are frequently small, non-profit, non-governmental organizations. 274

5. **The Long Journey of a Young Democracy,** *The Economist,* March 3, 2007. While signs of change are visible everywhere in South Africa, in many ways life has not improved substantially for many South Africans. Unemployment remains high, the country's leadership has bungled its handling of the HIV/AIDs

epidemic, crime is a major worry, and the government has found it difficult to deliver public services at adequate levels. Political corruption and the question of who will succeed the current president, Thabo Mbeki, also present serious challenges to the country's newly-acquired democratic institutions. 279

6. **Underwriting Liberian Rebirth,** Ellen Johnson-Sirleaf, *Harvard International Review,* Winter 2007. The author was elected president of Liberia in late 2005, making her the first democratically-elected woman president in African history. Assuming office following the end of a devastating 14-yr civil war, her focus is now on rebuilding Liberian society. Her administration and the country face several serious challenges including: side effects of the political impasse in neighboring Côte d'Ivoire, the vulnerability of war-affected youth, rebuilding the national infrastructure, and eliminating corruption. 282

7. **Toppling a Tyrant,** *The Economist,* March 17, 2007. Zimbabwe, once an African showcase, is now an economic basket case plagued by a shrinking economy, food shortages, and an 80% unemployment rate. This is largely a consequence of the heavy-handed political tactics taken by Robert Mugabe, the country's long-time president, in order to hold onto power. Mugabe must go for the well-being of the country, but support for the political opposition by neighboring African states has been conspicuously absent. 287

8. **Taking Care of Business,** Michael Klein, *Finance & Development,* December 2006. Peace and changes in economic policy have allowed the economies of many African countries to flourish, displaying growth rates that would have seemed unthinkable a decade earlier. Red tape and over-regulation, however, still constrain businesses in many countries, meaning that economic growth among traditional businesses is not occurring as efficiently as it could. This is changing, however, as African leaders consider ways of creating more business friendly environments. 288

9. **On the Brink,** Colin Macilwain, *Nature,* January 11, 2007. Bonny Island, strategically located at the mouth of the Niger River, has been an important trade center for centuries. In recent years it has also been the site of a major natural gas liquefaction plant serving the Nigerian petroleum industry. With the influx of outside workers to the area, however, comes the risk of a dramatic increase in the incidence of HIV/AIDS. To prevent this, the island has become the setting for Ibani-se, a comprehensive AIDS prevention and control project involving both local and international expertise designed to hold incidence rates to their current low levels. 291

Glossary of Terms and Abbreviations 295

Bibliography 299

Index 302

Using *Global Studies: Africa*

THE GLOBAL STUDIES SERIES

The Global Studies series was created to help readers acquire a basic knowledge and understanding of the regions and countries in the world. Each volume provides a foundation of information—geographic, cultural, economic, political, historical, artistic, and religious—that will allow readers to better assess the current and future problems within these countries and regions and to comprehend how events there might affect their own well-being. In short, these volumes present the background information necessary to respond to the realities of our global age.

Each of the volumes in the Global Studies series is crafted under the careful direction of an author/editor—an expert in the area under study. The author/editors teach and conduct research and have traveled extensively through the regions about which they are writing.

In this *Global Studies: Africa* edition, the author/editor has written an introductory essay on the continent as a whole, several regional essays, and country reports for each of the countries included.

MAJOR FEATURES OF THE GLOBAL STUDIES SERIES

The Global Studies volumes are organized to provide concise information on the regions and countries within those areas under study. The major sections and features of the books are described here.

Regional Essays

For *Global Studies: Africa,* the author/editor has written several essays focusing on the religious, cultural, sociopolitical, and economic differences and similarities of the countries and peoples in the various regions of Africa. Regional maps accompany the essays.

Country Reports

Concise reports are written for each of the countries within the region under study. These reports are the heart of each Global Studies volume. *Global Studies: Africa, Twelfth Edition,* contains 54 country reports.

The country reports are composed of five standard elements. Each report contains a detailed map visually positioning the country among its neighboring states; a summary of statistical information; a current essay providing important historical, geographical, political, cultural, and economic information; a historical timeline, offering a convenient visual survey of a few key historical events; and four "graphic indicators," with summary statements about the country in terms of development, freedom, health/welfare, and achievements.

A Note on the Statistical Reports

The statistical information provided for each country has been drawn from a wide range of sources. (The most frequently referenced are listed on page 299.) Every effort has been made to provide the most current and accurate information available.

However, sometimes the information cited by these sources differs to some extent; and, all too often, the most current information available for some countries is somewhat dated. Aside from these occasional difficulties, the statistical summary of each country is generally quite complete and up to date. Care should be taken, however, in using these statistics (or, for that matter, any published statistics) in making hard comparisons among countries. We have also provided comparable statistics for the United States and Canada, which can be found on pages x and xi.

World Press Articles

Within each Global Studies volume is reprinted a number of articles carefully selected by our editorial staff and the author/editor from a broad range of international periodicals and newspapers. The articles have been chosen for currency, interest, and their differing perspectives on the subject countries. There are 9 articles in *Global Studies: Africa, Twelfth Edition.*

WWW Sites

An extensive annotated list of selected World Wide Web sites can be found on the facing page viii in this edition of *Global Studies: Africa.* In addition, the URL addresses for country-specific Web sites are provided on the statistics page of most countries. All of the Web site addresses were correct and operational at press time. Instructors and students alike are urged to refer to those sites often to enhance their understanding of the region and to keep up with current events.

Glossary, Bibliography, Index

At the back of each Global Studies volume, readers will find a glossary of terms and abbreviations, which provides a quick reference to the specialized vocabulary of the area under study and to the standard abbreviations used throughout the volume.

Following the glossary is a bibliography, which lists general works, national histories, and current-events publications and periodicals that provide regular coverage on Africa.

The index at the end of the volume is an accurate reference to the contents of the volume. Readers seeking specific information and citations should consult this standard index.

Currency and Usefulness

Global Studies: Africa, like the other Global Studies volumes, is intended to provide the most current and useful information available necessary to understand the events that are shaping the cultures of the region today.

This volume is revised on a regular basis. The statistics are updated, regional essays and country reports revised, and world press articles replaced. In order to accomplish this task, we turn to our author/editor, our advisory boards, and—hopefully—to you, the users of this volume. Your comments are more than welcome. If you have an idea that you think will make the next edition more useful, an article or bit of information that will make it more current, or a general comment on its organization, content, or features that you would like to share with us, please send it in for serious consideration.

Selected World Wide Web Sites for Africa

(Some Web sites continually change their structure and content, so the information listed here may not always be available.)

GENERAL SITES

BBC World Service
http://www.bbc.co.uk/worldservice/index.shtml

The BBC, one of the world's most successful radio networks, provides the latest news from around the world, including news from almost all of the African countries. For individual country profiles and detailed time lines please visit: http://news.bbc.co.uk/1/hi/world/africa/country_profiles/.

C-SPAN ONLINE
http://www.c-span.org

Access C-SPAN International on the Web for International Programming Highlights and archived C-SPAN programs.

International Network Information Center at University of Texas
http://inic.utexas.edu

This gateway has pointers to international sites, including Africa, as well as African Studies Resources.

I-Trade International Trade Resources & Data Exchange
http://www.i-trade.com

Monthly exchange-rate data, U.S. Global Trade Outlook, and recent World Fact Book statistical demographic and geographic data for 180-plus countries can be found on this Web site.

Penn Library: African Collection
http://www.library.upenn.edu/collections/africa/

This vast site is rich in links to information about African studies, including demography and population.

ReliefWeb
http://www.reliefweb.int

The UN's Department of Humanitarian Affairs clearinghouse for international humanitarian emergencies presents daily news updates, including Reuters, VOA, PANA.

United Nations System
http://www.unsystem.org

The official Web site for the United Nations system of organizations can be found here. Everything is listed alphabetically, and examples include UNICC and the Food and Agriculture Organization.

UN Development Programme (UNDP)
http://www.undp.org

Publications and current information on world poverty, Mission Statement, UN Development Fund for Women, and more are available on this Web site. Be sure to see the Poverty Clock.

UN Environmental Programme (UNEP)
http://www.unep.org

This UNEP official site provides information on UN environmental programs, products, services, and events. A search engine is also available.

U.S. Agency for International Development (USAID)
http://www.usaid.gov/regions/afr/

The U.S. policy regarding assistance to African countries is presented at this site.

U.S. Central Intelligence Agency (CIA)
http://www.odci.gov

This site includes publications of the CIA, such as the World Fact Book, Factbook on Intelligence, Handbook of International Economic Statistics, and CIA maps.

U.S. Department of State
http://www.state.gov/countries/

Organized alphabetically, data on human rights issues, international organizations, and country reports as well as other data are available here.

World Bank Group
http://www.worldbank.org/html/extdr/regions.htm

News (press releases, summary of new projects, speeches), publications, topics in development, and reports on countries and regions can be accessed on this Web site. Links to other financial organizations are also provided.

World Health Organization (WHO)
http://www.who.int/en

Maintained by WHO's headquarters in Geneva, Switzerland, this site uses the Excite search engine to conduct keyword searches.

World Trade Organization (WTO)
http://www.wto.org

WTO's Web site topics include information on world trade systems, data on textiles, intellectual property rights, legal frameworks, trade and environmental policies, recent agreements, and other issues.

GENERAL AFRICA SITES

Africa News Web Site: Crisis in the Great Lakes Region
http://www.africanews.seeq.com

African News Web Site on Great Lakes (Rwanda, Burundi, Zaire, and Kenya, Tanzania, Uganda) can be found here with frequent updates and good links to other sites. It is possible to order e-mail crisis updates here.

Africa Action
http://www.africaaction.org/

Africa Action is a U.S.-based advocacy group that works for political, economic, and social justice throughout the African continent. Their Web site has links to articles on a wide number of key African current social, political, and economic issues.

Africa: South of the Sahara
http://www-sul.stanford.edu/depts/ssrg/africa/guide.html

On this site, Topics and Regions link headings will lead to a wealth of information.

African Studies WWW (U.Penn)
http://www.sas.upenn.edu/African_Studies/AS.html

This Web site provides facts about each African country, which includes news, statistics, and links to other Web sites.

AllAfrica Global Media
http://allafrica.com

From this page, explore African news by region or country. Topics covered include conflict and security; economy, business, and finance; environment and sustainable development; health; and human rights, plus many more.

Library of Congress Country Studies
http://lcweb2.loc.gov/frd/cs/cshome.html#toc

Of the 71 countries that are covered in the continuing series of books available at this Web site, at least a dozen of them are in Africa.

South African Government Index
http://www.gov.za/

This official site includes links to government agencies, data on structures of government, and links to detailed documents.

Mail & Guardian online

http://www.mg.co.za

This free electronic daily South African newspaper includes archived back issues as well as links to other related sites on Africa.

World History Archives

http://www.hartford-hwp.com/archives/

Hartford Web Publishing offers historical archives for the continent of Africa as a whole as well as for all the regions and countries in Africa. See individual country report pages for additional Web sites.

See individual country report pages for additional Web sites.

The United States (United States of America)

GEOGRAPHY

Area in Square Miles (Kilometers): 3,794,085 (9,826,630) (about 1/2 the size of Russia)

Capital (Population): Washington, DC (563,400)

Environmental Concerns: air and water pollution; limited freshwater resources, desertification; loss of habitat; waste disposal; acid rain

Geographical Features: vast central plain, mountains in the west, hills and low mountains in the east; rugged mountains and broad river valleys in Alaska; volcanic topography in Hawaii

Climate: mostly temperate, but ranging from tropical to arctic

PEOPLE
Population

Total: 301,139,947

Annual Growth Rate: 0.89%

Rural/Urban Population Ratio: 19/81

Major Languages: predominantly English; a sizable Spanish-speaking minority; many others

Ethnic Makeup: 82% white; 13% black; 4% Asian; 1% Amerindian and others

Religions: 52% Protestant; 24% Roman Catholic; 1% Jewish; 13% others; 10% none or unaffiliated

Health

Life Expectancy at Birth: 75 years (male); 81 years (female)

Infant Mortality: 6.37/1,000 live births

Physicians Available: 2.3/1000 people

HIV/AIDS Rate in Adults: 0.6%

Education

Adult Literacy Rate: 97% (official)

Compulsory (Ages): 7–16

COMMUNICATION

Telephones: 177,900,000 main lines

Daily Newspaper Circulation: 196.3/1,000 people

Televisions: 844/1,000 people

Internet Users: 208,000,000 (2006)

TRANSPORTATION

Highways in Miles (Kilometers): 3,986,827 (6,430,366)

Railroads in Miles (Kilometers): 140,499 (226,612)

Usable Airfields: 14,947

Motor Vehicles in Use: 229,620,000

GOVERNMENT

Type: federal republic

Independence Date: July 4, 1776

Head of State/Government: President George W. Bush is both head of state and head of government

Political Parties: Democratic Party; Republican Party; others of relatively minor political significance

Suffrage: universal at 18

MILITARY

Military Expenditures (% of GDP): 4.06%

Current Disputes: various boundary and territorial disputes; Iraq and Afghanistan; "war on terrorism"

ECONOMY

Per Capita Income/GDP: $43,800/$13.06 trillion

GDP Growth Rate: 2.9% (2006)

Inflation Rate: 3.2%

Unemployment Rate: 4.8%

Population Below Poverty Line: 12%

Natural Resources: many minerals and metals; petroleum; natural gas; timber; arable land

Agriculture: food grains; feed crops; fruits and vegetables; oil-bearing crops; livestock; dairy products

Industry: diversified in both capital and consumer-goods industries

Exports: $1.023 trillion (primary partners Canada, Mexico, Japan, China, U.K.)

Imports: $1.861 trillion (primary partners Canada, Mexico, Japan, China, Germany)

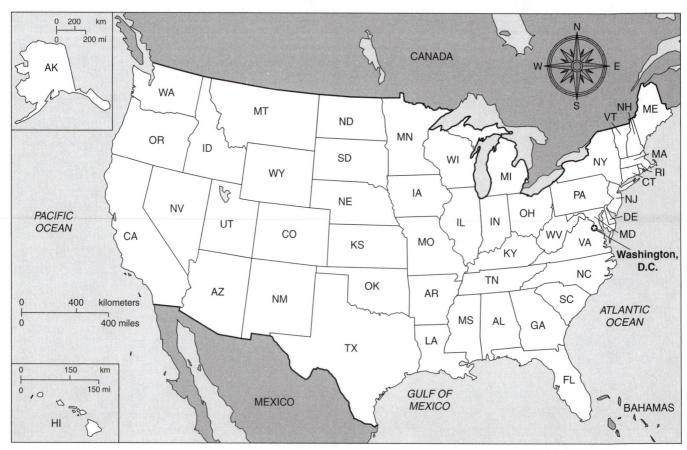

Canada

GEOGRAPHY
Area in Square Miles (Kilometers):
3,855,103 (9,984,670) (slightly larger than the United States)
Capital (Population): Ottawa (1,560,000)
Environmental Concerns: air and water pollution; acid rain; industrial damage to agriculture and forest productivity
Geographical Features: permafrost in the north; mountains in the west; central plains; lowlands in the southeast
Climate: varies from temperate to arctic

PEOPLE

Population
Total: 33,390,141(2007)
Annual Growth Rate: 0.87%
Rural/Urban Population Ratio: 20/80
Major Languages: both English and French are official
Ethnic Makeup: 28% British Isles origin; 23% French origin; 15% other European; 6% others; 2% indigenous; 26% mixed
Religions: 42.6% Roman Catholic; 27.7% Protestant; 12.7% others; 16% none.

Health
Life Expectancy at Birth: 77 years (male); 84 years (female)
Infant Mortality: 4.63/1,000 live births
Physicians Available: 2.1/1,000 people

HIV/AIDS Rate in Adults: 0

Education
Adult Literacy Rate: 97%
Compulsory (Ages): 6–16

COMMUNICATION
Telephones: 20,780,000 main lines
Daily Newspaper Circulation: 167.9/1,000 people
Televisions: 709/1,000 people
Internet Users: 22,000,000 (2006)

TRANSPORTATION
Highways in Miles (Kilometers): 646,226 (1,042,300)
Railroads in Miles (Kilometers): 29,802 (48,068)
Usable Airfields: 1,343
Motor Vehicles in Use: 18,360,000

GOVERNMENT
Type: federation with parliamentary democracy
Independence Date: July 1, 1867
Head of State/Government: Queen Elizabeth II; Prime Minister Stephen Harper
Political Parties: Conservative Party of Canada; Liberal Party; New Democratic Party; Bloc Québécois; Green Party
Suffrage: universal at 18

MILITARY
Military Expenditures (% of GDP): 1.1%
Current Disputes: maritime boundary disputes with the United States and Denmark (Greenland)

ECONOMY
Currency ($U.S. equivalent): 0.97 Canadian dollars = $1 (Oct. 2007)
Per Capita Income/GDP: $35,700/$1.181 trillion
GDP Growth Rate: 2.8%
Inflation Rate: 2%
Unemployment Rate: 6.4% (2006)
Labor Force by Occupation: 75% services; 14% manufacturing; 2% agriculture; and 8% others
Natural Resources: petroleum; natural gas; fish; minerals; cement; forestry products; wildlife; hydropower
Agriculture: grains; livestock; dairy products; potatoes; hogs; poultry and eggs; tobacco; fruits and vegetables
Industry: oil production and refining; natural-gas development; fish products; wood and paper products; chemicals; transportation equipment
Exports: $401.7 billion (primary partners United States, Japan, United Kingdom)
Imports: $356.5 billion (primary partners United States, China, Japan)

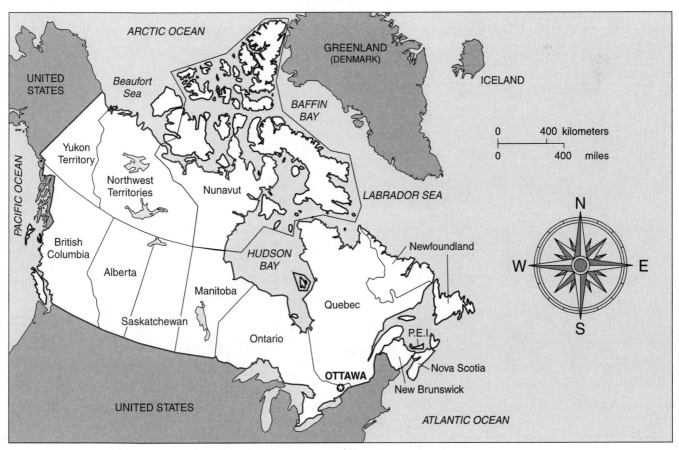

GLOBAL ●STUDIES

This map is provided to give you a graphic picture of where the countries of the world are located, the relationship they have with their region and neighbors, and their positions relative to major economic and political power blocs. We have focused on certain areas to illustrate these crowded regions more clearly. Africa is shaded for emphasis.

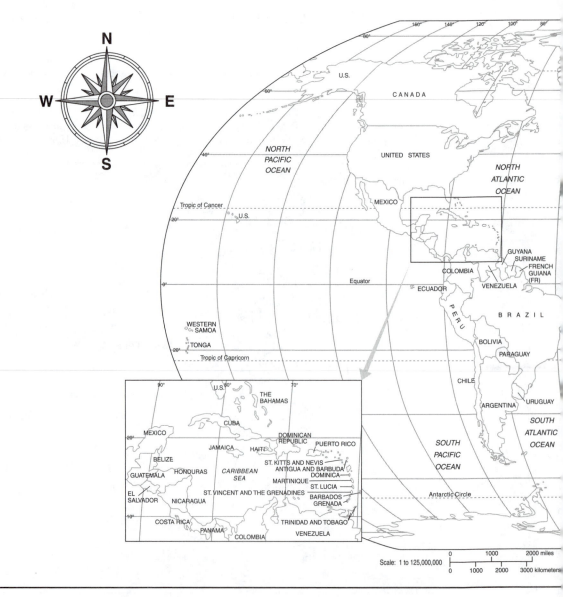

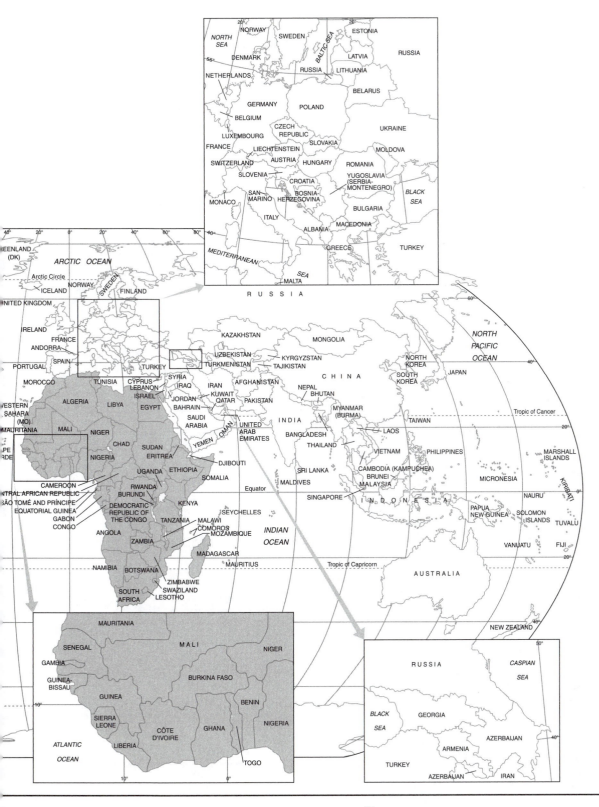

Africa

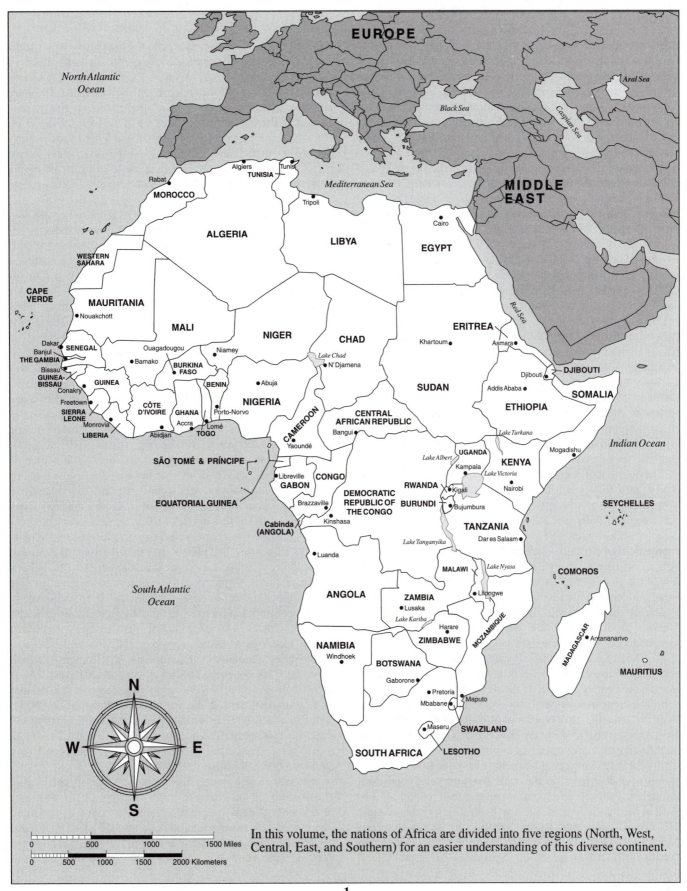

In this volume, the nations of Africa are divided into five regions (North, West, Central, East, and Southern) for an easier understanding of this diverse continent.

Africa   Looking for a Renaissance

At first glance the study of Africa and its people seems to be a monumental task, because the complexity and diversity of the cultural and geographic regions are astounding. However, within the myriad challenges of studying the continent there are wonderful stories to be told about each nation and the variety of people contained within it. What stands out about Africa and its heritage is its antiquity, and how this antiquity might rest peacefully inside a rapidly changing world. From Egypt to South Africa, the African countries present the oldest known civilizations and the point of origin of humanity itself, but each nation is also uniquely modern, facing the struggles of today and searching for a way to bring about development and improve the quality of life for the people.

All nations, including those in Africa, are built to bring about a better life for the population, and to avoid a government that actively kills their people in pursuit of nebulous, unattainable, and contradictory goals stated by corrupt leaders who are motivated by personal greed, that is disguised as religious or ethnic zealousy. Thus while the mainstream media continue to bring forward a vision of the continent that is full of tales of woe, it's important to remember that the vast majority of the African population holds out some semblance of hope for a better day. Contrary to many accounts, most African states are developing and building in their own way. There are wars, based on a variety of issues; religion, ethnicity, money, and simple differences of opinion, but for every country in violent conflict, there are two who strive to gain their niche against great odds in the contemporary global village.

The question of course is: what has happened in the last hundred years to this great continent—a continent that holds the key to the evolution of humanity, and a continent that developed the first language skills that allow us to communicate and evolve complex social structures? This text examines the history of the continent in an effort to understand how Africa has evolved and how it continues to struggle to develop. Because Africa, regardless of the glories of its past, is a continent hungry for development, and looking for a Renaissance.

During the early 1960s, most of the African continent was liberated from colonial rule. Seventeen nations gained their independence in the great *Uhuru* ("Freedom") year of 1960 alone. The times were electric. In country after country, the banners of new states, whose leaders offered idealistic promises to remake the continent and thus the world, replaced the flags of various European states and the United Nations. Hopes were high, and even the most ambitious of goals seemed obtainable. Non-Africans also spoke of the resource-rich continent as being on the verge of a developmental takeoff. Some of the old racist myths about Africa were at last being questioned.

Yet four decades after the great freedom year, conditions throughout Africa are sobering rather than euphoric. For most Africans, independence has been a desperate struggle for survival rather than an exhilarating path to development. Nowadays Africa is often described in the global media as a "continent in crisis," a "region in turmoil," "on a precipice,"

and "suffering"—phrases that echo the sensationalist writings of nineteenth-century missionaries eager to convince others of the continent's need for "salvation." Unfortunately, the modern headlines are too often accurate, and certainly far more accurate than the mission tracts of yesteryear. Today, millions of Africans are indeed seeking some form of salvation from the grinding poverty, pestilence, and in many areas, wars that afflict their lives. Added to these miseries is the ongoing HIV/AIDS pandemic, which is devastating much of the continent; the majority of AIDS sufferers and fatalities have been African.

Perhaps the scale of Africa's maladies helps to explain why contemporary evangelists are so much more successful in swelling their congregations than were their counterparts in the past. It is certainly not for lack of competition; Africa is a continent of many, often overlapping faiths. In addition to Islam, Christianity, and other spiritual paths, Africans have embraced a myriad of secular ideologies: Marxism, African socialism, people's capitalism, structural adjustment, pan-Africanism, authenticity, nonracialism, the one-party state, and the multiparty state. The list is endless, but salvation seems ever more distant.

Africa's current circumstances are indeed difficult, yet it is also true that the postcolonial era has brought progress as well as problems. The goals so optimistically pronounced at independence have, for the most part, not been abandoned. Even when the states have faltered, the societies that they encompass have remained dynamic and adaptable to shifting opportunities. The support of strong families continues to allow most Africans to overcome enormous adversity. There are starving children in Africa today, but there are also many more in school uniforms studying to make their dreams a reality. Africa as a whole remains a dynamic, ever-changing continent that in recent years has seen much progress as well as instances of regression. For example, the use of mobile wireless telephones (cell phones) has spread across the continent like wildfire, bringing mass-communications capacity to millions for the first time. While most Africans remain on the other side of the "digital divide" in terms of their capacity to participate in the "global information age," the introduction of new information technologies is bringing change. Textile businesses in such diverse places as Mauritius, Lesotho, and Ghana use the new technologies to monitor their niche markets in Europe and North America on a daily basis. This trend will probably grow if trade access between the developed and developing world continues to be liberalized through the World Trade Organization (WTO) and other multilateral agreements such as the African Growth and Opportunity Act (AGOA) and the Cotonou Convention, which, respectively, have helped to open up U.S. and European Union markets to African goods.

It is also worth noting that most of what appears in the global media about Africa is but a snapshot of the continent in moments of catastrophic deprivation, war, and degradation. The global flow of information is dominated by a small number of media companies that must for the most part capture the eyes and ears of consumers in the world's wealthier societies to

WOULD YOU BELIEVE?

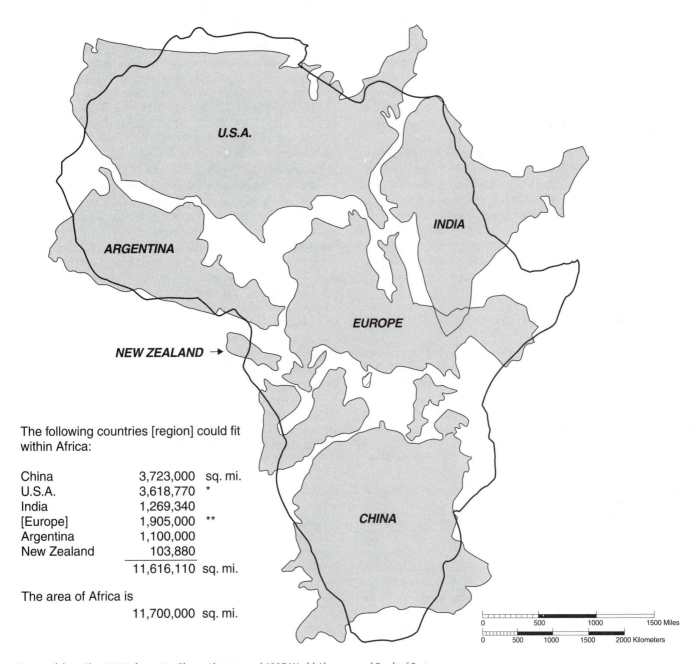

The following countries [region] could fit within Africa:

China	3,723,000	sq. mi.
U.S.A.	3,618,770	*
India	1,269,340	
[Europe]	1,905,000	**
Argentina	1,100,000	
New Zealand	103,880	
	11,616,110	sq. mi.

The area of Africa is

11,700,000	sq. mi.

Source of data: *The 1997 Information Please Almanac and 1997 World Almanac and Book of Facts.*
* Total, land and water, 50 states
** *1997 Information Please Almanac.* Includes Iceland. Excludes the former European Soviet Union and European Turkey.

capture market share and sell advertising. Incremental progress in improving the quality of life for ordinary Africans is rarely perceived by these media companies as newsworthy. Thus, events such as the building of a new school, road, or water system that can dramatically transform the lives of people in a particular African locality are rarely of interest to the international broadcasters that increasingly influence what appears on the air waves of Africa itself as well as the rest of the world. Outsiders also often simply lose sight of the fact that Africa is a vast continent and not a country.

It would be naïve to downplay the serious challenges that face what is, in per capita economic terms, the world's least-developed continent. According to the 2006 United Nations Human Development Report, 38 of the world's 50 least developed countries are in Africa. But it is also worth appreciating that, with the passing of time, many of the ills that were inherited from colonialism have been remedied. In the process, new perspectives on how to move forward are being tested. The corruption and lack of capacity that characterize many African governments are mitigated by the resilience of local communities. Africans not only seek salvation from deprivation but also actively work for the delivery of a better tomorrow in which their children can enjoy the material benefits of being participants, rather than onlookers, in their continent's integration into the process of globalization.

A prerequisite for the realization of such dreams is the maintenance of peace. Without peace, there can be no prospect of freedom and development. In this context, recent progress in bringing an end to the armed conflicts in Angola, Sierra Leone, the Horn of Africa, and, perhaps most significantly, Congo, along with the consolidation of stability in such other areas as Mozambique and South Africa, have become sources of renewed hope.

If the momentum for peace can be maintained by the continent's growing ranks of legitimately elected leaders, ongoing talk among statespeople and intellectuals about the onset of an era of rebirth for the continent will appear less as a pipedream and more as a realistic possibility. Such a renaissance is predicated upon faith in the commitment of post–Cold War Africa's capacity to resolve its internal problems in partnership with, but without undue interference from, nations outside Africa that have in the past contributed to the continent's instability.

A DIVERSE CONTINENT

Africa, which is almost four times the size of the United States (excluding Alaska), ranks just below Asia as the world's biggest continent. Well over one quarter of the membership of the United Nations consists of African states—53 in all. Such facts are worth noting, for even well-educated outsiders often lose sight of Africa's continental scope when they discuss its problems and prospects.

Not only is the African continent vast but, archaeology tells us, it was also the cradle of human civilization. (New evidence suggests that today's non-Africans are the descendants of Africans who moved out of the continent as recently as 80,000 years ago.) It should therefore not be surprising that the ways of life as well as genetic makeup of the 800 million or so contemporary inhabitants of Africa are characterized by extraordinary diversity. In southern Africa's Kalahari Desert (shared by South Africa, Namibia, and Botswana), a group of individuals, known to the outside world as Bushmen, continue to practice their ancient way of life as hunters and gatherers. Geneticists consider Bushmen to be the oldest surviving human beings—within their genetic structure, Bushman carry the original genes of the human race. To add majesty to their heritage, contemporary linguists claim that the click language spoken by the Bushmen is also the oldest known language in the world. Contemporary Africans speak more than 1,000 languages and live their lives according to a rich variety of household arrangements, kinship systems, and religious beliefs. The art and music styles of the continent are as varied as the people.

Given its diversity, it is not easy to generalize about Africa. For each statement, there is an exception. However, one aspect that is constant to all African societies is that they have always been changing, albeit in modern times at an ever-increasing rate. Cities have grown and people have moved back and forth between village and town, giving rise to new social groups,

institutions, occupations, religions, and forms of communication that have made their mark in the countryside as well as in the urban centers. All Africans, whether they be urban computer programmers or hunter-gatherers living in the remote corners of the Kalahari Desert, have taken on new practices, interests, and burdens, yet they have retained their African identity. Uniquely African institutions, values, and histories underlie contemporary lifestyles throughout the continent.

Memories of past civilizations are a source of pride and community. The medieval Mali and Ghana empires, the glory of Pharaonic Egypt, the Fulani caliphate of northern Nigeria, the knights of Kanem and Bornu, the Great Zimbabwe, and the Kingdom of the Kongo, among others, are all remembered. Africa is a paradox. Twenty-first century folks may be able to go to the moon, but nowhere are there monuments to challenge the greatest of the African past. Yet, even these wonders are under siege. In Sudan, the largest nation of the continent, cultures are under attack, and many of the oldest archeological sites, including pyramids, are threatened with extinction. The past is connected to the present through the generations and by ties to the land. In a continent where the majority of people are still farmers, land remains "the mother that never dies." It is valued for its fruits and because it is the place to which the ancestors came and were buried.

The art of personal relationships continues to be important. People typically live in large families. Children are considered precious, and large families are still desired for social as well as economic reasons. Elders are an important part of a household; nursing homes and retirement communities generally do not exist. People are not supposed to be loners. "I am because we are" remains a valued precept. In this age of nation-states, the "we" may refer to one's ethnic community, while obligations to one's extended family often take precedence over other loyalties.

Most Africans believe in a spiritual as well as a material world. The continent contains a rich variety of indigenous belief systems, which often coexist with the larger religions of Islam and various Christian sects. Many families believe that their lives are influenced by their ancestors. Africans from all walks of life will seek the services of professional "traditional" healers to explain an illness or suggest remedies for such things as sterility or bad fortune. But this pattern of behavior does not preclude one from turning to scientific medicine; all African governments face strong popular demands for better access to modern health-care facilities.

Islam has long been a strong force in Africa. Today that religion rivals Christianity as the fastest-growing faith on the continent. The followers of both religions often adapt their faiths to accommodate local traditions and values. Some people also join new religious movements and churches, such as the Brotherhood of the Cross and Star in Nigeria or the Church of Simon Kimbangu in Congo, that link Christian and indigenous beliefs with new ideas and rituals. Like other institutions in the towns and cities, the churches and mosques provide their followers with social networks.

Local art, like local religion, often reflects the influence of the changing world. An airplane is featured on a Nigerian gelede mask, the Apollo space mission inspires a Burkinabe carver, and an Ndebele dance wand is a beaded electric pole.

THE TROUBLED PRESENT

Some of the crises in Africa today threaten its peoples' traditional resiliency. The facts are grim: In material terms, the average African is poorer today than at independence, and it is predicted that poverty will only increase in the immediate future. Drought conditions in recent decades have led to food shortages across the continent. In the 1980s, widespread famine occurred in 22 African nations; the Food and Agriculture Organization (FAO) of the United Nations estimated that 70 percent of all Africans did not have enough to eat. An outpouring of assistance and relief efforts at the time saved as many as 35 million lives. Overall per capita food production in Africa dropped by 12 percent between 1961 and 1995. One factor in the decline has been the tendency of agricultural planners to ignore the fact that up to 70 percent of Africa's food crops are grown by women. It has also been estimated that up to 40 percent of the continent's food crops go uneaten as a result of inadequate transport and storage facilities. Although agricultural production rose modestly in the late 1990s, the food crisis continues. Since 1990, large parts of East and Southern Africa, in particular, have faced the prospect of renewed hunger. Other areas have become dependent on outside food aid. Declining commodity prices on world markets, explosive population growth, and recurring drought and locust infestations have often counterbalanced marginal advances in agricultural production through better incentives to farmers. Problems of climate irregularity, and obtaining and transporting needed goods and supplies require continued assistance and long-range planning. Wood, the average person's source of energy, grows scarcer every year, and most governments have had to contend with the rising cost of imported fuels.

Armed conflicts have devastated portions of Africa. Recent carnage in Angola, Djibouti, Sierra Leone, Somalia, and the Democratic Republic of the Congo (D.R.C., formerly Zaire), due to internal strife encouraged to greater or lesser degrees by outside forces, places them in a distinct class of suffering—a class that has also included (and that may yet again) Chad, Eritrea, Ethiopia, Mozambique, and Rwanda. By the end of 2002, civil war persisted in Burundi, Liberia, Sudan, Central African Republic, and northern Uganda, while threatening to ignite in long-stable Côte d'Ivoire. More than 3 million people have died in these countries over the past decade, while millions more have become refugees. Except for scattered enclaves, normal economic activities have been greatly disrupted or have ceased altogether.

Sudan today, in 2007, brings the whole issue of governance into sharp focus. Governance of whom, for what ends? In 2005, after more than two decades of civil war, a comprehensive peace agreement was reached between rebels from the country's southern region and the Sudanese government. At the same time the agreement was taking place, however, fighting broke out between the government and rebels in the country's western Darfur region; peacekeeping troops are currently trying to stabilize the region while tentative peace talks between rebels and the Sudanese government get underway. In the meantime, violence in the Darfur region is estimated to have killed more than 200,000 people and displaced 2 million more.

The Sudan is a test case that seems to be headed for continued disaster, and there are many throughout all of Africa who see no reason for it to remain unified as a country. What is clear is that there is no justification for Sudan's national unity, if that unity means the death and destruction of its people and their culture. The entire continent of Africa is unified by the need to develop its human and physical resources, and in order to do that the wars must stop.

Almost all African governments are deeply in debt. In 1991, the foreign debt owed by all the sub-Saharan African countries except South Africa already stood at about $175 billion.

MEASURING MISERY			
United Nations Human Development Index, 2006[*]: Ranking of African States Among World Nations. Total Number of States Ranked: 177 African States Not Ranked: Liberia, Somalia			
Rank	Country	Rank	Country
47	Seychelles	152	Kenya
63	Mauritius	153	Mauritania
64	Libya	155	Gambia
87	Tunisia	156	Senegal
102	Algeria	157	Eritrea
106	Cape Verde	158	Rwanda
111	Egypt	159	Nigeria
120	Equatorial Guinea	160	Guinea
121	South Africa	161	Angola
123	Morocco	162	Tanzania
124	Gabon	163	Benin
125	Namibia	164	Cote d'Ivoire
127	São Tomé and Príncipe	165	Zambia
131	Botswana	166	Malawi
132	Comoros	167	Democratic Republic of the Congo
136	Ghana	168	Mozambique
140	Congo	169	Burundi
141	Sudan	170	Ethiopia
143	Madagascar	171	Chad
144	Cameroon	172	Central African Republic
145	Uganda	173	Guinea-Bissau
146	Swaziland	174	Burkina Fasso
147	Togo	175	Mali
148	Djibouti	176	Sierra Leone
149	Lesotho	177	Niger
151	Zimbabwe		

[*]Standings among 177 countries, with the ranking 177 indicating the lowest development.

Source: UNDP, Human Development Report 2006.

THE AIDS PANDEMIC

Perhaps the greatest challenge currently facing Africa is the spread of HIV/AIDS. The statistics are chilling. According to the United Nations, of the 36 million people worldwide living with the HIV virus, some 24 million live in sub-Saharan Africa. Of the 5.3 million new infections estimated for the year 2000, 3.8 million were in Africa. AIDS is already the leading cause of death on the continent. In all, 2.4 million AIDS-related deaths were recorded for Africa in 2000, representing about 80 percent of the worldwide total. According to the 2006 United Nations Human Development Report, life expectancy is lower in sub-Saharan Africa today than it was three decades ago; HIV/AIDS is a major factor in this reversal.

AIDS-related fatalities have also resulted in a rapidly growing number of "AIDS orphans." According to Kingsley Amoako, executive secretary of the Economic Commission for Africa, more than 12 million children have been orphaned in Africa due to AIDS (out of the global estimate of just over 13 million). Speaking at a gathering of African leaders in November 2000, Amoako noted that, "Within the next 10 years, it is projected that there will be 40 million AIDS orphans in Africa. . . . The AIDS pandemic is undermining social and economic structures and reversing the fragile gains made since independence . . . in parts of Africa, AIDS is killing one in every three adults, making orphans out of every tenth child and decimating entire communities."

A growing concern is the feminization of HIV/AIDS in sub-Saharan Africa, where infection rates have been growing much more rapidly among women than men. According to the United Nations, women now account for 57% of HIV infections in the region, and young African women are estimated to be three times more likely than men to become infected. The reasons for this are unclear, although early sexual activity and age of marriage may increase the exposure of young girls to risk; possible gender bias in prevention and treatment may also be a factor.

The worst-hit parts of the continent in recent years have been East and Southern Africa, with some countries having infection rates of more than a fifth of their adult populations. According to published figures, the most affected countries are Botswana, South Africa, and Zimbabwe, where it is currently estimated that one in every two people under age 15 could die from the disease.

Inevitably, the spread of HIV/AIDS is having a devastating impact on economic and social development. For example, it is estimated that in the next decade, South Africa's gross domestic product will be 17 percent lower than it would have been without the pandemic.

Amid the gloom there is, nonetheless, grounds for hope that the scourge can ultimately be overcome. According to a UN report issued at the end of 2000, some parts of the continent are finally seeing a decrease in new HIV cases. The report notes that this has resulted in a modest overall decrease in the total number of new HIV cases in Africa as a whole. The decrease has been partially attributed to the gradual success of prevention programs, especially in the East African countries.

Africa's ability to fight HIV/AIDS is compromised by its debt burden and the high cost of HIV/AIDS treatment drugs. One of the most outspoken figures on the relationship between disease and debt on the continent has been Botswana's president, Festus Mogae. In a direct appeal to the wealthier nations, he observed:

Your wealth in recent years increased by trillions and therefore what we owe is peanuts. It will not affect anybody, not the balance sheets of banks or anybody. It's just a matter of principle. You are insisting on repayment as a matter of principle, but it has no financial consequences for anybody else except the debtor. For him it's a lot of money. . . . Pharmaceutical companies have come forward and offered us discounts. Some of these discounts are very generous but are still more than our faint means can allow us to afford, and therefore we are still not able to take full advantage of the offer. . . . We are saying the rest of the world, including and especially the United States and the rest of the G-7, at the governmental level should do something to make it possible for us to access these treatments that are currently available.

Although it is smaller in its absolute amount than that of Latin America, as a percentage of its economic output the continent's debt is the highest in the world and is rising swiftly. The combined gross national product (GNP) for the same countries, whose total populations are in excess of 500 million, was less than $150 billion, a figure that represents only 1.2 percent of the global GNP and is about equal to the GNP of Belgium, a country of 10 million people. In Zambia, an extreme example, the per capita foreign debt theoretically owed by each of its citizens is nearly $1,000, more than twice its annual per capita income.

In order to obtain money to meet debts and pay for their running expenses, many African governments have been obliged to accept the stringent terms of global lending agencies, most notably the World Bank and the International Monetary Fund (IMF). These lending terms have led to great hardship, especially in urban areas, through austerity measures such as the abandonment of price controls on basic foodstuffs and the freezing of wages. Many African governments and experts are questioning both the justice and practicality of these terms. In response there have been recent, though many would argue insufficient, moves by donor countries to arrange for debt relief in the poorest countries.

Another factor that helps to account for Africa's relative poverty is the low level of industrial output of all but a few of its countries. The decline of many commodity prices on the world market has further reduced national incomes. As a result, the foreign exchange needed to import food, machinery, fuel, and other goods is very limited in most African countries. In 1987, the continent's economy grew by only 0.8 percent, far below its population growth rate of about 3.2 percent. In the same year, cereal production declined 8 percent and overall agricultural production grew by only 0.5 percent. There has been some modest improvement in subsequent years. Recent estimates put the continent's economic growth rate at 1.5 percent—still the world's lowest, and far below that of the population growth rate. Perhaps more significant has been the high growth that has been recorded in those states, like Mozambique, that have managed to move away from civil war to governance based on democratic consensus.

But perhaps the greatest challenge facing Africa today is in the area of health. The HIV/AIDS pandemic has spread at an alarming rate over the past two decades, already claiming millions of lives and threatening millions more. Southern Africa has been especially hard hit in recent years, with more than one in five adults said to be HIV-positive in a number of countries. As a result, estimates of life expectancy have been declining dramatically. Botswana is a notable example. By the early 1990s, average overall life expectancy in the nation had risen to about 65 years, due to sustained public investment in providing universal access to primary health care. But the most recent estimate presented at the 2002 United Nations AIDS Conference in Spain suggest that average life expectancy in Botswana could drop to as little as 27 years by 2010. Put another way, unless the pandemic can be brought under control, it has been estimated that AIDS will eventually claim the lives of one out of every two Batswana (as the people of Botswana are known) born in the new millennium. The battle against AIDS in Africa has been complicated by the existence of multiple strains of the HIV virus, of which the most virulent is currently concentrated in Southern Africa. The spread of HIV/AIDS has contributed to the resurgence of diseases such as tuberculosis. Mortality due to malaria—Africa's traditional scourge—has also been rising in many areas, as has cholera. Diseases afflicting livestock, such as rinderpest and foot-and-mouth disease, have also been making a comeback in certain regions.

These issues take place in the context of a wide range of environmental challenges. Population pressure has led to the deterioration of arable land and increasing desertification in marginal environments. Moreover, Africa, like most other parts of the world, can expect to face the challenges of future climate change. This is perhaps best epitomized by recent shrinking of the fabled "snows of Kilimanjaro." Predictions call for significant changes in rainfall patterns, including moister conditions in West Africa's Sahel and increased drought in southern Africa.

THE EVOLUTION OF AFRICA'S ECONOMIES

Africa has seldom been rich, although it has vast resources, and some rulers and other elites have become very wealthy. In earlier centuries, the slave trade greatly contributed to limiting economic development in many African regions. During the period of European exploration and colonialism, Africa's involvement in the world economy greatly increased with the emergence of new forms of "legitimate" commerce. But colonial-era policies and practices assured that this development was of little long-term benefit to most of the continent's peoples.

During the 70 or so years of European colonial rule over most of Africa, its nations' economies were shaped to the advantage of the imperialists. Cash crops such as cocoa, coffee, and rubber began to be grown for the European market. Some African farmers benefited from these crops, but the cash-crop economy also involved large foreign-run plantations. It also encouraged the trends toward use of migrant labor and the decline in food production. Many people became dependent for their livelihood on the forces of the world market, which, like the weather, were beyond their immediate control.

Mining also increased during colonial times, again for the benefit of the colonial rulers. The ores were extracted from African soil by European companies. African labor was employed, but the machinery came from abroad. The copper, diamonds, gold, iron ore, and uranium were shipped overseas to be processed and marketed in the Western economies. Upon independence, African

governments received a varying percentage of the take through taxation and consortium agreements. But mining remained an enclave industry, sometimes described as a "state within a state" because such industries were run by outsiders who established communities that used imported machinery and technicians and exported the products to industrialized countries.

Inflationary conditions in other parts of the world have had adverse effects on Africa. The raw materials that Africans export today often receive low prices on the world market, while the manufactured goods that African countries import are expensive. Local African industries lack spare parts and machinery, and farmers frequently cannot afford to transport crops to market. As a result, the whole economy slows down. Thus, Africa, because of the policies of former colonial powers and current independent governments, is tied into the world economy in ways that do not always serve its peoples' best interests.

THE PROBLEMS OF GOVERNANCE

Outside forces are not the only cause of Africa's current crises. Too often, Africa has been a misgoverned continent. After independence, the idealism that characterized various nationalist movements, with their promises of popular self-determination, gave way in most states to cynical authoritarian regimes. By 1989, only Botswana, Mauritius, soon-to-be-independent Namibia, and, arguably, The Gambia and Senegal could reasonably claim that their governments were elected in genuinely free and fair elections.

During the 1980s, the government of Robert Mugabe in Zimbabwe, in Southern Africa, undoubtedly enjoyed majority support, but political life in the country was already seriously marred by violence and intimidation aimed at the Mugabe regime's potential opposition. Past multiparty contests in the North African nations of Egypt, Morocco, and Tunisia, as well as in the West African state of Liberia, had been manipulated to assure that the ruling establishments remained unchallenged. Elsewhere, the continent was divided between military and/or one-party regimes, which often combined the seemingly contradictory characteristics of weakness and absolutism at the top. While a few of the one-party states, most notably Tanzania, then offered people genuine, if limited, choices of leadership, most were, to a greater or lesser degree, simply vehicles of personal rule.

But since 1990 there has been a democratic reawakening in Africa, which has toppled the political status quo in some areas and threatened its survival throughout the continent. Whereas in 1989 some 35 nations were governed as single-party states, by 1994 there were none, though Swaziland and Uganda were experimenting with no-party systems. In a number of countries—Benin, Cape Verde, Central African Republic, Congo, Madagascar, Mali, Malawi, Niger, São Tomé and Príncipe, Senegal, South Africa, and Zambia—ruling parties were decisively rejected in multiparty elections, while elections in other areas led to a greater sharing of power between the old regimes and their formerly suppressed oppositions.

In many countries, the democratic transformation is still ongoing and remains fragile. There have been accusations of manipulation and voting fraud in a growing number of countries in the past decade; while in Algeria, The Gambia, Niger,

Nigeria, and Sierra Leone, the seeming will of the electorates has been overridden by military coups.

A very fragile democracy has since been restored to Nigeria, Africa's most populous state, where, in general elections in 2007, the first civilian-to-civilian transfer of power took place in the country's history. In Sierra Leone, a similar transfer of civilian-to-civilian power occurred after general elections in August, 2007. In The Gambia, where three decades of multiparty democracy were ended through a military coup, there have also been elections. But their legitimacy has been questioned.

Events in Benin have most closely paralleled the recent changes of Central/Eastern Europe. Benin's military-based, Marxist-Leninist regime of Mathieu Kérékou was pressured into relinquishing power to a transitional civilian government made up of technocrats and former dissidents. (Television broadcasts of this "civilian coup" enjoyed large audiences in neighboring countries.) In several other countries, such as Equatorial Guinea, Gabon, and Togo, mounting opposition has resulted in the semblance without the substance of free elections by long-ruling military autocrats. In the Democratic Republic of the Congo, attempts to establish a framework for reform through a multiparty consultative conference were overshadowed by the almost complete collapse of state structures. A victory by externally backed rebels in 1997 was followed by renewed civil war and foreign intervention. Continued conflict in the country has contributed to the further destabilization of neighboring states. Many people fear that these countries may soon experience turmoil similar to that which has engulfed Ethiopia, Liberia, Rwanda, Somalia, and Uganda, where military autocrats have been overthrown by armed rebels.

Why did most postcolonial African governments, until recently, take on autocratic forms? And why are these forms now being so widely challenged? There are no definitive answers to either of these questions. One common explanation for authoritarianism in Africa has been the weakness of the states themselves. Most African governments have faced the difficult task of maintaining national unity with diverse, ethnically divided citizenries. Although the states of Africa may overlay and overlap historic kingdoms, most are products of colonialism. Their boundaries were fashioned during the late-nineteenth-century European partition of the continent, which divided and joined ethnic groups by lines drawn in Europe. The successful leaders of African independence movements worked within the colonial boundaries; and when they joined together in the Organization of African Unity (OAU), they agreed to respect the territorial status quo.

While the need to stem interethnic and regional conflict has been one justification for placing limits on popular self-determination, another explanation can be found in the administrative systems that the nationalist leaderships inherited. All the European colonies in Africa functioned essentially as police states. Not only were various forms of opposition curtailed, but intrusive security establishments were created to watch over and control the indigenous populations. Although headed by Europeans, most colonial security services employed local staff members who were prepared to assume leadership roles at independence. A wave of military coups swept across West Africa during the 1960s; elsewhere, aspiring dictators like "Life President" Ngwazi Hastings Banda of Malawi were quick to appreciate the value of the inherited instruments of control.

Africa's economic difficulties have also frequently been cited as contributing to its political underdevelopment. On one hand, Nigeria's last civilian government, for example, was certainly undermined in part by the economic crisis that engulfed it due to falling oil revenues. On the other hand, in a pattern reminiscent of recent changes in Latin America, economic difficulties resulting in high rates of inflation and indebtedness seem to be tempting some African militaries, such as Benin's, to return to the barracks and allow civilian politicians to assume responsibility for the implementation of inevitably harsh austerity programs.

External powers have long sustained African dictatorships through their grants of military and economic aid—and, on occasion, direct intervention. For example, a local attempt in 1964 to restore constitutional rule in Gabon was thwarted by French paratroopers, while Joseph Desiré Mobutu's kleptocratic hold over Zaire (now the D.R.C.) relied from the very beginning on overt and covert assistance from the United States and other Western states. The former Soviet bloc and China also helped in the past to support their share of unsavory African allies, in places like Ethiopia, Equatorial Guinea, and Burundi. But the end of the Cold War has led to a reduced desire on the part of outside powers to prop up their unpopular African allies. At the same time, the major international lending agencies have increasingly concerned themselves with the perceived need to adjust the political as well as economic structures of debtor nations. This new emphasis is justified in part by the alleged linkage between political unaccountability and economic corruption and mismanagement.

The ongoing decline of socialism on the continent is also having a significant political effect. Some regimes have professed a Marxist orientation, while others have felt that a special African socialism could be built on the communal and cooperative traditions of their societies. In countries such as Guinea-Bissau and Mozambique, a revolutionary socialist orientation was introduced at the grassroots level during the struggles for independence, within areas liberated from colonialism. The various socialist governments have not been free of personality cults, nor from corruption and oppressive measures. And many governments that have eschewed the socialist label have, nonetheless, developed public corporations and central-planning methods similar to those governments that openly profess Marxism. In recent years, virtually all of Africa's governments, partly in line with IMF and World Bank requirements but also because of the inefficiency and losses of many of their public corporations, have placed greater emphasis on private-sector development.

REASONS FOR OPTIMISM

Although the problems facing African countries have grown since independence, so have the continent's collective achievements. The number of people who can read and write in local languages as well as in English, French, or Portuguese has increased enormously. More people can peruse newspapers, follow instructions for fertilizers, and read the labels on medicine bottles. The use of modern communications technology, particularly cellular phones and the Internet, has increased rapidly in the past decade. Professionals trained in modern technology who, for example, plan electrification schemes, organize large office staffs, or develop medical facilities are more available because of the large number of African universities that have developed since the end of colonialism. Health care has also expanded and improved in most areas. Outside of the areas that have been ravaged by war, life expectancy has generally increased and infant mortality rates have declined.

The problems besetting Africa have caused deep pessimism in some quarters, with a few observers going so far as to question whether the postcolonial division of the continent into multiethnic states is viable. But the states themselves have proved to be surprisingly resilient. Central authority has reemerged in such traumatized, once seemingly ungovernable countries as Uganda, Mozambique, and most recently Sierra Leone. Despite the terrible wars that are still being waged in a few nations, mostly in the form of civil wars, postwar African governments have been notably successful in avoiding armed conflict with one another (although this fact has been severely tested by external interventions in the Democratic Republic of the Congo). Of special significance is South Africa's recent transformation into a nonracial democracy, which has been accompanied by its emergence as the leading member of the Southern African Development Community and has brought an end to its previous policy of regional destabilization.

Another positive development is the increasing attention that African governments and intra-African agencies are giving to women, as was exemplified in a global population summit held in Cairo, Egypt, in 1994. The pivotal role of women in agriculture and other activities is increasingly being recognized and supported. In many countries, prenatal and hospital care for mothers and their babies have increased, conditions for women workers in factories have improved, and new cooperatives for women's activities have been developed. Women are also playing a more prominent role in the political life of many African countries.

The advances that have been made in Africa are important ones, but they could be undercut by continued economic decline. Africa needs debt relief and outside aid just to maintain the gains that have been made. Yet as an African proverb observes, "Someone else's legs will do you no good in traveling." Africa, as the individual country reports in this volume observe, is a continent of many and varied resources. There are mineral riches and a vast agricultural potential. However, the continent's people, the youths who make up more than half the population and the elders whose wisdom is revered, are its greatest resource. The rest of the world, which has benefited from the continent's material resources, can also learn from the social strengths of African families and communities.

Central Africa

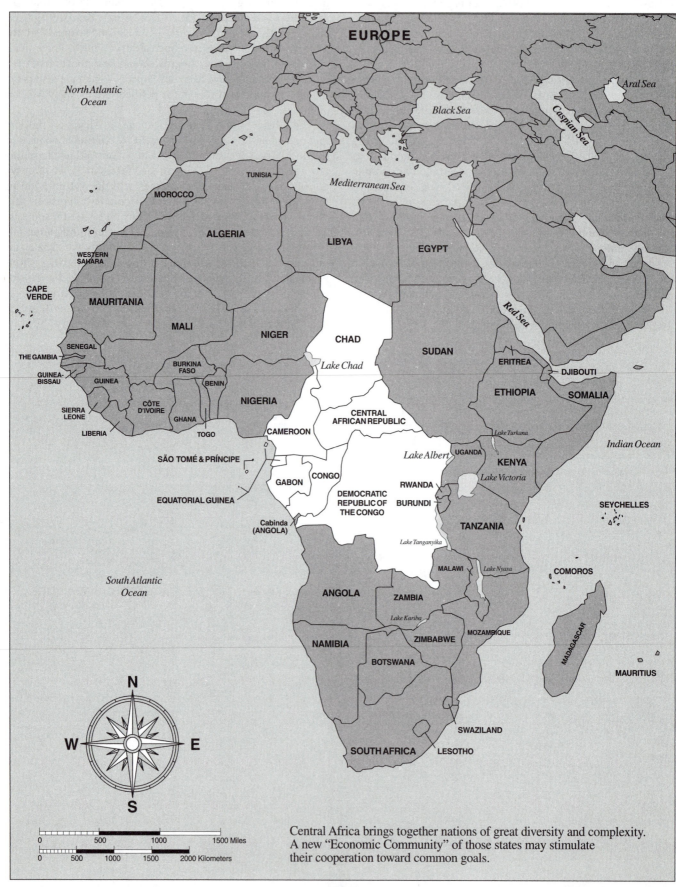

EUROPE

North Atlantic
Ocean

Black Sea

Aral Sea

Caspian Sea

Mediterranean Sea

TUNISIA

MOROCCO

ALGERIA

LIBYA

EGYPT

Red Sea

WESTERN
SAHARA

CAPE
VERDE

MAURITANIA

MALI

NIGER

CHAD

SUDAN

ERITREA

DJIBOUTI

SENEGAL

THE GAMBIA

GUINEA-
BISSAU

GUINEA

BURKINA
FASO

BENIN

Lake Chad

ETHIOPIA

SOMALIA

SIERRA
LEONE

CÔTE
D'IVOIRE

GHANA

NIGERIA

CENTRAL
AFRICAN REPUBLIC

Lake Turkana

Indian Ocean

LIBERIA

TOGO

CAMEROON

Lake Albert

UGANDA

SÃO TOMÉ & PRÍNCIPE

KENYA

EQUATORIAL GUINEA

GABON

CONGO

DEMOCRATIC
REPUBLIC OF
THE CONGO

RWANDA

BURUNDI

Lake Victoria

SEYCHELLES

Cabinda
(ANGOLA)

TANZANIA

Lake Tanganyika

South Atlantic
Ocean

ANGOLA

ZAMBIA

MALAWI

Lake Nyasa

COMOROS

Lake Kariba

MOZAMBIQUE

MADAGASCAR

NAMIBIA

ZIMBABWE

BOTSWANA

MAURITIUS

N

W   E

S

SWAZILAND

SOUTH AFRICA

LESOTHO

0   500   1000   1500 Miles

0   500   1000   1500   2000 Kilometers

Central Africa brings together nations of great diversity and complexity.
A new "Economic Community" of those states may stimulate
their cooperation toward common goals.

Central Africa   Possibilities for Cooperation

The Central African region, as defined in this book, brings together countries that have not shared a common past; nor do they necessarily seem destined for a common future. Cameroon, Chad, Central African Republic, Congo (Congo-Brazzaville), the Democratic Republic of the Congo (the D.R.C., or Congo-Kinshasa, formerly known as Zaire), Equatorial Guinea, Gabon, and São Tomé and Príncipe are not always grouped together as one region. Indeed, users of this volume who are familiar with the continent may also associate the label "Central Africa" with such states as Angola and Zambia rather than with some of the states mentioned here. Geographically, Chad is more closely associated with the Sahelian nations of West Africa than with the heavily forested regions of Central Africa to its south. Similarly, the southern part of Democratic Republic of Congo has long-standing cultural and economic links with Angola and Zambia, which in this text are associated with the states of Southern Africa, largely because of their political involvements.

Yet the eight countries that are designated here as belonging to Central Africa have much in common. French is a predominant language in all the states except Equatorial Guinea and São Tomé and Príncipe. All except São Tomé and Príncipe and the Democratic Republic of the Congo share a common currency, the CFA franc. And while Chad's current economic prospects appear to be exceptionally poor, the natural wealth found throughout the rest of Central Africa makes the region as a whole one of enormous potential. Finally, in the postcolonial era, all the Central African governments have made some progress in realizing their developmental possibilities through greater regional cooperation.

The countries of Central Africa incorporate a variety of peoples and cultures, resources, environments, systems of government, and national goals. Most of the modern nations overlay both societies that were village-based and localized, and societies that were once part of extensive state formations. Islam has had little influence in the region, except in Chad and northern Cameroon. In most areas, Christianity coexists with indigenous systems of belief. Sophisticated wooden sculptures are one of the cultural achievements associated with most Central African societies. To many people, the carvings are only material manifestations of the spiritual potential of complex local cosmologies. However, the art forms are myriad and distinctive, and their diversity is as striking as the common features that they share.

The postcolonial governments of Central Africa have ranged from outwardly conservative regimes (in Gabon and the Democratic Republic of Congo) to self-proclaimed revolutionary Marxist-Leninist orders (in Congo and São Tomé and Príncipe). More fundamentally, all of the states in the region have in the past fallen under the control of unelected autocracies, whose continued existence has been dependent on the coercive capacities of military forces—sometimes external ones. But the authoritarian status quo has been challenged in recent years. In Central African Republic, Congo, Democratic Republic of the Congo, and São Tomé and Príncipe, democratic openings have

(United Nations photo 117,717)

In Africa, cooperative work groups such as the one pictured above often take on jobs that would be done by machinery in industrialized countries.

resulted in the peaceful election of new governments. However, the elected government in Congo has since been overthrown by forces loyal to its former dictator. Elsewhere in the region, opposition parties have been legalized but otherwise have made limited progress.

GEOGRAPHIC DISTINCTIVENESS

All the states of the Central African region except Chad encompass equatorial rain forests. Citizens who live in these regions must cope with a climate that is hot and moist while facing the challenges of utilizing (and in some cases, unfortunately, clearing) the resources of the great forests. The problems of living in these areas account, in part, for the relatively low,

(United Nations photo)

Regional cooperation will be necessary to utilize the natural resources of Central African countries without damaging their precious but fragile environment. Environmentalists warn that the Central African forests are rapidly being destroyed.

albeit growing, population densities of most of the states. The difficulty of establishing roads and railroads impedes communication and thus economic development. The peoples of the rain-forest areas tend to cluster along riverbanks and existing rail lines. In modern times, largely because of the extensive development of minerals, many inhabitants have moved to the cities, accounting for a comparatively high urban population in all the states.

Central Africa's rivers have long been its lifelines. The watershed in Cameroon between the Niger and Congo (or Zaire) Rivers provides a natural divide between the West and Central African regions. The Congo River is the largest in the region,

but the Oubangi, Chari, Ogooue, and other rivers are important also for the communication and trading opportunities they offer. The rivers flow to the Atlantic Ocean, a fact that has encouraged the orientation of Central Africa's external trade toward Europe and the Americas.

Many of the countries of the region have similar sources of wealth. The rivers are capable of generating enormous amounts of hydropower. The rain forests are also rich in lumber, which is a major export of most of the countries. Other forest products, such as rubber and palm oil, are widely marketed.

Extensive lumbering and clearing activities for agriculture, have created worldwide concern about the depletion of the rain

(United Nations photo 71673)

Refugees from the conflict in the Republic of the Congo are seen here in the make-shift living quarters that they erected in the area allotted to them outside Elizabethville.

forests. As a result, in recent years there have been some organized boycotts in Europe of the region's hardwood exports, although far more trees are felled to process plywood.

As one might expect, Central Africa as a whole is one of the areas least affected by the drought conditions that periodically plague Africa. Nevertheless, serious drought is a well-known visitor in Chad, Central African Republic, and the northern regions of Cameroon, where it contributes to local food shortages. Savanna lands are found in some parts lying to the north and the south of the forests. Whereas rain forests have often inhibited travel, the savannas have long been transitional areas, great avenues of migration linking the regions of Africa, while providing agricultural and pastoral opportunities for their residents.

The Central African countries share other resources besides the products of the rain forest. Cameroon, Congo, and Gabon derive considerable revenues from their petroleum reserves. Other important minerals include diamonds, copper, gold, manganese, and uranium. The processes involved in the exploitation of these commodities, as well as the demand for them in the world market, are issues of common concern among the producing nations. Many of the states also share an interest in exported cash crops such as coffee, cocoa, and cotton, whose international prices are subject to sharp fluctuations.

The similarity of their environments and products provides an economic incentive for Central African cooperation.

LINKS TO FRANCE

Many of the different ethnic groups in Central Africa overlap national boundaries. Examples include the Fang, who are found in Cameroon, Equatorial Guinea, and Gabon; the Bateke of Congo and Gabon; and the BaKongo, who are concentrated in Angola as well as in Congo and the Democratic Republic of the Congo. Such cross-border ethnic ties are less important as sources of regional unity than the European colonial systems that the countries inherited. While Equatorial Guinea was controlled by Spain, São Tomé and Príncipe by Portugal, and the D.R.C. by Belgium, the predominant external power in the region remains France. Central African Republic, Chad, Congo, and Gabon were all once part of French Equatorial Africa. Most of Cameroon was also governed by the French, who were awarded the bulk of the former German colony of the Kamerun as a "trust territory" in the aftermath of World War I. French administration provided the five states with similar colonial experiences.

Early colonial development in the former French colonies and the Democratic Republic of the Congo was affected by

13

(United Nations photo 96708)

Here, in the Democratic Republic of the Congo, a bulldozer levels an access road to the Kamnyola Bridge over the Livumvi River.

European "concessions" companies, institutions that were sold extensive rights (often 99-year leases granting political as well as economic powers) to exploit such local products as ivory and rubber. At the beginning of the twentieth century, just 41 companies controlled 70 percent of all of the territory of contemporary Central African Republic, Congo, and Gabon. Mining operations as well as large plantations were established that often relied on forced labor. Individual production by Africans was also encouraged, often through coercion rather than economic incentives. While the colonial companies encouraged production and trade, they did little to aid the growth of infrastructure or long-term development. Only in the D.R.C. was industry promoted to any great extent.

In general, French colonial rule, along with that of the Belgians, Portuguese, and Spanish and the activities of the companies, offered few opportunities for Africans to gain training and education. There was also little encouragement of local entrepreneurship. An important exception to this pattern was the policies pursued by Felix Eboue, a black man from French Guiana (in South America) who served as a senior administrator in the Free French administration of French Equatorial Africa during the 1940s. Eboue increased opportunities for the urban elite in Central African Republic, Congo, and Gabon. He also played an important role in the Brazzaville Conference of 1944, which, recognizing the part that the people of the French colonies had played in World War II, abolished forced labor and granted citizenship to all. Yet political progress toward self-government was uneven. Because of the lack of local labor development, there

were too few people at independence who were qualified to shoulder the bureaucratic and administrative tasks of the regimes that took power. People who could handle the economic institutions for the countries' benefit were equally scarce. And in any case, the nations' economies remained for the most part securely in outside—largely French—hands.

The Spanish on the Equatorial Guinea island of Fernando Po, and the Portuguese of São Tomé and Príncipe, also profited from their exploitation of forced labor. Political opportunities in these territories were even more limited than on the African mainland. Neither country gained independence until fairly recently: Equatorial Guinea in 1968, São Tomé and Príncipe in 1975.

In the years since independence, most of the countries of Central Africa have been influenced, pressured, and supported by France and the other former colonial powers. French firms in Central African Republic, Congo, and Gabon continue to dominate the exploitation of local resources. Most of these companies are only slightly encumbered by the regulations of the independent states in which they operate, and all are geared toward European markets and needs. Financial institutions are generally branches of French institutions, and all the former French colonies as well as Equatorial Guinea are members of the Central African Franc (CFA) Zone. French expatriates occupy senior positions in local civil-service establishments and in companies; many more of them are resident in the region today than was true 30 years ago. In addition, French troops are stationed in Central African Republic, Chad, and Gabon, regimes that owe their very existence to past French military interventions. Besides being a major trading partner, France has contributed significantly to the budgets of its former possessions, especially the poorer states of Central African Republic and Chad.

Despite having been under Belgian rule, the Democratic Republic of the Congo is an active member of the Francophonic bloc in Africa. In 1977, French troops put down a rebellion in the southeastern part of Zaire (as the D.R.C. was then known). Zaire, in turn, sent its troops to serve beside those of France in Chad and Togo. Since playing a role in the 1979 coup that brought the current regime to power, France has also had a predominant influence in Equatorial Guinea.

REGIONAL COOPERATION AND CONFLICT

Although many Africans in Central Africa recognize that closer links among their countries would be beneficial, there have been fewer initiatives toward political unity or economic integration in this region than in East, West, or Southern Africa. In the years before independence, Barthelemy Boganda, of what is now Central African Republic, espoused and publicized the idea of a "United States of Latin Africa," which was to include Angola and Zaire as well as the territories of French Equatorial Africa, but he was frustrated by Paris as well as by local politicians. When France offered independence to its colonies in 1960, soon after Boganda's death, the possibility of forming a federation was discussed. But Gabon, which was wealthier than the other countries, declined to participate. Central African Republic, Chad, and Congo drafted an agreement that would have created a federal legislature and executive branch governing all three countries, but local jealousies defeated this plan.

There have been some formal efforts at economic integration among the former French states. The Customs and Economic Union of the Central African States (UDEAC) was established in 1964, but its membership has been unstable. Chad and Central African Republic withdrew to join Zaire in an alternate organization. (Central African Republic later returned, bringing the number of members to six.) The East and Central African states together planned an "Economic Community" in 1967, but it never materialized.

In the 1980s there were efforts to make greater progress toward economic cooperation. Urged on by the United Nations Economic Commission for Africa, and with the stimulus of the Lagos Plan of Action, representatives of Central African states met in 1982 to prepare for a new economic grouping. In 1983, all the Central African states as well as Rwanda and Burundi in East Africa signed a treaty establishing the Economic Community of Central African States (ECCA). ECCA's goals were broader than those of UDEAC. Members hoped that the union would stimulate industrial activity, increase markets, and reduce the dependence on France and other countries for trade and capital. But with dues often unpaid and meetings postponed, ECCA has so far failed to meet its potential.

Hopes that the Central African states could work collectively toward a brighter future have been further compromised by the spread in recent years of extreme political instability and brutal and far-reaching armed conflicts both within and between states in the region. This is particularly true of the ongoing civil war in the region's biggest state, the Democratic Republic of the Congo; this war has not only divided the region but has involved states as far afield as Libya, Nigeria, Zimbabwe, and South Africa.

In the mid-1990s, there was a growing optimism that democratization might enable the region to become a center of a continental renaissance. This view was greatly boosted by the fall of the corrupt, authoritarian regime of Mobutu Sese Seko, which led to the nominal transformation of Zaire into the Democratic Republic of the Congo. But such hopes suffered a serious setback with the resurgence of dictatorship and kleptocracy under Mobutu's successor, Laurent Kabila, who remained in power through external backers and through implicit appeals for genocide against ethnic groups perceived as his enemies. With such continued divide-and-misrule, the chances of Boganda's vision becoming a reality appeared more remote. But since the assassination of Laurent Kabila and the rise of his son Joseph Kabila in the D.R.C., prospects for peace in Central Africa's largest state seem realistic. After years of autocracy, there is an opportunity for a long-term cease-fire and cessation of hostilities among the warring factions within the region. Most notably, by the end of 2002, foreign state military forces had largely pulled out of the country. Regional initiatives may have failed in the past, but this is not to say that there will not be more effective cooperation in the future. The key element for the creation of new regional organizations rests in the ability of the Central African states to sit at a negotiating table and recognize the existence of their common interest. In this respect, peace in the D.R.C. represents the best hope for stability and development in Central Africa.

Cameroon (Republic of Cameroon)

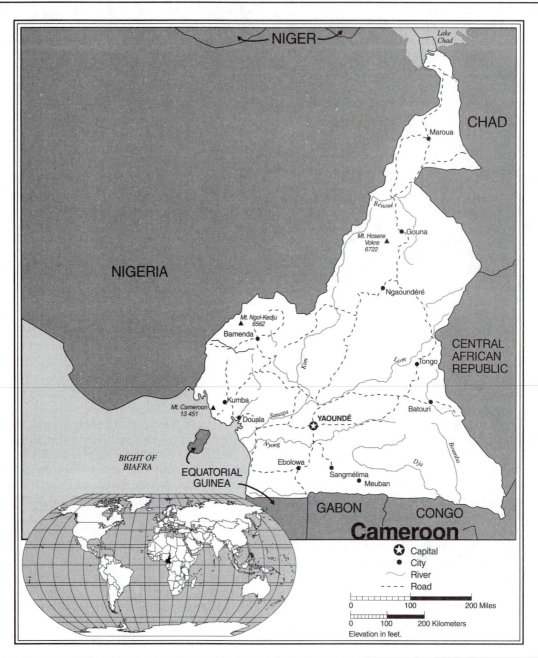

Cameroon Statistics

GEOGRAPHY

Area in Square Miles (Kilometers):
183,568 (475,400) (about the size of California)

Capital (Population): Yaoundé (1,248,200)

Environmental Concerns: deforestation; overgrazing; desertification; poaching; overfishing; water-borne disease

Geographical Features: diverse, with coastal plain in southwest, dissected plain in center, mountains in west, and plains in north

Climate: from tropical to semiarid

PEOPLE

Population

Total: 18.6 million

Annual Growth Rate: 2.2%

Rural/Urban Population Ratio: 53/47

Major Languages: English; French; Fulde; Ewondo; Duala; Bamelke; Bassa; Bali; others

Ethnic Makeup: 31% Cameroonian Highlander; 19% Equatorial Bantu; 11% Kirdi; 10% Fulani; 29% others

Religions: 40% indigenous beliefs; 40% Christian; 20% Muslim

Health

Life Expectancy at Birth: 52.15 years (male); 53.59 years (female)

Infant Mortality: 74/1,000 live births
Physicians Available: 1/11,848 people
HIV/AIDS Rate in Adults: 5.4%

Education

Adult Literacy Rate: 67.9%
Compulsory (Ages): 6–12; free

COMMUNICATION

Telephones: 100,300 main lines
Televisions: 72/1,000 people
Internet Users: 370,000

TRANSPORTATION

Highways in Miles (Kilometers): 30,000 (50,000)
Railroads in Miles (Kilometers): 693 (1,111)
Usable Airfields: 47
Motor Vehicles in Use: 173,000 (2003)

GOVERNMENT

Type: unitary republic
Independence Date: January 1, 1960 (from UN trusteeship under French administration)

Head of State/Government: President Paul Biya; Prime Minister Ephraim Inoni
Political Parties: Cameroonian Democratic Union; Cameroon People's Democratic Movement; Movement for the Defense of the Republic; Movement for the Liberation and Development of Cameroon; National Union for Democracy and Progress; others
Suffrage: universal at 20

MILITARY

Military Expenditures (% of GDP): 1.3%
Current Disputes: various border conflicts, especially with Nigeria

ECONOMY

Currency ($ U.S. equivalent): 464.16 CFA francs = $1
Per Capita Income/GDP: $1,700/$19.2 billion
GDP Growth Rate: 3.9%

Inflation Rate: 3.0%
Unemployment Rate: 30%
Labor Force by Occupation: 70% agriculture; 13% industry and commerce; 17% other
Population Below Poverty Line: 48%
Natural Resources: petroleum; timber; bauxite; iron ore; hydropower
Agriculture: coffee; cocoa; cotton; rubber; bananas; oilseed; grain; roots; livestock; timber
Industry: petroleum production and refining; food processing; light consumer goods; textiles; lumber
Exports: $4.32 billion (primary partners Spain, Italy, France, Netherlands)
Imports: $3.08 billion (primary partners France, Nigeria, China, Belgium)

SUGGESTED WEB SITES

http://www.sas.upenn.edu/African_Studies/Country_Specific/Cameroon.html
http://www.cameroon.net
http://www.telp.com/cameroon/home.htm

Cameroon Country Report

Over the past decade, Cameroonians have been united by at least two things: support for their world-class national soccer team, the Indomitable Lions, and condemnation of neighboring Nigeria about a long-simmering border dispute over the Bakassi Peninsula. The latter conflict was referred by both countries to the International Court of Justice for resolution. But when the Court ruled in Cameroon's favor in October 2002, the government of Nigeria reneged on its previous agreement to accept the verdict. In August 2003, after talks in Cameroon, Nigeria said that it would not hand over the Bakassi Peninsula for at least three years. Yet in December 2003, Nigeria did in fact hand over 32 villages to Cameroon as part of the 2002 International Court of Justice's ruling. In January 2004, Nigeria agreed to have joint border patrols with Cameroon.

Although it claims to operate a multi-party democracy, freedom of expression is severely limited in Cameroon. Politically, Cameroonians are deeply divided. During the October 2004 general elections, incumbent president Paul Biya was once again reelected by a large majority, even with many of the opposition parties boycotting. The poll, which was boycotted by the largest opposition parties, was a followup to the controversial elections of March 1992,

which ended a quarter-century of one-party rule by Biya's Cameroon People's Democratic Party (CPDM). Although the CPDM relinquished its monopoly of power, it retained control of the government. With a plurality of 88 out of 180 seats, the CPDM was able to form a coalition government with the Movement for the Defense of Democracy, which won six seats. Two other parties, the National Union for Democracy and Progress (UNDP) and the Union of Cameroonian Populations (UPC), divided most of the remaining seats.

DEVELOPMENT

The Cameroon Development Corporation coordinates more than half of the agricultural exports and, after the government, employs the most people. Cocoa and coffee comprise more than 50% of Cameroon's exports. Lower prices for these commodities in recent years have reduced the country's income.

Like the 1998 elections, the legitimacy of the 1992 poll was compromised by the boycott of some opposition parties—most notably the Social Democratic Front (SDF), the Democratic Union (CDU), and a faction of the UPC—allowing the CPDM

to win numerous constituencies by default. The situation was later aggravated, in October 1992, when the CPDM's Paul Biya was declared the victor in a snap election accompanied by opposition allegations of vote rigging. The overwhelming victory of the ruling party in the July 2007 legislative election has reinforced the position of the 74-year-old president, Paul Biya. It is expected that the ruling party will pass the constitutional amendments that will allow Mr. Biya to stand for re-election in 2011.

Cameroon's fractious politics is partially a reflection of its diversity. In geographical terms, the land is divided between the tropical forests in the south, the drier savanna of the north-central region, and the mountainous country along its western border, which forms a natural division between West and Central Africa. In terms of religion, the country has many Christians, Muslims, and followers of indigenous belief systems. More than a dozen major languages, with numerous dialects, are spoken. The languages of southern Cameroon are linguistically classified as Bantu. The "Bantu line" that runs across the country, roughly following the course of the Sanaga River, forms a boundary between the Bantu languages of Central, East, and Southern Africa and the non-Bantu tongues of North and

(United Nations photo 152,295 by Shaw McCutcheon)

Cameroon has experienced political unrest in recent years as various factions have moved to establish a stable form of government. At the heart of the political turmoil is the need to raise the living standards of the population through an increase in agricultural production. These farmers with their cattle herds are one part of this movement.

West Africa. Many scholars believe that the roots of the Bantu language tree are buried in Cameroonian soil. Cameroon is also unique among the continental African states in sharing two European languages, English and French, as its official mediums. Relations between Anglophone and Francophone Cameroon have been troubled in recent years. In October 2001, violence flared between government security forces and protesters favoring the separation of English-speaking Cameroon.

Cameroon's use of both English and French is a product of its unique colonial heritage. Three European powers have ruled over Cameroon. The Germans were the first. From 1884 to 1916, they laid the foundation of much of the country's communications infrastructure and, primarily through the establishment of European-run plantations, export agriculture. During World War I, the area was divided between the British and French, who subsequently ruled their respective zones as League of Nations (later the United Nations) mandates. French "Cameroun" included the eastern four fifths of the former German colony, while British "Cameroon" consisted of two narrow strips of territory that were administered as part of its Nigerian territory.

In the 1950s, Cameroonians in both the British and French zones began to agitate for unity and independence. At the core of their nationalist vision was the "Kamerun Idea," a belief that the period of German rule had given rise to a pan-Cameroonian identity. The largest and most radical of the nationalist movements in the French zone was the Union of the Cameroonian People, which turned to armed struggle. Between 1955 and 1963, when most of the UPC guerrillas were defeated, some 10,000 to 15,000 people were killed. Most of the victims belonged to the Bamileke and Bassa ethnic groups of southwestern Cameroon, which continues to be the core area of UPC support. (Some sources refer to the UPC uprising as the Bamileke Rebellion.)

FREEDOM

While Cameroon's human-rights record has improved since its return to multipartyism, political detentions and harassment continue. Amnesty International has drawn attention to the alleged starvation of detainees at the notorious Tchollire prison. Furthermore, the nation's vibrant free press has become a prime target of repression, with several editors arrested in 1998.

To counter the UPC revolt, the French adopted a dual policy of repression against the guerrillas' supporters and the devolution of political power to local non-UPC politicians. Most of these "moderate" leaders, who enjoyed core followings in both the heavily Christianized southeast and the Muslim north, coalesced as the Cameroonian Union, whose leader was Ahmadou Ahidjo, a northerner. In pre-independence elections, Ahidjo's party won just 51 out of the 100 seats. Ahidjo thus led a divided, war-torn state to independence in 1960.

In 1961, the southern section of British Cameroon voted to join Ahidjo's republic. The northern section opted to remain part of Nigeria. The principal party in the south was the Kamerun National Democratic Party, whose leader, John Foncha, became the vice president of the Cameroon republic, while Ahidjo served as president. The former British and French zones initially maintained their separate local parliaments, but the increasingly authoritarian Ahidjo pushed for a unified form of government. In 1966, all of Cameroon's legal political groups were dissolved into Ahidjo's new Cameroon National Union (CNU), creating a de facto one-party state. Trade unions and other mass organizations were also brought under CNU control. In

18

1972, Ahidjo proposed the abolition of the federation and the creation of a constitution for a unified Cameroon. This was approved by a suspiciously lopsided vote of 3,217,058 to 158.

In 1982, Ahidjo, believing that his health was graver than was actually the case, suddenly resigned. His handpicked successor was Paul Biya. To the surprise of many, the heretofore self-effacing Biya quickly proved to be his own man. He brought young technocrats into the ministries and initially called for a more open and democratic society. But as he pressed forward, Biya came into increasing conflict with Ahidjo, who tried to reassert his authority as CNU chairman. The ensuing power struggle took on overtones of an ethnic conflict between Biya's largely southern Christian supporters and Ahidjo's core following of northern Muslims. In 1983, Ahidjo lost and went into exile. The next year, he was tried and convicted, in absentia, for allegedly plotting Biya's overthrow.

HEALTH/WELFARE

The overall literacy rate in Cameroon, about 67.9%, is among the highest in Africa. There exists, however, great disparity in regional figures as well as between males and females. In addition to public schools, the government devotes a large proportion of its budget to subsidizing private schools.

In April 1984, only two months after the conviction, Ahidjo's supporters in the Presidential Guard attempted to overthrow Biya. The revolt was put down, but up to 1,000 people were killed. In the coup's aftermath, Biya combined repression with attempts to restructure the ruling apparatus. In 1985, the CNU was overhauled as the Cameroon People's Democratic Movement. However, President Biya became increasingly reliant on the support of his own Beti group.

An upsurge of prodemocracy agitation began in 1990. In March, the Social

Democratic Front was formed in Bamenda, the main town of the Anglophonic west, over government objections. In May, as many as 40,000 people from the vicinity of Bamenda, out of a total population of about 100,000, attended an SDF rally. Government troops opened fire on school children returning from the demonstration. This action led to a wave of unrest, which spread to the capital city of Yaoundé. The government media tried to portray the SDF as a subversive movement of "English speakers," but it attracted significant support in Francophonic areas. Dozens of additional opposition groups, including the UNDP (which is loyal to the now-deceased Ahidjo's legacy) and the long-underground UPC, joined forces with the SDF in calling for a transition government, a new constitution, and multiparty elections.

Throughout much of 1991, Cameroon's already depressed economy was further crippled by opposition mass action, dubbed the "Ghost Town Campaign." A series of concessions by Biya culminated in a November agreement between Biya and most of the opposition (the SDF being among the holdouts) to formulate a new constitution and prepare for elections.

ACHIEVEMENTS

The strong showing by Cameroon's national soccer team, the Indomitable Lions, in the 1990 and 1994 World Cup competitions is a source of pride for sports fans throughout Africa. Their success, along with the record numbers of medals won by African athletes in the 1988 and 1992 Olympics, is symbolic of the continent's coming of age in international sports competitions.

One unrealized hope has been that democratic reform would help move Cameroon away from its consistent Transparency International rating as one of the world's most corrupt countries. Endemic corruption has become associated with environmental degradation. In recent years

conservationists have been especially concerned about the construction of an oil pipeline, funded by the World Bank, without an environmental-impact study, and the allocation of about 80 percent of the country's forest for logging.

Timeline: PAST

1884
The establishment of the German Kamerun Protectorate

1916
The partition of Cameroon; separate British and French mandates are established under the League of Nations

1955
The UPC (formed in 1948) is outlawed for launching revolts in the cities

1960
The Independent Cameroon Republic is established, with Ahmadou Ahidjo as the first president

1961
The Cameroon Federal Republic reunites French Cameroon with British Cameroon after a UN-supervised referendum

1972
The new Constitution creates a unitary state

1980s
Ahidjo resigns and is replaced by Paul Biya; Lake Nyos releases lethal volcanic gases, killing an estimated 2,000 people

1990s
Nationwide agitation for a restoration of multiparty democracy; Biya retains the presidency in disputed elections

PRESENT

2000s
New clashes over the Bakassi Peninsula. Longtime leader Paul Biya won a new seven-year term in presidential elections in October 2004, with more than 70% of the vote. Opposition parties alleged widespread fraud; in August 2006, Nigeria handed over the disputed oil-rich Bakassi Peninsula to Cameroon. Nigerian troops completed their withdrawal and transferred control of the northern part of the territory.

Central African Republic

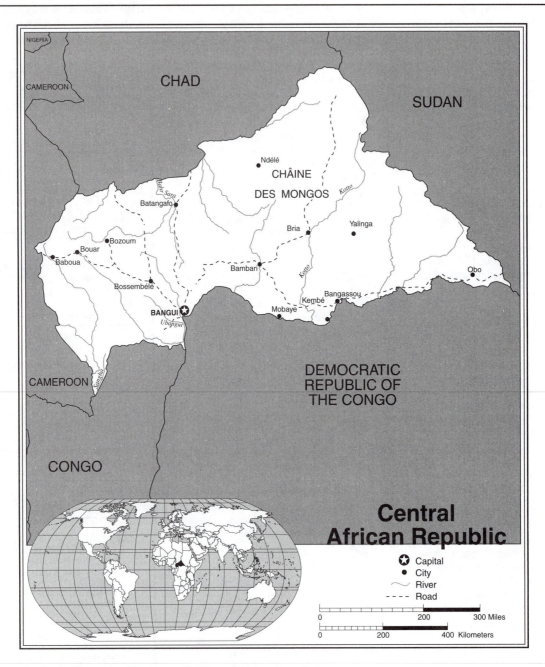

Central African Republic Statistics

GEOGRAPHY

Area in Square Miles (Kilometers): 240,324 (662,436) (about the size of Texas)
Capital (Population): Bangui (666,000)
Environmental Concerns: poaching; desertification; deforestation; potable water
Geographical Features: vast, flat to rolling, monotonous plateau; scattered hills in the northeast and southwest; landlocked
Climate: tropical

PEOPLE

Population

Total: 4,369,038
Annual Growth Rate: 1.51%
Rural/Urban Population Ratio: 62/38
Major Languages: French; Songo; Arabic; Hunsa; Swahili
Ethnic Makeup: 33% Baya; 27% Banda; 13% Mandja; 10% Sara; 17% others

Religions: 35% indigenous beliefs; 25% Protestant; 25% Roman Catholic; 15% Muslim

Health

Life Expectancy at Birth: 43.69 years (male); 43.79 years (female)
Infant Mortality: 83.97/1,000 live births
Physicians Available: 1/18,660 people
HIV/AIDS Rate in Adults: 13.5%

Education

Adult Literacy Rate: 51%
Compulsory (Ages): 6–14

COMMUNICATION

Telephones: 10,000 main lines
Televisions: 5/1,000 people
Internet Users: 13,000 (2006)

TRANSPORTATION

Highways in Miles (Kilometers): 14,286 (23,810)
Railroads in Miles (Kilometers): none
Usable Airfields: 51
Motor Vehicles in Use: 20,000

GOVERNMENT

Type: republic
Independence Date: August 13, 1960 (from France)

Head of State/Government: President Francois Bozize; Prime Minister Elie Dote
Political Parties: Movement for the Liberation of the Central African People; Central African Democratic Assembly; Movement for Democracy and Development; others
Suffrage: universal at 21

MILITARY

Military Expenditures (% of GDP): 1.1%
Current Disputes: internal strife

ECONOMY

Currency ($ U.S. Equivalent): 464.16 CFA francs = $1
Per Capita Income/GDP: $1,300/$4.6 billion
GDP Growth Rate: 3.5%
Inflation Rate: 6.7%

Unemployment Rate: 8%
Natural Resources: diamonds; uranium; timber; gold; petroleum; hydropower
Agriculture: cotton; coffee; tobacco; manioc; millet; corn; bananas; timber
Industry: diamond mining; sawmills; breweries; textiles; footwear; assembly of bicycles and motorcycles
Exports: $112 million (primary partners Benelux, Côte d'Ivoire, Spain)
Imports: $295.4 million (primary partners France, Cameroon, Benelux)

SUGGESTED WEB SITES

http://www.sas.upenn.edu/African_Studies/Country_Specific/Cent-A-R.html
http://www.emulateme.com/car.htm

Central African Republic Country Report

In March 2003, the government of the Central African Republic (CAR) was overthrown when rebels loyal to former Army chief-of-staff General François Bozize seized control of the capital, Bangui. The country's president, Ange-Félix Patassé, was out of the country at the time. For many years Patassé, elected in 1993 and reelected in 1998, had struggled to bring political and financial stability to the poor, landlocked country, following three decades of military dictatorship. He failed.

In 1996, the French military rescued the government from an army mutiny. The intervention was resented by many as a sign of France's continuing control. A national-reconciliation agreement was signed in March 1998 allowing UN peacekeepers to oversee elections in 1999 and the training of a new army.

DEVELOPMENT

C.A.R.'s timber industry has suffered from corruption and environmentally destructive forms of exploitation. However, the nation has considerable forestry potential, with dozens of commercially viable and renewable species of trees.

But in 2000, further unrest was sparked by government's failure to pay civil servants their back wages, resulting in a general strike

organized by 15 opposition groups. In May 2001, Patass survived an attempted coup, with the help of Libyan, Chadian, and Congolese rebel forces. Former president André Kolingba and Army chief-of-staff Bozize led the coup. Thereafter a curfew was instituted, which was lifted a year later. The lifting of the curfew was meant to signal the return of "security and peace." But in October 2002, rebels loyal to Bozize seized control of much of Bangui before being driven out by Libyan and progovernment forces.

Since gaining independence in 1960, the political, economic, and military presence of France has remained pervasive in C.A.R. At the same time, the country's natural resources, as well as French largess, have been dissipated. Yet with diamonds, timber, and a resilient peasantry, the country is better endowed than many of its neighbors. In recent years, Libya has taken a special interest in the country's mostly still untapped natural wealth.

C.A.R.'s population has traditionally been divided between the so-called river peoples and savanna peoples, but most are united by the Songo language. What the country has lacked is a leadership committed to national development rather than to internationally sanctioned waste.

BOGANDA'S VISION

In 1959, as Central African Republic moved toward independence, Barthelemy Boganda, a former priest and the leader of the territory's nationalist movement, did not share the

euphoria exhibited by many of his colleagues. To him, the French path to independence was a trap. Where there once had been a united French Equatorial Africa (A.E.F.), there were now five separate states, each struggling toward its own nationhood. Boganda had led the struggle to transform the territory into a true Central African Republic. But in 1958, French president Charles de Gaulle overruled all objections in forcing the breakup of the A.E.F. Boganda believed that, thus balkanized, the Central African states would each be too weak to achieve true independence, but he still hoped that A.E.F. reunification might prove possible after independence.

FREEDOM

C.A.R.'s human-rights record remains poor. Its security forces are linked to summary executions and torture. Other human-rights abuses include harsh prison conditions, arbitrary arrest, detention without trial, and restrictions on freedom of assembly. President Patassé granted amnesty to former senior officials of the Kolingba regime and mutineers.

In 1941, Boganda had founded the Popular Movement for the Social Evolution of Black Africa (MESAN). While Boganda was a pragmatist willing to use moderate means in his struggle, his vision was radical, for he hoped to unite French, Belgian, and Portuguese territories into an independent republic. His movement succeeded in gaining a local following among the peasantry as well as intellectuals. In 1958, Boganda led the territory to self-government, but he died in a mysterious plane crash just before independence.

Boganda's successors have failed to live up to his stature. At independence, David Dacko, a nephew of Boganda's who succeeded to the leadership of MESAN but also cultivated the political support of local French settlers who had seen Boganda as an agitator, led the country. Dacko's MESAN became the vehicle of the wealthy elite.

HEALTH/WELFARE

The literacy rate is low in Central African Republic—51%. Teacher training is currently being emphasized, especially for primary-school teachers. Poaching has diminished C.A.R.'s reputation as one of the world's last great wildlife refuges.

A general strike in December 1965 was followed by a military coup on New Year's Eve, which put Dacko's cousin, Army Commander Jean-Bedel Bokassa, in power. Dacko's overthrow was justified by the need to launch political and economic reforms. But more likely motives for the coup were French concern about Dacko's growing ties with China and Bokassa's own budding megalomania.

The country suffered greatly under Bokassa's eccentric rule. During the 1970s, he was often portrayed, alongside Idi Amin of Uganda, as an archetype of African leadership at its worst. It was more the sensational nature of his brutality—such as public torture and dismemberment of prisoners—rather than its scale that captured headlines. In 1972, he made himself "president-for-life." Unsatisfied with this position, in 1976 he proclaimed himself emperor, in the image of his hero Napoleon Bonaparte. The French government underwrote the $22 million spent on his coronation ceremony, which attracted widespread coverage in the global media.

In 1979, reports surfaced that Bokassa himself had participated in the beating deaths of schoolchildren who had protested his decree that they purchase new uniforms bearing his portrait. The French government

ACHIEVEMENTS

Despite recurrent drought, a poor infrastructure, and inefficient official marketing, the farmers of Central African Republic have generally been able to meet most of the nation's basic food needs.

finally decided that its ally had become a liability. While Bokassa was away on a state visit to Libya, French paratroopers returned Dacko to power. In 1981, Dacko was once more toppled, in a coup that installed Prime Minister (General) Andr Kolingba. In 1985, Kolingba's provisional military regime was transformed into a one-party state. But in 1991, under a combination of local and French pressure, he agreed to the legalization of opposition parties.

In March 2003, Rebel leader François Bozize seized the capital city, Bangui, and declared himself president, ousting President Ange-Felix Patasše, who was out of the country at the time. Upon assent to the presidency, Bozize drafted a new constitution followed by elections in 2005, in which François Bozize was named the winner of presidential elections. However, rebel factions disagreed with the results, and political instability continues to undermine the economy.

Thus, with an ongoing history of coups, army mutinies, and endemic corruption, CAR continues to lag behind as one of the least developed countries in Africa. The government continues to struggle to pay wages to those working for it. In 2003, a pan-African military force was put in place to restore order, but violence and lawlessness continues unabated in some parts of the country, especially in the northwest CAR with refugees forced to flee into Chad and Sudan.

Pressure for multiparty politics had increased as the government sank deeper into debt, despite financial intervention on the part of France, the World Bank, and the International Monetary Fund. Landlocked C.A.R.'s economy has long been constrained by high transport costs. But a perhaps greater burden has been the smuggling of its diamonds and other resources, including poached ivory, by officials who are high up in the government.

Timeline: PAST

1904
Separate French administration of the Oubangui-Chàri colony is established

1912–1913
Gold and diamonds are discovered

1949
Barthelemy Boganda sets up MESAN, which gains wide support

1960
Boganda dies; David Dacko, his successor, becomes president at independence

1966
Jean-Bedel Bokassa takes power after the first general strike

1976
Bokassa declares himself emperor

1979
Bokassa is involved in the massacre of schoolchildren; Dacko is returned as head of state

1981
André Kolingba takes power from Dacko

1990s
Ange-Félix Patassé wins the presidency; Patassé requires French intervention to overcome an army mutiny

PRESENT

2000s
General François Bozize overthrows the Patasše government

François Bozize is named the winner of presidential elections

Thousands flee lawlessness in northwest CAR for southern Chad

Rebels seize Birao, a town in the northeast. French fighter jets fire on rebel positions in support of government troops trying to regain control of areas in the northeast

The rebel People's Democratic Front, led by Abdoulaye Miskine, signs a peace accord with President Bozize in Libya and urges fighters to lay down their arms

Chad (Republic of Chad)

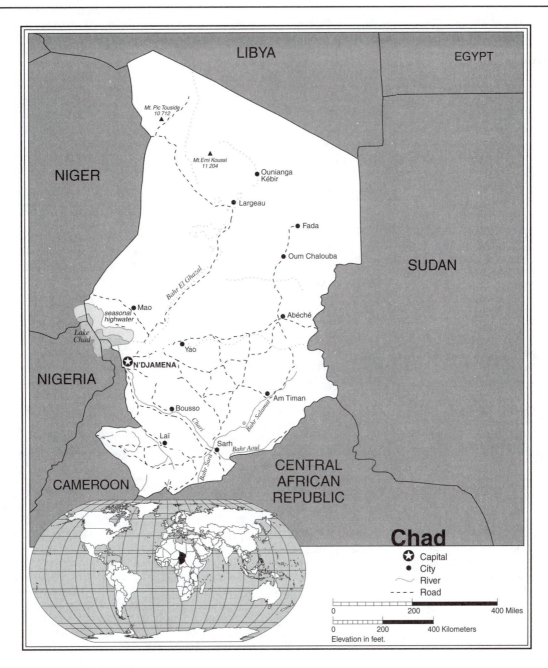

Chad Statistics

GEOGRAPHY

Area in Square Miles (Kilometers):
496,000 (1,284,634) (about 3 times the size of California)
Capital (Population): N'Djamena (826,000)
Environmental Concerns: soil and water pollution; desertification; insufficient potable water; waste disposal
Geographical Features: broad, arid plains in the center; desert in the north; mountains in the northwest; lowlands in the south; landlocked
Climate: tropical in the south; desert in the north

PEOPLE

Population

Total: 9,885,661
Annual Growth Rate: 2.32%
Rural/Urban Population Ratio: 79/21
Major Languages: French; Arabic; Sara; Sango; others
Ethnic Makeup: 200 distinct groups
Religions: 51% Muslim; 35% Christian; 7% animist; 7% others

Health

Life Expectancy at Birth: 46.17 years (male); 48.27 years (female)
Infant Mortality: 102.07/1,000 live births

GLOBAL STUDIES

Physicians Available: 1/27,765 people
HIV/AIDS Rate in Adults: 4.8%

Education

Adult Literacy Rate: 47.5%
Compulsory (Ages): 6–14

COMMUNICATION

Telephones: 13,000 main lines
Televisions: 8/1,000 people
Internet Users: 60,000 (2002)

TRANSPORTATION

Highways in Miles (Kilometers): 20,040
 (33,400 km)
Railroads in Miles (Kilometers): none
Usable Airfields: 52
Motor Vehicles in Use: 24,000

GOVERNMENT

Type: republic
Independence Date: August 11, 1960
 (from France)

Head of State/Government: President
 Idriss Déby; Prime Minister
 Nouradine Delwa Kassirek
 Koumakoye
Political Parties: Patriotic Salvation
 Movement; National Union for
 Development and Renewal; many
 others
Suffrage: universal at 18

MILITARY

Military Expenditures (% of GDP): 4.2%
Current Disputes: civil war; border
 conflicts over Lake Chad area

ECONOMY

Currency ($ U.S. equivalent): 465.51 CFA
 francs = $1
Per Capita Income/GDP: $1,500/$14.98
 billion
GDP Growth Rate: 8%
Inflation Rate: 3%

Labor Force by Occupation: 80%+
 agriculture
Population Below Poverty Line: 80%
Natural Resources: petroleum;
 uranium; natron; kaolin; fish (Lake
 Chad)
Agriculture: subsistence crops; cotton;
 peanuts; fish; livestock
Industry: livestock products; breweries;
 natron; soap; textiles; cigarettes;
 construction materials
Exports: $172 million (primary partners
 Portugal, Germany, Thailand)
Imports: $223 million (primary
 partners France, Nigeria,
 Cameroon)

SUGGESTED WEB SITES

http://www.chadembassy.org/site/index.cfm
http://www.sas.upenn.edu/African_
 Studies/Country_Specific/Chad
 .html

Chad Country Report

After decades of civil war between northern- and southern-based armed movements, in 1997 Chad completed its transition to civilian rule, under the firm guidance of its president, Idriss Déby. A former northern warlord who seized power in 1990, in 1996 Déby achieved a second-round victory in the country's first genuinely contested presidential elections since its independence in 1960. The result was seen as an endorsement of his government's gradual progress in rebuilding Chad's state structures, which had all but collapsed by the 1980s, when the fractured country was referred to as the "Lebanon of Africa."

DEVELOPMENT

Chad has potential petroleum and mineral wealth that would greatly help the economy if stable central government can be created. Deposits of chromium, tungsten, titanium, gold, uranium, and tin as well as oil are known to exist. Roads are in poor condition and are dangerous.

In June 2001, Chad's highest court confirmed Déby's reelection, after a controversial poll in which the results of about one quarter of the polling stations were cancelled due to alleged irregularities. Six unsuccessful candidates were briefly picked up for questioning by police after the poll. While

Déby's success—through both the ballot and bullet—in defeating, marginalizing, and/or reconciling rival factions has restored a semblance of statehood to Chad over the past five years, he continues to preside over a bankrupt government whose control over much of the countryside is tenuous.

In 1998, a new armed insurgency broke out in the north, led by former defense chief Youssouf Togoimi. In January 2002, a Libyan-brokered peace deal was agreed to by the government and Togoimi's rebels (known as the Movement for Democracy and Justice in Chad, or MDJT). But further clashes have put implementation of the peace agreement into jeopardy. The accord provides for a ceasefire, release of prisoners, integration of the rebels into the national army, and government positions for MDJT leaders.

Déby also faces continuing challenges to his control over the south, where there have been calls for Chad to become a federal, rather than unitary, state. Many in the south still resent the central government in the capital city of N'Djamena, believing it to represent predominantly northern interests. Ongoing fighting in Darfur in Sudan to the east and within the Central African Republic to the south could further destabilize the situation. In 2003 Chad received thousands of Sudanese refugees from Darfur fleeing ethnic Arab and ethnic African fighting who have now been

joined by thousands of Chadians fleeing rebel fighting within their own country. The fighting in Darfur has also spilled across the border into Chad.

CIVIL WAR

Chad's conflicts are partially rooted in the country's ethnic and religious divisions. It has been common for outsiders to portray the struggle as being between Arab-oriented Muslim northerners and black Christian southerners, but Chad's regional and ethnic allegiances are much more complex. Geographically, the country is better divided into three zones: the northern Sahara, a middle Sahel region, and the southern savanna.

FREEDOM

Despite some modest improvement, Chad's human-rights record remains poor. Its security forces are linked to torture, extra-judicial killings, beatings, disappearances, and rape. A recent Amnesty International report on Chad was entitled "Hope Betrayed." Antigovernment rebel forces are also accused of atrocities. The judiciary is not independent.

Within each of these ecological areas live peoples who speak different languages and engage in a variety of economic activities.

Wider ethno-regional and religious loyalties have emerged as a result of the Civil War, but such aggregates have tended to be fragile and their allegiances shifting.

At Chad's independence, France turned over power to François Tombalbaye, a Sara-speaking Christian southerner. Tombalbaye ruled with a combination of repression, ethnic favoritism, and incompetence, which quickly alienated his regime from broad sectors of the population. A northern-based coalition of armed groups, the National Liberation Front, or Frolinat, launched an increasingly successful insurgency. The intervention of French troops on Tombalbaye's behalf failed to stem the rebellion. In 1975, the army, tired of the war and upset by the president's increasingly conspicuous brutality, overthrew Tombalbaye and established a military regime, headed by Felix Malloum.

Malloum's government was also unable to defeat Frolinat; so, in 1978, it agreed to share power with the largest of the Frolinat groups, the Armed Forces of the North (FAN), led by Hissène Habré. This agreement broke down in 1979, resulting in fighting in N'Djamena. FAN came out ahead, while Malloum's men withdrew to the south. The triumph of the "northerners" immediately led to further fighting among various factions—some allied to Habré, others loyal to his main rival within the Frolinat, Goukkouni Oueddie. Earlier Habré had split from Oueddie, whom he accused of indifference toward Libya's unilateral annexation in 1976 of the Aouzou Strip, along Chad's northern frontier. At the time, Libya was the principal foreign backer of Frolinat.

In 1980, shortly after the last French forces withdrew from Chad, the Libyan Army invaded the country, at the invitation of Oueddie. Oueddie was then proclaimed the leader in a "Transitional Government of National Unity" (GUNT), which was established in N'Djamena. Nigeria and other neighboring states, joined by France and the United States, pressed for the withdrawal of the Libyan forces. This pressure grew in 1981 after Libyan leader Muammar al-Qadhafi announced the merger of Chad and Libya. Following a period of intense multinational negotiations, the Libyan military presence was reduced at Oueddie's request.

The removal of the Libyan forces from most of Chad was accompanied by revived fighting between GUNT and FAN, with the latter receiving substantial U.S. support, via Egypt and Sudan. A peacekeeping force assembled by the Organization of African Unity proved ineffectual. The collapse of GUNT in 1982 led to a second major Libyan invasion. The Libyan offensive was countered by the return of French forces, assisted by Zairian troops and by smaller contingents from several other Francophonic African countries. Between 1983 and 1987, the country was virtually partitioned along the 16th Parallel, with Habré's French-backed, FAN–led coalition in the south and the Libyan-backed remnants of GUNT in the north.

A political and military breakthrough occurred in 1987. Habré's efforts to unite the country led to a reconciliation with Malloum's followers and with elements within GUNT. Oueddie himself was apparently placed under house arrest in Libya. Emboldened, Habré launched a major offensive north of the 16th Parallel that rolled back the better-equipped Libyan forces, who by now included a substantial number of Lebanese mercenaries. A factor in the Libyan defeat was U.S.–supplied Stinger missiles, which allowed Habré's forces to neutralize Libya's powerful air force (Habré's government lacked significant air power of its own). A cease-fire was declared after the Libyans had been driven out of all of northern Chad with the exception of a portion of the disputed Aouzou Strip.

In 1988, Qadhafi announced that he would recognize the Habré government and pay compensation to Chad. The announcement was welcomed—with some skepticism—by Chadian and other African leaders, although no mention was made of the conflicting claims to the Aouzou Strip.

The long-running struggle for Chad took another turn in November 1990, with the sudden collapse of Habré's regime in the face of a three-week offensive by guerrillas loyal to his former army commander, Idriss Déby. Despite substantial Libyan (and Sudanese) backing for his seizure of power, Déby had the support of France, Nigeria, and the

Timeline: PAST

1960

Independence is achieved under President François Tombalbaye

1965–1966

Revolt breaks out among peasant groups; FROLINAT is formed

1978

Establishment of a Transitional Government of National Unity (GUNT) with Hissène Habré and Goukkouni Oueddie

1980s

Habré seizes power and reunites the country in a U.S.–supported war against Libya

1990s

Habré is overthrown by Idriss Déby; Déby promises to create a multiparty democracy, but conditions remain anarchic

PRESENT

2000s

Chad's northern provinces bordering Libya remain heavily landmined

Persistent armed insurgency in the north

Dèby is confirmed as reelected, after a controversial poll

Thousands of Sudanese refugees flee into Chad from Darfur in Sudan, and Chadian troops clash with pro-Sudanese government Arab Janjaweed militias as fighting in Sudan's Darfur region spills over the border and penetrates deeper into Chad

Chad and Sudan agree to stop conflict spilling across their borders, but violence continues unabated

Chad becomes an oil exporter through a pipeline connecting its oil fields to Cameroon

United States (Habré had supported Iraq's annexation of Kuwait). A 1,200-man French force began assisting Déby against rebels loyal to Habré and other faction leaders.

Between January and April 1993, Déby's hand was strengthened by the successful holding of a "National Convention," in which a number of formerly hostile groups agreed to cooperate with the government in drawing up a new constitution. In April 1994, his government was further boosted by Qadhafi's unexpected decision to withdraw his troops from the Aouzou Strip, leaving Chad in undisputed control of the territory. The move followed an International Court of Justice ruling in Chad's favor.

A BETTER FUTURE?

After a three-year-long civil war between various factions and the government, Chad seemed in 2003 to be on the verge of peace within the country after signing a set of peace accords with the National Resistance

Army (ANR) rebel movement (signed in January 2003), which was active in the east, and with the Movement for Democracy and Justice (signed in January 2002), who were operational in the north. Throughout 2004, violence broke out in Sudan's Darfur region, and Chad was faced with a major influx of more than 300,000 people who crossed its borders as refugees. By March 2004, the violence had reached such a high level that the United Nations Council for Refugees said that it was moving Sudanese refugees deeper into Chad to avoid attacks from Sudanese militias. Throughout April and May 2004, Chadian troops were occasionally fighting pro-Sudanese government militias, as fighting in Sudan's Darfur region spilled over the border. In 2006 Chad cut ties with Sudan, accusing it of supporting rebels bent on continued destabilization of Chad. The good news from Chad during this period of 2002 to 2004 was that in October 2003 Chad became an oil exporter with the opening of a pipeline connecting its oil fields with Cameroon.

The long, drawn-out conflict in Chad has led to immense suffering. Up to a half a million people—the equivalent of 10 percent of the total population—have been killed in the fighting.

Even if peace could be restored, the overall prospects for national development are bleak. The country has potential mineral wealth, but its geographic isolation and current world prices are disincentives to investors. Local food self-sufficiency should be obtainable despite the possibility of recurrent drought, but geography limits the potential of export crops. Chad thus appears to be an extreme case of the more general African need for a radical transformation of prevailing regional and global economic interrelationships. Had outside powers devoted half the resources to Chad's development over the past decades as they have provided to its civil conflicts, perhaps the country's future would appear brighter.

Congo (Republic of the Congo; Congo-Brazzaville)

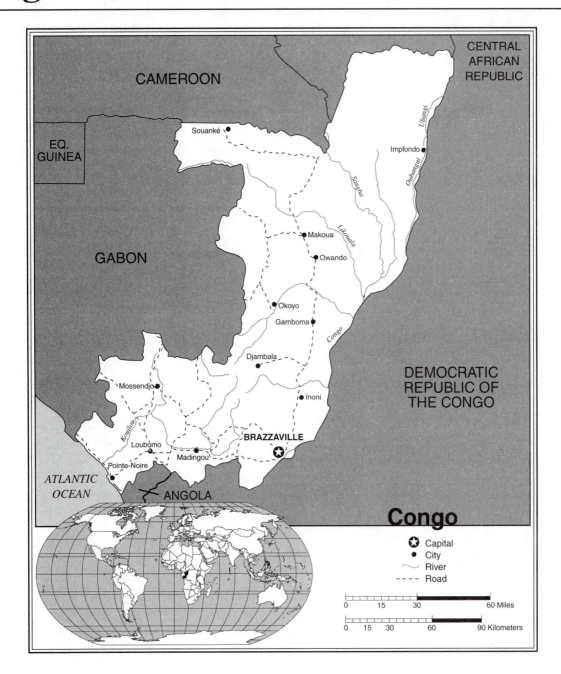

Congo Statistics

GEOGRAPHY

Area in Square Miles (Kilometers):
132,000 (342,000) (about the size of Montana)
Capital (Population): Brazzaville (1,360,000)
Environmental Concerns: air and water pollution; deforestation
Geographical Features: coastal plain; southern basin; central plateau; northern basin

Climate: tropical; particularly enervating climate astride the equator

PEOPLE

Population

Total: 3,800,610
Annual Growth Rate: 2.639%
Rural/Urban Population Ratio: 40/60
Major Languages: French; Lingala; Kikongo; Teke; Sangha; M'Bochi; others

Ethnic Makeup: 48% BaKongo; 20% Sangha; 17% Teke; 15% others
Religions: 50% Christian; 48% indigenous beliefs; 2% Muslim

Health

Life Expectancy at Birth: 52.1 years (male); 54.52 years (female)
Infant Mortality: 83.26/1,000 live births
Physicians Available: 1/3,873 people
HIV/AIDS Rate in Adults: 4.9%

27

GLOBAL STUDIES

Education

Adult Literacy Rate: 83.8%
Compulsory (Ages): 6–16

COMMUNICATION

Telephones: 15,900 main lines
Televisions: 17/1,000 people
Internet Users: 70,000 (2002)

TRANSPORTATION

Highways in Miles (Kilometers): 10,373 (17,289 km)
Railroads in Miles (Kilometers): 894 km
Usable Airfields: 32
Motor Vehicles in Use: 47,000

GOVERNMENT

Type: republic

Independence Date: August 15, 1960 (from France)
Head of State/Government: President Denis Sassou-Nguesso is both head of state and head of government
Political Parties: Democratic and Patriotic Forces; Congolese Movement for Democracy and Integral Development; many others
Suffrage: universal at 18

MILITARY

Military Expenditures (% of GDP): 3.1%
Current Disputes: civil conflicts; boundary issue with Democratic Republic of Congo

ECONOMY

Currency ($ U.S. Equivalent): 465.51 CFA francs = $1

Per Capita Income/GDP: $1,400/$2.5 billion
GDP Growth Rate: 6.1%
Inflation Rate: 2.6%
Natural Resources: timber; potash; lead; zinc; uranium; petroleum; natural gas; copper; phosphates
Agriculture: cassava; cocoa; coffee; sugarcane; rice; peanuts; vegetables; forest products
Industry: processing of agricultural and forestry goods; cement; brewing; petroleum
Exports: $5.996 billion (primary partners United States, South Korea, China)
Imports: $1.964 billion (primary partners France, United States, Italy)

SUGGESTED WEB SITES

http://www.sas.upenn.edu/African_ Studies/Country_Specific/Congo .html

Congo Country Report

Once considered one of Africa's most promising economies, over the past decade the Republic of the Congo—not to be confused with its larger neighbor the Democratic Republic of the Congo (D.R.C., the former Zaire)—has been afflicted by civil strife that has killed thousands while displacing up to one third of the population. In March 2002, the current president, General Denis Sassou-Nguesso, claimed 89 percent of the vote in presidential elections in which his two main political rivals, former president Pascal Lissouba and prime minister Bernard Kolelas, were barred from the contest. The poll was supposed to be the culmination of a two-year peace process that returned the country to democracy under a new Constitution. But in the same month, renewed fighting broke out between government forces and "Ninja" rebels loyal to Kolelas. In June, battles between government troops and the Ninja spread to Brazzaville, killing about 100 people.

The current round of political conflict in Congo began in 1997, when forces loyal to Sassou-Nguesso, who had previously ruled as a virtual dictator between 1979 and 1992, launched a rebellion. They seized control of Brazzaville in October 1997. The return of Sassou-Nguesso, who had garnered only 17 percent of the vote while losing the presidency to Lissouba just two years earlier, would not have been possible without the intervention of Angolan government forces, whose overt vio-

lation of Congolese sovereignty attracted little international comment. The Angolans were apparently motivated by allegations that Lissouba was supportive of UNITA rebels in their own country.

DEVELOPMENT

Congo's Niari Valley has become the nation's leading agricultural area, due to its rich alluvial soils. The government has been encouraging food-processing plants to locate in the region.

The fall of the capital did not end the fighting, which resulted in the Congolese Army as well as the country as a whole becoming largely split along north–south regional lines. Opposition to Sassou-Nguesso has been concentrated among the BaKongo people of the south, who make up about half of the total population. With continued Angolan backing, Sassou-Nguesso's forces were able to drive back those of his rivals.

At the end of 1999, many of the rebels agreed to a cease-fire accord. This was followed by a peace agreement that provided for a national dialogue; demilitarization of political parties; and the reorganization of the army, including the re-admission of rebel units into the security forces. By September 2001, some 15,000 rebels had been disarmed in a cash-for-arms scheme. This was rewarded by the International

Monetary Fund, which cancelled some $4 billion in debt. But other rebels have not as yet been bought off.

In December 2001, Lissouba was convicted in absentia by the High Court of treason and corruption charges, and sentenced to 30 years hard labor. Although Sassou-Nguesso's forces have maintained the upper hand, political stability and economic growth are unlikely to return to Congo in the absence of a truly inclusive process of reconciliation.

FREEDOM

Until 1990, political opposition groups, along with Jehovah's Witnesses and certain other religious sects, were vigorously suppressed. The new Constitution provides for basic freedoms of association, belief, and speech.

The overthrow of Lissouba was all the more unfortunate in that his government had seemed to have been making progress in negotiating an end to the violence among the political factions that has plagued the country for more than a decade. A 1995 agreement was supposed to lead to the disarmament of party militias. But instead, efforts to assure the disarmament of Sassou-Nguesso's men set off the revolt in June 1997. Previously, in November 1993, large sections of Brazzaville had been a battleground between troops

Since Congo achieved its independence in 1960, it has made enormous educational strides. Almost all children in the country now attend school, which has had a tremendous effect on helping to realize the potential of the country's natural resources.

loyal to the elected Pan-African Union of Social Democracy (UPADS) government of President Lissouba and the Ninjas—armed supporters of opposition leader Bernard Kolelas's Union for the Renewal of Democracy (URD). After several weeks of fighting, peace was finally restored with the intervention of an Organization of African Unity mediator. The crisis underscored the continuing fragility of Congo's difficult political transition into a multiparty democracy.

Sassou-Nguesso had previously ruled Congo as the head of a self-proclaimed, Marxist-Leninist one-party state. But in 1990, the ruling Congolese Workers Party (PCT) agreed to abandon both its past ideology and its monopoly of power. In 1991, a four-month-long "National Conference" met to pave the way for a new constitutional order. An interim government headed by Andre Milongo was appointed, pending elections, while Sassou-Nguesso was stripped of all but ceremonial power. In the

face of coup attempts by elements of the old order and a deteriorating economy, legislative and executive elections were finally held in the second half of 1992, resulting in Lissouba's election and a divided National Assembly.

A new National Assembly election in 1993 resulted in a decisive UPADS victory over a URD–PCT alliance, but the losers rejected the results for five months. With the economy experiencing a prolonged depression, political tensions remained high.

CONGO REPUBLIC

The Republic of the Congo takes its name from the river that forms its southeastern border with the Democratic Republic of Congo. Because Zaire prior to 1971 also called itself the Congo, the two countries are sometimes confused. Close historical and ethnic ties do in fact exist between the nations. The BaKongo are the largest

ethnolinguistic group in Congo and western former Zaire as well as in northern Angola. During the fifteenth and sixteenth centuries, this group was united under the powerful Kingdom of the Kongo, which ruled over much of Central Africa while establishing commercial and diplomatic ties with Europe. But the kingdom had virtually disappeared by the late nineteenth century, when the territory along the northwest bank of the Congo River—the modern republic—was annexed by France, while the southeast bank—Zaire—was placed under the brutal rule of King Leopold of Belgium.

Despite the establishment of this political division, cultural ties between Congo and the former Zaire, the former French and Belgian Congos, remained strong. Brazzaville sits across the river from the D.R.C. capital of Kinshasha. The metropolitan region formed by these two centers has, through such figures as the late Congolese artist Franco, given rise to *soukous,* a musical style that is now popular in such places as Tokyo and Paris as well as throughout much of Africa.

ECONOMIC DEVELOPMENT

Brazzaville, which today houses well over a third of Congo's population, was established during the colonial era as the administrative headquarters of French Equatorial Africa, a vast territory that included the present-day states of Chad, Central African Republic, Gabon, and Congo Republic. As a result, the city expanded, and the area around it developed as an imperial crossroads. The Congolese paid a heavy price for this growth. Thousands died while working under brutal conditions to build the Congo-Ocean Railroad, which linked Brazzaville with Pointe-Noire on the coast. Many more suffered as forced laborers for foreign concessionaires during the early decades of the twentieth century.

HEALTH/WELFARE

Almost all Congolese between ages 6 and 16 currently attend school. Adult-literacy programs have also proved successful, giving the country one of the highest literacy rates in Africa. However, 30% of Congolese children under age 5 are reported to suffer from chronic malnutrition.

While the economies of many African states stagnated or declined during the 1970s and 1980s, Congo generally experienced growth, a result of its oil wealth. Hydrocarbons account for 90 percent of the total value of the nation's exports. Congo is one of the main oil producers in sub-Saharan Africa. This resource forms the backbone of Congo's economy and, in recent years, the country has tried to increase financial transparency in the sector. But the danger of this dependence has been apparent since 1986, when falling oil prices led to a sharp decline in gross domestic product. An even greater threat to the nation's economic health is its mounting debt. As a result of heavy borrowing during the oil-boom years, by 1989 the total debt was estimated to be 50 percent greater than the value of the country's annual economic output. The annual cost of servicing the debt was almost equal to domestic expenditure.

The debt led to International Monetary Fund pressure on Congo's rulers to introduce austerity measures as part of a Structural Adjustment Program (SAP). The PCT regime and its interim successor were willing to move away from the country's emphasis on central planning toward a greater reliance on market economics. But after an initial round of severe budgetary cutbacks, both administrations found it difficult to reduce their spending further on such things as food subsidies and state-sector employment.

With nearly two thirds of Congo's population now urbanized, there has been deep concern about the social and political consequences of introducing harsher austerity measures. Many urban-dwellers are already either unemployed or underemployed; even those with steady formal-sector jobs have been squeezed by wages that fail to keep up with inflation. The country's powerful trade unions, which are hostile to SAP, have been in the forefront of the democratization process.

ACHIEVEMENTS

There are a number of Congolese poets and novelists who combine their creative efforts with teaching and public service. Tchicaya U'Tam'si, who died in 1988, wrote poetry and novels and worked for many years for UNESCO.

Although most Congolese are facing tough times in the short run, the economy's long-term prospects remain promising. Besides oil, the country is endowed with a wide variety of mineral reserves. Timber has long been a major industry. And after years of neglect, the agricultural sector is growing. The goal of a return to food self-sufficiency appears achievable. Cocoa, coffee, tobacco, and sugarcane are major cash crops, while palm-oil estates are being rehabilitated.

The small but well-established Congolese manufacturing sector also has much potential. Congo's urbanized population is relatively skilled, thanks to the enormous educational strides that have been made since independence. Almost all children in Congo now attend school. Prior to the devastation that occurred during the 1997 revolt, the infrastructure serving Brazzaville and Pointe-Noire, coupled with the previous government's emphasis on private-sector growth, was potentially attractive to outside investors.

LOOKING AHEAD

Civil wars and militia conflicts have plagued the Republic of Congo throughout its recent past, but hopes for stability were raised in 2003 when the government signed a peace accord with rebels in the south. After three relatively peaceful but coup-ridden decades of independence, the former French colony experienced the first of two destructive bouts of fighting in 1993 when disputed parliamentary elections led to bloody, ethnically based fighting between pro-government forces and the opposition. The finding and exploitation of oil has been a curse on the Congo, as the soldiers have moved out of the barrages and into the streets in a more or less continual struggle for political power during the last decade. However, in 2004 a cease-fire agreement followed by the inclusion of some opposition members in the government helped to restore peace. The government forces, who were backed by Angolan troops, held the upper hand until a peace deal was signed in March 2003 with remnants of the civil war militias, known as Ninjas. However, by 2007, Ninja militias were still active in the southern Pool region refusing to disarm and causing persistent instability through banditry.

Timeline: PAST

1910
Middle Congo becomes part of French Equatorial Africa

1944
Conference establishes French Union; Felix Eboue establishes positive policies for African advancement

1960
Independence is achieved, with Abbe Fulbert Youlou as the first president

1963
A general strike brings the army and a more radical government (National Revolutionary Movement) to power

1968–1969
A new military government under Marien Ngouabi takes over; the Congolese Workers' Party is formed

1977
Ngouabi is assassinated; Colonel Yhombi-Opango rules

1979–1992
Denis Sassou-Nguesso is president

1990s
Pascal Lissouba is elected president; former dictator Sassou-Nguesso again seizes power

PRESENT

2000s
Congo tries to recover from the civil conflict of the late 1990s

Security problems remain despite the peace process

Democratic Republic of the Congo

(Congo-Kinshasa; formerly Zaire)

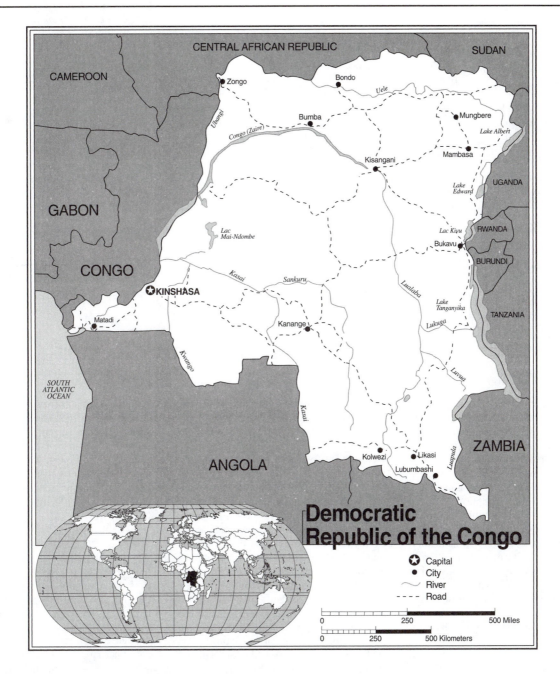

Democratic Republic of the Congo Statistics

GEOGRAPHY

Area in Square Miles (Kilometers):
905,063 (2,300,000) (1/4 the size of the United States)

Capital (Population): Kinshasa 7,273,947

Environmental Concerns: poaching; water pollution; deforestation; soil erosion; mining

Geographical Features: the vast central basin is a low-lying plateau; mountains in the east; dense tropical rain forest

Climate: tropical equatorial

PEOPLE

Population

Total: 65,751,512

Annual Growth Rate: 3.39%

Rural/Urban Population Ratio: 68/32

31

GLOBAL STUDIES

Major Languages: French; Lingala; Kingwana; others
Ethnic Makeup: Bantu majority; more than 200 African groups
Religions: 70% Christian; 20% indigenous beliefs; 10% Muslim

Health

Life Expectancy at Birth: 54.97 years (male); 59.5 years (female)
Infant Mortality: 65.52/1,000 live births
Physicians Available: 1/15,584 people
HIV/AIDS Rate in Adults: 4.2%

Education

Adult Literacy Rate: 65.5%
Compulsory (Ages): 6–12

COMMUNICATION

Telephones: 10,600 main lines
Daily Newspaper Circulation: 3/1,000 people
Internet Users: 180,000 (2002)

TRANSPORTATION

Highways in Miles (Kilometers): 95,168 (153,497 km)
Railroads in Miles (Kilometers): 5,139 km
Usable Airfields: 234
Motor Vehicles in Use: 530,000

GOVERNMENT

Type: Republic
Independence Date: June 30, 1960 (from Belgium)
Head of State/Government: President Joseph Kabila is both head of state and head of government
Political Parties: Popular Movement of the Revolution; Democratic Social Christian Party; others
Suffrage: universal and compulsory at 18

MILITARY

Military Expenditures (% of GDP): 2.5%
Current Disputes: civil war; boundary issues with surrounding states; military conflicts with neighboring states

ECONOMY

Currency ($ U.S. equivalent): 560 CDF = $1
Per Capita Income/GDP: $700/ $44.44 billion
GDP Growth Rate: −6.4%
Labor Force by Occupation: 65% agriculture; 19% services; 16% industry
Natural Resources: cobalt; copper; cadmium; petroleum; zinc; diamonds; manganese; tin; gold; silver; bauxite; iron ore; coal; hydropower; timber; others
Agriculture: coffee; palm oil; rubber; tea; manioc; root crops; corn; fruits; sugarcane; wood products
Industry: mineral mining and processing; consumer products; cement; diamonds
Exports: $1.108 billion (primary partners Belgium, United States, South Africa)
Imports: $1.319 billion (primary partners South Africa, Benelux, Nigeria)

SUGGESTED WEB SITE

http://www.sas.upenn.edu/African_ Studies/Country_Specific/DR_Congo .html

Democratic Republic of the Congo Country Report

Due to its geographical location and staggering mineral resources, the Democratic Republic of Congo (D.R.C.), also formerly known as Zaire, is perhaps the most strategically important nation in Africa, with the potential to become one of its richest. Unfortunately, after years of almost unbelievable levels of corruption, external interference, and greed, it suffers from the lack of a strong central government with credible structures. At times in its history, it has been difficult to imagine a nation in more distress than the D.R.C. After being ruled from 1965 to 1997 by the notoriously corrupt dictator Joseph Mobutu, in recent years the D.R.C. has all but fallen apart as armed internal and external forces have divided the country.

A series of agreements in 2002 led to the withdrawal of most external-state forces from Congolese soil and the promise of a "government of national unity." With an on-again, off-again peace process now bearing some fruit, there may be some grounds for cautious optimism.

The D.R.C.'s latest conflict began in August 1998, when rebels of the Congolese Assembly for Democracy, heavily backed by the Rwandan and Ugandan militaries, advanced rapidly from the east. This occurred shortly after the 15-month-old D.R.C. regime headed by Laurent Kabila, who had replaced Mobutu, called for the withdrawal of all foreign forces from Congolese soil. Early rebel hopes of a quick victory were frustrated by the intervention of Angolan, Namibian, and Zimbabwean forces. The fighting quickly became deadlocked, leading to mediation efforts under the chairmanship of Botswana's former president Sir Ketumile Masire, and backed by the United Nations and the Organization of African Unity. These negotiations appeared to be getting nowhere until January 2001, when Laurent Kabila was assassinated and replaced as president by his son Joseph. Meanwhile, the rebel forces had become divided, with their Rwandan and Ugandan mentors at times turning on each other. By May 2001, the International Rescue Committee, a New York–based refugee agency, had estimated that the war had directly and indirectly killed some 2.5 million people. In 2005, the Crisis Group, a Brussels-based think-tank, estimated that 1,000 people were dying every day from war-related causes, including disease, hunger, and violence.

Laurent Kabila had come to power as the leader of the Alliance of Democratic Forces for the Liberation of Congo-Zaire, a rebel movement that was itself heavily dependent on external support from Rwanda, Uganda, and Zimbabwe. In the final months of 1996, Kabila's forces seized control of eastern Zaire, and they arrived in Kinshasa in May 1997. Once in power, Kabila changed the name of the country from Zaire, an identity that had been imposed by Mobutu in 1971, to its former title: Democratic Republic of the Congo.

DEVELOPMENT

Western aid and development assistance were drastically reduced in 1992, but new aid was pledged in 1994 as a reward for Mobutu's cooperation in dealing with the Rwandan conflict. An agreement was signed with Egypt for the long-term development of Zaire's hydroelectric power.

Hopes that the new government would bring an end to the chronic corruption and mismanagement that have long plagued the country, or lead to an opening for democracy and improved human rights, soon proved misplaced. A leading Mobutu opponent, Etienne Tshisekedi wa Mulumba, was assaulted by Kabila's men within days of their victory. Tshisekedi remains the head of a nonviolent opposition coalition, the Union for Democracy and Social Progress, that is calling for a transition to democracy through a negotiated "government of national unity."

Meanwhile, the country's already decayed social and economic infrastructure continues to disintegrate. The informal sector now dominates the local economy. In the process, national unity is being challenged by the reemergence of secessionist tendencies in the mineral-rich provinces of Katanga (Shaba) and Kasai. Western and eastern former Zaire has been inundated by an influx of some 2 million refugees from the killing fields of Rwanda and Burundi. With its vast size and wealth, D.R.C.'s fate will ultimately affect the future of neighboring states as well as its own citizens. Since independence, its instability has been a destabilizing influence for its neighbors in Central, Eastern, and Southern Africa. At peace, it could become the hub of an African renaissance.

Geographically, the country is located at Africa's center. It encompasses the entire Congo River Basin, whose waters are the potential source of 13 percent of the world's hydroelectric power. This immense area, about one quarter the size of the United States, encompasses a variety of land forms. It contains good agricultural possibilities and a wide range of natural resources, some of which have been intensively exploited for decades.

The D.R.C. links Africa from west to east. Its very narrow coastline faces the Atlantic. Forces from the East African coast have long influenced the landlocked eastern D.R.C. In the mid-nineteenth century, Swahili, Arab, and Nyamwezi traders from Tanzania established their hegemony over much of southeastern Zaire, pillaging the countryside for ivory and slaves. While the slave trade has left bitter memories, the Swahili language has spread to become a lingua franca throughout the eastern third of the country.

The 66 million people of the Democratic Republic of the Congo belong to more than 200 different ethnic groups, speak some 700 languages and dialects, and have varied lifestyles. Boundaries established in the late nineteenth century hemmed in portions of the Azande, Konga, Chokwe, and Songye peoples, yet they maintain contact with their kin in other countries.

Many important precolonial states were centered here, including the Luba, Kuba, and Lunda kingdoms, the latter of which, in earlier centuries, exploited the salt and copper of southeastern Zaire. The Kingdom of the Kongo, located at the mouth of the Congo River, flourished during the fifteenth and sixteenth centuries, establishing

important diplomatic and commercial relations with Portugal. The elaborate political systems of these kingdoms are an important heritage for the Democratic Republic of the Congo.

LEOPOLD'S GENOCIDE

The European impact, like the Swahili and Arab influences from the east, had deeply destructive results. The Congo Basin was explored and exploited by private individuals before it came under Belgian domination. As a private citizen, King Leopold of Belgium sponsored H. M. Stanley's expeditions to explore the basin. In 1879, Leopold used Stanley's "treaties" as a justification for setting up the "Congo Independent State" over the whole region. This state was actually a private proprietary colony. To turn a profit on his vast enterprise, Leopold acted under the assumption that the people and resources in the territory were his personal property. His commercial agents and various concessionaires, to whom he leased portions of his colony, began to brutally coerce the local African population into providing ivory, wild rubber, and other commodities. The armed militias sent out to collect quotas of rubber and other goods committed numerous atrocities against the people, including destroying whole villages.

FREEDOM

The regimes in the Democratic Republic of the Congo have shown little respect for human rights. One Amnesty International report concluded that all political prisoners were tortured, and death squads were active.

No one knows for sure how many Africans perished in Congo Independent State as a result of the brutalities of Leopold's agents. Some critics estimate that the territory's population was reduced by 10 *million* people over a period of 20 years. Many were starved to death as forced laborers. Others were massacred in order to induce survivors to produce more rubber. Women and children were suffocated in "hostage houses" while their men did their masters' bidding. Thousands fled to neighboring territories.

For years the Congo regime was able to keep information of its crimes from leaking overseas, but eventually reports from missionaries and others did emerge. Public outrage was stirred by accounts such as E. D. Morel's *Red Rubber* and Mark Twain's caustic *King Leopold's Soliloquy*, as well

as gruesome pictures of men, women, and children whose hands had been severed by troops (who were expected to produce the hands for their officers as evidence of their diligence). Joseph Conrad's fictionalized account of his experiences, *The Heart of Darkness*, became a popular literary classic. Finally even the European imperialists, during an era when their racial arrogance was at its height, could no longer stomach Leopold, called by some "the king with ten million murders on his soul."

During the years of Belgian rule, 1908 to 1960, foreign domination was less genocidal, but a tradition of abuse had nevertheless been established. The colonial authorities still used armed forces for "pacification" campaigns, tax collection, and labor recruitment. Local collaborators were turned into chiefs and given arbitrary powers that they would not have had under indigenous political systems. Concessionary companies continued to use force to recruit labor for their plantations and mines. The colonial regime encouraged the work of Catholic missionaries. Health facilities as well as a paternalistic system of education were developed. A strong elementary-school system was part of the colonial program, but the Belgians never instituted a major secondary-school system, and there was no institution of higher learning. By independence, only 16 Congolese had been able to earn university degrees, all but two in non-Belgian institutions. A small group of high-school–educated Congolese, known as *évolués* ("evolved ones"), served the needs of an administration that never intended nor planned for Congo's independence.

In the 1950s, the independence movements that were emerging throughout Africa affected the Congolese, especially townspeople. The Belgians began to recognize the need to prepare for a different future. Small initiatives were allowed; in 1955, nationalist associations were first permitted, and a 30-year timetable for independence was proposed. This sparked heated debate. Some évolués agreed with the Belgians' proposal. Others, including the members of the Alliance of the Ba-Kongo (ABAKO), an ethnic association in Kinshasa, and the National Congolese Movement (MNC), led by Prime Minister Patrice Lumumba, rejected it.

A serious clash at an ABAKO demonstration in 1959 resulted in some 50 deaths. In the face of mounting unrest, further encouraged by the imminent independence of the French Congo (Republic of the Congo), the Belgians conceded a rapid transition to independence. A constitutional conference in January 1960 established a federal-government system for the future independent state. But there was no real preparation for this far-reaching political change.

THE CONGO CRISIS

Democratic Republic of the Congo became independent on June 30, 1960, under the leadership of President Joseph Kasavubu and Prime Minister Patrice Lumumba. Within a week, an army mutiny had stimulated widespread disorder. The scars of Congo's uniquely bitter colonial experience showed. Unlike in Africa's other postcolonial states, hatred of the white former masters turned to violence in Congo, resulting in the hurried flight of the majority of its large European community. Ethnic and regional bloodshed took a much greater toll among the African population. The wealthy Katanga Province (now Shaba) and South Kasai seceded.

Lumumba called upon the United Nations for assistance, and troops came from a variety of countries to serve in the UN force. Later, as a result of a dispute with President Kasavubu, Lumumba sought Soviet aid. Congo could have become a Cold War battlefield, but the army, under Lumumba's former confidant, Joseph Desiré Mobutu, intervened. Lumumba was arrested and turned over to the Katanga rebels; he was later assassinated. Western interests and, in particular, the U.S. Central Intelligence Agency (CIA) played a substantial if not fully revealed role in the downfall of the idealistic Lumumba and the rise of his cynical successor, Mobutu. Rebellions by Lumumbists in the northeast and Katanga secessionists, supported by foreign mercenaries, continued through 1967.

MOBUTUISM

Mobutu seized full power in 1965, ousting Kasavubu in a military coup. With ruthless energy, he eliminated the rival political factions within the central government and crushed the regional rebellions. Mobutu banned party politics. In 1971, he established the Second Republic as a one-party state in which all power was centralized around the "Founding President." Every citizen, at birth, was legally expected to be a disciplined member of Mobutu's Popular Revolutionary Movement (MPR). With the exception of some religious organizations, virtually all social institutions were to function as MPR organs. The official ideology of the MPR republic became "Mobutuism"—the words, deeds, and decrees of "the Guide" Mobutu. All citizens were required to sing his praises daily at the workplace, at schools, and at social gatherings. In hymns and prayers, the name Mobutu was often substituted for that of Jesus. A principal slogan of Mobutuism was "authenticity." Supposedly this meant a rejection of European values and norms for African ones.

But it was Mobutu alone who defined what was authentic. He added to his own name the title *Sese Seko* ("the All Powerful") while declaring all European personal names illegal. He also established a national dress code; ties were outlawed, men were expected to wear his abacost suit, and women were obliged to wear the *paigne,* or wrapper. (The former Zaire was perhaps the only place in the world where the necktie was a symbol of political resistance.) The name of the country was changed from Congo to *Zaire,* a word derived from the sixteenth-century Portuguese mispronunciation of the (Ki)Kongo word for "river."

HEALTH/WELFARE

In 1978, more than 5 million students were registered for primary schools and 35,000 for college. However, the level of education has since declined. Many teachers were laid off in the 1980s, though nonexistent "ghost teachers" remained on the payroll. The few innovative educational programs that do manage to exist are outside of the state system.

Outside of Zaire, some took Mobutu's protestations of authenticity at face value, while a few other African dictators, such as Togo's Gnassingbé Eyadéma, emulated aspects of his fascist methodology. But the majority of Zairians grew to loathe his "cultural revolution."

Authenticity was briefly accompanied by a program of nationalization. Union Miniére and other corporations were placed under government control. In 1973 and 1974, plantations, commercial institutions, and other businesses were also taken over, in what was called a "radicalizing of the Zairian Revolution."

But the expropriated businesses simply enriched a small elite. In many cases, Mobutu gave them away to his cronies, who often sold off the assets. Consequently, the economy suffered. Industries and businesses were mismanaged or ravaged. Some individuals became extraordinarily wealthy, while the population as a whole became progressively poorer with each passing year. Mobutu allegedly became the wealthiest person in all of Africa, with a fortune estimated in excess of $5 billion (about equal to Zaire's national debt), most of which was invested and spent outside of Africa. He and his relatives owned mansions all over the world.

Until his last year in power, no opposition to Mobutu was allowed. Those critical of the regime faced imprisonment, torture, or death. The Roman Catholic Church and the Kimbanguist Church of Jesus Christ Upon This Earth were the only institutions able to speak out. Strikes were not allowed. In 1977 and 1978, new revolts in the Shaba Province were crushed by U.S.–backed Moroccan, French, and Belgian military interventions. Thus in 1997, rebels under Laurent Kabila ousted the ailing Mobutu and renamed the country the Democratic Republic of the Congo.

ECONOMIC DISASTER

The country's economic potential was developed by and for the Belgians, but by 1960, that development had gone further than in most other African colonial territories. It started with a good economic base, but the chaos of the early 1960s brought development to a standstill, and the Mobutu years were marked by regression. Development projects were initiated, but often without careful planning. World economic conditions, including falling copper and cobalt prices, contributed to Zaire's difficulties.

But the main obstacle to any sort of economic progress was the rampant corruption of Mobutu and those around him. The governing system in Zaire was a kleptocracy (rule by thieves). A well-organized system of graft transferred wealth from ordinary citizens to officials and other elites. With Mobutu stealing billions and those closest to him stealing millions, the entire society operated on an invisible tax system; for example, citizens had to bribe nurses for medical care, bureaucrats for documents, principals for school admission, and police to stay out of jail. For most civil servants, who were paid little or nothing, accepting bribes was a necessary activity. This fundamental fact also applied to most soldiers, who thus survived by living off the civilian population.

ACHIEVEMENTS

Kinshasha has been called the dance-music capital of Africa. The most popular sound is *souskous,* or "Congo rumba." The grand old man of the style is Rochereau Tabu Ley. Other artists, like Papa Wemba, Pablo Lubidika, and Sandoka, have joined him in spreading its rhythms internationally.

Ordinary people have suffered. By 1990, real wages of urban workers in the country were only 2 percent of what they were in 1960. Rural incomes had also deteriorated. The official 1990 price paid to coffee farmers, for example, was only one fifth of what it was in 1954 under the hugely exploitive Belgian regime. The situation has worsened since, due to periods of hyperinflation.

Much of the state's coffee and other cash crops have long been smuggled, more often than not through the connivance of senior government officials. Thus, although the country's agriculture has great economic potential, the returns from this sector continue to shrink. Despite its immense size and plentiful rainfall, it must import about 60 percent of its food requirements. Rural people move to the city or, for lack of employment, move back to the country and take up subsistence agriculture, rather than cash-crop farming, in order to ensure their own survival. The deterioration of roads and bridges has led to the decline of all trade.

In 1983, the government adopted International Monetary Fund austerity measures, but this only cut public expenditures. It had no effect on the endemic corruption, nor did it increase taxes on the rich. Under Mobutu's regime, more than 30 percent of former Zaire's budget went for debt servicing.

In June 1997, Kabila announced short-term economic priorities, including job creation, road and hospital rebuilding, and a national fuel-supply pipeline. But it was unclear where the money would come from to implement these plans.

U.S. SUPPORT FOR MOBUTU

Mobutu's regime was able to sidestep its financial crises and maintain power through the support of foreign powers, especially Belgium, France, Germany, and the United States. A U.S. intelligence report prepared in the mid-1950s concluded that the then–Belgian Congo was indeed the hub of Africa and thus vital to America's strategic interests. U.S. policy was thus the first to promote and then to perpetuate Mobutu as a pro-Western source of stability in the region. Mobutu himself skillfully cultivated this image.

Mobutu collaborated with the United States in opposing the Marxist-oriented Popular Movement for the Liberation of Angola. By so doing, he not only set himself up as an important Cold War ally but also was able to pursue regional objectives of his own. The National Front for the Liberation of Angola, long championed by the CIA as a counterforce to the MPLA, was led by an in-law of Mobutu, Holden Roberto. Mobutu also long coveted Angola's oil-rich enclave

of Cabinda and thus sought CIA and South African assistance for the "independence" movement there. In recent years, millions of U.S. dollars were spent upgrading the airstrip at Kamina in Shaba Province, used by the CIA to supply the guerrillas of the National Union for the Total Independence of Angola, another faction opposed to the MPLA government. In 1989, Mobutu attempted to set himself up as a mediator between the government and the UNITA rebels, but even the latter grew to distrust him.

The United States had long known of Mobutu's human-rights violations and of the oppression and corruption that characterized his regime; high-level defectors as well as victims had publicized its abuses. Since 1987, Mobutu responded with heavily financed public-relations efforts aimed at lobbying U.S. legislators. U.S. support for Mobutu continued, but the eventual collapse of his authority led Washington belatedly to search for alternatives.

Mobutu also allied himself with other conservative forces in Africa and the Middle East. Moroccan troops came to his aid during the revolts in Shaba Province in 1977 and 1978. For his part, Mobutu was a leading African supporter of Morocco's stand with regard to the Western Sahara dispute. Under his rule the country was also an active member of the Francophonic African bloc. In 1983, Mobutu dispatched 2,000 Zairian troops to Chad in support of the government of Hissène Habré, then under attack from Libya, while in 1986, his men again joined French forces in propping up the Eyadéma regime in Togo. He also maintained and strengthened his ties with South Africa (today, the former Zaire imports almost half its food from that state). In 1982, he renewed the diplomatic ties with Israel that had been broken after the Arab–Israeli War of 1973. Israelis subsequently joined French and Belgians as senior advisers and trainers working within the former Zairian Army. In 1990, the outbreak of violent unrest in Kinshasha once more led to the intervention of French and Belgian troops.

Despite Mobutu's cultivation of foreign assistance to prop up his dictatorship, internal opposition grew. In 1990, he tried to head off his critics both at home and abroad by promising to set up a new Third Republic, based on multiparty democracy. Despite this step, repression intensified.

In October 1996, while Mobutu was in Europe recovering from cancer surgery, rebel troops under the leadership of Laurent Kabila seized their first major town, Uvira. Thousands of Rwandan Hutu refugees were forced to flee back to Rwanda. When Mobutu returned home in April

1997, he declared a nationwide state of emergency. Kabila's supporters then closed down Kinshasa as part of the campaign to oust Mobutu. Following negotiations with South Africa's Mandela, Mobutu left Kinshasa and went into exile.

THE STRUGGLE CONTINUES

Although the history of the Democratic Republic of Congo (D.R.C.) has been one of civil war and corruption, signs of change are on the horizon. A vast country with

Timeline: PAST

1879
Leopold sets up the Congo Independent State as his private kingdom

1906
Congo becomes a Belgian colony

1960
Congo gains independence; civil war begins; a UN force is involved; Patrice Lumumba is murdered

1965
Joseph Desiré Mobutu takes command in a bloodless coup

1971
The name of the state is changed to Zaire

1990s
Central authority crumbles; millions of Rwandan and Burundian refugees flood into Zaire; Mobutu is overthrown

PRESENT

2000s
Civil war continues, but hopes of a permanent cease-fire have emerged

Laurent Kabila is assassinated and replaced by his son, Joseph Kabila

New constitution, with text agreed by former warring factions, adopted by parliament and voters ushering in hopes for a stable future

The first free presidential and parliamentary polls are held in four decades. Joseph Kabila is declared winner in October 2006 run-off presidential election over opposition candidate Jean-Pierre Bemba

DRC, Rwanda, and Burundi relaunch the regional economic bloc Great Lakes Countries Economic Community, known under its French acronym CEPGL

immense economic resources, the D.R.C. has been at the centre of what could be termed Africa's international war. But a peace deal, and the formation of a transitional government in 2003 appeared to signal the end of the five-year conflict which pitted government forces, supported by Angola, Namibia, and Zimbabwe, against rebels backed by Uganda and Rwanda. In April 2003, President Laurent Kabila signed a new constitution, under which an interim government would rule for two years, pending elections in 2005. The constitution was drawn up at talks in South Africa between D.R.C.'s warring factions. In May 2003, the last Ugandan troops left eastern D.R.C. as reports of bloody clashes between rival militias in Bunia emerged. The French arrived in Bunia to fill the vacuum left by the Ugandans as part of a UN-mandated rapid-reaction force.

D.R.C. leaders of the main former rebel groups were sworn in as vice presidents in July 2003 with an interim parliament inaugurated in August 2003.

By December 2003, former government soldiers of the Mobutu regime and those of two main rebel groups formed a united force. This led in March 2004 to gunmen attacking military bases in Kinshasa in an apparent coup attempt. In June 2004, rebel soldiers occupied the eastern border town of Bukavu for a week. The government accused Rwanda of supporting the rebels. Popular protests in Kinshasa over the UN's failure to prevent the town's capture turned violent. A second reported coup attempt by rebel guards was neutralized in June 2004.

The political and military situation in D.R.C. is stable. The fact that there were mass popular protests in support of the transitional government against the slow speed of the UN's response and opposing a coup, indicates that there is a certain degree of maturity amongst the population. The people of the D.R.C. will not stand for radical changes brought about by violence from any minority group. Moreover, without majority participation in some form of democratic election, no government can expect to achieve a mandate to rule the country.

The war claimed an estimated three million lives, either as a direct result of fighting or because of disease and malnutrition. It has been called possibly the worst emergency to unfold in Africa in recent decades. The war had an economic as well as a political side. Fighting was fueled by the country's vast mineral wealth, with all sides taking advantage of the anarchy to plunder its natural resources. Although the eastern regions are still plagued by militia violence, the DRC is now poised for a new beginning as former rebels have joined a power-sharing government. In spite of recent coup attempts and sporadic violence, a fragile peace has held since the formal end of the war. Joseph Kabila, who became Congo's president when his father Laurent Kabila was assassinated in 2001, gained a new mandate through the ballot box to rule the vast country as its elected leader in an election in 2006. The vote was praised by international monitors as free and fair. Kabila has promised to rule by consensus to try to heal the still raw scars of Congo's many conflicts.

Equatorial Guinea (Republic of Equatorial Guinea)

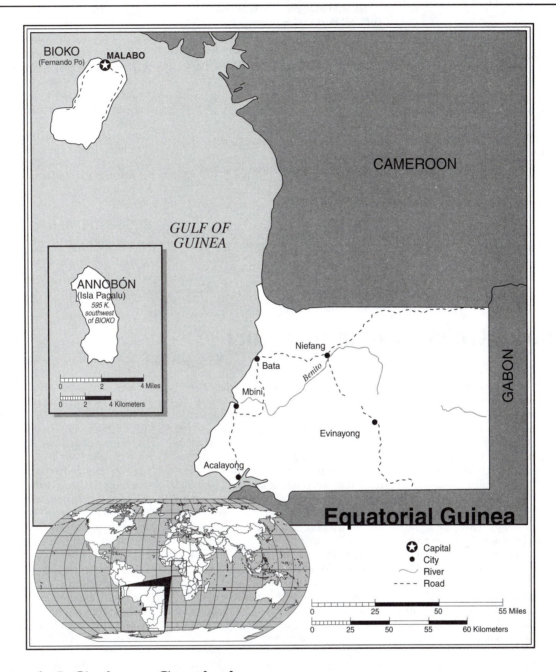

Equatorial Guinea Statistics

GEOGRAPHY

Area in Square Miles (Kilometers): 10,820
 (28,023) (about the size of Maryland)
Capital (Population): Malabo (60,065)
Environmental Concerns: desertification;
 lack of potable water
Geographical Features: coastal plains
 rise to interior hills; volcanic islands;
 mainland portion and 5 inhabited islands
Climate: tropical

PEOPLE

Population

Total: 551,201
Annual Growth Rate: 2.47%
Rural/Urban Population Ratio: 61/39
Major Languages: Spanish; French; Bubi;
 Fang; Ibo
Ethnic Makeup: primarily Bioko, Rio
 Muni; fewer than 1,000 Europeans

Religions: nominally Christian,
 predominantly Roman Catholic;
 indigenous beliefs

Health

Life Expectancy at Birth: 48.11 years
 (male); 50.95 years (female)
Infant Mortality: 87.15/1,000 live births
Physicians Available: 1/3,532 people
HIV/AIDS Rate in Adults: 3.4%

Education

Adult Literacy Rate: 85.7%
Compulsory (Ages): 6–11; free

COMMUNICATION

Telephones: 10,000 main lines
Televisions: 88/1,000 people
Internet Users: 8,000 (2002)

TRANSPORTATION

Highways in Miles (Kilometers): 1,789 (2,885 km)
Railroads in Miles (Kilometers): none
Usable Airfields: 4
Motor Vehicles in Use: 7,600

GOVERNMENT

Type: republic
Independence Date: October 12, 1968
(from Spain)

Head of State/Government: President
(Brigadier General) Teodoro Obiang
Nguema Mbasogo; Prime Minister
Ricardo Mangue obama Nfubea
Political Parties: Democratic Party
for Equatorial Guinea; Progressive
Democratic Alliance; Popular Action
of Equatorial Guinea; Convergence
Party for Social Democracy; others
Suffrage: universal at 18

MILITARY

Military Expenditures (% of GDP):
0.1%
Current Disputes: maritime boundary
disputes with Cameroon, Gabon, and
Nigeria

ECONOMY

Currency ($ U.S. Equivalent): 465.51
CFA francs = $1

Per Capita Income/GDP: $50,200/
$25.6 billion
GDP Growth Rate: 18.6%
Inflation Rate: 6%
Unemployment Rate: 30%
Natural Resources: timber; petroleum;
gold; manganese; uranium
Agriculture: cocoa; coffee; timber;
rice; yams; cassava; bananas;
palm oil; livestock
Industry: fishing; sawmilling; petroleum;
natural gas
Exports: $8.96 billion (primary partners
China, Japan, United States)
Imports: $2.543 billion (primary
partners United States, France,
Spain)

SUGGESTED WEB SITE

http://www.sas.upenn.edu/ African_
Studies/E-Guinea.html

Equatorial Guinea Country Report

Few countries have been more consistently misruled than Equatorial Guinea. Having been traumatized during its first decade of independence by the sadistic Macias Nguema (1968–1979), the country continues to decay under his nephew and former security chief, Obiang Nguema Mbasogo. Mr Obiang Nguema overthrew and executed his uncle, President Francisco Nguema, in 1979. These two men hailing from the same family have been at the helm of Equatorial Guinea. Both men have ruled the country with an iron fist, committing some of the worst human rights violations in Africa.

In June 2002, the country's High Court handed 68 people prison sentences of up to 20 years for an alleged coup plot against President Obiang Nguema. Those jailed included a main opposition leader, Placido Mico Abogo. The European Union noted with concern that alleged "confessions" from among the accused seemed to have been obtained under duress.

DEVELOPMENT

The exploitation of oil and gas by U.S., French, and Spanish companies should greatly increase government revenues. The U.S. company Walter International recently finished work on a gas-separation plant.

Many observers look upon the trial as another betrayal of repeated promises

of political reform. Since the last (1999) elections, which were characterized by widespread intimidation, including arrest and torture against the opposition, Obiang has sought to encourage exiled opponents to return to Equatorial Guinea. A few returned to register their parties for elections that were scheduled for 2003, and eight of the principal opposition groups formed a coalition to try to remove Obiang from power. In response, the president tried to distance himself from his own government. In 2001, he replaced his cabinet for failing to "respect the majority opinion of the people," immediately prior to the formation of the opposition's coalition of eight parties.

Obiang officially transformed his regime into a multiparty democracy back in 1992. But this gesture is now dismissed as a thinly disguised sham for the benefit of the French, Spanish, and Americans who provide assistance to his regime. Outside interest in the country is focused on its new-found oil wealth, which in recent years has fueled economic growth that has so far been of little benefit to ordinary people.

As a result of the government's failure to honor its commitments, all the significant opposition groups boycotted 1993 elections, describing them as a farce. Subsequent opposition attempts to come to an accommodation with the government were set back in 1995, when a prominent opposition leader was arrested. In 1996,

Obiang claimed 97.85 percent of the vote in a new presidential poll.

In December 2002, President Obiang Nguema was unanimously re-elected, with 100 percent of the vote. The opposition leaders had pulled out of the poll, citing fraud and irregularities. However, by August 2003, exiled opposition leaders had formed a self-proclaimed government-in-exile with their base in Madrid, Spain. This led to the government releasing opposition leader Placido Mico Abogo and 17 other political prisoners. In March 2004, President Obiang said that 15 mercenaries (linked to the suspected mercenaries detained in Zimbabwe at the same time) were responsible for an alleged coup attempt. The trial of the 14 accused coup plotters from South Africa and Armenia took place in April 2004. A crackdown on immigrants followed the alleged coup attempt, with hundreds of foreigners deported.

FREEDOM

In September 1998, Amnesty International cautiously welcomed a decree by President Obiang Nguema Mbasogo commuting the death sentences of 15 political opponents, including 4 exiles judged in absentia, who had been convicted in a summary trial the previous June. The reprieves were considered a vindication of those arguing for the continued need to put international pressure on the regime.

In April 2004, during the parliamentary and municipal elections, President Obiang's ruling Democratic Party of Equatorial Guinea (PDGE) and allied parties took 98 of 100 seats in parliament, and all but seven of 244 municipal posts. Foreign independent election observers criticized both the poll and election result. Indeed, the ruling party and its leader have been able to garner some of the highest voting figures in the history of world democratic politics. One certainly must look closely at election results of 100 percent for the president and 98 percent for parliamentary and municipal candidates from the ruling party—these results show either an amazing degree of popularity for the man and his party, or else something is obviously desperately wrong in Equatorial Guinea. In most countries throughout the world, even announcing such electoral results would bring the population protesting into the streets, with mass riots and police killings resulting.

Equatorial Guinea's current suffering contrasts with the mood of optimism that characterized the country when it gained its independence from Spain in 1968. Confidence was then buoyed by a strong and growing gross domestic product, potential mineral riches, and exceptionally good soil.

HEALTH/WELFARE

At independence, Equatorial Guinea had one of the best doctor-to-population ratios in Africa, but Macias's rule left it with one of the lowest. Health care is gradually reviving, however, with major assistance coming from public and private sources.

The republic is comprised of two small islands, Fernando Po (now officially known as Bioko) and Annobón, and the larger and more populous coastal enclave of Rio Muni. Before the two islands and the enclave were united, during the 1800s, as Spain's only colony in sub-Saharan Africa, all three areas were victimized by their intense involvement in the slave trade.

Spain's major colonial concern was the prosperity of the large cocoa and coffee plantations that were established on the islands, particularly on Fernando Po. Because of resistance from the local Bubi, labor for these estates was imported from elsewhere in West Africa. Coercive recruitment and poor working conditions led to frequent charges of slavery.

Despite early evidence of its potential riches, Rio Muni was largely neglected by

the Spanish, who did not occupy its interior until 1926. In the 1930s and 1940s, much of the enclave was under the political control of the Elar-ayong, a nationalist movement that sought to unite the Fang, Rio Muni's principal ethnic group, against both the Spanish and the French rulers in neighboring Cameroon and Gabon. The territory has remained one of the world's least developed areas.

In 1968, then–Fascist-ruled Spain entrusted local power to Macias Nguema, who had risen through the ranks of the security service. Under his increasingly deranged misrule, virtually all public and private enterprise collapsed; indeed, between 1974 and 1979, the country had no budget. One third of the nation's population went into exile; tens of thousands of others were either murdered or allowed to die of disease and starvation. Many of the survivors were put to forced labor, and the rest were left to subsist off the land. Killings were carried out by boys conscripted between the ages of seven and 14.

Although no community in Equatorial Guinea was left unscarred by Macias's tyranny, the greatest disruption occurred on the islands. By 1976, the entire resident-alien population had left, along with most surviving members of the educated class. On Annobón, the government blocked all international efforts to stem a severe cholera epidemic in 1973. The near-total depopulation of the island was completed in 1976, when all able-bodied men on Annobón, along with another 20,000 from Rio Muni, were drafted for forced labor on Fernando Po.

ACHIEVEMENTS

At independence, 90% of all children attended school, but the schools were closed under Macias. Since 1979, primary education has revived and now incorporates most children.

If Equatorial Guinea's first decade of independence was hell, the years since have at best been purgatory. No sector of the economy is free of corruption. Uncontrolled—and in theory illegal—logging is destroying Rio Muni's environment, while in Malabo, the police routinely engage in theft. Food is imported and malnutrition commonplace. It has been reported that the remaining population of Annobón is being systematically starved while Obiang Nguema Mbasogo collects huge payments from international

companies that use the island as a toxic-waste dump.

At least one fifth of the Equato-Guinean population continue to live in exile, mostly in Cameroon and Gabon. This community has fostered a number of opposition groups. The government relies financially on French and Spanish aid. But Madrid's commitment has been strained by criticism from the Spanish press, which has been virtually alone in publicizing the continued suffering of Equatorial Guinea's people.

Timeline: PAST

1500s
Europeans explore modern Equatorial Guinea

1641
The Dutch establish slave-trading stations

1778
Spain claims the area of Equatorial Guinea; de facto control is not completed until 1926

1930
The League of Nations investigates charges of slavery on Fernando Po

1958
The murder of nationalist leader Acacio Mane leads to the founding of political parties

1963
Local autonomy is granted

1968
Independence; Macias Nguema begins his reign

1979
A coup ends the dictatorial regime of Macias Nguema; Obiang Nguema Mbasogo becomes the new ruler

1990s
A shift to multipartyism is accompanied by wave of political detentions; Obiang Nguema Mbasogo claims electoral victory

PRESENT

2000s
The exploitation of large oil reserves boosts the economy, but ordinary people still suffer

Suspected mercenaries arrested over alleged coup attempt; group is linked to suspected mercenaries detained in Zimbabwe; the accused foreign coup plotters to overthrow President Obiang are tried in Malabo, and their South African leader is sentenced to 34 years in jail

Hundreds of foreigners are deported under an immigration crackdown

Gabon (Gabonese Republic)

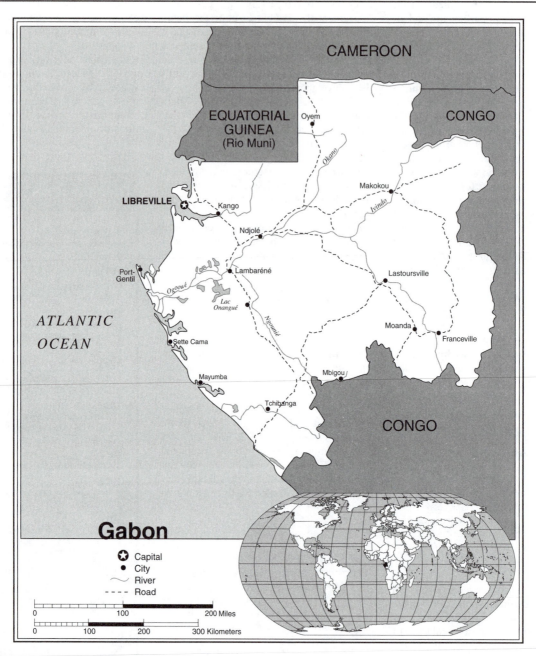

Gabon Statistics

GEOGRAPHY

Area in Square Miles (Kilometers):
102,317 (264,180) (about the size of
Colorado)

Capital (Population): Libreville
(573,000)

Environmental Concerns: deforestation;
poaching

Geographical Features: narrow coastal
plain; hilly interior; savanna in the east
and south

Climate: tropical

PEOPLE

Population

Total: 1,454,867

Annual Growth Rate: 2.036%

Rural/Urban Population Ratio: 16/84

Major Languages: French; Fang;
Myene; Eshira; Bopounou; Bateke;
Bandjabi

Ethnic Makeup: about 95% African,
including Eshira, Fang, Bapounou, and
Bateke; 5% European

Religions: 55%–75% Christian; less than 1%
Muslim; remainder indigenous beliefs

Health

Life Expectancy at Birth: 52.85 years
(male); 55.17 years (female)

Infant Mortality: 53.65/1,000 live births

Physicians Available: 1/2,337 people

HIV/AIDS Rate in Adults: 8.1%

Education

Adult Literacy Rate: 63.2%
Compulsory (Ages): 6–16

COMMUNICATION

Telephones: 36,500 main lines
Televisions: 35/1,000 people
Internet Users: 81,000 (2002)

TRANSPORTATION

Highways in Miles (Kilometers): 5,685
   (9,170 km)
Railroads in Miles (Kilometers): 814 km
Usable Airfields: 56
Motor Vehicles in Use: 33,000

GOVERNMENT

Type: republic; multiparty presidential
   regime
Independence Date: August 17, 1960
   (from France)

Head of State/Government: President El
   Hadj Omar Bongo; Prime Minister
   Jean Eyeghe Ndong
Political Parties: Gabonese Democratic
   Party; Gabonese Party for Progress;
   National Woodcutters Rally; others
Suffrage: universal at 21

MILITARY

Military Expenditures (% of GDP):
   3.4%
Current Disputes: maritime boundary
   dispute with Equatorial Guinea

ECONOMY

Currency ($ U.S. equivalent): 465.51 CFA
   francs = $1
Per Capita Income/GDP: $7,100/$10.19
   billion
GDP Growth Rate: 1.2%
Inflation Rate: 1.5%
Unemployment Rate: 21%

Labor Force by Occupation: 60%
   agriculture; 25% services and
   government; 15% industry and
   commerce
Natural Resources: petroleum; iron ore;
   manganese; uranium; gold; timber;
   hydropower
Agriculture: cocoa; coffee; palm oil
Industry: petroleum; lumber; mining;
   chemicals; ship repair; food
   processing; cement; textiles
Exports: 6.677 billion (primary partners
   United States, France, China)
Imports: $1.607 billion (primary partners
   France, Côte d'Ivoire, United States)

SUGGESTED WEB SITES

http://www.gabonnews.com
http://www.sas.upenn.edu/African_
   Studies/Country_Specific/Gabon
   .html
http://www.presidence-gabon.com/
   index-a.html

Gabon Country Report

Since independence, Gabon has achieved one of the highest per capita gross domestic products in Africa, due to exploitation of the country's natural riches, especially its oil. Oil exports and a small population have ensured more wealth per head of population than many of its neighbors. But there is a wide gap between such statistical wealth and the real poverty that still shapes the lives of most Gabonese. Disparities in income have helped fuel crime. In a controversial response, in July 2002 the government razed four village suburbs of the capital city

Libreville, saying that the areas had become havens for foreign criminal gangs.

Guided by only two presidents since independence from France in 1960, Gabon has proven to be one of the most stable nations in Africa. With more than 40 tribal groups in the nation the country has managed to avoid the ethnic violence that has frequently wrecked havok on many of the other African states. At the top of the local governing elite is President Omar Bongo, whose main palace, built a decade ago at a reported cost of $300 million, symbolizes his penchant for grandeur. Shortly after taking office in 1967, Bongo institutionalized his personal rule as the head of a one-party state. Until recently, his Democratic Party of Gabon (PDG) held a legal monopoly of power. In office since 1967, Bongo is currently Africa's longest serving leader. But, although the PDG's Constitution restricted the presidency to the "Founder President," for many years it was Gabon's former colonial master, France, not the ruling party's by-laws, that upheld the Bongo regime. After a landslide victory for the Gabonese Democratic Party in January 2002, parliament changed the constitution to allow President Bongo to run for office as many times as he wishes.

The French colonial presence in Gabon dates back to 1843. Between 1898 and 1930, many Gabonese were subject to long periods of forced labor, cutting timber for

French concessions companies. World War II coincided with a period of political liberalization in the territory under the Free French government of Felix Emboue, a black man born in French Guiana. Educated Gabonese were promoted for the first time to important positions in the local administration. In the 1950s, two major political parties emerged to compete in local politics: the Social Democratic Union of Gabon (UDSG), led by Jean-Hilaire Aubame; and the Gabonese Democratic Bloc (BDG) of Indjenjet Gondjout and Leon M'ba.

In the 1957 elections, the UDSG received 60 percent of the popular vote but gained only 19 seats in the 40-seat Assembly. Leon M'ba, who had the support of French logging interests, was elected leader by 21 BDG and independent deputies. As a result, it was M'ba who was at the helm when Gabon gained its independence, in 1960. This birth coincided with M'ba's declaration giving himself emergency powers, provoking a period of prolonged constitutional crisis.

DEVELOPMENT

The Trans-Gabonais Railway is one of the largest construction projects in Africa. Work began in 1974 and, after some delays, most of the line is now complete. The railway has opened up much of Gabon's interior to commercial development. The Chinese have become very important foreign investors in Gabon in recent years. In April 2004 the French oil firm Total signed a contract to export Gabonese oil to China. As oil reserves diminish, Gabon is trying to diversify away from oil. In September 2004 yet another agreement was signed with a Chinese company, this time to exploit iron ore. Both contracts represent a major boost for the Gabonese economy as they will generate thousands of jobs.

FREEDOM

Since 1967 Bongo has maintained power through a combination of repression and the deft use of patronage. The current transition to a multiparty process, however, has led to an improvement in human rights.

In January 1964, M'ba dissolved the Assembly over its members' continued refusal to accept a one-party state under his leadership. In February, the president himself was forced to resign by a group of army officers. Power was transferred to a civilian "Provisional Government," headed by Aubame, which also included BDG politicians such as Gondjout and several prominent, unaffiliated citizens. However, no sooner had the Provisional Government been installed than Gabon was invaded by French troops. Local military units were massacred in the surprise attack, which returned M'ba to office. Upon his death, M'ba was succeeded by his hand-picked successor, Omar Bongo.

HEALTH/WELFARE

The government claims to have instituted universal, compulsory education for Gabonese up to age 16. Independent observers doubt the government's claim but concur that major progress has been made in education. Health services have also expanded greatly.

It has been suggested that France's 1964 invasion was motivated primarily by a desire to maintain absolute control over Gabon's uranium deposits, which were then vital to France's nuclear-weapons program. Many Gabonese have since believed that their country has remained a de facto French possession. France has maintained its military presence, and the Presidential Guard, mainly officered by Moroccan and French mercenaries, outguns the Gabonese Army. France dominates Gabon's resource-rich economy.

In recent decades, Gabon's status quo has been challenged by its increasingly urbanized population. Although Bongo was able to co-opt or exile many of the figures who had once opposed M'ba, a new generation of opposition has emerged both at home and in exile. During the 1980s, the underground Movement for National Recovery (MORENA) emerged as the leading opposition group. In 1989, Bongo began talks with some elements within MORENA,

which led to a division within its ranks. But the breakup of MORENA failed to stem the emergence of new groups calling for a return to multiparty democracy.

Demonstrations and strikes at the beginning of 1990 led to the legalization of opposition parties. But the murder of a prominent opposition leader in May led to serious rioting at Port-Gentil, Gabon's second city. In response, France sent troops to the area. Multiparty elections for the National Assembly, in September–October 1990, resulted in a narrow victory for the PDG, amid allegations of widespread fraud. In 1992, most opposition groups united as the Coordination of Democratic Opposition. Bongo's victory claim in the December 1993 presidential elections was widely disbelieved. In September 1994, he agreed to the formation of a coalition "Transitional Government" and the drafting of a new Constitution, which was approved by 96 percent of the voters in July 1995.

ACHIEVEMENTS

Gabon will soon have a second private television station, funded by a French cable station. Profits will be used to fund films that will be shown on other African stations. Gabon's first private station is funded by Swiss and Gabonese capital.

In 1996, the PDG won a sweeping, but controversial, victory in parliamentary elections. This was followed up in 1998 by a landslide reelection victory for Bongo. The PDG's continuing hold on power was reconfirmed in the 2002 parliamentary elections. Following the poll, the National Woodcutters Rally, a party that has strong support in Libreville, agreed to take up Bongo's offer to serve as junior partners with the PDG in Gabon's first coalition government. Although opposition politicians claimed that the results had been rigged, independent observers have credited the PDG with success in retaining support of the rural base while co-opting opponents into its fold. In 2005, President

Omar Bongo was re-elected as president for a seven-year term, which resulted in the opposition supporters protesting and clashing with police in the capital. In the parliamentary elections that followed in December 2006, President Bongo's party once again comfortably won parliamentary elections amid opposition protests and accusation of fraud.

Timeline: PAST

1849
Libreville is founded by the French as a settlement for freed slaves

1910
Gabon becomes a colony within French Equatorial Africa

1940
The Free French in Brazzaville seize Gabon from the pro-Vichy government

1960
Independence is gained; Leon M'ba becomes president

1967
Omar Bongo becomes Gabon's second president after M'ba's death

1968
The Gabonese Democratic Party (PDG) becomes the only party of the state

1990s
Bongo agrees to multiparty elections but seeks to put limits on the opposition; riots in Port-Gentil

PRESENT

2000s
The PDG retains power amid opposition accusations of fraud

Constitution changed to allow President Bongo to run for president as many times as he wishes

Gabon and Equatorial Guinea agree to start talks over disputed islands in potentially oil-rich waters in the Gulf of Guinea

São Tomé and Príncipe (Democratic Republic of São Tomé and Príncipe)

PRÍNCIPE
Santo Antonio

SÃO TOMÉ
Neves
SÃO TOMÉ
Santa Cruz
Porto Alegre

São Tomé
and Príncipe

- ✪ Capital
- • City
- ~ River
- --- Road

0   20   40   50 Miles
0   20   40   60 Kilometers

São Tomé and Príncipe Statistics

GEOGRAPHY

Area in Square Miles (Kilometers): 387
(1,001) (about 5 times the size of
Washington, D.C.)

Capital (Population): São Tomé
(67,000)

Environmental Concerns: deforestation;
soil erosion; soil exhaustion

Geographical Features: volcanic;
mountainous; islands in the Gulf of
Guinea; the smallest country in Africa

Climate: tropical

PEOPLE

Population

Total: 199,579
Annual Growth Rate: 3.1%
Rural/Urban Population Ratio: 42/58
Major Languages: Portuguese; Fang; Kriolu

GLOBAL STUDIES

Ethnic Makeup: Portuguese-African mixture; African minority
Religions: 80% Christian; 20% others

Health

Life Expectancy at Birth: 66.03 years (male); 69.3 years (female)
Infant Mortality: 40.54/1,000 live births
Physicians Available: 1/1,881 people

Education

Adult Literacy Rate: 84.9%
Compulsory (Ages): for 4 years between ages 7–14

COMMUNICATION

Telephones: 7,100 main lines
Televisions: 154/1,000 people
Internet Users: 23,000 (2002)

TRANSPORTATION

Highways in Miles (Kilometers): 198 (320)
Railroads in Miles (Kilometers): none
Usable Airfields: 2

GOVERNMENT

Type: republic
Independence Date: July 12, 1975 (from Portugal)
Head of State/Government: President Fradique de Menezes; Prime Minister Tome Soares da Vera Cruz
Political Parties: Party for Democratic Convergence; Movement for the Liberation of São Tomé and Príncipe–Social Democratic Party; others
Suffrage: universal at 18

MILITARY

Military Expenditures (% of GDP): 0.8%
Current Disputes: none

ECONOMY

Currency ($ U.S. equivalent): 13,704 dobras = $1
Per Capita Income/GDP: $1,200/$278 million

GDP Growth Rate: 4.7%
Inflation Rate: 7%
Labor Force by Occupation: mainly engaged in subsistence agriculture and fishing
Natural Resources: fish; hydropower
Agriculture: cacao; coconut palms; coffee; bananas; palm kernels; copra
Industry: light construction; textiles; soap; beer; fish processing; timber
Exports: $9.773 million (primary partners Netherlands, Portugal, Spain)
Imports: $48.87 million (primary partners Portugal, France, United Kingdom)

SUGGESTED WEB SITES

http://www.sao-tome.com
http://www.state.gov/ www.background_notes/ sao_tome_0397_bgn.html
http://www.emulateme.com/saotome .htm
http://www.sas.upenn.edu/African_Studies/ Country_Specific/Sao_Tome.html

São Tomé and Príncipe Country Report

In August 1995, soldiers in the small island-nation of São Tomé and Príncipe briefly deposed Miguel Trovoada, the country's first democratically elected president. The coup quickly collapsed, however, in the face of domestic and international opposition. While the country's new democracy survived, it was vulnerable to a weak economy, which showed little prospect of significant improvement anytime soon.

DEVELOPMENT

Local food production has been significantly boosted by a French-funded plan. Japan is assisting in fishery development. There is concern that tourist fishermen may adversely affect the local fishing industry.

The islands held their first multiparty elections in January 1991. The elections resulted in the defeat of the former ruling party, the Liberation Movement of São Tomé and Príncipe–Social Democratic Party (MLSTP–PSD), by Trovoada's Party for Democratic Convergence–Group of Reflection (PDC–GR). Subsequent elections in December 1992, however, reversed the PDC–GR advantage in Parliament, leading to an uneasy division of power. This division was reinforced with Trovoada's reelection in 1996, followed by an even greater MLSTP–PSD parliamentary victory in 1998.

In the July 2001 presidential elections businessman Fradique de Menezes was declared the winner. He was sworn into office in early September. However, the victory of the opposition MLSTP–PSD party in the March 2002 parliamentary elections led de Menezes to appoint Gabriel da Costa as prime minister, and both main political parties agreed to share power and form a broad-based government. de Menezes is the country's third president after Miguel Trovoada who served two five-year terms, the maximum permitted by the constitution.

The government was confronted with a massive civil-servants strike in 2001 to press for higher pay. Officials said the country's external debt in 1998 amounted to U.S. $270 million, far more than the country's annual gross domestic product.

São Tomé and Príncipe gained its independence in 1975, after a half-millennium of Portuguese rule. During the colonial era, economic life centered around the interests of a few thousand Portuguese settlers, particularly a handful of large-plantation owners who controlled more than 80 percent of the land. After independence, most of the Portuguese fled, taking their skills and capital and leaving the economy in disarray. But production on the plantations has since been revived.

The Portuguese began the first permanent settlement of São Tomé and Príncipe in the late 1400s. Through slave labor, the islands developed rapidly as one of the world's leading exporters of sugar. Only a small fraction of the profits from this boom were consumed locally; and high mortality rates, caused by brutal working conditions, led to an almost insatiable demand for more slaves. Profits from sugar declined after the mid-1500s due to competition from Brazil and the Caribbean. A period of prolonged depression set in.

FREEDOM

Before 1987, human rights were circumscribed in São Tomé and Príncipe. Gradual liberalization has now given way to a commitment to political pluralism. The current government has a good record of respect for human rights. Major problems are an inefficient judicial system, harsh prison conditions, and acts of police brutality. Outdated labor practices on the plantations limit worker rights.

In the early 1800s, a second economic boom swept the islands, when they became leading exporters of coffee, and, more important, cocoa. (São Tomé and Príncipe's position in the world market has since declined, yet these two cash crops, along with copra, have continued to be economic mainstays.) Although slavery was officially abolished during the nineteenth century, forced labor was maintained by the Portuguese into modern times. Involuntary contract workers, known as *serviçais,* were imported to labor on the islands' plantations, which had notoriously high mortality rates. Sporadic labor unrest and occasional incidents of international outrage led to some improvement in working conditions, but fundamental reforms came about only after independence. A historical turning point for the islands was the Batepa Massacre in 1953, when several hundred African laborers were killed following local resistance to labor conditions.

HEALTH/WELFARE

Since independence, the government has had enormous progress in expanding health care and education. The Sãotoméan infant mortality rate is now among the lowest in Africa, and average life expectancy is among the highest. About 65% of the population between 6 and 19 years of age now attend school.

Between 1975 and 1991, São Tomé and Príncipe was ruled by the MLSTP–PSD, which had emerged in exile as the island's leading anticolonial movement, as a one-party state initially committed to Marxist-Leninism. But in 1990, a new policy of *abertura,* or political and economic "opening," resulted in the legalization of opposition parties and the introduction of direct elections with secret balloting. Press restrictions were also lifted, and the nation's security police were purged. The democratization process was welcomed by previously exiled opposition groups, most of which united as the PDC–GR. The changed political climate was also reflected in the establishment of an independent labor movement. Previously, strikes were forbidden.

The move toward multiparty politics was accompanied by an evolution to a market economy. Since 1985, a "Free Trade Zone" was established, state farms were privatized, and private capital was attracted to build up a tourist industry. These moves were accompanied by a major expansion of Western loans and assistance to the islands—an inflow of capital that now accounts for nearly half of the gross domestic product.

The government also focused its development efforts on fishing. In 1978, a 200-mile maritime zone was declared over the tuna-rich waters around the islands. The state-owned fishing company, Empesca, began upgrading the local fleet, which still consists mostly of canoes using old-fashioned nets. The influx of aid and investment

has resulted in several years of sustained economic growth.

ACHIEVEMENTS

São Tomé and Príncipe shares in a rich Luso-African artistic tradition. The country is particularly renowned for poets such as Jose de Almeida and Francisco Tenreiro, who were among the first to express in the Portuguese language the experiences and pride of Africans.

The current inhabitants of São Tomé and Príncipe are primarily of mixed African and European descent. During the colonial period, the society was stratified along racial lines. At the top were the Europeans —mostly Portuguese. Just below them were the mesticos or *filhos da terra,* the mixed-blood descendants of slaves. Descendants of slaves who arrived later were known as *forros.* Contract workers were labeled as *serviçais,* while their children became known as *tongas.* Still another group was the *angolares,* who reportedly were the descendants of shipwrecked slaves. All of these colonial categories were used to divide and rule the local population; the distinctions have begun to diminish, however, as an important sociological factor on the islands.

THE FUTURE

The nation of São Tomé and Príncipe is precariously balanced between financial stability and social chaos. The stability arises from the recent discovery and exploitation of large offshore oil fields. In August 2002 President Fraque de Menezes announced plans for a U.S. naval base in the country, which would aim to protect São Tomé's oil interests. Yet the social chaos still lingers and the possibility of it rising up from the ranks of the army still exists.

On July 16, 2003 a military coup toppled the government. The coup occurred largely as a result of the yet to be realized oil wealth and its future distribution. President de Menezes, who was in Nigeria at the time, returned to São Tomé a week later, after an agreement had been reached with the junta. Although a general amnesty was given to the coup leaders, conditions have not improved so the threat of yet another coup still lingers.

By October 2003 oil companies bid for offshore oil blocs controlled by São Tomé and Nigeria, which are expected to generate hundreds of millions of dollars in licensing money for São Tomé. During March 2004 the government was on the verge of collapse as a major conflict arose between the president and prime minister over control of the oil deals. Four cabinet ministers were

replaced. In September 2004, President de Menezes replaced Prime Minister Gabriel Arcanjo Ferreira da Costa and changed the government Cabinet after a series of corruption scandals. A new Prime Minister, Damiao Vaz De Almeida, was immediately sworn in. In July 2006, President de Menezes was re-elected. The president's party, the Democratic Movement of Forces for Change (MDFM), also won the March 2006 elections, which made it possible for the president to appoint an ally as prime minister. Previous governments have been cohabited by rival presidents and prime ministers.

The outlook for this island nation is quite promising. The government hopes to reduce dependence on donors and cocoa exports by exploiting offshore oil. Falls in production and prices have left the island state heavily reliant on foreign aid. The government has been encouraging economic diversification, and oil drilling for commercial production is expected to begin within a few years. Also one way to diversify the economy is to promote tourism given the islands natural beauty, which has hitherto not been aggressively exploited. In short, the country's fortunes could change once again by a prospective oil boom in the near future.

Timeline: PAST

1500s
The Portuguese settle São Tomé and Príncipe

1876
Slavery is abolished, but forced labor continues

1953
The Portuguese massacre hundreds of islanders

1972
Factions within the liberation movement unite to form the MLSTP in Gabon

1975
Independence

1979
Manuel Pinto da Costa deposes and exiles Miguel Trovoada, the premier and former number-two man in the MLSTP

1990s
Economic and political liberalization; multiparty elections

PRESENT

2000s
Fradique de Menezes wins the presidency

São Tomé and Nigeria share offshore oil fields, which have yet to be exploited

São Tomé hopes to reduce dependence on donors and cocoa exports by exploiting offshore oil

East Africa

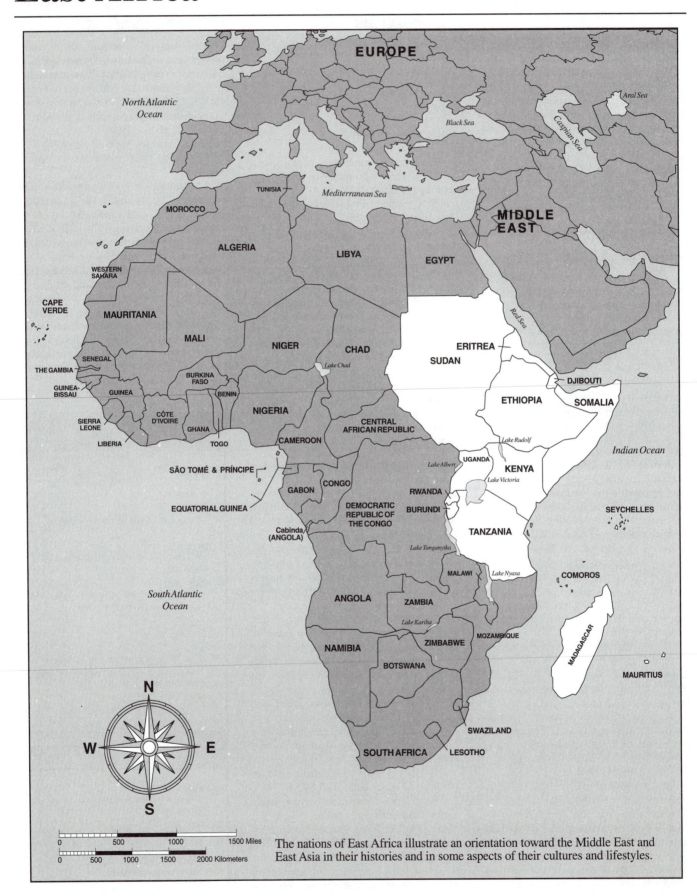

The nations of East Africa illustrate an orientation toward the Middle East and East Asia in their histories and in some aspects of their cultures and lifestyles.

East Africa   A Mixed Inheritance

The vast East African region, ranging from Sudan in the north to Tanzania and the Indian Ocean islands in the south, is an area of great diversity. Although the islands are the homes of distinctive civilizations with ties to Asia, their interactions with the African mainland give their inclusion here validity. Ecological features such as the Great Rift Valley, the prevalence of cattle-herding lifestyles, and long-standing participation in the Indian Ocean trading networks are some of the region's unifying aspects.

CATTLE-HERDING SOCIETIES

A long-horned cow would be an appropriate symbol for East Africa. Most of the region's rural inhabitants, who make up the majority of people from the Horn, to Lake Malawi, to Madagascar, value cattle for their social as well as economic importance. The Nuer of Sudan, the Somalis near the Red Sea (who, like many other peoples of the Horn, herd camels as well as cattle, goats, and sheep), and the Maasai of Tanzania and Kenya are among the pastoral peoples whose herds provide their livelihoods. Farming communities such as the Kikuyu of Kenya, the Baganda of Uganda, and the Malagasy of Madagascar also prize cattle.

Much of the East African landmass is well suited for herding. Whereas the rain forests of West and Central Africa are generally infested with tsetse flies, whose bite is fatal to livestock, most of East Africa is made up of belts of tropical and temperate savanna, which are ideal for grazing. Thus pastoralism has long been predominant in the savanna zones of West and Southern, as well as East, Africa. Tropical rain forests are found in East Africa only on the east coast of Madagascar and scattered along the mainland's coast. Much of the East African interior is dominated by the Great Rift Valley, which stretches from the Red Sea as far south as Malawi. This geological formation is characterized by mountains as well as valleys, and it features the region's great lakes, such as Lake Albert, Lake Tanganyika, and Lake Malawi.

People have been moving into and through the East African region since the existence of humankind; indeed, most of the earliest human fossils have been unearthed in this region. Today, almost all the mainland inhabitants speak languages that belong to either the Bantu or Nilotic linguistic families. There has been much historical speculation about the past migration of these peoples, but recent research indicates that both linguistic groups have probably been established in the area for a long time, although oral traditions and other forms of historical evidence indicate locally important shifts in settlement patterns into the contemporary period. Iron working and, in at least a few cases, small-scale steel production have been a part of the regional economy for more than 2,000 years. Long-distance trade and the production of various crafts have also existed since ancient times.

The inhabitants of the region have had to deal with insufficient and unreliable rainfall. Drought and famine in the Horn and in areas of Kenya and Tanzania have in recent years changed lifestyles and dislocated many people.

ISLAMIC INFLUENCE

Many of the areas of East Africa have been influenced—since at least as far back as Roman times and perhaps much further—by the Middle East and other parts of Asia. Over the past thousand years, most parts of East Africa, including the Christian highlands of Ethiopia and the inland interlake states such as Buganda, Burundi, and Rwanda, became familiar to the Muslim Arab traders of the Swahili and Red Sea coasts and the Sudanese interior. Somalia, Djibouti, and Sudan, which border the Red Sea and are close to the Arabian Peninsula, have been the countries most influenced by Arab Islamic culture. Mogadishu, the capital of Somalia, began as an Islamic trading post in the tenth century A.D. The Islamic faith, its various sects or brotherhoods, the Koran, and the Shari'a (the Islamic legal code) are predominant throughout the Horn, except in the Ethiopian and Eritrean highlands and southern Sudan. In recent years, many Somalis, Sudanese, and others have migrated to the oil-rich states of Arabia to work.

Farther south, in the communities and cultures on the perimeters of the east coast, Arabs and local Bantu-speaking Africans combined, from as early as the ninth century but especially during the 1200s to 1400s, to form the culture and the language that we now call Swahili. In the first half of the nineteenth century, Seyyid Said, the sultan of Oman, transferred his capital to Zanzibar, in recognition of the outpost's economic importance. Motivated by the rapid expansion of trade in ivory and slaves, many Arab–Swahili traders began to establish themselves and build settlements as far inland as the forests of eastern Democratic Republic of the Congo. As a result, some of the non-coastal peoples also adopted Islam, while Swahili developed into a regional lingua franca.

The whole region from the Horn to Tanzania continued to be affected by the slave trade through much of the nineteenth century. Slaves were sent north from Uganda and southern Sudan to Egypt and the Middle East, and from Ethiopia across the Red Sea. Others were taken to the coast by Arab, Swahili, or African traders, either to work on the plantations in Zanzibar or to be transported to the Persian Gulf and the Indian Ocean islands.

In the late 1800s and early 1900s, South Asian laborers from what was then British India were brought in by the British to build the East African railroad. South Asian traders already resided in Zanzibar; others now came and settled in Kenya and Tanzania, becoming shopkeepers and bankers in inland centers, such as Kampala and Nairobi, as well as on the coast, in Mombasa and Dar es Salaam or in smaller stops along the railroad. South Asian laborers were also sent in large numbers to work on the sugar plantations of Mauritius; their descendants there now make up about two thirds of that island's population.

(United Nations photo 131,312 by Ray Witlin)

In the drought-affected areas of East Africa, people must devote considerable time and energy to the search for water.

The subregions of East Africa include the following: the countries of the Horn, East Africa proper, and the islands. The Horn includes Djibouti, Ethiopia, Eritrea, Somalia, and Sudan, which are associated here with one another not so much because of a common heritage or on account of any compatibility of their governments (indeed, they are often hostile to one another), but because of the movements of peoples across borders in recent times. *East Africa proper* is comprised of Kenya, Tanzania, and Uganda, which do have underlying cultural ties and a history of economic relations, in which Rwanda and Burundi have also shared. The *Indian Ocean islands* include the Comoros, Madagascar, Mauritius, and Seychelles, which, notwithstanding the expanses of ocean that separate them, have certain cultural aspects and current interests in common.

THE HORN

Ethiopia traditionally has had a distinct, semi-isolated history that has separated the nation from its neighbors. This early Christian civilization, which was periodically united by a strong dynasty but at other times was disunited, was centered in the highlands of the interior, surrounded by often hostile lowland peoples. Before the nineteenth century, it was in infrequent contact with other Christian societies. In the 1800s, however, a series of strong rulers reunified the highlands and went on to conquer surrounding peoples such as the Afar, Oromo, and Somali. In the process, the state expanded to its current boundaries. While the empire's expansion helped it to preserve its independence during Africa's colonial partition, sectarian and ethnic divisions—a legacy of the imperial state-building process—now threaten to tear the polity apart.

Ethiopia and the rest of the Horn have been influenced by outside powers, whose interests in the region have been primarily rooted in its strategic location. In the nineteenth century, both Britain and France became interested in the Horn, because the Red Sea was the link between their countries and the markets of Asia. This was especially true after the completion of the Suez Canal in 1869. Both of the imperial powers occupied ports on the Red Sea at the time. They then began to compete over the upper Nile in modern Sudan. In the 1890s, French forces, led by Captain Jean Baptiste Marchand, literally raced from the present-day area of Congo to reach the center of Sudan before the arrival of a larger British expeditionary force, which had invaded the region from Egypt. Ultimately, the British were able to consolidate their control over the entire Sudan.

Italian ambitions in the Horn were initially encouraged by the British, in order to counter the French. Italy's defeat by the Ethiopians at the Battle of Adowa in 1896 did not deter its efforts to dominate the coastal areas of Eritrea and southeastern Somalia. Later, under Benito Mussolini, Italy briefly (1936–1942) occupied Ethiopia itself.

During the Cold War, great-power competition for control of the Red Sea and the Gulf of Aden, with their strategic locations near the oil fields of the Middle East as well as along the Suez shipping routes, continued between the United States and the Soviet Union. Local events sometimes led to shifts in alignments. Before 1977, for instance, the United States was closely allied with Ethiopia, and the Soviet Union with Somalia. However, in 1977–1978, Ethiopia, having come under a self-proclaimed Marxist-Leninist government, allied itself with the Soviet Union, receiving in return the support of Cuban troops and billions of dollars' worth of Socialist-bloc military aid, on loan, for use in its battles against Eritrean and Somali rebels. The latter group, living in Ethiopia's Ogaden region, were seeking to become part of a greater Somalia. In this irredentist adventure, they had the direct support of invading Somalia troops. Although the United States refused to counter the Soviets by in turn backing the irredentists, it subsequently established relations with the Somali government at a level that allowed it virtually to take over the former Soviet military facility at Berbera.

Discord and Drought

The countries of the Horn, unlike the other states in the region, are politically alienated from one another. There is thus little prospect of an effective regional community emerging among them in the foreseeable future. Although the end of the Cold War has reduced the interest of external powers, local animosities continue to wreak havoc in the region. The Horn continues to be bound together and torn apart by millions of refugees fleeing armed conflicts in all of the states. Ethiopia, Somalia, and Sudan have suffered under especially vicious authoritarian regimes that resorted to the mass murder of dissident segments of their populations. Although the old regimes have been overthrown in Ethiopia and Somalia, peace has yet to come to either society. Having gained its independence only in 1993, Eritrea, Africa's newest nation, has struggled to overcome the devastating legacy of its 30-year liberation struggle against Ethiopia. Eritrea's well-being has been further compromised by reverses in a border war with Ethiopia. Recent battlefield victories against the Eritreans have revived the passions of some Ethiopians who have never fully accepted Eritrea's secession. The stability of neighboring Djibouti, once a regional enclave of calm, has also been compromised in recent years by sometimes violent internal political conflicts.

The horrible effects of these wars have been magnified by recurrent droughts and famines. Hundreds of thousands of people have starved to death in the past decade, while many more have survived only because of international aid efforts.

Ethiopians leave their homes for Djibouti, Somalia, and Sudan for relief from war and famine. Sudanese and Somalis flee to Ethiopia for the same reasons. Today, every country harbors not only refugees but also dissidents from neighboring lands and has a citizenry related to those who live in adjoining countries. Peoples such as the Afar minority in Djibouti often seek support from their kin in Eritrea and Ethiopia. Many Somali guerrilla groups have used Ethiopia as a base, while Somali factions have continued to give aid and comfort to Ethiopia's rebellious Ogaden population. Ethiopian factions allegedly continue to assist southern rebels against the government of Sudan, which had long supported the Tigray and Eritrean rebel movements of northern Ethiopia.

At times, the states of the region have reached agreements among themselves to curb their interference in one another's affairs. But they have made almost no progress in the more fundamental task of establishing internal peace, thus assuring that the region's violent downward spiral continues.

THE SOUTHERN STATES OF EAST AFRICA

The peoples of Kenya, Tanzania, and Uganda as well as Burundi and Rwanda have underlying connections rooted in the past. The kingdoms of the Lakes Region of Uganda, Rwanda, and Burundi, though they have been politically superseded in the postcolonial era, have left their legacies. For example, myths about a heroic dynasty of rulers, the Chwezi, who ruled over an early Ugandan-based kingdom, are widespread. Archaeological evidence attests to the actual existence of the Chwezi, probably in the sixteenth century. Peoples in western Kenya and Tanzania, who have lived under less centralized systems of governance but nonetheless have rituals similar to those of the Ugandan kingdoms, also share the traditions of the Chwezi dynasty, which have become associated with a spirit cult.

The precolonial kingdoms of Rwanda and Burundi, both of which came under German and, later, Belgian control during the colonial era, were socially divided between a ruling warrior class, the Tutsis, and a much larger peasant class, the Hutus. Although both states are now independent republics, their societies remain bitterly divided along these ethnoclass lines. In Rwanda, the feudal hegemony of the Tutsis was overthrown in a bloody civil conflict in 1959, which led to the flight of many Tutsis. But in 1994, the sons of these Tutsi exiles came to power, after elements in the former Hutu-dominated regime organized a genocidal campaign against all Tutsis. In the belief that the Tutsis were back on top, millions of Hutus then fled the country. In Burundi, Tutsi rule was maintained for decades through a repressive police state, which in 1972 and 1988 resorted to the mass murder of Hutus. Elections in 1993 resulted in the country's first Hutu president at the head of a government that included members of both groups, but he was murdered by the predominantly Tutsi army. Since then, the country has been teetering on the brink of yet another catastrophe, as some of its politicians try to promote reconciliation.

Kenya and Uganda were taken over by the British in the late nineteenth century, while Tanzania, originally conquered by Germany, became a British colony after World War I. In Kenya, the British encouraged the growth of a settler community. Although never much more than 1 percent of the colony's resident population, the British settlers were given the best agricultural lands in the rich highlands region around Nairobi; and throughout most of the colonial era, they were allowed to exert a political and economic hegemony over the local Africans. The settler populations in Tanzania and Uganda were smaller and less powerful. While the settler presence in Kenya led to land alienation and consequent immiseration for many Africans, it also fostered a fair amount of colonial investment in infrastructure. As a result, Kenya had a relatively sophisticated economy at the time of its independence, a fact that was to complicate proposals for its economic integration with Tanzania and Uganda.

In the 1950s, the British established the East African Common Services Organization to promote greater economic cooperation among its Kenyan, Tanganyikan (Tanzanian), and Ugandan territories. By the early 1960s, the links among the states were so close that President Julius Nyerere of Tanzania proposed that his country delay its independence until Kenya also gained its freedom, in hopes that the two countries would then join together. This did not occur.

In 1967, the Common Services Organization was transformed by its three (now independent) members into a full-fledged "common market," known as the East African Community (EAC). The EAC collectively managed the railway system, development of harbors, and international air, postal, and telecommunication facilities. It also maintained a common currency, development bank, and other economic, cultural, and scientific services. Peoples moved freely across the borders of the three EAC states. However, the EAC soon began to unravel, as conflicts over its operations grew. It finally collapsed in 1977. The countries disputed the benefits of the association, which seemed to have been garnered primarily by Kenya. The ideologies and personalities of its leaders at the time—Nyerere, Jomo Kenyatta of Kenya, and Idi Amin of Uganda—differed greatly. Relations between Kenya and Tanzania deteriorated to the point that the border between them was closed for several years.

In 1984, Kenya, Tanzania, and Uganda signed an "East African Mediation Agreement," which allowed for the division of the EAC's assets and liabilities, along with the reopening of the Kenya–Tanzania border. This final chapter of the old Community laid the groundwork for renewed cooperation, which ultimately, in late 2001, led to the EAC's reestablishment in a lavish ceremony at Arusha, Tanzania.

By the end of the 1980s, the value of the Community to the three economies has become clear. But political factors continued to complicate the quest for integration. In 1986, Kenya and Tanzania, along with Rwanda, Burundi, Sudan, and then Zaire (today the Democratic Republic of the Congo) pledged to prevent their territories from being used by exiles seeking to destabilize their neighbors. While this broader agreement went unenforced, political relations among Kenya, Tanzania, and Uganda (which in 1986 came under the control of Yoweri Museveni's National Resistance Movement, after years of suffering under the brutal regimes of Amin and Milton Obote) began to improve.

From 1981, the three states were also linked in a loose nineteen-member state "Preferential Trade Area" for southern and eastern Africa. This body laid the basis for further cooperation in the areas of security, trade, and joint hydroelectric projects. Although members of the Economic Community of Central African States, Rwanda and Burundi were also linked with Kenya, Tanzania, and Uganda as a subregion of the UN Commission for Africa.

In 1993, the three states established a "Permanent Tripartite Commission" to look into reviving the East African Community. By then the leaders of all three countries—Daniel Mkapa of Tanzania, Daniel Arap Moi of Kenya, and Museveni—had been implementing confidence-building measures. The 1993 agreement had the goal of establishing a common market and currency zone for the region. But both Tanzania and Uganda were reluctant to move forward due to Kenya's continued industrial

advantages. The 2001 treaty has allayed these concerns by dropping a strict time frame for the removal of trade restrictions.

While full economic and political union for the EAC members (who are likely to be expanded to include Rwanda, Burundi, and perhaps Ethiopia) remains a long-term goal, some important structures have already been put in place: the East African Court of Justice, the East African Legislative Assembly, and the Secretariat. In 1998, a common East African passport was introduced that allows citizens of the three nations to cross one another's borders freely. Progress is also reportedly being made toward free currency convertibility, reduced tariffs, and in the areas of defense and foreign policy. All of these steps have generally been greeted with popular support. As the Tanzanian statesman Salim Salim noted: "You can choose a friend but you cannot choose a brother. . . . In this case Kenyans and Ugandans are our brothers."

THE ISLANDS

The Comoros, Madagascar, Mauritius, and Seychelles each have their own unique characteristics. They all have some important traits in common. All four island nations have been strongly influenced historically by contacts with Asia as well as with mainland Africa and Europe. Madagascar and the Comoros have populations that originated in Indonesia and the Middle East as well as in Africa; the Malagasy language is related to Indonesian Malay. The citizens of Mauritius and Seychelles are of European as well as African and Asian origin.

All four island groups have also been influenced by France. Mauritius and Seychelles were not permanently inhabited until the 1770s, when French settlers arrived with their African slaves. The British subsequently took control of these two island groups and, during the 1830s, abolished slavery. Thereafter the British encouraged migration from South Asia and, to a lesser extent, from China to make up for labor shortages on the islands' plantations. Local French-based creoles remain the major languages on the islands.

In 1978, all the islands, along with opposition groups from the French possession of Réunion, formed the Indian Ocean Commission. Originally a body with a socialist orientation, the commission campaigned for the independence of Réunion and the return of the island of Diego Garcia by Britain to Mauritius, as well as the dismantling of the U.S. naval base located there. By the end of the 1980s, however, the export-oriented growth of Mauritius and the continuing prosperity of Seychelles' tourist-based economy were helping to push all nations toward a greater emphasis on market economics in their multilateral, as well as internal, policy initiatives. Madagascar and the Comoros have recently offered investment incentives for Mauritius-based private firms. Mauritians have also played prominent roles in the development of tourism in the Comoros.

In addition to their growing economic ties, the Comoros and Mauritius, and to a somewhat lesser extent, Madagascar and Seychelles, have created linkages with South Africa. In 1995, Mauritius followed South Africa's lead to become the 12th member of the Southern African Development Community (SADC).

Burundi (Republic of Burundi)

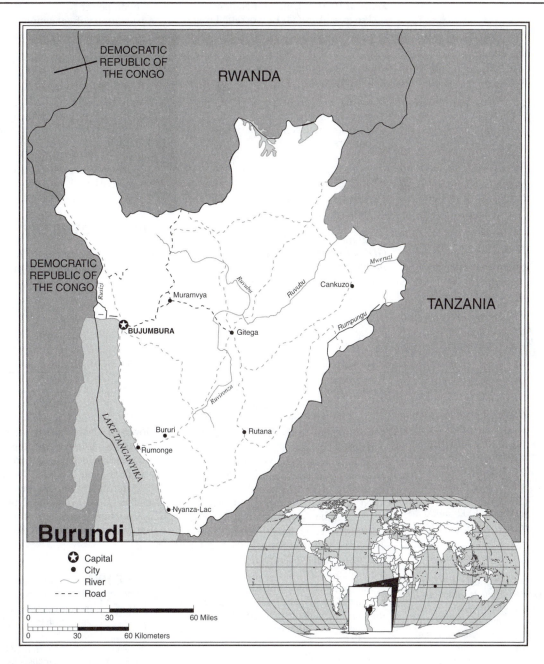

Burundi Statistics

GEOGRAPHY

Area in Square Miles (Kilometers): 10,759 (27,834) (about the size of Maryland)
Capital (Population): Bujumbura (346,000)
Environmental Concerns: soil erosion; deforestation; habitat loss
Geographical Features: hilly and mountainous, dropping to a plateau in the east; some plains; landlocked

Climate: tropical to temperate; temperature varies with altitude

PEOPLE

Population

Total: 8,390,505
Annual Growth Rate: 3.593%
Rural/Urban Population Ratio: 90/10
Major Languages: Kirundi; French; Swahili; others

Ethnic Makeup: 85% Hutu; 14% Tutsi; 1% Twa and others
Religions: 67% Christian; 23% indigenous beliefs; 10% Muslim

Health

Life Expectancy at Birth: 50.48 years (male); 52.12 years (female)
Infant Mortality: 61.93/1,000 live births
Physicians Available: 1/31,777 people
HIV/AIDS Rate in Adults: 6%

51

GLOBAL STUDIES

Education

Adult Literacy Rate: 59.3%
Compulsory (Ages): 7–13; free

COMMUNICATION

Telephones: 31,100 main lines
Televisions: 7/1,000 people
Internet Users: 60,000 (2003)

TRANSPORTATION

Highways in Miles (Kilometers): 7,393
   (12,322 km)
Railroads in Miles (Kilometers): none
Usable Airfields: 8
Motor Vehicles in Use: 20,000

GOVERNMENT

Type: republic
Independence Date: July 1, 1962
   (from UN trusteeship under Belgian
   administration)

Head of State/Government: President
   Pierre Nkurunziza is both head of state
   and head of government
Political Parties: Union for National
   Progress; Burundi Democratic Front;
   others
Suffrage: universal for adults

MILITARY

Military Expenditures (% of GDP): 5.9%
Current Disputes: severe interethnic
   conflict, transcending national
   borders

ECONOMY

Currency ($ U.S. equivalent): 1,104.20
   francs = $1
Per Capita Income/GDP: $700/$5.854
   billion
GDP Growth Rate: 5.1%
Inflation Rate: 10.7%
Population Below Poverty Line: 70%

Natural Resources: nickel; uranium; rare
   earth oxides; peat; cobalt; copper;
   platinum; vanadium; arable land;
   hydropower
Agriculture: coffee; cotton; tea; corn;
   sorghum; sweet potatoes; bananas;
   manioc; livestock
Industry: light consumer goods;
   assembly of imported components;
   public-works construction; food
   processing
Exports: $24 million (primary partners
   European Union, United States,
   Kenya)
Imports: $125 million (primary
   partners European Union, Tanzania,
   Zambia)

SUGGESTED WEB SITE

http://www.sas.upenn.edu/African_
   Studies/Country_Specific/Burundi.html

Burundi Country Report

Notwithstanding the tireless diplomatic efforts of South African mediators, Burundi has in recent years remained divided between the forces loyal to its transitional government and the predominantly ethnic-Hutu rebels of the Forces for the Defense of Democracy (FDD) and the National Liberation Forces (FNL). Talks among the groupings throughout 2002 failed to achieve national reconciliation.

DEVELOPMENT

Burundi's sources of wealth are limited. There is no active development of mineral resources, although nickel has been located and may be mined soon. There is little industry, and the coffee industry, which contributes 75% to 90% of export earnings, has declined.

Hutu rebels have been fighting with Burundi's government since 1993, when Tutsi paratroopers assassinated the small Central African country's first democratically elected president, who was a Hutu. Despite being in the minority, Tutsis have effectively controlled the nation of 8 million people for all but a few months since independence in 1961. The current transitional government took office in November 2001 to implement a power-sharing agreement, mediated in August 2000 by

former South African president Nelson Mandela, between Hutu and Tutsi political parties. But the rebels maintain that true power remains in the hands of the Tutsi-dominated military.

Burundi's current divisions have deeper roots. In 1972 and again in 1988, tens of thousands of people, mostly Hutus, perished in genocidal attacks. In more recent years, the situation has been further complicated by the escalation of conflict between Tutsis and Hutus in the neighboring states of Rwanda and the Democratic Republic of the Congo (D.R.C.).

In the past the violence was initiated by members of the Tutsi governing elite seeking to maintain their privileged status through brutal military control. Today, the army's hold on the countryside is increasingly being challenged by an armed movement of the FDD and FNL. This movement is spreading counterterror in the name of the country's Hutu majority. What has remained the same over the years is the general indifference of the outside world to Burundi's horrific record of ethnic conflict.

In 1993, the country seemed poised to enter a bright new era when, in their first democratic elections, Burundians chose their first Hutu head of state, Melchior Ndadaye, and a Parliament dominated by the Hutu Front for Democracy in Burundi (FRODEBU) party. But within months Ndadaye was assassinated, setting the scene for subsequent Hutu–Tutsi violence, in which

at least 200,000 people have been killed. In early 1994, Parliament elected another Hutu, Cyprien Ntaryamira, as president. However, he was killed when a plane he was traveling in was sabotaged in April—the same incident that killed the reformist president of neighboring Rwanda.

After talks among the main parties, another Hutu, Sylvestre Ntibantunganya, was appointed president in October 1994. But within months the mainly Tutsi Union

FREEDOM

Beset by on-going genocide, there is currently no genuine freedom in Burundi, for either its ethnic majority or minority populations. People continue to flee the country by the tens of thousands.

for National Progress (UPRONA) party withdrew from the government and Parliament, sparking off a new wave of ethnic violence. In the process the capital city, Bujumbura, was largely emptied of its Hutu majority, while many ordinary Tutsis fled from much of the countryside. In July 1996, the army overthrew Ntibantunganya, bringing back to power the Tutsi general Pierre Buyoyo, who had ruled the country from 1987 to 1993. Subsequent talks among the Burundian political parties, mediated first by former Tanzanian president Julius Nyerere and then by Mandela, failed to reach agreement on crucial issues. These included the role of the Burundian Army and the dismantling of "regroupment camps," which are said to hold more than 800,000 Hutu civilians.

A DIVIDED SOCIETY

Burundi's population is ethnosocially divided into three distinctive groups. At the bottom of the social hierarchy are the Twa, commonly stereotyped as "pygmies." Believed to be the earliest inhabitants of the country, today the Twa account for only about 1 percent of the population. The largest group, constituting 85 percent of the population, are the Hutus, most of whom subsist as farmers. The dominant group are the Tutsis, 14 percent of the population.

Among the Tutsis, who are subdivided into clans, status has long been associated with cattle-keeping. Leading Tutsis continue to form an aristocratic ruling class over the whole of Burundi society. Until 1966, the leader of Burundi's Tutsi aristocracy was the *Mwami,* or king.

The Burundi kingdom goes back at least as far as the sixteenth century. By the late 1800s, when the kingdom was incorporated into German East Africa, the Tutsis had subordinated the Hutus, who became clients of local Tutsi aristocrats, herding their cattle and rendering other services. The Germans and subsequently the Belgians, who assumed paramount authority over the kingdom after World War I, were content to rule through Burundi's established social hierarchy. But many Hutus as well as Tutsis were educated by Christian missionaries.

HEALTH/WELFARE

Much of the educational system has been in private hands, especially the Roman Catholic Church. Burundi lost many educated and trained people during the Hutu massacres in the 1970s and 1980s.

In the late 1950s, Prince Louis Rwagazore, a Tutsi, tried to accommodate Hutu as well as Tutsi aspirations by establishing the nationalist reform movement known as UPRONA. Rwagazore was assassinated before independence, but UPRONA led the country to independence in 1962, with King Mwambutsa IV retaining considerable power as head of state. The Tutsi elite remained dominant, but the UPRONA cabinets contained representation from the two major groups. This attempt to balance the interests of the Tutsis and Hutus broke down in 1965, when Hutu politicians within both UPRONA and the rival People's Party won 80 percent of the vote and the majority of the seats in both houses of the bicameral Legislature. In response, the king abolished the Legislature before it could convene. A group of Hutu army officers then attempted to overthrow the government. Mwambutsa fled the country, but Tutsi officers, led by Michel Micombero, crushed the revolt in a countercoup.

In the aftermath of the uprising, Micombero took power amid a campaign of reprisals in which, it is believed, some 5,000 Hutus were killed. He deposed Mwambutsa's son, Ntare V, from the kingship and set up a "Government of Public Safety," which set about purging Hutu members from the government and the army. The political struggle involved interclan competition among the Tutsis as well as the maintenance of their hegemony over the Hutus.

Under Micombero, Burundi continued to be afflicted with interethnic violence, occasional coup attempts, and pro-monarchist agitation. A major purge of influential Hutus was carried out in 1969. In 1972, Ntare V was lured to Uganda by Idi Amin, who turned him over to Micombero. Ntare was placed under arrest upon his arrival and was subsequently murdered by his guards.

ACHIEVEMENTS

Burundians were briefly united in July 1996 by the victory of their countryman Venuste Niyongabo in the men's 5,000-meter race at the Atlanta Summer Olympic Games. He dedicated his gold medal (the first for a Burundi citizen) to the hope of national reconciliation.

A declaration of martial law then set off another explosion of violence. In response to an alleged uprising involving the deaths of up to 2,000 Tutsis, government supporters began to massacre large numbers of Hutus. Educated Hutus were especially targeted in a two-month campaign of selective genocide, which is generally estimated to have claimed 200,000 victims (estimates range from 80,000 to 500,000 deaths for the entire period, with additional atrocities being reported through 1973). More than 100,000 Hutus fled to Uganda, Rwanda, Zaire (present-day D.R.C.), and Tanzania. Among the governments of the world, only Tanzania and Rwanda showed any deep concern for the course of events. China, France, and Libya used the crisis to significantly upgrade their military aid to the Burundi regime.

In 1974, Micombero formally transformed Burundi into a single-party state

Timeline: PAST

1795
Mwami Ntare Rugaamba expands the boundaries of the Nkoma kingdom

1919
The area is mandated to Belgium by the League of Nations after the Germans lose World War I

1958–1961
Prince Louis Rwagazore leads a nationalist movement and founds UPRONA

1961
Rwagazore is assassinated; independence is achieved

1965–1966
A failed coup results in purges of Hutus in the government and army; Michel Micombero seizes power

1972
Government forces massacre 200,000 Hutu

1976
Jean-Baptiste Bagaza comes to power in a military coup

1987
Bagaza is overthrown in a military coup led by Pierre Buyoyo

1990s
Buyoyo loses in multiparty elections; Melchior Ndadye becomes Burundi's first Hutu president; Buyoyo regains power in a military coup

PRESENT

2000s
Unrest in neighboring states complicates the ethnic conflict in Burundi
Nelson Mandela mediates for national reconciliation
Pierre Nkurunziza, from the Hutu FDD group, is elected as president by the two houses of parliament, replacing Domitien Ndayizeye
The Forces for National Liberation (FNL) continues as the remaining active rebel group, in spite of signing a ceasefire with the government
The Democratic Republic of the Congo, Rwanda, and Burundi relaunch the regional economic bloc—Great Lakes Countries Economic Community—known under its French acronym CEPGL

under UPRONA. Although Micombero was replaced two years later in a military coup by Colonel Jean-Baptiste Bagaza, power remained effectively in the hands of members of the Tutsi elite who controlled UPRONA, the civil service, and the army. In 1985, Bagaza widened existing state persecution of Seventh Day Adventists and Jehovah's Witnesses to include the Roman Catholic Church, to which a majority of Burundi's population belong, suspecting it of fostering seditious—that is, pro-Hutu—sympathies. (The overthrow of Bagaza by Pierre Buyoyo, in a 1987 military coup, led to a lifting of the anti-Catholic campaign.)

Ethnic violence erupted again in 1988. Apparently some Tutsis were killed by Hutus in northern Burundi, in response to rumors of another massacre of Hutus. In retaliation, the army massacred between 5,000 and 25,000 Hutus. Another 60,000 Hutus took temporary refuge in Rwanda, while more than 100,000 were left homeless. In 1991, the revolutionary Party for the Liberation of the Hutu People, or Palipehutu, launched its own attacks on Tutsi soldiers and civilians, leading to further killing on all sides.

LAND ISSUES

Burundi is one of the poorest countries in the world, despite its rich volcanic soils and generous international development assistance (it has been one of the highest per capita aid recipients on the African continent). In addition to the dislocations caused by cycles of interethnic violence, the nation's development prospects are seriously compromised by geographic isolation and population pressure on the land. About 25 percent of Burundi's land is under cultivation—generally by individual farmers trying to subsist on plots of no more than three acres. Another 60 percent of the country is devoted to pasture for mostly Tutsi livestock. Hutu farmers continue to be tied by patron–client relationships to Tutsi overlords.

In the 1980s, the government tied its rural development efforts to an unpopular villagization scheme. This issue has complicated on-going attempts to reach some kind of accommodation between the Tutsi elite and Hutu masses. Having cautiously increased Hutu participation in his government while reserving ultimate power in the hands of the all-Tutsi Military Commit-

tee of National Salvation, Buyoyo agreed to the restoration of multiparty politics in 1991. A new Constitution was approved in March 1992; it allowed competition between approved, ethnically balanced, parties. In the resulting July 1993 elections, Buyoyo's UPRONA was defeated by the Front for Democracy in Burundi. FRO-DEBU's leader, Ndadaye, was sworn in as the head of a joint FRODEBU–UPRONA government. His subsequent assassination by Tutsi hard-liners in the military set off a new wave of interethnic killings. The firm stand against the coup by Buyoyo and the Tutsi/UPRONA prime minister, Sylvie Kinigi, helped to calm the situation, but attempts to make a fresh start collapsed in 1994 when a plane carrying Ntaryamira, Burundi's newly elected head of state, and his Rwandan counterpart was shot down over Rwanda. The latest coup followed UPRONA's withdrawal from the government following the massacre of more than 300 Tutsis by FDD, who by September 1996 were attempting to besiege the capital.

During a four-week period from late October to November 1996, the Tutsi-led Burundian military massacred at least 1,000 civilians. The government forces fought with Hutu rebels, as some 50,000 Hutus returned from camps that had been closed in Zaire. The Tutsi-dominated military set up more than a dozen "protection zones" for Hutu civilians while soldiers continued battling Hutu rebels. Strife continued as an estimated 200,000 Burundians were living in refugee camps in Tanzania.

BURUNDI TODAY

Burundi is a nation in search of its national identity. The country has been torn by ethnic violence since independence in 1961. Throughout the post independence era the dominant Tutsi minority and the Hutu majority have not been able to find a way to live together in peace. A ceasefire between

the warring groups was signed in 2002 but the fighting continues.

Another South African power-sharing deal was signed in 2004, allocating government and national assembly posts to members of the Hutu majority and the Tutsi minority. During June 2004 the UN took over peacekeeping duties from African Union troops. After years of war and the installation of a new provisional president, Domitien Ndayizeye, most of the country is now beginning to reap the dividends of a peace process.

With only one rebel group remaining active in the countryside around the capital and a strong effort by the international community, there is hope that negotiations to resolve differences will succeed. During his tenure, President Ndayizeye, a senior figure in the largest Hutu party Frodebu, faced the formidable challenge of maintaining good relations with Burundi's Tutsi-led government army while persuading Hutu rebels to stop fighting.

Today, uneasy peace is slowly returning to Burundi. In the elections held in June 2005, the Hutu FDD group won parliamentary elections. As a result, Pierre Nkurunziza, from the FDD group, was subsequently elected as president by the two houses of parliament. In 2006 the remaining active rebel group, the Forces for National Liberation (FNL), and the government signed a ceasefire at talks in Tanzania. The UN went ahead to wind down its peacekeeping mission, choosing to refocus its operations on helping with reconstruction efforts. Although the future looks promising for peace, some factions of the FNL have continued to stage sporadic raids in Bujumbura, the capital city, and in other parts of the country. Nkurunziza is faced with the daunting challenges of reassuring the Tutsi minority and of reviving the economy after a 12-year ethnic-based civil war. It is gratifying to note that stability is in sight, attributed partly to international mediation and support.

Comoros (Union of Comoros)

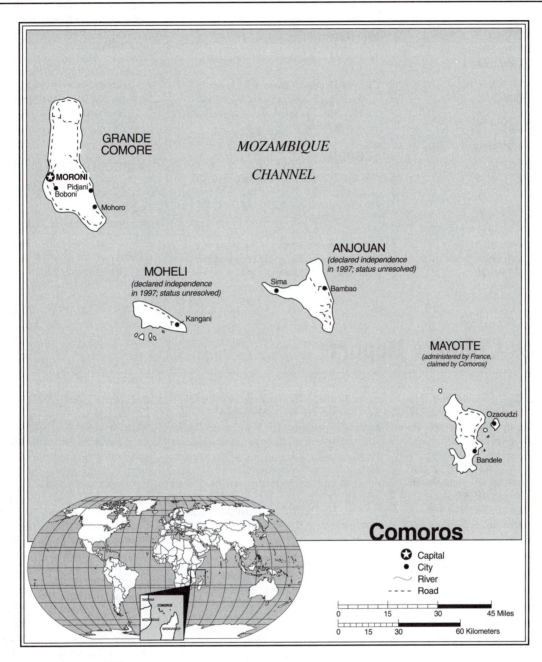

GRANDE COMORE

MOZAMBIQUE

CHANNEL

★ MORONI
Pidjani
Boboni
Mohoro

MOHELI
(declared independence in 1997; status unresolved)

Kangani

ANJOUAN
(declared independence in 1997; status unresolved)

Sima
Bambao

MAYOTTE
(administered by France, claimed by Comoros)

Ozaoudzi

Bandele

Comoros

- ★ Capital
- ● City
- ～ River
- - - - Road

0	15	30	45 Miles
0	15	30	60 Kilometers

Comoros Statistics

GEOGRAPHY

Area in Square Miles (Kilometers): 838 (2,171) (about 12 times the size of Washington, D.C.)

Capital (Population): Moroni (60,200)

Environmental Concerns: soil degradation and erosion; deforestation

Geographical Features: volcanic islands; interiors vary from steep mountains to low hills

Climate: tropical marine

PEOPLE

Population

Total: 711,417

Annual Growth Rate: 2.84%

Rural/Urban Population Ratio: 63/37

Major Languages: Arabic; French; Comoran

Ethnic Makeup: Antalote; Cafre; Makoa; Oimatsaha; Sakalava

Religions: 98% Sunni Muslim; 2% Roman Catholic

Health

Life Expectancy at Birth: 60.37 years (male); 65.15 years (female)

Infant Mortality: 70.66/1,000 live births

Physicians Available: 1/6,600 people

HIV/AIDS Rate in Adults: 0.12%

Education

Adult Literacy Rate: 56.5%
Compulsory (Ages): 7–16

COMMUNICATION

Telephones: 16,900 main lines
Internet Users: 21,000 (2003)

TRANSPORTATION

Highways in Miles (Kilometers): 528 (880 km)
Railroads in Miles (Kilometers): none
Usable Airfields: 4

GOVERNMENT

Type: republic
Independence Date: July 6, 1975 (from France)
Head of State/Government: President Ahmed Abdallah Sambi

Political Parties: Rassemblement National pour le Development; Front National pour la Justice
Suffrage: universal at 18

MILITARY

Military Expenditures (% of GDP): 2.8%
Current Disputes: Comoros claims the French-administered island of Mayotte; Moheli and Anjouan seek independence

ECONOMY

Currency ($ U.S. Equivalent): 349.33 francs = $1
Per Capita Income/GDP: $600/$1.275 billion
GDP Growth Rate: 3%
Inflation Rate: 3.5%
Unemployment Rate: 20%; extreme underemployment

Labor Force by Occupation: 80% agriculture
Population Below Poverty Line: 60%
Natural Resources: negligible
Agriculture: perfume essences; copra; coconuts; cloves; vanilla; bananas; cassava
Industry: tourism; perfume distillation
Exports: $34 million (primary partners France, United States, Singapore)
Imports: $115 million (primary partners France, South Africa, Kenya)

SUGGESTED WEB SITES

http://www.arabji.com/Comoros/index.htm
http://www.sas.upenn.edu/ African_Studies/Country_Specific/Comoros.html
http://www.cia.gov/cia/ publications/factbook/geos/ cn.html

Comoros Country Report

A small archipelago consisting of three main islands—Grande Comore, Moheli, and Anjouan (a fourth island, Mayotte, has voluntarily remained under French rule)—in recent years Comoros has struggled to maintain its fragile unity. In 1997, separatists seized control of Anjouan and Moheli, subsequently declaring independence. But after years of failed mediation efforts by other African states, in December 2001 voters throughout Comoros were able to overwhelmingly agree on a new Constitution designed to reunite their country as a loose federation. This followed the seizure of power by a "military committee" on Anjouan that was committed to reunification. In April 2002, Azali Assoumani, who had previously seized power on Grande Comore, was sworn in as the president of the new "Union of Comoros," and Prime Minister Bolero was appointed Minister of External Defense and Territorial Security. But his authority was soon challenged by Mze Abdou Soule Elbak, who a month later was elected as the president of Grande Comore. A military standoff thereafter developed on Grande Comore between followers of Azali and Elbak, further threatening the islands' prospects of ever achieving political stability. President Azali has not yet appointed a Prime Minister.

The years since independence from France, in 1975, have not been kind to Comoros, which has been consistently listed by the United Nations as one of the world's least-developed countries. Lack of economic development has been compounded at times by natural disasters, eccentric and authoritarian leadership, political violence, and external interventions. The 1990 restoration of multiparty democracy, along with subsequent elections in 1992–1993, has so far failed to provide a basis for national consensus.

DEVELOPMENT

One of the major projects undertaken since independence has been the ongoing expansion of the port at Mutsamundu, to allow large ships to visit the islands. Vessels of up to 25,000 tons can now dock at the harbor. In recent years, there has been a significant expansion of tourism to Comoros.

Meanwhile, the entire archipelago remains impoverished. While many Comorans remain underemployed as subsistence farmers, more than half of the country's food is imported. As a result, many Comorans have questioned the wisdom of independence, but appeals by Anjouan and Moheli islanders for a return of French control have been rejected by Paris.

The Comoros archipelago was populated by a number of Indian Ocean peoples, who—by the time of the arrival of Europeans during the early 1500s—had combined to form the predominantly Muslim, Swahili-speaking society found on the islands today. In 1886, the French proclaimed a protectorate over the three main islands that currently constitute the Union of Comoros (France had ruled Mayotte since 1843). Throughout the colonial period, Comoros was especially valued by the French for strategic reasons. A local elite of large landholders prospered from the production of cash crops. Life for most Comorans, however, remained one of extreme poverty.

A month after independence, the first Comoran government, led by Ahmed Abdullah Abderemane, was overthrown by mercenaries, who installed Ali Soilih in power. He promised a socialist transformation of the nation and began to implement land reform, but he rapidly lost support both at home and abroad—under his leadership, gangs of undisciplined youths terrorized society, while the basic institutions and services of government all but disappeared. In 1977, the situation was made even worse

FREEDOM

Freedom was abridged after independence under both Ahmed Abdullah and Ali Soilih. The government elected in 1990 ended human-rights abuses.

by a major volcanic eruption, which left 20,000 people homeless, and by the arrival of 16,000 Comoran refugees following massacres in neighboring Madagascar.

In 1978, another band of mercenaries—this time led by the notorious Bob Denard, whose previous exploits in Zaire (present-day Democratic Republic of the Congo or D.R.C.), Togo, and elsewhere had made his name infamous throughout Africa—overthrew Soilih and restored Abdullah to power. Denard, however, remained the true power behind the throne.

HEALTH/WELFARE

Health statistics improved during the 1980s, but a recent World Health Organization survey estimated that 10% of Comoran children ages 3 to 6 years are seriously malnourished and another 37% are moderately malnourished.

The Denard–Abdullah government enjoyed close ties with influential right-wing elements in France and South Africa. Connections with Pretoria were manifested through the use of Comoros as a major conduit for South African supplies to the Renamo rebels in Mozambique. Economic ties with South Africa, especially in tourism and sanctions-busting, also grew. The government also established good relations with Saudi Arabia, Kuwait, and other conservative Arab governments while attracting significant additional aid from the international donor agencies.

In 1982, the country legally became a one-party state. Attempted coups in 1985 and 1987 aggravated political tensions. Many Comorans particularly resented the overbearing influence of Denard and his men. By November 1989, this group included President Abdullah himself. With the personal backing of President François Mitterand of France and President F. W. de Klerk of South Africa, Abdullah moved to replace Denard's mercenaries with a French-approved security unit. But before this move could be implemented, Abdullah was murdered following a meeting with Denard.

The head of the Supreme Court, Said Mohamed Djohar, was appointed interim president in the wake of the assassination. After a period of some confusion, during which popular protests against Denard

swelled, Djohar quietly sought French intervention to oust the mercenaries. With both Paris and Pretoria united against him, Denard agreed to relinquish power, in exchange for safe passage to South Africa. The removal of Denard and temporary stationing of a French peacekeeping force was accompanied by the lifting of political restrictions in preparation for presidential elections. In 1990, a runoff resulted in a 55 percent electoral mandate for Djohar.

ACHIEVEMENTS

Comoros has long been the world's leading exporter of ylang-ylang, an essence used to make perfume. It is also the second-leading producer of vanilla and a major grower of cloves. Together, these cash crops account for more than 95% of export earnings. Unfortunately, the international prices of these crops have been low for the past 2 decades.

In September 1995, Denard's men returned to overthrow Djohar. But the mercenaries were soon forced to surrender to French forces, who installed Caambi el Yachourtu, rather than Djohar, as acting president. At the end of 1996, Mohamed Taki Abdulkarim replaced Yachourtu as president. In November 1998, Taki died suddenly and was replaced by Tadjiddine Ben Said Massounde as the head of a ruling military committee. Massounde's government was overthrown in a bloodless coup on April 30, 1999. Azali Assoumani was subsequently installed as president.

As noted earlier, to bring the breakaway islands back into the fold, Moheli, Anjouan, and the largest island, Grande Comore, were granted their own presidents and greater autonomy under a 2001 constitution. The loose federation was renamed "The Union of the Comoros," which retained control of security and financial matters. The constitution also stipulated a rotation of the presidency of the union between the three islands. In the 2006 presidential elections, Ahmed Abdallah Mohamed Sambi, an Iranian-trained Sunni Muslim cleric, won the election with 58% of the vote. His predecessor, Azali Assoumani, was from Grande Comore, while he represents the island of Anjouan, and the next president is slated to come from the third island, Moheli, in 2010. This is hopeful news for Comoros.

After a history of coups and secession bids, the island nation experienced its first peaceful change of power in the country's post-independence history. Nevertheless, as the Comoros attempt to stabilize its political situation, it faces the daunting challenges of a poor economy with high unemployment rates and corruption.

While at the federal level, there was a peaceful transfer of power, local politics on the three islands is a different case altogether. For example, in May 2007, the African Union sent troops to help keep the peace in June 2007 elections after Anjouan President Mohamed Bacar refused to stand down. In defiance of the federal government and the African Union, Anjouan went ahead with local elections. The defiant Mohamed Bacar was inaugurated as Anjouan's president after the elections in contravention of the new constitution.

Timeline: PAST

1500s
Various groups settle in the islands, which become part of a Swahili trading network

1886
A French protectorate over the remaining Comoros islands is proclaimed

1914–1946
The islands are ruled as part of the French colony of Madagascar

1975
Independence is followed by a mercenary coup, which installs Ali Soilih

1978
Ali Soilih is overthrown by mercenaries; Ahmed Abdullah is restored

1980s
Abdullah proclaims a one-party state; real power remains in the hands of mercenary leader Bob Denard

1990s
The assassination of Abdullah leads to the removal of Denard and to multiparty elections

PRESENT

2000s
The country is renamed "Union of Comoros"

Despite the name change, Comoros's political unity has not been achieved

Djibouti (Republic of Djibouti)

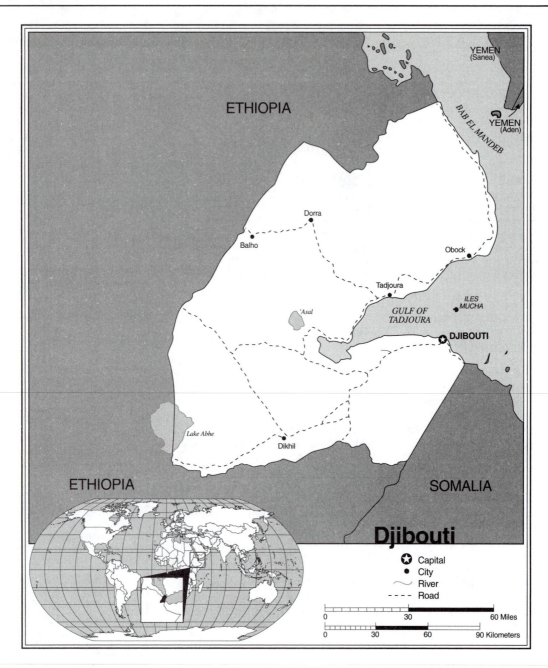

Djibouti Statistics

GEOGRAPHY

Area in Square Miles (Kilometers):
8,492 (22,000) (about the size of Massachusetts)

Capital (Population): Djibouti (542,000)

Environmental Concerns: insufficient potable water; desertification

Geographical Features: coastal plain and plateau, separated by central mountains

Climate: desert

PEOPLE

Population

Total: 496,374
Annual Growth Rate: 1.984%

Rural/Urban Population Ratio: 18/82

Major Languages: French; Arabic; Somali; Afar

Ethnic Makeup: 60% Issa/Somali; 35% Afar; 5% French, Arab, Ethiopian, Italian

Religions: 94% Muslim; 6% Christian

Health

Life Expectancy at Birth: 41.88 years
   (male); 44.65 years (female)
Infant Mortality: 100.77/1,000 live births
Physicians Available: 1/3,790 people
HIV/AIDS Rate in Adults: 2.9%

Education

Adult Literacy Rate: 67.9%

COMMUNICATION

Telephones: 10,800 main lines
Televisions: 43/1,000 people
Internet Users: 11,000 (2003)

TRANSPORTATION

Highways in Miles (Kilometers): 1,740
   (2,809 km)
Railroads in Miles (Kilometers): 100 km
Usable Airfields: 13
Motor Vehicles in Use: 16,000

GOVERNMENT

Type: republic
Independence Date: June 27, 1977 (from
   France)
Head of State/Government: President
   Ismail Omar Guellah; Prime Minister
   Dileita Mohamed Dileita
Political Parties: People's Progress
   Assembly; Democratic Renewal Party;
   Democratic National Party; others
Suffrage: universal for adults

MILITARY

Military Expenditures (% of GDP): 3.8%
Current Disputes: ethnic conflict; border
   clashes with Eritrea

ECONOMY

Currency ($ U.S. Equivalent): 176.22
   francs = $1

Per Capita Income/GDP: $1,000/$1.878
   billion
GDP Growth Rate: 3.2%
Inflation Rate: 2%
Unemployment Rate: 50%
Population Below Poverty Line: 50%
Natural Resources: geothermal areas
Agriculture: livestock; fruits; vegetables
Industry: port and maritime support;
   construction
Exports: $250 million (primary partners
   Somalia, Yemen, Ethiopia)
Imports: $987 million (primary partners
   France, Ethiopia, Italy)

SUGGESTED WEB SITES

http://www.sas.upenn.edu/ African_
   Studies/ Country_Specific/Djibouti
   .html
http://www.republique-djibouti
   .com
http://www.cia.gov/cia/ publications/
   factbook/geos/ dj.html

Djibouti Country Report

After a decade of civil unrest, Djibouti has settled down under the leadership of its second president, Ismail Omar Guelleh. In April 1999, Guelleh succeeded the aging Hassan Gouled Aptidon, who stepped down due to ill health. While Guelleh's main opponent, Musa Ahmed Idriss, was arrested after claiming massive electoral fraud, the new president has since consolidated his authority by building on the process of national reconciliation that had begun under his predecessor. In February 2000, this resulted in a peace agreement between the government and armed rebel holdouts of the Front for the Restoration of Democratic Unity (FRUD), resulting in the return of the rebel leader Ahmad Dini. A subsequent coup attempt, allegedly orchestrated by the chief of police, was crushed.

DEVELOPMENT

Recent discoveries of natural-gas reserves in Djibouti could result in a surplus for export. A number of small-scale irrigation schemes have been established. There is also a growing, though still quite small, fishing industry.

Political conflict in Djibouti has mirrored the country's ethnic tensions between the Somali-speaking Issas and the Afar-speakers. An earlier, 1997, power-sharing

agreement was reached between the long-ruling, Issa-dominated Popular Rally for Progress Party (RPP) and a more moderate faction of the Afar-dominated FRUD. Although the FRUD moderates went on to win all 65 seats in December 1997 legislative elections, more radical elements of FRUD continued their armed resistance to President Aptidon. While the conflict has now ended, suspicions between Afars and Issas continue to threaten Djibouti's fragile political unity.

FREEDOM

The government continues to harass and detain its critics. Prison conditions are harsh, with the sexual assault of female prisoners being commonplace.

Since achieving its independence from France, Djibouti has also had to strike a cautious balance between the competing interests of its larger neighbors, Ethiopia and Somalia. In the past, Somalia has claimed ownership of the territory, based on the numerical preponderance of Djibouti's Somali population, variously estimated at 50 to 70 percent. However, local Somalis as well as Afars also have strong ties to communities in Ethiopia. Furthermore, Djibouti's location at the crossroads of Africa and Eurasia has made it a focus of continuing

strategic concern to nonregional powers, particularly France, which maintains a large military presence in the country.

In January 2002, German warships and 1,000 sailors arrived in Djibouti to patrol shipping lanes in the Red Sea area, in support of U.S. actions in Afghanistan. Although Djibouti says it won't be used as a base for attacks against another country in the region, some 900 U.S. troops also set up camp in support of the U.S.-led war on terror. The effort by Djibouti's government to fight the war on terror had one major political consequence as the government, in September 2002, passed a law allowing three other parties to compete in elections, thus opening the way for full multiparty politics.

In January 2003, the Union for Presidential Majority Coalition candidate Ismail Omar Guelleh won Djibouti's first free multiparty elections since independence in 1977. Ismael Omar Guelleh succeeded his uncle and Djibouti's first president, Hassan Gouled Aptidon, in April 1999, at the age of 52. He took office after being elected in a multiparty ballot, which was not contested by Mr. Aptidon. A former head of security, he worked for many years in his uncle's office. He is known to favor continuing Djibouti's traditionally strong ties with France, and has played an important role in trying to reconcile the different factions in neighbouring Somalia. In

September 2003, one of President Guelleh's first actions after assuming office was to begin a drive to detain and expel illegal immigrants, thought to make up 15 percent of the population.

In April 2005, Guelleh won a second term in presidential elections where he was the only candidate because the opposition failed to field a candidate. He campaigned on reducing poverty and becoming self-sufficient in food production, rather than relying heavily on food imports from abroad. As mandated by the constitution, he has indicated that he will step down at the end of his second term.

Modern Djibouti's colonial genesis is a product of mid-nineteenth-century European rivalry over control of the Red Sea. In 1862, France occupied the town of Obock, across the harbor from the city of Djibouti. This move was taken in anticipation of the 1869 opening of the Suez Canal, which transformed the Red Sea into the major shipping route between Asia, East Africa, and Europe. In 1888, Paris, having acquired Djibouti city and its hinterland, proclaimed its authority over French Somaliland, the modern territory of Djibouti.

HEALTH/WELFARE

Progress has been made in reducing infant mortality, but health services are strained in this very poor country. However, on the positive side, school enrollment has expanded by nearly one third since 1987.

The independence of France's other mainland African colonies by 1960, along with the formation in that year of the Somali Democratic Republic, led to local agitation for an end to French rule. To counter the effects of Somali nationalism, the French began to favor the Afar minority in local politics and employment. French presi-dent Charles de Gaulle's 1966 visit was accompanied by large, mainly Somali, pro-independence demonstrations. As a result, a referendum was held on the question of independence. Colonial control of voter registration assured a predominantly Afar electorate, who, fearful of Somali domination, opted for continued French rule. French Somaliland was then transformed into the self-governing "Territory of Afars and Issas." The name reflected a continuing colonial policy of divide-and-rule; members of the Issas clan constituted just over half of the area's Somali-speakers.

ACHIEVEMENTS

Besides feeding its own refugees, the government of Djibouti has played a major role in assisting international efforts to relieve the effects of recurrent famines in Ethiopia, Somalia, and Sudan.

By the 1970s, neither Ethiopia nor France was opposed to Djibouti's independence but, for their own strategic reasons, both countries backed the Afar community in its desire for assurances that the territory would not be incorporated into Somalia. An ethnic power-sharing arrangement was established that in effect acknowledged local Somali preponderance. The empowerment of local Somalis, in particular Issas, was accompanied by diminished pan-Somali sentiment. On June 27, 1977, the Republic of Djibouti became independent. French troops remained in the country, however, supposedly as a guarantee of its sovereignty. Internally, political power was divided by means of ethnically balanced cabinets.

War broke out between Ethiopia and Somalia a few months after Djibouti's independence. Djibouti remained neutral, but ethnic tensions mounted with the arrival of Somali refugees. In 1981, the Afar-dominated Djiboutian Popular Movement was outlawed. The Issa-dominated Popular Rally for Progress (RPP) then became the country's sole legal party.

Refugees have poured into Djibouti for years now, fleeing conflict and famine in Ethiopia, Somalia, and Sudan. The influx has swelled the country's population by about one third and has deepened Djibouti's dependence on external food aid. Massive unemployment among Djibouti's largely urban population remains a critical problem.

Timeline: PAST

1862
France buys the port of Obock

1888
France acquires the port of Djibouti

1917
The Addis Ababa-Djibouti Railroad is completed

1958
Djibouti votes to remain part of Overseas France

1977
Independence; the Ogaden War

1980s
The underground Union of Movements for Democracy is formed as an interethnic, antigovernment coalition

1990s
Civil war rends the country; Ismail Omar Guelleh is elected to replace President Hassan Gouled Aptidon

PRESENT

2000s
Ethnic conflict continues

Eritrea (State of Eritrea)

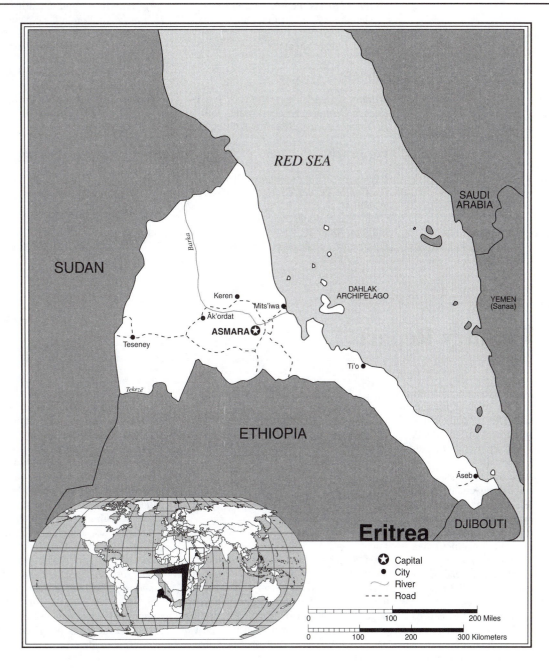

Eritrea Statistics

GEOGRAPHY

Area in Square Miles (Kilometers):
46,829 (121,320) (about the size of Pennsylvania)
Capital (Population): Asmara (503,000)
Environmental Concerns: deforestation; desertification; soil erosion; overgrazing
Geographical Features: north-south–trending highlands, descending on the east to a coastal desert plain, on the northwest to hilly terrain, and on the southwest to flat-to-rolling plains

Climate: hot, dry desert on the seacoast; cooler and wetter in the central highlands; semiarid in western hills and lowlands

PEOPLE

Population

Total: 4,906,585
Annual Growth Rate: 2.461%
Rural/Urban Population Ratio: 81/19
Major Languages: various, including Tigrinya, Tigre, Kunama, Arabic, Amharic, and Afar

Ethnic Makeup: 50% ethnic Tigrinya; 40% Tigre and Kunama; 4% Afar; 3% Saho; 3% others
Religions: Muslim; Coptic Christian; Roman Catholic; Protestant

Health

Life Expectancy at Birth: 57.88 years (male); 61.28 years (female)
Infant Mortality: 45.24/1,000 live births
Physicians Available: 1/36,000 people
HIV/AIDS Rate in Adults: 2.7%

Education

Adult Literacy Rate: 58.6%
Compulsory (Ages): 7–13; free

COMMUNICATION

Telephones: 37,700 main lines
Televisions: 6/1,000 people
Internet Users: 100,000 (2003)

TRANSPORTATION

Highways in Miles (Kilometers): 2,486
  (4,010 km)
Railroads in Miles (Kilometers): 306 km
Usable Airfields: 17

GOVERNMENT

Type: transitional government
Independence Date: May 24, 1993 (from
  Ethiopia)

Head of State/Government: President
  Isaias Aferweki (or Afworki) is both
  head of state and head of government
Political Parties: People's Front for
  Democracy and Justice (only
  recognized party)
Suffrage: universal at 18

MILITARY

Military Expenditures (% of GDP): 6.3%
Current Disputes: border disputes with
  Yemen; uneasy cease-fire with Ethiopia

ECONOMY

Currency ($ U.S. Equivalent): 15 nakfa
Per Capita Income/GDP: $1,000/$4.751
  billion
GDP Growth Rate: 2%
Inflation Rate: 12.3%
Labor Force by Occupation: 80%
  agriculture

Natural Resources: gold; potash; zinc;
  copper; salt; possibly petroleum and
  natural gas; fish
Agriculture: sorghum; lentils; vegetables;
  maize; cotton; tobacco; coffee; sisal;
  livestock; fish
Industry: food processing; beverages;
  clothing and textiles
Exports: $17.65 million (primary partners
  Sudan, Ethiopia, Japan)
Imports: $701.8 million (primary
  partners Italy, United Arab Emirates,
  Germany)

SUGGESTED WEB SITES

http://www.sas.upenn.edu/
  African_Studies/Country_Specific/
  Eritrea.html
http://www.eritrea.org
http://www.cia.gov/cia/
  publications/factbook/geos/
  er.html

Eritrea Country Report

In 1998, a border dispute between Eritrea and Ethiopia, around the town of Badme, erupted into open war. This formally ended with a cease-fire agreement in June 2000, but not before leaving thousands of soldiers dead on both sides. In December of that year, Eritrea and Ethiopia signed a further agreement establishing commissions to mark the border, exchange prisoners, return displaced people, and hear compensation claims. On February 6, 2001, Eritrea accepted the United Nations' plan for a temporary demilitarized zone along its border with Ethiopia. By the end of the month, Ethiopia had completed its troop withdrawal. A key provision of the peace agreement was met in April when Eritrea announced that its forces had pulled out of the border zone with Ethiopia. In May, Eritrea and Ethiopia agreed on a UN-proposed mediator to try to demarcate their disputed border. The completion of this task in 2002 has resulted in what will hopefully be a lasting peace between Eritrea and Ethiopia, after decades of conflict.

Eritrea became Africa's newest nation in May 1993, ending 41 years of union with Ethiopia. The origins of Eritrea's separation date back to September 1961, when a small group of armed men calling themselves the Eritrean Liberation Front (ELF) began a bitter independence struggle that would last for three decades.

Between 60,000 and 70,000 people perished as a result of that war, while another

DEVELOPMENT

Since liberation, the government has concentrated its efforts on restoring agricultural and communications infrastructure. The railway and ports of Assab and Massawa are being rehabilitated. In 1991, 80% of the country was dependent on food aid, but subsequent good rains helped boost crop production.

700,000—then about one fifth of the total population—went into exile. What had been one of the continent's most sophisticated light-industrial infrastructures was largely reduced to ruins. Yet the war has also left a positive legacy, in the spirit of unity, self-reliance, and sacrifice that it engendered among Eritreans.

There is no clear-cut reason why a nationalist sentiment should have emerged in Eritrea. Like most African countries, the boundaries of Eritrea are an artificial product of the late-nineteenth-century European scramble for colonies. Between 1869 and 1889, the territory fell under the rule of Italy. Italian influence survives today, especially in the overcrowded but elegant capital city of Asmara, which was developed as a showcase of neo-Roman imperialism. Italian rule came to an abrupt end in 1941, when British troops occupied the territory in World War II. The British withdrew only in 1952. In accordance with the wishes

of the UN Security Council, the territory was then federated as an autonomous state within the "Empire of Ethiopia."

The federation did not come about through the wishes of the Eritreans. It was, rather, based on the dubious Ethiopian claim that Eritrea was an integral part of the Empire that had been alienated by the Italians. Among the Christians, there were historic cultural ties with their Ethiopian coreligionists, though the Tigrinya-speaking Copts of Eritrea were ethnically distinct from the Empire's then–politically dominant Amharic-speakers. The Muslim lowland areas had never been under any form of Ethiopian control. But, perhaps more important, developments under Italian rule had laid the basis for a sense that Eritrea had its own identity.

FREEDOM

The Eritrean government has pledged to uphold a bill of rights. While the government is dominated by the former EPLF, other parties and organizations participate in the 105-seat Provisional Council. Multiparty elections in 1997 confirmed former EPLF leader Isaias Aferweki as president.

In the face of growing dissatisfaction inside the territory, Ethiopia's emperor, Haile Selassie, ended Eritrea's autonomous status in 1962. Fighting intensified in the early 1970s, after a faction ultimately known as the Eritrean Popular Liberation Front (EPLF) split from the ELF. The 1974 overthrow of Selassie briefly brought hopes of a peaceful settlement. But Ethiopia's new military rulers, known as the Dergue, committed themselves to securing the area by force. The ELF faded as the EPLF became increasingly effective in pinning down larger numbers of Ethiopian troops. In a major break with tradition, a large proportion of the EPLF's "Liberation Army," including many in command positions, was made up of women. In areas liberated by the EPLF, women were given the right to own land and choose their husbands, while the practice of female circumcision was discouraged.

HEALTH/WELFARE

A major challenge for the government has been the repatriation of hundreds of thousands of war refugees, mostly from neighboring Sudan. Rebuilding efforts were spearheaded by ex-combatants of the Liberation Army, who continued to work for virtually no pay. The EPLF established its own medical and educational services during the war.

Had it not been for the massive military support that the Dergue received from the Soviet Union and its allies, the conflict would have ended sooner. In the late 1980s, the EPLF began to work more closely with other groups inside Ethiopia proper that had taken up arms against their government. This resulted in an alliance between the EPLF and the Ethiopian People's Revolutionary Democratic Front (EPRDF), which was facilitated by the fact that leading members of both groups spoke Tigrinya. In May 1991, the Dergue collapsed, with the EPLF taking Asmara in the same month that EPRDF troops entered the Ethiopian capital of Addis Ababa. In July, the new EPRDF government agreed in principle to Eritrea's right to self-determination.

ACHIEVEMENTS

Eritrea's independence struggle and on-going national development efforts have been carried out against overwhelming odds, and with very little external support. During the war, self-reliance was manifested in the fact that most weapons and ammunition used by the EPLF were captured from Ethiopian forces.

In 1997, the EPLF, transformed as the People's Front for Democracy and Justice, claimed an overwhelming mandate in elections in which there was little effective opposition. A number of smaller parties, including remnants of the ELF, had joined the Front. Former EPLF leader Isaias Aferweki was confirmed as president of Eritrea.

The renewal of war in Ethiopia has had a devastating effect on Eritrea's economy, which had been making significant progress in the years following independence. The rehabilitation of the port of Massawa and other infrastructure had boosted trade. Light industries, mostly based in Asmara, had recovered. International investors have shown increased interest in the country's mineral wealth, especially offshore oil. In July 1997, the country introduced its own currency, the nakfa, which replaced the Ethiopian birr. Resulting exchange disputes between the two nations led to a souring of relations prior to the outbreak of the border war.

Some of the difficulties of the border dispute include Eritrea's inability to provide enough food for its population as efforts are focused on the fighting with Ethiopia rather than development. It is estimated that over two-thirds of the population of Eritrea is dependent on international food aid. This situation is made worse by recurrent drought and by the fact that much of the workforce is locked down in the military rather than in gainful employment.

Timeline: PAST

1869
Italians occupy the Eritrean port of Assab

1889
Italians occupy all of Eritrea

1935–1936
Italians use Eritrea as a springboard for conquest of Ethiopia

1941–1952
Great Britain occupies Eritrea

1952
Eritrea is federated with Ethiopia

1961
The ELF begins the liberation struggle

1962
Federation ends; Eritrea is a province of Ethiopia

1990s
99.8% vote yes for Eritrea's independence; Isaias Aferweki becomes the newly independent nation's first president

PRESENT

2000s
Eritrea and Ethiopia try to forge lasting peace but with little success

The border dispute that turned into a full-scale war with Ethiopia in 1998 continues to be a source of tension

Ethiopia (Federal Democratic Republic of Ethiopia)

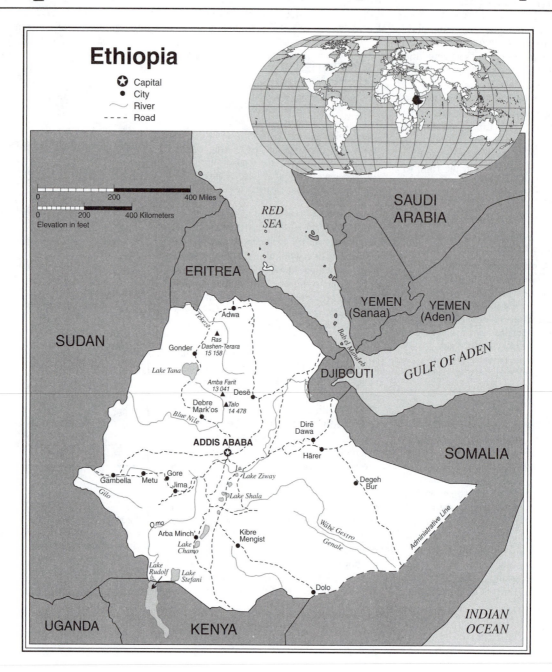

Ethiopia Statistics

GEOGRAPHY

Area in Square Miles (Kilometers):
435,071 (1,127,127) (about twice the size of Texas)

Capital (Population): Addis Ababa (2,973,000)

Environmental Concerns: deforestation; overgrazing; soil erosion; desertification

Geographical Features: a high plateau with a central mountain range divided by the Great Rift Valley; landlocked

Climate: tropical monsoon with wide topographic-induced variation

PEOPLE

Population

Total: 76,511,887
Annual Growth Rate: 2.272%

Rural/Urban Population Ratio: 84/16

Major Languages: Amharic; Tigrinya; Oromo; Somali; Arabic; Italian; English

Ethnic Makeup: 40% Oromo; 32% Amhara and Tigre; 9% Sidamo; 19% others

Religions: 45%–50% Muslims; 35%–40% Ethiopian Orthodox Christian; 12% animist; remainder others

Health

Life Expectancy at Birth: 48.06 years (male); 50.44 years (female)
Infant Mortality: 91.92/1,000 live births
Physicians Available: 1/36,600 people
HIV/AIDS Rate in Adults: 4.4%

Education

Adult Literacy Rate: 42.7%
Compulsory (Ages): 7–13; free

COMMUNICATION

Telephones: 725,000 main lines
Televisions: 4/1,000 people
Internet Users 164,000 (2003)

TRANSPORTATION

Highways in Miles (Kilometers): 21,881 (36,469 km)
Railroads in Miles (Kilometers): 669 km
Usable Airfields: 84
Motor Vehicles in Use: 66,000

GOVERNMENT

Type: federal republic

Independence Date: oldest independent country in Africa (at least 2,000 years)
Head of State/Government: President Girma Woldegiorgis; Prime Minister Meles Zenawi
Political Parties: Ethiopian People's Revolutionary Democratic Front; many others
Suffrage: universal at 18

MILITARY

Military Expenditures (% of GDP): 12.6%
Current Disputes: border conflicts with Somalia; uneasy cease-fire with Eritrea

ECONOMY

Currency ($ U.S. Equivalent): 9.08 birrs = $1
Per Capita Income/GDP: $1,000/$73.79 billion
GDP Growth Rate: 10.6%
Inflation Rate: 17.8%
Labor Force by Occupation: 80% agriculture; 12% government and services; 8% industry

Population Below Poverty Line: 64%
Natural Resources: gold; platinum, copper; potash; natural gas; hydropower
Agriculture: cereals; pulses; coffee; oilseed; sugarcane; vegetables; livestock
Industry: food processing; beverages; textiles; cement; building materials; hydropower
Exports: $1.085 billion (primary partners Germany, Japan, Djibouti)
Imports: $4.105 billion (primary partners Saudi Arabia, United States, Japan)

SUGGESTED WEB SITES

http://www.ethiopians.com
http://www.ethiopianembassy.org
http://www.ethiopianspokes.net
http://www.ethiopiadaily.com
http://www.state.gov/www/ background_notes/ethiopia_0398_bgn .html
http://www.cia.gov/cia/ publications/factbook/geos/et .html

Ethiopia Country Report

The end of the year 2000 witnessed two major events in Ethiopia. In November, Haile Selassie, the former emperor of Ethiopia, was officially buried in Addis Ababa's Trinity Cathedral. And in December, Ethiopia and Eritrea signed a peace agreement in Algeria, formally ending two years of bloody armed conflict. The agreement, which followed a successful Ethiopian military offensive, established commissions to delineate the disputed border between the countries and provided for the exchange of prisoners and the return of displaced people. Subsequently the two countries officially accepted a new common border, drawn up by an independent commission in The Hague. But both sides made claims to the town of Badme.

In April 2001, thousands of demonstrators clashed with police in Addis Ababa, in protest against police brutality and in support of calls for political and academic freedom. A year earlier, President Meles Zenawi's Ethiopian People's Revolutionary Democratic Front (EPRDF) had won an easy victory in legislative elections against some 25 opposition parties. In almost half of the constituencies, EPRDF candidates ran unopposed. In 2005, Meles Zenawi's EPRDF won bitterly contested elections, paving the way for his third five-year term as prime minister. The opposition cried foul, and in the violent protests that followed, dozens were killed and hundreds arrested and charged with treason.

Following equally overwhelming and controversial election victories in 1994–1995, the EPRDF remains the country's dominant political group. The movement initially came to power in 1991 as an armed movement, following the successful overthrow of Ethiopia's Marxist-oriented military dictatorship, after years of struggle.

Since coming to power, the EPRDF has faced a wide spectrum of opponents. Some critics see its transformation of Ethiopia into a multiethnic federation of 14 self-governing regions as a threat to national unity. Others contend that its devolutionary structures are a sham designed to obscure its own determination to rule from the center as a virtual one-party state. International as well as domestic supporters, however, see Ethiopia's new Constitution as a bold experiment in institutionalizing a new model of multiethnic statehood.

The EPRDF had emerged in the 1980s as an umbrella movement fighting to liberate Ethiopia from the repressive misrule by the Provisional Military Administrative Council, popularly known as the *Dergue* (Amharic for "Committee"). The Dergue had come to power through a popular uprising against the country's

DEVELOPMENT

There has been some progress in the country's industrial sector in recent years, after a sharp decline during the 1970s. Soviet-bloc investment resulted in the establishment of new enterprises in such areas as cement, textiles, and farm machinery.

FREEDOM

Despite its public commitment to freedom of speech and association, the EPRDF government has resorted to authoritarian measures against its critics. In 1995, Ethiopia had the highest number of jailed journalists in Africa. Basic freedoms are also compromised.

(United Nations photo 122,841 by Muldoon)

From 1916 to 1974, Ethiopia was ruled by Haile Selassie, also known as Ras Tafari (from which today's term *Rastafarian* is derived). He is pictured above, on the left, shaking hands with the now infamous Idi Amin of Uganda.

HEALTH/WELFARE

Ethiopia's progress in increasing literacy during the 1970s was undermined by the severe dislocations of the 1980s. By 1991, Ethiopia had some 500 government soldiers for every teacher.

MODERN HISTORY

Modern Ethiopian history began in the nineteenth century, when the highlands became politically reunited by a series of kings, culminating in Menilik II, who built up power by importing European armaments. Once the Coptic core of his kingdom was intact, Menilik began to spread his authority across the lowlands, thus uniting most of contemporary Ethiopia. In 1889 and 1896, Menilik also defeated invading Italian armies, thus preserving his empire's independence during the European partition of Africa.

From 1916 to 1974, Ethiopia was ruled by Ras Tafari (from which is derived the term *Rasta,* or *Rastafarian*), who, in 1930, was crowned Emperor Haile Selassie. The late Selassie remains a controversial figure. For many decades, he was seen both at home and abroad as a reformer who was modernizing his state. In 1936, after his kingdom had been occupied by Benito Mussolini, the leader of Italy, he made a memorable speech before the League of Nations, warning the world of the price it would inevitably pay for appeasing Fascist aggression. At the time, many African-Americans and Africans outside of Ethiopia saw Selassie as a great hero in the struggle of black peoples everywhere for dignity and empowerment. Selassie returned to his throne in 1941 and thereafter served as an elder statesman to the African nationalists of the 1950s and 1960s. However, by the latter decade, his own domestic authority was increasingly being questioned.

In his later years, Selassie could not, or would not, move against the forces that were undermining his empire. Despite its trappings of progress, the Ethiopian state remained quasi-feudal in character. Many of the best lands were controlled by the nobility and the Church, whose leading members lived privileged lives at the expense of the peasantry. Many educated people grew disenchanted with what they perceived as a reactionary monarchy and social order. Urban workers resented being paid low wages by often foreign owners. Within the junior ranks of the army and civil service, there was also great dissatisfaction with the way in which their

former imperial order. It is still uncertain whether Ethiopia's second revolution in two decades will succeed where its first one failed.

Political instability has reduced Ethiopia from a developing breadbasket to a famine-ridden basket case. Interethnic conflict among an increasingly desperate population, many of whom have long had better access to arms and ammunition than to food and medicine, could lead to the state's disintegration. In the late 1990s, the problems facing the EPRDF government were intensified by the outbreak of the border war with Eritrea, which compromised the landlocked country's access to the sea.

AN IMPERIAL PAST

Ethiopia rivals Egypt as Africa's oldest country. For centuries, its kings claimed direct descent from the biblical King Solomon and the Queen of Sheba. Whether Ethiopia was the site of Sheba is uncertain, as is the local claim that, prior to the birth of Christ, the country became the final resting place of the Ark of the Covenant holding the original Ten Commandments given

to Moses (the Ark is said to survive in a local monastery).

Local history is better established from the time of the Axum Empire, which prospered from the first century. During the fourth century, the Axumite court adopted the Coptic Christian faith, which has remained central to the culture of Ethiopia's highland region. The Church still uses the Geez, the ancient Axumite tongue from which the modern Ethiopian languages of Amharic and Tigrinya are derived, in its services.

From the eighth century A.D., much of the area surrounding the highlands fell under Muslim control, all but cutting off the Copts from their European coreligionists. (Today, most Muslim Ethiopians live in the lowlands.) For many centuries, Ethiopia's history was characterized by struggles among the groups inhabiting these two regions and religions. Occasionally a powerful ruler would succeed in making himself truly "King of Kings" by uniting the Christian highlands and expanding into the lowlands. At other times, the mountains would be divided into weak polities that were vulnerable to the raids of both Muslim and non-Muslim lowlanders.

(United Nations photo 164612 by John Isaac)

Ethiopians experienced a brutal civil war from 1974 to 1991. The continuous fighting displaced millions of people. The problems of this forced migration were compounded by drought and starvation. The drought victims pictured above are gathered at one of the many relief camps.

superiors were able to siphon off state revenues for personal enrichment. But the empire's greatest weakness was its inability to accommodate the aspirations of the various ethnic, regional, and sectarian groupings living within its borders.

Ethiopia is a multiethnic state. Since the time of Menilik, the dominant group has been the Coptic Amhara-speakers, whose preeminence has been resented by their Tigrinya coreligionists as well as by predominantly non-Coptic groups such as the Afars, Gurages, Oromo, and Somalis. In recent years, movements fighting for ethnoregional autonomy have emerged among the Tigrinya of Tigray, the Oromo, and, to a lesser extent, the Afars, while many Somalis in Ethiopia's Ogaden region have long struggled for union with neighboring Somalia. Somali irredentism led to open warfare between the two principal Horn of Africa states in 1963–1964 and again in 1977–1978.

The former northern coastal province of Eritrea was a special case. From the late nineteenth century until World War II, it was an Italian colony. After the war, it was integrated into Selassie's empire. Thereafter, a local independence movement, largely united as the Eritrean People's Liberation Front (EPLF), waged a successful

armed struggle, which led to Eritrea's full independence in 1993.

ACHIEVEMENTS

With a history spanning 2 millennia, the cultural achievements of Ethiopia are vast. Today, Addis Ababa is the site of the headquarters of the Organization of African Unity. Ethiopia's Kefe Province is the home of the coffee plant, from whence it takes its name.

REVOLUTION AND REPRESSION

In 1974, Haile Selassie was overthrown by the military, after months of mounting unrest throughout the country. A major factor triggering the coup was the government's inaction in 1972–1974, when famine swept across the northern provinces, claiming 200,000 lives. Some accused the Amhara government of using the famine as a way of weakening the predominantly Tigrinya areas of the empire. Others saw the tragedy simply as proof of the venal incompetence of Selassie's administration.

The overthrow of the old order was welcomed by most Ethiopians. Unfortunately, what began as a promising revolutionary

transformation quickly degenerated into a repressive dictatorship, which pushed the nation into chronic instability and distress. By the end of 1974, after the first in a series of bloody purges within its ranks, the Dergue had embraced Marxism as its guiding philosophy. Revolutionary measures followed. Companies and lands were nationalized. Students were sent into the countryside to assist in land reforms and to teach literacy. Peasants and workers were organized into cooperative associations, called *kebeles*. Initial steps were also taken to end Amhara hegemony within the state.

Progressive aspects of the Ethiopian revolution were offset by the murderous nature of the regime. Power struggles within the Dergue, as well as its determination to eliminate all alternatives to its authority, contributed to periods of "red terror," during which thousands of supporters of the revolution as well as those associated with the old regime were killed. By 1977, the Dergue itself had been transformed from a collective decision-making body to a small clique loyal to Colonel Mengistu Haile Mariam, who became a presidential dictator.

Mengistu sought for years to legitimize his rule through a commitment to Marxist-Leninism. He formally presided over a Commission for Organizing the Party of the Working People of Ethiopia, which, in 1984, announced the formation of a single-party state, led by the new Workers' Party. But real power remained in the hands of Mengistu's Dergue.

CIVIL WAR

From 1974 to 1991, Ethiopians suffered through civil war. In the face of oppressive central authority, ethnic-based resistance movements became increasingly effective in their struggles throughout much of the country. In the late 1970s, the Mengistu regime began to receive massive military aid from the Soviet bloc in its campaigns against the Eritreans and Somalis. Some 17,000 Cuban troops and thousands of other military personnel from the Warsaw Pact countries allowed the government temporarily to gain the upper hand in the fighting. The Ethiopian Army grew to more than 300,000 men under arms at any given time, the largest military force on the continent. Throughout the 1980s, military expenditures claimed more than half of the national budget.

Despite the massive domestic and international commitment on the side of the Mengistu regime, the rebels gradually gained the upper hand. Before 1991, almost all of northern Eritrea, except its besieged capital city of Asmara, had fallen to the EPLF, which had built up its own powerful arsenal, largely from captured government equipment. Local rebels had also liberated the province of Tigray and, as part of the EPRDF coalition, pushed south toward Ethiopia's capital city of Addis Ababa. In the south, independent Oromo and Somali rebels challenged government authority. There was also resistance to Mengistu from within the ranks of the national army. A major rebellion against his authority in 1989 was crushed, devastating military morale in the process. The regime was further undermined by the withdrawal of remaining Cuban and Soviet-bloc support.

Ethiopians have paid a terrible price for their nation's conflicts. Tens of thousands have been killed in combat, while many more have died from the side effects of war. In 1984–1985, the conscience of the world was moved by the images of mass starvation in the northern war zone. (At the time, however, the global media and concerned groups like Band Aid paid relatively little attention to the nonenvironmental factors that contributed to the crisis.) Up to 1 million lives were lost before adequate relief supplies reached the famine areas. Although drought and other environmental factors, such as soil erosion, contributed to the catastrophe, the fact that people continued to starve despite the availability of international relief can be attributed only to the use of food as a weapon of war.

There were other political constraints on local crop production. Having seized the lands of the old ruling class, the Mengistu regime, in accordance with its Marxist-Leninist precepts, invested most of its agricultural inputs in large state farms, whose productivity was abysmal. Peasant production also fell in nondrought areas, due to insecure tenure, poor producer prices, lack of credit, and an absence of consumer goods. Ethiopia's rural areas were further disrupted by the government's heavy-handed villagization and relocation schemes. In 1984–1985, thousands died when the government moved some 600,000 northerners to what were supposedly more fertile regions in the southwest. Many considered the scheme to be part of the central government's war effort against local communities resistant to its authority. By the same token, villagization has long been associated with counterinsurgency efforts; concentrated settlements allow occupying armies to exert greater control over potentially hostile populations.

UNCERTAIN PROSPECTS

The Dergue's demise has not as yet been accompanied by national reconciliation. Opposition to the EPRDF's attempt to transform Ethiopia into a multiethnic federation has been especially strong among Amharas, many of whom support the All-Amhara People's Organization. Others accuse the EPRDF—or, more especially, former Stalinists within the Tigrean People's Liberation Front (TPLF), which has been its predominant element—of trying to create its own monopoly of power.

In 1992, fighting broke out between the EPRDF and the forces of its former rebel partner, the Oromo Liberation Front (OLF), which claims to represent Ethiopia's largest ethnic group (Oromos constitute 40 percent of the population). The OLF was prominent among those who boycotted June 1992 local-government elections, which were further marred by allegations of vote-rigging and intimidation on behalf of the EPRDF. In December 1993, the OLF joined a number of other movements in a Council of Alternative Forces for Peace and Democracy (CAFPD). At its inaugural meeting, seven CAFPD delegates were detained for allegedly advocating the armed overthrow of the government. In April, another antigovernment coalition, the Ethiopian National Democratic party, was formed. Both movements called for an election boycott.

Another source of resistance to the EPRDF was the Ogadeni National Liberation Front (ONLF), which won strong support from Ogadeni Somalis in the June 1992 elections. In April, the Transitional Government removed ONLF's Hassan Jireh from power as the Ogaden region's elected administrator; in May, he was arrested. As a result, clashes occurred between the ONLF and EPRDF in the area, with the former boycotting the subsequent polls. Smaller uprisings and acts of terror, such as a January 1996 bombing of an Addis Ababa hotel, have posed further challenges for the government, which has also had to cope with drought. But while the extent of its electoral mandate is disputed, the EPRDF has demonstrated that it retains strong popular support, while its opposition is divided.

However, ongoing internal strife and sour relations with its neighbors of Eritrea and Somalia do not bode well for Ethiopia's political stability. The UN notes that the ongoing disputes over the demarcation of the border with Eritrea threaten peace. At the end of 2006, Ethiopia sent between 5,000 and 10,000 troops into Somalia to expel the Islamists and offer tacit support to a pro-Ethiopia and pro-Western weak transitional government. The fierce fights in Somalia resulted in over 50,000 Somali refugees moving into Ethiopia between 2006 and 2007, fleeing the instability in their homeland.

Timeline: PAST

1855
Emperor Tewodros begins the conquest and development of modern Ethiopia

1896
Ethiopia defeats Italian invaders at the Battle of Adowa

1936
Fascist Italy invades Ethiopia and rules until 1941

1961
The Eritrean liberation struggle begins

1972–1973
Famines in Tigray and Welo Provinces result in up to 200,000 deaths

1974
Emperor Haile Selassie is overthrown; the PMAC is established

1977
Diplomatic realignment and a new arms agreement with the Soviet Union

1980s
Massive famine, resulting from both drought and warfare

1990s
The Mengistu regime is overthrown by EPRDF rebels; Eritrea achieves independence of Ethiopia

PRESENT

2000s
Interethnic political tensions continue

Ethiopia and Eritrea work to forge a lasting peace, but the impasse over the demarcation of their shared border continues

Ethiopian military forces help to oust Somalia's Islamists

Kenya (Republic of Kenya)

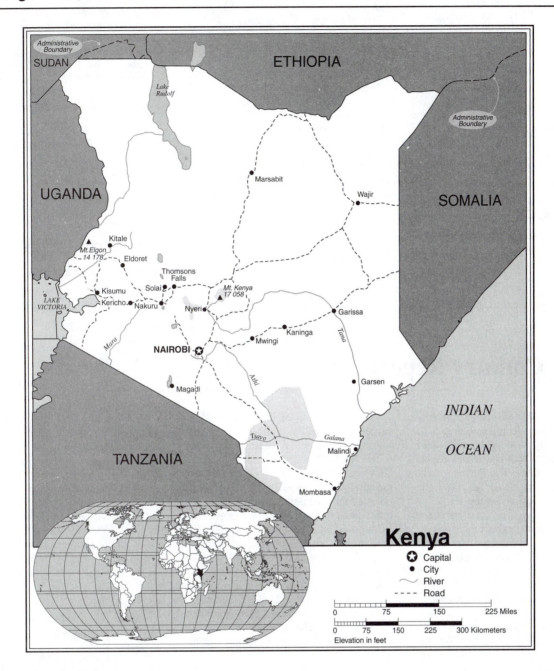

Kenya Statistics

GEOGRAPHY

Area in Square Miles (Kilometers):
224,900 (582,488) (twice the size of Nevada)

Capital (Population): Nairobi
(2,845,400)

Environmental Concerns: water pollution;
deforestation; soil erosion; poaching;
water-hyacinth infestation in Lake
Victoria

Geographical Features: low plains rise to
central highlands bisected by the Great
Rift Valley; fertile plateau in the west
Climate: tropical to arid

PEOPLE

Population

Total: 36,913,721
Annual Growth Rate: 2.799%

Rural/Urban Population Ratio:
81/19

Major Languages: English; Kiswahili;
Maasai; others

Ethnic Makeup: 22% Kikuyu; 14%
Luhya; 13% Luo; 12% Kalenjin; 11%
Kamba; 28% others

Religions: 38% Protestant; 28%
Catholic; 26% indigenous beliefs; 8%
others

GLOBAL STUDIES

Health

Life Expectancy at Birth: 55.24 years
(male); 55.37 years (female)
Infant Mortality: 57.44/1,000 live births
Physicians Available: 1/5,999 people
HIV/AIDS Rate in Adults: 6.7%

Education

Adult Literacy Rate: 85.1%
Compulsory (Ages): 6–14; free

COMMUNICATION

Telephones: 293,400 main lines
Televisions: 18/1,000 people
Internet Users: 2.77 million (2002)

TRANSPORTATION

Highways in Miles (Kilometers): 37,959
(63,265 km)
Railroads in Miles (Kilometers):
(2,778 km)
Usable Airfields: 225
Motor Vehicles in Use: 357,000

GOVERNMENT

Type: republic
Independence Date: December 12, 1963
(from the United Kingdom)
Head of State/Government: President
Mwai Kibaki is both head of state and
head of government
Political Parties: Kenya African National
Union; Forum for the Restoration of
Democracy; Democratic Party of Kenya;
others
Suffrage: universal at 18

MILITARY

Military Expenditures (% of GDP): 2.8%
Current Disputes: border conflict with
Sudan; civil unrest and interethnic
violence; tensions with Somalia

ECONOMY

Currency ($ U.S. Equivalent): 66.64
shillings = $1
Per Capita Income/GDP: $1,200/$41.48 billion

GDP Growth Rate: 6.1%
Inflation Rate: 9.8%
Unemployment Rate: 40%
Labor Force by Occupation: 75%–80%
agriculture
Population Below Poverty Line: 50%
Natural Resources: gold; limestone; soda
ash; salt barites; rubies; fluorspar;
garnets; wildlife; hydropower
Agriculture: coffee; tea; corn; wheat;
sugarcane; fruit; vegetables; livestock
and dairy products
Industry: small-scale consumer goods;
agricultural processing; oil refining;
cement; tourism
Exports: $3.614 billion (primary partners
Uganda, United Kingdom, Tanzania)
Imports: $6.602 billion (primary partners
United Kingdom, United Arab
Emirates, Japan)

SUGGESTED WEB SITES

http://www.kenyaweb.com
http://www.kenyaembassy.com
http://www.kentimes.com

Kenya Country Report

In December 2002, the 24-year rule of Kenya's second president, Daniel arap Moi, ended when Kenyans elected a new leader. Opposition-party candidate Mwai Kibaki won by a landslide. The defeat of the former ruling party under Moi will undoubtedly have a wide ranging set of implications for Kenya. The most important steps taken by the new government was the July 2004 proposal of a new constitution which is aimed at curtailing the powers of the president and creating a new post of Prime Minister.

Late in 2002, Moi had informed Kenyans that Uhuru Kenyatta, the son of Kenya's first president, Jomo Kenyatta, would serve as the ruling Kenyan African National Union (KANU) party presidential candidate. Uhuru Kenyatta had entered politics a year earlier, when Moi appointed him to both the Parliament and the cabinet.

DEVELOPMENT

Under its director Richard Leakey, the Kenyan Wildlife Service during the early 1990s cracked down on poachers while placing itself in the forefront of the global campaign to ban all ivory trading. As a result, local wildlife populations began to recover.

The designation of Kenyatta as Moi's successor caused a number of resignations by members of cabinet and other senior KANU leaders, who then formed a "National Rainbow Coalition." In October, the grouping combined with most of the other established opposition parties in rallying around former vice-president Kibaki as its presidential candidate.

The elections took place against a backdrop of economic adversity. With a major portion of its economy devoted to tourism, since the terrorist attacks in the United States on September 11, 2001, Kenya has been faced with the worst recession since independence. The election took place during a period of stress for the Kenyan tourism sector after the November 2002 bomb attack in which ten Kenyans and 3 Israelis were killed. A simultaneous rocket attack on an Israeli airliner failed. A statement, reportedly from Al-Qaeda, claimed responsibility. In addition, years of drought in northern and central Kenya have left more than 1 million people dependent on food supplies from the government.

The designation of Uhuru Kenyatta as his successor was but the latest in a series of surprise political moves by Moi. In June 2001, he reshuffled the cabinet, appointing opposition-party leader Raila Odinga as energy minister in the first coalition government in Kenya's history. Earlier, in

1999, President Moi had surprised many by appointing one of his best-known critics, the internationally renowned archaeologist and conservationist Richard Leakey, as head of Kenya's civil service, with an apparent mandate to restore the country's flagging economic fortunes by rooting out endemic corruption and lethargy in the public sector. While Leakey and his "Recovery Team" could claim some progress in shaking up the system, entrenched interests had largely frustrated its efforts.

FREEDOM

In 1997–1998, Kenya's already poor human-rights record deteriorated, with extra-judicial killings, beatings, and torture by the police. The National Youth Service, intended to provide young Kenyans with vocational training, was co-opted to block opposition political meetings. The worst atrocities, however, were linked to interethnic violence.

In August 1998, the world's attention had focused on the bombing of the U.S. Embassy building in Nairobi, Kenya's capital city. Scores of people in the vicinity of the blast were killed or injured. For Kenyans, it was an unprecedented act of international terrorism on their soil. It was also a further blow to the country's already troubled tourist industry, which had been hard hit by a continuing upward spiral of both criminal and political violence. The strength of the tourist industry—a critical foreign-exchange earner—coupled with years of growth in manufacturing and services had made Kenya, and especially Nairobi, the commercial center of East Africa. But today, after four decades of independence, most Kenyans remain the impoverished citizens of a state struggling to develop as a nation. And the recent restoration of multiparty politics has so far served only to intensify interethnic conflict.

In the precolonial past, Kenyan communities belonged to relatively small-scale, but economically interlinked, societies. Predominantly pastoral groups, such as the Maasai and Turkana, exchanged cattle for the crops of the Kalinjin, Kamba, Kikuyu, Luo, and others. Swahili city-states developed on the coast. In the 1800s, caravans of Arab as well as Swahili traders stimulated economic and political changes. However, the outsiders who had the greatest modern impact on the Kenyan interior were European settlers, who began to arrive in the first decade of the twentieth century. By the 1930s, much of the temperate hill country around Nairobi had become the "White Highlands." More than 6 million acres of land—Maasai pasture and Kikuyu and Kamba farms—were stolen by the settlers. African communities were often displaced to increasingly overcrowded reserves. Laborers, mostly Kikuyu migrants from the reserves, worked for the new European owners, sometimes on lands that they had once farmed for themselves.

HEALTH/WELFARE

Kenya's social infrastructure has been burdened by the influx of some 300,000 refugees from the neighboring states of Ethiopia, Somalia, and Sudan. Circumcision of girls under age 17 was banned in 2001. The lack of rainfall during the last four years has caused major crop failure and a major food crisis for consumers.

By the 1950s, African grievances had been heightened by increased European settlement and the growing removal of African "squatters" from their estates. There were also growing class and ideological differences among Africans, leading to tensions between educated Christians with middle-class aspirations and displaced members of the rural underclass. Many members of the latter group, in particular, began to mobilize themselves in largely Kikuyu oathing societies, which coalesced into the Mau Mau movement.

Armed resistance by Mau Mau guerrillas began in 1951, with isolated attacks on white settlers. In response, the British proclaimed a state of emergency, which lasted for 10 years. Without any outside support, the Mau Mau held out for years by making effective use of the highland forests as sanctuaries. Nonetheless, by 1955, the uprising had largely been crushed. Although the name Mau Mau became for many outsiders synonymous with antiwhite terrorism, only 32 European civilians actually lost their lives during the rebellion. In contrast, at least 13,000 Kikuyu were killed. Another 80,000 Africans were detained by the colonial authorities, and more than 1 million were resettled in controlled villages. While the Mau Mau were overwhelmed by often ruthless counterinsurgency measures, they achieved an important victory: The British realized that the preservation of Kenya as a white-settler–dominated colony was militarily and politically untenable.

In the aftermath of the emergency, the person who emerged as the charismatic leader of Kenya's nationalist movement was Jomo Kenyatta, who had been detained and accused by the British—without any evidence—of leading the resistance movement. At independence, in 1963, he became the president. He held the office until his death in 1978.

ACHIEVEMENTS

Each year, Kenya devotes about half of its government expenditures to education. Most Kenyan students can now expect 12 years of schooling. Tertiary education is also expanding.

To many, the situation in Kenya under Kenyatta looked promising. His government encouraged racial harmony, and the slogan Harambee (Swahili for "Pull together") became a call for people of all ethnic groups and races to work together for development. Land reforms provided plots to 1.5 million farmers. A policy of Africanization created business opportunities for local entrepreneurs, and industry grew. Although the Kenya African National Union was supposedly guided by a policy of "African Socialism," the nation was seen by many as a showcase of capitalist development.

POLITICAL DEVELOPMENT

Kenyatta's Kenya quickly became a de facto one-party state. In 1966, the country's first vice-president, Oginga Odinga, resigned to form an opposition party, the Kenyan People's Union (KPU). Three years later, however, the party was banned and its leaders, including Odinga, were imprisoned. Thereafter KANU became the focus of political competition, and voters were allowed to remove sitting members of Parliament, including cabinet ministers. But politics was marred by intimidation and violence, including the assassinations of prominent critics within government, most notably Economic Development Minister Tom Mboya, in 1969, and Foreign Affairs Minister J. M. Kariuki, in 1975. Constraints on freedom of association were justified in the interest of preventing ethnic conflict—much of the KPU support came from the Luo group. However, ethnicity has always been important in shaping struggles within KANU itself.

Under Daniel arap Moi, Kenyatta's successor, the political climate grew steadily more repressive. In 1982, his government was badly shaken by a failed coup attempt, in which about 250 people died and approximately 1,500 others were detained. The air force was disbanded and the university, whose students came out in support of the coup-makers, was temporarily closed.

In the aftermath of the coup, all parties other than KANU were formally outlawed. Moi followed this step by declaring, in 1986, that KANU was above the government, the Parliament, and the judiciary. Press restrictions, detentions, and blatant acts of intimidation became common. Those members of Parliament brave enough to be critical of Moi's imperial presidency were removed from KANU and thus Parliament. Political tensions were blamed on the local agents of an ever-growing list of outside forces, including Christian missionaries and Muslim fundamentalists, foreign academics and the news media, and Libyan and U.S. meddlers.

A number of underground opposition groups emerged during the mid-1980s, most notably the socialist-oriented Mwakenya movement, whose ranks included such prominent exiles as the writer Ngugi wa Thiong'o. In 1987, many of these groups came together to form the United Movement for Democracy, or UMOJA (Swahili for "unity"). But in the immediate aftermath of the 1989 KANU elections, which in many areas were blatantly rigged, Moi's grip on power appeared strong.

The early months of 1990, however, witnessed an upsurge in antigovernment unrest. In February, the murder of Foreign Minister Robert Ouko touched off rioting in Nairobi and his home city of Kisumu. Another riot occurred when squatters were forcibly evicted from the Nairobi shantytown of Muoroto. Growing calls for the restoration of multiparty democracy fueled a cycle of unrest and repression. The detention in July of two former cabinet ministers, Kenneth Matiba and Charles Rubia, for their part in the democracy agitation sparked nationwide rioting, which left at least 28 people dead and 1,000 arrested. Opposition movements, most notably the Forum for the Restoration of Democracy (FORD), began to emerge in defiance of the government's ban on their activities.

Under mounting external pressure from Western donor countries as well as from his internal opponents, Moi finally agreed to the legalization of opposition parties, in December 1991. Unfortunately, this move failed to diffuse Kenya's increasingly violent political, social, and ethnic tensions.

Continued police harassment of the opposition triggered renewed rioting throughout the country. There was also a rise in interethnic clashes in both rural and urban areas, which many, even within KANU, attributed to government incitement. In the Rift Valley, armed members of Moi's own Kalinjin grouping attacked other groups for supposedly settling on their land. Hundreds were killed and thousands injured and displaced in the worst violence since the Mau Mau era. In the face of the government's cynical resort to divide-and-rule tactics, the fledgling opposition movement betrayed the hopes of many of its supporters by becoming hopelessly splintered. New groups, such as the Islamic Party of Kenya, openly appealed for support along ethnoreligious lines. More significantly, a leadership struggle in the main FORD grouping between Matiba and the veteran Odinga split the party into two, while a proposed alliance with Mwai Kibaki's Democratic Party failed to materialize. Although motivated as much by personal ambitions and lingering mistrust between KANU defectors and long-term KANU opponents, the FORD split soon took on an ethnic dimension, with many Kikuyu backing Matiba, while Luo remained solidly loyal to Odinga.

Taking skillful advantage of his opponents' disarray, Moi called elections in December 1992, which resulted in his plurality victory, with 36 percent of the vote. KANU was able to capture 95 of the 188 parliamentary seats that were up for grabs. The two FORD factions won 31 seats each, while the Democratic Party captured 23 seats. Notwithstanding voting irregularities, most independent observers blamed the divided opposition for sowing the seeds of its own defeat. The death of the widely respected Odinga in January 1994 coincided with renewed attempts to form a united opposition to KANU. In 1996, a group of opposition Members of Parliament was established.

Kenya's politics reflects class as well as ethnic divisions. The richest 10 percent of the population own an estimated 40 percent of the wealth, while the poorest 30 percent own only 10 percent. Past economic growth has failed to alleviate poverty. Kenya's relatively large middle class has grown resentful of increased repression and the evident corruption at the very top, but it is also fearful about perceived anarchy from below.

Although its rate of growth has declined during much of the past two decades, the Kenyan economy has expanded since independence. Nairobi is now the leading center of industrial and commercial activity in East Africa. While foreign capital has played an important role in industrial development, the largest share of investment has come from government and the local private sector.

A significant percentage of foreign-exchange earnings has come from agriculture. A wide variety of cash crops is exported, a diversity that has buffered the nation's economy to some degree from the uncertainties associated with single-commodity dependence. While large plantations—now often owned by wealthy Kenyans—have survived from the colonial era, much of the commercial production is carried out by small landholders.

A major challenge to Kenya's well-being has been its rapidly expanding population. Although there are some hopeful signs that women are beginning to plan for fewer children than in the past, the nation has been plagued with one of the highest population growth rates in the world, until very recently hovering around 3 percent per year (it is now estimated at 1.15 percent). More than half of all Kenyans are under age 15. Pressure on arable land is enormous. It will be difficult to create nonagricultural employment for the burgeoning rural-turned-urban workforce, even in the context of democratic stability and renewed economic growth.

THE ROAD AHEAD

Since the election there have been major steps taken to eliminate corruption in Kenya. Immediately following the election in January 2003, the government presented, and passed, a bill creating an anti-corruption commission. Subsequently, a Moi critic John Githongo was appointed as anti-graft czar. In appreciation for their efforts, in November 2003 the International Monetary Fund (IMF) resumed lending after a three-year gap, citing effective anti-corruption measures. One month later in an effort for peace and reconciliation, the government decided to grant former president Daniel arap Moi immunity from prosecution on corruption charges.

Timeline: PAST

1895
The British East African Protectorate is proclaimed

1900–1910
British colonists begin to settle in the Highlands area

1951
Mau Mau, a predominantly Kikuyu movement, resists colonial rule

1963
Kenya gains independence under the leadership of Jomo Kenyatta

1978
Daniel arap Moi becomes president upon the death of Kenyatta

1980s
A coup attempt by members of the Kenyan Air Force is crushed; political repression grows

1990s
Prodemocracy agitation leads to a return of multiparty politics; interethnic violence threatens democratic transition; President Daniel arap Moi is reelected; the U.S. Embassy building in Nairobi is bombed

PRESENT

2000s
Kenya seeks to root out public corruption

Kenya works to strengthen its economy and international reputation

Opposition candidate Mwai Kibaki wins the presidency, ending KANU rule

Wangari Maathi wins the Nobel Prize for her contribution towards the preservation of the Kenyan natural environment

Voters reject a proposed new constitution

Sustained economic growth has been realized under Kibaki's leadership. In 2006, Kenya's economy grew at a commendable rate of 6.1% compared to 0.6% when he took over in 2002. However, in spite of this good showing and in spite of the tough talk about corruption, his government has been implicated in a major corruption scandal. It is alleged that former and current ministers have been involved in a scam of shadowy deals amounting to over a billion dollars of public money. International donors have questioned Kibaki's efforts at rooting corruption given these allegations. There has also been political wrangle with respect to the new constitution. In 2005 Parliament approved a draft constitution after days of violent protests in Nairobi over aspects of the draft, which demonstrators said gave too much power to the president. In a follow-up referendum, the voters rejected the proposed constitution, a move that was seen as a protest against President Kibaki and his government.

Madagascar (Republic of Madagascar)

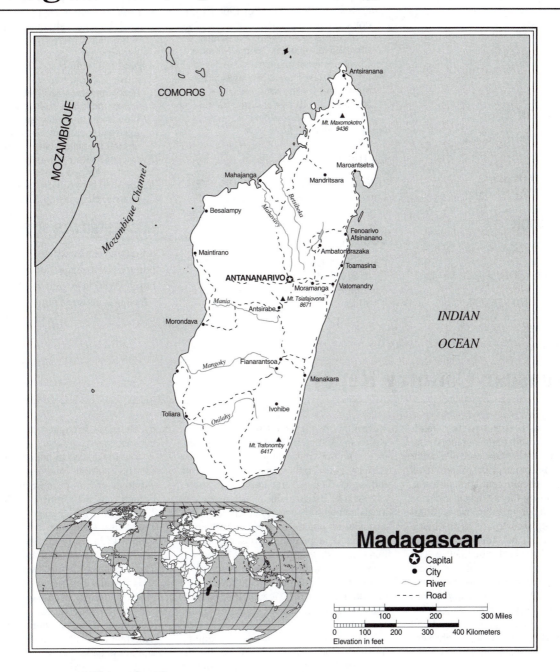

Madagascar Statistics

GEOGRAPHY

Area in Square Miles (Kilometers):
226,658 (587,041) (about twice the size of Arizona)

Capital (Population): Antananarivo (1,689,000)

Environmental Concerns: soil erosion resulting from deforestation and overgrazing; desertification; water contamination; endangered species

Geographical Features: narrow coastal plain; high plateau and mountains in the center; the world's fourth-largest island

Climate: tropical along the coast; temperate inland; arid in the south

PEOPLE

Population

Total: 19,448,815
Annual Growth Rate: 3.00%

Rural/Urban Population Ratio: 74/26
Major Languages: Malagasy; French
Ethnic Makeup: Malayo Indonesian; Cotiers; French; Indian; Creole; Comoran
Religions: 52% indigenous beliefs; 41% Christian; 7% Muslim

Health

Life Expectancy at Birth: 60.23 years (male); 64.1 years (female)

Infant Mortality: 57.02/1,000 live
  births
Physicians Available: 1/8,628 people
HIV/AIDS Rate in Adults: 1.7%

Education

Adult Literacy Rate: 68.9%
Compulsory (Ages): for 5 years
  between 6–13

COMMUNICATION

Telephones: 129,800 main lines
Daily Newspaper Circulation: 4/1,000
  people
Televisions: 20/1,000 people
Internet Users: 110,000 (2006)

TRANSPORTATION

Highways in Miles (Kilometers): 29,894
  (49,827 km)
Railroads in Miles (Kilometers): 854 km
Usable Airfields: 116
Motor Vehicles in Use: 76,000

GOVERNMENT

Type: republic
Independence Date: June 26, 1960 (from
  France)
Head of State/Government: President
  Marc Ravalomanana; Prime Minister
  Charles Rabemananjara
Political Parties: I Love Madagascar;
  Movement for the Progress of
  Madagascar; Renewal of the Social
  Democratic Party; others
Suffrage: universal at 18

MILITARY

Military Expenditures (% of GDP): 1%
Current Disputes: territorial disputes over
  islands administered by France; civil strife

ECONOMY

Currency ($ U.S. Equivalent): 1,815.00
  Ariary = $1
Per Capita Income/GDP: $900/$17.27
  billion

GDP Growth Rate: 4.7%
Inflation Rate: 8%
Population Below Poverty Line: 70%
Natural Resources: graphite; chromite;
  coal; bauxite; salt; quartz; tar sands;
  semiprecious stones; mica; fish;
  hydropower
Agriculture: coffee; vanilla; sugarcane;
  cloves; cocoa; rice; cassava (tapioca);
  beans; bananas; livestock products
Industry: meat processing; soap;
  breweries; tanneries; sugar; textiles;
  glassware; cement; automobile
  assembly; paper; petroleum; tourism
Exports: $993.5 million (primary partners
  France, United States, Germany)
Imports: $1.544 billion (primary partners
  France, Hong Kong, China)

SUGGESTED WEB SITES

http://www.embassy.org
http://www.madagascarnews.com
http://www.cia.gov/cia/publications/
  factbook/geos/ma.html

Madagascar Country Report

Madagascar has been called the "small-est continent"; indeed, many geologists believe that it once formed the core of a larger landmass, whose other principal remnants are the Indian subcontinent and Australia. The world's fourth-largest island remains a world unto itself in other ways. Botanists and zoologists know it as the home of flora and fauna not found elsewhere. The island's culture is also distinctive. The Malagasy language, which with dialectical variations is spoken throughout the island, is related to the Malay tongues of distant Indonesia. But despite their geographic separation from the African mainland and their Asiatic roots, the Malagasy are very aware of their African identity.

DEVELOPMENT

In 1989, "Export Processing Zones" were established to attract foreign investment through tax and currency incentives. The government especially hopes to attract business from neighboring Mauritius, whose success with such zones has led to labor shortages and a shift toward more value-added production.

While the early history of Madagascar is the subject of much scholarly debate, it is clear that by the year A.D. 500, the island was being settled by Malay-speaking peoples, who may have migrated via the East African coast rather than directly from Indonesia. The cultural imprint of Southeast Asia is also evident in such aspects as local architecture, music, cosmology, and agricultural practices. African influences are equally apparent. During the precolonial period, the peoples of Madagascar were in communication with communities on the African mainland, and the waves of migration across the Mozambique channel contributed to the island's modern ethnic diversity.

During the early nineteenth century, most of Madagascar was united by the rulers of Merina. In seeking to build up their realm and preserve the island's independence, the Merina kings and queens welcomed European (mostly English) missionaries, who helped introduce new ideas and technologies. As a result, many Malagasy, including the royalty, adopted Christianity. The kingdom had established diplomatic relations with the United States and various European powers and was thus a recognized member of the international community. Foreign businesspeople were attracted to invest in the island's growing economy, while the rapid spread of schools and medical services, increasingly staffed by Malagasy, brought profound changes to the society.

The Merina court hoped that its "Christian civilization" and modernizing army would deter European aggression. But the French were determined to rule the island. The 1884–1885 Franco–Malagasy War ended in a stalemate, but a French invasion in 1895 led to the Merina kingdom's destruction. It was not an easy conquest. The Malagasy Army, with its artillery and modern fortifications, held out for many months; eventually, however, it was outgunned by the invaders. French sovereignty was proclaimed in 1896, but "pacification" campaigns continued for another decade.

FREEDOM

Respect for human rights has improved since 1993, and there has been little political violence since the 1996 election. There are isolated reports of police brutality against criminal suspects and detainees, as well as instances of arbitrary arrest and detention. Prison conditions are often life threatening, with women experiencing abuse, including rape. New judges are being appointed in an effort to relieve the overburdened judiciary.

(United Nations photo 140091 by L. Rajaonina)

Madagascar has a unique ethnic diversity, created by migrations from the African mainland and Southeast Asia. The varied ethnic makeup of the population can be seen in the faces of these schoolchildren.

French rule reduced what had been a prospering state into a colonial backwater. The pace of development slowed as the local economy was restructured to serve the interests of French settlers, whose numbers had swelled to 60,000 by the time of World War II. Probably the most important French contribution to Madagascar was the encouragement their misrule gave to the growth of local nationalism. By the 1940s, a strong sense of Malagasy identity had been forged through common hatred of the colonialists.

HEALTH/WELFARE

Primary-school enrollment is now universal. Thirty-six percent of the appropriate age group attend secondary school, while 5% of those ages 20 to 24 are in tertiary institutions. Malaria remains a major health challenge. Madagascar's health and education facilities are underfunded.

The local overthrow of Vichy power by the British in 1943 created an opening for Malagasy nationalists to organize themselves into mass parties, the most prominent of which was the Malagasy Movement for Democratic Renewal (MRDM). In 1946, the MRDM elected two overseas deputies to the French National Assembly, on the basis of its call for immediate independence. France responded by instructing its administrators to "fight the MRDM by every means." Arrests led to resistance. In March 1947, a general insurrection began. Peasant rebels, using whatever weapons they could find, liberated large areas from French control. French troops countered by destroying crops and blockading rebel areas, in an effort to starve the insurrectionists into surrendering. Thousands of Malagasy were massacred. By the end of the year, the rebellion had been largely crushed, although a state of siege was maintained until 1956. No one knows precisely how many Malagasy lost their lives in the uprising, but contemporary estimates indicate about 90,000.

INDEPENDENCE AND REVOLUTION

Madagascar gained its independence in 1960. However, many viewed the new government, led by Philibert Tsiranana of the Social Democratic Party (PSD), as a vehicle for continuing French influence; memories of 1947 were still strong. Lack of economic and social reform led to a peasant uprising in 1971. This Maoist-inspired rebellion was suppressed, but the government was left weakened. In 1972, new unrest, this time spearheaded by students and workers in the towns, led to Tsiranana's overthrow by the military. After a period of confusion, radical forces consolidated power around Lieutenant Commander Didier Ratsiraka, who assumed the presidency in 1975.

Under Ratsiraka, a new Constitution was adopted that allowed for a controlled process of multiparty competition, in which all parties were grouped within the National Front. Within this framework, the largest party was Ratsiraka's Vanguard of the Malagasy Revolution (AREMA). Initially, all parties were expected to support the president's Charter of the Malagasy Revolution, which called for a Marxist-oriented socialist transformation. In accordance with the Charter, foreign-owned banks and financial institutions were nationalized. A series of state enterprises were also established to promote industrial development, but few proved viable.

Although 80 percent of the Malagasy were employed in agriculture, investment in rural areas and concerns was modest. The government attempted to work through *fokonolas* (indigenous village-management bodies). State farms and collectives were also established on land expropriated from French settlers. While these efforts led to some improvements, such as increased mechanization, state marketing monopolies and planning constraints contributed to shortfalls. Efforts to keep consumer prices low were blamed for a drop in rice production, the Malagasy staple, while cash-crop production, primarily coffee, vanilla, and cloves, suffered from falling world prices.

ACHIEVEMENTS

A recently established wildlife preserve will allow the unique animals of Madagascar to survive and develop. Sixty-six species of land animals are found nowhere else on earth, including the aye-aye, a nocturnal lemur that has bat ears, beaver teeth, and an elongated clawed finger, all of which serve the aye-aye in finding food.

Since 1980, Madagascar has experienced grave economic difficulties, which have given rise to political instability. Food shortages in towns have led to rioting, while frustrated peasants have abandoned their fields. Ratsiraka's government turned increasingly from socialism to a greater reliance on market economics. But the economy has remained impoverished.

In 1985, having abandoned attempts to make the National Front into a vehicle for a single-party state, Ratsiraka presided over a loosening of his once-authoritarian control. In February 1990, most remaining restrictions on multiparty politics were lifted. But the regime's opponents, including a revived PSD, became militant in their demands for a new constitution. After six months of crippling strikes and protests, Ratsiraka formally ceded many of his powers to a transitional government, headed by Albert Zafy, in November 1991. In February 1993, Zafy won the presidency by a large margin. But subsequent divisions with Parliament over his rejection of an International Monetary Fund austerity plan, accompanied by allegations of financial irregularities, led to his impeachment in August 1996. In elections held at the end of the year, Ratsiraka made a comeback, narrowly defeating Zafy. More than half of the population, however, stayed away from the polls.

Marc Ravalomanana shocked most outside observers when, under the banner of his newly organized I Love Madagascar (TIM) party, he claimed outright victory in presidential elections in December 2001. A bitter seven-month struggle for power ensued with the president of 27 years, Didier Ratsiraka.

Ravalomanana argued that, having won a majority of the votes in the first round of the elections, there need not be another round of voting. Ratsiraka, on the other hand, sought solace in the Constitution and demanded another round of voting. Since many saw the elections as rigged in favor of Ratsiraka, it was widely perceived in Madagascar that Ravalomanana was the winner and that Ratsiraka was merely stalling for time and acting as an impediment to hold onto power. In April 2002, after a recount, the High Constitutional Court named Ravalomanana the winner of the December 2001 polls, but Ratsiraka ignored the verdict.

Once the demand for new elections was turned down, Ratsiraka mobilized the army and took over various areas of Madagascar. Without Madagascar Army support, Ravalomanana organized a motley crew of reserves and attacked the army-held positions. The result was chaotic. For seven months the country had two presidents and two capitals. Widespread demonstrations and worker strikes paralyzed trade, commerce, and industry, with political discourse becoming intransigent. The dispute caused immediate economic depression, as Ratsiraka's allies put up economic barricades throughout much of the country. Gasoline and medical supplies were in short supply, as foreign reserves held in U.S. banks were frozen.

In July 2002, shortly after the United States and France recognized Ravalomanana as the legitimate leader, Ratsiraka and various family members flew into exile in the Seychelles, and his forces on the island either surrendered or switched sides. Ravalomanana has promised to use his entrepreneurial flair to fight the poverty and unemployment that afflict many Madagascans. But he has inherited an economy that is suffering after months of economic disruption and political violence.

The African Union has so far refused to accept Ravalomanana's presidency and did not admit him to the initiation of the organization in September 2002. The AU had demanded that new elections be held to resolve the issue. The lack of AU recognition, however, has been offset by recognition from France, Britain, and the United States.

New elections were not held and as the president took office he began to search out and prosecute corruption in the country. During February 2003 the former head of the

armed forces was arrested and charged with attempting a coup against President Ravalomanana. In August 2003, exiled former president Didier Ratsiraka was sentenced to 10 years hard labor for embezzling public funds. In December former Prime Minister Tantely Andrianarivo was also sentenced to 12 years hard labor for abuse of office. For his efforts at rooting out corruption, the World Bank and International Monetary Fund wrote off nearly half of Madagascar's debt—around two billion dollars.

In March 2005, the United States gave development aid to Madagascar under a scheme to reward nations considered by Washington to be promoting democracy and market reforms. In the most recent elections of May 2006, Marc Ravalomanana, the incumbent, was declared the winner of the presidential elections. In April 2007, voters in a referendum endorsed constitutional reforms to increase presidential powers and make English an official language. The consolidation of power by Ravalomanana has raised questions about his authoritarian tendencies.

Timeline: PAST

1828
Merina rulers gain sovereignty over other peoples of the island

1884–1885
Franco–Malagasy War

1904
The French complete the conquest of the island

1947–1948
A revolt is suppressed by the French, with great loss of life

1960
Independence from France; Philibert Tsiranana becomes the first president

1972
A coup leads to the fall of the First Malagasy Republic

1975
Didier Ratsiraka becomes president by military appointment

1980s
Economic problems intensify

1990
Elections in 1989–1990 strengthen multiparty democracy

PRESENT

2000s
Ratsiraka finally cedes power to Marc Ravalomanana

Mauritius (Republic of Mauritius)

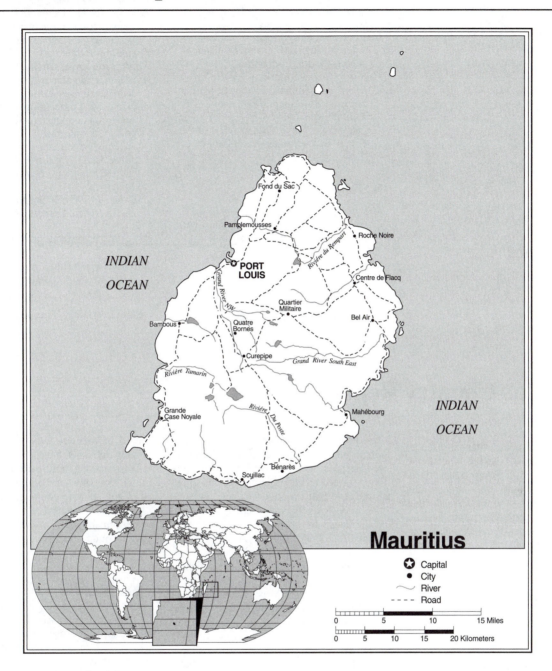

Mauritius Statistics

GEOGRAPHY

Area in Square Miles (Kilometers): 720 (1,865) (about 11 times the size of Washington, D.C.)

Capital (Population): Port Louis (176,000)

Environmental Concerns: water pollution; population pressures on land and water resources

Geographical Features: a small coastal plain rising to discontinuous mountains encircling a central plateau

Climate: tropical

PEOPLE

Population

Total: 1,250,882

Annual Growth Rate: 0.798%

Rural/Urban Population Ratio: 58/42

Major Languages: English; Creole; French; Hindi; Urdu; Hakka; Bojpoori

Ethnic Makeup: 68% Indo-Mauritian; 27% Creole; 3% Sino-Mauritian; 2% Franco-Mauritian

Religions: 52% Hindu; 28% Christian; 17% Muslim; 3% others

Health

Life Expectancy at Birth: 72.98 years
   (male); 76.9 years (female)
Infant Mortality: 14.14/1,000 live births
Physicians Available: 1/1,182 people
HIV/AIDS Rate in Adults: 0.1%

Education

Adult Literacy Rate: 84.4%
Compulsory (Ages): 5–12

COMMUNICATION

Telephones: 357,300 main lines
Daily Newspaper Circulation: 49/1,000
   people
Televisions: 150/1,000 people
Internet Users: 182,000 (2006)

TRANSPORTATION

Highways in Miles (Kilometers): 1,212
   (2,020 km)
Railroads in Miles (Kilometers): none
Usable Airfields: 6
Motor Vehicles in Use: 82,500

GOVERNMENT

Type: parliamentary democracy
Independence Date: March 12, 1968
   (from the United Kingdom)
Head of State/Government: President Sir
   Anerood Jugnauth; Prime Minister
   Navinchandra Ramgoolam
Political Parties: Mauritian Labor Party;
   Mauritian Militant Movement; Militant
   Socialist Movement; Mauritian
   Militant Renaissance; Mauritian Social
   Democratic Party; Organization of the
   People of Rodrigues; Hizbullah; others
Suffrage: universal at 18

MILITARY

Military Expenditures (% of GDP): 0.3%
Current Disputes: territorial disputes with
   France and the United Kingdom

ECONOMY

Currency ($ U.S. equivalent): 29.80
   rupees = $1
Per Capita Income/GDP: $13,700/$17.02
   billion

GDP Growth Rate: 5%
Inflation Rate: 4.2%
Unemployment Rate: 9.8%
Labor Force by Occupation: 36%
   construction and industry; 24%
   services; 14% agriculture; 26% others
Population Below Poverty Line: 10%
Natural Resources: arable land; fish
Agriculture: sugarcane; tea; corn; potatoes;
   bananas; pulses; cattle; goats; fish
Industry: food processing; textiles;
   apparel; chemicals; metal products;
   transport equipment; nonelectrical
   machinery; tourism
Exports: $2.138 billion (primary partners
   United Kingdom, France, United
   States)
Imports: $3.391 billion (primary partners
   South Africa, France, India)

SUGGESTED WEB SITES

http://www.mauritius-info.com
http://www.ncb.intnet.ma/govt/
http://www.sas.upenn.edu/African_
   Studies/Country_Specific/Mauritius
   .html

Mauritius Country Report

Although it was not permanently settled until 1722, today Mauritius is home to 1.2 million people of South Asian, Euro-African, Chinese, and other origins. Out of this extraordinary human diversity has emerged a society that in recent decades has become a model of democratic stability and economic growth as well as ethnic, racial, and sectarian tolerance.

DEVELOPMENT

The success of the Mauritian EPZ along with the export-led growth of various Asian economies has encouraged a growing number of other African countries, such as Botswana, Cape Verde, and Madagascar, to launch their own export zones.

Mauritius was first settled by the French, some of whom achieved great wealth by setting up sugar plantations. From the beginning, the plantations prospered through their exploitation of slave labor imported from the African mainland. Over time, the European and African communities merged into a common Creole culture; that membership currently accounts for

one quarter of the Mauritian population. A small number claim pure French descent. For decades, members of this latter group have formed an economic and social elite. More than half the sugar acreage remains the property of 21 large Franco–Mauritian plantations; the rest is divided among nearly 28,000 small land-holdings. French cultural influence remains strong. Most of the newspapers on the island are published in French, which shares official-language status with English. Most Mauritians also speak a local, French-influenced, Creole language. Most Mauritian Creoles are Roman Catholics.

In 1810, Mauritius was occupied by the British; they ruled the island until 1968. (After years of debate, in 1992, the country cut its ties with Great Britain to become a republic.) When the British abolished slavery, in 1835, the plantation owners turned to large-scale use of indentured labor from what was then British India. Today nearly two thirds of the population are of South Asian descent and have maintained their home languages. Most are Hindu, but a substantial minority are Muslim. Other faiths, such as Buddhism, are also represented.

Although the majority of Mauritians gained the right to vote after World War II, the island has maintained an uninterrupted

record of parliamentary rule since 1886. Ethnic divisions have long been important in shaping political allegiances. But ethnic constituency-building has not led, in recent years, to communal polarization. Other factors—such as class, ideology, and opportunism—have also been influential. All postindependence governments have been multiethnic coalitions.

FREEDOM

Political pluralism and human rights are respected on Mauritius, but problem areas remain. There are reports of police abuse of suspects and delayed access to defense counsel. Child labor exists. Legislation outlawing domestic violence has been passed recently. The nation has more than 30 political parties, of which about a half dozen are important at any given time. The Mauritian labor movement is one of the strongest in all of Africa.

While government in Mauritius has been characterized by shifting coalitions, with no single party winning a majority of seats, there has been relative stability in leadership at the top. Over the past half-century, Mauritius has had only three prime ministers. In September 2000, a coalition led by former prime minister Sir Aneerood Jugnauth won a landslide victory, ousting the rival coalition of Navin Ramgoolam, who had ousted Jugnauth five years earlier. Jugnauth had first come to power in 1982 by defeating Seewoosagar Ramgoolam, Navin's father.

HEALTH/WELFARE

Medical and most educational expenses are free. Food prices are heavily subsidized. Rising government deficits, however, threaten future social spending. Mauritius has a high life expectancy rate and a low infant mortality rate. Human-rights education has been introduced in secondary schools.

In February 2002 a major turn of political events occurred. Political power changed hands in Mauritius as Cassam Uteem resigned as president after refusing to sign the controversial anti-terrorism bill. The vice president, who also refused to sign the bill, resigned as well. Later in the year Karl Hoffman was elected president by National Assembly, but stepped down in September 2003. President Aneerood Jugnauth took his place on October 7, 2003.

With reference to the premiership, former Prime Minister Navin Ramgoolam of the Social Alliance returned to power after defeating Paul Berenger of the Mauritian Militant Movement in elections in July 2005. The new premier campaigned on a platform to tackle rising inflation and unemployment by trade agreements that would give preference to Mauritian exports, including sugar and textiles. Navin Ramgoolam had already held the post from 1995 to 2000. His predecessor, Paul Berenger, a white Mauritian of French descent, was the island's first non-Hindu prime minister in 2003.

Although most major political parties have in the past espoused various shades of socialism, Mauritius's economic success in recent decades has created a strong consensus in favor of export-oriented market economics. Until the 1970s, the Mauritian economy was almost entirely dependent on sugar. While 45 percent of the island's total landmass continues to be planted with the crop, sugar now ranks below textiles and

tourism in its contribution to export earnings and gross domestic product. The transformation of Mauritius from monocrop dependency into a FledgLing industrial state with a strong service sector has made it one of the major economic success stories of the developing world. Mauritian growth has been built on a foundation of export-oriented manufacturing. At the core of the Mauritian take-off is its island-wide Export Processing Zone (EPZ), which has attracted industrial investment through a combination of low wages, tax breaks, and other financial incentives. Although most of the EPZ output has been in the field of cheap textiles, the economy has begun to diversify into more capital- and skill-intensive production. The year 2002 saw the Cyber Cities plan launched to create concentrations of hi-tech facilities and to boost the economy by adding thousands of jobs. In 1989, Mauritius also entered the international financial services market by launching Africa's first offshore banking center.

ACHIEVEMENTS

Perhaps Mauritius's most important modern achievement has been its successful efforts to reduce its birth rate. This has been brought about by government-backed family planning as well as by increased economic opportunities for women.

The success of the Mauritian economy is measured in relative terms. Mauritius is still considered a middle-income country. In reality, however, there are, as with most developing societies, great disparities in the distribution of wealth. Nonetheless, quality-of-life indicators confirm a rising standard of living for the population as a whole. While great progress has been made toward eliminating poverty and disease, concern has also grown about the environmental capacity of the small, crowded country to sustain its current rate of development. There is also a general recognition that Mauritian prosperity is—and will for the foreseeable future remain—extremely vulnerable to global-market forces. This was demonstrated after the September 11, 2001, terrorist attacks in the United States, when tourism took a precipitous dive, and previously with the declining level of sugar

production caused by the cyclone in 1999. The much-acclaimed ethnic diversity of Mauritius also came under examination as there were racially inspired riots in 2000 between Creoles and Hindu communities after the death while in police custody of a Creole Rastafarian pop star, Rasta Karya.

Timeline: PAST

1600s
The Dutch claim, but abandon, Mauritius

1722
French settlers arrive, and slaves imported from the African mainland

1814
The Treaty of Paris formally cedes Mauritius to the British

1835
Slavery is abolished; South Asians arrive

1937
Rioting on sugar estates shakes the political control of the Franco-Mauritian elite

1948
An expanded franchise allows greater democracy

1968
Independence

1979
A cyclone destroys homes as well as much of the sugar crop

1982
Aneerood Jugnauth replaces Seewoosagar Ramgoolam as prime minister

1990s
Mauritius becomes a republic; Mauritius becomes the 12th member of the SADC

PRESENT

2000s
Jugnauth regains the prime ministership in a landslide electoral victory

Mauritius continues its focus on market economics

Aneerood Jugnauth is made president after Karl Hoffmann steps down

One hundred former residents of the Chagos Archipelago—claimed by Mauritius—make a return visit nearly 40 years after being evicted to make way for a U.S. military base on the island of Diego Garcia

Rwanda (Rwandese Republic)

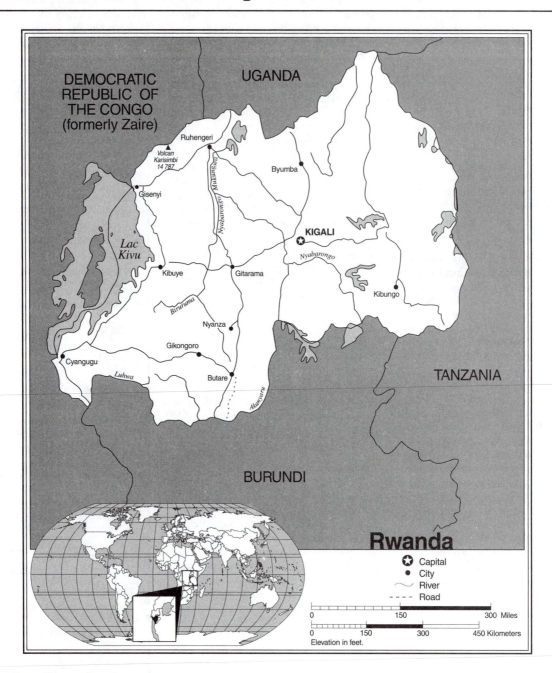

Rwanda Statistics

GEOGRAPHY

Area in Square Miles (Kilometers): 10,169
(26,338) (about the size of Maryland)
Capital (Population): Kigali (603,049)
Environmental Concerns: deforestation;
overgrazing; soil exhaustion and
erosion; poaching
Geographical Features: mostly grassy
uplands and hills; landlocked
Climate: temperate

PEOPLE

Population

Total: 9,907,509
Annual Growth Rate: 2.766%
Rural/Urban Population Ratio: 83/17
Major Languages: Kinyarwanda; French;
Kiswahili; English
Ethnic Makeup: 84% Hutu; 15% Tutsi;
1% Twa

Religions: 95% Christian; 4% Muslim;
2% none or other

Health

Life Expectancy at Birth: 47.87 years
(male); 50.16 years (female)
Infant Mortality: 85.27/1,000 live
births
Physicians Available: 1/50,000 people
HIV/AIDS Rate in Adults: 5.1%

Education

Adult Literacy Rate: 70.4%
Compulsory (Ages): 7–14

COMMUNICATION

Telephones: 22,000 main lines
Internet Users: 65,000 (2006)

TRANSPORTATION

Highways in Miles (Kilometers): 8,405 (14,008)
Railroads in Miles (Kilometers): none
Usable Airfields: 9
Motor Vehicles in Use: 28,000

GOVERNMENT

Type: republic
Independence Date: July 1, 1962 (from Belgian-administered UN trusteeship)

Head of State/Government: President Paul Kagame; Prime Minister Bernard Makuza
Political Parties: Rwanda Patriotic Front; Democratic Republican Movement; Liberal Party; Democratic Socialist Party; others
Suffrage: universal at 18

MILITARY

Military Expenditures (% of GDP): 2.9%
Current Disputes: continued internal ethnic violence; conflict in the Democratic Republic of the Congo

ECONOMY

Currency ($ U.S. equivalent): 543.15 francs
Per Capita Income/GDP: $1,600/$13.7 billion
GDP Growth Rate: 5.8%
Inflation Rate: 7.5%

Labor Force by Occupation: 90% agriculture
Population Below Poverty Line: 70%
Natural Resources: tungsten ore; tin; cassiterite; methane; hydropower; arable land
Agriculture: coffee; tea; pyrethrum; bananas; sorghum; beans; potatoes; livestock
Industry: agricultural-products processing; mining; light consumer goods; cement
Exports: $135.4 million (primary partners Europe, Pakistan, United States)
Imports: $390.4 million (primary partners Kenya, Europe, United States)

SUGGESTED WEB SITES

http://www.rwanda1.com/government/
http://www.rwandanews.org
http://www.cia.gov/cia/publications/factbook/geos/rw.html

Rwanda Country Report

In July 2002, the presidents of Rwanda and the Democratic Republic of the Congo (D.R.C.) signed a peace agreement to end their four-year war. With South Africa and the United Nations acting as guarantors, the deal committed Rwanda to the withdrawal of troops from eastern D.R.C., and the D.R.C. to helping disarm Rwandan Hutu refugees in its territory who were responsible for the 1994 genocide that targeted Rwanda's Tutsi minority. By October 2002, Rwanda had honored its commitment, bringing cautious hope for a lasting peace.

DEVELOPMENT

Hydroelectric stations meet much of the country's energy needs. Before the 1994 genocide, plans were being made to exploit methane-gas reserves under Lake Kivu.

Rwandans have been living a nightmare. The 1994 genocide ranks as one of the world's greatest tragedies. A small country, only about the size of Maryland, Rwanda had 8 million inhabitants early in 1994, making it continental Africa's most densely populated state. This population was divided into three groups: the Hutu majority (89 percent); the Tutsis (10 percent); and the Twa, commonly stereotyped as "Pygmies" (1 percent). By September 1994, civil war involving genocidal con-

flict between Hutus and Tutsis had nearly halved the country's resident population while radically altering its group demography. Up to 1 million people, including women and children, were killed and an additional 2 million displaced. The international community, especially France, the United States, and the United Nations, did little to stop the genocide.

Rebel forces of the ousted government that initiated the genocide have continued to threaten Rwanda, from the D.R.C. In response, since 1997 Rwanda has intervened against its opponents in the D.R.C. as well as in Rwanda itself. In the process, much of eastern D.R.C. has come under Rwandan occupation. Rwanda's ability to send and sustain some 50,000 well-armed troops into the D.R.C. would probably not have been possible without the tacit support of its donors. A UN report released in October 2002 confirmed the involvement of the Rwandan, as well as the Ugandan and Zimbabwean, militaries in the exploitation of the D.R.C.'s natural resources.

The dominant figure in Rwanda over the past decade has been Paul Kagame, who in April 2000 was inaugurated as president, following the resignation of Pasteur Bizimungu. The change at the top had little immediate effect. As vice-president and minister of defense, Kagame, through his largely Tutsi-controlled Rwanda Patriotic Front (RPF), had dominated the "Government of National Unity" since its instal-

lation in 1994. While the resignation of Bizimungu and other members of the mainly Hutu Republican Democratic Movement (RDM) raised eyebrows, the RDM itself opted to remain within the government.

FREEDOM

The Rwandan government and its opponents continue to be responsible for serious human-rights abuses, including massacres. More than 120,000 prisoners are in overcrowded jails, most accused of participating in the 1994 genocide. Genocide trials, which began at the end of 1996, have made little progress and are expected to take years to complete. Hutu death squads, composed of members of the defeated former Rwandan Armed Forces and Interahamwe genocide gangs, continue to target Tutsis and foreigners.

At the end of 2001, voting to elect members of traditional *gacaca* (courts) began. The courts, in which ordinary Rwandans judge their peers, aim to clear the backlog of 1994 genocide cases. Just as important, justice can be seen to be done by the people themselves, based on their traditional standards.

THE 1994 GENOCIDE

The genocide began within a half-hour of the April 6, 1994, death of the country's democratizing dictator, President

Juvenal Habyarimana. Along with president Cyprien Ntaryamira of neighboring Burundi, Habyarimana was killed when his plane was shot down. While the identity of the culprits remains a matter of speculation, Belgian troops reported that rockets were fired from Kanombe military base, which was then controlled by the country's Presidential Guard, known locally as the Akuza. In broadcasts over the independent Radio Libre Mille Collins, Hutu extremists then openly called for the destruction of the Tutsis—"The graves are only half full, who will help us fill them up?" Because the tirades were in idiomatic Kinyarwanda, the national language, they initially escaped the attention of most international journalists on the spot. Meanwhile, Akuza and regular army units set up roadblocks and began systematically to massacre Tutsi citizens in the capital, Kigali. Even greater numbers perished in the countryside, because their names appeared on death lists that had been prepared with the help of local Hutu chiefs.

By July, more than 500,000 people had been murdered. While most were Tutsis, Hutus who had supported moves toward ethnic reconciliation and democratization had also been targeted. During December 2003, three former media directors were found guilty of inciting Hutus to kill Tutsis during the 1994 genocide and received lengthy jail sentences. In addition to elements within the Hutu-dominated military, the killings were carried out by youth-wing militias of the ruling party, the National Revolutionary Movement for Development (MRND) and the Coalition for Defense of Freedom (CDR). Known respectively as the Interahamwe and Impuzamugambi, the ranks of these two all-Hutu militias had mushroomed in the aftermath of an August 1993 agreement designed to return the country to multiparty rule. The extent of the killings was apparent in neighboring Tanzania, where thousands of corpses were televised being carried downstream by the Kagara River. At a rate of 80 an hour, they entered Lake Victoria, more than 100 miles from the Rwandan border.

SYSTEMATIC PLANS FOR MASS MURDER

Preparations for the genocide had been going on for months. According to Amnesty International, Hutu "Zero Network" death squads had already murdered some 2,300 people in the months leading up to the crisis. Although this information was the subject of press reports, no action was taken by the 2,500 peacekeeping troops who had been stationed in the country since June 1993 as the United Nations Assistance Mission to Rwanda (UNAMIR). Once the crisis began, most of UNAMIR's personnel

were hastily withdrawn. French and Belgian paratroopers arrived for a brief time to evacuate their nationals.

Rwanda's genocide did not end with the destruction of a third or more of the Tutsi minority. Enraged by the massacres of their brethren, the 14,000-man Tutsi-dominated Rwanda Patriotic Front, which had been waging an armed struggle against the Habyarimana regime since October, launched a massive offensive. The 35,000-man regular army, along with the militias, crumbled. In July 1994, the RPF took full control of Kigali and drove the remnants of the government and its army into eastern Zaire (since 1997, the D.R.C.). Two million panic-stricken Hutu civilians also fled across the border. By then, about 1 million Rwandans were already in exile. Another 2.5 million people were crowded into a "safe zone" created by the French military. As the French prepared to pull out, the fate of these refugees was uncertain.

In depopulated Kigali, the RPF set up a "Provisional Government" with a Hutu president, Pasteur Bizimungu, and prime minister Faustin Twagiramungu. Its most powerful figure, however, was the RPF commander, Major General Paul Kagame, who became both the vice-president and minister of defense. In June 2004, former president Pasteur Bizimungu was sentenced to 15 years in jail for embezzlement, inciting violence and associating with criminals. He was released from jail in April 2007, three years into his 15-year sentence, after receiving a presidential pardon from Paul Kagame.

HUTUS AND TUTSIS

The roots of Hutu–Tutsi animosity in Rwanda (as well as Burundi) run deep. Yet it is not easy for an outsider to differentiate between the two groups. Their members both speak Kinyarwanda and look the same physically, notwithstanding the stereotype of the Tutsis being exceptionally tall; intermarriage between the two groups has taken place for centuries. By some accounts, the Tutsi arrived as northern Nilotic conquerors, perhaps in the fifteenth century. But others believe that the two groups have always been defined by class or caste rather than by ethnicity.

In the beginning, according to one epic Kinyarwanda poem, the godlike ruler Kigwa fashioned a test to choose his successor. He gave each of his sons a bowl of milk to guard during the night. His son Gatwa drank the milk. Yahutu slept and spilled the milk. Only Gatutsi guarded it well. The myth justifies the old Rwandan social order, in which the Twas were the outcasts, the Hutus servants, and the Tutsis aristocrats. Historically, Hutu serfs herded cattle and performed various other services for their Tutsi "protectors." At the top of the hierarchy was the Mwami, or king.

THE COLONIAL ERA: HUTU AND TUTSI ANIMOSITIES CONTINUE

Rwanda's feudal system survived into the colonial era. German and, later, Belgian administrators opted to rule through the existing order. But the social order was subtly destabilized by the new ideas emanating from the Catholic mission schools and by the colonialists' encouragement of the predominantly Hutu peasantry to grow cash crops, especially coffee. Discontent also grew due to the ever-increasing pressure of people and herds on already crowded lands.

In the late 1950s, under UN pressure, Belgium began to devolve political power to Rwandans. The death of the Mwami in 1959 sparked a bloody Hutu uprising against the Tutsi aristocracy. Tens of thousands, if not hundreds of thousands, were killed. Against this violent backdrop, pre-independence elections were held in 1961. These resulted in a victory for the first president, Gregoire Kayibanda's, Hutu Emancipation Movement (better known as Parmehutu). Thus, at independence, in 1962, Rwanda's traditionally Tutsi-dominated society was suddenly under a Hutu-dominated government.

In 1963 and 1964, the continued inter-ethnic competition for power exploded into more violence, which resulted in the flight of hundreds of thousands of ethnic Tutsis to neighboring Burundi, Tanzania, and Uganda. Along with their descendants, this refugee population today numbers about 1 million. Successive Hutu-dominated governments have barred their return, questioning their citizenship and citing extreme land pressure as barriers to their re-absorption. But the implied hope that the refugees would integrate into their host societies has failed to materialize. The RPF was originally formed in Uganda by Tutsi exiles, many of whom were hardened veterans of that country's past conflicts. The repatriation of all Rwandan Tutsis has been a key RPF demand.

HABYARIMANA TAKES POWER

Major General Juvenal Habyarimana, a Hutu from the north, seized power in a military coup in 1973. Two years later, he institutionalized his still army-dominated regime as a one-party state under the MRND, in the name of overcoming ethnic divisions. Yet hostility between the Hutus and Tutsis remained. Inside the country, a system of ethnic quotas was introduced, which formally limited the remaining Tutsi minority to a maximum of 14 percent of the positions in schools and at the workplace. In reality, the Tutsis were often allocated less, while the MRND's critics maintained that the best opportunities were reserved for Hutus from Habyarimana's northern home area of Kisenyi.

POPULAR DISCONTENT

In the 1980s, many Hutus, as well as Tutsis, grew impatient with their government's corrupt authoritarianism. The post-1987 international collapse of coffee prices, Rwanda's major export-earner, led to an economic decline, further fueling popular discontent. Even before the armed challenge of the RPF, the MRND had agreed to give up its monopoly of power, though this pledge was compromised by continued repression. Prominent among the new parties that then emerged were the Democratic Republic Movement (MDR), the Social Democrats (PSD), and the Liberals (PL). The PL and PSD were able to attract both Hutu and Tutsi support. As a result, many of their Hutu as well as Tutsi members were killed in 1994. The MDR was associated with southern-regional Hutu resentment at the MRND's supposed northern bias.

A political breakthrough occurred in March 1992 with the formation of a "Transitional Coalition Government," headed by the MDR's Dismas Nsengiyaremye, which also included MRND, PSD, and PL ministers. Habyarimana remained as president. With French military assistance, including the participation of several hundred French "advisers," Habyarimana's interim government of national unity was able to halt the RPF's advance in 1992. A series of ceasefires was negotiated with the RPF, leading up to the promise of (but never-realized) UN–supervised elections. But from the

beginning, progress toward national reconciliation was compromised by hard-line Hutus within the ruling military/MRND establishment and the extremist CDR. Ironically, these elements, who conspired to carry out the anti-Tutsi genocide in order to maintain control, were pushed out of the country by the RPF. These Hutu officials, soldiers, and militarymen, thought to be responsible for massacring hundreds of thousands of Tutsis and moderate Hutus during the 1994 Civil War, were exiled to camps in Zaire (D.R.C.) and Tanzania. Soon these militants returned and began a two-month wave of killings in western Rwanda in an apparent attempt to stop the Tutsis from testifying at genocide trials being conducted by the Rwandan government and the United Nations.

As Rwanda civil unrest intensified, refugees continued to flow into strife-torn Zaire. Estimates are that between 100,000 and 350,000 Hutu citizens are still in camps there. In March 1997, some 70,000 Rwandan Hutu refugees were gathered in Ubunda, a town 80 miles south of Kisangani on the Zaire River. But civil war in the D.R.C. has caused these people to be pushed back into Rwanda, where they are faced with the persistent and serious unrest in their home country. In October 2004 the government sent nearly 400 Rwandan troops as part of a peacekeeping mission in Sudan's Darfur region.

RWANDA TODAY

The years 2002–2007 were extremely important in Rwanda. During this period a new constitution, designed to prevent another genocide, was approved by the electorate. The document bans the incitement of ethnic hatred and calls for regular elections of political officials. In August 2003, in the first presidential elections since the 1994 genocide, Paul Kagame won a landslide victory. With his election as president, Kagame's role in Rwandan life became legitimized. October 2003 witnessed the first multiparty parliamentary elections, and President Kagame's Rwandan Patriotic Front won an absolute majority of the seats.

Although the election results seem to indicate support for President Kagame and his ruling party, they came with a tremendous amount of controversy. European Union (EU) observers noted that the 2003 elections had been marred by massive fraud and irregularities. During March 2004 an independent French report concluded that President Kagame ordered the 1994 attack on the president's plane, which in turn sparked the genocide. Although President Kagame immediately rejected the conclusion of the French report, its implications shall haunt the nation for many years to come. In November 2006, Paul Kagame

broke off diplomatic relations with France after a French judge issued an international arrest warrant for him based on the allegation that he was involved in bringing down Habyarimana's plane.

Under Kagame's leadership, Rwanda has been relatively stable. He has set the country on a path to recovery in spite of sporadic strife with rebels. The country is in the process of rebuilding its economy, with coffee and tea production being among its main sources of foreign exchange. Economic growth rates have exceeded 5% in recent years. Kagame has also tried to blur the ethnic divisions by replacing the 12 provinces by a smaller number of regions with the aim of creating ethnically diverse administrative areas. In spite of these achievements, the Crisis Group—a conflict-prevention agency— reported in 2002 that the RPF tolerated no criticism or challenge to its authority. Furthermore, over two-thirds of the population lives below the poverty line.

Timeline: PAST

A.D. 1860–1895
Mwami Kigeri Rwabugiri expands and consolidates the kingdom

1916
Belgium rules Rwanda as a mandate of the League of Nations

1959
The Hutu rebellion

1962
Rwanda becomes independent; Gregoire Kayibana is president

1973
Juvenal Habyarimana seizes power

1975
The National Revolutionary Movement for Development is formed

1978
A new Constitution is approved in a nationwide referendum; Habyarimana is reelected president

1990s
Genocidal conflict results in a dramatic drop in the country's resident population; millions are killed or displaced; French relief workers withdraw from Rwanda; Tutsi massacre of Hutu at Kibeho refugee camp

PRESENT

2000s
Paul Kagame becomes president

Rwandans occupy much of eastern Democratic Republic of the Congo but later withdraws its massive force of 50,000 troops

Government begins the mass release of thousands of prisoners involved in the 1994 genocide

Seychelles (Republic of Seychelles)

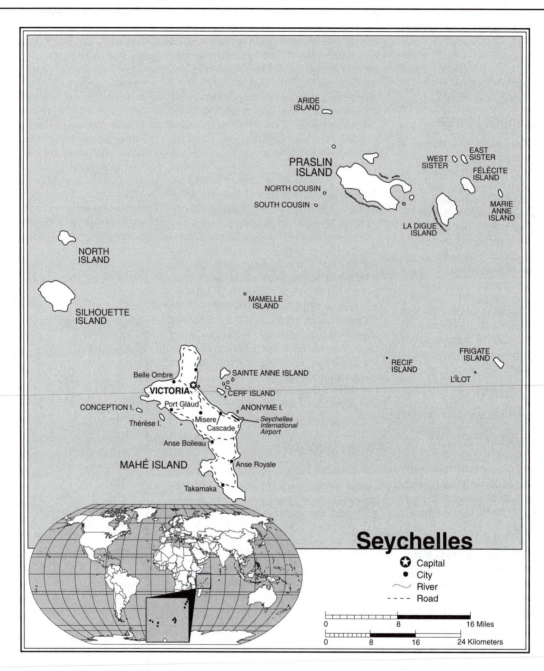

Seychelles Statistics

GEOGRAPHY

Area in Square Miles (Kilometers):
185 (455) (2.5 times the size of
Washington, D.C.)
Capital (Population): Victoria (30,000)
Environmental Concerns: uncertain
freshwater supply
Geographical Features: Mahé Group is
granitic, narrow coastal strip; rocky,
hilly; other islands are coral, flat,
elevated reefs
Climate: tropical marine

PEOPLE

Population

Total: 81,195
Annual Growth Rate: 0.432%
Rural/Urban Population Ratio: 47/53

Major Languages: English; French;
Creole
Ethnic Makeup: Seychellois (mixture of
Asians, Africans, and Europeans)
Religions: 96% Christian; 4% others

Health

Life Expectancy at Birth: 66.98 years
(male); 77.86 years (female)
Infant Mortality: 14.75/1,000 live births

Physicians Available: 1/906 people
HIV/AIDS Rate in Adults: na

Education

Adult Literacy Rate: 91.8%
Compulsory (Ages): 6–15; free

COMMUNICATION

Telephones: 20,700 main lines
Daily Newspaper Circulation: 41/1,000 people
Televisions: 173/1,000 people
Internet Users: 29,000 (2006)

TRANSPORTATION

Highways in Miles (Kilometers): 162 (270)
Railroads in Miles (Kilometers): none
Usable Airfields: 15
Motor Vehicles in Use: 8,600

GOVERNMENT

Type: republic
Independence Date: June 29, 1976 (from the United Kingdom)

Head of State/Government: President James Michel is both head of state and head of government
Political Parties: Seychelles People's Progressive Front; Seychelles National Party; Democratic Party
Suffrage: universal at 17

MILITARY

Military Expenditures (% of GDP): 2%
Current Disputes: claims Chagos Archipelago

ECONOMY

Currency ($ U.S. Equivalent): 8.03 rupees = $1
Per Capita Income/GDP: $7,800/$626 million
GDP Growth Rate: −1%
Inflation Rate: 3.3%
Labor Force by Occupation: 71% services; 19% industry; 10% agriculture
Natural Resources: fish; copra; cinnamon trees

Agriculture: vanilla; coconuts; sweet potatoes; cinnamon; cassava; bananas; chickens; fish

Industry: tourism; fishing; copra and vanilla processing; coconut oil; boat building; printing; furniture; beverages

Exports: $365.1 million (primary partners United Kingdom, Italy, France)

Imports: $570.6 million (primary partners Italy, South Africa, France)

SUGGESTED WEB SITES

http://www.seychelles-online.com/sc

http://www.sas.upenn.edu/African_Studies/Country_Specific/Seychelles.html

http://www.cia.gov/cia/publications/factbook/geos/se.html

Seychelles Country Report

Africa's smallest country in terms of both size and population, the Republic of Seychelles consists of a number of widely scattered archipelagos off the coast of East Africa. Over the last quarter-century, Seychellois have enjoyed enormous economic and social progress. According to the United Nations, today they enjoy the highest standard of living in Africa.

DEVELOPMENT

Seychelles has declared an Exclusive Economic Zone of 200 miles around all of its islands in order to promote the local fishing industry. Most of the zone's catch is harvested by foreign boats, which are supposed to pay licensing fees to Seychelles.

But for many years, the country's politics was bitterly polarized between supporters of President James Mancham and his successor, Albert René. The holding of multiparty elections in 1992 and 1993, after 15 years of single-party rule under René, has been accompanied by a significant degree of reconciliation between the partisans of these two long-time rivals.

The roots of Seychelles' modern political economy go back to 1963, when

FREEDOM

Since the restoration of multiparty democracy, there has been greater political freedom in Seychelles. The opposition nonetheless continues to complain of police harassment and to protest about the government's control over the broadcast media.

Mancham's Democratic Party and René's People's United Party were established. The former originally favored private enterprise and the retention of the British imperial connection, while the latter advocated an independent socialist state. Electoral victories in 1970 and 1974 allowed Mancham to pursue his dream of turning Seychelles into a tourist paradise and a financial and trading center by aggressively seeking outside investment. Tourism began to flourish following the opening of an international airport on the main island of Mahe in 1971, fueling an economic boom. Between 1970 and 1980, per capita income rose from nearly $150 to $1,700 (today it is about $7,600).

In 1974, Mancham, in an about-face, joined René in advocating the islands' independence. The Democratic Party, despite its modest electoral and overwhel-

ming parliamentary majority, set up a coalition government with the People's United Party. On June 29, 1976, Seychelles became independent, with Mancham as president and René as prime minister.

HEALTH/WELFARE

A national health program has been established; private practice has been abolished. Free-lunch programs have raised nutritional levels among the young. Education is also free, up to age 15.

On June 5, 1977, with Mancham out of the country, René's supporters, with Tanzanian assistance, staged a successful coup in which several people were killed. Thereafter René assumed the presidency and suspended the Constitution. A period of rule by decree gave way in 1979, without the benefit of referendum, to a new constitutional framework in which the People's Progressive Front Seychelles (SPPF), successor to the People's United Party, was recognized as the nation's sole political voice. The first years of one-party government were characterized by continued economic growth, which allowed for an impressive expansion of social-welfare programs.

Political power since the coup has largely remained concentrated in the hands of René. The early years of his regime, however, were marked by unrest. In 1978, the first in a series of unsuccessful countercoups was followed, several months later, by violent protests against the government's attempts to impose a compulsory National Youth Service, which would have removed the nation's 16- and 17-year-olds from their families in order to foster their sociopolitical indoctrination in accordance with the René government's socialist ideals. Another major incident occurred in 1981, when a group of international mercenaries, who had the backing of authorities in Kenya and South Africa as well as exiled Seychellois, were forced to flee in a hijacked jet after an airport shootout with local security forces. Following this attempt, Tanzanian troops were sent to the islands. A year later, the Tanzanians were instrumental in crushing a mutiny of Seychellois soldiers.

Despite its success in creating a model welfare state, which undoubtedly strengthened its popular acceptance, for years René continued to govern in a repressive manner. Internal opposition was not tolerated by his government, and exiled activists were largely neutralized. About one fifth of the islands' population now live overseas (not all of these people left the country, however, for political reasons).

In 1991, René gave in to rising internal and external pressures for a return to multiparty democracy. In July 1992, his party won 58 percent of the vote for a commission to rewrite the Constitution. Mancham's Democrats received just over a third of the vote. But in November 1992, voters heeded Mancham's call, rejecting the revised constitution proposed by the pro-René commission. Faced with a possible deadlock, the two parties reached consensus on new proposals, which were ratified in a June 1993 referendum. Presidential and parliamentary elections held the following month confirmed majority support for René's party.

In elections in 1998 and 2001, the SPPF gained renewed mandates. These latter contests are perhaps more significant for the emergence of the United Opposition coalition, led by Wavel Ramkalawan, as the main opposition party in place of the aging Mancham's Democrats. Increasing support of the United Opposition coalition was apparent in September 2001, when President René won another term in office, with 54 percent of the votes, against 45 percent for Ramkalawan.

In April 2004, James Michel succeeded France Albert René, who led the country for almost three decades before stepping down. In July 2006, Michel won a five-year term in presidential elections. In the 2006 elections, he received 54% of the vote, compared with 46% by Wavel Ramkalawan. Michel is not new to Seychelles politics, given that he was a former vice president who served alongside veteran politician René since 1977, when a bloodless coup brought the long-term leader to power. In the parliamentary elections that took place in May 2007, the ruling party, the Seychelles People's Progressive Front, won 23 of the 34 seats in the national assembly, with the opposition Seychelles National Party (SNP) taking the remainder.

Timeline: PAST

1771
French settlement begins

1814
British rule is established

1830
The British end slavery

1903
Seychelles is detached from Mauritius by the British and made a Crown colony

1948
Legislative Council with qualified suffrage is introduced

1967
Universal suffrage

1976
Independence

1977
An Albert René coup against James Mancham

1980s
An Amnesty International report alleges government fabrication of drug-possession cases for political reasons

1990s
René agrees to a multiparty system; René and his party are approved in presidential and parliamentary elections

PRESENT

2000s
The tourism sector accounts for 30% of Seychellois employment and 70% of hard-currency earnings

The government seeks to diversify the economy

France Albert René steps down as president

Somalia

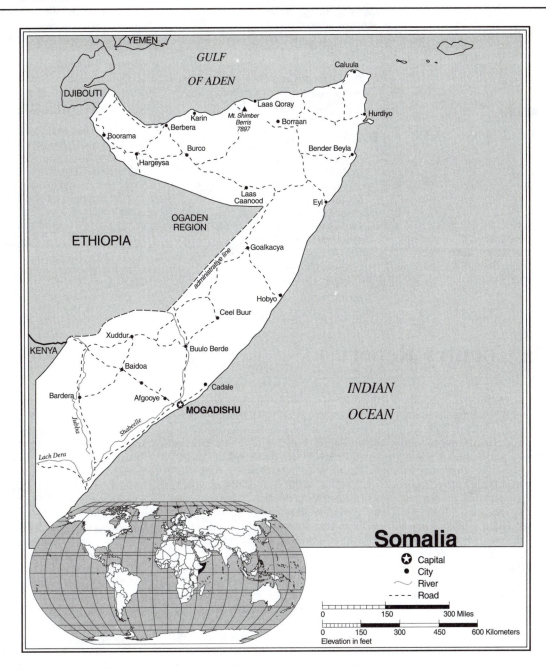

Somalia Statistics

GEOGRAPHY

Area in Square Miles (Kilometers):
246,331 (638,000) (about the size of Texas)

Capital (Population): Mogadishu (1,320,000)

Environmental Concerns: famine; contaminated water; deforestation; overgrazing; soil erosion; desertification

Geographical Features: principally desert; mostly flat to undulating plain, rising to hills in the north

Climate: arid to semiarid

PEOPLE

Population

Total: 9,118,773

Annual Growth Rate: 2.832%

Rural/Urban Population Ratio: 66/34

Major Languages: Somali; Arabic; Italian; English

Ethnic Makeup: 85% Somali; Bantu; Arab

Religion: Sunni Muslim

Health

Life Expectancy at Birth: 47.06 years (male); 50.69 years (female)

Infant Mortality: 113.08/1,000 live births

Physicians Available: 1/19,071 people

Education

Adult Literacy Rate: 37.8%
Compulsory (Ages): 6–14; free

COMMUNICATION

Telephones: 100,000 main lines
Televisions: 18/1,000 people
Internet Users: 94,000 (2006)

TRANSPORTATION

Highways in Miles (Kilometers): 13,702
(22,100)
Railroads in Miles (Kilometers): none
Usable Airfields: 65
Motor Vehicles in Use: 20,000

GOVERNMENT

Type: "Transitional National Government"
Independence Date: July 1, 1960 (from
a merger of British Somaliland and
Italian Somaliland)

Head of State/Government: President
Abdullahi Yusuf Ahmed; Prime
Minister Ali Muhammad Ghedi
Political Parties: none
Suffrage: universal at 18

MILITARY

Military Expenditures (% of GDP): 0.9%
Current Disputes: civil war; border and
territorial disputes with Ethiopia

ECONOMY

Currency ($ U.S. Equivalent): 1,308.00
shillings = $1
Per Capita Income/GDP: $600/$5.259
billion
Inflation Rate: NA
Labor Force by Occupation: 71%
agriculture; 29% industry and services
Natural Resources: uranium; iron ore; tin;
gypsum; bauxite; copper; salt
Agriculture: livestock; bananas;

sugarcane; cotton; cereals; corn;
sorghum; mangoes; fish
Industry: sugar refining; textiles; limited
petroleum refining
Exports: $241 million (primary partners
Saudi Arabia, United Arab Emirates,
Yemen)
Imports: $576 million (primary partners
Djibouti, Kenya, India)

SUGGESTED WEB SITES

http://www.unsomalia.org
http://www.somalianews.com
http://somalinet.com
http://somaliawatch.org
http://www.cia.gov/cia/
publications/factbook/geos/
so.html

*Note: Population statistics in Somalia are
complicated by the large number of nomads and
by refugee movements in response to famine and
clan warfare.

Somalia Country Report

Wracked by violence, ruled by warlords, torn asunder not just by tribal but also petty clan disputes (some of which go back centuries), there seems to be nowhere to look for a spark of hope towards peace in Somalia. The list of transgressions committed by Somalia's leaders over the last fifteen years is immense. The country has thrown out their traditional allies, waged war with their regional neighbors, killed numerous international volunteers (who were supplying the starving residents with food and medical supplies), and fought viciously with one another in an unprecedented anarchy.

In what looked like a chance for peace in Somalia, there was a breakthrough in January 2004 at peace talks held in Kenya when the warlords and a few politicians signed a deal to set up a new parliament. Within four months however, renewed fighting broke out, killing 100 people as ethnic militias clashed in the southern town of Bula Hawo. The violence notwithstanding, a new transitional parliament was inaugurated in August 2004 at a ceremony in Kenya. In October, the body elected Abdullahi Yusuf as president of Somalia. The election took place in Kenya because the Somali capital was regarded as being too dangerous.

President Yusuf pledged to do his best to promote reconciliation and to set about rebuilding the country. He called on the international community to provide aid and peacekeepers. The former army officer and faction leader led a guerrilla movement in

the 1970s aimed at ousting the Somali dictator Siad Barre. In the 1990s President Yusuf emerged as the pre-eminent leader of his native Puntland region, which he declared autonomous in 1998. President Yusuf's leadership style is said to be authoritarian. Clearly, in the eyes of the assembled representatives of Somalia, what the country needed in 2004 was another separatist dictator, who arose from the ranks of the warlords themselves, to resolve the pressing issues of the Somalian state.

The newly formed government returned home from Kenya in February 2005. The divisive question for the new government was where to sit the new parliament. Mogadishu was still very unstable with the ongoing clan fights. To underscore the instability in Mogadishu, in November 2005, there was an assassination attempt on Prime Minister Ali Mohammed Ghedi in which gunmen killed six people in his convoy. In February 2006 the decision was reached to let the parliament meet for the first time since its return from Kenya in 2004 in the central town of Baidoa.

Mogadishu continued to be unstable by mid 2006 with scores of people killed and hundreds injured in fights between rival militias. At this point in time, Sheikh Aweys' Islamic militia had the upper hand in the fights and controlled Mogadishu and much of the south of Somalia, further eroding the authority of the new but fledgling government. The Islamists militias were

successful in kicking out the warlords who had ruled this part of Somalia for 15 years. However, with the backing of Ethiopian troops, forces loyal to the interim administration seized control from the Islamists at the end of 2006. A period of uncertainty looms large with thousands of Somalis escaping drought, strict Islamist rule, and the possibility of war, fleeing to Kenya as refugees since the start of 2006. In 2007 the United States joined the fighting by carrying out air strikes in southern Somalia, which it said targeted al-Qaeda figures, and which reportedly killed an unknown number of civilians. It is the first known direct U.S. military intervention in Somalia since 1993. Under pressure from Ethiopian forces and American bombardments, the Islamists abandoned their stronghold, the port town of Kismayo. President Abdullahi Yusuf entered Mogadishu in January 2007 for the first time since taking office in 2004.

DEVELOPMENT

Most development projects have ended. Somalia's material infrastructure has largely been destroyed by war and neglect, though some local rebuilding efforts are under way, especially in the more peaceful central and northern parts of the country. In 1996, the European Union agreed to finance the reconstruction of the port of Berbera.

Somalia has in effect been without a central government since 1991, when after the overthrow of President Siad Barre, the country entered a period of chaos from which it has never recovered. The country has been dominated by "warlords" reponsible for small fiefdoms supported by heavily armed militias under their control. The resulting intermilitia fighting, added to the inability to deal with famine and disease, has led to the deaths of up to 1 million people. There appears to be little hope for an early resolution to the continuing conflicts in Somalia. The international donor community has long vanished, fundamentally giving up efforts to work out a peaceful solution to the problems of the nation. To compound matters, the northern portion of the country has broken away from the south and is now called Somaliland.

A "Transitional National Government" led by Abdiqassim Salah Hassan was put in place in August 2000. Hassan was elected by a "Transitional National Assembly," which had been formed at an internationally backed peace conference in neighboring Djibouti. After months of negotiations, the new government was accepted by a broad cross-section of Somali society. But a number of key groupings, in addition to still-powerful military leaders, remained outside of the accord. The northern "Puntland" and "Somaliland" governments were among those that boycotted the talks. The latter administration has declared itself an independent state, despite international opposition. In the breakaway Somaliland, Dahir Riyale Kahin was selected as president during May 2002 after the death of Mohamed Ibrahim Egal. He pledged to preserve the sovereignty of the state after narrowly winning the presidential election.

For much of the outside world, Somalia has become a symbol of failure of both international peacekeeping operations and the postcolonial African state. For the Somalis themselves, Somalia is an ideal that has ceased to exist—but may yet be re-created. Literally hundreds of thousands of Somalis starved to death in 1991–1992 before a massive U.S.-led United Nations intervention—officially known as UNITAF but labeled "Operation Restore Hope" by the Americans—assured the delivery of relief supplies. The 1994 withdrawal of most UN forces (the last token units left in March 1995), following UNITAF's failure to disarm local militias while supporting the creation of a "Transitional National Council," led to the termination of relief efforts in many areas, but widespread famine was averted in 1994–1995. Repeated attempts to reach a settlement between the various armed factions have continued to fail, despite the death in August 1996 of Somalia's most powerful warlord, General Mohammed Farah Aideed.

SOMALI SOCIETY

The roots of Somalia's suffering run deep. Somalis have lived with the threat of famine for centuries, as the climate is arid even in good years. Traditionally, most Somalis were nomadic pastoralists, but in recent years, this way of life has declined dramatically. Prior to the 1990s crisis, about half the population were still almost entirely reliant on livestock. Somali herds have sometimes been quite big: In the early 1980s, more than 1 million animals, mostly goats and sheep, were exported annually. Large numbers of cattle and camels have also been kept. But hundreds of thousands of animals were lost due to lack of rain during the mid-1980s; and since 1983, reports of rinderpest led to a sharp drop in exports, due to the closing of the once-lucrative Saudi Arabian market to East African animals.

A quarter of the Somali population have long combined livestock-keeping with agriculture. Cultivation is possible in the area between the Juba and Shebelle Rivers and in portions of the north. Although up to 15 percent of the country is potentially arable, only about 1 percent of the land has been put to plow at any given time. Bananas, cotton, and frankincense have been major cash crops, while maize and sorghum are subsistence crops. Like Somali pastoralists, farmers walk a thin line between abundance and scarcity, for locusts as well as drought are common visitors.

The delicate nature of Somali agriculture helps to explain recent urbanization. One out of every four Somalis lives in the large towns and cities. The principal urban center is Mogadishu, which, despite being divided by war, still houses well over a million people. Unfortunately, as Somalis have migrated in from the countryside, they have found little employment. Even before the recent collapse, the country's manufacturing and

service sectors were small. By 1990, more than 100,000 Somalis had become migrant workers in the Arab/Persian Gulf states. (In 1990–1991, many were repatriated as a result of the regional conflict over Kuwait.)

Until recently, many outsiders assumed that Somalia possessed a greater degree of national coherence than most other African states. Somalis do share a common language and a sense of cultural identity. Islam is also a binding feature. However, competing clan and subclan allegiances have long played a divisive political role in the society. Membership in all the current armed factions is congruent with blood loyalties. Traditionally, the clans were governed by experienced, wise men. But the authority of these elders has now largely given way to the power of younger men with a surplus of guns and a surfeit of education and a lack of moral decency.

Past appeals to greater Somali nationalism have also been a source of conflict by encouraging irredentist sentiments against Somalia's neighbors. During the colonial era, contemporary Somalia was divided. For about 75 years, the northern region was governed by the British, while the southern portion was subject to Italian rule. These colonial legacies have complicated efforts at nation-building. Many northerners feel that their region has been neglected and would benefit from greater political autonomy or independence.

Somalia became independent on July 1, 1960, when the new national flag, a white, five-pointed star on a blue field, was raised in the former British and Italian territories. The star symbolized the five supposed branches of the Somali nation—that is, the now-united peoples of British and Italian Somalilands and the Somalis still living in French Somaliland (modern Djibouti), Ethiopia, and Kenya.

THE RISE AND FALL OF SIAD BARRE

Siad Barre came to power in 1969, through a coup promising radical change. As chairman of the military's Supreme Revolutionary Council, Barre combined Somali nationalism and Islam with a commitment to "scientific socialism." Some genuine efforts were made to restructure society through the development of new local councils and worker management committees. New civil and labor codes were written. The Somali Revolutionary Socialist Party was developed as the sole legal political party.

Initially, the new order seemed to be making progress. The Somali language was alphabetized in a modified form of Roman script, which allowed the government to launch mass-literacy campaigns. Various rural-development projects were also implemented. In particular, roads were built, which helped to break down isolation among regions.

The promise of Barre's early years in office gradually faded. Little was done to follow through the developments of the early 1970s, as Barre increasingly bypassed the participatory institutions that he had helped to create. His government became one of personal rule; he took on emergency powers, relieved members of the governing council of their duties, surrounded himself with members of his own Marehan branch of the Darod clan, and isolated himself from the public. Barre also isolated Somalia from the rest of Africa by pursuing irredentist policies in order to unite the other points of the Somali star under his rule. To accomplish this task, he began to encourage local guerrilla movements among the ethnic Somalis living in Kenya and Ethiopia.

ACHIEVEMENTS

Somalia has been described as a "nation of poets." Many scholars attribute the strength of the Somali poetic tradition not only to the nomadic way of life, which encourages oral arts, but to the role of poetry as a local social and political medium.

In 1977, Barre sent his forces into the Ogaden region to assist the local rebels of the Western Somali Liberation Front. The invaders achieved initial military success against the Ethiopians, whose forces had been weakened by revolutionary strife and battles with Eritrean rebels. However, the intervention of some 17,000 Cuban troops and other Soviet-bloc personnel on the side of the Ethiopians quickly turned the tide of battle. At the same time, the Somali incursion was condemned by all members of the Organization of African Unity.

The intervention of the Soviet bloc on the side of the Ethiopians was a bitter disappointment to Barre, who had enjoyed Soviet support for his military buildup. In exchange, he had allowed the Soviets to establish a secret base at the strategic northern port of Berbera. However, in 1977, the Soviets decided to shift their allegiances decisively to the then–newly established revolutionary government in Ethiopia. Barre in turn tried to attract U.S. support with offers of basing rights at Berbera, but the Carter administration was unwilling to jeopardize its interests in either Ethiopia or Kenya by backing Barre's irredentist adventure. American–Somali relations became closer during the Reagan administration, which signed a 10-year pact giving U.S. forces access to air and naval facilities at Berbera, for which the United States increased its aid to Somalia, including limited arms supplies.

In 1988, Barre met with Ethiopian leader Mengistu Mariam. Together, they pledged to respect their mutual border.

This understanding came about in the context of growing internal resistance to both regimes. By 1990, numerous clan-based armed resistance movements were enjoying success against Barre.

Growing resistance was accompanied by massive atrocities on the part of government forces. Human-rights concerns were cited by the U.S. and other governments in ending their assistance to Somalia. In March 1990, Barre called for national dialogue and spoke of a possible end to one-party rule. But continuing atrocities, including the killing of more than 100 protesters at the national stadium, fueled further armed resistance.

In January 1991, Barre fled Mogadishu, which was seized by resistance forces of the United Somali Congress (USC). The USC set up an interim administration, but its authority was not recognized by other groups. By the end of the year, the USC itself had split into two warring factions. A 12-faction "Manifesto Group" recognized Ali Mahdi as the country's president. But Mahdi's authority was repudiated by the four-faction Somali National Alliance (SNA), led by Farah Aideed. Much of Mogadishu was destroyed in inconclusive fighting between the two groupings. Other militias, including forces still loyal to Barre (that is, the Somali National Front, or SNF), also continued to fight one another. In the north, the Somali National Movement (SNM) declared its zone's sovereign independence as "Somaliland."

Continued fighting coincided with drought. As failed crops and dying livestock resulted in countrywide famine, international relief efforts were unable to supply sufficient quantities of outside food to those most in need, due to the prevailing state of lawlessness. In mid-1992, the International Red Cross estimated that, of southern Somalia's 4.5 million people, 1.5 million were in danger of starvation. Another 500,000 or so had fled the country. More than 300,000 children under age five were reported to have perished.

As Somalia's suffering grew and became publicized in the Western media, many observers suggested the need for the United Nations to intervene. A small UN presence, known as UNISOM, was established in August 1992, but its attempts to police the delivery of relief supplies proved to be ineffectual. Conceived as a massive U.S.–led military operation, initially consisting of 30,000 troops (22,000 Americans), UNITAF averted catastrophe by assuring the delivery of food and medical supplies to Somalia's starving millions. Still, the foreign troops' mission was unclear.

In 1993, a bloody clash between Aideed's SNA militia and Pakistani troops in Mogadishu led to full-scale armed conflict. Efforts by UNITAF forces to capture Aideed and neutralize his men were unsuccessful. After

a U.S. helicopter was shot down in October 1993, President Bill Clinton decided to end American involvement in UNITAF by March 1994. By then, much higher losses had been suffered by several other nations participating in the UNITAF–UNISOM coalition, causing them also to reassess their commitments. Outgunned and demoralized, the remaining UN forces (officially labeled UNISOM II) remained largely confined to their compounds until their withdrawal.

Timeline: PAST

1886–1887
The British take control of northern regions of present-day Somalia

1889
Italy establishes a protectorate in the eastern areas of present-day Somalia

1960
Somalia is formed through a merger of former British and Italian colonies under UN Trusteeship

1969
Siad Barre comes to power through an army coup; the Supreme Revolutionary Council is established

1977–1978
The Ogaden war in Ethiopia results in Somalia's defeat

1980s
SNM rebels escalate their campaign in the north; government forces respond with genocidal attacks on the local Issaq population

1990s
The fall of Barre leaves Somalia without an effective central government; U.S.–led UN intervention feeds millions while attempting to restore order In the face of mounting losses, foreign troops pull out of Somalia

PRESENT

2000s
Chaos still reigns in Somalia, causing untold suffering

Abdiqassim Salah Hassan is named interim president

2004
275-member Transitional Federal Government replaces the Transitional National Government

2006
Militias loyal to the Union of Islamic Courts take control of Mogadishu and other parts of the south after defeating clan warlords

Ethiopian troops and government forces rout and evict Islamist militias from Mogadishu

2007
Unites States carries out air strikes in southern Somalia and in Puntland, which it says targeted al-Qaeda figures

Sudan (Republic of the Sudan)

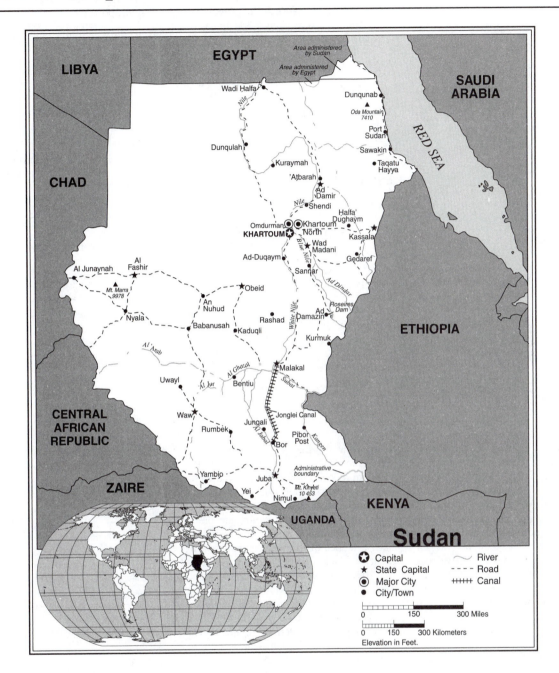

Sudan Statistics

GEOGRAPHY

Area in Square Miles (Kilometers):
967,247 (2,505,810) (about 1/4 the size of the United States)
Capital (Population): Khartoum (2,853,000)
Environmental Concerns: insufficient potable water; excessive hunting of wildlife; soil erosion; desertification
Geographical Features: generally flat, featureless plain; mountains in the east and west
Climate: arid desert to tropical

PEOPLE

Population

Total: 39,379,358
Annual Growth Rate: 2.082%
Rural/Urban Population Ratio: 59/41

Major Languages: Arabic; Sudanic languages; Nubian; English; others
Ethnic Makeup: 52% black; 39% Arab; 6% Beja; 3% others
Religions: 70% Sunni Muslim, especially in north; 25% indigenous beliefs; 5% Christian

Health

Life Expectancy at Birth: 48.24 years (male); 50.03 years (female)

GLOBAL STUDIES

Infant Mortality: 91.78/1,000 live births
Physicians Available: 1/11,300 people
HIV/AIDS Rate in Adults: 2.3%

Education

Adult Literacy Rate: 61.1%

COMMUNICATION

Telephones: 636,900 main lines
Daily Newspaper Circulation: 21/1,000 people
Televisions: 8.2/1,000 people
Internet Users: 3.5 million (2006)

TRANSPORTATION

Highways in Miles (Kilometers): 7,378 (11,900 km)
Railroads in Miles (Kilometers): 5,978 km
Usable Airfields: 88
Motor Vehicles in Use: 75,000

GOVERNMENT

Type: transitional
Independence Date: January 1, 1956 (from Egypt and the United Kingdom)

Head of State/Government: President Umar Hasan Ahmad al-Bashir is both head of state and head of government
Political Parties: National Congress Party; Popular National Congress; Umma; Sudan People's Liberation Movement (Army); others
Suffrage: universal at 17

MILITARY

Military Expenditures (% of GDP): 3%
Current Disputes: civil war; border disputes and clashes with Egypt and Kenya

ECONOMY

Currency ($ U.S. Equivalent): 2.07 pounds = $1
Per Capita Income/GDP: $2,400/$97.19 billion
GDP Growth Rate: 9.3%
Inflation Rate: 8.8%
Unemployment Rate: 18.7%
Labor Force by Occupation: 80% agriculture; 13% government; 7% industry and commerce

Natural Resources: petroleum; iron ore; chromium ore; copper; zinc; tungsten; mica; silver; gold; hydropower

Agriculture: cotton; sesame; gum arabic; sorghum; millet; wheat; sheep; groundnuts

Industry: textiles; cement; cotton ginning; edible oils; soap; sugar; shoes; petroleum refining

Exports: $7.505 billion (primary partners Japan, China, Saudi Arabia)

Imports: $8.693 billion (primary partners China, Saudi Arabia, United Kingdom)

SUGGESTED WEB SITES

http://www.sudan.net
http://sudanhome.com
http://www.sudmer.com
http://www.sunanews.net
http://www.cia.gov/cia/publications/factbook/geos/su.html

Sudan Country Report

The name Sudan comes from the Arabic *bilad al-sudan,* or "land of the blacks." Today, Sudan is Africa's largest country. Apart from an 11-year period of peace, it has been torn since its indpendence in 1956 by civil war between the mainly Muslim north and the animist and Christian south. Sudan's tremendous size as well as its great ethnic and religious diversity have frustrated the efforts of successive postindependence governments to build a lasting sense of national unity.

DEVELOPMENT

Many ambitious development plans have been launched since independence, but progress has been limited by political instability. The periodic introduction and redefinition of "Islamic" financial procedures have complicated long-term planning.

The current president, Omar Bashir, was reelected in 2001 for another five years. The elections were boycotted by the main opposition parties. The Machakos Protocol of July 2002, which was signed by both the government and the two largest southern rebel groups, calls for a six-year interval period, after which there will be a referendum held on self-determination for the

south. However, the Muslim-led Sudanese government has continued to attack the southern rebels; through the age-old tactic of divide-and-conquer, it has been able to make periodic inroads into the rebels' African strongholds. Ethnic groups are pitted against one another. Meanwhile, there has been evidence of the widespread enslavement of blacks in the south. In December 2001, for example, more than 14,550 slaves, mainly blacks, were freed following campaigning by human-rights activists.

Listed by the U.S. government as a major supporter of terrorism, until 1997 Sudan's Islamic fundamentalist government provided refuge for Osama bin Laden. Since then, the government has been keen to overcome its image as a pariah state. The challenges facing Sudan have also been complicated by the discovery of major oil fields in the south. The government has sought to establish safe enclaves for the exploitation of the oil fields, at the cost of relocating people who were living in the area. The oil fields may make Sudan rich, but they remain a primary source of alienation, as funds generated by the government from oil revenues have been used to purchase weapons against the southern rebels.

The future looks like continued civil war until Sudan ceases to enslave its people, grants the southerners self-determination,

brings peace to Darfur, and ceases trying to impose an Islamic state on its religiously mixed population.

FREEDOM

The current regime rules through massive repression. In 1992, Africa Watch accused it of practicing genocide against the Nuba people. Elsewhere, tales of massacres, forced relocations, enslavement, torture, and starvation are commonplace. The insurgent groups have also been responsible for numerous atrocities.

HISTORY

Sudan, like its northern neighbor Egypt, is a gift of the Nile. The river and its various branches snake across the country, providing water to most of the 80 percent of Sudanese who survive by farming. From ancient times, the Upper Nile region of northern Sudan has been the site of a series of civilizations whose histories are closely intertwined with those of Egypt. There has been constant human interaction between the two zones. Some groups, such as the Nubians, expanded northward into the Egyptian lower Nile.

The last ruler to unite the Nile Valley politically was the nineteenth-century

(United Nations photo 157661 by Milton Grant)

Millions of Sudanese have been displaced by war and drought. The effects on the population have been devastating, and even the best efforts of the international community have met with only limited success.

Turko–Egyptian ruler Muhammad Ali. After absorbing northern Sudan, by then predominantly Arabized Muslim, into his Egyptian state, Ali gradually expanded his authority to the south and west over non-Arabic and, in many cases, non-Muslim groups. This process, which was largely motivated by a desire for slave labor, united for the first time the diverse regions that today make up Sudan. In the 1880s, much of Sudan fell under the theocratic rule of the Mahdists, a local anti-Egyptian Islamic movement. The Mahdists were defeated by an Anglo–Egyptian force in 1898. Thereafter, the British dominated Sudan until its independence, in 1956.

Sudanese society has remained divided ever since. There has been strong pan-Arab sentiment in the north, but 60 percent of Sudanese, concentrated in the south and west, are non-Arab. About a third of Sudanese, especially in the south, are also non-Muslim. Despite this fact, many, but by no means all, Sudanese Muslims have favored the creation of an Islamic state. Ideological divisions among various socialist- and nonsocialist-oriented factions have also been important. Sudan has long had a strong Communist Party (whether legal or not), drawing on the support of organized labor, and an influential middle class.

The division between northern and southern Sudan has been especially deep.

A mutiny by southern soldiers prior to independence escalated into a 17-year rebellion by southerners against what they perceived to be the hegemony of Muslim Arabs. Some 500,000 southerners perished before the Anya Nya rebels and the government reached a compromise settlement, recognizing southern autonomy in 1972.

HEALTH/WELFARE

Civil strife and declining government expenditures have resulted in rising rates of infant mortality. Warfare has also prevented famine relief from reaching needy populations, resulting in instances of mass starvation.

In northern Sudan, the first 14 years of independence saw the rule of seven different civilian coalitions and six years of military rule. Despite this chronic instability, a tradition of liberal tolerance among political factions was generally maintained. Government became increasingly authoritarian during the administration of Jaafar Nimeiri, who came to power in a 1969 military coup.

Nimeiri quickly moved to consolidate his power by eliminating challenges to his government from the Islamic right and the Communist left. His greatest success was ending the Anya Nya revolt, but his subsequent tampering with the provisions of the

peace agreement led to renewed resistance. In 1983, Nimeiri decided to impose Islamic law throughout Sudanese society. This led to the growth of the Sudanese People's Liberation Army (SPLA), under the leadership of John Garang, which quickly seized control of much of the southern Sudanese countryside. Opposition to Nimeiri had also been growing in the north, as more people became alienated by the regime's increasingly heavy-handed ways and inability to manage the declining economy. Finally, in 1985, he was toppled in a coup.

The holding of multiparty elections in 1986 seemed to presage a restoration of Sudan's tradition of pluralism. With the SPLA preventing voting in much of the south, the two largest parties were the northern-based Umma and Democratic Union (DUP). The National Islamic Front was the third-largest vote-getter, with eight other parties plus a number of independents gaining parliamentary seats. The major challenge facing the new coalition government, led by Umma, was reconciliation with the SPLA. Because the SPLA, unlike the earlier Anya Nya, was committed to national unity, the task did not appear insurmountable. However, arguments within the government over meeting key SPLA demands, such as the repeal of Islamic law, caused the war to drag on. A hard-line faction within Umma and the NIF sought to resist a return to secularism. In March 1989, a new government, made up of Umma and the DUP, committed itself to accommodating the SPLA. However, a month later, on the day the cabinet was to ratify an agreement with the rebels, there was a coup by pro-NIF officers.

ACHIEVEMENTS

Although his music is banned in his own country, Mohammed Wardi is probably Sudan's most popular musician. Now living in exile, he has been imprisoned and tortured for his songs against injustice, which also appeal to a large international audience, especially in North Africa and the Middle East.

Besides leading to a breakdown in all efforts to end the SPLA rebellion, the NIF/military regime has been responsible for establishing the most intolerant, repressive government in Sudan's modern history. Extra-judicial executions have become commonplace. Instances of pillaging and enslavement of non-Muslim communities by government-linked militias have increased. NIF-affiliated security groups have become a law unto themselves, striking out at their perceived enemies and intimidating Muslims and non-Muslims alike to conform to their fundamentalist norms. Islamic norms are also being invoked to justify a radical campaign to undermine the status of women.

In 1990, most of the now-banned political parties (including Umma, the DUP, and the Communists) aligned themselves with the SPLA as the National Democratic Alliance. But opposition by the northern-based parties proved ineffectual, leading to the formation of a new, Eritrean-based armed movement—the Sudan Alliance of Forces, headed by Abdul Azizi Khalid.

Beginning in 1991, the SPLA was weakened by a series of splits. Two factions—Kerubino Kuanyin Bol's SPLA–Bahr al-Ghazal group and Riek Macher's Southern Sudan Independence Army (SSIA)—accepted a government peace plan in April 1996. But the plan was rejected by John Garang's SPLA (Torit faction), which remains the most powerful southern group. After a number of years of being on the defensive, Garang's forces began making significant advances in 1996, partially as a result of increased support from neighboring countries that have come to look upon the Khartoum regime as a regional threat. (In June 1995, the regime was implicated in an attempt to assassinate Egyptian president Hosni Mubarak in Ethiopia, which resulted in the imposition of UN antiterrorism sanctions. Border clashes have since occurred with Eritrea, Kenya, and Uganda as well as Egypt.)

In January 2005 a comprehensive landmark peace deal was signed between the government and southern rebels, after years of negotiations and fighting. In this deal, the south was given greater autonomy and a promise to share in the oil revenues. The south has large oil reserves that are being exploited by the government in Khartoum without any benefits trickling down to the south. The peace deal was followed by the formation of a power-sharing government of national unity in which the first vice president would come from the South. Former southern rebel leader John Garang was sworn in as first vice president. However, his tenure as vice president was cut short when he was killed in a plane crash.

Garang's death sparked deadly clashes in the capital between southern Sudanese and northern Arabs. He was succeeded by Salva Kiir, who soon formed an autonomous government in the south, in line with the January 2005 peace deal. The administration is dominated by former rebels. The peace deal effectively ended 20 years of southern civil war. This ushered in bright prospects for peace in the troubled Sudan, given its vast resources, including large areas of cultivatable land, gold, cotton and vast oil reserves that could bring large amounts of revenues to the peoples of Sudan. This wealth could be focused toward the pressing need for reconstruction of the infrastructure, much of which was destroyed during years of fighting, and the resettlement of millions of displaced southerners that have returned.

As the government was celebrating this newfound peace, trouble broke out in the region of Darfur in western Sudan in 2003, when rebels in Darfur rose up against government, claiming the region was being neglected by Khartoum. Government troops and pro-Sudanese government Arab Janjaweed militias countered the rebels and began a campaign of systematic killings of non-Arab African villagers in this region. The United Nations notes that the conflict has resulted in more than 2 million people fleeing their homes, and more than 200,000 have been killed. Pro-government Arab militias are accused of carrying out a campaign of ethnic cleansing against non-Arab groups in the region. The conflict has spilled over international borders into Chad to the west, which has strained relations between the two countries. Both countries have accused each other of cross-border incursions. The Darfur conflict has the potential to escalate into a wider, regional war.

ECONOMIC PROSPECTS

Although it has great potential, political conflict has left Sudan one of the poorest nations in the world. Persistent warfare and lack of financing are blocking needed infrastructure improvements. Sudan's unwillingness to pay its foreign debt has led to calls for its expulsion from the International Monetary Fund.

Nearly 7 million Sudanese (out of a total population then of 23 million) had been displaced by 1988—more than 4 million by warfare, with drought and desertification contributing to the remainder. Sudan has been a major recipient of international emergency food aid for years, but warfare, corruption, and genocidal indifference have often blocked help from reaching the needy. In 1994, the United Nations estimated that 700,000 southern Sudanese faced the prospect of starvation.

Timeline: PAST

1820
Egypt invades northern Sudan

1881
The Mahdist Revolt begins

1956
Independence

1969
Jaafar Nimeiri comes to power

1972
Hostilities end in southern Sudan

1980s
Islamic law replaces the former penal code; renewed civil war in the south; Nimeiri is overthrown in a popular coup; an elected government is installed

1990s
The hard-line Islamic fundamentalist regime becomes increasingly repressive

PRESENT

2000s
Famine threatens large segments of the population

Omar al-Bashir claims victory in boycotted elections

2005
Government and southern rebels sign a peace deal that guarantees autonomy to the south including wealth and power sharing

UN report accuses the government and militias of systematic abuses in Darfur, but stops short of calling the violence genocide

2006
Sudan rejects a UN resolution calling for a UN peacekeeping force in Darfur, saying it would compromise sovereignty

2007
The SPLM accuses Khartoum of failing to honor the 2005 peace deal with the southern rebels and suspends its involvement in the national unity government

Tanzania (United Republic of Tanzania)

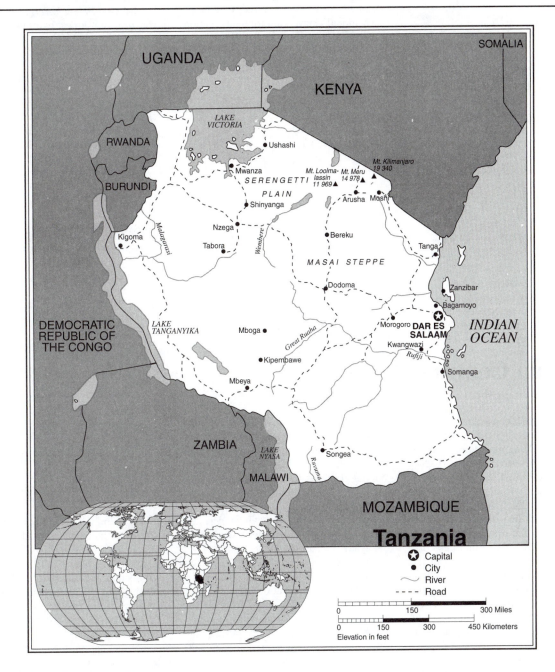

Tanzania Statistics

GEOGRAPHY

Area in Square Miles (Kilometers):
363,950 (939,652) (about twice the size of California)

Capital (Population): Dar es Salaam (2,347,000); Dodoma (to be new capital) (180,000)

Environmental Concerns: soil degradation; deforestation; desertification; destruction of coral reefs and marine environment

Geographical Features: plains along the coast; central plateau; highlands in the north and south

Climate: tropical to temperate

PEOPLE

Population

Total: 39,384,223
Annual Growth Rate: 2.091%
Rural/Urban Population Ratio: 77/23

Major Languages: Kiswahili; Chagga; Gogo; Ha; Haya; Luo; Maasai; English; others

Ethnic Makeup: 99% African; 1% others

Religions: indigenous beliefs; Muslim; Christian; Hindu

Health

Life Expectancy at Birth: 49.44 years (male); 52.04 years (female)
Infant Mortality: 71.69/1,000 live births

95

GLOBAL STUDIES

Physicians Available: 1/20,511 people
HIV/AIDS Rate in Adults: 8.8%

Education

Adult Literacy Rate: 69.4%
Compulsory (Ages): 7–14; free

COMMUNICATION

Telephones: 169,135 main lines
Televisions: 2.8/1,000 people
Internet Users: 384,300 (2006)

TRANSPORTATION

Highways in Miles (Kilometers): 48,913
   (78,891 km)
Railroads in Miles (Kilometers): 3,690 km
Usable Airfields: 124
Motor Vehicles in Use: 134,000

GOVERNMENT

Type: republic
Independence Date: December 9, 1961
   (from United Nations trusteeship)

Head of State/Government: President
   Jakaya Kikwete is both head of state
   and head of government
Political Parties: Revolutionary Party;
   National Convention for Construction
   and Reform; Civic United Front;
   Union for Multiparty Democracy;
   Democratic Party; United Democratic
   Party; others
Suffrage: universal at 18

MILITARY

Military Expenditures (% of GDP):
   0.2%
Current Disputes: boundary disputes with
   Malawi; civil strife

ECONOMY

Currency ($ U.S. Equivalent): 1,200
   shillings = $1
Per Capita Income/GDP: $800/$29.64
   billion
GDP Growth Rate: 5.9%
Inflation Rate: 4.4%

Labor Force by Occupation: 80%
   agriculture; 20% services and
   industry
Population Below Poverty Line: 51%
Natural Resources: hydropower;
   tin; phosphates; iron ore; coal;
   diamonds; gemstones; gold; natural
   gas; nickel
Agriculture: coffee; sisal; tea; cotton;
   pyrethrum; cashews; tobacco; cloves;
   wheat; fruits; vegetables; livestock
Industry: agricultural processing; mining;
   oil refining; shoes; cement; textiles;
   wood products; fertilizer; salt
Exports: $1.831 billion (primary partners
   United Kingdom, India, Germany)
Imports: $3.18 billion (primary partners
   South Africa, Japan, United Kingdom)

SUGGESTED WEB SITES

http://www.tanzania.go.tz
http://www.tanzanianews.com
http://www.cia.gov/cia/ publications/
   factbook/geos/ tz.html
http://www.tanzania_online.gov.uk

Tanzania Country Report

After winning a second term of office in 2000, taking nearly 72 percent of the vote, President Benjamin Mkapa and the ruling Chama Cha Mapinduzi (CCM) party were confronted with a series of challenges. The government banned opposition rallies, which were demanding new elections. Police staged a raid in January 2001 on the offices of the Civic United Front (CUF), the main opposition party in Zanzibar, and killed two in the process. Widepread protests in Zanzibar ensued, during which at least 31 people were killed. One hundred were arrested, and CUF chairman Ibrahim Lupimba was charged with unlawful assembly and disturbing the peace.

The government sent in troop reinforcements, but the solution to the unrest ultimately was to prove to be a political one. CCM and the CUF agreed in March 2001 to the formation of a joint committee to restore calm to Zanzibar, and also to encourage the return of around 2,000 refugees who had fled to Kenya.

Still, tensions remained high throughout Tanzania, and the opposition parties picked up a great deal of support. In April, opposition parties staged the first major political demonstrations against the government in more than 20 years. Some 50,000 supporters of the opposition marched in Dar es Salaam.

In 2005, Benjamin Mkapa retired after 10 years in power. During the elections of December 2005, ruling party candidate Jakaya Kikwete decisively won presidential elections. During his tenure, Benjamin Mkapa is credited with being the driving force behind Tanzania's extensive economic liberalization, which was well received by the IMF and World Bank. Jakaya Kikwete vowed to continue this policy and was rewarded by the African Development Bank, which announced in 2006 the cancellation of more than $640,000,000 of debt owed by Tanzania, saying it was impressed with Tanzania's economic record and the level of accountability of public finance. Between 2000 and 2006, the annual growth rate averaged 5.8%, a commendable performance in these times of economic turbulence. However, most Tanzanians continue to live below the poverty level.

In November 2001 the presidents of Tanzania, Uganda, and Kenya launched a regional parliament and court of justice in Arusha. They will legislate on matters of common interest such as trade and immigration rules.

In October 1999, more than 3 million Tanzanians joined leaders from around the world in filing through a temporary mausoleum housing the body of the country's late first president, Julius Nyerere. It was an

DEVELOPMENT

The Bulyanhulu gold mine near the northern town of Mwanza opens, making Tanzania Africa's third-largest producer of gold.

overwhelming tribute to the man who was known at home and abroad as *Mwalimu*— Swahili for "teacher." Nyerere voluntarily relinquished power in 1985, but the legacy of his nation-building efforts can be found throughout the country. After independence, until recently Tanzania enjoyed internal unity and an expansion of social services. The Kiswahili language helped bind the nation together. But economic growth has remained modest; Tanzania continues to be one of the poorest nations in the world.

After a period of harsh German rule followed by paternalistic British trusteeship, the Tanzanian mainland gained its independence, as Tanganyika, in 1961. In 1964, it merged with the small island state of Zanzibar, which had been a British protectorate, to form the "United Republic of Tanzania." Political activity in Tanzania was restricted to the Chama Cha Mapinduzi party, which joined the former Tanganyika African National Union with its Zanzibar partner, the Afro-Shirazi Party.

(UN photo 154919 by Ray Witlin)

The Tanzanian economy is primarily agriculture-based. However, rainfall for most of the country is sporadic. This, coupled with wide swings in world-market demand for its cash crops, has led to economic pressures. These men in the village of Lumeji are receiving seed grains needed to develop Tanzania's food production.

FREEDOM

Civil rights in Tanzania, especially on the island of Zanzibar, remain circumscribed, with police often harassing supporters of the political opposition. Arbitrary arrest and torture remain commonplace on the island, but on the mainland there has been a steady opening up of society since 1995, though there still exist restrictions on freedoms of speech and association.

In February 1992, the CCM agreed to compete with other "national parties"—provided they did not "divide the people along tribal, religious or racial lines." Multiparty elections were held in October–December 1995, with the CCM claiming victory over a divided opposition in a poll characterized by massive irregularities. The disputed official results were CCM, 60 percent of the vote and 187 members of Parliament (MPs), including 128 seats where the results were still being legally

contested months later; the National Committee for Constitutional Reform (NCCR), 25 percent of the vote and 15 MPs; and the Civic United Front, 24 MPs but only a small percentage of the vote, concentrated in Zanzibar and Pemba Islands. The new CCM leader, Ben Mkapa, replaced as president Ali Hassan Mwinyi, who was forced to step down after having served two terms. The dominant personality in the CCM, however, remained former president Nyerere.

By 1967, the CCM's predecessors had already eliminated legal opposition, when they proclaimed their commitment to the Arusha Declaration, a blueprint for "African Socialism." At the time, Tanzania was one of the least-developed countries in the world. It has remained so. Beyond this fact, there is much controversy over the degree to which the goals of the declaration have been achieved. To some critics, the Arusha experiment has been responsible for reducing a potentially well-off country to ruin. Supporters often counter that it has led to a stable society in which major strides

have been made toward greater democracy, equality, and human development. Both sides exaggerate.

HEALTH/WELFARE

The Tanzanian Development Plan calls for the government to give priority to health and education in its expenditures. This reflects a recognition that early progress in these areas has been undermined to some extent in recent years. Malnutrition remains a critical problem.

Like many African states, Tanzania has a primarily agrarian economy that is constrained by a less than optimal environment. Although some 80 percent of the population are employed in agriculture, only 8 percent of the land is under cultivation. Rainfall for most of the country is low and erratic, and soil erosion and deforestation are critical problems in many areas. But geography and environmental problems are only one facet of Tanzania's low agricultural productivity. There has also been instability in world-market demand for the nation's principal cash crops: coffee, cotton, cloves, sisal, and tobacco. The cost of imported fuel, fertilizers, and other inputs has risen simultaneously.

Government policies have also been responsible for underdevelopment. Perhaps the greatest policy disaster was the program of villagization. Tanzania hoped to relocate its rural and unemployed urban populations into *ujaama* (Swahili for "familyhood") villages, which were to become the basis for agrarian progress. In the early 1970s, coercive measures were adopted to force the pace of resettlement. Agricultural production is estimated to have fallen as much as 50 percent during the initial period of ujaama dislocation, transforming the nation from a grain exporter to a grain importer.

Another policy constraint was the exceedingly low official produce prices paid by the government to farmers. Many peasants withdrew from the official market, while others turned to black-market sales. Since 1985, the official market has been liberalized, and prices have risen. This has been accompanied by a modest rise in production, yet the lack of consumer goods in rural areas is widely seen as a disincentive to greater development.

All sectors of the Tanzanian economy have suffered from deteriorating infrastructure. Here again there are both external and internal causes. Balanced against rising imported-energy and equipment costs have been inefficiencies caused by poor planning, barriers to capital investment, and a relative neglect of communications and transport. Even when crops or goods are available, they often cannot reach their destination. Tanzania's few bituminized roads have long been in a chronic state of disrepair, and there have been frequent shutdowns of its railways. In particular, much of the southern third of the country is isolated from access to even inferior transport services.

ACHIEVEMENTS

The government has had enormous success in its program of promoting the use of Kiswahili (Swahili) as the national language throughout society. Mass literacy in Kiswahili has facilitated the rise of a national culture, helping to make Tanzania one of the more cohesive African nations.

Manufacturing declined from 10 to 4 percent of gross domestic product in the 1980s, with most sectors operating at less than half of their capacity. Inefficiencies also grew in the nation's mining sector. Diamonds, gold, iron, coal, and other minerals are exploited, but production has been generally falling and now accounts for less than 1 percent of GDP. Lack of capital investment has led to a deterioration of existing operations and an inability to open up new deposits.

As with agriculture, the Tanzanian government has in recent years increasingly abandoned socialism in favor of market economics, in its efforts to rehabilitate and expand the industrial and service sectors of the economy. A number of state enterprises are being privatized, and better opportunities are being offered to outside investors. Tourism is now being actively promoted, after decades of neglect. As the country liberalized its economy it has begun to play a more active role in regional economic affairs. During March 2004 the presidents of Tanzania, Uganda, and Kenya signed a protocol in Arusha over proposed customs unions, intended to boost trade.

Tanzania has made real progress in extending health, education, and other social services to its population since independence, though the statistical evidence is inadequate and official claims exaggerated. Some 1,700 health centers and dispensaries have been built since 1961, but they have long been plagued by shortages of medicines, equipment, and even basic supplies such as bandages and syringes. Although the country has a national health service, patients often end up paying for material costs.

Much of the progress that has been made in human services is a function of outside donations. Despite the Arusha Declaration's emphasis on self-reliance, Tanzania has for decades been either at or near the top of the list of African countries in per capita receipt of international aid.

Even before the recent opening to multipartyism, Tanzania's politics was in a state of transition. Political life was dominated from the 1950s by Julius Nyerere, who was the driving personality behind the Arusha experiment. However, in 1985, he gave up the presidency in favor of Ali Hassan Mwinyi, and, in 1990, Nyerere resigned as chairman of the CCM, without having to give up his leading influence in the party.

The move to multiparty politics is complicated by the omnipresent CCM. The party has sought to control all organized social activity outside of religion. A network of community and workplace cells has assured that all Tanzanians have at least one party official responsible for monitoring their affairs.

In 1993, a dozen new opposition parties were registered, though others, notably the Democratic Party of Reverend Christopher Mtikila, remain banned. Opposition disunity contributed to subsequent CCM election victories. In addition, the CCM still enjoys a near media monopoly, occasionally invoking the National Security Act to harass independent journalists. Overt political repression has been most notable on Zanzibar and Pemba Islands.

Timeline: PAST

1820

The sultan of Oman transfers the capital to Zanzibar as Arab commercial activity increases

1885

Germany declares a protectorate over the area

1905–1906

The Maji Maji rebellion unites many ethnic groups against German rule

1919

Tanganyika becomes a League of Nations mandate under the United Kingdom

1961

Tanganyika becomes independent; Julius Nyerere is the leader

1964

Tanzania is formed of Tanganyika and Zanzibar

1967

The Arusha Declaration establishes a Tanzanian socialist program for development

1985

Nyerere retires; Ali Hassan Mwinyi succeeds as president

1990s

The CCM wins disputed multiparty elections

PRESENT

2000s

Tanzania continues to look for ways to diversify its economy

Tensions erupt between the government and the opposition

President Ben Mkapa is criticized for ordering a $21 million presidential plane

Uganda (Republic of Uganda)

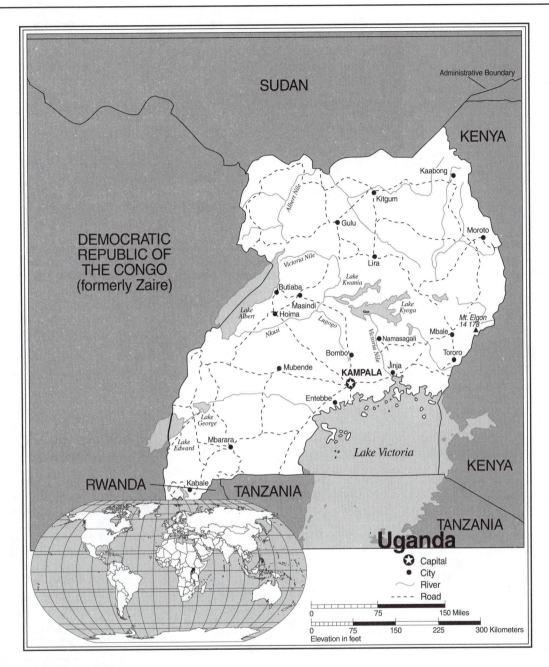

Uganda Statistics

GEOGRAPHY

Area in Square Miles (Kilometers): 91,076 (235,885) (about the size of Oregon)

Capital (Population): Kampala (1,274,000)

Environmental Concerns: draining of wetlands; deforestation; overgrazing; soil erosion; widespread poaching

Geographical Features: mostly plateau, with a rim of mountains

Climate: generally tropical, but semiarid in the northeast

PEOPLE

Population

Total: 30,262,610

Annual Growth Rate: 3.572%

Rural/Urban Population Ratio: 87/13

Major Languages: English; Swahili; Bantu languages; Nilotic languages

Ethnic Makeup: Bantu; Nilotic; Nilo-Hamitic; Sudanic

Religions: 66% Christian; 18% indigenous beliefs; 16% Muslim

Health

Life Expectancy at Birth: 50.78 years (male); 52.73 years (female)

Infant Mortality: 67.22/1,000 live births

Physicians Available: 1/20,700 people

HIV/AIDS Rate in Adults: 4.1%

Education

Adult Literacy Rate: 66.8%

COMMUNICATION

Telephones: 108,100 main lines
Televisions: 27/1,000 people
Internet Users: 750,000 (2006)

TRANSPORTATION

Highways in Miles (Kilometers): 42,448
  (70,746 km)
Railroads in Miles (Kilometers): 745
  1,244 km
Usable Airfields: 31
Motor Vehicles in Use: 51,000

GOVERNMENT

Type: republic
Independence Date: October 9, 1962
  (from the United Kingdom)

Head of State/Government: President
  Yoweri Kaguta Museveni is both head
  of state and head of government
Political Parties: National Resistance
  Movement (only organization allowed
  to operate unfettered)
Suffrage: universal at 18

MILITARY

Military Expenditures (% of GDP): 2.2%
Current Disputes: continuing ethnic strife
  in the region

ECONOMY

Currency ($ U.S. Equivalent): 1,765
  Uganda shillings = $1
Per Capita Income/GDP: $1,900/$52.93
  billion
GDP Growth Rate: 5.3%
Inflation Rate: 7.9%
Labor Force by Occupation: 82%
  agriculture; 13% services; 5% industry

Population Below Poverty Line: 35%
Natural Resources: copper; cobalt;
  salt; limestone; hydropower; arable
  land
Agriculture: coffee; tea; cotton; tobacco;
  cassava; potatoes; corn; millet; pulses;
  livestock
Industry: sugar; brewing; tobacco;
  textiles; cement
Exports: $961.7 million (primary partner
  Europe)
Imports: $1.945 billion (primary partners
  Kenya, United States, India)

SUGGESTED WEB SITES

http://www.ugandaweb.com
http://www.government.go.ug
http://www.monitor.co.ug
http://www.mbendi.co.za/
  cyugcy.htm
http://www.uganda.co.ug/
http://www.cia.gov/cia/publications/
  factbook/geos/ug.html

Uganda Country Report

In 2000, Ugandans voted to reject multiparty politics in favor of continuing President Yoweri Museveni's "no-party" system. This action was followed in 2001 by another victory for Museveni in the presidential elections, in which he defeated his rival, Kizza Besigye, by 69 percent to 28 percent. In the first multiparty elections in 25 years, Yoweri Museveni was declared winner of the elections in 2006. He won 59% of the vote, while his main rival, Kizza Besigye of the opposition Forum for Democratic Change, garnered 37% of the votes. To pave way for Museveni to seek a third elected term, parliament abolished a constitutional limit on presidential terms in 2005. Museveni has remained in power since 1985 through his tight control over the military and governing institutions. But his position has been challenged by his involvement in regional conflicts as well as by domestic rebels, most notably the Lords Resistance Army (LRA), which continues to terrorize northern Uganda. This led to a series of significant diplomatic initiatives in 2002.

DEVELOPMENT

In the past few years, Uganda's economy has been growing at an average annual rate of about 5%, boosted by increased investment. Foreign economic assistance nonetheless accounts for approximately 29% of government spending.

In March 2002, Sudan and Uganda signed an agreement aimed at containing the LRA, which was active along their common border. The deal allowed Uganda to carry out limited operations in Sudan. Although the LRA thereafter came under sustained attack in what the Ugandan military dubbed "Operation Iron Fist," the movement not only survived but also was able to regain control over areas in northern Uganda. In July, the Ugandan government broke off the offensive and agreed to begin negotiations with the LRA to end the war.

Finding common ground with the LRA may not be easy. A self-proclaimed "prophet" named Joseph Kony, who says he wants to run Uganda in conformity with the biblical Ten Commandments, leads the movement. But, in practice, the LRA has been responsible for the abduction of thousands of boys and girls. The boys are indoctrinated to kill and rape, while the girls are consigned to serve as laborers and targets of sexual gratification.

Over the past five years, Uganda's army has also been heavily involved in fighting in the Democratic Republic of the Congo (D.R.C., the former Zaire). In March 2001, Uganda classified Rwanda—its former ally in the D.R.C.'s civil war—as a hostile nation after several months of clashes between the two countries' armed forces over key areas of eastern D.R.C., which they had collectively occupied since 1998. Both countries, along with Zimbabwe, have been accused

of pillaging the D.R.C.'s natural wealth. Tensions were eased between the two states in February 2002, when Museveni met the Rwandan president, Paul Kagame, as part of an on-going, British-backed effort to defuse tensions.

In August 2002, Museveni signed a peace accord with D.R.C. president Joseph Kabila, which had been brokered by the Angolan president Jose Eduardo dos Santos. This resulted in the rapid withdrawal of Ugandan forces from Eastern D.R.C. Uganda pulled out the last of its troops from eastern D.R.C. in May 2004 as tens of thousands of D.R. Congo civilians seek asylum in Uganda.

FREEDOM

The human-rights situation in Uganda remains poor, with government security forces linked to torture, extra-judicial executions, and other atrocities. Freedom of speech and association are curtailed. Insurgent groups are also associated with atrocities; the Lord's Resistance Army continues to kill, torture, maim, and abduct large numbers of civilians, enslaving numerous children.

Uganda's foreign and domestic conflicts pose a potential threat to the very real progress that the country has made since the coming to power of Museveni's National

Resistance Movement (NRM). After years of repressive rule accompanied by massive interethnic violence, Uganda is still struggling for peace and reconciliation. A land rich in natural and human resources, Uganda suffered dreadfully during the despotic regimes of Milton Obote (1962–1971, 1980–1985) and Idi Amin (1971–1979). Under these two dictators, hundreds of thousands of Ugandans were murdered by the state. Former dictator Idi Amin died in a hospital in Jedaah, Saudi Arabia in August 2003. Amin was not mourned in Uganda and had no state funeral.

HEALTH/WELFARE

Millions of Ugandans live below the poverty line. Uganda's traditionally strong school system was damaged but not completely destroyed under Amin and Obote. In 1986, some 70% of primary-school children attended classes. The killing and exiling of teachers have resulted in a serious drop of standards at all levels of the education system, but progress is under way. The adult literacy rate has risen to 62%.

The country had reached a state of general social and political collapse by 1986, when the NRM seized power. The new government soon made considerable progress in restoring a sense of normalcy in most of the country, except for the north. In May 1996, Museveni officially received 74 percent of the vote in a contested presidential poll. Despite charges of fraud by his closest rival, Paul Ssemogerere, most independent observers accepted the poll as an endorsement of Museveni's leadership, including his view that politics should remain organized on a nonparty basis. There has since, however, emerged growing international criticism of his intolerance of genuine political pluralism.

HISTORIC GEOGRAPHY

The breakdown of Uganda is an extreme example of the disruptive role of ethnic and sectarian competition, which was fostered by policies of both its colonial and postcolonial governments. Uganda consists of two major zones: the plains of the northeast and the southern highlands. It has been said that you can drop anything into the rich volcanic soils of the well-watered south and it will grow. Until the 1960s, the area was divided into four kingdoms—Buganda, Bunyoro, Ankole, and Toro—populated by peoples using related Bantu languages. The histories of these four states stretch back hundreds of years. European visitors of the nineteenth century were impressed by their sophisticated social orders, which

the Europeans equated with the feudal monarchies of medieval Europe.

When the British took over, they integrated the ruling class of the southern highlands into a system of "indirect rule." By then, missionaries had already succeeded in converting many southerners to Christianity; indeed, civil war among Protestants, Catholics, and Muslims within Buganda had been the British pretext for establishing their overrule.

The Acholi, Langi, Karamojang, Teso, Madi, and Kakwa peoples, who are predominant in the northeast, lack the political heritage of hierarchical state-building found in the south. These groups are also linguistically separate, speaking either Nilotic or Nilo-Hamitic languages. The British united the two regions as the Uganda Protectorate during the 1890s (the word *Uganda,* which is a corruption of "Buganda," has since become the accepted name for the larger entity). But the zones developed separately under colonial rule.

Cash-crop farming, especially of cotton, by local peasants spurred an economic boom in the south. The Bugandan ruling class benefited in particular. Increasing levels of education and wealth led to the European stereotype of the "progressive" Bugandans as the "Japanese of Africa." A growing class of Asian entrepreneurs also played an important role in the local economy, although its prosperity, as well as that of the Bugandan elite, suffered from subordination to resident-British interests.

The south's growing economy stood in sharp contrast to the relative neglect of the northeast. Forced to earn money to pay taxes, many northeasterners became migrant workers in the south. They were also recruited, almost exclusively, to serve in the colonial security forces.

ACHIEVEMENTS

The Ugandan government was one of the first countries in Africa (and the world) to acknowledge the seriousness of the HIV/AIDS epidemic within its borders. It has instituted public-information campaigns and welcomed outside support.

As independence approached, many Bugandans feared that other groups would compromise their interests. Under the leadership of their king, Mutesa II, they sought to uphold their separate status. Other groups feared that Bugandan wealth and educational levels could lead to their dominance. A compromise federal structure was agreed to for the new state. At independence, the southern kingdoms retained their autonomous status within the "United

Kingdom of Uganda." The first government was made up of Mutesa's royalist party and the United People's Congress (UPC), a largely non-Bugandan coalition, led by Milton Obote, a Langi. Mutesa was elected president and Obote prime minister.

Timeline: PAST

1500s
Establishment of the oldest Ugandan kingdom, Bunyoro, followed by the formation of Buganda and other kingdoms

1893
A British protectorate over Uganda is proclaimed

1962
Uganda becomes independent

1966
Milton Obote introduces a new unitary Constitution and forces Bugandan compliance

1971
Idi Amin seizes power

1978–1979
Amin invades Tanzania; Tanzania invades Uganda and overturns Amin's government

1980s
The rise and fall of the second Obote regime; the NRM takes power under Yoweri Museveni

1990s
Recovery produces slow gains; unrest continues in the northeast

PRESENT

2000s
Uganda addresses the HIV/AIDS pandemic

Museveni retains power

Uganda pulls out last of its troops from eastern DR Congo

Government and LRA rebels hold their first face-to-face talks without any concrete agreement on how to end the insurgency

Parliament approves a constitutional amendment that scraps presidential term limits

Voters in a referendum overwhelmingly back a return to multiparty politics

THE REIGN OF TERROR

In 1966, the delicate balance of ethnic interests was upset when Obote used the army—still dominated by fellow northeasterners—to overthrow Mutesa and the Constitution. In the name of abolishing "tribalism," Obote established a one-party state and ruled in an increasingly dictatorial fashion. However, in 1971, he was overthrown by his army chief, Idi Amin. Amin began his regime with widespread public support but alienated himself by favoring fellow Muslims and Kakwa. He expelled the 40,000-member Asian community and distributed their property to his cronies. The Langi, suspected of being pro-Obote, were also early targets of his persecution, but his attacks soon spread to other members of Uganda's Christian community, at the time about 80 percent of the total population. Educated people in particular were purged. The number of Ugandans murdered by Amin's death squads is unknown; the most commonly cited figure is 300,000, but estimates range from 50,000 to 1 million. Many others went into exile. Throughout the world, Amin's name became synonymous with despotic rule.

A Ugandan military incursion into Tanzania led to war between the two countries in 1979. Many Ugandans joined with the Tanzanians in defeating Amin's army and its Libyan allies.

Unfortunately, the overthrow of Amin, who fled into exile, did not lead to better times. In 1980, Obote was returned to power, through a fraudulent vote count. His second administration was characterized by a continuation of the violence of the Amin years. Obote's security forces massacred an estimated 300,000 people, mostly southerners, while an equal number fled the country. Much of the killing occurred in the Bugandan area known as the Luwero triangle, which was completely depopulated; its fields are still full of skeletons today. As the killings escalated, so did the resistance of Museveni's NRM guerrillas, who had taken to the bush in the aftermath of the failed election. In 1985, a split between Ancholi and Langi officers led to Obote's overthrow and yet another pattern of interethnic recrimination. Finally, in 1986, the NRM gained the upper hand.

Thereafter a new political order began to emerge based on Museveni's vision of a "no-party government." His position was strengthened in March 1994, when elections to a Constituent Assembly resulted in his supporters' capturing more than two thirds of the seats. In another controversial initiative, Museveni allowed the restoration of traditional offices, including Bugandan kingship.

THE STRUGGLE CONTINUES

Museveni's National Resistance Movement administration has faced enormous challenges in trying to bring about national reconstruction. The task has been complicated by continued warfare in the northeast by armed factions representing ele-ments of the former regimes, independent Karamojong communities, and followers of prophetic religious movements. In 1987, an uprising of the Holy Spirit rebels of Alice Lakwena was crushed, at the cost of some 15,000 lives.

The restoration of peace to most of the country has promoted economic growth. Western-backed economic reforms produced an annual growth rate of 13 percent between 1990 and 1998. The rate of inflation also improved, falling from 200 to 7 percent in the same period. On the regional level, Museveni has championed the formation of a new "East African Community" (EAC), which is intended to lay the groundwork for economic and ultimately monetary integration with Tanzania and Kenya.

While rebuilding their shattered country, Ugandans have had to cope with an especially severe outbreak of HIV/AIDS. Thousands have died of the disease in the last decade; it is believed that literally hundreds of thousands of Ugandans are HIV-positive. The government's bold acknowledgment and proactive efforts to address the crisis, however, have been credited with helping to contain the pandemic. Indeed the vigorous campaign against HIV/AIDS has paid great dividends in tackling this disease. The campaign is credited with reducing the HIV prevalence rate from a high of 30% in the 1990s to a low of 4.1% in 2007. Uganda shows that, with good leadership and government commitment, HIV can be curtailed.

North Africa

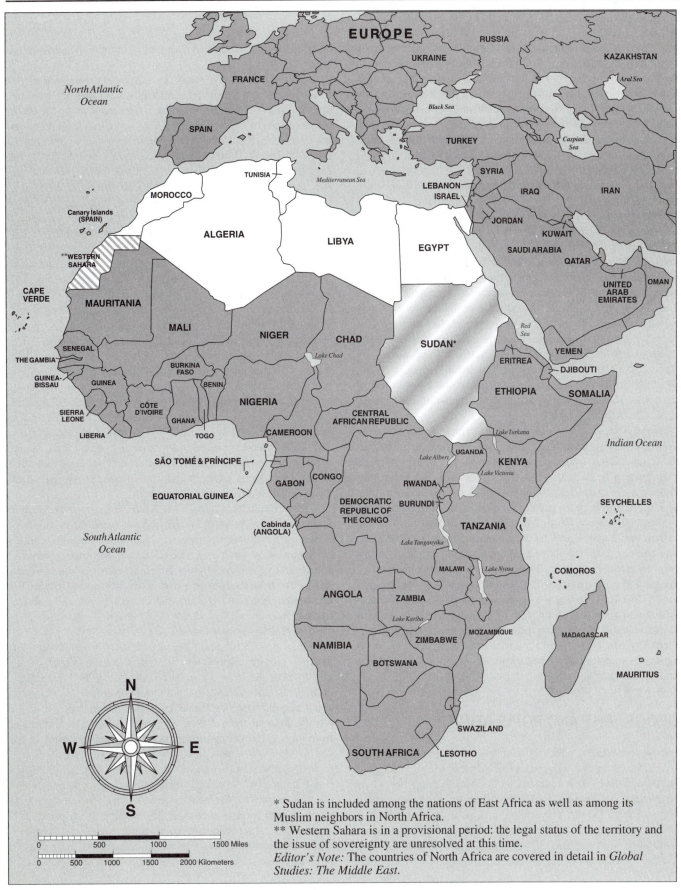

EUROPE

RUSSIA

KAZAKHSTAN

Aral Sea

North Atlantic Ocean

FRANCE

UKRAINE

Black Sea

Caspian Sea

SPAIN

TURKEY

Mediterranean Sea

TUNISIA

SYRIA

LEBANON
ISRAEL

IRAQ

IRAN

MOROCCO

Canary Islands
(SPAIN)

ALGERIA

LIBYA

EGYPT

JORDAN

KUWAIT

SAUDI ARABIA

QATAR

**WESTERN
SAHARA

UNITED
ARAB
EMIRATES

OMAN

CAPE
VERDE

MAURITANIA

MALI

NIGER

CHAD

*Red
Sea*

SUDAN*

YEMEN

ERITREA

DJIBOUTI

Lake Chad

SENEGAL

THE GAMBIA

BURKINA
FASO

ETHIOPIA

SOMALIA

GUINEA-
BISSAU

GUINEA

BENIN

NIGERIA

CENTRAL
AFRICAN REPUBLIC

Lake Turkana

SIERRA
LEONE

CÔTE
D'IVOIRE

GHANA

Indian Ocean

LIBERIA

TOGO

CAMEROON

UGANDA

Lake Albert

KENYA

SÃO TOMÉ & PRÍNCIPE

Lake Victoria

EQUATORIAL GUINEA

GABON

CONGO

RWANDA

SEYCHELLES

South Atlantic Ocean

Cabinda
(ANGOLA)

DEMOCRATIC
REPUBLIC OF
THE CONGO

BURUNDI

TANZANIA

Lake Tanganyika

MALAWI

Lake Nyasa

COMOROS

ANGOLA

ZAMBIA

Lake Kariba

MOZAMBIQUE

MADAGASCAR

NAMIBIA

ZIMBABWE

MAURITIUS

BOTSWANA

SWAZILAND

SOUTH AFRICA

LESOTHO

N
W E
S

0   500   1000   1500 Miles
0   500   1000   1500   2000 Kilometers

* Sudan is included among the nations of East Africa as well as among its
Muslim neighbors in North Africa.
** Western Sahara is in a provisional period: the legal status of the territory and
the issue of sovereignty are unresolved at this time.
Editor's Note: The countries of North Africa are covered in detail in *Global
Studies: The Middle East.*

North Africa   The Crossroads of the Continent

Located at the geographical and cultural crossroads between Europe, Asia, and the rest of Africa, North Africa has served since ancient times as a link between the civilizations of sub-Saharan Africa and the rest of the world. Traders historically carried the continent's products northward, either across the Sahara Desert or up the Nile River and Red Sea, to the great port cities of the Mediterranean coast. Goods also flowed southward. In addition, the trade networks carried ideas: Islam, for example, spread from coastal North Africa across much of the rest of the continent to become the religion of at least one third of all Africans.

While there are millions of people now living in the countries of North Africa who claim that they are Arabs, it is important to remember that the designation Arab is cultural and ethnolinguistic in origin. The people of North Africa are also Africans, no matter where their particular ethnic group might originally have come from. North Africans occupy a geographically integral part of Africa, but due to the color of their skins they may look like they are foreigners to the continent. In fact, they have been living in Africa for thousands of years. The Arabs are merely another ethno-linguistic people living in Africa. The pyramids are African, built by Africans in Africa, to worship African gods and spiritual entities that reflected a particular cosmological view of the world. The Arabs who now rule Egypt are in this sense guardians of the African temples.

North Africa's role as the continent's principal window to the Western world gradually declined after the year A.D. 1500, as the trans-Atlantic trade increased. (The history of East Africa's participation in Indian Ocean trade goes back much further.) However, the countries of North Africa have continued to play an important role in the greater development of the continent.

The countries of North Africa—Morocco, Algeria, Tunisia, Libya, and Egypt—and their millions of people differ from one another, but they share a predominant, overarching Arab-Islamic culture that both distinguishes them from the rest of Africa and unites them with the Arabic-speaking countries of the Middle East. To begin to understand the societies of North Africa and their role in the rest of the continent, it is helpful to examine the area's geography. The region's diverse environment has long encouraged its inhabitants to engage in a broad variety of economic activities: pastoralism, agriculture, trading, crafts, and, later, industry.

GEOGRAPHY AND POPULATION

Except for Tunisia, which is relatively small, the countries of North Africa are sprawling societies. Algeria, Libya, and Egypt are among the biggest countries on the African continent. Their sizes can be misleading, for much of their territories are largely barren Sahara Desert. The approximate populations of the five states today range from Egypt's 80 million people to Libya's 6 million; Morocco has 33 million, Algeria 31 million, and Tunisia 10 million citizens. All these populations are increasing at a rapid rate; indeed, well over half of the region's citizens are under age 30.

Due to its scarcity, water is the region's most precious resource, so most people live either in valleys near the Mediterranean coast or along the Nile. The latter runs through the desert for thousands of miles, creating a narrow green ribbon that is the home of 95 percent of Egypt's population who live within 12 miles of its banks. More than 90 percent of the people of Algeria, Libya, Morocco, and Tunisia live within 200 miles of either the Mediterranean or, in the case of Morocco, the Atlantic coast.

Besides determining where people live, the temperate, if often too dry, climate of North Africa has always influenced local economies and lifestyles. There is intensive agriculture along the coasts and rivers. Algeria, Morocco, and Tunisia are well known for their citrus fruits, olives, and wine grapes. The intensively irrigated Nile Valley has been a leading source of high-quality cotton as well as locally consumed foodstuffs since the time of the American Civil War, which temporarily removed U.S.–produced fiber from the world market. In the oases that dot the Sahara Desert, date palms are grown for their sweet fruits, which are almost a regional staple. Throughout the steppelands between the fertile coasts and the desert, pastoralists follow flocks of sheep and goats or herds of cattle and camels in constant search of pasture. Although now few in number, it was these nomads who in the past developed the trans-Saharan trade. As paved roads and airports have replaced their caravan routes, long-distance nomadism has declined. But the traditions it bred, including a love of independence, remain an important part of North Africa's cultural heritage.

Urban culture has flourished in North Africa since the ancient times of the Egyptian pharaohs and the mercantilist rulers of Carthage. Supported by trade and local industries, the region's medieval cities, such as Cairo, Fez, and Kairouan, were the administrative centers of great Islamic empires, whose civilizations shined during Europe's dark ages. In the modern era, the urban areas are bustling industrial centers, ports, and political capitals.

Geography—or, more precisely, geology—has helped to fuel economic growth in recent decades. Although agriculture continues to provide employment in Algeria and Libya for as much as a third of the labor force, discoveries of oil and natural gas in the 1950s dramatically altered these two countries' economic structures. Between 1960 and 1980, Libya's annual per capita income jumped from $50 to almost $10,000, transforming it from among the poorest to among the richest countries in the world. Algeria has also greatly benefited from the exploitation of hydrocarbons, although less dramatically than Libya. Egypt and Tunisia have developed much smaller oil industries, which nonetheless provide for their domestic energy needs and generate much-needed foreign exchange. The decline in oil prices during the 1980s, however, reduced revenues, increased unemployment, and contributed to social and political unrest, especially in Algeria. While it has no oil, Morocco profits from its possession

(Photo by Wayne Edge)

Camels are still used in North Africa to move through the desert.

of much of the world's phosphate production, which is concentrated in the Moroccan-occupied territory of Western Sahara.

CULTURAL AND POLITICAL HERITAGES

The vast majority of the inhabitants of North Africa are Arabic-speaking Muslims. Islam and Arabic both became established in the region between the seventh and eleventh centuries A.D. By the time of the Crusades in the eastern Mediterranean, the societies of North Africa were thoroughly incorporated into the Muslim world, even though the area had earlier been the home of many Christians. Except for Egypt, where about 6 percent of the population belong to the Coptic Church, there are very few Christians in the rest of the North Africa. Until recently, important Jewish communities existed in all the region's countries, but their numbers have dwindled as a result of mass emigration to Israel.

With Islam came Arabic, the language of the Qur'an—the holy book of Islam. Today, Egypt and Libya are almost exclusively Arabic-speaking. In Algeria, Morocco, and Tunisia, besides the widely spoken Arabic language, Berber (Tamazight)

is the primary language of many people. As many as a third of the Moroccans and a fourth of the Algerians speak a form of Berber as their first language. Centuries of interaction between the Arabs and Berbers as well as their common adherence to Islam have promoted a sense of cultural unity between the two communities, although disputes have developed in Algeria and Morocco over demands that Berber be included in local school curriculums and an official and national language. As was the case almost everywhere else on the continent, the linguistic situation in North Africa was further complicated by the introduction of European languages during the colonial era. Today, French is particularly important as a language of science and administration in Algeria, Morocco, and Tunisia.

In 2001, the king of Morocco, Mohamed VI, established the Royal Institute of the Amazigh Culture, whose official goal is the promotion of the Berber culture an language. In Algeira, the government established in 1995 the High Council for the Berber language with a similar aim.

By the seventeenth century, all the countries of North Africa, except Morocco, were autonomous provinces of the Ottoman Empire, which was based in present-day Turkey and also incorporated most of the Middle East. Morocco was an independent state; indeed, it was one of the earliest to recognize the independence of the United States from Britain. From 1830, the European powers gradually encroached upon the Ottoman Empire's North African realm. Thus, like most of their sub-Saharan counterparts, all the states of North Africa fell under European imperial control. Algeria's conquest by the French began in 1830 but took decades to accomplish, due to fierce local resistance. France also seized Tunisia in 1881 and, along with Spain, partitioned Morocco in 1912. Britain occupied Egypt in 1882, and Italy invaded Libya in 1911, although anti-Italian resistance continued until World War II, when the area was liberated by Allied troops.

The differing natures of their European occupations have influenced the political and social characters of each North African state. Algeria, which was directly incorporated into France as a province for 120 years, did not win its independence until 1962, after a protracted war of liberation. Morocco,

by contrast, was accorded independence in 1956, after only 44 years of French–Spanish control, during which the local monarchy continued to exist. Tunisia's 75 years of French rule also ended in 1956, as a strong nationalist party took the reins of power. Egypt, although formally independent of Great Britain, did not win genuine self-determination until 1952, when a group of nationalist army officers came to power by overthrowing the British-supported monarchy. Libya became a temporary ward of the United Nations after Italy was deprived of its colonial empire during World War II. The country was granted independence by the United Nations in 1951, under a monarch whose religious followers had led much of the anti-Italian resistance.

Editor's Note—The countries of North Africa are covered in detail in *Global Studies: The Middle East.*

Algeria (Peoples' Democratic Republic of Algeria)

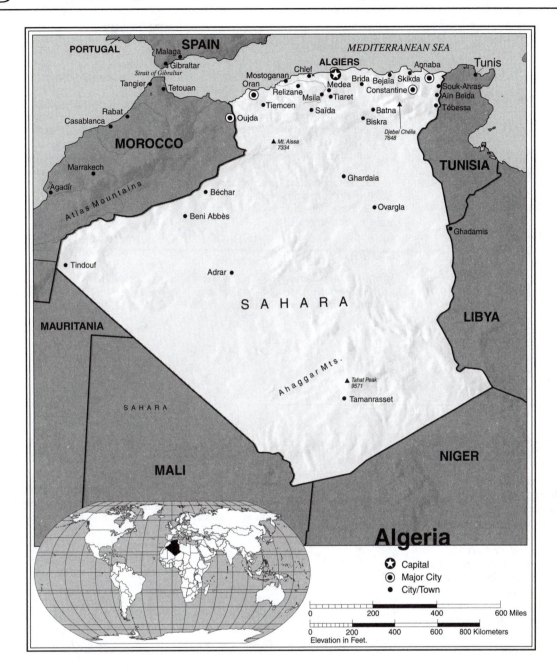

Algeria Statistics

GEOGRAPHY

Area in Square Miles (Kilometers):
919,352 (2,381,740) (about 3½ times the size of Texas)
Capital (Population): Algiers (3,705,000)
Environmental Concerns: soil erosion; desertification; water pollution; inadequate potable water
Geographical Features: mostly high plateau and desert; some mountains; narrow, discontinuous coastal plain

Climate: arid to semiarid; mild winters and hot summers on coastal plain; less rain and cold winters on high plateau; considerable temperature variation in desert

PEOPLE
Population

Total: 33,333,216
Annual Growth Rate: 1.216%
Rural/Urban Population Ratio: 44/56

Major Languages: Arabic; Berber dialects; Ahaggar (Tuareg); French
Ethnic Makeup: 99% Arab-Berber; less than 1% European
Religions: 99% Sunni Muslim (Islam is the state religion); 1% Shi'a Muslim, Christian, and Jewish

Health

Life Expectancy at Birth: 71.94 years (male); 75 years (female)

107

Infant Mortality Rate (Ratio): 28.78/1,000
live births

Education

Adult Literacy Rate: 70%
Compulsory (Ages): 6–15

COMMUNICATION

Telephones: 2,572,000 plus 1,447,310 cell
phones
Daily Newspaper Circulation: 52 per
1,000 people
Televisions: 71 per 1,000 people
Internet Users: 2 (2000)

TRANSPORTATION

Highways in Miles (Kilometers): 63,605
(102,424)
Railroads in Miles (Kilometers): 2,963
(4,772)
Usable Airfields: 137
Motor Vehicles in Use: 920,000

GOVERNMENT

Type: republic
Independence Date: July 5, 1962 (from
France)
Head of State/Government: President
Abdelaziz Bouteflika; Prime Minister
Abdelaziz Belkhadem
Political Parties: With the move toward
representative government the Algerian
National Front (FNA) has become
the majority party in recent elections.
Minority (opposition) parties include
the National Democratic Rally (RND),
National Entente Movement, National
Reform Movement, and En-Nahda
(Renaissance). The Islamic Salvation
Front (FIS) remains outlawed due to its
religious orientation.
Suffrage: universal at 18

MILITARY

Military Expenditures (% of GDP): 3.2%
Current Disputes: disputed southeastern
border with Libya; Algeria supports

Polisario Front which seeks to
establish an independent Western
Sahara, currently occupied by Morocco

ECONOMY

Currency ($U.S. Equivalent): 72 Algerian
dinars = $1
Per Capita Income/GDP: $7,700/$77
billion
GDP Growth Rate: 5.6%
Inflation Rate: 3%
Unemployment Rate: 15.7%
Labor Force: 9,300,000
Natural Resources: petroleum; natural
gas; iron ore; phosphates; uranium;
lead; zinc
Agriculture: wheat; barley; oats; grapes;
olives; citrus fruits; sheep; cattle
Industry: petroleum; natural gas;
light industries; mining; electrical;
petrochemicals; food processing
Exports: $55.6 billion (primary partners
United States, Italy, Spain)
Imports: $15.25 billion (primary partners
France, Italy, Spain)

Algeria Country Report

The modern state of Algeria occupies the central part of North Africa, a geographically distinctive and separate region of Africa that includes Morocco, Tunisia, and Libya. The name of the country comes from the Arabic word *al-Jaza'ir,* "the islands," because of the rocky islets along this part of the Mediterranean coast. The name of the capital, Algiers, has the same origin.

The official name of the state is the Democratic and Popular Republic of Algeria. It is the second-largest nation in Africa (after Sudan). The overall population density is low, but the population is concentrated in the northern third of the country. The vast stretches of the Algerian Sahara are largely unpopulated. The country had an extremely high birth rate prior to 1988, but government-sponsored family-planning programs have significantly reduced the rate.

GEOGRAPHY

Algeria's geography is a formidable obstacle to broad economic and social development. About 80 percent of the land is uncultivable desert, and only 12 percent is arable without irrigation. Most of the population live in a narrow coastal plain and in a fertile, hilly inland region called the Tell (Arabic for "hillock"). The four

Saharan provinces have only 3 percent of the population but comprise more than half the land area.

The mineral resources that made possible Algeria's transformation in two decades from a land devastated by civil war to one of the developing world's success stories are all located in the Sahara. Economic growth, however, has been uneven, generally affecting the rural and lower-class urban populations unfavorably. The large-scale exodus of rural families into the cities, with consequent neglect of agriculture, has resulted in a vast increase in urban slums. Economic disparities were a major cause of riots in 1988, that led to political reforms and the dismantling of the socialist system responsible for Algerian development since independence.

Algeria is unique among newly independent Middle Eastern countries in that it gained its independence through a civil war. For more than 130 years (1830–1962), it was occupied by France and became a French department (similar to a U.S. state). With free movement from mainland France to Algeria and vice versa, the country was settled by large numbers of Europeans, who became the politically dominant group in the population although they were a minority. The modern Algerian nation is the product of the interaction of native

Muslim Algerians with the European settlers, who also considered Algeria home.

Algeria's geography is a key to the country's past disunity. In addition to its vast Saharan territory, Algeria is broken up into discontinuous regions by a number of rugged mountain ranges. The Mediterranean coastline is narrow and is backed throughout its length by mountains, notably the imposing Kabyle range. The Algerian Atlas range, a continuation of the Moroccan Atlas, is a complex system of deep valleys, high plateaux, and peaks ranging up to 6,000 feet. In south central Algeria is the most impressive range in the country, the Aurès, a great mountain block.

The original inhabitants of the entire North African region were Berbers, a people of unknown origin grouped into various tribes. Berbers make up about 30 percent of the total population. The majority live in the eastern Kabylia region and the Aures (Chaouia), with a small, compact group in the five cities of the Mzab, in the Algerian Sahara. The Tuareg, a nomadic Berber people spread across southern Algeria, Mali, and Niger, are the only ones with a written script, called Tifinagh. In the past, they were literally "lords of the desert," patrolling the caravan routes on their swift camels and collecting tolls for safe passage as guides for caravaneers. They were a colorful sight in their tents with their indigo robes (which tinted their skin blue, hence the name for them, the "Blue Men"). But Saharan droughts, motorized transport, and the development of the oil industry have largely destroyed their traditional role and lifestyle. Today, Tuareg are more likely to be found pumping gas in cities or doing low-wage work in the oil fields than patrolling the desert.

The Arabs, who brought Islam to North Africa in the seventh century A.D., converted the Algerian Berbers after a fierce resistance. The Arabs brought their language as a unifying feature, and religion linked the Algerians with the larger Islamic world. Today, most follow Sunni Islam, but a significant minority, about 100,000, are Shi'a Muslims. They refer to themselves as *Ibadis,* from their observance of an ancient Shi'a rite, and live in five "holy cities" clustered in a remote Saharan valley where centuries ago they took refuge from Sunni rulers of northern Algeria. Their valley, the Mzab, has always maintained religious autonomy from Algerian central governments. The much larger Berber population of Kabylia has also resisted central authority, whether Islamic or French, throughout Algerian history. One of many pressures on the government today is that of an organized Kabyle movement, which seeks greater autonomy for the region and an emphasis on Berber language in schools, along with the revitalization of Kabyle culture.

HISTORY

The Corsair Regency

The foundations of the modern Algerian state were laid in the sixteenth century, with the establishment of the Regency of Algiers, an outlying province of the Ottoman Empire. Algiers in particular, due to its natural harbor, was developed for use by the Ottomans as a naval base for wars against European fleets in the Mediterranean. The Algerian coast was the farthest westward extent of Ottoman power. Consequently, Algiers and Oran, the two major ports, were exposed to constant threats of attack by Spanish and other European fleets. They could not easily be supported, or governed directly, by the Ottomans. The regency, from its beginnings, was a state geared for war.

The regency was established by two Greek-born Muslim sea captains, Aruj and Khayr al-Din (called Barbarossa by his European opponents because of his flaming red beard). The brothers obtained commissions from the Ottoman sultan for expeditions against the Spanish. They made their principal base at Algiers, then a small port, which Khayr al-Din expanded into a powerful fortress and naval base. His government consisted of a garrison of Ottoman soldiers sent by the sultan to keep order, along with a naval force called the corsairs.

Corsairing or piracy (the choice of term depended upon one's viewpoint) was a common practice in the Mediterranean, but the rise to power of the Algerine corsairs converted it into a more or less respectable profession.[1] The cities of Tetuan, Tunis, Salé (Morocco), and Tripoli (Libya) also had corsair fleets, but the Algerian corsairs were so effective against European shipping that for 300 years (1500–1800), European rulers called them the "scourge of the Mediterranean." One factor in their success was their ability to attract outstanding sea captains from various European countries. Renegades from Italy, Greece, Holland, France, and Britain joined the Algerian fleet, converted to Islam, and took Muslim names as a symbol of their new status. Some rose to high rank.

The corsair states, particularly Algiers and Tripoli, were a major factor in the establishment of U.S. naval power and by extension American foreign policy. Prior to independence American merchant vessels traveled under the protection of the Union Jack, England having paid regular tribute in return for exemption of its ships from corsair capture. This protective cover was no longer valid after 1782, and the United States found itself paying huge sums for ransom of its crews and return of cargoes where possible. The very notion of tribute, then as now, was anathema to American policymakers, and in 1804 President Jefferson ordered and Congress approved construction of 6 naval frigates, the first units in the U.S. Navy, to patrol the Mediterranean and protect American merchant shipping there.

Government in Algiers passed through several stages and eventually became a system of deys. The deys were elected by the Divan, a council of the captains of the Ottoman garrison. Deys were elected for life, but most of them never fulfilled their tenure due to constant intrigue, military coups, and assassinations. Yet the system provided considerable stability, security for the population, and wealth and prestige for the regency. These factors probably account for its durability; the line of deys governed uninterruptedly from the late 1600s to 1830.

Outside of Algiers and its hinterland, authority was delegated to local chiefs and religious leaders, who were responsible for tax collection and remittances to the dey's treasury. The chiefs were kept in line with generous subsidies. It was a system well adapted to the fragmented society of Algeria and one that enabled a small military group to rule a large territory at relatively little cost.[2]

The French Conquest

In 1827, the dey of Algiers, enraged at the French government's refusal to pay an old debt incurred during Napoleon's wars, struck the French consul on the shoulder with a fly-whisk in the course of an interview. The king of France, Charles X, demanded an apology for the "insult" to his representative. None was forthcoming, so the French blockaded the port of Algiers in retaliation. But the dey continued to keep silent. In 1830, a French army landed on the coast west of the city, marched overland, and entered it with almost no resistance. The dey surrendered and went into exile.[3]

The French, who had been looking for an excuse to expand their interests in North Africa, now were not sure what to do with Algiers. The overthrow of the despotic Charles X in favor of a constitutional monarchy in France confused the situation even further. But the Algerians considered the French worse than the Turks, who were at least fellow Muslims. In the 1830s, they rallied behind their first national leader, Emir Abd al-Qadir.

Abd al-Qadir was the son of a prominent religious leader and, more important, was a descendant of the Prophet Muhammad. Abd al-Qadir had unusual qualities of leadership, military skill, and physical courage. From 1830 to 1847, he carried on guerrilla warfare against a French army of more than 100,000 men with such success that at one point the French signed a formal treaty recognizing him as head of an Algerian nation in the interior. Abd al-Qadir described his strategy in a prophetic letter to the king of France:

> France will march forward, and we shall retire. But France will find it necessary to retire, and we shall return. We shall weary and harry you, and our climate will do the rest.[4]

In order to defeat Abd al-Qadir, the French commander used "total war" tactics, burning villages, destroying crops, killing livestock, and levying fines on peoples who continued to support the emir. These measures, called "pacification" by France, finally succeeded. In 1847, Abd al-Qadir surrendered to French authorities. He was imprisoned for several years, in violation of a solemn commitment, and was then released by Emperor Napoleon III. He spent the rest of his life in exile.

Although he did not succeed in his quest, Abd al-Qadir is venerated as the first

Algerian nationalist, able by his leadership and Islamic prestige to unite warring groups in a struggle for independence from foreign control. Abd al-Qadir's green and white flag was raised again by the Algerian nationalists during the second war of independence (1954–1962), and it is the flag of the republic today.

Algérie Française

After the defeat of Abd al-Qadir, the French gradually brought all of present-day Algerian territory under their control. The Kabyles, living in the rugged mountain region east of Algiers, were the last to submit. The Kabyles had submitted in 1857, but they rebelled in 1871 after a series of decrees by the French government had made all Algerian Muslims subjects but not citizens, giving them a status inferior to French and other European settlers.

The Kabyle rebellion had terrible results, not only for the Kabyles but for all Algerian Muslims. More than a million acres of Muslim lands were confiscated by French authorities and sold to European settlers. A special code of laws was enacted to treat Algerian Muslims differently from Europeans, with severe fines and sentences for such "infractions" as insulting a European or wearing shoes in public. (It was assumed that a Muslim caught wearing shoes had stolen them.)

In 1871, Algeria legally became a French department. But in terms of exploitation of natives by settlers, it may as well have remained a colony. One author notes that "the desire to make a settlement colony out of an already populated area led to a policy of driving the indigenous people out of the best arable lands."[5] Land confiscation was only part of the exploitation of Algeria by the *colons* (French settlers). They developed a modern Algerian agriculture integrated into the French economy, providing France with much of its wine, citrus, olives, and vegetables. Colons owned 30 percent of the arable land and 90 percent of the best farmland. Special taxes were imposed on the Algerian Muslims; the colons were exempted from paying most taxes.

The political structure of Algeria was even more favorable to the European minority. The colons were well represented in the French National Assembly, and their representatives made sure that any reforms or laws intended to improve the living conditions or rights of the Algerian Muslim population would be blocked.

In fairness to the colons, it must be pointed out that many of them had come to Algeria as poor immigrants and worked hard to improve their lot and to develop the country. By 1930, the centenary of the French conquest, many colon families had lived in Algiers for two generations or more. Colons had drained malarial swamps south of Algiers and developed the Mitidja, the country's most fertile region. A fine road and rail system linked all parts of the country, and French public schools served all cities and towns. Algiers even had its own university, a branch of the Sorbonne. It is not surprising that to the colons, Algeria was their country, "Algérie Française." Throughout Algeria they rebaptized Algerian cities with names like Orléansville and Philippeville, with paved French streets, cafes, bakeries, and little squares with flower gardens and benches where old men in berets dozed in the hot sun.

Jules Cambon, governor general of Algeria in the 1890s, once described the country as having "only a dust of people left here." What he meant was that the ruthless treatment of the Algerians by the French during the pacification had deprived them of their natural leaders. A group of leaders developed slowly in Algeria, but it was made up largely of *evolués*—persons who had received French educations, spoke French better than Arabic, and accepted French citizenship as the price of status.[6]

Other Algerians, several hundred thousand of them, served in the French Army in the two world wars. Many of them became aware of the political rights that they were supposed to have but did not. Still others, religious leaders and teachers, were influenced by the Arab nationalist movement for independence from foreign control in Egypt and other parts of the Middle East.

Until the 1940s, the majority of the evolués and other Algerian leaders did not want independence. They wanted full assimilation with France and Muslim equality with the colons. Ferhat Abbas, a French-trained pharmacist who was the spokesman for the evolués, said in 1936 that he did not believe that there was such a thing as an Algerian nation separate from France.

Abbas and his associates changed their minds after World War II. In 1943, they had presented to the French government a manifesto demanding full political and legal equality for Muslims with the colons. It was blocked by colon leaders, who feared that they would be drowned in a Muslim sea. On May 8, 1945, the date of the Allied victory over Nazi Germany, a parade of Muslims celebrating the event but also demanding equality led to violence in the city of Sétif. Several colons were killed; in retaliation, army troops and groups of colon vigilantes swept through Muslim neighborhoods, burning houses and slaughtering thousands of Muslims. From then on, Muslim leaders believed that independence through armed struggle was the only choice left to them.

The War for Independence

November 1 is an important holiday in France. It is called Toussaint (All Saints' Day). On that day, French people remember and honor all the many saints in the pantheon of French Catholicism. It is a day devoted to reflection and staying at home.

In the years after the Sétif massacre, there had been scattered outbreaks of violence in Algeria, some of them created by the so-called Secret Organization (OS), which had developed an extensive network of cells in preparation for armed insurrection. In 1952, French police accidentally uncovered the network and jailed most of its leaders. One of them, a former French Army sergeant named Ahmed Ben Bella, subsequently escaped and went to Cairo, Egypt.

As the day of Toussaint 1954 neared, Algeria seemed calm. But appearances were deceptive. Earlier in the year, nine former members of the OS had laid plans in secret for armed revolution. They divided Algeria into six *wilayas* (departments), each with a military commander. They also planned a series of coordinated attacks for the early morning hours of November 1, when the French population would be asleep and the police preparing for a holiday. Bombs exploded at French Army barracks, police stations, storage warehouses, telephone offices, and government buildings. The revolutionaries circulated leaflets in the name of the National Liberation Front (FLN), warning the French that they had acted to liberate Algeria from the colonialist yoke and calling on Algerian Muslims to join in the struggle to rebuild Algeria as a free Islamic state.

There were very few casualties as a result of the Toussaint attacks; for some time the French did not realize that they had a revolution on their hands. But as violence continued, regular army troops were sent to Algeria to help the hard-pressed police and the colons. Eventually there were 400,000 French troops in Algeria, as opposed to just 6,000 guerrillas. But the

Agriculture is important in raising the living standards of Algeria. These farmers are harvesting forage peas, which will be used for animal feed.

French consistently refused to consider the situation in Algeria a war. They called it a "police action." Others called it the "war without a name."[7] Despite their great numerical superiority, they were unable to defeat the FLN.

Elsewhere the French tried various tactics. They divided the country into small sectors, with permanent garrisons for each sector. They organized mobile units to track down the guerrillas in caves and hideouts. About 2 million villagers were moved into barbed-wire "regroupment camps," with a complete dislocation of their way of life, in order to deny the guerrillas the support of the population.

The war was settled not by military action but by political negotiations. The French people and government, worn down by the effects of World War II and their involvement in Indochina, grew sick of the slaughter, the plastic bombs exploding in public places (in France as well as Algeria), and the brutality of the army in dealing with guerrilla prisoners. A French newspaper editor expressed the general feeling: "Algeria is ruining the spring. This land of sun and earth has never been so near us. It invades our hearts and torments our minds."[8]

The colons and a number of senior French Army officers were the last to give up their dream of an Algeria that would be forever French. Together the colons and the army forced a change in the French government. General Charles de Gaulle, the French wartime resistance hero, returned to power after a dozen years in retirement. But de Gaulle, a realist, had no intention of keeping Algeria forever French. He began secret negotiations with FLN leaders for Algerian independence.

By 1961 the battlefield had extended into metropolitan France, with plastic bombs set off in cafés and other public places, killing hundreds of people. On its side, the French military routinely used torture and gang-style executions without trial to crush the rebellion. Some 3,000 of those arrested simply disappeared.[9] Clashes between FLN fighters and those of its rival, the Algerian Nationalist Movement, caused further disruptions. In October, the shooting of Paris police officers led to the deaths of several hundred Algerians by the police during a peaceful protest march (an error not revealed by the French government until its archives for the period were opened in 1999).

Subsequently, colon and dissident military leaders united in a last effort to keep Algeria French. They staged an uprising against de Gaulle in Algiers, seizing government buildings and demanding his removal from office. But the bulk of the French Army remained loyal to him.

An attempted assassination of the French president in 1962 was unsuccessful. The colon–military alliance, calling itself the Secret Army Organization (OAS), then launched a savage campaign of violence against the Muslim population, gunning down people or shooting them at random on streets and in public markets. The OAS expected that the FLN would break the cease-fire in order to protect its own people. But it did not do so.

THE AGONY OF INDEPENDENCE

With the collapse of the OAS campaign against the FLN as well as its own government, the way was clear for Algeria to become an independent nation for the first time in its history. This became a reality on July 5, 1962, with the signing of a treaty with France. However, few modern nations have become self-governing with so many handicaps. Several hundred thousand people—French, Algerian Muslims, men, women, and children—were casualties of the conflict. An even more painful loss was the departure of the entire European community. Panicked colons and their families boarded overcrowded ships to cross the Mediterranean, most of them to France, a land they knew only as visitors. Nearly all of the skilled workers, managers, landowners, and professionals in all fields were French, and they had done little to train Algerian counterparts.

The new Algerian government was also affected by factional rivalries among its leaders. The French writer Alexis de Tocqueville once wrote, "In rebellion, as in a novel, the most difficult part to invent is the end." The FLN revolutionaries had to invent a new system, one that would bring dignity and hope to people dehumanized by 130 years of French occupation and eight years of savage war.

The first leader to emerge from intraparty struggle to lead the nation was Ahmed Ben Bella, who had spent the war in exile in Egypt but had great prestige as the political brains behind the FLN. Ben Bella laid the groundwork for an Algerian political system centered on the FLN as a single legal political party, and in September 1963, he was elected president. Ben Bella introduced a system of *autogestion* (workers' self-management), by which tenant farmers took over the management of farms abandoned by their colon owners and restored them to production as cooperatives. Autogestion became the basis

United Nations Photo (UN102110)

The rapid growth in the population of Algeria, coupled with urban migration, has created a serious housing shortage, as this crowded apartment building in Algiers testifies.

for Algerian socialism—the foundation of development for decades.

Ben Bella did little else for Algeria, and he alienated most of his former associates with his ambitions for personal power. In June 1965, he was overthrown in a military coup headed by the defense minister, Colonel Houari Boumedienne. Ben Bella was sentenced to house arrest for 15 years; he was pardoned and exiled in 1980. While in exile, he founded the Movement for a Democratic Algeria, in opposition to the regime. In 1990, he returned to Algeria and announced plans to lead a broad-based opposition party in the framework of the multiparty system. He retired from political and public life in 1997, and the Movement was dissolved.

Boumedienne declared that the coup was a "corrective revolution, intended to reestablish authentic socialism and put an end to internal divisions and personal rule."[10] The government was reorganized under

a Council of the Revolution, all military men, headed by Boumedienne, who subsequently became president of the republic. After a long period of preparation and gradual assumption of power by the reclusive and taciturn Boumedienne, a National Charter (Constitution) was approved by voters in 1976. The Charter defined Algeria as a socialist state with Islam as the state religion, basic citizens' rights guaranteed, and leadership by the FLN as the only legal political party. A National Popular Assembly (the first elected in 1977) was responsible for legislation.

In theory, the Algerian president had no more constitutional powers than the U.S. president. However, in practice, Boumedienne was the ruler of the state, being president, prime minister, and commander of the armed forces rolled into one. In November 1978, he became ill from a rare blood disease; he died in December. For a time, it appeared that factional rivalries

would again split the FLN, especially as Boumedienne had named neither a vice-president nor a prime minister, nor had he suggested a successor.

The Algeria of 1978 was a very different nation from that of 1962. The scars of war had mostly healed. The FLN closed ranks and named Colonel Chadli Bendjedid to succeed Boumedienne as president for a five-year term. In 1984, Bendjedid was reelected. But the process of ordered socialist development was abruptly and forcibly interrupted in October 1988. A new generation of Algerians, who had come of age long after the war for independence, took to the streets, protesting high prices, lack of jobs, inept leadership, a bloated bureaucracy, and other grievances.

The riots accelerated the process of Algeria's "second revolution" toward political pluralism and dismantling of the single-party socialist system. President Bendjedid initially declared a state of emergency; and for the first time since independence, the army was called in to restore order. Some 500 people were killed in the rioting, most of them jobless youths. But the president moved swiftly to mobilize the nation in the wake of the violence. In a national referendum, voters approved changes in the governing system to allow political parties to form outside the FLN. Another constitutional change, also effective in 1989, made the cabinet and prime minister responsible to the National Assembly.

The president retained his popularity during the upheaval and was reelected for a third term, winning 81 percent of the votes. A number of new parties were formed in 1989 to contest future Assembly elections. They represented a variety of political and social positions. Thus, the People's Movement for Algerian Renewal advocated a "democratic Algeria, representative of moderate Islam," while the National Algerian Party, more fundamentalist in its views, had a platform of full enforcement of Islamic law and the creation of 2 million new jobs. The Socialist Forces Front (FFS), founded many years earlier by exiled FLN leader Hocine Ait Ahmed, resurfaced with a manifesto urging Algerians to support "the irreversible process of democracy."

For its part, the government sought to revitalize the FLN as a genuine mass party on the order of the Tunisian Destour, while insisting that it would not duplicate its neighbor country's *démocratie de façade* but would instead embark on real political reforms. Recruitment of new members was extended to rural areas. Although press freedom was confirmed in the constitutional changes approved by the voters, control of the major newspapers and media was shifted from the government to the FLN, to provide greater exposure.

FOREIGN POLICY

During the first decade of independence, Algeria's foreign policy was strongly nationalistic and anti-Western. Having won their independence from one colonial power, the Algerians were vocally hostile toward the United States and its allies, calling them enemies of popular liberation. Algeria supported revolutionary movements all over the world, providing funds, arms, and training. The Palestine Liberation Organization, rebels against Portuguese colonial rule in Mozambique, Muslim guerrillas fighting the Christian Ethiopian government in Eritrea—all benefited from active Algerian support.

The government broke diplomatic relations with the United States in 1967, due to American support for Israel, and did not restore them for a decade. In the mid-1970s, Algeria moderated its anti-Western stance in favor of nonalignment and good relations with both East and West. Relations improved thereafter to such a point that Algerian mediators were instrumental in resolving the 1979–1980 American hostage crisis in Iran, since Iran regarded Algeria as a suitable mediator—Islamic yet nonaligned. However, Algeria's subsequent alignment with Iraq (in sympathy for Iraq as a fellow-Arab state) during the Iran–Iraq War caused a break in diplomatic relations with the Islamic Republic. They were not restored until 2000.

Until recently, Algeria's relations with Morocco were marked by suspicion, hostility, and periodic conflict. The two countries clashed briefly in 1963 over ownership of iron mines near Tindouf, on the border. Algeria also supported the Western Saharan nationalist movement fighting for independence for the former Spanish colony against Moroccan occupation. After Morocco annexed the territory, Algeria provided bases, sanctuary, funds, and weapons to the Polisario Front, the military wing of the movement. The Bendjedid government recognized the self-declared Sahrawi Arab Democratic Republic in 1980 and sponsored SADR membership in the Organization for African Unity (OAU).

Algeria's own economic difficulties plus the slow progress led by Bouteflika from military to civilian leadership and restoration of the parliamentary system helped reduce support for the Polisario. The Polisario office in Algiers was ordered closed. However the government continued its economic support for the 80,000 to 160,000 Sahrawis (even these figures are disputed) crowded into refugee camps in its Saharan territory.

THE ECONOMY

Algeria's oil and gas resources were developed by the French. Commercial production and exports began in 1958 and continued through the war for independence; they were not affected, since the Sahara was governed under a separate military administration. The oil fields were turned over to Algeria after independence but continued to be managed by French technicians until 1970, when the industry was nationalized.

During President Boumedienne's period in office, all sectors of the Algerian economy were governed under the 1976 National Charter. This document set forth provisions for national development under a uniquely Algerian form of state socialism. However, persistent economic difficulties caused by a combination of lower oil prices and global oversupply led the Bendjedid government to scrap the Charter. Since then, Algeria has borrowed heavily and regularly from international lenders to pay for continued industrial growth.

After a number of years of negative economic growth, the government initiated an austerity program in 1992. Imports of luxury products were prohibited and several new taxes introduced. The program was approved by the International Monetary Fund, Algeria's main source of external financing. In 1995, the IMF loaned $1.8 billion to cover government borrowing up to 60 percent under the approved austerity program to make the required "structural adjustment." In August of that year, the Paris Club—the international consortium that manages most of Algeria's foreign indebtedness—rescheduled $7 billion of the country's foreign debts due in 1996–1997, including interest payments, to ease the strain on the economy.

The agricultural sector employs 47 percent of the labor force and accounts for 12 percent of gross domestic product. But inasmuch as Algeria must import 70 percent of its food, better agricultural production is essential to overall economic development. Overall agricultural production growth has averaged 5 percent annually since 1990. The autogestion system introduced as a stop-gap measure after independence and enshrined later in FLN economic practice, when it seemed to work, was totally abandoned. In 1988, some 3,500 state farms were converted to collective farms, with individuals holding title to lands.

The key features of Bouteflika's economic reform program, one designed to attract foreign investment, include banking reforms, reduction of the huge government

bureaucracy, favorable terms for foreign companies and privatization of state-owned enterprises. The telecommunications industry was privatized in 2000 and the government-owned cement and steel industries in 2002.

Privatization of state-owned enterprises is a key feature of the government's plan to attract foreign investment. The telecommunications sector was privatized in August 2000, and some 200 other public enterprises were in process of transfer to private ownership.

THE FUNDAMENTALIST CHALLENGE

Despite the growing appeal of Islamic fundamentalism in numerous Arab countries in recent years, Algeria until very recently seemed an unlikely site for the rise of a strong fundamentalist movement. The country's long association with France, its lack of historic Islamic identity as a nation, and several decades of single-party socialism militated against such a development. But the failure of successive Algerian governments to resolve severe economic problems, plus the lack of representative political institutions nurtured within the ruling FLN, brought about the rise of fundamentalism as a political. Fundamentalists took an active part in the 1988 riots; and with the establishment of a multiparty system, they organized a political party, the Islamic Salvation Front (FIS). It soon claimed 3 million adherents among the then 25 million Algerians.

FIS candidates won 55 percent of urban mayoral and council seats in the 1989 local and municipal elections. The FLN conversely managed to hold on to power largely in the rural areas. Fears that FIS success might draw army intervention and spark another round of revolutionary violence led the government to postpone for six months the scheduled June 1991 elections for an enlarged 430-member National People's Assembly. An interim government, under the technocrat prime minister Sid Ahmed Ghozali, was formed to oversee the transition process.

HEALTH/WELFARE

The 1984 Family Law improved women's rights in marriage, education and work opportunities. But professional women and, more recently, rural women and their children have become special targets of Islamic violence. Some 400 professional women were murdered in 1995 and more than 400 were killed in a one-day rampage in January 1998.

In accordance with President Bendjedid's commitment to multiparty democracy, the first stage of Assembly elections took place on December 26, 1991, with FIS candidates winning 188 out of 231 contested seats. But before the second stage could take place, the army stepped in. FIS leaders were arrested, and the elections were postponed indefinitely. President Bendjedid resigned on January 17, 1992, well ahead of the expiration (in 1993) of his third five-year term. He said that he did so as a sacrifice in the interest of restoring stability to the nation and preserving democracy. Mohammed Boudiaf, one of the nine historic chiefs of the Revolution, returned from years of exile in Morocco to become head of the Higher Council of State, set up by military leaders after the abortive elections and resignation of President Bendjedid. FIS headquarters was closed and the party declared illegal by a court in Algiers. Local councils and provincial assemblies formed by the FIS after the elections were dissolved and replaced by "executive delegations" appointed by the Higher Council.

Subsequently, Boudiaf named a 60-member Consultative Council to work with the various political factions to reach a consensus on reforms. However, the refusal of such leaders as former president Ben Bella and Socialist Forces Front (FFS) leader Hocine Ait Ahmed to participate limited its effectiveness. Boudiaf was also suspected of using it to build a personal power base. On June 29, 1992, he was assassinated,

reportedly by a member of his own presidential guard.

With Boudiaf gone, Algeria's generals turned to their own ranks for new leadership. In 1994, General Liamine Zeroual, the real strongman of the regime, was named head of state by the Higher Council. Zeroual pledged that elections for president would be held in November 1995 as a first step toward the restoration of parliamentary government. The top FIS leaders, Abbas Madani and Ali Belhaj, who had been given 12-year jail sentences for "endangering state security" were released but had their sentences commuted to house arrest, on the assumption that in return for dialogue, they would call a halt to the spiraling violence.

However, the dialogue proved inconclusive, and Zeroual declared that the presidential elections would be held on schedule. Earlier, leaders of the FIS, FFS, FLN, and several smaller parties had met in Rome, Italy, under the sponsorship of Sant-Egidio, a Catholic service agency, and announced a "National Contract." It called for the restoration of FIS political rights in return for an end to violence, multiparty democracy, and exclusion of the military from government. The Algerian "personality" was defined in the Contract as Islamic, Arab, and Berber.

Military leaders rejected the National Contract out of hand, due to the FIS's participation. However, the November 1995 presidential election was held as scheduled, albeit under massive army protection—soldiers were stationed within 65 feet of every polling place. Zeroual won handily, as expected, garnering 61 percent of the votes. But the fact that the election was held at all, despite a boycott call by several party leaders and threats of violence from the Armed Islamic Group (GIA), was impressive.[11]

THE KILLING FIELDS

Algeria's modern history has been well described as one of excesses. Thus "the colonial period was unusually harsh, the war for independence particularly costly . . . . the insistence on one-party rule initially unwavering and the projects for industrialization overly ambitious," as specialists on the country have noted.[12] Extremes of violence are nothing new in Algerian life. But in addition to horrifying violence, the real tragedy of the conflict has been to pit "an inflexible regime and a fanatical opposition" against "innocent victims doomed by their secular lifestyle or their piety."[13]

Shortly before the 1995 election, Ahmed Ben Bella, Algeria's first president and the leader of the now-dissolved Movement for a Democratic Algeria, wrote a thoughtful analysis of the "dialogue at Rome" in which he had participated and that pro-

duced the National Contract. He noted: "A mad escalation of violence is the hallmark of everyday life. Nobody is safe: journalists, intellectuals, women, children and old people are all equally threatened. Yet the use of force, the recourse to violence, will not allow any of the protagonists to solve the problem to their advantage, and the solution must be a political one." The dialogue at Rome, he added, "was meant to lead to a consensus that would bring together everyone—including the regime in power—within the framework of the current Constitution, which stipulates political pluralism, democracy, respect for all human rights and freedoms."[14]

The conflict between the armed wing of the FIS, the Armed Islamic Group (GIA), and the military regime reached a level of violence in the period after the 1995 "election" that left no room for compromise. The GIA targeted not only the army and police but also writers, journalists, government officials and other public figures, professional women, even doctors and dentists. Ironically, one of its victims was the head of the Algerian League for Human Rights, which had protested the detention without trial of some 9,000 FIS members in roofless prisons deep in the Sahara, under unbelievably harsh conditions.

The GIA widened its circle of violence in the rest of the decade and on into the new century. In addition to Algerians it carried out attacks on foreigners, killing tourists as well as long-term foreign residents, notably Trappist monks. Rural villages were a favorite target, since they had neither police nor army protection. Entire village populations were massacred in a manner eerily reminiscent of the war for independence. The army and security forces did their share of killings, often arresting people and holding them indefinitely without charges. In 2003 the international organization Human Rights Watch reported that in addition to 120,000 deaths, some 7,000 persons had simply disappeared, never to be seen again by their families.

ACHIEVEMENTS

A new pipeline from the vast Hassi Berkine oil field, the African continent's largest, went into production in 1998, with exports of 300,000 barrels per day. Increased foreign investment due to expansion of the hydrocarbons sector, privatization of state-owned enterprises, and favorable terms for foreign companies increased GDP growth to 5 percent in 2001, with small annual increases thereafter, reaching 5.6 percent in 2006.

As the violence continued, the GIA also attacked foreigners, killing among others seven Trappist monks and the bishop of Oran. Rural villages were a favorite target since they lacked police or army protection. Men, women, and children in these villages were massacred under conditions of appalling brutality. A UN Human Rights subcommittee visited the country in 2000 and reported that the GIA and government troops were almost equally responsible for the casualties.

Through two referenda, President Bouteflika enacted two amnesty programs (2000 and 2005) that allowed Islamic militants who did not commit blood crimes to give up the fight and surrender their weapons without being prosecuted. The Islamic Army of Salvation (AIS), one of the largest armed groups, was first to take advantage of the new law. Thousands of fighters accepted the amnesty deal and hundreds more were freed from jail while several exiled leaders returned to the country. The Salafist Group for Preaching and Combat (GSPC) is a small ultra-conservative faction which rejected the amnesty deal. It still seeks radical change through violence and occasionally attacks military and civilian targets. In a probable survival effort, it officially declared in January 2007 that it had become part of al-Qaeda and renamed itself al-Qaeda in the Islamic Land of the Maghreb.

WHAT PRICE DIALOGUE?

The "colonial legacy" that France bequeathed to Algeria in over a century of effort to make the country an outpost of French culture and values continues to hamper the development of a specifically Algerian identity, one which is primarily Muslim and Arab. However, progress toward this goal is undermined by France's status as Algeria's main trading partner and the favorite destination in Europe for Algerian emigrants. (Some 700,000 emigrated there in 2004–2005). The 1962 constitution defines the country as Arab and Islamic. Its lack of success in building a strong economy, a vigorous multi-party political system and a sense of national pride in Algerian accomplishments has prompted rethinking, particularly among intellectuals, about their French heritage. Historian James McDougall observed recently that "French is coming back. For social mobility you need French." Another scholar commented that "Algeria has had to create itself without a sense of its Algerian-ness."[15,16]

Zeroual next set June 5, 1997, for elections to the 380-member Assembly, the first national election since the abortive 1992 one. Despite a meager 65.5 percent voter turnout due to fears of violence, Zeroual's newly formed party, the National Democratic Rally, won 115 seats. Along with the FLN's 64 seats, the results gave the regime a slim majority.

Two "moderate" Islamist parties (so called because they rejected violence) also participated in the elections. The Movement for a Peaceful Society ran second to the government party, with 69 seats; and An-Nahdah won 34 seats, giving at least a semblance of opposition in the Assembly. The first local and municipal elections in Algeria's modern history were held in 1997 as well, continuing the trend as government-backed candidates won the majority of offices.

In 1999, Zeroual resigned and scheduled open presidential elections for April. Seven candidates filed; they included former foreign minister Abdelaziz Bouteflika, who had lived in Switzerland for many years. Subsequently all the other candidates withdrew, citing irregularities in the election process. But the election went off as scheduled, and Bouteflika was declared the winner, with 74 percent of the vote. The names of the other candidates remained on the ballot (the two "moderate" Islamist candidates received 17 percent of the vote).

Bouteflika's good intentions and early success became mired in 2000 and 2001, however, in a power struggle with military leaders. And with neither the campaign against the GIA nor moves toward reconciliation with the Islamists yielding much in the way of results, the Algerian people have become more disillusioned than ever.

Recent riots in Kabylia have compounded Bouteflika's difficulties. The Berber people of that region have chafed since independence against Arab political and economic domination, and have fought to preserve their culture and language. The death of a young Berber while in police custody sparked riots during April and May 2001, which soon spread over the whole country. Rioters clashed with police in Bejaia and Tizi Ouzou, the regional capitals, after heavy-handed police actions had killed some 80 persons. The crackdown generated public criticism abroad, particularly in France, where a government spokesman condemned "the violence of the repression" and urged a peaceful dialogue with the Berber population.

Another blow to the embattled regime came with the walkout from the Assembly of members of the Rally for Culture and Democracy (RCD), the main Berber party represented in the ruling coalition.

1518–1520
Establishment of the Regency of Algiers

1827–1830
The French conquest, triggered by the "fly-whisk incident"

1847
The defeat of Abd al-Qadir by French forces

1871
Algeria becomes an overseas department of France

1936
The Blum-Viollette Plan, for Muslim rights, is annulled by colon opposition

1943
Ferhat Abbas issues the Manifesto of the Algerian People

1954–1962
Civil war, ending with Algerian independence

1965
Ben Bella is overthrown by Boumedienne

1976
The National Charter commits Algeria to revolutionary socialist development

1978
President Boumedienne dies

1980s
Land reform is resumed with the breakup of 200 large farms into smaller units; Arabization campaign

1990s
President Bendjedid steps down; the Islamic Salvation Front becomes a force and eventually is banned; the economy undergoes an austerity program; civil war

1999
Abdelaziz Bouteflika elected by voters as new president. Bicameral legislature elected with multi-party participation in 2001.

PRESENT

2000s
Efforts to restore the multiparty system; continued civil conflict

2005
Bouteflika issues Charter for Peace and Reconciliation approved in national referendum

Its leaders cited government failure to address Berber demands for official recognition of their language, affordable housing and job opportunities for youth as the main reasons for their withdrawal. Such issues as these, notably those of housing and jobs, affect the entire population. "Reconciliation, in my view, must protect us from experiencing once again the two evil phenomena of terrorist violence and extremism," Bouteflika said in his address to the nation.[17]

In May 2007 voters went to the polls for the third time since the abortive 1992 parliamentary elections. The FLN won a majority of seats, but the results were tainted by the fact that only 35.51 percent of the electorate participated. This lack of interest suggests that most Algerians have lost faith in the political process, parties and leaders, who have failed to address their pressing problems. Reports of recent visitors indicate that the main concerns for most Algerians today are the cost of living, security and their personal safety.

NOTES

1. See William Spencer, *Algiers in the Age of the Corsairs* (Norman, OK: University of Oklahoma Press, 1976), Centers of Civilization Series. "The corsair, if brought to justice in maritime courts, identified himself as *corsale* or *Korsan,* never as fugitive or criminal; his occupation was as clearly identifiable as that of tanner, goldsmith, potter or tailor," p. 47.

2. Raphael Danziger, *Abd al-Qadir and the Algerians* (New York: Holmes and Meier, 1977), notes that Turkish intrigue kept the tribes in a state of near-constant tribal warfare, thereby preventing them from forming dangerous coalitions, p. 24.

3. The usual explanation for the quick collapse of the regency after 300 years is that its forces were prepared for naval warfare but not for attack by land. *Ibid.,* pp. 36–38.

4. Quoted in Harold D. Nelson, *Algeria, A Country Study* (Washington, D.C.: American University, Foreign Area Studies, 1979), p. 31.

5. Marnia Lazreg, *The Emergence of Classes in Algeria* (Boulder, CO: Westview Press, 1976), p. 53.

6. For Algerian Muslims to become French citizens meant giving up their religion, for all practical purposes, since Islam recognizes only Islamic law and to be a French citizen means accepting French laws. Fewer than 3,000 Algerians became French citizens during the period of French rule. Nelson, *op. cit.,* pp. 34–35.

7. John E. Talbott, *The War Without a Name: France in Algeria, 1954–1962* (New York: Alfred A. Knopf, 1980).

8. Georges Suffert, in *Esprit,* 25 (1957), p. 819.

9. The opening of French historical archives in 1999 and recent interviews with leading generals in Algiers at the time, such as Jacques Massu, have reopened debate in France about the conduct of the war. In December 2000, members of the French Communist Party, which had backed the FLN, urged formation of a special commission to investigate charges of torture and provide compensation for victims' families. Suzanne Daley, in *The New York Times* (December 30, 2000). Retired general Paul Aussarress was fined $6,500 in 2001 for his 1999 book, *Algeria Special Forces 1955–1957,* in which he admitted the torture and execution of many Algerians and the disappearance of some 3,000 suspects while in custody; he was charged with "trying to justify war."

10. Nelson, *op. cit.,* p. 68.

11. Robert Mortimer, "Algeria: The Dialectic of Elections and Violence," *Current History* (May 1997), p. 232.

12. Frank Ruddy, who was assigned to Tindouf by the United Nations as a member of the observer group monitoring the referendum in the Western Sahara, comments on the town's national-history museum, "the one cultural attraction." However, "most of its space is devoted to especially grisly photos of terrible things the French did to Algerians during the Algerian war of independence." *The World & I* (August 1997), p. 138.

13. Robert Fisk, in *The Independent* (London) (March 16, 1995).

14. Ahmed Ben Bella, "A Time for Peace in Algeria," *The World Today* (November 1995), p. 209.

15. "Algerians' Awkward Embrace of France," by Jill Carroll. *Christian Science Monitor,* June 6, 2007.

16. Michael Slackman, *New York Times,* September 26, 2005.

17. Although the famed Casbah of Algiers, named by UNESCO as a World Heritage site, with its unique Ottoman-era architecture, is seriously threatened by neglect on the part of the Algerian government and its failure to carry out development under a U.S. government preservation development grant. See Joshua Hammer, "Saving the Casbah," *Smithsonian,* July 2007, pp. 34–42.

Egypt (Arab Republic of Egypt)

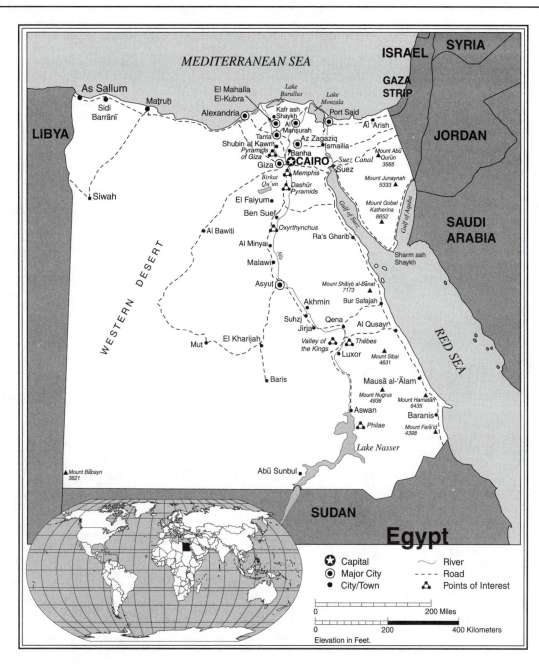

Egypt Statistics

GEOGRAPHY

Area in Square Miles (Kilometers): 386,258 (1,001,258) (about 3 times the size of New Mexico)

Capital (Population): Cairo (6,800,000)

Environmental Concerns: loss of agricultural land; increasing soil salinization; desertification; oil pollution threatening coral reefs and marine habitats; other water pollution; rapid population growth

Geographical Features: a vast desert plateau interrupted by the Nile Valley and Delta

Climate: desert; dry, hot summers; moderate winters

PEOPLE

Population

Total: 80,335,036

Annual Growth Rate: 1.7%

Rural/Urban Population Ratio: 55/45

Major Languages: Arabic; English widely used by educated classes

Ethnic Makeup: 99% Eastern Hamitic (Egyptian, Bedouin, Arab, Nubian); 1% others

Religions: 94% Muslim (mostly Sunni); 6% Coptic Christian and others

Health

Life Expectancy at Birth: 69 years (male), 74 years (female)

Infant Mortality Rate (Ratio): 29.5/1,000 live births

Education

Adult Literacy Rate: 59.7%

Compulsory (Ages): for 5 years between 6 and 13

COMMUNICATION

Telephones: 9,600,000 main lines
Daily Newspaper Circulation: 43 per 1,000 people
Televisions: 110 per 1,000 people
Internet Users: 4,200,000

TRANSPORTATION

Highways in Miles (Kilometers): 39,744 (64,000)
Railroads in Miles (Kilometers): 2,973 (4,955)
Usable Airfields: 92
Motor Vehicles in Use: 1,703,000

GOVERNMENT

Type: presidential republic
Independence Date: July 23, 1952, for the republic; February 28, 1922, marking the end of British rule
Head of State/Government: President Mohammed Hosni Mubarak; Prime Minister Ahmad Nazif

Political Parties: National Democratic Party (NDP), majority Party; approved opposition parties include New Wafd, National Progressive Unionist Group (Tagammu), Socialist Liberal Party. The Muslim Brotherhood is prohibited from functioning as a political party but its members take part in elections running as independents.
Suffrage: universal and compulsory at 18

MILITARY

Military Expenditures (% of GDP): 3.4%
Current Disputes: Sudan continues to claim the Egyptian-administered Hala'ib Triangle, a small territory north of The 22nd parallel of latitude. It was originally included in British-controlled Sudan in the 1899 treaty defining the Egyptian-Sudanese border.

ECONOMY

Currency: 5.725 Egyptian pounds = $1
Per Capita Income/GDP: $4,200/$328.1 billion

GDP Growth Rate: 5.7%
Inflation Rate: 6.5%
Unemployment Rate: 10.3%
Labor Force: 21,800,000 (note: a substantial number of Egyptian workers, especially skilled ones, are employed in nearby Arab countries)
Labor Force: 20,600,000
Natural Resources: petroleum; natural gas; iron ore; phosphates; manganese; limestone; gypsum; talc; asbestos; lead; zinc
Agriculture: cotton; sugarcane; rice; corn; wheat; beans; fruits; vegetables; livestock; fish
Industry: textiles; food processing; tourism; chemicals; petroleum; construction; cement; metals
Exports: $24.22 billion (primary partners United States, Italy, Spain)
Imports: $35.86 billion (primary partners United States, Germany, China)

SUGGESTED WEB SITE

http://lcweb2.loc.gov/frd/cs/ egtoc.htm

Egypt Country Report

The Arab Republic of Egypt is located at the extreme northeastern corner of Africa, with part of its territory—the Sinai Peninsula—serving as a land bridge to Southwest Asia. The country's total land area is approximately 386,000 square miles. However, 96 percent of this is uninhabitable desert. Except for a few scattered oases, the only settled and cultivable area is a narrow strip along the Nile River. The vast majority of Egypt's population is concentrated in this strip, resulting in high population density. Migration from rural areas to cities has intensified urban density; Cairo's population is currently 6.8 million, with millions more in the greater metropolitan area. It is a city that is literally "bursting at the seams."

Egypt today identifies itself as an Arab nation and is a founding member of the League of Arab States (which has its headquarters in Cairo). But its "Arab" identity is relatively new. It was first defined by the late president Gamal Abdel Nasser, who as a schoolboy became aware of his "Arabness" in response to British imperialism and particularly Britain's establishment of a national home for Jews in Arab Palestine. But Egypt's incredibly long history as a distinct society has given its people a separate Egyptian identity and a sense of superiority

over other peoples, notably desert people such as the Arabs of old.[1] Also, its development under British tutelage gave the country a headstart over other Arab countries or societies. Despite its people's overall low level of adult literacy, Egypt has more highly skilled professionals than do other Arab countries.

HISTORY

Although Egypt is a modern nation in terms of independence from foreign control, it has a distinct national identity and a rich culture that date back thousands of years. The modern Egyptians take great pride in their brilliant past; this sense of the past gives them patience and a certain fatalism that enable them to withstand misfortunes that would crush most peoples. The Egyptian peasants, the *fellahin,* are as stoic and enduring as the water buffaloes they use to do their plowing. Since the time of the pharaohs, Egypt has been invaded many times, and it was under foreign control for most of its history. When Nasser, the first president of the new Egyptian republic, came to power in 1954, he said that he was the first native Egyptian to rule the country in nearly 3,000 years.

It is often said that Egypt is the "gift of the Nile." The mighty river, flowing north

DEVELOPMENT

Egypt's GDP growth rate, which held steady at 4–5 percent in the 90s, was affected by external events, notably the 9/11 terrorist attacks in the U.S. and the 2003 invasion of Iraq. The tourist industry, which generates 12 percent of revenues, saw a downturn but rebounded strongly in the early 2000s. However multiple bomb-blasts at the Sharm El-Shaikh Red Sea resort and in Cairo in 2004–2005, the first in 7 years, posed a new threat to the industry. The Sharm El-Shaikh attack in particular killed 88 persons and injured 119, mostly Egyptians but some foreigners.

to the Mediterranean with an enormous annual spate that deposited rich silt along its banks, attracted nomadic peoples to settle there as early as 6000 B.C. They developed a productive agriculture based on the river's seasonal floods. They lived in plastered mud huts in small, compact villages. Their villages were not too different from those one sees today in parts of the Nile Delta.

Each village had its "headman," the head of some family more prosperous or industrious (or both) than the others. The arrival of other nomadic desert peoples

© Royalty-Free/CORBIS (DILCB015947)

These pyramids at Giza are among the most famous mementos of Egypt's past.

gradually brought about the evolution of an organized system of government. Since the Egyptian villagers did not have nearby mountains or wild forests to retreat into, they were easily governable.

The institution of kingship was well established in Egypt by 2000 B.C., and in the time of Ramses II (1300–1233 B.C.), Egyptian monarchs extended their power over a large part of the Middle East. All Egyptian rulers were called pharaohs, although there was no hereditary system of descent and many different dynasties ruled during the country's first 2,000 years of existence. The pharaohs had their capital at Thebes, but they built other important cities on the banks of the Nile. Recent research by Egyptologists indicate that the ancient Egyptians had an amazingly accurate knowledge of astronomy. The Pyramids of Giza, for example, were built so as to be aligned with true north. Lacking modern instruments, their builders apparently used two stars, Thaban and Draconis, in the Big Dipper, for their alignment, with a point equidistant from them to mark their approximation of true north. Only centuries later was the North Star identified as such. Recent excavations at the Great Pyramid of Giza indicate that some 2,500 years ago Egyptian builders used concrete technology in their work, mixing lime, sand and clay to form concrete blocks for both the outer and inner casings of this and other massive structures. The archaeological evidence suggests that concrete blocks, rather than the much heavier limestone

ones, would have enabled the builders to work much faster and thus speeded up construction.

Another important discovery, in November 1999, was that of inscriptions on the walls of *Wadi Hoi* ("Valley of Terror") that may well be the world's oldest written language, predating the cuneiform letters developed by the Sumerians in Mesopotamia.

In the first century B.C., Egypt became part of the Roman Empire. The city of Alexandria, founded by Alexander the Great, became a center of Greek and Roman learning and culture. Later, it became a center of Christianity. The Egyptian Coptic Church was one of the earliest organized churches. The Copts, direct descendants of the early Egyptians, are the principal minority group in Egypt today. (The name Copt comes from *aigyptos,* Greek for "Egyptian.") The Copts welcomed the Arab invaders who brought Islam to Egypt, preferring them to their oppressive Byzantine Christian rulers. Muslim rulers over the centuries usually protected the Copts as "Peoples of the Book," leaving authority over them to their religious leaders, in return for allegiance and payment of a small tax. But in recent years, the rise of Islamic fundamentalism has made life more difficult for Egypt's Coptic minority. Coptic-Muslim friction declined significantly in the 1990s, but the 10 million Copts continue to complain of petty discrimination (such as university admission) and political disenfranchisement. To its credit, the government has eased building restrictions on new churches and allowed

broadcasting of Christian services on state TV. Recently it restored property expropriated by the Nasser regime in 1950s to Coptic Church ownership.

THE INFLUENCE OF ISLAM

Islam was the major formative influence in the development of modern Egyptian society. Islamic armies from Arabia invaded Egypt in the seventh century A.D. Large numbers of nomadic Arabs followed, settling the Nile Valley until, over time, they became the majority in the population. Egypt was under the rule of the caliphs ("successors" of the Prophet Muhammad) until the tenth century, when a Shi'a group broke away and formed a separate government. The leaders of this group also called themselves caliphs. To show their independence, they founded a new capital in the desert south of Alexandria. The name they chose for their new capital was prophetic: *al-Qahira*—"City of War"—the modern city of Cairo.

In the sixteenth century, Egypt became a province of the Ottoman Empire. It was then under the rule of the Mamluks, originally slaves or prisoners of war who were converted to Islam. Many Mamluk leaders had been freed and then acquired their own slaves. They formed a military aristocracy, constantly fighting with one another for land and power. The Ottomans found it simpler to leave Egypt under Mamluk control, merely requiring periodic tribute and taxes.

EGYPT ENTERS THE MODERN WORLD

At the end of the eighteenth century, rivalry between Britain and France for control of trade in the Mediterranean and the sea routes to India involved Egypt. The French general Napoleon Bonaparte led an expedition to Egypt in 1798. However, the British, in cooperation with Ottoman forces, drove the French from Egypt. A confused struggle for power followed. The victor was Muhammad Ali, an Albanian officer in the Ottoman garrison at Cairo. In 1805, the Ottoman sultan appointed him governor of Egypt.

Although he was not an Egyptian, Muhammad Ali had a vision of Egypt under his rule as a rich and powerful country. He began by forming a new army consisting of native Egyptians instead of mercenaries or slave-soldiers. This army was trained by European advisers and gave a good account of itself in campaigns, performing better than the regular Ottoman armies.[2] His successor, Ismail, went a step further by hiring some 50 demobilized veterans of

Two young Egyptian boys gaze in wonder at the language of their ancestors, Karnak.

the American Civil War, both Yankees and rebels, who brought discipline and military experience to the training of Egyptian recruits. These mercenaries remained in Egypt after the end of the campaigns of Ismail and his successors in the Middle East, and when they died they were buried in the long-forgotten and neglected American cemetery in a corner of Cairo.

Muhammad Ali set up an organized, efficient tax-collection system. He suppressed the Mamluks and confiscated all the lands that they had seized from Egyptian peasants over the years, lifting a heavy tax burden from peasant backs. He took personal charge of all Egypt's exports. Cotton, a new crop, became the major Egyptian export and became known the world over for its high quality. Dams and irrigation canals were dug to improve cultivation and expand arable land. Although Muhammad Ali grew rich in the process of carrying out these policies, he was concerned for the welfare of the peasantry. He once said, "One must guide this people as one guides children; to leave them to their own devices

would be to render them subject to all the disorders from which I have saved them."[3]

Muhammad Ali's successors were named *khedives* ("viceroys"), in that they ruled Egypt in theory on behalf of their superior, the sultan. In practice, they acted as independent rulers. Under the khedives, Egypt was again drawn into European power politics, with unfortunate results. Khedive Ismail, the most ambitious of Muhammad Ali's descendants, was determined to make Egypt the equal of Western European nations. His major project was the Suez Canal, built by a European company and opened in 1869. The Italian composer Verdi was invited to compose the opera *Aida* for its inauguration. He refused to do so at first, saying that Egypt was a country whose civilization he did not admire. Eventually he was persuaded (with the help of the then-princely bonus of $20,000!) and set to music the ancient Egyptian legend of imperialism and grand passion. Verdi's task was eased by the fact that Auguste Mariette, the preeminent Egyptologist of the period, wrote the libretto and designed sets and

costumes with absolute fidelity to pharaonic times.

However, the expense of this and other grandiose projects bankrupted the country. Ismail was forced to sell Egypt's shares in the Suez Canal Company—to the British government!—and his successors were forced to accept British control over Egyptian finances. In 1882, a revolt of army officers threatened to overthrow the khedive. The British intervened and established a de facto protectorate, keeping the khedive in office in order to avoid conflict with the Ottomans.

EGYPTIAN NATIONALISM

The British protectorate lasted from 1882 to 1956. An Egyptian nationalist movement gradually developed in the early 1900s, inspired by the teachings of religious leaders and Western-educated officials in the khedives' government. They advocated a revival of Islam and its strengthening to enable Egypt and other Islamic lands to resist European control.

United Nations Photo (UN67110)

In 1952, the Free Officers organization persuaded Egypt's King Farouk to abdicate. The monarchy was formally abolished in 1954, when Gamal Abdel Nasser (pictured above) became Egypt's president, prime minister, and head of the Revolutionary Command Council.

During World War I, Egypt was a major base for British campaigns against the Ottoman Empire. The British formally declared their protectorate over Egypt in order to "defend" the country, since legally it was still an Ottoman province. The British worked with Arab nationalist leaders against the Turks and promised to help them form an independent Arab nation after the war. Egyptian nationalists were active in the Arab cause, and although at that time they did not particularly care about being a part of a new Arab nation, they wanted independence from Britain.

At the end of World War I, Egyptian nationalist leaders organized the *Wafd* (Arabic for "delegation"). In 1918, the Wafd presented demands to the British for the complete independence of Egypt. The British rejected the demands, saying that Egypt was not ready for self-government. The Wafd then turned to violence, organizing boycotts, strikes, and terrorist attacks on British soldiers and on Egyptians accused of cooperating with the British.

Under pressure, the British finally abolished the protectorate in 1922. But they retained control over Egyptian foreign policy, defense, and communications as well as the protection of minorities and foreign residents and of Sudan, which had been part of Egypt since the 1880s. Thus, Egypt's "independence" was a hollow shell.

Egypt did regain control over internal affairs. The government was set up as a constitutional monarchy under a new king, Fuad. Political parties were allowed, and in elections for a Parliament in 1923, the Wafd emerged as the dominant party. But nei-ther Fuad nor the son who succeeded him, Farouk, trusted Wafd leaders. They feared that the Wafd was working to establish a republic. For their part, the Wafd leaders did not believe that the rulers were seriously interested in the good of the country. So Egypt waddled along for two decades with little progress.

THE EGYPTIAN REVOLUTION

During the years of the monarchy, the Egyptian Army gradually developed a corps of professional officers, most of them from lower- or middle-class Egyptian backgrounds. They were strongly patriotic and resented what they perceived to be British cultural snobbery as well as Britain's continual influence over Egyptian affairs.

The training school for these young officers was the Egyptian Military Academy, founded in 1936. Among them was Gamal Abdel Nasser, the eldest son of a village postal clerk. Nasser and his fellow officers were already active in anti-British demonstrations by the time they entered the academy. During World War II, the British, fearing a German takeover of Egypt, reinstated the protectorate. Egypt became the main British military base in the Middle East. This action galvanized the officers into forming a revolutionary movement. Nasser said at the time that it roused in him the seeds of revolt. "It made [us] realize that there is a dignity to be retrieved and defended."[4]

When Jewish leaders in Palestine organized Israel in May 1948, Egypt, along with other nearby Arab countries, sent troops to destroy the new state. Nasser and several of his fellow officers were sent to the front. The Egyptian Army was defeated; Nasser himself was trapped with his unit, was wounded, and was rescued only by an armistice. Even more shocking to the young officers was the evident corruption and weakness of their own government. The weapons that they received were inferior and often defective, battle orders were inaccurate, and their superiors proved to be incompetent in strategy and tactics.

Nasser and his fellow officers attributed their defeat not to their own weaknesses but to their government's failures. When they returned to Egypt, they were determined to overthrow the monarchy. They formed a secret organization, the Free Officers. It was not the only organization dedicated to the overthrow of the monarchy, but it was the best disciplined and had the general support of the army.

On July 23, 1952, the Free Officers launched their revolution. It came six months after "Black Saturday," the burning of Cairo by mobs protesting the continued presence of British troops in Egypt. The Free Officers persuaded King Farouk to abdicate, and they declared Egypt a republic. A nine-member Revolutionary Command Council (RCC) was established to govern the country.

EGYPT UNDER NASSER

In his self-analytical book *The Philosophy of the Revolution,* Nasser wrote, "I always imagine that in this region in which we live there is a role wandering aimlessly about in search of an actor to play it."[5] Nasser saw himself as playing that role. Previously, he had operated behind the scenes, but always as the leader to whom the other Free Officers looked upto. By 1954, Nasser had emerged as Egypt's leader. When the monarchy was formally abolished in 1954, he became president, prime minister, and head of the RCC. Cynics said that Nasser came along when Egypt was ready for another king; the Egyptians could not function without one!

Nasser came to power determined to restore dignity and status to Egypt, to eliminate foreign control, and to make his country the leader of a united Arab world. It was an ambitious set of goals, and Nasser was only partly successful in attaining them. But in his struggles to achieve these goals, he brought considerable status to Egypt. The country became a leader of the "Third World" of Africa and Asia, developing nations newly freed from foreign control.

Nasser was successful in removing the last vestiges of British rule from Egypt. British troops were withdrawn from the Suez Canal Zone, and Nasser nationalized the canal in 1956, taking over the management from the private foreign company that had operated it since 1869. That action made the British furious, since the British government had a majority interest in the company. The British worked out a secret plan with the French and the Israelis, neither of whom liked Nasser, to invade Egypt and overthrow him. British and French paratroopers seized the canal in October 1956, but the United States and the Soviet Union, in an unusual display of cooperation, forced them to withdraw. It was the first of several occasions when Nasser turned military defeat into political victory. It was also one of the few times when Nasser and the United States were on the same side of an issue.

Between 1956 and 1967, Nasser developed a close alliance with the Soviet Union—at least, it seemed that way to the United States. Nasser's pet economic project was the building of a dam at Aswan, on the upper Nile, to regulate the annual flow of river water and thus enable Egypt to reclaim new land and develop its agriculture. He applied for aid from the United States through the World Bank to finance the project, but he was turned down, largely due to his publicly expressed hostility toward Israel. Again Nasser turned defeat into a victory of sorts. The Soviet Union agreed to finance the dam, which was completed in 1971, and subsequently to equip and train the Egyptian Army. Thousands of Soviet advisers poured into Egypt, and it seemed to U.S. and Israeli leaders that Egypt had become a dependency of the Soviet Union.

The lowest point in Nasser's career came in June 1967. Israel invaded Egypt and defeated his Soviet-trained army, along with those of Jordan and Syria, and occupied the Sinai Peninsula in a lightning six-day war. The Israelis were restrained from marching on Cairo only by a United Nations cease-fire. Nasser took personal responsibility for the defeat, calling it *al-Nakba* ("The Catastrophe"). He announced his resignation, but the Egyptian people refused to accept it. The public outcry was so great that he agreed to continue in office. One observer wrote, "The irony was that Nasser had led the country to defeat, but Egypt without Nasser was unthinkable."[6]

Nasser had little success in his efforts to unify the Arab world. One attempt, for example, was a union of Egypt and Syria, which lasted barely three years (1958–1961). Egyptian forces were sent to support a new republican government in Yemen after the overthrow of that country's autocratic ruler, but they became bogged down in a civil war there and had to be withdrawn. Other efforts to unify the Arab world also failed. Arab leaders respected Nasser but were unwilling to play second fiddle to him in an organized Arab state. In 1967, after the Arab defeat, Nasser lashed out bitterly at the other Arab leaders. He said, "You issue statements, but we have to fight. If you want to liberate [Palestine] then get in line in front of us."[7]

Inside Egypt, the results of Nasser's 18-year rule were also mixed. Although he talked about developing representative government, Nasser distrusted political parties and remembered the destructive rivalries under the monarchy that had kept Egypt divided and weak. The Wafd and all other political parties were declared illegal. Nasser set up his own political organization to replace them, called the Arab Socialist Union (ASU). It was a mass party, but it had no real power. Nasser and a few close associates ran the government and controlled the ASU. The associates took their orders directly from Nasser; they called him *El-Rais*—"The Boss."

As he grew older, Nasser, plagued by health problems, became more dictatorial,

secretive, and suspicious. The Boss tolerated no opposition and ensured tight control over Egypt with a large police force and a secret service that monitored activities in every village and town.

Nasser died in 1970. Ironically, his death came on the heels of a major policy success: the arranging of a truce between the Palestine Liberation Organization and the government of Jordan. Despite his health problems, Nasser had seemed indestructible, and his death came as a shock. Millions of Egyptians followed his funeral cortege through the streets of Cairo, weeping and wailing over the loss of their beloved Rais.

ANWAR AL-SADAT

Nasser was succeeded by his vice-president, Anwar al-Sadat, in accordance with constitutional procedure. Sadat had been one of the original Free Officers and had worked with Nasser since their early days at the Military Academy. In the Nasser years, Sadat had come to be regarded as a lightweight, always ready to do whatever The Boss wanted.

Many Egyptians did not even know what Sadat looked like. A popular story was told of an Egyptian peasant in from the country to visit his cousin, a taxi driver. As they drove around Cairo, they passed a large poster of Nasser and Sadat shaking hands. "I know our beloved leader, but who is the man with him?" asked the peasant. "I think he owns that café across the street," replied his cousin.

When Sadat became president, however, it did not take long for the Egyptian people to learn what he looked like. Sadat introduced a "revolution of rectification," which he said was needed to correct the errors of his predecessor.[8] These included too much dependence on the Soviet Union, too much government interference in the economy, and failure to develop an effective Arab policy against Israel. He was a master of timing, taking bold action at unexpected times to advance Egypt's international and regional prestige. Thus, in 1972 he abruptly ordered the 15,000 Soviet advisers in Egypt to leave the country, despite the fact that they were training his army and supplying all his military equipment. His purpose was to reduce Egypt's dependence on one foreign power, and as he had calculated, the United States now came to his aid.

A year later, in October 1973, Egyptian forces crossed the Suez Canal in a surprise attack and broke through Israeli defense lines in occupied Sinai. The attack was coordinated with Syrian forces invading Israel from the east, through the Golan Heights. The Israelis were driven back with heavy casualties on both fronts, and although they

United Nations Photo (UN122838)

Nasser died in 1970 and was succeeded by Vice-President Anwar al-Sadat. Sadat, initially virtually unknown by the Egyptian people, took many bold steps in cementing his role as leader of Egypt.

eventually regrouped and won back most of the lost ground, Sadat felt he had won a moral and psychological victory. After the war, Egyptians believed that they had held their own with the Israelis and had demonstrated Arab ability to handle the sophisticated weaponry of modern warfare. On the 25th anniversary of the 1973 October War, Egypt held its first military parade in 17 years, and 250 young couples were married in a mass public wedding ceremony at the Pyramids to remind the new generation—a third of the population are under age 15—of Egypt's great "victory."

Anwar al-Sadat's most spectacular action took place in 1977. It seemed to him that the Arab–Israeli conflict was at a stalemate. Neither side would budge from its position, and the Egyptian people were angry at having so little to show for the 1973 success. In November, he addressed a hushed meeting of the People's Assembly and said, "Israel will be astonished when it hears me saying . . . that I am ready to go to their own house, to the Knesset itself, to talk to them."[9] And he did so, becoming for a second time the "Hero of the Crossing,"[10] but this time to the very citadel of Egypt's enemy.

Sadat's successes in foreign policy, culminating in the 1979 peace treaty with Israel, gave him great prestige internationally. Receipt of the Nobel Peace Prize, jointly with Israeli prime minister Menachem Begin, confirmed his status as a peacemaker. His pipe-smoking affability and sartorial elegance endeared him to U.S. policymakers.

The view that more and more Egyptians held of their world-famous leader was less flattering. Religious leaders and conservative Muslims objected to Sadat's luxurious style of living. The poor resented having to pay more for basic necessities. The educated classes were angry about Sadat's claim that the political system had become more open and democratic when, in fact, it had not. The Arab Socialist Union was abolished and several new political parties were allowed to organize. But the ASU's top leaders merely formed their own party, the National Democratic Party, headed by Sadat. For all practical purposes, Egypt under Sadat was even more of a single-party state under an authoritarian leader than it had been in Nasser's time.

Sadat's economic policies also worked to his disadvantage. In 1974, he announced a new program for postwar recovery, *Infitah* ("Opening"). It would be an open-door policy, bringing an end to Nasser's state-run socialist system. Foreign investors would be encouraged to invest in Egypt, and foreign experts would bring their technological knowledge to help develop industries. Infitah, properly applied, would bring an economic miracle to Egypt.

Rather than spur economic growth, however, Infitah made fortunes for just a few, leaving the great majority of Egyptians no better off than before. Chief among those who profited were members of the Sadat family. Corruption among the small ruling class, many of its members newly rich contractors, aroused anger on the part of the Egyptian people. In 1977, the economy was in such bad shape that the government increased bread prices. Riots broke out, and Sadat was forced to cancel the increase.

On October 6, 1981, President Sadat and government leaders were reviewing an armed-forces parade in Cairo to mark the eighth anniversary of the Crossing. Suddenly, a volley of shots rang out from one of the trucks in the parade. Sadat fell, mortally wounded. The assassins, most of them young military men, were immediately arrested. They belonged to *Al Takfir Wal Hijra* ("Repentance and Flight from Sin"), a secret group that advocated the reestablishment of a pure Islamic society in Egypt—by violence, if necessary. Their leader declared that the killing of Sadat was an essential first step in this process.

Islamic fundamentalism developed rapidly in the Middle East after the 1979 Iranian Revolution. The success of that revolution was a spur to Egyptian fundamentalists. They accused Sadat of favoring Western capitalism through his Infitah policy, of making peace with the "enemy of Islam" (Israel), and of not being a good Muslim. At their trial, Sadat's assassins

said that they had acted to rid Egypt of an unjust ruler, a proper action under the laws of Islam.

Sadat may have contributed to his early death (he was 63) by a series of actions taken earlier in the year. About 1,600 people were arrested in September 1981 in a massive crackdown on religious unrest. They included not only religious leaders but also journalists, lawyers, intellectuals, provincial governors, and leaders of the country's small but growing opposition parties. Many of them were not connected with any fundamentalist Islamic organization. It seemed to most Egyptians that Sadat had overreacted, and at that point, he lost the support of the nation. In contrast to Nasser's funeral, few tears were shed at Sadat's. His funeral was attended mostly by foreign dignitaries. One of them said that Sadat had been buried without the people and without the army. In October 2006 Sadat's nephew Talaat was given a one-year jail sentence and stripped of his parliamentary immunity on charges he blamed the military for negligence in his uncle's death.[12]

MUBARAK IN POWER

Vice-President Hosni Mubarak, former Air Force commander and designer of Egypt's 1973 success against Israel, succeeded Sadat without incident. Mubarak dealt firmly with Islamic fundamentalism at the beginning of his regime. He was given emergency powers and approved death sentences for five of Sadat's assassins in 1982. But he moved cautiously in other areas of national life, in an effort to disassociate himself from some of Sadat's more unpopular policies. The economic policy of Infitah, which had led to widespread graft and corruption, was abandoned; stiff sentences were handed out to a number of entrepreneurs and capitalists, including Sadat's brother-in-law and several associates of the late president.

Mubarak also began rebuilding bridges with other Arab states that had been damaged after the peace treaty with Israel. Egypt was readmitted to membership in the Islamic Conference, the Islamic Development Bank, the Arab League, and other Arab regional organizations. In 1990, the Arab League headquarters was moved from Tunis back to Cairo, its original location. Egypt backed Iraq with arms and advisers in its war with Iran, but Mubarak broke with Saddam Hussein after the invasion of Kuwait, accusing the Iraqi leader of perfidy. Some 35,000 Egyptian troops served with the UN–U.S. coalition during the Gulf War; and as a result of these efforts, the country resumed its accustomed role as the focal point of Arab politics.

Despite the peace treaty, relations with Israel continued to be difficult. One bone of contention was removed in 1989 with the return of the Israeli-held enclave of Taba, in the Sinai Peninsula, to Egyptian control. It had been operated as an Israeli beach resort.

The return of Taba strengthened the government's claim that the 10-year-old peace treaty had been valuable overall in advancing Egypt's interests. The sequence of agreements between the Palestine Liberation Organization and Israel for a sovereign Palestinian entity, along with Israel's improved relations with its other Arab neighbors, contributed to a substantial thaw in the Egyptian "cold peace" with its former enemy. In March 1995, a delegation from Israel's Knesset arrived in Cairo, the first such parliamentary group to visit Egypt since the peace treaty.

But relations worsened after the election in 1996 of Benjamin Netanyahu as head of a new Israeli government. Egypt had strongly supported the Oslo accords for a Palestinian state, and it had set up a free zone for transit of Palestinian products in 1995. The Egyptian view that Netanyahu was not adhering to the accords led to a "war of words" between the two countries. Israeli tourists were discouraged from visiting Egypt or received hostile treatment when visiting Egyptian monuments, and almost no Egyptians opted for visits to Israel. The newspaper *Al-Ahram* even stopped carrying cartoons by a popular Israeli-American cartoonist because he had served in the Israeli Army. The two governments cooperated briefly in the return of a small Bedouin tribe, the Azazma, to its Egyptian home area in the Sinai. The tribe had fled into Israel following a dispute with another tribe that turned into open conflict.

The election of Ehud Barak as Israel's new prime minister was well received in Eygpt, notably due to his resumption of peace negotiations with the then-Palestinian leader Yassir Arafat. However the breakdown of those negotiations and Barak's defeat by Ariel Sharon in the 2000 Israeli elections re-established the "deep freeze" between the two countries. In 2004 President Mubarak declared Sharon incapable of making peace. However Israel's withdrawal from the Gaza Strip in 2005 helped improve Sharon's image in Egypt as peacemaker rather than butcher. One result was a prisoner swap. Mubarak released an Israeli Arab convicted of espionage in Egypt in return for 6 Egyptian students who had been studying in Israel.

Internal Politics

Although Mubarak's unostentatious lifestyle and firm leadership encouraged confidence among the Egyptian regime, the system that he inherited from his predecessors remained largely impervious to change. The first free multiparty national elections held since the 1952 Revolution took place in 1984—although they were not entirely free, because a law requiring political parties to win at least 8 percent of the popular vote limited party participation. Mubarak was reelected easily for a full six-year term (he was the only candidate), and his ruling National Democratic Party won 73 percent of seats in the Assembly. The New Wafd Party was the only party able to meet the 8 percent requirement.

New elections for the Assembly in 1987 indicated how far Egypt's embryonic democracy had progressed under Mubarak. This time, four opposition parties aside from his own party presented candidates. Although the National Democratic Party's plurality was still a hefty 69.6 percent, 17 percent of the electorate voted for opposition candidates. The New Wafd increased its percentage of the popular vote to 10.9 percent, and a number of Muslim Brotherhood members were elected as independents. The National Progressive Unionist Group, the most leftist of the parties, failed to win a seat.

Mubarak was re-elected for a fourth six-year term in 1999, receiving 94 percent of the vote, as 79 percent of the country's 24 million voters cast their ballots. Again, he was the only candidate. But in February 2005 he announced that henceforth Egypt's presidential elections would be multi-party, with other candidates allowed to run for the office. The voters subsequently "approved" this constitutional change, although only 27 percent actually did so.

In September Mubarak was re-elected for his fifth term in office against token opposition. (His main opponent, Ayman Nour, had been jailed earlier on charges seen generally to be politically motivated.) Elections followed in three stages for the 444-seat National Assembly (Parliament). The NDP won 311 seats, while its main opponent, the Muslim Brotherhood, although disallowed as a political party and its members required to run as independents, won 88.

FREEDOM

The Islamic fundamentalist challenge to Egypt's secular government has caused the erosion of many rights and freedoms enshrined in the country's Constitution. A state of emergency first issued in 1981 is still in effect; it was renewed in 2001 for a 3-year period. In June 2003 the Peoples' Assembly approved establishment of a National Council for Human Rights that would monitor violations or misuse of government authority.

AT WAR WITH FUNDAMENTALISM

Egypt's seemingly intractable social problems—high unemployment, an inadequate job market flooded annually by new additions to the labor force, chronic budgetary deficits, and a bloated and inefficient bureaucracy, to name a few—have played into the hands of Islamic fundamentalists, those who would build a new Egyptian state based on the laws of Islam. Although they form part of a larger fundamentalist movement in the Islamic world, one that would replace existing secular regimes with regimes that adhere completely to spiritual law and custom (Shari'a), Egypt's fundamentalists do not harbor expansionist goals. Their goal is to replace the Mubarak regime with a more purely "Islamic" one, faithful to the laws and principles of the religion and dominated by religious leaders.

Egypt's fundamentalists are broadly grouped under the organizational name al-Gamaa al-Islamiya, with the more militant ones forming subgroups such as the Vanguard of Islam and Islamic Jihad, itself an outgrowth of al-Takfir wal-Hijra, which had been responsible for the assassination of Anwar Sadat. Ironically, Sadat had formed Al-Gamaa to counter leftist political groups. However, it differs from its parent organization, the Muslim Brotherhood, in advocating the overthrow of the government by violence in order to establish a regime ruled under Islamic law. During Mubarak's first term, he kept a tight lid on violence. But in the 1990s, the increasing strength of the Islamists and their popularity with the large number of educated but unemployed youth led to an increase in violence and destabilized the nation.

Violence was initially aimed at government security forces, but starting in 1992, the fundamentalists' strategy shifted to vulnerable targets such as foreign tourists and the Coptic Christian minority. A number of Copts were killed and many Copt business owners were forced to pay "protection money" to al-Gamaa in order to continue in operation. Subsequently the Copts' situation improved somewhat, as stringent security measures were put in place to contain Islamic fundamentalist violence. Gun battles in 1999 between Muslim and Copt villagers in southern Egypt resulted in 200 Christian deaths and the arrests of a number of Muslims as well as Copts. Some 96 Muslims were charged with violence before a state-security court, but only four were convicted, and to short jail terms. However, Muslim–Coptic relations remained unstable. Early in 2002, two Coptic weekly newspapers, Al Nabaa and Akbar Nabaa, were shut down after the Superior Press Council, a quasi-government body, filed a lawsuit charging them with "offending Egyptians and undermining national unity."

Islamic Jihad, the major fundamentalist organization and the one responsible for Sadat's assassination, subsequently shifted its locale and objectives in order to evade the repression of the Mubarak government. Many of its members joined the fighters in Afghanistan who were resisting the Soviet occupation of that country. After the Soviet withdrawal in 1989, some 300 of them remained, forming the core of the Taliban force that eventually won control of 90 percent of Afghanistan. In that capacity, they became associated with Osama bin Laden and his al-Qaeda international terror network. Two of their leaders, Dr. Ayman al-Zawahiri (a surgeon) and Muhammad Atif, are believed to have planned the September 11, 2001, terrorist bombings in the United States. However, Islamic Jihad's chief aim is the overthrow of the Mubarak government and its replacement by an Islamic one. Its hostility to the United States stems from American support for that government and for the U.S. alliance with Israel against the Palestinians.

In targeting tourism in their campaign to overthrow the regime, fundamentalists have attacked tourist buses. Four tourists were killed in the lobby of a plush Cairo hotel in 1993. In November 1997, 64 tourists were gunned down in a grisly massacre at the Temple of Hatshepsut near Luxor, in the Valley of the Kings, one of Egypt's prize tourist attractions. Aftershocks from the terrorist attacks on the United States have decimated the tourist industry, which is Egypt's largest source of income ($4.3 billion in 2000, with 5.4 million visitors in that year). Egyptair, the national airline, lost $56 million in October 2001 alone; and cancellations of package tours, foreign-airline bookings, and hotel reservations led to a 45 percent drop in tourist revenues.

One important reason for the rise in fundamentalist violence stems from the government's ineptness in meeting social crises. After the disastrous earthquake of October 1992, Islamic fundamentalist groups were first to provide aid to the victims, distributing $1,000 to each family made homeless, while the cumbersome, multilayered government bureaucracy took weeks to respond to the crisis. Similarly, al-Gamaa established a network of Islamic schools, hospitals, clinics, daycare centers, and even small industries in poor districts such as Cairo's Imbaba quarter.

The Mubarak government's response to rising violence has been one of extreme repression. The death penalty may be imposed for "antistate terrorism." The state of emergency that was established after Anwar Sadat's assassination in 1981 has been renewed regularly, most recently in 2001 for a three-year extension, over the vehement protests of opposition deputies in the Assembly. Some 770 members of the Vanguard of Islam were tried and convicted of subversion in 1993. The crackdown left Egypt almost free from violence for several years. But in 1996, al-Gamaa and two other hitherto unknown Islamic militant groups, Assiut Terrorist Organization and Kotbion (named for a Muslim Brotherhood leader executed in 1966 for an attempt to kill President Nasser), resumed terrorist activities. Eighteen Greek tourists were murdered in April, and the State Security Court sentenced five Assiut members to death for killing police and civilians in a murderous rampage. At their trial they chanted "God make a staircase of our skulls to Your glory," waving Korans in their cage, in an eerie replay of the trials of Sadat's assassins.

An unfortunate result of government repression of the militants is that Egypt, traditionally an open, tolerant, and largely nonviolent society, has taken on many of the features of a totalitarian state. Human rights are routinely suspended, the prime offenders being officers of the dreaded State Security Investigation (SSI). Indefinite detention without charges is a common practice, and torture is used extensively to extract "confessions" from suspects or their relatives. All of al-Gamaa's leaders are either in prison, in exile, or dead; and with 20,000 suspected Islamists also jailed, the government could claim with some

justification that it had broken the back of the 1990s insurgency. Its confidence was enhanced in March 1999 when al-Gamaa said that it would no longer engage in violence. Two previous cease-fire offers had been spurned, but this newest offer resulted in the release of several hundred Islamists to "test its validity."

Due to the extremism of methods employed by both sides, the conflict between the regime and the fundamentalists has begun to polarize Egyptian society. The fundamentalists, in struggling to overthrow the regime and replace it with a more legitimately Islamic one (in their view) have at times attacked intellectuals, journalists, writers and others who do not openly advocate similar views or even oppose them. The novelist Farag Foda, who strongly criticized Egypt's "creeping Islamization" in his works, was killed outside of his Cairo home in the early 1990s, and Haguib Mahfouz, the Arab world's only Nobel laureate in literature, was critically wounded in 1994 by a Gamaa gunman.

In 1995, the regime imposed further restrictions on Egypt's normally freewheeling press and journalistic bodies. A law would impose fines of up to $3,000 and five-year jail sentences for articles "harmful to the state." The long arm of the law reached into the educational establishment as well. A university professor and noted Koranic scholar was charged with apostasy by clerics at Al-Azhar University, on the grounds that he had argued in his writings that the Koran should be interpreted in its historical/linguistic context alongside its identification as the Word of God. The charge came under the Islamic principle of *hisba,* "accountability." He was found guilty and ordered to divorce his wife, since a Muslim woman may not be married to an apostate. A 1996 law prohibited the use of hisba in the courts, but the damage had been done; the professor and his wife were forced into exile to preserve their marriage.

Another distinguished professor ran afoul of the government's Al-Azhar–imposed limits on free speech, as Saad Eddine Ibrahim, director of the American University at Cairo's Ibn Khaldoun Center for Democracy, was arrested in July 2000. He was charged with "defaming" Egypt abroad. The charge resulted from a documentary film produced at the Center which was critical of parliamentary electoral process for encouraging fraud. Due in part to widespread criticism in Europe and particularly the United States—Ibrahim holds dual Egyptian-American citizenship—he was released. In May 2001 he was rearrested, tried and convicted by a special court, and given a 7-year jail sentence. After strong

international criticism and a warning by U.S. president Bush that his administration would oppose any increase in the $2 billion annual aid program to Egypt, the Court of Cassation, the country's highest court, threw out the conviction and ordered him released.

While Ibrahim's release suggests that the Egyptian government is sensitive to charges of misuse of human rights from abroad, its posture internally toward its citizens has changed little since emergency laws went into effect. Recently the head of the Group for Developing Democracy, a civil rights watchdog agency in Cairo, noted that "Egypt doesn't want real democracy. The state wants us puppets in its big show of paper democracy." And in July 2003 the director of the Cairo office of the UN Development Program told a reporter: "People seem to be accepting an immoral tradeoff between human rights and security."

A small but significant step toward reawakening the country's moribund political system was taken in September 2005 with an open presidential election. The incumbent was opposed by 9 candidates, the most prominent being Ayman Nour, leader of the Al Ghad ("Tomorrow") opposition party. Mubarak was re-elected but won "only" 88.6 percent of the popular vote. However voting irregularities charged by opposition leaders led to a further crackdown. In December Ayman Nour was given a 5-year forced labor sentence for what U.S. officials later described as false charges. He had finished second to Mubarak in the popular vote.

Elections for the Shura, the upper house of the National Assembly, in June 2007 re-emphasized the flawed nature of Egypt's political system. (The Shura lacks law-making powers but members have parliamentary immunity and other perquisites that make membership attractive particularly to business owners and wealthy investors.)

Despite government claims that the election marked a "great leap forward" for public participation, obstacles such as limited access to polling places, stuffed ballot boxes, voter intimidation and the pre-election arrest of some 800 Muslim Brotherhood members kept the turnout low. One Muslim Brotherhood leader noted sadly, "the regime is incapable of honest political competition. Its aim is to marginalize the Brotherhood and prevent us from moving forward toward successful reforms and change through legal and constructive means."[13]

As is noted elsewhere in this book (see Heartland of Islam essay), government repression and arrests of hundreds of its activists along with those of Kifaya (which would remove President Mubarak), and more recently a number of opposition editors for articles critical of the regime, has forced the Muslim Brotherhood to rethink its position in terms of "forceful negativism." In October 2007 its leaders issued a draft platform. This platform would establish a Majlis Ulama (Council of Islamic Scholars), selected by the membership rather than in a popular election. The Council would have veto power over legislation passed by the National Assembly (Parliament) that it considered incompatible with Islamic law. Under its terms Egypt would be no longer a republic but a "Civic Islamic State."[14]

In a further effort to blunt the opposition, Mubarak in February 2006 abruptly postponed local council elections scheduled for April, canceling a promise he had made during the presidential campaign to promote greater democracy. While these councils have little actual power, a constitutional change in 2005 will give them control over nomination of candidates for president in 2011, when Mubarak is prohibited from running or serving.

ACHIEVEMENTS

Alexandria, founded in 332 B.C. by Alexander the Great, was one of the world's great cities in antiquity, with its Library, its Pharos (Lighthouse), its palaces, and other monuments. Most of them were destroyed by fire or sank into the sea long ago, as the city fell into neglect. Then, in 1995, underwater archeologists discovered the ruins of the Pharos; its location had not been known previously. Other discoveries followed—the palace of Cleopatra, the remains of Napoleon's fleet (sunk by the British in the Battle of the Nile), Roman and Greek trading vessels filled with amphorae, etc. The restoration of the Library was completed in 2000, with half of its 11 floors under the Mediterranean; visitors in the main reading room are surrounded by water cascading down its windows. After centuries of decay, Alexandria is again a magnet for tourists.

A STRUGGLING ECONOMY

Egypt's economy rests upon a narrow and unstable base, due to rapid demographic growth and limited arable land and because political factors have adversely influenced national development. The country has a relatively high level of education and, as a result, is a net exporter of skilled labor to other Arab countries. But the overproduction of university graduates has produced a bloated and inefficient bureau-cracy, as the government is required to provide a position for every graduate who cannot find other employment.

Agriculture is the most important sector of the economy, accounting for about one third of national income. The major crops are long-staple cotton and sugarcane. Egyptian agriculture since time immemorial has been based on irrigation from the Nile River. In recent years, greater control of irrigation water through the Aswan High Dam, expansion of land devoted to cotton production, and improved planting methods have begun to show positive results.

A new High Dam at Aswan, completed in 1971 upstream from the original one built in 1906, resulted from a political decision by the Nasser government to seek foreign financing for its program of expansion of cultivable land and generation of electricity for industrialization. When Western lending institutions refused to finance the dam, also for political reasons, Nasser turned to the Soviet Union for help. By 1974, just three years after its completion, revenues had exceeded construction costs. The dam made possible the electrification of all of Egypt's villages as well as a fishing industry at Lake Nasser, its reservoir. It proved valuable in providing the agricultural sector with irrigation water during the prolonged 1980–1988 drought, although at sharply reduced levels. However, the increased costs of land reclamation and loss of the sardine fishing grounds along the Mediterranean coast have made the dam a mixed blessing for Egypt.

Egypt was self-sufficient in foodstuffs as recently as the 1970s but now must import 60 percent of its food. Such factors as rapid population growth, rural-to-urban migration with consequent loss of agricultural labor, and Sadat's open-door policy for imports combined to produce this negative food balance. Subsidies for basic commodities, which cost the government nearly $2 billion a year, are an important cause of inflation, since they keep the budget continuously in deficit. Fearing a recurrence of the 1977 Bread Riots, the government kept prices in check. However, inflation, which had dropped to 8 percent in 1995 due to International Monetary Fund stabilization policies required for loans, rose to 37 percent in 1999 as the new free-market policy produced a tidal wave of imports. As a result, the foreign trade deficit increased drastically.

Egypt has important oil and natural-gas deposits, and new discoveries continue to strengthen this sector of the economy. Oil reserves increased to 3.3 billion barrels in 2001, due to new fields being brought on stream in the Western Desert. Proven natural-gas reserves are 51 trillion cubic feet, sufficient to meet domestic needs for 30 years at current rates of consumption.

A 2001 agreement with Jordan would guarantee Jordan's purchase of Egyptian natural-gas supplies, contingent on completion of the pipeline under the Red Sea from Al-Arish to Aqaba. But an earlier agreement with Israel, Egypt's closest and potentially most lucrative gas market, has been put on hold due to the renewed Palestinian–Israeli conflict. Under the agreement, Egypt would have provided $300 million a year in gas, meeting 15 percent of Israel's electric-power needs.

Egypt also derives revenues from Suez Canal tolls and user fees, from tourism, and from remittances from Egyptian workers abroad, mostly working in Saudi Arabia and other oil-producing Gulf states. The flow of remittances from the approximately 4 million expatriate workers was reduced and then all but cut off with the Iraqi invasion of Kuwait. Egyptians fled from both countries in panic, arriving home as penniless refugees. With unemployment already at 20 percent and housing in short supply, the government faced an enormous assimilation problem apart from its loss of revenue. The United States helped by agreeing to write off $4.5 billion in Egyptian military debts. However the imprisonment and unduly harsh sentence of dissident presidential candidate Ayman Nour led the U.S. in January 2006 to suspend a projected trade and tariff elimination agreement between the two countries.

One encouraging sign of brighter days ahead is the expansion of local manufacturing industries, in line with government efforts to reduce dependence upon imported goods. A 10-year tax exemption plus remission of customs duties on imported machinery have encouraged a number of new business ventures, notably in the clothing industry.

Unfortunately one of the few enterprises affecting Egypt's poor directly was literally "dumped" in January 2003 when the government stopped renewing licenses to the Zabbaleen, a 60,000-member Coptic community that traditionally collects a third of Cairo's 10,000 daily tons of garbage and trash. Future collections of all garbage and trash are to be made by foreign companies under contract. The new system would have certain advantages of the Zabbaleen system, mainly in terms of sanitation. But the economic impact on them will be severe. Over the years the Zabbaleen have used profits from trash collection to fund neighborhood improvements, schools and jobs for a great number of women.

In 1987, Mubarak gained some foreign help for Egypt's cash-strapped economy when agreement was reached with the International Monetary Fund for a standby credit of $325 million over 18 months to allow the country to meet its balance-of-payments deficit. The Club of Paris, a group of public and private banks from various industrialized countries, then rescheduled $12 billion in Egyptian external debts over a 10-year period.

Expanded foreign aid and changes in government agricultural policy required by the World Bank for new loans helped spur economic recovery in the 1990s, especially in agriculture. Production records were set in 1996 in wheat, corn, and rice, meeting 50 percent of domestic needs. The cotton harvest for that year was 350,000 tons, with 50,000 tons exported. However, a new agricultural law passed in 1992 but not implemented until 1997 ended land rents, allowing landlords to set their own leases and in effect reclaim their properties taken over by the government during the Nasser era. The purpose is to provide an incentive for tenant farmers to grow export crops such as cotton and rice. But as a result, Egypt's 900,000 tenant farmers have faced the loss of lands held on long-term leases for several generations.

However, these economic successes must be balanced against Egypt's chronic social problems and the lack of an effective representative political system. The head of the Muslim Brotherhood made the astute observation in a 1993 speech that "the threat is not in the extremist movement. It is in the absence of democratic institutions." Until such institutions are firmly in place, with access to education, full employment, broad political participation, civil rights, and the benefits of growth spread evenly across all levels of society, unrest and efforts to Islamize the government by force are likely to continue.

By 2000, the government's harsh repression had seriously weakened the fundamentalist movement, albeit at a heavy cost. Some 1,200 police officers and militants had been killed during the 1990s, and 16,000 persons remained jailed without charges on suspicion of membership in Islamic Jihad or other organizations. However, public disaffection continues to grow and to involve increasing numbers of nonfundamentalists. In May 2000, a demonstration by several hundred Al-Azhar students protesting the reprinting of a 1983 novel by Syrian writer Haider Haider was broken up by police. The demonstrators charged that the novel was insulting both to the Prophet Muhammad and to Islam; it had been reprinted as part of a Ministry of Culture project to promote modern Arabic literature. In 2001, the Cairo Book Fair, one of the Arab world's

Timeline: PAST

2500–671 B.C.
Period of the pharaohs

671–30 B.C.
The Persian conquest, followed by Macedonians and rule by Ptolemies

30 B.C.
Egypt becomes a Roman province

A.D. 641
Invading Arabs bring Islam

969
The founding of Cairo

1517–1800
Egypt becomes an Ottoman province

1798-1831
Napoleon's invasion, followed by the rise to power of Muhammad Ali

1869
The Suez Canal opens to traffic

1882
The United Kingdom establishes a protectorate

1952
The Free Officers overthrow the monarchy and establish Egypt as a republic

1956
Nationalization of the Suez Canal

1958–1961
Union with Syria into the United Arab Republic

1967
The Six-Day War with Israel ends in Israel's occupation of the Gaza Strip and the Sinai Peninsula

1970
Gamal Abdel Nasser dies; Anwar Sadat succeeds as head of Egypt

1979
A peace treaty is signed at Camp David between Egypt and Israel

1980s
Sadat is assassinated; he is succeeded by Hosni Mubarak; a crackdown on Islamic fundamentalists

1990s
The government employs totalitarian tactics in its battle with fundamentalists

PRESENT

2000s
Deep social and economic problems persist

had banned a number of books. They were declared to be pornographic by Muslim Brotherhood members of the Legislature and criticized by Al-Azhar faculty as being offensive to Islam.

Egypt's own difficulties with fundamentalists caused some reluctance on its part when support for the U.S.–led international coalition against terrorism formed after the September 11, 2001, bombings of the World Trade Center in New York City and the Pentagon near Washington, D.C. The reluctance stemmed in part from public anger over continued American support for Israel against the Palestinians and the suffering of Iraq's fellow Arabs under the 11-year sanctions imposed on that country.

In March 2004 the government reached agreement with Israel to set up a number of Qualifying Industrial Zones (Q.I.Z.) in an effort to boost its flagging economy. Egyptian manufacturers, notable of textiles, will be able to export goods duty-free to the U.S. provided that 35 percent of goods exported were locally produced and a percentage reserved for Israeli products. Egypt's total exports to the U.S. of $3.3 billion included $336 million in textiles and clothing. The Q.I.Z.s will add significantly to this total.

Encouraged by a *fatwa* (Islamic religious ruling) on its lawfulness under Shari'a law given by a scholar at Al-Azhar University, Egypt's In Vitro Fertilization Center in Cairo became in October 2005 the first in the Arab world to conduct stem-cell research.

NOTES

1. Leila Ahmed, in *A Border Passage* (New York: Farrar, Strauss & Giroux, 1999), deals at length with Egyptian vs. Arab identity from the perspective of growing up in British-controlled Egypt.

2. An English observer said, "In arms and firing they are nearly as perfect as European troops." Afaf L. Marsot, *Egypt in the Reign of Muhammad Ali* (Cambridge, England: Cambridge University Press, 1984), p. 132.

3. *Ibid.*, p. 161.

4. Quoted in P. J. Vatikiotis, *Nasser and His Generation* (New York: St. Martin's Press, 1978), p. 35.

5. Gamal Abdel Nasser, *The Philosophy of the Revolution* (Cairo: Ministry of National Guidance, 1954), p. 52.

6. Derek Hopwood, *Egypt: Politics and Society 1945–1981* (London: George Allen and Unwin, 1982), p. 77.

7. Quoted in Vatikiotis, *op. cit.,* p. 245.

8. Hopwood, *op. cit.,* p. 106.

9. David Hirst and Irene Beeson, *Sadat* (London: Faber and Faber, 1981), p. 255.

biggest cultural events, was boycotted by many Egyptian writers and editors, after its sponsor, the same Ministry of Culture,

10. "Banners slung across the broad thoroughfares of central Cairo acclaimed The Hero of the Crossing (of the October 1973 War)." *Ibid.,* pp. 17–18.

11. With unemployment at 10 percent and 30 percent of the population under age 15, most young graduates must struggle to find a job, let alone get married. To do so a man must provide shelter, jewelry and gifts for his bride and proof to her family that he can support her and their future children. Marriages must also be registered with the government. Increasingly young couples are entering into "temporary (*urfi*) marriages," essentially common-law partnerships, involving witnesses, consent of the guardian of the bride, and public declaration that they meet Islamic standards. Some 3 million such arrangements are registered with notaries public, but given Egypt's economic instability there are probably three times the number in the country.

12. Reported by Jano Charbel and Michael Slackman in *The New York Times,* November 1, 2006. Sadat's nephew had also charged the government with secretly releasing his uncle's chief assassin.

13. Mohammed Habib, quoted in Dan Murphy, "Egypt vote shows unease with democracy," *The Christian Science Monitor,* June 12, 2007.

14. Mohammed Elmenshawy, "The Muslim Brotherhood Shows its True colors," *The Christian Science Monitor,* October 12, 2007.

Libya (Socialist People's Libyan Arab Jamahiriyya)

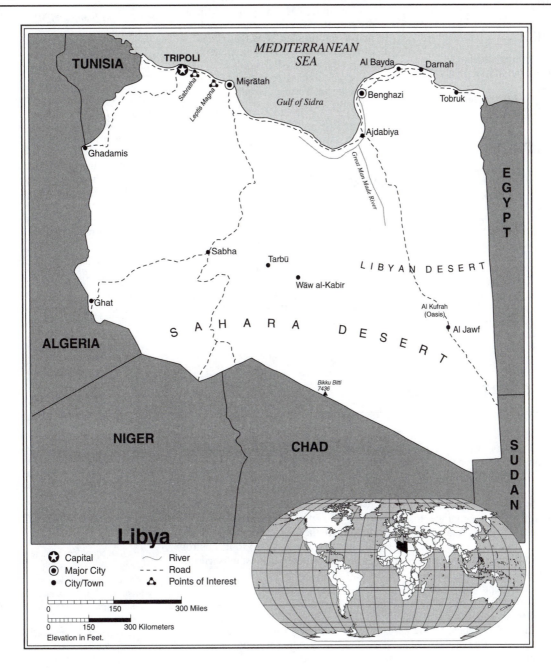

Libya Statistics

GEOGRAPHY

Area in Square Miles (Kilometers):
679,147 (1,759,450) (about the size of Alaska)

Capital (Population): Tripoli (1,681,000)

Environmental Concerns: desertification; very limited freshwater resources

Geographical Features: mostly barren, flat to undulating plains, plateaus, depressions

Climate: Mediterranean along the coast; dry, extreme desert in the interior

PEOPLE

Population

Total: 6,036,914 (includes 166,510 non-nationals)

Annual Growth Rate: 2.26%

Rural/Urban Population Ratio: 14/86

Major Languages: Arabic; English; Italian

Ethnic Makeup: 97% Berber and Arab; 3% others

Religions: 97% Sunni Muslim; 3% others

Health

Life Expectancy at Birth: 74.6 years (male); 79 years (female)

Infant Mortality Rate: 22.8/1,000 live births

Education

Adult Literacy Rate: 82.6%
Compulsory (Ages): 6–15

COMMUNICATION

Telephones: 380,000 main lines
Daily Newspaper Circulation: 15 per
   1,000 people
Televisions: 105 per 1,000 people
Internet Users: 1 (2000)

TRANSPORTATION

Highways in Miles (Kilometers): 15,180
   (24,484)
Railroads in Miles (Kilometers): none
Usable Airfields: 139
Motor Vehicles in Use: 904,000

GOVERNMENT

Type: officially a *Jamahiriyya* ("state
   belonging to the people") with
   government authority exercised by a
   General Peoples' Congress

Independence Date: December 24, 1951
   (from Italy)
Head of State/Government: Leader of
   the Revolution Muhammad al-Minyar
   al-Qadhafi ("Brother Leader") holds
   no official title but is de facto head
   of state. Ali al-Mahmoudi, General
   Secretary of the GPC, holds a
   position comparable to that of Prime
   Minister in Western parliamentary
   systems
Political Parties: none
Suffrage: universal and compulsory at 18

MILITARY

Military Expenditures (% of GDP): 3.9%

Current Disputes: Libya claims
   32,000 square kilometers of land in
   southeastern Algeria and 25,000 square
   kilometers in the Tommo region of
   Niger, both claims resulting from the
   1899 treaty establishing France's West
   African colonies. Both claims are
   presently dormant.

ECONOMY

Currency ($U.S. Equivalent): 1.305
   dinars = $1
Per Capita Income/GDP: $12,700/$74.97
   billion
GDP Growth Rate: 8.1%
Inflation Rate: 3.1%
Unemployment Rate: 3%
Labor Force: 1,787,000
Natural Resources: petroleum; natural
   gas; gypsum
Agriculture: wheat; barley; olives; dates;
   citrus fruits; vegetables; peanuts; beef;
   eggs
Industry: petroleum; food processing;
   textiles; handicrafts; cement
Exports: $37-billion (primary partners
   Italy, Germany, Spain)
Imports: $14.47 billion (primary partners
   Italy, Germany, Tunisia)

SUGGESTED WEB SITES

http://lcweb2.loc.gov/frd/cs/
   lytoc.html
http://home.earthlink.net/
   ~dribrahim/

Libya Country Report

The Socialist People's Libyan Arab Jamahiriyya (Republic), commonly known as Libya, is the fourth largest of the Arab countries. Since it became a republic in 1969, it has played a role in regional and international affairs more appropriate to the size of its huge territory than to its small population.

Libya consists of three geographical regions: Tripolitania, Cyrenaica, and the Fezzan. Most of the population live in Tripolitania, the northwestern part of the country, where Tripoli, the capital and major port, is located. Cyrenaica, in the east along the Egyptian border, has a narrow coastline backed by a high plateau (2,400-feet elevation) called the Jabal al-Akhdar ("Green Mountain"). It contains Libya's other principal city, Benghazi. The two regions are separated by the Sirte, an extension of the Sahara Desert that reaches almost to the Mediterranean Sea. Most of Libya's oil fields are in the Sirte.

The Fezzan occupies the central part of the country. It is entirely desert, except for a string of widely scattered oases. Its borders are with Chad, Algeria, Niger, and Sudan. The border with Chad, established during French colonial rule in sub-Saharan Africa, was once disputed by Libya. The

matter was settled through international mediation, with the border formally demarcated in 1994. Libya also claims areas in northern Niger and southeastern Algeria left over from the colonial period, when they formed part of the French West African empire. In the Libyan view, these areas should have been transferred to its control under the peace treaty that established the Libyan state.

HISTORY

Until modern times, Libya did not have a separate identity, either national or territorial. It always formed a part of some other territorial unit and in most cases was controlled by outsiders. However, control was usually limited to the coastal areas. The Berbers of the interior were little affected by the passing of conquerors and the rise and fall of civilizations.

Libya's culture and social structure have been influenced more by the Islamic Arabs than by any other invaders. The Arabs brought Islam to Libya in the early seventh century. Arab groups settled in the region and intermarried with the Berber population to such an extent that the Libyans became one of the most thoroughly Arabized peoples in the Islamic world.

DEVELOPMENT

Restoration of full diplomatic relations with the United States and the end of sanctions now permits American firms, particularly oil companies, to invest in Libya's renewed economic development. Similarly European countries, notably those that are heavy purchasers of Libyan oil, have become active investors in the country's infrastructure. Italy's export credit agency recently agreed to write off $230 million in Libyan debts in exchange for investments by Italian companies. The Bush administration in 2007 allocated $1.15 million in aid to the Libyan economy in "normalizing" relations.

Coastal Libya, around Tripoli, was an outlying province of the Ottoman Empire for several centuries. Like its urban neighbors Tunis and Algiers, Tripoli had a fleet of corsairs that made life dangerous for European merchant ships in the Mediterranean. When the United States became a Mediterranean trading nation, the corsairs of Tripoli included American ships among their targets. The USS *Philadelphia* was sent to Tripoli to "teach the corsairs a lesson" in 1804, but it got stuck on a sandbar

The Fezzan occupies the central part of Libya and is entirely desert, except for some widely scattered oases. This oasis is called Bu Gheilan.

and was captured. Navy Lieutenant Stephen Decatur led a commando raid into Tripoli harbor and blew up the ship, inspiring the words to what would become the official U.S. Marine hymn: "From the halls of Montezuma to the shores of Tripoli. . . . " Ironically the Marines never reached Tripoli, although a land campaign led by the itinerant American soldier of fortune William Eaton, who had been hired by a dispossessed member of the ruling dynasty to recover his throne, got only as far as Darna, well east of the capital.

This ruling dynasty, founded by an ex-Ottoman officer named Ahmad Karamanli, controlled Tripoli and its coastline from the 18th century on. Its corsair fleet was allied with the Ottoman navy. In 1815, at the end of the Napoleonic Wars, British and French naval forces defeated the Tripolitan corsairs and forced the Karamanli ruler of that time to end payment of tribute. Lacking its main source of revenue, his population rebelled. By 1835 France had seized control of Algiers and Tunis, the other main corsair states. To forestall further territorial losses the Ottoman sultan, Tripoli's nominal ruler, sent forces to occupy the city and

for the first time place it under direct Ottoman rule.

The Sanusiya Movement

At various stages in Islam's long history, new groups or movements have appeared committed to purifying or reforming Islamic society and taking it back to its original form of a simple community of believers led by just rulers. Several of these movements, such as the Wahhabis of Saudi Arabia, were important in the founding of modern Islamic states. The movement called the Sanusiya was formed in the nineteenth century. In later years, it became an important factor in the formation of modern Libya.

The founder, the Grand Sanusi, was a religious teacher from Algeria. He left Algeria after the French conquest and settled in northern Cyrenaica. The Grand Sanusi's teachings attracted many followers. He also attracted the attention of the Ottoman authorities, who distrusted his advocacy of a strong united Islamic world in which Ottomans and Arabs would be partners. In 1895, to escape from the Ottomans, the Grand Sanusi's son and successor moved

Sanusiya headquarters to Kufra, a remote oasis in the Sahara.

The Sanusiya began as a peaceful movement interested only in bringing new converts to Islam and founding a network of *zawiyas* ("lodges") for contemplation and monastic life throughout the desert. But when European countries began to seize territories in North and West Africa, the Sanusi became warrior-monks and fought the invaders.

Italy Conquers Libya

The Italian conquest of Libya began in 1911. The Italians needed colonies, not only for prestige but also for the resettlement of poor and landless peasants from Italy's crowded southern provinces. The Italians expected an easy victory against a weak Ottoman garrison; Libya would become the "Fourth Shore" of a new Roman Empire from shore to shore along the Mediterranean. But the Italians found Libya a tougher land to subdue than they had expected. Italian forces were pinned to Tripoli and a few other points on the coast by the Ottoman garrison and the fierce Sanusi warrior-monks.

After the 1969 Revolution, the government strove to develop many aspects of the country. These local chiefs are meeting to plan community development.

The Italians were given a second chance after World War I. The Italian government of swaggering dictator Benito Mussolini sent an army to occupy Tripolitania. When the Italians moved on Cyrenaica, the Grand Sanusi crossed the Egyptian border into exile under British protection. The Italians found Cyrenaica much more difficult to control than Tripolitania. It is ideal guerrilla country, from the caves of Jabal al-Akhdar to the stony plains and dry, hidden *wadis* (river beds) of the south. It took nine years (1923–1932) for Italy to overcome all of Libya, despite Italy's vast superiority in troops and weapons. Sanusi guerrilla bands harried the Italians, cutting supply lines, ambushing patrols, and attacking convoys. Their leader, Shaykh Omar Mukhtar, became Libya's first national hero.

The Italians finally overcame the Sanusi by the use of methods that do not shock us today but seemed unbelievably brutal at the time. Cyrenaica was made into a huge concentration camp, with a barbed-wire fence along the Egyptian border. Nomadic peoples were herded into these camps, guarded by soldiers to prevent them from aiding the Sanusi. Sanusi prisoners were pushed out of airplanes, wells were plugged to deny water to the people, and flocks were slaughtered. In 1931, Omar Mukhtar was captured, court-martialed, and hanged in public. The resistance ended with his death.

The Italians did not have long to cultivate their Fourth Shore. During the 1930s, they poured millions of lire into the colony. A paved highway from the Egyptian to the Tunisian border along the coast was completed in 1937; in World War II, it became a handy invasion route for the British. A system of state-subsidized farms was set up for immigrant Italian peasants. Each was given free transportation, a house, seed, fertilizers, a mule, and a pair of shoes as inducements to come to Libya. By 1940, the Italian population had reached 110,000, and about 495,000 acres of land had been converted into productive farms, vineyards, and olive groves.[1]

Independent Libya

Libya was a major battleground during World War II, as British, German, and Italian armies rolled back and forth across the desert. The British defeated the Germans and occupied northern Libya, while a French army occupied the Fezzan. The United States later built an important air base, Wheelus Field, near Tripoli. Thus the three major Allied powers all had an interest in Libya's future. But they could not agree on what to do with occupied Libya.

Italy wanted Libya back. France wished to keep the Fezzan as a buffer for its African colonies, while Britain preferred self-government for Cyrenaica under the Grand Sanusi, who had become staunchly pro-British during his exile in Egypt. The Soviet Union favored a Soviet trusteeship over Libya, which would provide the Soviet Union with a convenient outlet in the Mediterranean. The United States waffled but finally settled on independence, which would at least keep the Soviet tentacles from enveloping Libya.

Due to lack of agreement, the Libyan "problem" was referred to the United Nations General Assembly. Popular demonstrations of support for independence in Libya impressed a number of the newer UN members; in 1951, the General Assembly approved a resolution for an independent Libyan state, a kingdom under the Grand Sanusi, Idris.

THE KINGDOM OF LIBYA

Libya has been governed under two political systems since independence: a constitutional monarchy (1951–1969); and a Socialist republic (1969–), which has no constitution because all power "belongs" to the people. Qadhafi's Libyan Arab Jamahiriyya has lasted more than twice as long as its monarchical predecessor, and its aggressive forays into foreign affairs are significantly different from foreign policy under King Idris.

At independence, Libya was an artificial union of the three provinces. The Libyan people had little sense of national identity or unity. Loyalty was to one's family, clan, village, and, in a general sense, to the higher authority represented by a tribal confederation. The only other loyalty linking Libyans was the Islamic religion. The tides of war and conquest that had washed over them for centuries had had little effect on their strong, traditional attachment to Islam.[2]

Political differences also divided the three provinces. Tripolitanians talked openly of abolishing the monarchy. Cyrenaica was the home and power base of King Idris; the king's principal supporters were the Sanusiya and certain important families. The distances and poor communication links between the provinces contributed to the impression that they should be separate countries. Leaders could not even agree on the choice between Tripoli and Benghazi for the capital. For his part, the king distrusted both cities as being corrupt and overly influenced by foreigners. He had his administrative capital at Baida, in the Jabal al-Akhdar.

Libya at the start of independence was an extremely poor country. Per capita income in 1951 was about $30 per year; in 1960, it was about $100 per year. Approximately 5 percent of the land was marginally usable for agriculture, and only 1 percent could be cultivated on a permanent basis. Most economists considered Libya to be a hopeless case, almost totally dependent on foreign aid for survival. (It is interesting to note that the Italians were seemingly able to force more out of the soil, but one must remember that the Italian government poured a great deal of money into the country to develop the plantations, and credit must also be given to the extremely hard-working Italian farmer.)

Despite its meager resources and lack of political experience, Libya was valuable to the United States and Britain in the 1950s and 1960s because of its strategic location. The United States negotiated a long-term lease on Wheelus Field in 1954, as a vital link in the chain of U.S. bases built around the southern perimeter of the Soviet Union due to the Cold War. In return, U.S. aid of $42 million sweetened the pot, and Wheelus became the single largest employer of Libyan labor. The British had two air bases and maintained a garrison in Tobruk.

Political development in the kingdom was minimal. King Idris knew little about parliamentary democracy, and he distrusted political parties. The 1951 Constitution provided for an elected Legislature, but a dispute between the king and the Tripolitanian National Congress, one of several Tripolitanian parties, led to the outlawing of all political parties. Elections were held every four years, but only property-owning adult males could vote (women were granted the vote in 1963). The same legislators were reelected regularly. In

United Nations Photo (UN81801)

Muammar al-Qadhafi led a group of army officers in the military coup of 1969 that deposed King Idris. In later years, Qadhafi gained world-wide notoriety for his apparent sanction of terrorism.

the absence of political activity, the king was the glue that held Libya together.

THE 1969 REVOLUTION

At dawn on September 1, 1969, a group of young, unknown army officers abruptly carried out a military coup in Libya. King Idris, who had gone to Turkey for medical treatment, was deposed, and a "Libyan Arab Republic" was proclaimed by the officers. These men, whose names were not known to the outside world until weeks after the coup, were led by Captain Muammar Muhammad al-Qadhafi. He went on Benghazi radio to announce to a startled Libyan population: "People of Libya . . . your armed forces have undertaken the overthrow of the reactionary and corrupt regime. . . . From now on Libya is a free, sovereign republic, ascending with God's help to exalted heights."[3]

Qadhafi's new regime made a sharp change in policy from that of its predecessor. Wheelus Field and the British air bases were evacuated and returned to Libyan control. Libya took an active part in Arab affairs and supported Arab unity, to the extent of working to undermine other Arab leaders whom Qadhafi considered undemocratic or unfriendly to his regime.[4]

REGIONAL POLICY

To date, Qadhafi's efforts to unite Libya with other Arab states have not been successful. A 1984 agreement for a federal union with Morocco, which provided for separate sovereignty but a federated Assembly and unified foreign policies, was abrogated unilaterally by the late King Hassan II, after Qadhafi had charged him with "Arab treason" for

meeting with Israeli leader Shimon Peres. Undeterred, Qadhafi tried again in 1987 with neighboring Algeria, receiving a medal from President Chadli Bendjedid but no other encouragement.

Although distrustful of the mercurial Libyan leader, other North African heads of state have continued to work with him on the basis that it is safer to have Qadhafi inside the circle than isolated outside. Tunisia restored diplomatic relations in 1987, and Qadhafi agreed to compensate the Tunisian government for lost wages of Tunisian workers expelled from Libya during the 1985 economic recession. Qadhafi also accepted International Court of Justice arbitration over Libya's dispute with Tunisia over oil rights in the Gulf of Gabes. But Qadhafi continued to be unpredictable in his Arab policy. In 2007, for example, he refused to attend the Arab summit meeting, saying that other Arab countries were now serving American "imperial" interests. He added that Libya had now turned its back on the Arabs and become an African nation.

Libya's "re-formation" as an African nation was underscored by an open-ended invitation to sub-Saharan African leaders to send their workers to work in the country. By 2000, nearly a million had arrived, most of them from Nigeria, Chad, and Ghana. Economic problems in sub-Saharan Africa caused thousands more to use Libya as an escape route for Europe, many of them also fleeing from civil war in Côte d' Ivoire and Sierra Leone. The flood of migrants generated tension between them and Libyan natives; the latter viewed the migrants as agents of social misbehavior ranging from prostitution to drug usage and AIDS. In August 2000, the Libyan government deported several thousand African workers. They were hauled to the Niger border in trucks and dumped across the border there. Qadhafi had announced earlier that a "United States of Africa" would come into existence in March 2001 under Libyan sponsorship. But for once the Libyan people did not agree with him; "We are native Arabs, not Africans," they told their leader.

SOCIAL REVOLUTION

Qadhafi's desert upbringing and Islamic education gave him a strong, puritanical moral code. In addition to closing foreign bases and expropriating properties of Italians and Jews, he moved forcefully against symbols of foreign influence. The Italian cathedral in Tripoli became a mosque, street signs were converted to Arabic, nightclubs were closed, and the production and sale of alcohol were prohibited.

But Qadhafi's revolution went far beyond changing names. In a three-volume work entitled *The Green Book,* he described his vision of the appropriate political system for Libya. Political parties would not be allowed, nor would constitutions, legislatures, even an organized court system. All of these institutions, according to Qadhafi, eventually become corrupt and unrepresentative. Instead, "people's committees" would run the government, business, industry, and even the universities. Libyan embassies abroad were renamed "people's bureaus" and were run by junior officers. (The takeover of the London bureau in 1984 led to counterdemonstrations by Libyan students and the killing of a British police officer by gunfire from inside the bureau. The Libyan bureau in Washington, D.C., was closed by the U.S. Federal Bureau of Investigation and the staff deported on charges of espionage and terrorism against Libyans in the United States.) The country was renamed the Socialist People's Libyan Arab Jamahiriyya, and titles of government officials were eliminated. Qadhafi became "Leader of the Revolution," and each government department was headed by the secretary of a particular people's committee.

Qadhafi then developed a so-called Third International Theory, based on the belief that neither capitalism nor communism could solve the world's problems. What was needed, he said, was a "middle way" that would harness the driving forces of human history—religion and nationalism—to interact with each other to revitalize humankind. Islam would be the source of that middle way, because "it provides for the realization of justice and equity, it does not allow the rich to exploit the poor."[5]

THE ECONOMY

Modern Libya's economy is based almost entirely on oil exports. Concessions were granted to various foreign companies to explore for oil in 1955, and the first oil strikes were made in 1957. Within a decade, Libya had become the world's fourth-largest exporter of crude oil. During the 1960s, pipelines were built from the oil fields to new export terminals on the Mediterranean coast. The lightness and low sulfur content of Libyan crude oil make it highly desirable to industrialized countries, and, with the exception of the United States, differences in political viewpoint have had little effect on Libyan oil sales abroad.

After the 1969 Revolution, Libya became a leader in the drive by oil-producing countries to gain control over their petroleum industries. The process began in 1971, when the new Libyan government took over the interests of British Petroleum in Libya. The Libyan method of nationalization was to proceed against individual companies rather than to take on the "oil

giants" all at once. It took more than a decade before the last company, Exxon, capitulated. However, the companies' $2 billion in assets were left in limbo in 1986, when the administration of U.S. president Ronald Reagan imposed a ban on all trade with Libya to protest Libya's involvement in international terrorism. Sanctions were continued under Reagan's successors until 2004, when the United States, the last holdout, lifted them in acknowledgement of Libya's improved international respectability. Among other actions the country has closed down its unconventional weapons program and permitted Libyan agents allegedly involved in the 1988 Lockerbie, Scotland airline bombing to be tried in a neutral court.

Libya's oil reserves are estimated at 36 billion barrels, along with 52 trillion cubic feet of recoverable natural gas reserves. The low sulfur content of Libyan oil and its proximity to the Mediterranean coast, which keeps transport costs low, have made its oil highly marketable. With oil production reaching a record 1.4 million barrels per day, Libya has been able to build a strong petrochemical industry. The Marsa Brega petrochemical complex is one of the world's largest producers of urea, although a major contract with India was canceled in 1996 due to UN sanctions on trade with Libya.

Until recently, industrial-development successes based on oil revenues enabled Libyans to enjoy an ever-improving standard of living, and funding priorities were shifted from industry to agricultural development in the budget. But a combination of factors—mismanagement, lack of a

cadre of skilled Libyan workers, absenteeism, low motivation of the workforce, and a significant drop in revenues (from $22 billion in 1980 to $7 billion in 1988)—cast doubts on the effectiveness of Qadhafi's *Green Book* socialistic economic policies.

In 1988, the leader began closing the book. As production incentives, controls on both imports and exports were eliminated, and profit sharing for employees of small businesses was encouraged. In 1990, the General People's Congress (GPC), Libya's equivalent of a parliament, began a restructuring of government, adding new secretariats (ministries) to help expand economic development and diversify the economy.

In January 2000, Qadhafi marched into a GPC meeting waving a copy of the annual budget. He tore up the copy and ordered most of the secretariats abolished. Their powers would be transferred to "provincial cells" outside of Tripoli. Only five government functions—finance, defense, foreign affairs, information, and African unity—would remain under central-government control. In October of that year, Qadhafi ordered further cuts, continuing his direct management of national affairs. For the first time he named a prime minister, Mubarak al-Shamekh, to head the stripped-down government. The secretariat for information was abolished, and the heads of the justice and finance secretariats summarily dismissed. The head of the National Oil Company (NOC), Libya's longest-serving government official, was transferred to a new post; Qadhafi had criticized the NOC for mismanagement of the oil industry and lack of vision.

Libya also started developing its considerable uranium resources. A 1985 agreement with the Soviet Union provided the components for an 880-megawatt nuclear-power station in the Sirte region. Libya has enough uranium to meet its foreseeable domestic needs. The German-built chemical-weapons plant at Rabta, described by Libyans as a pharmaceutical complex but confirmed as to its real function by visiting scientists, was destroyed in a mysterious fire in the 1980s. A Russian-built nuclear reactor at Tajoora, 30 miles from Tripoli, suffered a similar fate, not from fire but due to faulty ventilation and high levels of radiation. But the Libyans have pressed on. An underground complex at Mount Tarhuna, south of Tripoli, was completed in 1998 and closed subsequently to international inspection. Libya claims that it is part of the Great Man-Made River (GMR) project and thus not subject to such inspections.

The GMR, a vast $30 billion complex of pipelines to draw water from underground Saharan aquifers, was begun in 1983. A component of Qadhafi's vision of a self-sufficient sovereign Libya, its goals were to expand irrigation in the fertile coastal agricultural area and improve the potable water supply in Libyan cities. It was planned in five stages. As of 2006–07 it was in full operation, with one set of pipelines serving the Jefara agricultural plain through Jebel Nafusah, a network of lines serving Tripoli from three aquifers deep in the Sahara, and separate lines serving Benghazi and Tobruk. The GMR may never bring economic benefits sufficient to offset its cost, but aside from providing potable water to Libya's cities it has helped build national unity and given Libyans a strong sense of national pride.

In addition to its heavy dependence on oil revenues, another obstacle to economic development in Libya is derived from an unbalanced labor force. One author observed, "Foreigners do all the work. Moroccans clean houses, Sudanese grow vegetables, Egyptians fix cars and drive trucks. Iraqis run the power stations and American and European technicians keep the equipment and systems humming. All the Libyans do is show up for makework government jobs."[6] Difficult climatic conditions and little arable land severely limit agricultural production; the country must import 75 percent of its food.

AN UNCERTAIN FUTURE

The revolutionary regime has been more successful than the monarchy was in making the wealth from oil revenues available to ordinary Libyans. Per capita income, which was $2,170 the year after the revolution, had risen to $10,900 by 1980. U.S sanctions and the drop in global oil prices have resulted in sharp reductions; per capita income was $8,900 in 2001 and $6,700 in 2005.

This influx of wealth changed the lives of the people in a very short period of time. Semi-nomadic tribes such as the Qadadfas of the Sirte (Qadhafi's kin) have been provided with permanent homes, for example. Extensive social-welfare programs, such as free medical care, free education, and low-cost housing, have greatly enhanced the lives of many Libyans. However, this wealth has yet to be spread evenly across society. The economic downturn of the 1990s produced a thriving black market, along with price gouging and corruption in

HEALTH/WELFARE

Shortages of adequately educated Libyans remains a major obstacle to national development. A recent survey of government managers found that only 3–5 percent had had leadership training. As a starting point in dealing with educational inadequacy the government approved in October 2006 a project with One Laptop Per Child, a U.S. firm, to provide wireless laptop computers to all Libyan school children by June 2008. In return for its $250 million investment Libya will receive 1.2 million computers, one server per school, technical advisers, satellite internet service and other infrastructure elements for the school system.

the public sector. In 1996, Libya organized "purification committees," mostly staffed by young army officers, to monitor and report instances of black-market and other illegal activities.

Until recently, opposition to Qadhafi was confined almost entirely to exiles abroad, centered on former associates living in Cairo, Egypt, who had broken with the Libyan leader for reasons either personal or related to economic mismanagement. But economic downturns and dissatisfaction with the leader's wildly unsuccessful foreign-policy ventures increased popular discontent at home. In 1983, Qadhafi had introduced two domestic policies that also generated widespread resentment: He called for the drafting of women into the armed services, and he recommended that all children be educated at home until age 10. The 200 basic "people's congresses," set up in 1977 to recommend policy to the national General People's Congress (which in theory is responsible for national policy), objected strongly to both proposals. Qadhafi then created 2,000 more people's congresses, presumably to dilute the opposition, but withdrew the proposals. In effect, suggested one observer, *The Green Book* theory had begun to work, and Qadhafi didn't like it.

Qadhafi's principal support base rests on the armed forces and the "revolutionary committees," formed of youths whose responsibility is to guard against infractions of *The Green Book* rules. "Brother Colonel" also relies upon a small group of collaborators from the early days of the Revolution, and his own relatives and members of the Qadadfa form part of the inner power structure. This structure is highly informal, and it may explain why Qadhafi is able to disappear from public view from time to time,

as he did after the United States conducted an air raid on Tripoli in 1986, and emerge having lost none of his popularity and charismatic appeal.

In recent years, disaffection within the army has led to a number of attempts to overthrow Qadhafi. The most serious coup attempt took place in 1984, when army units allied with the opposition Islamic Front for the Salvation of Libya, based in Cairo and headed by several of Qadhafi's former associates, attacked the central barracks in Tripoli where he usually resides. The attackers were defeated in a bloody gun battle. A previously unknown opposition group based in Geneva, Switzerland, claimed in 1996 that its agents had poisoned the camel's milk that Qadhafi drinks while eating dates on his desert journeys, but proof of this claim is lacking.

INTERNAL CHANGES

Qadhafi has a talent for the unexpected that has made him an effective survivor. In 1988, he ordered the release of all political prisoners and personally drove a bulldozer through the main gate of Tripoli's prison to inaugurate "Freedom Day." Exiled opponents of the regime were invited to return under a promise of amnesty, and a number did so.

In June of that year, the GPC approved a "Charter of Human Rights" as an addendum to *The Green Book*. The charter outlaws the death penalty, bans mistreatment of prisoners, and guarantees every accused person the right to a fair trial. It also permits formation of labor unions, confirms the right to education and suitable employment for all Libyan citizens, and places Libya on record as prohibiting production of nuclear and chemical weapons. In March 1995, the country's last prison was destroyed and its inmates freed in application of the charter's guarantees of civil liberty.

With political reform unlikely given Qadhafi's hold on the levers of power and his general popularity, the most likely changes in Libyan life and prospects appear to be socioeconomic. Apart from its educational deficiencies mentioned above, the country still lacks an effective legal system, hospitals and clinics, broad-based leadership and other components of successful state-building. In an effort to move in this direction, the government in 2007 announced layoffs for 400,000 workers, nearly all of them employed by the state. The reduction will save some $3 billion in salaries. Dismissed employees would be guaranteed $40,000 in individual loans, to be used in starting a business or working in the almost nonexistent private sector.

THE WAR WITH CHAD

Libyan forces occupied the Aouzou Strip in northern Chad in 1973, claiming it as an integral part of the Libyan state. Occupation gave Libya access also to the reportedly rich uranium resources of the region. In subsequent years, Qadhafi played upon political rivalries in Chad to extend the occupation into a de facto one of annexation of most of its poverty-stricken neighbor.

But in late 1986 and early 1987, Chadian leaders patched up their differences and turned on the Libyans. In a series of spectacular raids on entrenched Libyan forces, the highly mobile Chadians, traveling mostly in Toyota trucks, routed the Libyans and drove them out of northern Chad. Chadian forces then moved into the Aouzou Strip and even attacked nearby air bases inside Libya. The defeats, with casualties of some 3,000 Libyans and loss of huge quantities of Soviet-supplied military equipment, exposed the weaknesses of the overequipped, undertrained, and poorly motivated Libyan Army.

ACHIEVEMENTS

The Great Man-Made River (GMR) called by Qadhafi the world's eighth wonder, is in the third stage of completion as noted above. In addition to the network of pipes, each one 13 feet in diameter, excess water pumped will be stored in the Kufra basin, which has a capacity for 5000 cubic meters. The water flow to Tripoli and Benghazi is presently 200 million cubic feet per day, sufficient to meet the needs of residents of both cities.

In 1989, after admitting his mistake, Qadhafi signed a cease-fire with then-Chadian leader Hissène Habré and agreed to submit the dispute over ownership of Aouzou to the International Court of Justice (ICJ). The ICJ affirmed Chadian sovereignty in 1994 on the basis of a 1955 agreement arranged by France as the occupying power there. Libyan forces withdrew from Aouzou in May, and since then the two countries have enjoyed a peaceful relationship. In 1998, the border was opened completely, in line with Qadhafi's policy of "strengthening neighborly relations."

FOREIGN POLICY

Libya's relations with the United States have remained hostile since the 1969 Revolution, which not only overthrew King Idris but also resulted in the closing of the important Wheelus Field air base. Despite Qadhafi's efforts in more recent years to portray himself and Libya as respectable members of the world of nations, the country remains on the U.S. Department of State's list as one of the main sponsors of international terrorism. In 1986, U.S. war planes bombed Tripoli and Benghazi in retaliation for the bombing of a disco in Berlin, Germany, which killed two U.S. servicemen and injured 238 others. The retaliatory U.S. air attack on Libya killed 55 Libyan civilians, including Qadhafi's adopted daughter. After numerous delays and conflicting evidence about Libya's role in the Berlin bombing, a trial began in 1998 for four persons implicated in the attack. Only one, a diplomat in the embassy in East Berlin (now closed), was a Libyan national. The trial ended in 2001 with the conviction of the four; they were given 12- to 14-year sentences.

Libya resumed its old role of "pariah state" in 1992 by refusing to extradite two officers of its intelligence service suspected of complicity in the 1988 bombing of a Pan American jumbo jet over Lockerbie, Scotland. The United States, France, and Britain had demanded the officers' extradition and introduced a resolution to that effect in the UN Security Council; in the event of noncompliance on Libya's part, sanctions would be imposed on the country. *Resolution 748* passed by a 10-to-zero vote, with five abstentions. A concurrent ruling by the ICJ ordered Libya to turn over the suspects or explain in writing why it was not obligated to do so.

Qadhafi, however, refused to comply with *Resolution 748.* He argued that the suspects should be tried (if at all) in a neutral country, since they could not be given a fair trial either in Britain or the United States.

The Security Council responded by imposing partial sanctions on Libya. Despite the partial embargo, Libya's leader continued to reject compliance with the resolution. As a result, the Security Council in 1993 passed *Resolution 883,* imposing much stiffer sanctions on the country. The new sanctions banned all shipments of spare parts and equipment sales and froze Libyan foreign bank deposits. International flights to Libya were prohibited. The only area of the economy not affected was that of oil exports, since Britain and other Western European countries are dependent on low-sulfur Libyan crude for their economies.

The tug-of-war between the United Nations and its recalcitrant member went on for six years. In March 1998, the United Nations set a 60-day deadline for compliance. Subsequently Qadhafi reversed his stance on the Lockerbie suspects. While he insisted that the Libyan government was not involved, he agreed to turn over the suspects to be tried in a neutral court under Scottish law. The two were then flown to the Netherlands, where they were tried in a court set up in an abandoned Dutch air base, Camp Zeist. The trial was marked by intricate legal maneuverings and some questionable evidence. In 2000, one of the suspects was acquitted. The other, former Libyan intelligence agent Abdel Basset al-Megrahi, was found guilty and sentenced to life imprisonment. However several Scottish judges involved in the trial recently declared that prosecution and conviction were flawed by flimsy or fabricated evidence. This would be grounds for a new trial.

In 2003 the Libyan leader formally admitted the country's involvement in the issue and agreed to compensate the families of the victims. Each of the 270 families would receive between $5 million and $10 million under a $2.7 billion settlement, with the funds deposited in an international bank. The agreement resulted in the end of sanctions on the country.

PROSPECTS

The tide of fundamentalism sweeping across the Islamic world and challenging secular regimes has largely spared Libya thus far, although there were occasional clashes between fundamentalists and police in the 1980s, and in 1992, some 500 fundamentalists were jailed briefly. However, the bloody civil uprisings against the regimes in neighboring Algeria and Egypt caused Qadhafi in 1994 to reemphasize Libya's Islamic nature. New laws passed by the General People's Congress would apply Islamic law (Shari'a) and punishments in such areas as marriage and divorce, wills and inheritance, crimes of theft and violence (where the Islamic punishment is cutting off a hand), and for apostasy. Libya's tribal-based society and Qadhafi's own interpretation of

Timeline: PAST

1835

Tripoli becomes an Ottoman province with the Sanusiya controlling the interior

1932

Libya becomes an Italian colony, Italy's "Fourth Shore"

1951

An independent kingdom is set up by the UN under King Idris

1969

The Revolution overthrows Idris; the Libyan Arab Republic is established

1973–1976

Qadhafi decrees a cultural and social revolution with government by people's committees

1980s

A campaign to eliminate Libyan opponents abroad; the United States imposes economic sanctions in response to suspected Libya-terrorist ties; U.S. planes attack targets in Tripoli and Benghazi; Libyan troops are driven from Chad, including the Aouzou Strip

1990s

Libya's relations with its neighbors improve; the UN votes to impose sanctions on Libya for terrorist acts; Qadhafi comes to an agreement with the UN regarding the trial of the PanAm/Lockerbie bombing suspects

Islamic law to support women's rights and to deal with other social issues continue to serve as obstacles to Islamic fundamentalism.

Resolution of the Lockerbie issue and other positive steps taken by Qadhafi have gained Libya international respectability. A more recent incident involved the sentencing by a Libyan court of Bulgarian nurses and a Palestinian doctor (later given Bulgarian citizenship) on charges of infecting children in a hospital in Benghazi with H.I.V. The court first sentenced them to death, but after an international outcry plus credible evidence that unsanitary conditions in the hospital were responsible for the outbreak the sentences were commuted to life imprisonment. Eventually after further international pressure, including warnings by Britain and France, Libya's largest oil recipients, and continued U.S. sanctions, the nurses and doctor were released to Bulgaria, under the terms of a 1984 treaty which allows citizens of one country convicted of crimes in the other to serve out their sentences in their home country. The pot was further "sweetened" by payments of some $460 million to the victims' families from an unspecified international fund.

Despite his continued hostility toward Israel, Qadhafi has sought to cultivate an image of international respectability in recent years. He has emphasized in particular Libya's role in African unity. With support from other African states, Libya was elected to the chairmanship of the UN Commission on Human Rights (UNCHR) in 2003.

In September 2007 Qadhafi's African policy took another major step forward when the Libyan leader agreed to mediate in Sudan's Darfur conflict. Wearing a brown shirt patterned in green patches in the shape of Africa, he met with UN Secretary-General Ban Ki-Moon in his desert tent in Sirte, his desert home, and agreed to host Darfur peace talks in Tripoli on October 27. The Libyan Minister for African Affairs struck the tone for the forthcoming talks: "We have three-quarters of a million Darfuris working in Libya, and our security is united with Sudan and Darfur."[7]

On September 7, 1999, the Libyan leader celebrated his 30th year in power with a parade of thousands of footsoldiers, along with long-range missiles and tanks, through the streets of Tripoli. Libyan jets, many of them piloted by women, flew overhead.

Qadhafi's excellent health and commitment to the rather unrealistic ideas of the *Green Book* make forecasting Libya's political future dubious at best. His eldest son, Sayf, recently formed an Economic Development Board charged with developing the private sector. Another son, El-Saadi, made an official visit to Japan in 2001. But lacking either monarchical or dictatorial strongman traditions, it seems likely that the structure of authority established in 1969 will continue for the foreseeable future.

The lifting of UN sanctions on the country resulted from Qadhafi's acceptance of international jurisdiction in the Lockerbie case. As a result, relations with Europe have been normalized. The moribund tourist industry is also beginning to show signs of life, offering desert oases, splendid beaches and well-preserved Roman ruins to prospective visitors. In December 2003 Qadhafi again confounded his critics by agreeing to discontinue Libya's nuclear weapons development program and open its facilities to international inspection. The country also signed the Nuclear Non-Proliferation Treaty. In March 2004 the Libyan leader ordered 3,300 chemical bombs destroyed and agreed to halt further production.

NOTES

1. "[I]rrigation, colonization and hard work have wrought marvels. Everywhere you see plantations forced out of the sandy, wretched soil." A. H. Broderick, *North Africa* (London: Oxford University Press, 1943), p. 27.

2. Religious leaders issued a *fatwa* ("binding legal decision") stating that a vote against independence would be a vote against religion. Omar el Fathaly, et al., *Political Development and Bureaucracy in Libya* (Lexington, KY: Lexington Books, 1977).

3. See *Middle East Journal,* vol. 24, no. 2 (Spring 1970), Documents Section.

4. John Wright, *Libya: A Modern History* (Baltimore, MD: Johns Hopkins University Press, 1982), pp. 124–126. Qadhafi's idol was former Egyptian president Nasser, a leader in the movement for unity and freedom among the Arabs. While he was at school in Sebha, in the Fezzan, he listened to Radio Cairo's Voice of the Arabs and was later expelled from school as a militant organizer of demonstrations.

5. *The London Times* (June 6, 1973).

6. Khidr Hamza, with Jeff Stein, *Saddam's Bombmaker* (New York: Scribner's, 2000), p. 289. The author was head of the Iraqi nuclear-weapons program before defecting to Libya and eventually the United States.

7. Quoted by Warren Hoge, *The New York Times,* Sept. 8, 2007.

Morocco (Kingdom of Morocco)

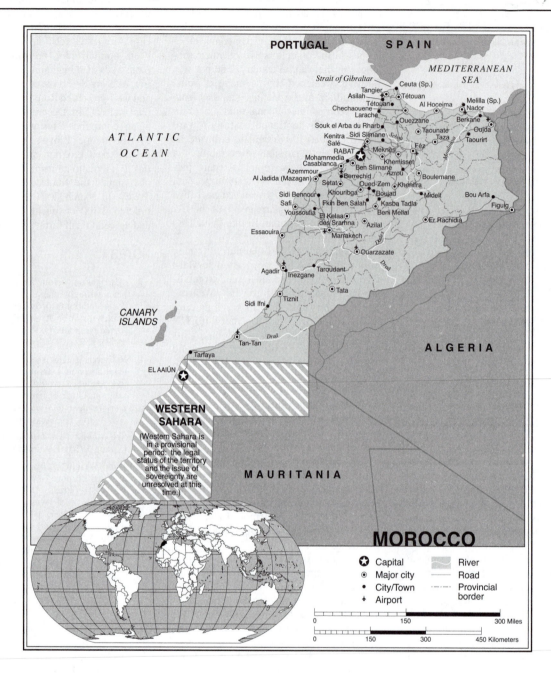

Morocco Statistics

GEOGRAPHY

Area in Square Miles (Kilometers):
274,400 (710,850) including the
Western Sahara (102,675 square
miles-266,000 sq.km.) about the size
of California
Capital (Population): Rabat (1,293,000)
Environmental Concerns: land
degradation; desertification; soil
erosion; overgrazing; contamination of
water supplies; oil pollution of coastal
waters
Geographical Features: the northern
coast and interior are mountainous,
with large areas of bordering plateaux,
intermontane valleys, and rich coastal
plains; south, southeast and entire
Western Sahara is desert
Climate: varies from Mediterranean to
desert

PEOPLE

Population

Total: 33,757,175
Annual Growth Rate: 1.5%
Rural/Urban Population Ratio: 47/53
Major Languages: Arabic; Tamazight
(name for spoken Berber Languages
with 3 main dialects), Tashelheit
(south), Tarifit (north) and Tamazight

(central). French widely used and understood
Ethnic Makeup: 64% Arab; 35% Berber; 1% non-Moroccan and Jewish
Religions: 99% Sunni Muslim; 1% Christian and Jewish

Health

Life Expectancy at Birth: 68.8 years (male), 73.6 years (female)
Infant Mortality Rate (Ratio): 38.85/1,000 live births

Education

Adult Literacy Rate: 51.7%
Compulsory (Ages): 7–13

COMMUNICATION

Telephones: 1,515,000 main lines
Daily Newspaper Circulation: 13 per 1,000 people
Televisions: 93 per 1,000 people
Internet Service Providers: 8 (2000)

TRANSPORTATION

Highways in Miles (Kilometers): 37,649 (60,626)

Railroads in Miles (Kilometers): 1,184 (1,907)
Usable Airfields: 69
Motor Vehicles in Use: 1,278,000

GOVERNMENT

Type: constitutional monarchy
Independence Date: March 2, 1956 (from France)
Head of State/Government: King Muhammad VI; Prime Minister Driss Jettou
Political Parties: National Rally of Independents; Popular Movement; National Democratic Party; Constitutional Union; Socialist Union of Popular Forces; Istiqlal; Kutla Bloc; Party of Progress and Socialism; others
Suffrage: universal at 18

MILITARY

Military Expenditures (% of GDP): 5%
Current Disputes: final resolution on the status of Western Sahara remains to be worked out; from time to time Morocco demands the retrocession of Ceuta and Melilla, cities located

physically within its territory but considered extensions of mainland Spain (plazas de soberaniá by the Spanish government)

ECONOMY

Currency ($U.S. Equivalent): 8.77 dirhams = $1
Per Capita Income/GDP: $4,400/ $147 billion
GDP Growth Rate: 6.7%
Inflation Rate: 2.8%
Unemployment Rate: 7.7%
Labor Force: 11,250,000
Natural Resources: phosphates; iron ore; manganese; lead; zinc; fish; salt
Agriculture: barley; wheat; citrus fruits; wine; vegetables; olives; livestock
Industry: phosphate mining and processing; food processing; leather goods; textiles; construction; tourism
Exports: $11.72 billion (primary partners France, Spain, United Kingdom)
Imports: $21.22 billion (primary partners France, Spain, Germany)

Morocco Country Report

The Kingdom of Morocco is the western-most country in North Africa. Morocco's population is the second largest (after Egypt) of the Arab states. The country's territory includes the Western Sahara (a claim made under dispute), formerly two Spanish colonies, Rio de Oro and Saguia al-Hamra. Morocco annexed part in 1976 and the balance in 1978, after Mauritania's withdrawal from its share, as decided in an agreement with Spain. Since then, Morocco has incorporated the Western Sahara into the kingdom as its newest province.

Two other territories physically within Morocco remain outside Moroccan control. They are the cities of Ceuta and Melilla, both located on rocky peninsulas that jut out into the Mediterranean Sea. They have been held by Spain since the fifteenth century. (Spain also owns several small islands off the coast in Moroccan territorial waters in the Mediterranean.) Spain's support for Morocco's admission to the European Union (EU) as an associate member has eased tensions between them over the enclaves. An additional economic advantage to Morocco is that each day some 40,000 Moroccans cross legally into them for work.

In 1986 a Spanish law excluding Moroccan Muslim residents from Spanish citizenship led to protests among them. The Moroccan government did not pursue the protests, and in 1988 the question of citizenship became moot when the Spanish Cortes (Parliament) passed a law formally incorporating Ceuta and Melilla into Spain as overseas territories.

DEVELOPMENT

Morocco has important reserves of phosphate rock. It also has exportable supplies of certain rare metal, such as antimony. Unfortunately it lacks oil resources. An oil strike in the Sahara in 2000 proved abortive. Abundant rainfall has improved agricultural production; GDP growth presently averages 5 percent annually.

In the last couple of years the two cities have been all but overwhelmed by migrants, most of them undocumented, from sub-Saharan Africa seeking to cross into Europe, where they hope to find jobs and a better life than is available in their own countries of origin. Some 15,000 attempted the hazardous crossing in 2004

as compared with 350 in all in the previous 6-year period. A mass breakthrough in October, which resulted in many casualties as the migrants scaled the razor-wire fences around the enclaves, led the Spanish government to send military units to guard the borders. On its side, the Moroccan government stepped up efforts to block illegal migration through its territory and break up the criminal networks bringing the migrants northward. Some 1,000 of them were captured and interned in the desert town of Bou Arfa, near Goulimine, prior to their deportation. The UN and human rights groups, notably Doctors Without Borders, criticized the deportations. In a response in October 2005, large-scale demonstrations took place in Rabat, with marchers carrying signs that read "we are all Africans; Morocco cannot become Europe's immigration policeman."[1]

Although Morocco is better off than many of its African neighbors who provide the bulk of would-be immigrants, its growing youth population and lack of jobs continue to encourage Moroccans particularly in the lower age groups to attempt the often risky crossing into Europe in search of employment. Thus in December 2005 Italy reported a 15 percent increase

Hamilton Wright/Government of Morocco (GM001)

Morocco has a rich history. The Karawiyyin Mosque at Fez was founded in the ninth century A.D. and is the largest mosque in North Africa. It is also the seat of one of Africa's oldest universities.

in illegal immigrants; a third of them were Moroccans. This was due largely to the closure of Ceuta and Melilla. As an example of this economic pressure, a coal mine in the rural east near Jerada, operated by a Russian company, was closed abruptly in the late 1990s as the company shifted its operations to Poland and the Ukraine. As a result the community found itself with no jobs and no prospects.

Morocco is a rugged land, dominated by several massive mountain ranges. The Rif Range, averaging 7,000 feet in elevation, runs parallel to the Mediterranean, isolating the northern region from the rest of the country. The Atlas Mountains dominate the interior of Morocco. The Middle Atlas begins south of the Rif, separated by the Taza Gap (the traditional gateway for invaders from the east), and extends from northeast to southwest to join the High Atlas, a snow capped range containing North Africa's highest peak. A third range, the Anti-Atlas, walls off the desert from the rest of Morocco. These ranges and the general inaccessibility of the country have isolated Morocco throughout most of its history, not only from outside invaders but internally as well, because of the geographical separation of peoples.

Moroccan geography explains the country's dual population structure. A significant number are Berbers, descendants of

the region's original inhabitants, who were called *Barbari* by the Romans when they arrived in North Africa, due to their lack of a written language (i.e. Latin) and their ignorance of Roman culture and laws. The Berbers were, until recently, grouped into tribes, often taking the name of a common ancestor, such as the Ait ("Sons of") 'Atta of southern Morocco.[2] Invading Arabs converted them to Islam in the eighth century but made few other changes in Berber life. Unlike the Berbers, the majority of the Arabs who settled in Morocco were, and are, town-dwellers. The Berbers, more than the Arabs, derived unity and support from their extended families rather than from state control, whether real or putative.

The fact that the Arabs were invaders caused the majority of the Berbers to withdraw into mountain areas. They accepted Islam but held stubbornly to their basic independence. Much of Morocco's past history consisted of efforts by various rulers, both Berber and Arab, to control Berber territory. The result was a kind of balance-of-power political system. The rulers had their power bases in the cities, while the rural groups operated as independent units. Moroccan rulers made periodic military expeditions into Berber territory to collect tribute and if possible to secure full obedience from the Berbers. When the ruler was strong, the Berbers paid up and submitted;

when he was weak, they ignored him. At times Berber leaders might invade "government territory," capturing cities and replacing one ruler with another more to their liking. When they were not fighting with urban rulers, different Berber groups fought among themselves, so the system did little to foster Moroccan national unity.

HISTORY

Morocco has a rich cultural history, with many of its ancient monuments more or less intact. It has been governed by some form of monarchy for over a thousand years, although royal authority was frequently limited or contested by rivals. The current ruling dynasty, the Alawis, assumed power in the 1600s. One reason for their long rule is the fact that they descend from the Prophet Muhammad. Thus, Moroccans have had a real sense of Islamic traditions and history through their rulers.

The first identifiable Moroccan "state" was established by a descendant of Muhammad named Idris, in the late eighth century. Idris had taken refuge in the far west of the Islamic world to escape civil war in the east. Because of his piety, learning, and descent from Muhammad, he was accepted by a number of Berber groups as their spiritual and political leader. His son and successor, Idris II, founded the first Moroccan capital, Fez. Father and son established the principle whereby descent from the Prophet was an important qualification for political power as well as social status in Morocco.

The Idrisids ruled over only a small portion of the current Moroccan territory, and, after the death of Idris II, their "nation" lapsed into decentralized family rule. In any case, the Berbers had no real idea of nationhood; each separate Berber group thought of itself as a nation. But in the eleventh and twelfth centuries, two Berber confederations developed that brought imperial grandeur to Morocco. These were the Almoravids and the Almohads. Under their rule, North Africa developed a political structure separate from that of the eastern Islamic world, one strongly influenced by Berber values.

The Almoravids began as camel-riding nomads from the Western Sahara who were inspired by a religious teacher to carry out a reform movement to revive the true faith of Islam. (The word *Almoravid* comes from the Arabic *al-Murabitun*, "men of the ribat," rather like the crusading religious orders of Christianity in the Middle Ages.) Fired by religious zeal, the Almoravids conquered all of Morocco and parts of western Algeria.

A second "imperial" dynasty, the Almohads, succeeded the Almoravids but improved on their performance. They were the first, and probably the last, to unite all of North Africa and Islamic Spain under one government. Almohad monuments, such as the Qutubiya tower, the best-known landmark of Marrakesh, and the Tower of Hassan in Rabat, still stand as reminders of their power and the high level of the Almohads' architectural achievements.

The same fragmentation, conflicts, and Berber/Arab rivalries that had undermined their predecessors brought down the Almohads in the late thirteenth century. From then on, dynasty succeeded dynasty in power. An interesting point about this cyclical pattern is that despite the lack of political unity, a distinctive Moroccan style and culture developed. Each dynasty contributed something to this culture, in architecture, crafts, literature, and music. The interchange between Morocco and Islamic Spain was constant and fruitful. Poets, musicians, artisans, architects, and others traveled regularly between Spanish and Moroccan cities. One can visit the city of Fez today and be instantly transported back into the Hispano-Moorish way of life of the Middle Ages.

Mulay Ismail

The Alawis came to power and established their rule partly by force, but also as a result of their descent from the Prophet Muhammad. This link enabled them to win the support of both Arab and Berber populations. The real founder of the dynasty was Mulay Ismail, one of the longest-reigning and most powerful monarchs in Morocco's history.

Mulay Ismail unified the Moroccan nation. The great majority of the Berber groups accepted him as their sovereign. The sultan built watchtowers and posted permanent garrisons in Berber territories to make sure they continued to do so. He brought public security to Morocco also; it was said that in his time, a Jew or an unveiled woman could travel safely anywhere in the land, which was not the case in most parts of North Africa, the Middle East, and Europe.

Mulay Ismail was a contemporary of Louis XIV, and the reports of his envoys to the French court at Versailles convinced him that he should build a capital like it. He chose Meknes, not far from Fez. The work was half finished when he died of old age. The slaves and prisoners working on this "Moroccan Versailles" threw down their shovels and ran away. The enormous unfinished walls and arched Bab al-Mansur ("Gate of the Victorious") still stand today as reminders of Mulay Ismail's dream.

Mulay Ismail had many wives and left behind 500 sons but no instructions as to which should succeed him. His eventual successor, Sultan Muhammad II, was the first foreign sovereign to recognize U.S. independence (in 1777). However the removal of British naval protection for U.S. merchant shipping after the Revolution led to attacks by corsairs from Morocco and other North African states. In 1784 the brig *Betsy* was seized by Moroccan corsairs and its crew taken hostage. The sultan had allowed this to happen because of delays in Congress in signing a formal peace treaty. In 1786, "armed with Innocence and the Olive Branch," Thomas Jefferson, John Adams and Benjamin Franklin collectively negotiated the first U.S. treaty with a foreign power, admittedly sweetened by a $20,000 "gift" to the sultan. Under its terms the United States was allowed to set up a consulate (or legation) in Tangier, and although it is now a museum it remains the only national landmark abroad.[3]

The French Protectorate

In the 1800s and early 1900s, Morocco became increasingly vulnerable to outside pressures. The French, who were established in neighboring Algeria and Tunisia, wanted to complete their conquests. The nineteenth-century sultans were less and less able to control the mountain Berbers and were forced to make constant expeditions into the "land of dissidence," at great expense to the treasury. They began borrowing money from European bankers, not only to pay their bills but also to finance arms purchases and the development of ports, railroads, and industries to create a modern economy and prove to the European powers that Morocco could manage its own affairs. Nothing worked; by 1900, Morocco was so far in debt that the French took over the management of its finances. (One sultan, Abd al-Aziz, had bought one of everything he was told about by European salesmen, including a gold-plated toy train that carried food from the kitchen to the dining room of his palace.) Meanwhile, the European powers plotted the country's downfall.

In 1904, France, Britain, Spain, and Germany signed secret agreements partitioning the country. The French would be given the largest part of the country, while Spain would receive the northern third as a protectorate plus some territory in the Western Sahara. In return, the French and Spanish agreed to respect Britain's claim to Egypt and Germany's claim to East African territory.

The ax fell on Morocco in 1912. French workers building the new port of Casablanca were killed by Moroccans. Mobs attacked foreigners in Fez, and the sultan's

FREEDOM

Elections in 2002 for the new Chamber of Representatives were cited by observers as free and fair, with a balance of seats among various parties. New King Muhammad VI's "National Action Plan" raises the legal marriageable age for women to 18 and gives other rights to them. In 2003 the king proposed revisions to the 1957 *Mudawanna* (Family Law) which were approved by the Chamber. They now have the right to file for divorce, share equally in family property, and travel without prior consent from male family members.

troops could not control them. French troops marched to Fez from Algeria to restore order. The sultan, Mulay Hafidh (Hafiz), was forced to sign the Treaty of Fez, establishing a French protectorate over southern Morocco. The sultan believed that he had betrayed his country and died shortly thereafter, supposedly of a broken heart. Spain then occupied the northern third of the country, and Tangier, the traditional residence of foreign consuls, became an international city ruled by several European powers.

The French protectorate over Morocco covered barely 45 years (1912–1956). But in that brief period, the French introduced significant changes into Moroccan life. For the first time, southern Morocco was brought entirely under central government control, although the "pacification" of the Berbers was not complete until 1934. French troops also intervened in the Spanish Zone to help put down a rebellion in the Rif led by Abd al-Krim, a *Qadi* ("religious judge") and leader of the powerful Ait Waryaghar tribe.[4]

The organization of the protectorate was largely the work of the first French resident-general, Marshal Louis Lyautey. Lyautey had great respect for Morocco's past and its dignified people. His goal was to develop the country and modernize the sultan's government while preserving Moroccan traditions and culture. He preferred the Berbers to the Arabs and set up a separate administration under Berber-speaking French officers for Berber areas.[5]

Lyautey's successors were less respectful of Moroccan traditions. The sultan, supposedly an independent ruler, became a figurehead. French *colons* (settlers) flocked to Morocco to buy land at rock-bottom prices and develop vineyards, citrus groves, and orchards. Modern cities sprang up around the perimeters of Rabat, Fez, Marrakesh, and other cities. In rural areas, particularly in the Atlas Mountains, the French worked with powerful local chiefs (*qaids*). Certain qaids used the arrangement to become enormously wealthy. One qaid, al-Glawi, as he was called, strutted about like a rooster in his territory and often said that he was the real sultan of Morocco.[6]

Morocco's Independence Struggle

The movement for independence in Morocco developed slowly. The only symbol of national unity was the sultan, Muhammad ibn Yusuf. But he seemed ineffectual to most young Moroccans, particularly those educated in French schools, who began to question the right of France to rule a people against their will.

The hopes of these young Moroccans got a boost during World War II. The Western Allies, Great Britain and the United States, had gone on record in favor of the right of subject peoples to self-determination after the war. When U.S. president Franklin D. Roosevelt and British prime minister Winston Churchill came to Casablanca for an important wartime conference, the sultan was convinced to meet them privately and get a commitment for Morocco's independence. The leaders promised their support.

However, Roosevelt died before the end of the war, and Churchill was defeated for reelection. The French were not under any pressure after the war to end the protectorate. When a group of Moroccan nationalists formed the Istiqlal ("Independence") Party and demanded the end of French rule, most of them were arrested. A few leaders escaped to the Spanish Zone or to Tangier, where they could operate freely. For several years, Istiqlal headquarters was the home of the principal of the American School at Tangier, an ardent supporter of Moroccan nationalism.

With the Istiqlal dispersed, the sultan represented the last hope for national unity and resistance. Until then, he had gone along with the French; but in the early 1950s, he began to oppose them openly. The French began to look for a way to remove him from office and install a more cooperative ruler.

In 1953, the Glawi and his fellow qaids decided, along with the French, that the time was right to depose the sultan. The qaids demanded that he abdicate; they said that his presence was contributing to Moroccan instability. When he refused, he was bundled into a French plane and sent into exile. An elderly uncle was named to replace him.

The sultan's departure had the opposite effect from what was intended. In exile, he became a symbol for Moroccan resistance to the protectorate. Violence broke out, French settlers were murdered, and a Moroccan Army of Liberation began battling French troops in rural regions. Although the French could probably have contained the rebellion in Morocco, they were under great pressure in neighboring Algeria and Tunisia, where resistance movements were also under way. In 1955, the French abruptly capitulated. Sultan Muhammad ibn Yusuf returned to his palace in Rabat in triumph, and the elderly uncle retired to potter about his garden in Tangier.

INDEPENDENCE

Morocco became independent on March 2, 1956. (The Spanish protectorate ended in April, and Tangier came under Moroccan control in October, although it kept its free-port status and special banking and currency privileges for several more years.) It began its existence as a sovereign state with a number of assets—a popular ruler, an established government, and a well-developed system of roads, schools, hospitals, and industries inherited from the protectorate. Against these assets were the liabilities of age-old Arab-Berber and inter-Berber conflicts, little experience with political parties or democratic institutions, and an economy dominated by Europeans.

The sultan's goal was to establish a constitutional monarchy. His first action was to give himself a new title, King Muhammad V, symbolizing the end of the old autocratic rule of his predecessors. He also pardoned the Glawi, who crawled into his presence to kiss his feet and crawled out backwards as proof of penitence. (He died soon thereafter.) However, the power of the qaids and pashas ended; "they were compromised by their association with the French, and returned to the land to make way for nationalist cadres, many . . . not from the regions they were assigned to administer."[7]

Muhammad V did not live long enough to reach his goal. He died unexpectedly in 1961 and was succeeded by his eldest son, Crown Prince Hassan. Hassan II ruled until his death in 1999. While he fulfilled his father's promise immediately with a Constitution, in most other ways Hassan II set his own stamp on Morocco.

The Constitution provided for an elected legislature and a multiparty political system. In addition to the Istiqlal, a number of other parties were organized, including one representing the monarchy. But the results of the French failure to develop a satisfactory party system soon became apparent. Berber-Arab friction, urban-rural distrust, city rivalries, and inter-Berber hostility all intensified. Elections failed to produce a clear majority for any party, not even the king's.

In 1965, riots broke out in Casablanca. The immediate cause was labor unrest, but the real reason lay in the lack of effective leadership by the parties. The king declared a state of emergency, dismissed the legislature, and assumed full powers under the Constitution.

For the next dozen years, Hassan II ruled as an absolute monarch. He continued to insist that his goal was a parliamentary system, a "government of national union." But he depended on a small group of cronies, members of prominent merchant families, the large Alawi family, or powerful Berber leaders as a more reliable group than the fractious political parties. The dominance of "the king's men" led to growing dissatisfaction and the perception that the king had sold out to special interests. Gradually, unrest spread to the army, previously loyal to its commander-in-chief. In 1971, during a diplomatic reception, cadets from the main military academy invaded the royal palace near Rabat. A number of foreign diplomats were killed and the king held prisoner briefly before loyal troops could crush the rebellion. The next year, a plot by air-force pilots to shoot down the king's plane was narrowly averted. The two escapes helped confirm in Hassan's mind his invincibility under the protection of Allah.

But they also prompted him to reinstate the parliamentary system. A new Constitution issued in 1972 defined Morocco "as a democratic and social constitutional monarchy in which Islam is the established religion."[8] However, the king retained the constitutional powers that, along with those derived from his spiritual role as "Commander of the Faithful" and lineal descendant of Muhammad, undergirded his authority.

HEALTH/WELFARE

In October 2000, the International Labor Organization (ILO) ranked Morocco as the 3rd-highest country in the world, after China and India, in the exploitation of child labor. Moroccan children as young as 5, all girls, are employed in the carpet industry. In addition to Moroccan and other African illegal immigrants to Europe, the Spanish government tries to control illegal immigration through a new program of recruitment of Moroccan women to leave their families for short-term work on Spanish farms.

INTERNAL POLITICS

Morocco's de facto annexation of the Western Sahara has important implications for future national development due to the territory's size, underpopulation, and mineral resources, particularly shale

Hamilton Wright/Government of Morocco (GM002)

Tangier was once a free city and port. Just across the Strait of Gibraltar from Spain, it now is Morocco's northern metropolis. Modernization and expansion of port facilities to accommodate large cruise ships and tankers got under way in 1999.

oil and phosphates. But the annexation has been equally important to political unity. The "Green March" of 350,000 unarmed Moroccans into Spanish territory in 1975 to dramatize Morocco's claim was organized by the king and supported by all segments of the population and the opposition parties. In 1977, opposition leaders agreed to serve under the king in a "government of national union." The first elections in 12 years were held for a new Legislature; several new parties took part.

The 1984 elections continued the national unity process. The pro-monarchist Constitutional Union (CU) party won a majority of seats in the Chamber of Representatives (Parliament). A new party, the National Rally of Independents (RNI), formed by members with no party affiliations, emerged as the chief rival to the CU.

New elections were scheduled for 1989 but were postponed three times; the king said that extra time was needed for the economic-stabilization program to show results and generate public confidence. The elections finally took place in two stages in 1993: the first for election of party candidates, and the second for trade-union and professional-association candidates. The final tally showed 195 seats for center-right (royalist) candidates, to 120 for the Democratic-bloc opposition. As a result, coalition government became necessary. The two leading opposition parties,

however—the Socialist Union of Popular Forces (USFP) and the Istiqlal—refused to participate, claiming election irregularities. Opposition from members of these parties plus the Kutla Bloc, an alliance formed by several parties, blocked legislative action until 1994. At that point, the entire opposition bloc walked out of the Legislature and announced a boycott of the government.

King Hassan resolved the crisis by appointing then-USFP leader Abdellatif Filali as the new prime minister, thus bringing the opposition into the government. The king continued with this method of political reconciliation by appointing the new head of the USFP, Abderrahmane Youssoufi, to the position after the latter's return from political exile in 1998.

A referendum in 1996 approved several amendments to the constitution. One in particular replaced the unicameral legislature by a bicameral one. The upper house (Chamber of Counselors) has 270 seats, elected indirectly by municipal councils, professional associations, and labor syndicates for 9-year terms. The lower house (Chamber of Representatives) has 325 seats, 295 elected by popular vote for 5-year terms, with 30 seats reserved for women. The first lower house election was held in 2002; the next is scheduled for October 2007.

The 2002 elections underlined the broad spectrum of Moroccan politics. The Socialist Union of Popular Forces (USFP) won 50 seats, the venerable Istiqlal 48, the National

Rally of Independents (RNI) 41 and the Popular Movement 27. The relatively new Islamist party, Party of Justice and Development (PJD) won 42 seats, becoming thereby the third party in the country.

In the September 7, 2007 parliamentary elections the Istiqlal won the largest number of seats (52) while the PJD increased its representation to 46, lower than expected. The USFP ran fifth with 38 seats after the Popular Movement (41) and the RNI (39). The voter turnout was the lowest ever, at 37 percent, and as usual there were claims of electoral fraud, vote buying, and manipulation of the results by the state and the monarchy in order to block the rise of a single party and more importantly, to prevent the Islamists from gaining the upper hand in the rough-and-tumble game of Moroccan politics.

FOREIGN RELATIONS

During his long reign, King Hassan II served effectively in mediating the long-running Arab-Israeli conflict. He took an active part in the negotiations for the 1979 Egyptian-Israeli peace treaty and for the treaty between Israel and Jordan in 1994. For these services he came to be viewed by the United States and by European powers as an impartial mediator. However, his absolute rule and suppression of human rights at home caused difficulties with Europe. The European Union suspended $145 million in aid in 1992; it was restored only after Hassan had released long-time political prisoners and pardoned 150 alleged Islamic militants. In 1995, Morocco became the second African country, after Tunisia, to be granted associate status in the EU.

Thus far, Morocco's only venture in "imperial politics" has been in the Western Sahara. This California-size desert territory, formerly a Spanish protectorate and then a colony after 1912, was never a part of the modern Moroccan state. Its only connection is historical—it was the headquarters and starting point for the Almoravid dynasty, camel-riding nomads who ruled western North Africa and southern Spain in the eleventh century. But the presence of so much empty land, along with millions of tons of phosphate rock and potential oil fields, encouraged the king to "play international politics" in order to secure the territory. In October 1975 the king led a "Green March" of half a million Moroccans armed only with Korans into the Spanish Sahara "to recover sacred Moroccan territory. As a result, Spain agreed in 1976 to cede it jointly to Morocco and Mauritania, in two zones, one-third to Mauritania and two-thirds to Morocco. After the overthrow of the Mauritanian government by a military coup in 1978, its new leaders turned over its zone to Morocco.

Since then Morocco's control has been challenged by Polisario, an acronym for the military wing of the Saharan nationalist movement. The latter's goal is a sovereign state, the Sahrawi Arab Democratic Republic (S.A.D.R.) It has been recognized as such by a number of African countries. However the territory remains under Moroccan control; it has been defined as the country's newest province. As a frontier province, over the past three decades thousands of Moroccan settlers have moved there, encouraged by free land, farm equipment, subsidized housing and other inducements.

Conflict between the Moroccan army and Polisario forces operating from Algerian bases with Algerian support for their cause continued throughout the 1980s. It eventually led the army to construct a 350-mile "Sand Wall" from the Atlantic Ocean around the province's land border. Meanwhile some 140,000 Sahrawis became refugees, crowded into four small camps in southern Algeria.

The dispute eventually came before the UN in 1991. In 1995 the Security Council, prodded by Algeria, approved *Resolution 995*. It called for voter registration for a referendum to determine the future of the territory. The two parties agreed to a cease-fire, and a UN Observer Force,

MINURSO, was established to monitor the cease-fire and supervise voter registration. Due largely to Morocco's intransigence, the referendum has yet to be held, despite efforts at mediation by ex-U.S. Secretary of State James Baker and others.

The "glacial chill" between Morocco and the Polisario thawed a bit in 2005, when the latter released 404 Moroccan prisoners in a "humanitarian gesture." But with the demographic balance tipped in its favor by large-scale Moroccan settlement, it seemed that nothing short of strong international pressure would move the country toward acceptance of *Resolution 995*.

A decade later, the referendum seems less and less likely to be held. King Hassan II unilaterally named the territory Morocco's newest province, and by 2001 Moroccan settlers formed a majority in the population of 244,593. In December 2001, French president Jacques Chirac made an official visit to Morocco and saluted the country for the development of its "southern provinces." Earlier, the United Nations had appointed former U.S. secretary of state James Baker as mediator between Morocco and the Polisario. After several failed attempts at mediation, Baker submitted a plan for postponement of the referendum until 2006. In the interim, the Sahrawis would elect an autonomous governing body, with its powers limited to local and provincial affairs. The voting list would include all residents. Large-scale Moroccan settler movement into the territory with government inducements such as free housing and land have changed Western Saharan demography. Any future referendum is unlikely to result in a vote for separation or independence. Moroccan and Polisario negotiators continue to meet under UN auspices from time to time, most recently in 2007, but with inconclusive results. The Moroccans did agree to "consider" local autonomy for the Western Sahara province, but Polisario's representatives held firmly to a referendum which would include the Sahrawis in Algerian refugee camps. Even if one were held, the preponderance of Moroccans in the voter population would undoubtedly result in its continued attachment to Morocco.

THE ECONOMY

Morocco has many of certain resources but too little of other, critical ones. It has two thirds of the world's known reserves of phosphate rock and is the top exporter of phosphates. The major thrust in industrial development is in phosphate-related industries. Access to deposits was one

reason for Morocco's annexation of the Western Sahara, although to date there has been little extraction there due to the political conflict. The downturn in demand and falling prices in the global phosphates market brought on a debt crisis in the late 1980s. Increased phosphate demand globally and improved crop production following the end of several drought years have strengthened the economy. Privatization of the government-owned tobacco monopoly, the first industry to be so affected, generated a budgetary surplus in 2002.

ACHIEVEMENTS

A Moroccan runner, Abdelkader Mouaziz, won the 31st New York City Marathon, two and one-half minutes ahead of his nearest rival. Another Moroccan, Youssef el Aynaoui, had become one of the world's premier tennis players and competed well in major tournaments before his retirement.

The country also has important but undeveloped iron-ore deposits and a small but significant production of rare metals such as mercury, antimony, nickel, and lead. In the past, a major obstacle to development was the lack of oil resources. Prospects for oil improved in 2000 when the U.S. oil company Skidmore Energy was thought to have struck oil near Talsinnt, in the eastern Sahara. But the find, which the king had declared to be God's gift to Morocco, turned out to be mud. In 2001, the French oil company TotalFinaElf and Kerr-McGee of Texas were granted parallel concessions of 44,000 square miles offshore in Western Saharan waters near Dakhla.

Although recurring droughts have hampered improvement of the agricultural sector, it still accounts for 20 percent of gross domestic product and employs 50 percent of the labor force. Production varies widely from year to year, due to fluctuating rainfall. Abundant rains in 2001 resulted in bumper crops and a 25 percent increase in agricultural output, with 8 percent growth in GDP for that year.

The fisheries sector is equally important to the economy, with 2,175 miles of coastline and half a million square miles of territorial waters to draw from. Fisheries account for 16 percent of exports; annual production is approximately 1 million tons. The agreement with the European Union for associate status has been very beneficial to the industry. Morocco received $500 million in 1999–2001 from European countries in return for fishing rights for their vessels in Moroccan territorial waters.

But the economic outlook and social prospects remain bleak for most people. Although the birth rate has been sharply reduced, job prospects are limited for the large number of young Moroccans entering the labor force each year. The "suicide bombers," who attacked a Jewish community center, a hotel, foreign consulates and other structures in Casablanca in May 2003, killing some 41 persons, were said to belong to the radical Islamist organization al-Sirat al-Mustakim (Righteous Path), believed to be linked with al Qaeda. However, the fact that they came mostly from the impoverished Thomasville slum area of the city suggests that they acted not out of a desire to overthrow the monarchy, but out of frustration with the problems that face Morocco's youth today, namely unemployment, poverty and lack of opportunities in the workplace. As one observer noted of those arrested (only 12 were suicide bombers), little distinguished them from the group of young men idling in the streets or hawking designer sunglasses at intersections around town.

PROSPECTS

King Hassan II died in July 1999. The monarch had ruled his country for 38 years—the second-longest reign in the Middle East. Like King Hussein of Jordan, Hassan became identified with his country to such a degree that "Hassan was Morocco, and Morocco was Hassan." But unlike Jordan's ruler, Hassan combined religious with secular authority. Among his many titles was that of "Commander of the Faithful," and the affection felt for him by most Moroccans, particularly women and youth, was amply visible during his state funeral. His frequent reminders to the nation in speeches and broadcasts that "I am the person entrusted by God to lead you" clearly identified him in the public mind not only as their religious leader but also as head of the family.

The king's eldest son, Crown Prince Muhammad, succeeded him without incident as Muhammad VI. Morocco's new ruler began his reign with public commitments to reform human-rights protections and an effort to atone for some aspects of Hassan's autocratic rule. One of his first actions was the dismissal of Interior Minister Driss Basri, the acknowledged "power behind the throne." He had been considered largely responsible for the "Years of Lead" during Hassan's rule, when human rights were routinely violated and opposition political leaders jailed on various pretexts by the police, army and security services.

Muhammad VI also publicly admitted the existence of the Tazmamat "death camp" and other camps in the Sahara, where rebel army officers and political prisoners were held, often for years and without trial or access to their families. (The family of General Oufkir, leader of the 1972 attempted coup who was later executed, were among those held, but they managed to escape.)[8] The new king also committed $3.8 million in compensation to the families of those who had been imprisoned.

The expansion of what has been variously described as "Islamism", "Islamic fundamentalism" and "Islamic radicalism" in the Muslim world has not escaped Morocco entirely. Hassan II kept the movement on a tight rein during his years in power. He outlawed the main Islamist party, Adl wa Ihsan ("Justice and Charity") and locked its leader away in a mental institution. After his accession Muhammad VI established the Equity and Reconciliation Commission, headed by human rights activist Driss Benezkri, to investigate rights violations during the Years of Lead. By April 2005, when it was disbanded, the Commission had investigated 22,000 cases and compensated the families involved on behalf of the victims. Unfortunately because it had been established as only an investigative body, it could not prosecute defendants. Any such action would have to be taken through the judiciary.

Mohammed VI also issued in 2000 a "National Action Plan" which included women's rights, a free press, and other elements lacking in the country's social structure. But actions attributed to Islamic fundamentalists, such as the Casablanca bombings, provoked a heavy reaction particularly in the security services. Independent publications such as *Le Journal,* the most popular French-language magazine, and newspapers were closed. The head of the Moroccan Association for Human Rights was arrested and beaten, and riot police broke up demonstrations protesting the restrictions, arresting 800 persons. A police officer noted that "we don't want the chaos of a second intifada," a reference to the current Palestinian uprising against Israel.

The king's major social reform effort to date is the Family Code of Laws, approved by the Chamber of Representatives in 2003. Among other provisions it makes wives equal to their husbands in ownership of property and allows them to initiate divorce proceedings. In a separate action, Muhammad VI appointed the first female Royal Counselor, and reserved 30 seats for women in the Chamber.

Reform in Morocco continues to face numerous obstacles, nonetheless. A 2005 Report by Reporters Without Borders indicated that 80 percent of the country's jour-

nalists did not feel free to write about many issues, despite the protection presumably afforded by the Action Plan. One reporter noted in the Report that "while the practice of freedom is clear, the legal guarantee is not there. I would not necessarily say that we are in a process of democratization. I would say we are in a process."[9]

Despite their significant numbers and tradition as Morocco's first inhabitants, the Berbers (called Amazigh in their native language) have felt themselves increasingly excluded from the political process in recent years and their culture marginalized. Their language, called Tamazight although it comprises three closely-related dialects, is not recognized in the Moroccan constitution. Protests in Berber areas, notably the Rif, led the king in July 2001 to establish

---

a Royal Amazigh Language and Culture Institute. Its goals are to standardize the language, teach it in school curricula, and develop media programs devoted to cultural preservation. The important carpet industry, mostly represented by women, is being expanded through technology and global marketing. An Amazigh satellite TV channel was launched in 2007 and the important Moroccan tourism industry reoriented to emphasize Amazigh dance, restoration of Berber *qasbas* (fortresses) and other elements in traditional Berber culture.[10]

NOTES

1. Sue Miller, "Migration Station," *Christian Science Monitor,* June 26, 2003.

2. See David M. Hart, *Dadda 'Atta and His Forty Grandsons* (Cambridge, England: Menas Press, 1981), pp. 8–11. Dadda 'Atta was a historical figure, a minor saint or marabout.

3. Michael B. Oren, *Power, Faith and Fantasy: America and The Middle East Since 1776* (New York: W.W. Norton, 2007, p. 28).

4. The oldest property owned by the U.S. government abroad is the American Consulate in Tangier; a consul was assigned there in 1791.

5. See David Woolman, *Rebels in the Rif: Abd 'al Krim and the Rif Rebellion* (Palo Alto, CA: Stanford University Press, 1968). On the Ait Waryaghar, see David M. Hart, *The Ait Waryaghar of the Moroccan Rif: An Ethnography and a History* (Tucson, AZ: University of Arizona Press, 1976). Abd 'al Krim had annihilated a Spanish army and set up a Republic of the Rif (1921–1926).

6. For a detailed description of protectorate tribal administration, see Robin Bidwell, *Morocco Under Colonial Rule* (London: Frank Cass, 1973).

7. Mark Tessler, "Morocco: Institutional Pluralism and Monarchical Dominance," in W. I. Zartman, ed., *Political Elites in North Africa* (New York: Longman, 1982), p. 44.

8. See Malika Oufkir, with Michele Fitoussi, *Stolen Lives: Twenty Years in a Desert Jail* (New York: Hyperion Books, 1999). Another prisoner, Ahmed Marzouki, recently published his memoir of life there. Entitled *Cell 10,* it has sold widely in Morocco.

9. Geoff Pingree and Lisa Abend, "Morocco moves gradually to address past repression." *The Christian Science Monitor,* September 23, 2005.

10. Shaina Adams and Brahim El Guabli, "The Amazigh People of Morocco," *Fellowship,* Vol. 73, No.7–9, Fall 2007, pp. 21–24.

Tunisia (Republic of Tunisia)

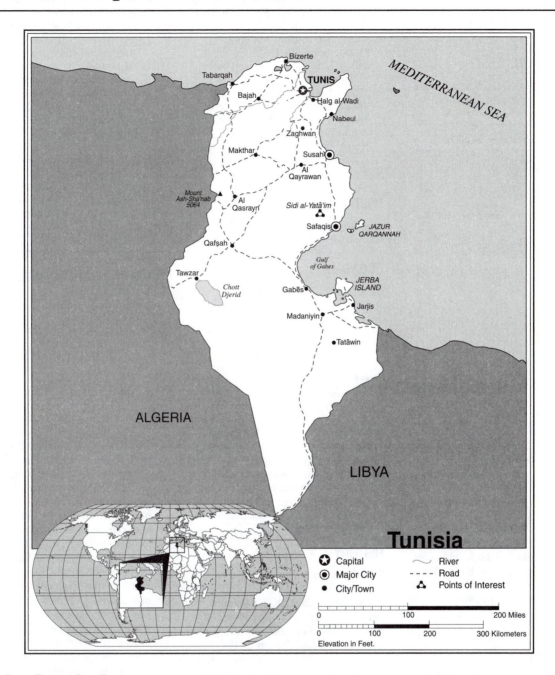

Tunisia Statistics

GEOGRAPHY

Area in Square Miles (Kilometers):
63,153 (163,610) (about the size of Georgia)

Capital (Population): Tunis (675,000)

Environmental Concerns: hazardous-waste disposal; water pollution; limited fresh water resources; deforestation; overgrazing; soil erosion; desertification

Geographical Features: mountains in north; hot, dry central plain; semiarid south merges into Sahara

Climate: hot, dry summers; mild, rainy winters; desert in the south; temperate in the north

PEOPLE

Population

Total: 10,276,158

Annual Growth Rate: 0.98%

Rural/Urban Population Ratio: 37/63

Major Languages: Arabic; French

Ethnic Makeup: 98% Arab-Berber; 1% European; 1% others

Religions: 98% Muslim; 1% Christian; less than 1% Jewish

Health

Life Expectancy at Birth: 73.6 years (male); 77 years (female)

Infant Mortality Rate: 22.94/1,000 live
  births

Education

Adult Literacy Rate: 74.2%
Compulsory (Ages): 6–16

COMMUNICATION

Telephones: 1,313,000 main lines
Daily Newspaper Circulation: 45 per
  1,000 people
Televisions: 156 per 1,000 people
Internet Service Provider: 1 (2000)

TRANSPORTATION

Highways in Miles (Kilometers): 14,345
  (23,100)
Railroads in Miles (Kilometers): 1,403
  (2,260)
Usable Airfields: 32
Motor Vehicles in Use: 531,000

GOVERNMENT

Type: republic

Independence Date: March 20, 1956
  (from France)
Head of State/Government: President Zine
  El Abidine Ben Ali; Prime Minister
  Mohammed Ghannouchi
Political Parties: Constitutional
  Democratic Rally (RCD), official
  ruling party, other approved parties
  include Green Party for Progress
  (PVP), Liberal Socialist Party
  (PSL), Movement for Democratic
  Socialism (MDS), Progressive
  Democratic Party. An-Nahda
  (Renaissance), an Islamist party,
  remains outlawed
Suffrage: universal at 20

MILITARY

Military Expenditures (% of GDP): 1.5%
Current Disputes: none

ECONOMY

Currency ($U.S. Equivalent): 1.33
  dinars = $1

Per Capita Income/GDP: $8,600/
  $87.88 billion
GDP Growth Rate: 4%
Inflation Rate: 4.6%
Unemployment Rate: 13.9%
Labor Force: 3,502,000 (note: the
  decrease in this figure from the 11th
  edition may be due to an increase in
  the number of expatriate workers)
Natural Resources: petroleum;
  phosphates; iron ore; lead; zinc; salt
Agriculture: olives; dates; oranges;
  almonds; grain; sugar beets; grapes;
  poultry; beef; dairy products
Industry: petroleum; mining; tourism;
  textiles; footwear; food; beverages
Exports: $11.6 billion (primary partners
  Germany, France, Italy)
Imports: $13.89 billion (primary partners
  France, Germany, Italy)

SUGGESTED WEB SITES

http://www.cia.gov/cia/ publications/
  factbook/index.html
http://www.tunisiaonline.com

Tunisia Country Report

Tunisia, the smallest of the North African countries, is less than one tenth the size of Libya, its neighbor to the east. However, its population is nearly twice the size of Libya's.

Tunisia's long coastline has exposed it over the centuries to a succession of invaders from the sea. The southern third of the country is part of the Sahara Desert; the central third consists of high, arid plains. Only the northern region has sufficient rainfall for agriculture. This region contains Tunisia's single permanent river, the Medjerda.

DEVELOPMENT

Associate membership in the European Union has resulted in a number of advantages to Tunisia. One important one is favorable terms for its agricultural exports. Privatization of some 140 state-owned industries, a liberal investment code and tax reform have made possible a GDP growth rate averaging 4.5 to 5 percent annually.

The country is predominantly urban. There is almost no nomadic population, and there are no high mountains to provide refuge for independent mountain peo-

ples opposed to central government. The Tunis region and the Sahel, a coastal plain important in olive production, are the most densely populated areas. Tunis, the capital, is not only the dominant city but also the hub of government, economic, and political activity.

HISTORY

Tunisia has an ancient history that is urban rather than territorial. Phoenician merchants from what is today Lebanon founded a number of trading posts several thousand years ago. The most important one was Carthage, founded in 814 B.C. It grew wealthy through trade and developed a maritime empire. Its great rival was Rome; after several wars, the Romans defeated the Carthaginians and destroyed Carthage. Later, the Romans rebuilt the city, and it became great once again as the capital of the Roman province of Africa. Rome's African province was one of the most prosperous in the empire. The wheat and other commodities shipped to Rome from North African farms were vitally needed to feed the Roman population. When the ships from Carthage were late due to storms, lost at sea, or seized by pirates, the Romans suffered hardship. Modern Tunisia has yet to reach the level of prosperity it had under Roman rule.

The collapse of the Roman Empire in the fifth century A.D. affected Roman Africa as well. Cities were abandoned; the irrigation system that had made the farms prosperous fell into ruin. A number of these Roman cities, such as Dougga, Utica, and Carthage itself, which is now a suburb of Tunis, have been preserved as historical monuments of this period.

Arab armies from the east brought Islam to North Africa in the late seventh century. After some resistance, the population accepted the new religion, and from that time on the area was ruled as the Arab-Islamic province of *Ifriqiya*. The Anglicized form of this Arabic word, "Africa," was eventually applied to the entire continent.

The Arab governors did not want to have anything to do with Carthage, since they associated it with Christian Roman rule. They built a new capital on the site of a village on the outskirts of Carthage, named Tunis. The fact that Tunis has been the capital and major city in the country for 14 centuries has contributed to the sense of unity and nationhood among most Tunisians.[1]

The original Tunisian population consisted of Berbers, a people of unknown origin. During the centuries of Islamic rule, many Arabs settled in the country. Other waves of immigration brought Muslims from Spain, Greeks, Italians, Maltese, and many other nationalities. Until recently, Tunisia also had a large community of Jews, most of whom emigrated to the State of Israel when it was founded in 1948. The blending of ethnic groups and nationalities over the years has created a relatively homogeneous and tolerant society, with few of the conflicts that marked other societies in the Islamic world.

From the late 1500s to the 1880s, Tunisia was a self-governing province of the Ottoman Empire. It was called a regency because its governors ruled as "regents" on behalf of the Ottoman sultan. Tunis was already a well-established, cosmopolitan city when it became the regency capital. Its rulers, called beys, were supported by an Ottoman garrison and a corsair fleet of fast ships that served as auxiliaries to the regular Ottoman navy. The corsairs, many of them Christian renegades, ruled the Mediterranean Sea for four centuries, raiding the coasts of nearby European countries and preying on merchant vessels, seizing cargoes and holding crews for ransom. The newly independent United States was also affected, with American merchant ships seized and cargoes taken by the corsairs. In 1799, the United States signed a treaty with the bey, agreeing to pay an annual tribute in return for his protection of American ships.

In the nineteenth century, European powers, particularly France and Britain, began to interfere directly in the Ottoman Empire and to seize some of its outlying provinces. France and Britain had a "gentleman's agreement" about Ottoman territories in Africa—the French were given a free hand in North Africa and the British in Egypt. In 1830, the French seized Algiers, capital of the Algiers Regency, and began to intervene in neighboring Tunisia in order to protect their Algerian investment.

The beys of Tunis worked very hard to forestall a French occupation. In order to do this, they had to satisfy the European powers that they were developing modern political institutions and rights for their people. Ahmad Bey (1837–1855) abolished slavery and piracy, organized a modern army (trained by French officers), and established a national system of tax collection. Muhammad al-Sadiq Bey (1859–1882) approved in 1861 the first written Constitution in the Islamic world. This Constitution had a declaration of rights and provided for a hereditary (but not an absolute) monarchy under the beys. The Constitution worked better in theory than in practice. Provincial landowners and local chiefs opposed the Constitution because it undermined their authority. The peasants, whom it supposedly was designed to protect, opposed the Constitution because it brought them heavy new taxes, collected

by government troops sent from Tunis. In 1864, a popular rebellion broke out against the bey, and he was forced to suspend the Constitution.

In 1881, a French army invaded and occupied all of Tunisia, almost without firing a shot. The French said that they had intervened because the bey's government could not meet its debts to French bankers and capitalists, who had been lending money for years to keep the country afloat. There was concern also about the European population. Europeans from many countries had been pouring into Tunisia, ever since the bey had given foreigners the right to own land and set up businesses.

The bey's government continued under the French protectorate, but it was supplemented by a French administration, which held actual power. The French collected taxes, imposed French law, and developed roads, railroads, ports, hospitals, and schools. French landowners bought large areas and converted them into vineyards, olive groves, and wheat farms. For the first time in 2,000 years, Tunisia exported wheat, corn, and olive oil to the lands on the other side of the Mediterranean.

Because Tunisia was small, manageable, and primarily urban, its society, particularly in certain regions, was influenced strongly by French culture. An elite developed whose members preferred the French language to their native Arabic. They were encouraged to enroll their sons in Sadiki College, a European-type high school set up in Tunis by the French to train young Tunisians and expose them to Western subjects. After completing their studies at Sadiki, most were sent to France to complete their education in such institutions as the Sorbonne (University of Paris). The experience helped shape their political thinking, and on their return to Tunisia a number of them formed a movement for self-government that they called Destour (*Dustur* in Arabic), meaning "Constitution." The name was logical, since these

young men had observed that independent countries such as France based their sovereignty on such a document. They were convinced that nationalism, "in order to be effective against the French, had to break loose from its traditional power base in the urban elite and mobilize mass support."[2] In 1934, a group of young nationalists quit the Destour and formed a new party, the Neo-Destour. The goal of the Neo-Destour Party was Tunisia's independence from France. From the beginning, its leader was Habib Bourguiba.

HABIB BOURGUIBA

Habib Ben Ali Bourguiba, born in 1903, once said he had "invented" Tunisia, not historically but in the sense of shaping its existence as a modern sovereign nation. The Neo-Destour Party, under Bourguiba's leadership, became the country's first mass political party. It drew its membership from shopkeepers, craftspeople, blue-collar workers, and peasants, along with French-educated lawyers and doctors. The party became the vanguard of the nation, mobilizing the population in a campaign of strikes, demonstrations, and violence in order to gain independence. It was a long struggle. Bourguiba spent many years in prison. But eventually the Neo-Destour tactics succeeded. On March 20, 1956, France ended its protectorate and Tunisia became an independent republic, led by Habib Bourguiba.

One of the problems facing Tunisia today is that its political organization has changed very little since independence. A Constitution was approved in 1959 that established a "presidential republic"—that is, a republic in which the elected president has great power. Bourguiba was elected president in 1957.

Bourguiba was also the head of the Neo-Destour Party, the country's only legal political party. The Constitution provided for a National Assembly, which is responsible for enacting laws. But to be elected to the Assembly, a candidate had to be a member of the Neo-Destour Party. Bourguiba's philosophy and programs for national development in his country were often called Bourguibism. It was tailored to the particular historical experience of the Tunisian people. Since ancient Carthage, Tunisian life has been characterized by the presence of a strong central government able to impose order and bring relative stability to the people. The predominance of cities and villages over nomadism reinforced this sense of order. The experience of Carthage, and even more so that of Rome, set the pattern. "The Beys continued the pattern of strong order while the French developed a strongly bourgeois, trade-oriented society, adding humanitarian and some authoritarian values contained in French political philosophy."[3] Bourguiba considered himself the tutor of the Tunisian people, guiding them toward moral, economic, and political maturity.

In 1961, Bourguiba introduced a new program for Tunisian development that he termed "Destourian Socialism." It combined Bourguibism with government planning for economic and social development. The name of the Neo-Destour Party was changed to the Destour Socialist Party (PSD) to indicate its new direction. Destourian Socialism worked for the general good, but it was not Marxist; Bourguiba stressed national unanimity rather than class struggle and opposed communism as the "ideology of a godless state." Bourguiba took the view that Destourian Socialism was directly related to Islam. He said once that the original members of the Islamic community (in Muhammad's time in Mecca) "were socialists . . . and worked for the common good."[4] For many years after independence, Tunisia appeared to be a model among new nations because of its stability, order, and economic progress. Particularly notable were Bourguiba's reforms in social and political life. Islamic law was replaced by a Western-style legal system, with various levels of courts. Women were encouraged to attend school and enter occupations previously closed to them, and they were given equal rights with men in matters of divorce and inheritance.

Bourguiba strongly criticized those aspects of Islam that seemed to him to be obstacles to national development. He was against women wearing the veil, polygyny, and ownership of lands by religious leaders, which kept land out of production. He even encouraged people not to fast during the holy month of Ramadan, because their hunger made them less effective in their work.

There were few challenges to Bourguiba's leadership. His method of alternately dismissing and reinstating party leaders who disagreed with him effectively maintained Destourian unity. But in later years Bourguiba's periodic health problems, the growth of Islamic fundamentalism, and the disenchantment of Tunisian youth with the single-party system raised doubts about Tunisia's future under the PSD.

The system was provided with a certain continuity by the election of Bourguiba as president-for-life in 1974, when a constitutional amendment was approved specifying that at the time of his death or in the event of his disability, the prime minister would succeed him and hold office pending a general election. One author observed: "Nobody is big enough to replace Bourguiba. He created a national liberation movement, fashioned the country and its institutions."[5] Yet he failed to recognize or deal with changing political and social realities in his later years.

The new generation coming of age in Tunisia is deeply alienated from the old. Young Tunisians (half the population are under age 15) increasingly protest their inability to find jobs, their exclusion from the political decision-making process, the unfair distribution of wealth, and the lack of political organizations. It seems as if there are two Tunisias: the old Tunisia of genteel politicians and freedom fighters; and the new one of alienated youths, angry peasants, and frustrated intellectuals. Somehow the two have gotten out of touch with each other.

The division between these groups has been magnified by the growth of Islamic fundamentalism, which in Bourguiba's view was equated with rejection of the secular, modern Islamic society that he created. The Islamic Tendency Movement (MTI) emerged in the 1980s as the major fundamentalist group. MTI applied for recognition as a political party after Bourguiba had agreed to allow political activity outside of the Destour Party and had licensed two opposition parties. But MTI's application was rejected.

THE END OF AN ERA

In 1984, riots over an increase in the price of bread signaled a turning point for the regime. For the first time in the republic's history, an organized Islamic opposition challenged Bourguiba, on the grounds that he had deformed Islam to create a secular society. Former Bourguiba associates urged a broadening of the political process and formed political movements to challenge the Destour monopoly on power. Although they were frequently jailed and their movements proscribed or declared illegal, they continued to press for political reform.

However, Bourguiba turned a deaf ear to all proposals for political change. Having survived several heart attacks and other illnesses to regain reasonably good health, he seemed to feel that he was indestructible. His personal life underwent significant change as he became more authoritarian. He had divorced his French wife, apparently in response to criticism that a true Tunisian patriot would not have a French spouse. His second wife, Wassila, a member of the prominent Ben Ammar family, soon became the power behind the throne. As Bourguiba's mental state deteriorated, he divorced her arbitrarily in 1986. At that time the president-for-life assumed direct control over party and government. As he did so, his actions became increasingly irrational. He would appoint a cabinet minister one day and forget the next that he had done so. Opposition became an obsession with him. The two legal opposition parties were forced out of local and national elections by arrests of leaders and a shutdown of opposition newspapers. The Tunisian Labor Confederation (UGTT) was disbanded, and the government launched a massive purge of fundamentalists.

The purge was directed by General Zine el-Abidine Ben Ali, the minister of the interior, regarded by Bourguiba as one of the few people he could trust. There were mass arrests of Islamic militants, most of them belonging to the outlawed Islamic Tendency Movement, a fundamentalist organization that Bourguiba outlawed as subversive. (It was later reorganized as a political party, Ennahda—"Renaissance"—but was again banned by Ben Ali after he became president.)

Increasingly, it seemed to responsible leaders that Bourguiba was becoming senile as well as paranoid. "The government lacks all sense of vision," said a long-time observer. "The strategy is to get through the day, to play palace parlor games." A student leader was more cynical: "There is no logic to [Bourguiba's] decisions; sometimes he does the opposite of what he did the day before."[6]

A decision that would prove crucial to the needed change in leadership was made by Bourguiba in September 1987, when he named Ben Ali as prime minister. Six weeks later, Ben Ali carried out a bloodless coup, removing the aging president under the 1974 constitutional provision that allows the prime minister to take over in the event of a president's "manifest incapacity" to govern. A council of medical doctors affirmed that this was the case. Bourguiba was placed under temporary house arrest in his Monastir villa, but he was allowed visitors and some freedom of movement within the city (after 1990).

Habib Bourguiba died in April 2001, at the age of 96. He was buried next door to this villa, in a mausoleum of white marble.

The words inscribed on its door—"Liberator of women, builder of modern Tunisia"—seem an appropriate inscription for the "inventor" of his country.

NEW DIRECTIONS

President Ben Ali (elected to a full five-year term in April 1989) initiated a series of bold reforms designed to wean the country away from the one-party system. Political prisoners were released under a general amnesty. Prodded by Ben Ali, the Destour-dominated National Assembly passed laws ensuring press freedom and the right of political parties to form as long as their platforms are not based exclusively on language, race, or religion. The Assembly also abolished the constitutional provision establishing the position of president-for-life, which had been created expressly for Bourguiba. Henceforth Tunisian presidents would be limited to three consecutive terms in office.

Ben Ali also undertook the major job of restructuring and revitalizing the Destour Party. In 1988, it was renamed the Constitutional Democratic Rally (RCD). Ben Ali told delegates to the first RCD Congress that no single party could represent all Tunisians. There can be no democracy without pluralism, fair elections, and freedom of expression, he said.

Elections in 1988 underscored Tunisia's fixation on the single-party system. RCD candidates won all 141 seats in the Chamber of Deputies, taking 80 percent of the popular vote. Two new opposition parties, the Progressive Socialist Party and the Progressive Socialist Rally, participated but failed to win more than 5 percent of the popular vote, the minimum needed for representation in the Chamber. MTI candidates, although required to run as independents because of the ban on "Islamic" parties under the revised election law, dominated urban voting, taking 30 percent of the popular vote in the cities. However, the winner-take-all system of electing candidates shut them out as well.

Local and municipal elections have confirmed the RCD stranglehold on Tunisian political life; its performance was the exact opposite of that of the National Liberation Front in neighboring Algeria, where the dominant party was discredited over time and finally defeated in open national elections by a fundamentalist party. In the 1995 local and municipal council elections, RCD candidates won 4,084 out of 4,090 contested seats, with 92.5 percent of Tunisia's 1,865,401 registered voters casting their ballots.

Efforts to mobilize an effective opposition movement earlier were hampered

when Ahmed Mestiri, the long-time head of the Movement of Socialist Democrats (MDS), the major legal opposition party, resigned in 1992. In the 1994 elections, the only opposition party to increase its support was the former Tunisian Communist Party, renamed the Movement for Renewal. It won four seats in the Chamber as Tunisia continued its slow progress toward multi-party democracy.

After the election the Chamber of Deputies was enlarged from the present 144 to 160 deputies. Twenty seats would be reserved for members from opposition parties. In the presidential election, Ben Ali was re-elected for a third term and again in 1999 for a fourth term. In the latter election he faced modest opposition, and as a result his victory margin was a "bare" 99.44 percent.[7]

The Chamber was enlarged again in time for the 1999 elections, this time to 182 seats, to broaden representation for Tunisia's growing population. The results were somewhat different from the previous election. The RCD won 148 seats to 13 for the MDS, the largest opposition party. However, opposition parties all together increased their representation from 19 seats to 34.

THE ECONOMY

The challenge to Ben Ali lies not only in broadening political participation but also in improving the economy. After a period of impressive expansion in the 1960s and 1970s, the growth rate began dropping steadily, largely due to decreased demand and lowered prices for the country's three main exports (phosphates, petroleum, and olive oil). Tunisia is the world's fourth-ranking producer of phosphates, and its most important industries are those related to production of superphosphates and fertilizers.

Problems have dogged the phosphate industry. The quality of the rock mined is poor in comparison with that of other phosphate producers, such as Morocco. The Tunisian industry experienced hard times in the late 1980s with the drop in global

phosphate prices; a quarter of its 12,000-member workforce were laid off in 1987. However, improved production methods and higher world demand led to a 29 percent increase in exports in 1990.

Tunisia's oil reserves are estimated at 1.65 billion barrels. The main producing fields are at El Borma and offshore in the Gulf of Gabes. New offshore discoveries and a 1996 agreement with Libya for 50/50 sharing of production from the disputed Gulf of Gabes oil field have improved oil output, currently about 4.3 million barrels annually.

Tunisia became an associate member of the European Union in 1995, the first Mediterranean country to do so. The terms of the EU agreement require the country to remove trade barriers over a 10-year period. In turn, Tunisian products such as citrus and olives receive highly favorable export terms in EU countries. The EU also provides technical support and training for the government's Mise A Nouveau (Upgrading and Improvement) program intended to enhance productivity in business and industry and compete internationally.

Tunisia's political stability—albeit one gained at the expense of human rights—and its economic reforms have made it a favored country for foreign aid over the years. During the period 1970–2000 it received more World Bank loans than any other Arab or African country. Its economic reform program, featuring privatization of 140 state-owned enterprises since 1987, liberalizing of prices, reduction of tariffs and other reforms, is lauded as a model for development by international financial institutions.

The country's political stability and effective use of its limited resources for development have made it a favored country for foreign aid. Since the 1970s it has received more World Bank loans than any other Arab or African country. The funding has been equitably distributed, so that 60 percent of the population are middle class, and 80 percent own their own homes.

THE FUTURE

Tunisia's progress as an economic beacon of stability in an unstable region has been somewhat offset by a decline in its long-established status as a successful example of a secular, progressive Islamic state. Following President Ben Ali's ouster of his predecessor in 1987, he proclaimed a new era for Tunisians, based on respect for law, human rights, and democracy. Tunisia's Islamic nature was reaffirmed by such actions as the reopening of the venerable Zitouna University in Tunis, a center for Islamic scholarship, along with its counterpart in Kairouan. But like other Islamic countries, it has not been free from the scourge of militant Islamic fundamentalism. The fundamentalist movement Al-Nahda ("Renaissance"), which advocates a Tunisian government based on Islamic law, attacked RCD headquarters in February 1991. Many of its members, including the leader, were subsequently arrested and it was outlawed as a political party.

Militant Islam, represented by Al-Qaeda and its various subsidiary organizations, has not entirely spared Tunisia despite its government's extreme repression of fundamentalist groups. In April 2003 a bomb attack on the ancient Jewish synagogue on Djerba Island, a popular tourist destination, killed 17 people, striking a blow at the country's important tourist industry. Subsequently, in 2007, a plan to attack the American and British embassies in Tunis was uncovered and thwarted in a series of gun battles between militants and security forces, with 12 militants and 2 security officers killed. The plan had been developed by members of the Salafist Group for Preaching and Combat (GSPC), an Algerian group which has joined al-Qaeda in January 2007 and renamed itself al-Qaeda in the land of the Islamic Maghreb.

In subsequent years, Tunisia has become an increasingly closed society. The press is heavily censored. Bourguiba's death was not even reported in Tunisia, and the obligatory seven days of mourning were countered by instructions to banks and government offices to keep regular hours. Telephones are routinely tapped. More than 1,000 Ennahda members have been arrested and jailed without trial. In December 2000, a dozen members of another Islamic fundamentalist group were given 17-year jail sentences for forming an illegal organization; their lawyers walked out of the trial to protest the court's bias and procedural abuses.

The regime's repression of Islamic groups, even moderate nonviolent ones, has changed its former image as a tolerant, progressive Islamic country. The Tunisian League for Human Rights, oldest in the Arab world, has been shut down from time to time by the government. Until recently opposition political leaders were given no coverage in the mainstream press, and press censorship remains routine. The UN-sponsored "World Summit on the Information Society" held in Tunis in November 2005 offered opposition groups a rare opportunity to air their protests against the government's repressive policies. Leaders of the groups—the Progressive Democratic Party, Tunisian Communist Party and Human Rights League, along with the unrecognized Tunisian Journalists' Union,

addressed the conference and called for freedom of the press, the right to free public association, and the release of the country's 600 political prisoners.

Following his "tainted" election victory in 1999, Ben Ali announced a new program designed to provide full employment by 2004. Called the 21–21 program, it would supplement an earlier 26–26 one that had brought the public and private sectors together to end poverty and increase home ownership, notably among the poor. In his address announcing the new program, Ben Ali stated: "Change comes from anchoring the democratic process in a steady and incremental progress aimed at avoiding setbacks or losing momentum."[8]

Ironically, the Ben Ali government's ruthless crackdown on Islamist parties, beginning with the ban on Al-Nahda after its success in the 1989 elections and continuing up to the present, has generated a largely non-violent but politically effective opposition, particularly among university students. To some extent, the radicalization of Tunisian youth stems from anger over U.S. wars in Iraq and Afghanistan, as is the case elsewhere in the Arab world. But heavy-handed government methods used in the crackdown are also a factor. In 2004 six youths were given 19-year jail sentences for downloading bomb-making instructions on the Internet, after a trial described as unfair by human rights lawyers. (The six were released in 2006). But as the leader of the Tunisian Journalists' Union commented in launching a hunger strike by opposition leaders on the eve of the Tunis Summit, "It is the only means open to protest, because the authorities have closed all other avenues of dialogue and negotiation."[9]

The government's harsh and restrictive policies were eased somewhat in 2004–2006. They included approval for the International Committee of the Red Cross to visit Tunisian prisons and a limiting of censorship of newspaper and magazine articles. But any return to Tunisia's traditionally open, secular society as formed by Habib Bourguiba seemed doubtful. A senior Tunisian university professor publicly questioned the moderating of repressive government policies: "Is the government able to endorse secular regulations and rules of law? Is the secular leadership strong enough to resist an Islamic (sic) uprising? And would this be an invitation to danger or a credible and reliable step toward a liberal system?"[10]

NOTES

1. Harold D. Nelson, ed., *Tunisia: A Country Study* (Washington, D.C.: American University, Foreign Area Studies, 1979), p. 68.

2. *Ibid.,* p. 42.

3. *Ibid.,* p. 194. What Nelson means, in this case, by "authoritarianism" is that the French brought to Tunisia the elaborate bureaucracy of metropolitan France, with levels of administration from the center down to local towns and villages.

4. *Ibid.,* p. 196.

5. Jim Rupert, in *The Christian Science Monitor* (November 23, 1984).

6. Louise Lief, in *The Christian Science Monitor* (April 10, 1987).

7. Mamoun Fandy, in *The Christian Science Monitor* (October 25, 1999).

8. Georgie Ann Geyer, in *The Washington Post* (October 23, 1999).

9. "Hunger for Change," *The Economist,* November 12, 2005.

10. Quoted by Jill Carroll, "Secular Tunisia may face new, younger Islamist challenge," *The Christian Science Monitor,* October 10, 2007, p. 1.

Timeline: PAST

264–146 B.C.

Wars between Rome and Carthage, ending in the destruction of Carthage and its rebuilding as a Roman city

800–900

The establishment of Islam in Ifriqiya, with its new capital at Tunis

1200–1400

The Hafsid dynasty develops Tunisia as a highly centralized urban state

1500–1800

Ottoman Turks establish Tunis as a corsair state to control Mediterranean sea lanes

1881–1956

French protectorate

1956

Tunisia gains independence, led by Habib Bourguiba

1974

An abortive merger with Libya

1980s

Bourguiba is removed from office in a "palace coup;" he is succeeded by Ben Ali

1990s

Tunisia's economic picture brightens; Ben Ali seeks some social modernization; women's rights are expanded

PRESENT

2000s

Human-rights abuses continue

The Western Sahara   Whose Desert?

It is a fearsome place, swept by sand-laden winds that sting through layers of clothing, scorched by 120°F temperatures, its flat, monotonous landscape broken occasionally by dried-up *wadis* (river beds). The Spanish called it Rio de Oro, "River of Gold," in a bitter jest, for it has neither. Rainfall averages two to eight inches a year in a region twice the size of Colorado but without mountains, only rolling dunes swept constantly by sand-laden winds that fill tents, clothing and food with gritty particles of sand. The region had no name until the twentieth century; it was simply the "western" part of the Sahara. For a brief period in the eleventh century A.D. a Berber tribal confederation, the Almoravids, rode out of the territory to find a powerful Islamic sultanate in Morocco and Spain. But after they were overthrown by another tribal confederation, the Almohads, the Western Sahara reverted to political obscurity.

As a political entity, the Western Sahara resulted from European colonization in Africa in the late nineteenth century. Britain and France had a head start in establishing colonies. Spain was a latecomer. By the time the Spanish joined the race for colonies, little was left for them in Africa. Since they already controlled the Canary Islands, off the West African coast, it was natural for them to claim Rio de Oro, the nearest area on the coast.

In 1884, Spain claimed Rio de Oro and its adjoining region, Saguia al-Hamra, in a note to other European powers. The Spanish claim was based on the principle that "occupation of a territory's coast entitled a colonial power to control over the interior."[1] But Spanish rights to the Saharan interior clashed with French claims to Mauritania and efforts to control the independent Sultanate of Morocco to the north. After the establishment of a joint Franco—Spanish protectorate over Morocco in 1912, Rio de Oro and Saguia al-Hamra were recognized as a single Spanish colony, with its boundaries fixed with the French colony of Mauritania on the south and east and Morocco to the north. The nomads of the Western Sahara now found themselves living within fixed boundaries defined by outsiders.

The Spanish moved very slowly into the interior. The entire Western Sahara was not "pacified" until 1934. Spain invested heavily in the development of the important Western Sahara phosphate deposits but did little else to develop the colony. The Spanish population was essentially a garrison community, living apart from the Sahrawis, the indigenous Saharan population, in towns or military posts. A few Sahrawis went to Spain or other European countries, where they received a modern education; upon their return, they began to organize a Saharan nationalist movement. Other Sahrawis traveled to Egypt and returned with ideas of organizing a Saharan Arab independent state. A real sense of either a Spanish Saharan or an independent Sahrawi identity was slow to emerge.[2]

Serious conflict over the Spanish Sahara developed in the 1960s. By that time, both Morocco and Mauritania had become independent. Algeria, the third African territory involved in the conflict, won its independence after a bloody national liberation war against France. All three new states were highly nationalist and were opposed to the continuation of colonial rule over any African people, particularly Muslim peoples. They encouraged the Sahrawis to fight for liberation from Spain, giving arms and money to guerrilla groups and keeping their borders open.

However, the three states had different motives. Morocco claimed the Western Sahara on the basis of historical ties dating back to the Almoravids, plus the oath of allegiance sworn to Moroccan sultans by Saharan chiefs in the nineteenth and twentieth centuries. Kinship was also a factor; several important Saharan families have branches in Morocco, and both the mother and the first wife of the founder of Morocco's current ruling dynasty, Mulay Ismail, were from Sahrawi families.

The Mauritanian claim to the Spanish Sahara was based not on historical sovereignty but on kinship. Sahrawis have close ethnic ties with the Moors, the majority of the population of Mauritania. Also, Mauritania feared Moroccan expansion, since its territory had once been included in the Almoravid state. A Saharan buffer state between Mauritania and Morocco would serve as protection for the Mauritanians.

Algeria's interest in Spanish Sahara was largely a matter of support for a national liberation movement against a colonial power. The Algerians made no territorial claim to the colony. Algeria's foreign policy has rested on two pillars since independence: the right to self-determination of subject peoples and the principle of self-determination through referendum. Algeria consistently maintains that the Saharan people should have these rights.

In the 1960s, Spain came under pressure from the United Nations to give up its colonies. After much hesitation, the Spanish announced in August 1974 that a referendum would be held under UN supervision to decide the colony's future.

The Spanish action brought the conflict to a head. King Hassan II declared that 1975 would mark the restoration of Moroccan sovereignty over the territory. The main opposition to this claim came from Polisario (an acronym for the Popular Front for the Liberation of Saguia al-Hamra and Rio de Oro, the two divisions of the Spanish colony). This organization, formed by Saharan exiles based initially in Mauritania, issued a declaration of independence, and Polisario guerrillas began attacking Spanish garrisons, increasing the pressure on Spain to withdraw. In October 1975, King Hassan announced that he would lead a massive, peaceful march of civilians, "armed" only with Korans, into the Spanish Sahara to recover sacred Moroccan territory. This "Green March" of half a million unarmed Moroccan volunteers into Spanish territory seemed an unusual, even risky, method of validating a territorial claim, but it worked. In 1976, Spain reached agreement with Morocco and Mauritania to partition the territory into two zones, one-third going to Mauritania and two-thirds to Morocco. The Moroccan zone included the important phosphate deposits.

The Polisario rejected the partition agreement. It announced the formation of the Sahrawi Arab Democratic Republic

(S.A.D.R.), "a free, independent, sovereign state governed by a national democratic system, of a unionist orientation, progressive and of Islamic faith, on the base of the free popular will founded at the beginnings of the democratic option."[3]

In the early stages of the war, Polisario tactics of swift-striking attacks from hidden bases in the vast desert were highly effective against the Moroccan and Mauritanian occupation forces. Mauritania withdrew from the war in 1978 when a military coup overthrew its government. The new Mauritanian rulers signed a peace treaty with Polisario representatives. Morocco, not to be outdone, promptly annexed the Mauritanian share of the territory and beefed up its military forces. A fortified "Sand Wall," which was built in stages from the former border with Rio de Oro down to the Moroccan—Mauritanian border and in 1987 extended about 350 miles to the Atlantic Ocean, providing the Moroccan Army with a strong defensive base from which to launch punitive raids against its elusive foe. The new segment also cut off the Polisario's access to the sea; Polisario raiders had begun to intercept and board fishing vessels in attempts to disrupt development of that important Moroccan resource and to bring pressure on foreign countries (such as Spain) that use the fishing grounds to push Morocco toward a settlement.

Although a large number of member states of the Organization of African Unity (OAU) subsequently recognized the Sahrawi Republic, Morocco blocked its admission to the OAU, on the grounds that it was part of Moroccan territory. However, the drain on Moroccan resources of indefinitely maintaining a 100,000-man army in the desert led King Hassan II to soften his obduracy, particularly in relation to Algeria. With both countries affected by severe economic problems and some political instability, a rapprochement became possible in the late 1980s. Diplomatic relations were restored in 1988 and in 1989, Morocco joined Algeria, Libya, Tunisia, and Mauritania in the creation of the Arab Maghrib Union (known by its French acronym UMA). The new regional organization aimed at integrating all five states in the future.

Algeria's preoccupation with internal affairs and the withdrawal of Algerian and Libyan financial aid placed the Polisario in a difficult position. Two of its founders, Omar Hadrami and Noureddine Belali, defected in 1989 and acknowledged Moroccan sovereignty over the territory. A 1990 amnesty offer by King Hassan for all Polisario members and Saharan exiles was accepted by nearly 1,000 persons; these included S.A.D.R.'s foreign minister, Brahim Hakim.

Later, Polisario leaders reached an agreement in principle with the king to settle the dispute by referendum. Participants in the referendum would be limited to the original inhabitants of the territory. But with the Moroccan Army entrenched behind its Sand Wall and the Polisario in control of the open desert, there was little chance for the implementation of the referendum.

UN mediation produced a formal cease-fire in 1991 until a referendum is organized. A UN observer force, the Mission for the Referendum in the Western Sahara (MINURSO), proceeded to the territory to supervise voter registration. By that time, thousands of Moroccan settlers had moved there to take advantage of free land, housing, and other inducements offered by the government to help "Moroccanize" the country's newest

province. The new residents changed the population balance, thereby complicating registration procedures. Morocco insisted that they should be eligible to vote in the referendum. A further complication arose from the fact that some 140,000 of the original inhabitants included in the 1974 Spanish census had become refugees in Algeria.

In May 1995, the UN Security Council, prodded by Algeria and Sahrawi activists, approved *Resolution 995*, which called for prompt registration of voters in the territory under the supervision of MINURSO. By December 1998, 147,000 voters were registered. However, the Moroccan government insisted that 85,000 others, belonging to three Saharan tribes residing there in the past, should be included in the registration rolls. Former U.S. secretary of state James Baker was appointed as a "high-profile" UN envoy to mediate between Morocco and the Polisario to resolve the registration deadlock and promote a final settlement for the territory.

In 2003, after several unproductive mediation efforts, Baker submitted a proposal to break the deadlock. The "Baker Plan" suggested that the referendum be postponed until 2006 and that, in the interim, the resident Sahrawi population would elect an autonomous governing body with powers limited to local and provincial affairs. Morocco rejected the plan at once while the Sahrawis first rejected it but later accepted it.

In July 2005, UN Secretary General Kofi Annan appointed Dutch Ambassador Peter Van Walsum to replace James Baker as his personal envoy for the Western Sahara.

In 2006, Morocco proposed a "third path" to settlement: it would give the Western Sahara a special autonomy within the kingdom. The Polisario rejected the idea outright and, in spring 2007, the UN Security Council asked the two parties to negotiate directly.

The first direct negotiations brokered by the UN took place in June 2007 in Manhasset, New York; another set of negotiations took place in August. Both were inconclusive. Morocco kept insisting on a referendum that asks people to accept or reject autonomy, while the Polisario requested that the referendum offers the independence option as well.

Before the third set of negotiations took place in early January 2008, the Polisario's 12th Congress decided in mid-December 2007 that it would consider resuming its armed struggle for independence if negotiations fail again.

Given Western Sahara's economic importance to Morocco and its political importance to the Monarchy, it seemed unlikely that an amicable solution is possible in the current conditions. The territory acquired a Moroccan majority in its population; its important phosphate rock deposits should give Morocco's economy a major boost when they are developed. It also offers the possibility of offshore oil discoveries, and its vast empty space could easily absorb settlers from Morocco's overcrowded cities.

On their side the Sahrawi refugees crowded into four refugee camps near Tindouf, Algeria, have developed, surprisingly, a representative democratic system with an elected parliament, a 95 percent literacy rate and a constitution guaranteeing gender equality and respect for all religions. Elected local councils undergird the parliament, and there is a high degree of volunteerism to take care of needed public services such as trash collection and food rations distribution. "We may well have developed a blueprint for an independent Western Sahara," says a tribal leader. "But we have been landless for so long, I don't know if the UN is just waiting for us to disappear, or what?"[4] Despite its recognition by 75 countries, global collective memory seems thus far to have failed to hold the SADR in its sight.

One of the key obstacles to deciding the fate of this territory is the absence of the will to do so among major international powers such as France, the United States and Spain. They all gain from the current status-quo and all stand to lose something if the situation evolves counter to Morocco's stability. These outside powers do not wish to undermine their economic and security interests by antagonizing Morocco and Algeria, two key competing regional powers.

NOTES

1. John Damis, Conflict in Northwest Africa: The Western Sahara Dispute (Palo Alto, CA: Hoover Institution Press, 1983), P. 110.
2. *Ibid*, p. 13, notes that a tribal Assembly (Jama'a) was formed in 1967 for the Sahrawis but that its 43 members were all tribal chiefs or their representatives; it had only advisory powers.
3. Proclamation of The Saharawi Arab Democratic Republic, February 27, 1976. Online at http://www.wsahara.net/sadr.html
4. John Thorne, "Sahara refugees from a progressive sodety." *Christian Science Monitor,* March 26, 2004.

Southern Africa

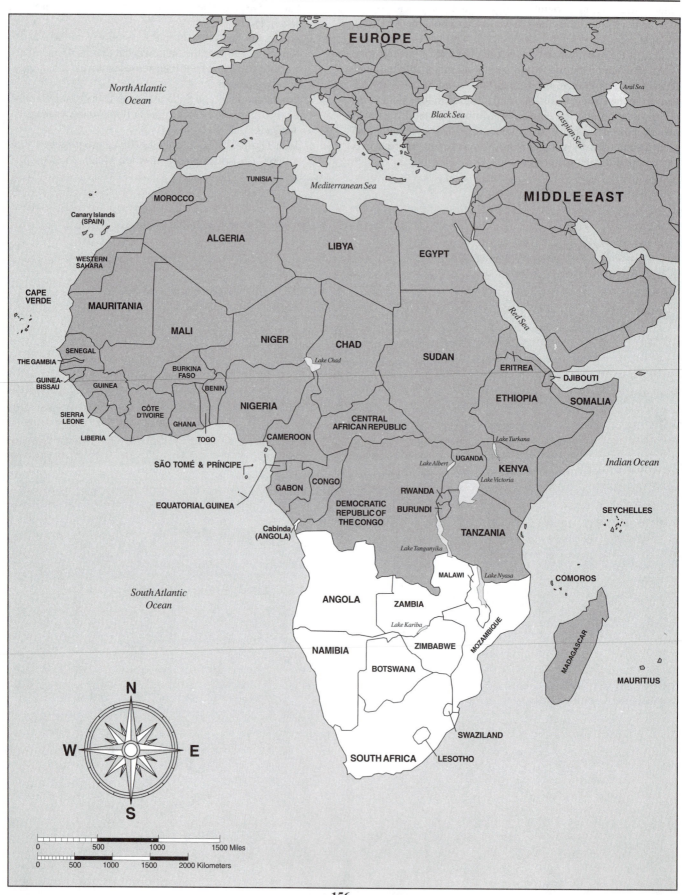

Southern Africa: The Continuing Struggle for Self-Determination

Southern Africa—which includes the nations of Angola, Botswana, Lesotho, Malawi, Mozambique, Namibia, South Africa, Swaziland, Zambia, and Zimbabwe—is a diverse region made up of savannas and forest, snow-topped mountains and desert, temperate Mediterranean and torrid tropical climates. Until recently much of the region was marred by armed conflict. But the wars and civil conflicts that have long plagued Angola, Mozambique, Lesotho, Namibia, and South Africa in particular have for now ended. In the case of Angola, this has been facilitated by developments in the Democratic Republic of the Congo (D.R.C., the former Zaire), which for decades had served as a source of, often Western-backed, regional destabilization. The more recent involvement of the governments of Namibia, Angola, and Zimbabwe in the D.R.C.'s internal conflicts appears to be coming to a close with a peace agreement initiated by South Africa. As a result, military complexes can be scaled down in favor of diverting more resources to the challenges of economic development while addressing the very serious challenge of the HIV/AIDS pandemic.

Southern African identity is as much defined by the region's peoples and their past and present interactions as by the region's geographic features. An appreciation of local history is crucial to understanding the forces that both divide and unite the region today. Throughout the twentieth century the dominant theme in the history of Southern Africa was the evolving struggle of the region's indigenous black African majority to free itself of the racial hegemony of white settlers from Europe and their descendants. With the end of the liberation wars, however, the major themes of the twenty-first century are peace and development. It is the pace and style of this development which is the key feature of Southern Africa today. War is the enemy of development. One of the primary themes in Southern Africa today is land, and the domination of the land by various groups of Europeans. Much of the history of Southern Africa has been shaped by the loss of land by indigenous communities to European settlers. The resulting imbalance in land distribution has not been resolved by the establishment of black-majority rule in the former settler-dominated states of Zimbabwe, Namibia, and South Africa. The resulting land shortage for the majority of rural dwellers in those states remains a major constraint to socioeconomic development.

EUROPEAN MIGRATION AND DOMINANCE

A dominant theme in the modern history of Southern Africa has been the evolving struggle of the region's indigenous black African majority to free itself of the racial hegemony of white settlers from Europe and their descendants. By the eighth century A.D., but probably earlier, the southernmost regions of the continent were populated by a variety of black African ethnic groups who spoke languages belonging to the Bantu as well as the Khoisan linguistic classifications. Members of these two groupings practiced both agriculture and pastoralism; archaeological evidence indicates that livestock keeping in Southern Africa pre-dates the time of Christ. Some, such as the BaKongo of northern Angola and the Shona peoples of the Zimbabwean plateaux, had, by the fifteenth century, organized strong states; others, like most Nguni-speakers prior to the early 1800s, lived in smaller communities. Trade networks existed throughout the region, linking various local peoples not only to one another but also to the markets of the Indian Ocean and beyond. For example, porcelains from China have been unearthed in the grounds of the Great Zimbabwe, a stone-walled settlement that flourished in the fifteenth century.

In the 1500s, small numbers of Portuguese began settling along the coasts of Angola and Mozambique. A century later, in 1652, the Dutch established a settlement at Africa's southernmost tip, the Cape of Good Hope. While the Portuguese flag generally remained confined to coastal enclaves until the late 1800s, the Dutch colony expanded steadily into the interior throughout the 1700s, seizing the land of local Khoisan communities. Unlike the colonial footholds of the Portuguese and other Europeans on the continent, which prior to the 1800s were mostly centers for the export of slaves, the Dutch Cape Colony imported slaves from Asia as well as from elsewhere in Africa. Although not legally enslaved, conquered Khoisan were also reduced to servitude. In the process, a new society evolved at the Cape. Much like the American South before the U.S. Civil War, the Cape Colony was racially divided between free white settlers and subordinated peoples of mixed African and Afro-Asian descent.

During the Napoleonic Wars, Britain took over the Cape Colony. Shortly thereafter, in 1820, significant numbers of English-speaking colonists began arriving in the region. The arrival of the British coincided with a period of political realignment throughout much of Southern Africa that is commonly referred to as the "Mfecane." Until recently, the historical literature has generally attributed this upheaval to dislocations caused by the rise of the Zulu state, under the great warrior prince Shaka. However, more recent scholarship on the Mfecane has focused on the disruptive effects of increased traffic in contraband slaves from the interior to the Cape and the Portuguese stations of Mozambique, following the international ban on slave trading.

In the 1830s, the British abolished slavery throughout their empire and extended limited civil rights to nonwhites at the Cape. In response, a large number of white Dutch-descended Boers, or Afrikaners, moved into the interior, where they founded two republics that were free of British control. This migration, known as the Great Trek, did not lead the white settlers into an empty land. The territory was home to many African groups, who lost their farms and pastures to the superior firepower of the early Afrikaners, who often coerced local communities into

(United Nations photo 131283 by J. P. Laffont)

Angolan youths celebrated when the nation became independent in 1974.

supplying corvee labor for their farms and public works. But a few African polities, like Lesotho and the western Botswana kingdoms, were able to preserve their independence by acquiring their own firearms.

In the second half of the nineteenth century, white migration and dominance spread throughout the rest of Southern Africa. The discovery of diamonds and gold in northeastern South Africa encouraged white exploration and subsequent occupation farther north. In the 1890s, Cecil Rhodes's British South Africa Company occupied modern Zambia and Zimbabwe, which then became known as the Rhodesias. British traders, missionaries, and settlers also invaded the area now known as Malawi. Meanwhile, the Germans seized Namibia, while the Portuguese began to expand inland from their coastal enclaves. Thus, by 1900, the entire region had fallen under white colonial control.

With the exception of Lesotho and Botswana, which were occupied as British "protectorates," all of the European colonies in Southern Africa had significant populations of white settlers, who in each case played a predominant political and economic role in their respective territories. Throughout the region, this white supremacy was fostered and maintained through racially discriminatory policies of land alienation, labor regulation, and the denial of full civil rights to nonwhites. In South Africa, where the largest and longest-settled white population resided, the Afrikaners and English-speaking settlers were granted full self-government in 1910—with a Constitution that left the country's black majority virtually powerless.

Yet despite the many changes that have occurred throughout African history, there is one thing that remains constant. In Southern Africa's Kalahari Desert (shared by South Africa, Namibia, and Botswana), a group of Khoisan individuals, known to the outside world as Bushmen, continue to practice their ancient way of life as hunters and gatherers. Geneticists say the Bushmen are the oldest surviving human beings. Within their genetic structure they carry the original genes of the human race. To add majesty to their heritage, contemporary linguist claim that the click language spoken by the Bushmen is also the oldest known language in the world. Hunters and gatherers in the ancient world, they survive today with a variety of skills and have intermingled with the more recent arrivals to form a rich blend of diverse cultures.

BLACK NATIONALISM AND SOUTH AFRICAN DESTABILIZATION

After World War II, new movements advocating black self-determination gained ascendancy throughout the region. However, the progress of these struggles for majority rule and independence was gradual. By 1968, the countries of Botswana, Lesotho, Malawi, Swaziland, and Zambia had gained their independence. The area was then polarized between liberated and nonliberated nations. In 1974, a military uprising in Portugal brought statehood to Angola and Mozambique, after long armed struggles by liberation forces in the two territories. Wars of liberation also led to the overthrow of white-settler rule in Zimbabwe, in 1980, and the independence of Namibia, in 1990. Finally, in 1994, South Africa completed a negotiated transition to a nonracial government.

South Africa's liberation has far-reaching implications for the entire Southern African subcontinent as well as the country's own historically oppressed masses. Since the late nineteenth century, South Africa has been the region's economic hub. Today, it accounts for about 80 percent of the total Southern African gross domestic product. Most of the subcontinent's roads and rails also run through South Africa. For generations, the country has recruited expatriate as well as local black African workers for its industries and mines. Today, it is the most economically developed country on the continent, with manufactured goods and agricultural surpluses that are in high demand elsewhere. By the late 1980s, when the imposition of economic sanctions against the then-apartheid regime was at its height, some 46 African countries were importing South African products. With sanctions now lifted, South Africa's economic role on the continent is likely to increase substantially.

(United Nations photo 128704 by Jerry Frank)

South Africa's economic and military dominance overshadows the region's planning. Pictured above is Cape Town, South Africa's chief port and the country's legislative capital.

A significant milestone was South Africa's admittance in 1994 as the 11th member of the Southern African Development Community (SADC). This organization's ultimate goal is to emulate the European Union (formerly called the European Community or Common Market) by promoting economic integration and political coordination among Southern Africa's states (including Tanzania). While South Africa is expected to be at the center of the Community, SADC's roots lie in past efforts by its other members to reduce their ties to that country. The organization grew out of the Southern African Development Coordination Conference (SADCC), which was created by the region's then–black-ruled states in 1980 to lessen their dependency on white-ruled South Africa. Each SADCC government assumed responsibility for research and planning in a specific developmental area: Angola for energy, Mozambique for transport and communication, Tanzania for industry, and so on.

In its first decade, SADCC succeeded in attracting considerable outside aid for building and rehabilitating its member states' infrastructure. The organization's greatest success was the Beira corridor project, which enabled the Mozambican port to serve once more as a major regional transit point. Other successes included telecommunications independence of South Africa, new regional power grids, and the upgrading of Tanzanian roads to carry Malawian goods to the port of Dar es Salaam. In 1992, with South Africa's liberation on the horizon, the potential for a more ambitious and inclusive SADC grouping became possible.

In 1996, South African president Nelson Mandela replaced Botswana's president, Sir Ketumile Masire, as SADC chairman, while Pretoria became the headquarters of a new SADC "Organ for Politics Defense and Security." The new South Africa's role as security coordinator within SADC was especially ironic: Before 1990, it had been the violent destabilizing policies of South Africa's military that had sabotaged efforts toward building greater regional cooperation. SADCC members, especially those that were further linked as the so-called Frontline States (Angola, Botswana, Mozambique, Tanzania, Zambia, and Zimbabwe), were then hostile to South Africa's racial policies. To varying degrees, they provided havens for those oppressed by these policies. South Africa responded by striking out against its exiled opponents through overt and covert military operations, while encouraging insurgent movements among some of its neighbors, most notably in Angola and Mozambique.

In Angola, South Africa (along with the United States) backed the rebel movement UNITA, while in Mozambique, it assisted RENAMO. Both of these movements resorted to the destruction of the railways and roads in their operational areas, a tactic that greatly increased the dependence on South African communications of the landlocked states of Botswana, Malawi, Zambia, and Zimbabwe. It is estimated that in the 1980s, the overall monetary cost to the Frontline States of South Africa's destabilization campaign was about $60 billion. (The same countries' combined annual gross national product was only about $25 billion in 1989.) The human costs were even greater: Hundreds of thousands of people were killed; at least equal numbers were maimed; and in Mozambique alone, more than 1 million people became refugees.

In the Southern African context, South Africa remains a military superpower. Despite the imposition of a United Nations arms embargo between 1977 and 1994, the country's military establishment was able to secure both the arms and sophisticated technology needed to develop its own military/industrial complex. Now a global arms exporter, South Africa is nearly self-sufficient in basic munitions, with a vast and advanced arsenal of weapons. Whereas in 1978 it imported 75 percent of its weapons, today that figure is less than 5 percent. By the 1980s, the country had also developed a nuclear arsenal, which it now claims to have dismantled. However, the former embargo was not entirely ineffective—while South African industry produced many sophisticated weapons systems, it found it increasingly difficult to maintain its regional superiority in such high-technology fields as fighter aircraft. By 1989, the increasing edge of Angolan pilots and air-defense systems was a significant factor in the former South African regime's decision to disengage from the Angolan Civil War. The economic costs of South African militarization were also steep. In addition to draining some 20 percent of its total budget outlays, the destabilization campaign contributed to increased international economic sanctions, which between 1985 and 1990 cost its own economy at least $20 billion. Today, both South Africa and its neighbors hope to benefit from a "peace dividend." But after a generation of militarization, progress in shifting resources from lethal to peaceful pursuits will be gradual.

Throughout the 1980s, South Africa justified its acts of aggression by claiming that it was engaged in counterinsurgency operations against guerrillas of the African National Congress (ANC) and Pan Africanist Congress (PAC), which

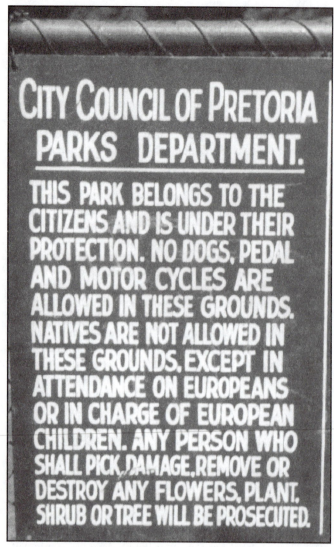

This sign, once displayed in a park in Pretoria, South Africa, reflected the restrictions of apartheid, formerly the South African government's official policy of racial discrimination.

Maize and cereal production suffered everywhere. South Africa and Zimbabwe, which are usually grain exporters, had to import food. The countries of Angola, Botswana, and Lesotho each had more than half a million people who were affected by the shortfalls, while some 2 million were malnourished in Mozambique. But in 1988, the rains returned to the region, raising cereal production by 40 percent. Zimbabwe was able not only to export but also to provide food aid to other African countries. However, South African destabilization contributed to continuing food scarcities in many parts of Angola and Mozambique.

In 1991–1992, the entire region was once more pushed toward catastrophe, with the onset of the worst single drought year in at least a century. While rainfall improved somewhat in the second half of the 1990s, climate-related disasters have continued to plague the region. In 2000–2001, Mozambique experienced severe flooding that displaced large numbers of people, disrupted agricultural production, and required the country to seek international food relief. Then, in 2003–2004 and again in 2006–2007, large portions of Southern Africa were once again subject to drought, in some cases the most severe in 50 years. It's been estimated that as many as 6 million people have been threatened by hunger as a result. Some climate models suggest that drought may be an increasingly frequent occurrence in Southern Africa for the foreseeable future.

A NEW ERA

Recent events have given rise to hopes for a new era of peace and progress in the region. In 1988, Angola, Cuba, and South Africa reached an agreement, with U.S. and Soviet support, that led to South Africa's withdrawal from Namibia and the removal of Cuban troops from Angola, where they had been supporting government forces. In 1990, Namibia gained its independence under the elected leadership of SWAPO—the liberation movement that had fought against local South African occupation for more than a quarter of a century. In Mozambique, two decades of fighting between the FRELIMO government and South African–backed RENAMO rebels ended in a peace process that has resulted in the successful holding of two multiparty elections. In Zambia and Malawi, multiparty democracy was restored, resulting in the electoral defeat of long-serving authoritarian rulers. The most significant development in the region, however, has been South Africa's transformation. There, the 1990 release of prominent political prisoners, particularly Nelson Mandela, the unbanning of the ANC and PAC, and the lifting of internal state-of-emergency restrictions resulted in extended negotiations that led to an end to white-minority rule.

Southern Africa has also experienced some reversals in recent years. After an on-again, off-again start, direct negotiations between the Angolan government and UNITA rebels led in 1991 to a UN–supervised peace process. But this agreement collapsed in 1992, when UNITA rejected multiparty election results. Although external support for UNITA declined, the movement was able to continue to wreak havoc on much of the Angolan countryside through its trafficking of illegal diamonds and other commodities across the uncontrolled border between Angola and the D.R.C. This in turn encouraged Angola

were then struggling for the regime's overthrow. In fact, the various Frontline States took a cautious attitude toward the activities of South African political refugees, generally forbidding them from launching armed attacks from within their borders. In 1984, both Angola and Mozambique formally signed agreements of mutual noninterference with South Africa. But within a year, these accords had repeatedly and blatantly been violated by South Africa.

Drought, along with continued warfare, has resulted in recurrent food shortages in much of Southern Africa in recent decades—again especially in Angola and Mozambique. The early 1980s' drought in Southern Africa neither lasted as long as nor was as widely publicized as those of West Africa and the Horn, yet it was as destructive. Although some countries, such as Botswana, Mozambique, and Zimbabwe, as well as areas of South Africa, suffered more from nature than others, the main features of the crisis were the same: water reserves were depleted; cattle and game died; and crop production declined, often by 50 percent or more.

to intervene in the D.R.C. on behalf of the government against UNITA–aligned rebels. By thus effectively encircling UNITA, the Angolan government was ultimately able to achieve military victory where mediation had failed.

The political and economic collapse of Zimbabwe under the leadership of Robert Mugabe over the past decade has also been discouraging. After achieving its independence in 1980, the country was viewed by many as an economic and political role model for the region. At present, however, Mugabe's policies have become increasingly oppressive, directed primarily at retaining political power, and the Zimbabwe's economy has become a basket case, forcing many to flee to neighboring countries for economic survival.

Having finally come to the end of its epoch of struggle against white-minority rule, Southern Africa as a whole may be on the threshold of sustained growth. In South Africa the 1990 release of Nelson Mandela and other political prisoners, followed by the adoption of a new constitution in 1994 that provided for majority rule brought the era of apartheid to a close, ending the era of white-minority rule throughout the region. Besides their now-shared commitment to nonracialism, cooperation among the states is being facilitated by their new-found, yet still tenuous, commitment to democracy. Economic thinking within the region has also converged toward a consensus favorable to the growth of market economies. While Angola, Mozambique, Tanzania, Zambia, and Zimbabwe have all moved away from past commitments to various shades of state-centered socialism, the South African economy is being freed from the statist distortions of apartheid. While reconstruction will take time, its resource base and human as well as physical infrastructure could make Southern Africa a major global nexus in the twenty-first century.

Angola (Republic of Angola)

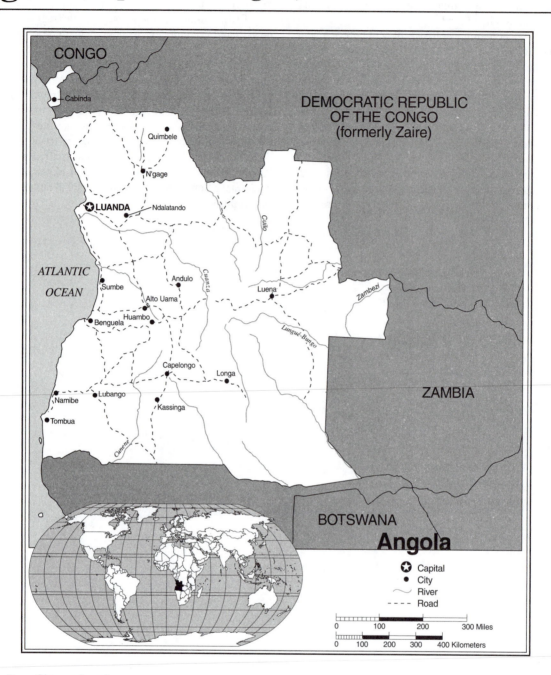

Angola Statistics

GEOGRAPHY

Area in Square Miles (Kilometers):
481,351 (1,246,699) (about twice the size of Texas)
Capital (Population): Luanda (2,819,000)
Environmental Concerns: soil erosion; desertification; deforestation; loss of habitat and biodiversity; water pollution
Geographical Features: a narrow coastal plain rises abruptly to a vast interior plateau

Climate: semiarid in south and along coast to Luanda; the north has a cool, dry season and then a hot, rainy season

PEOPLE

Population

Total: 12,263,596
Annual Growth Rate: 2.18%
Rural/Urban Population Ratio: 66/34
Major Languages: Portuguese; Bantu and other African languages
Ethnic Makeup: 37% Ovimbundu; 25% Kimbundu; 13% Bakongo; 25% others
Religions: 47% indigenous beliefs; 38% Roman Catholic; 15% Protestant

Health

Life Expectancy at Birth: 37 years (male); 39 years (female)
Infant Mortality: 184/1,000 live births
Physicians Available: 1/15,136 people
HIV/AIDS Rate in Adults: 3.9%

Education

Adult Literacy Rate: 42%
Compulsory (Ages): 7–15; free

COMMUNICATION

Telephones: 98,200 main lines; 2,264,000 cellular/mobile
Daily Newspaper Circulation: 11/1,000 people
Televisions: 48/1,000 people
Internet Users: 85,000 (2005)

TRANSPORTATION

Highways in Miles (Kilometers): 51,429 (76,626)
Railroads in Miles (Kilometers): 1,982 (3,189)
Usable Airfields: 232
Motor Vehicles in Use: 223,000

GOVERNMENT

Type: republic
Independence Date: November 11, 1975 (from Portugal)

Head of State/Government: President José Edouardo dos Santos is both head of state and head of government
Political Parties: Popular Movement for the Liberation of Angola; National Front for the Liberation of Angola; others
Suffrage: universal at 18

MILITARY

Military Expenditures (% of GDP): 5.7%
Current Disputes: apparent end of civil war

ECONOMY

Currency ($ U.S. Equivalent): 80.4 new kwanzas = $1
Per Capita Income/GDP: $3,399/$53.9 billion
GDP Growth Rate: 16.1%
Inflation Rate: 13%
Unemployment Rate: unemployment and underemployment affect more than half the population
Labor Force by Occupation: 85% agriculture; 15% industry and services

Natural Resources: petroleum; diamonds; phosphates; iron ore; copper; feldspar; gold; bauxite; uranium
Agriculture: coffee; sisal; cotton; sugarcane; tobacco; vegetables; bananas; plantains; livestock; forest products; fish
Industry: petroleum; minerals; fish processing; brewing; tobacco products; textiles; food processing; construction; others
Exports: $31.4 billion (primary partners United States, European Union, China)
Imports: $11.28 billion (primary partners European Union, South Korea, South Africa)

SUGGESTED WEB SITES

http://www.angola.org
http://www.angolapress-angop .ao/index-e.asp
http://www.angolanews.com
http://www.sas.upenn.edu/African_ Studies/Country_Specific/Angola. html

Angola Country Report

In April 2002, after the death of Jonas Savimbi, the leader of the rebel Union for Total Independence of Angola (UNITA) forces, and the concurrent decimation of his army, a cease-fire was signed in Luanda between UNITA and the governing Popular Movement for the Liberation of Angola (MPLA). After 27 years, the war in Angola was over. The death of Savimbi in a gunfight with government forces in February 2002 rendered UNITA ineffective.

DEVELOPMENT

Most of Angola's export revenues currently come from oil. There are important diamond and iron mines, but their output has suffered due to the war, which also prevented the exploitation of the country's considerable reserves of other minerals. Angola has enormous agricultural potential, but only about 2% of its arable land is under cultivation.

By early 2002 UNITA had been driven out of the Democratic Republic of the Congo (D.R.C.), its rear base, by the combined forces of Angola, Zimbabwe, Namibia, and the D.R.C. Without its rear base of support, funds derived from diamond sales after the Blood diamonds campaign, and leader

Savimbi, UNITA was largely a spent force. In February 2003 the UN mission overseeing the peace process ended, and by June the UNITA had transformed itself into a political party, electing Isaias Samakuva as its new leader.

A peace accord had been signed in 1994, after which the United Nations sent in peacekeepers. But the fighting steadily worsened again, and the MPLA government requested in 1999 that the UN withdraw its peacekeeping forces. The peacekeepers withdrew, and sanctions were instituted against UNITA that froze the European bank accounts for UNITA's leaders and isolated funds used to trade in gems.

Angola, however, remains with large quantities of land mines spread throughout the countryside, and the physical infrastructure has been left in tatters. It will take years to recover from the effects of the civil war, but the country's mineral resources will provide the foundation for development in the future.

In 1996, hopes for a cease-fire had been raised when UNITA agreed in principle to join the MPLA in forming a "Government of National Unity," but a settlement was never implemented. Instead, both sides maintained their military capacities while supporting proxy forces in neighboring states.

FREEDOM

Despite new constitutional guarantees, pessimists note that neither UNITA nor MPLA has demonstrated a strong commitment to democracy and human rights in the past. Within UNITA, Jonas Savimbi's word was law; he was known to have critics within his movement burned as "witches." For a time UNITA had its own Internet address, perhaps the first armed faction to do so.

Since 1975, more than half a million Angolans perished as a result of fighting between the two movements, including many passive victims of land mines. Up to 1 million others fled the country, while another 1 million or so were internally displaced. According to a report by the human-rights organization Africa Watch, tens of thousands of Angolans have lost their limbs "because of the indiscriminate use of landmines by both sides of the conflict." Angola's small and impoverished population could not have perpetuated such carnage were it not for decades of external interference in the nation's internal affairs. The United States, the Soviet Union, South Africa, Cuba, Zaire, and many others helped to create and sustain this tragedy.

(United Nations photo 131277 by J. P. Laffont)

Angola's war for independence from Portugal led to the creation of a one-party state.

After the end of the Cold War and the demise of South Africa's apartheid regime, there was an almost complete cutoff of outside support for the conflict. An agreement in April 1991 between the MPLA and UNITA to participate in United Nations–sponsored elections led to a dramatic decline in violence during 16 months of "phony peace." The successful holding of elections in September 1992 further raised hopes of a new beginning for Angola. While the MPLA appeared to have topped the poll, UNITA and the smaller National Front for the Liberation of Angola (FNLA) secured a considerable vote. But hopes for a new beginning under an all-party government of national unity were quickly dashed by UNITA's rejection of the election result. As a result, the country was plunged into renewed civil war.

THE COLONIAL LEGACY

The roots of Angola's long suffering lie in the area's colonial underdevelopment. The Portuguese first made contact with the peoples of the region in 1483. They initially established peaceful trading contact with the powerful Kongo kingdom and other coastal peoples, some of whom were converted to Catholicism by Jesuit missionaries. But from then to the mid-1800s, the outsiders primarily saw the area as a source of slaves. Angola has been called the "mother of Brazil" because up to 4 million Angolans were carried away from its shores to that land, chained in the holds of slave ships. With the possible exception of Nigeria, no African territory lost more of its people to the trans-Atlantic slave trade.

Following the nineteenth-century suppression of the slave trade, the Portuguese introduced internal systems of exploitation that very often amounted to slavery in all but name. Large numbers of Angolans were pressed into working on coffee plantations owned by a growing community of white settlers. Others were forced to labor in other sectors, such as diamond mines or public-works projects.

HEALTH/WELFARE

Civil war caused a serious deterioration of Angola's health services, resulting in lower life expectancy and one of the highest infant mortality rates in the world.

Although the Portuguese claimed that they encouraged Angolans to learn Portuguese and practice Catholicism, thus becoming "assimilated" into the world of the colonizers, they actually made little effort to provide education. No more than 2 percent of the population ever achieved the legal status of *assimilado*. The assimilados, many of whom were of mixed race, were concentrated in the coastal towns. Of the few interior Angolans who became literate, a large proportion were the products of Protestant, non-Portuguese, mission schools. Because each mission tended to operate in a particular region and teach from its own syllabus, usually in the local language, an unfortunate by-product of these schools was the reinforcement (the creation, some would argue) of ethnic rivalries among the territory's educated elite.

In the late colonial period, the FNLA, MPLA, and UNITA emerged as the three major liberation movements challenging Portuguese rule. Although all three sought a national following, each built up an ethnoregional core of support by 1975. The FNLA grew out of a movement whose original focus was limited to the northern Kongo-speaking population, while UNITA's principal stronghold was the largely Ovimbundu-speaking south-central plateaux. The MPLA had its strongest following among assimilados and Kimbundu-speakers, who are predominant in Luanda, the capital, and the interior to the west of the city. From the beginning, all three movements cultivated separate sources of external support.

ACHIEVEMENTS

Between 1975 and 1980, the Angolan government claimed that it had tripled the nation's primary-school enrollment, to 76%. That figure subsequently dropped as a result of war.

The armed struggle against the Portuguese began in 1961, with a massive FNLA–inspired uprising in the north and MPLA–led unrest in Luanda. To counter the northern rebellion, the Portuguese resorted to the saturation bombing of villages. In the first year of fighting, this left an estimated 50,000 dead (about half the total number killed throughout the anticolonial struggle). The liberation forces were as much hampered by their own disunity as by the brutality of Portugal's counterinsurgency tactics. Undisciplined rebels associated with the FNLA, for example, were known to massacre not only Portuguese plantation owners but many of their southern workers as well. Such incidents contributed to UNITA's split from the FNLA in 1966. There is also evidence of UNITA forces cooperating with the Portuguese in attacks on the MPLA. Besides competition with its two rivals, the MPLA also encountered some difficulty in keeping its urban and rural factions united.

CIVIL WAR

The overthrow of Portugal's Fascist government in 1974 led to Angola's rapid decolonization. Attempts to create a transitional government of national unity among the three major nationalist movements failed. The MPLA succeeded in seizing Luanda, which led to a loose alliance between the FNLA and UNITA. As fighting between the groups escalated, so did the involvement of their foreign backers. Meanwhile, most of Angola's 300,000 or more white settlers fled the country, triggering the collapse of much of the local economy. With the notable exception of Angola's offshore oil industry, most economic sectors have since failed to recover their preindependence output as a result of the war.

While the chronology of outside intervention in the Angolan conflict is a matter of dispute, it is nonetheless clear that, by October 1975, up to 2,000 South African troops were assisting the FNLA–UNITA forces in the south. In response, Cuba dispatched a force of 18,000 to 20,000 to assist the MPLA, which earlier had gained control of Luanda. These events proved decisive during the war's first phase. On the one hand, collaboration with South Africa led to the withdrawal of Chinese and much of the African support for the FNLA–UNITA cause. It also contributed to the U.S. Congress' passage of the Clarke Amendment, which abruptly terminated the United States' direct involvement. On the other hand, the arrival of the Cubans allowed the MPLA quickly to gain the upper hand on the battlefield. Not wishing to fight a conventional war against the Cubans by themselves, the South Africans withdrew their conventional forces in March 1976.

By 1977, the MPLA's "People's Republic" had established itself in all of Angola's provinces. It was recognized by the United Nations and most of its membership as the nation's sole legitimate government, the United States numbering among the few that continued to withhold recognition. However, the MPLA's apparent victory did not bring an end to the hostilities. Although the remaining pockets of FNLA resistance were overcome following an Angola–Zaire rapprochement in 1978, UNITA maintained its largely guerrilla struggle. Until 1989, UNITA's major supporter was South Africa, whose destabilization of the Luanda government was motivated by its desire to keep the Benguela railway closed (thus diverting traffic to its own system) and harass Angola-based SWAPO forces. Besides supplying UNITA with logistical support, the South Africans repeatedly invaded southern Angola and on occasion infiltrated sabotage units into other areas of the country. South African aggression in turn justified Cuba's maintenance (by 1988) of some 50,000 troops in support of the government. In 1986, the U.S. Congress approved the resumption of "covert" U.S. material assistance to UNITA via Zaire.

An escalation of the fighting in 1987 and 1988 was accompanied by a revival of negotiations for a peace settlement among representatives of the Angolan government, Cuba, South Africa, and the United States. In 1988, South African forces were checked in a battle at the Angolan town of Cuito Cuanavale. South Africa agreed to withdraw from Namibia and end its involvement in the Angolan conflict. It was further agreed that Cuba would complete a phased withdrawal of its forces from the region by mid-1991.

THE FUTURE

With the end of the war, Angola now faces the daunting task of rebuilding its devastated infrastructure and resettling the hundreds of thousands of refugees who fled the fighting. Many Angolans remain dependent on food aid. Angola's Cabinda province is one of Africa's largest petroleum producers, and the rise in world oil prices since 2004 has led to a large influx of foreign currency; one consequence has been that the country's domestic inflation rate has dropped dramatically in recent years. Nonetheless Angola remains one of the world's poorest countries, with the average life expectancy among the lowest on the continent. The extreme deprivations of the war have led to problems in Angola with far-reaching social, political, and economic implications. Angola has denied allegations that oil revenue has been squandered through corruption and mismanagement. However, corruption has long been viewed as a major problem within Angola, with numerous high level military and government officials implicated in illicit activities. In 2003 the International Monetary Fund (IMF) dispatched investigators to track down missing oil money. By April 2004 more than 3,000 people were arrested in a crackdown on illegal diamond mining and trafficking. The government stated that 11,000 people were expelled since December 2003 in a campaign against exploitation of economic resources. The vast majority of these individuals were diamond traders.

Timeline: PAST

1400s
The Kongo state develops

1483
The Portuguese make contact with the Kongo state

1640
Queen Nzinga defends the Mbundu kingdom against the Portuguese

1956
The MPLA is founded in Luanda

1961
The national war of liberation begins

1975
Angola gains independence from Portugal

1976
South African-initiated air and ground incursions into Angola

1979
President Agostinho Neto dies; José dos Santos becomes president

1986
Jonas Savimbi visits the United States; U.S. "material and moral" support for UNITA resumes

1990s
Talks for national reconciliation break down; multiparty elections are held

PRESENT

2002
Savimbi is killed in a gun battle with government forces. End of civil war

2007
Elections announced for 2008 and 2009

Botswana (Republic of Botswana)

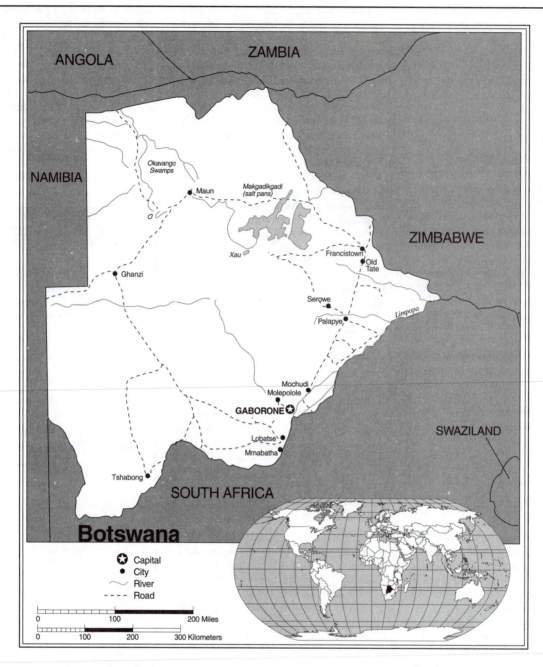

Botswana Statistics

GEOGRAPHY

Area in Square Miles (Kilometers):
231,804 (600,372) (about the size of Texas)

Capital (Population): Gaborone (248,000)

Environmental Concerns: overgrazing; desertification; limited freshwater resources

Geographical Features: mainly flat to gently rolling tableland; Kalahari sandvelt covers 50% of the country; wetlands in the north

Climate: semiarid; warm winters and hot summers

PEOPLE

Population

Total: 1,815,508

Annual Growth Rate: 0.6%

Rural/Urban Population Ratio: 52/48

Major Languages: English; Setswana

Ethnic Makeup: 80% Tswana; 12% Kalanga; 18% others

Religions: 85% indigenous beliefs; 15% Christian

Health

Life Expectancy at Birth: 35 years (male); 33 years (female)

Infant Mortality: 69.98/1,000 live births

Physicians Available: 1/4,395 people
HIV/AIDS Rate in Adults: 37.3%

Education

Adult Literacy Rate: 81.2%

COMMUNICATION

Telephones: 136,900 main lines; 979,800 cellular/mobile
Daily Newspaper Circulation: 29/1,000 people
Televisions: 24/1,000 people
Internet Users: 60,000 (2005)

TRANSPORTATION

Highways in Miles (Kilometers): 6,130 (10,217)
Railroads in Miles (Kilometers): 544 (888)
Usable Airfields: 85
Motor Vehicles in Use: 150,000

GOVERNMENT

Type: parliamentary republic
Independence Date: September 30, 1966 (from the United Kingdom)
Head of State/Government: President Festus Mogae is both head of state and head of government
Political Parties: Botswana Democratic Party; Botswana Alliance Movement; Botswana National Front; Botswana Congress Party; others
Suffrage: universal at 18

MILITARY

Military Expenditures (% of GDP): 3.3%
Current Disputes: none

ECONOMY

Currency ($ U.S. Equivalent): 5.84 pulas = $1
Per Capita Income/GDP: $10,900/$17.9 billion

GDP Growth Rate: 5.4%
Inflation Rate: 11.5%
Unemployment Rate: 23.8%
Population Below Poverty Line: 30.3%
Natural Resources: diamonds; copper; nickel; salt; soda ash; potash; coal; iron ore; silver
Agriculture: sorghum; maize; pulses; peanuts; cowpeas; beans; sunflower seeds; livestock
Industry: diamonds; copper; nickel; salt; soda ash; potash; tourism; livestock processing
Exports: $4.6 billion (primary partners Europe, Southern Africa)
Imports: $2.6 billion (primary partners Southern Africa, Europe)

SUGGESTED WEB SITES

http://www.gov.bw
http://www.info.bw
http://www.cia.gov/library/ publications/the-world-Factbook/ geos/bc.html

Botswana Country Report

Since its independence in 1966, Botswana has enjoyed one of the highest average economic growth rates in the world. This has resulted in a better life for many of its citizens. But serious challenges remain if the country is to realize the ambitious goals contained within its "Vision 2016" program of national development. Economic growth has not been accompanied by equity. More than 40 percent of households remain below the official poverty line. Another concern is the feeling of many Botswana that their country's economy continues to be dominated by noncitizens, while many locals remain unemployed or underemployed.

As Africa's longest continuous multiparty democracy, Botswana has a long tradition of lively and unimpeded public debate and is among the continent's most stable countries. Relatively free of corruption, and with a good human rights record, the country is known for its fiscally conservative economic policies, utilized to sustain the most profitable diamond mines in the world and shift the income derived from the mines towards social development projects. Botswana protects some of the continent's largest areas of wilderness. The Kalahari Desert, home to the dwindling group of Bushman hunter gatherers, makes up much of the country and most areas are too arid to sustain any agriculture other than cattle.

Perhaps the greatest challenge currently facing Botswana is its sad distinction of having the world's highest recorded rate of HIV/AIDS infection. About one third of all Batswana between the ages of 15 and 40 are believed to be living with HIV/AIDS. Known to some as "Africa for Beginners," Botswana has become a victim of its own economic success, as foreign investment has lead to better transport links which in turn have aided the spread of HIV/AIDS. The disease has left many thousands of children orphaned and has dramatically reduced the national life expectancy rate, from 69 years in 1995 to just under 40 years today. Based on current trends, UN-AIDS estimates that overall life expectancy could drop further to as low as 27 years by 2010.

DEVELOPMENT

The United Nations' 1990 Human Development Report singles out Botswana among the nations of Africa for significantly improving the living conditions of its people. In 1989, President Masire was awarded The Hunger Project's leadership prize, based on Botswana's record of improving rural nutritional levels during the 1980s despite 7 years of severe drought.

The man currently leading Botswana in the face of the above challenges is the country's third president, Festus Mogae, who was inaugurated in April 1998 following the retirement of the long-serving Sir Ketumile Masire (1980–1998). In October 1999, Mogae and his Botswana Democratic Party won an easy victory in national elections, against a divided opposition. But his government was subsequently rocked by conflict between several veteran members of the cabinet and the youthful, charismatic vice-president, Ian Khama, a former army commander and the son of the country's first president, Sir Seretse Khama (1966–1980). In August 2000, it was announced that Ian Khama would be given a new coordinating role to assure adequate performance by various ministries, leading many local commentators to proclaim him as Botswana's first "prime minister." President Festus Mogae's party scored a landslide victory in the October 2004 elections, winning a new five-year mandate to rule. Upon being sworn in, President Mogae promised to tackle poverty and unemployment, and pledged to tackle the spread of HIV/AIDS; he has said that he aims to achieve an AIDS-free Botswana by 2016.

Over the past four decades, Botswana has been hailed as a model of postcolonial development in Africa. When the country emerged from 81 years of British colonial occupation, it was ranked as one of the 10 poorest countries in the world, with an annual per capita income of just $69.

(Photo by Wayne Edge)

Three blocks away from the game park with these monkeys you'll find one of the largest shopping centers in South Africa.

In the years since, the nation's economy has grown at an average annual rate of 9 percent. Social services have been steadily expanded, and infrastructure has been created. Whereas at independence the country had no significant paved roads, most major towns and villages are now interlinked by ribbons of asphalt and tarmac. The nation's capital, Gaborone, has emerged as a vibrant city. Schools, hospitals, and businesses dot the landscape, while the country's all-digital telecommunications network is among the most advanced in the world. But the failure of such growth to promote greater equity has also led to a rise in social tensions.

FREEDOM

Democratic pluralism has been strengthened by the growth of a strong civil society and an independent press. Concern has been voiced about social and economic discrimination against Khoisan-speaking communities living in remote areas of the Kalahari, who are known to many outsiders as "Bushmen." In particular, controversy has arisen over recent government efforts to encourage remaining Khoisan groups to leave their ancestral lands in the Kalahari Game Reserve and settle in nearby towns.

Botswana's economic success has come in the context of its unbroken postindependence commitment to political pluralism, respect for human rights, and racial and ethnic tolerance. Freedoms of speech and association have been upheld. In October 1999, the nation held its eighth successive multi-party election. The Botswana Democratic Party, which has ruled since independence, increased its majority in part due to a split in the main opposition party, the left-leaning opposition Botswana National Front.

Most of Botswana's people share Setswana as their first language, which is understood by about 95% of the population. There also exist a number of sizable minority communities—Kalanga, Herero, Kalagari, Khoisan groups, and others—but contemporary ethnic conflict is relatively modest. In 2002, Parliament agreed to amend the Constitution to remove all references to "tribes" while widening the representation within the Ntlo ya Dikgosi, an advisory house of traditional leaders. In the nineteenth century, most of Botswana was incorporated into five Tswana states, each centering around a large settlement of 10,000 people or more. These states, which incorporated non-Tswana communities, survived through agropastoralism, hunting, and their control of trade routes linking Southern and Central Africa.

Lucrative dealing in ivory and ostrich feathers allowed local rulers to build up their arsenals and thus deter the aggressive designs of South African whites. An attempt by white settlers to seize control of southeastern Botswana was defeated in an 1852–1853 war. However, European missionaries and traders were welcomed, leading to a growth of Christian education and the consumption of industrial goods.

HEALTH/WELFARE

After years of being praised as a model of primary health-care delivery, Botswana's public-health service has come under increased criticism for a perceived decline in quality. Botswana's high HIV-positive rate has placed the system under serious stress.

A radical transformation took place after the imposition of British overrule in 1885. Colonial taxes and economic decline stimulated the growth of migrant labor to the mines and industries of South Africa. (In a few regions, migrant earnings remain the major source of income to this day.) Although colonial rule brought much hardship and little benefit, the twentieth-century relationship between the people of

Botswana and the British was complicated by local fears of being incorporated into South Africa. For many decades, leading nationalists championed continued rule from London as a shield against their powerful, racially oppressive neighbor.

ECONOMIC DEVELOPMENT

Economic growth since independence has been largely fueled by the rapid expansion of mining activity. Botswana has become one of the world's leading producers of diamonds, which typically account for 80 percent of its export earnings. Local production is managed by Debswana Corporation, an even partnership between the Botswana government and DeBeers, a South Africa–based global corporation; DeBeers' Central Selling Organization has a near monopoly on diamond sales worldwide. The Botswana government has a good record of maximizing the local benefits of Debswana's production.

ACHIEVEMENTS

In 1999, Botswana's Mpule Kwelagobe was crowned as Miss Universe. In July 2000, Botswana launched its first national television service. A UN report ranked Botswana first in Africa in its percentage of women holding middle- and senior-level managerial positions.

The nickel/copper/cobalt mining complex at Selibi-Pikwe is the largest nongovernment employer in Botswana. Falling metal prices and high development costs have reduced the mine's profitability. Despite high operating efficiency, it is expected to close by the end of the decade. Given that mining can make only a modest contribution to local employment, and because of the potential vulnerability of the diamond market, Botswana is seeking to expand its small manufacturing and service sectors. Meat processing is currently the largest industrial activity outside minerals, but efforts are under way to attract overseas investment in both private and parastatal production. Botswana already has a liberal foreign-exchange policy and has established Bedia as an agency to promote foreign direct investment.

Although it has been negatively affected by events in neighboring Zimbabwe (in September 2003 Botswana begin erecting a fence along its border with Zimbabwean illegal immigrants), tourism is of growing importance. Northern Botswana is particularly noted for its bountiful wildlife and stunning scenery. The region includes the Okavango Delta, a vast and uniquely beautiful swamp area, and the Chobe National Park, home of the world's largest elephant herds.

Agriculture is still a leading economic activity for many Botswana. The standard Tswana greeting, *Pula* ("Rain"), reflects the significance attached to water in a society prone to its periodic scarcity. Botswana suffered severe droughts between 1980 and 1987 and again in 1991 and 1992, which—despite the availability of underground water supplies—had a devastating effect on both crops and livestock. Up to 1 million cattle are believed to have perished. Small-scale agropastoralists, who make up the largest segment of the population, were particularly hard hit. However, government relief measures prevented famine. The government provides generous subsidies to farmers, but environmental constraints hamper efforts to achieve food self-sufficiency even in nondrought years.

Commercial agriculture is dominated by livestock. The Lobatse abbatoir, opened in 1954, stimulated the growth of the cattle industry. Despite periodic challenges from disease and drought, beef exports have become relatively stable. Much of the output of the Botswana Meat Commission has preferential access to the European Union. There is some concern about the potential for future reductions in the European quota. Because most of Botswana's herds are grazed in communal lands, questions about the allocation of pasture are a source of local debate. There is also a growing, but largely misinformed, international concern that wildlife are being threatened by overgrazing livestock.

SOUTH AFRICA

Before 1990, Botswana's progress took place against a backdrop of political hostility on the part of its powerful neighbor, South Africa. Since the nineteenth century, Botswana has sheltered many South African refugees fleeing racist oppression. This led to periodic acts of aggression against the country, especially during the 1980s, when Botswana became the repeated victim of overt military raids and covert terrorist operations. The establishment of a nonracial democracy in South Africa has led to a normalization of relations.

Gaborone is the headquarters of the Southern African Development Community, which was originally conceived to reduce the economic dependence of its 10 member nations on the South African apartheid state. With South Africa now a member, SADC now plans to transform itself into a common market. Despite the countries' past political differences, Botswana has maintained a customs union with South Africa that dates back to the colonial era.

Timeline: PAST

700s
Emergence of the Tswana trading center at Toutswemogala

1820s
Kololo and Ndebele invaders devastate the countryside

1830s
Tswana begin to acquire guns through trade in ivory and other game products

1852–1853
Batswana defeat Boer invaders

1885
The British establish colonial rule over Botswana

1966
Botswana regains its independence

1980s
Elections in 1984 and 1989 result in landslide victories for the Democratic Party; the National Front is the major opposition party

1990s
The ruling Democratic Party wins the 1994 and 1999 elections; the opposition National Front makes gains in 1994 but loses seats in 1999

PRESENT

2000s
Despite astounding national economic growth, many Botswana remain poor

HIV/AIDS crisis

Lesotho (Kingdom of Lesotho)

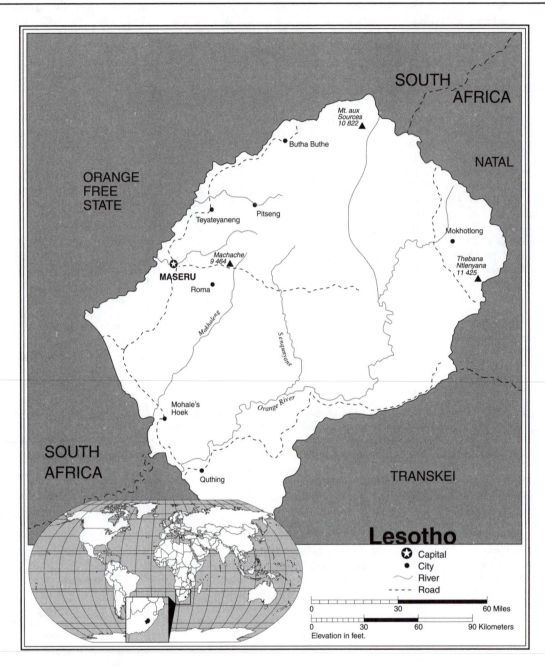

Lesotho Statistics

GEOGRAPHY

Area in Square Miles (Kilometers): 11,716 (30,344) (about the size of Maryland)
Capital (Population): Maseru (271,000)
Environmental Concerns: overgrazing; soil erosion; soil exhaustion; desertification; water pressures
Geographical Features: mostly highland, with plateaus, hills, and mountains; landlocked

Climate: temperate

PEOPLE

Population

Total: 1,865,040
Annual Growth Rate: 0.14%
Rural/Urban Population Ratio: 73/27
Major Languages: English; Sesotho
Ethnic Makeup: 99.7% Sotho

Religions: 80% Christian; 20% indigenous beliefs

Health

Life Expectancy at Birth: 35 years (male); 36 years (female)
Infant Mortality: 91/1,000 live births
Physicians Available: 1/14,306 people
HIV/AIDS Rate in Adults: 28.9%

170

Education

Adult Literacy Rate: 84.8%
Compulsory (Ages): 6–13; free

COMMUNICATION

Telephones: 48,000 main lines; 249,800 cellular/mobile
Daily Newspaper Circulation: 7/1,000 people
Televisions: 7/1,000 people
Internet Users: 51,500 (2005)

TRANSPORTATION

Highways in Miles (Kilometers): 3,638 (5,940)
Railroads in Miles (Kilometers): 1.6 (2.6)
Usable Airfields: 28
Motor Vehicles in Use: 23,000

GOVERNMENT

Type: parliamentary constitutional monarchy

Independence Date: October 4, 1966 (from the United Kingdom)
Head of State/Government: King Letsie III; Prime Minister Pakalitha Mosisili
Political Parties: Lesotho Congress for Democracy; Basotho National Party; Basutoland Congress Party; Marematlou Freedom Party; others
Suffrage: universal at 18

MILITARY

Current Disputes: none
Military Expenditures (% of GDP): 2.3%

ECONOMY

Currency ($ U.S. Equivalent): 6.85 malotis = $1
Per Capita Income/GDP: $2,700/$5.4 billion
GDP Growth Rate: 6.2%
Inflation Rate: 6.1%
Unemployment Rate: 45%
Population below poverty line: 49%

Labor Force by Occupation: 86% subsistence agriculture; 35% of male wage earners work in South Africa
Natural Resources: water; agricultural and grazing land; some diamonds and other minerals
Agriculture: corn; wheat; sorghum; pulses; barley; livestock
Industry: food and beverages; textiles; handicrafts; construction; tourism
Exports: $752 million (primary partners Southern Africa, North America)
Imports: $1.4 billion (primary partners Southern Africa, Asia)

SUGGESTED WEB SITES

http://www.mbendi.co.za/cylecy.htm
http://library.stanford.edu/africa/leso.html
http://www.cia.gov/library/publications/the-world-factbook/geos/lt.html

Lesotho Country Report

In 2002, the Lesotho Congress for Democracy (LCD) party returned to power after securing a majority of parliamentary seats in elections. The elections, which were endorsed as free and fair by international election observers, were held under a revised Constitution designed to give smaller parties a voice in Parliament.

DEVELOPMENT

Despite an infusion of international aid, Lesotho's economic dependence on South Africa has not decreased since independence; indeed, it has been calculated that the majority of outside funds have actually ended up paying for South African services.

As a result of the election Prime Minister Mosisili was sworn-in for a second five-year term in June 2002. Throughout the independence era Lesotho has had a number of highly visible corruption cases, the most important of which was the May 2002 conviction of Masupha Sole, ex-chief executive of Lesotho Highlands Development Authority. Sole, who was found guilty of accepting bribes from foreign construction companies, was paid millions over a 10-year span in return for business

on the Lesotho Highlands Water Project, which supplies water to South Africa. The small farmers throughout Lesotho, who are not supplied with water through irrigation, receive their main source of water through rain, and the rains in the highlands are sporadic.

During February 2004 Prime Minister Mosisili declared a state of emergency and appealed for food aid. Aid officials say hundreds of thousands face shortages after a three-year struggle against drought. Paradoxically in March 2004 the official opening of the first phase of the multi-billion-dollar Lesotho Highlands Water Project, which supplies water to South Africa, took place.

FREEDOM

In Lesotho, basic freedoms and rights are compromised by continuing political instability. Basotho journalists have come out against proposed measures that they say will gag Lesotho's vigorous independent press.

From October 1998 until the new government took over in 2002, Lesotho was ruled by a transitional executive, put into place following the intervention of Botswana and South African troops in support of the previous LCD–led government,

which was being threatened by a military coup. Large segments of Lesotho's defense force resisted the intervention, causing scores of deaths on both sides. In the process, many businesses in the capital city, Maseru, and other centers were heavily looted by rioters, who directed much of their anger against Asians.

Listed by the United Nations as one of the world's least developed nations, Lesotho's domestic economy remains primarily based around subsistence agriculture, especially the raising of livestock. This has been hit particularly hard by drought in recent years. As a consequence, each year up to half of Lesotho's adult males seek employment in neighboring South Africa, where jobs are becoming increasingly scarce. The retrenchment of Basotho mine-workers has led to a local unemployment rate of nearly 50 percent. This dire economic situation is aggravated by Lesotho's chronic political instability.

Lesotho is one of the most ethnically homogeneous nations in Africa; almost all of its citizens are Sotho. The country's emergence and survival were largely the product of the diplomatic and military prowess of its nineteenth-century rulers, especially its great founder, King Moshoeshoe I. In the 1860s, warfare with South African whites led to the loss of land and people as well as an acceptance of British overrule. For nearly a century, the British preserved the country but also taxed the inhabitants and generally neglected their interests. Consequently, Lesotho remained dependent on South Africa. However, despite South African attempts to incorporate the country politically as well as economically, Lesotho's independence was restored by the British in 1966.

Lesotho's politicians were bitterly divided at independence. The conservative Basotho National Party (BNP) had won an upset victory in preindependence elections, with strong backing from the South African government and the local Roman Catholic Church—Lesotho's largest Christian denomination. The opposition, which walked out of the independence talks, was polarized between a pro-royalist faction, the Marematlou Freedom Party (whose regional sympathies largely lay with the African National Congress of South Africa), and the Basotho Congress Party (or BCP, which was allied with the rival Pan-Africanist Congress).

HEALTH/WELFARE

With many of Lesotho's young men working in the mines of South Africa, much of the resident population relies on subsistence agriculture. Despite efforts to boost production, malnutrition, aggravated by drought, is a serious problem.

Soon after independence, the BNP prime minister, Leabua Jonathan, placed the king, Moshoeshoe II, under house arrest. (Later, the king was temporarily exiled.) The BCP won the 1970 elections, but Jonathan, possibly at the behest of South Africa, declared a state of emergency and nullified the results.

In the early 1980s, armed resistance to Jonathan's dictatorship was carried out by the Lesotho Liberation Army (LLA), an armed faction of the BCP. The Lesotho government maintained that the LLA was aided and abetted by South Africa as part of that country's regional destabilization efforts. By 1983, both the South African government and the Catholic Church hier-

archy were becoming nervous about Jonathan's establishment of diplomatic ties with various Communist-ruled countries and the growing sympathy within the BNP, in particular its increasingly radical youth wing, for the ANC. South African military raids and terrorist attacks targeting anti-apartheid refugees in Lesotho became increasingly common. Finally, a South African blockade of Lesotho in 1986 led directly to Jonathan's ouster by his military.

Lesotho's new ruling Military Council, initially led by Major General Justinus Lekhanya, was closely linked to South Africa. In 1990, Lekhanya had Moshoeshoe II exiled (for the second time), after he refused to agree to the dismissals of several senior officers. Moshoeshoe's son Letsie was installed in his place. In 1991, Lekhanya was himself toppled by the army. The new leader, General Elias Rameama, promised to hold multiparty elections. In 1992, Moshoeshoe returned, to a hero's welcome, but he was prevented from resuming his role as monarch. His status was uncertain after elections in March 1993 brought the BCP back to power.

ACHIEVEMENTS

Lesotho has long been known for the high quality of its schools, which for more than a century and a half have trained many of the leading citizens of Southern Africa.

Under its aging leader, Ntsu Mokhele, the BCP faced military opposition to its rule. An outbreak of internal fighting within the Royal Lesotho Defense Force (RLDF) culminated, in April 1994, in the assassination of the deputy prime minister and the kidnapping of cabinet members by mutinous soldiers. In August, King Letsie tried to dismiss the government and suspend the constitution. In the face of growing unrest, Botswana, South Africa, and Zimbabwe acted on behalf of the Southern African Development Community as mediators—and subsequently as guarantors—of constitutional rule. The BCP and Moshoeshoe

were both restored to power; the latter was killed in January 1996 in an auto accident. In June 1997, a schism in the BCP's ranks led Mokhele to establish the new Lesotho Congress for Democracy party, taking most of the BCP with him. The LCD won a landslide victory in May 1998 elections, but the remnants of the BCP and other opposition parties refused to accept the result, inciting King Letsie and the military to intervene. The resulting mutiny within the RLDF led to the South African/Botswana intervention to restore order.

Timeline: PAST

1820s
Lesotho emerges as a leading state in Southern Africa

1866
Afrikaners annex half of Lesotho

1870–1881
The Sotho successfully fight to preserve local autonomy under the British

1966
Independence is restored

1970
The elections and Constitution are declared void by Leabua Jonathan

1974
An uprising against the government fails

1979
The Lesotho Liberation Army begins a sabotage campaign

1986
South African destabilization leads to the overthrow of Jonathan by the military

1990s
Troops from South Africa and Botswana intervene in Lesotho to avert a coup

PRESENT

2000s
The Lesotho Congress for Democracy is returned to power in parliamentary elections

Malawi (Republic of Malawi)

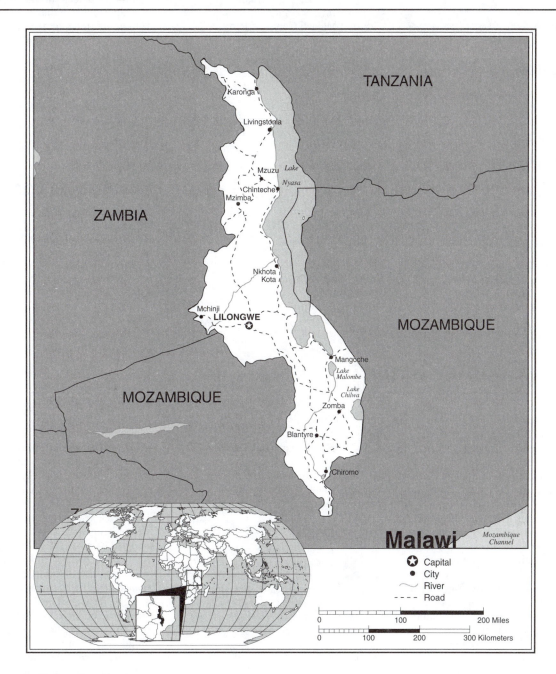

Malawi Statistics

GEOGRAPHY

Area in Square Miles (Kilometers):
45,747 (118,484) (about the size of
Pennsylvania)
Capital (Population): Lilongwe (523,000)
Environmental Concerns: deforestation;
land degradation; water pollution;
siltation of fish spawning grounds
Geographical Features: narrow,
elongated plateau with rolling plains,
rounded hills, some mountains;
landlocked
Climate: subtropical

PEOPLE

Population

Total: 13,603,181 (2007)
Annual Growth Rate: 2.38%
Rural/Urban Population Ratio: 83/17

Major Languages: Chichewa; English;
regional languages
Ethnic Makeup: 90% Chewa; 10%
Nyanja, Lomwe, other Bantu groups
Religions: 79.9% Christian; 12.8%
Muslim; 7.3% other

Health

Life Expectancy at Birth: 40 years (male);
40 years (female)
Infant Mortality: 96/1,000 live births

GLOBAL STUDIES

Physicians Available: 1/47,634 people
HIV/AIDS Rate in Adults: 14.2%

Education

Adult Literacy Rate: 62.7%
Compulsory (Ages): 6–14

COMMUNICATION

Telephones: 102,700 main lines; 429,300
  cellular/mobile

TRANSPORTATION

Highways in Miles (Kilometers): 8,756
  (14,594)
Railroads in Miles (Kilometers): 494 (797)
Usable Airfields: 39
Motor Vehicles in Use: 55,000

GOVERNMENT

Type: multiparty democracy
Independence Date: July 6, 1964 (from
  the United Kingdom)

Head of State/Government: President
  Binguwa Mutharika is both head of
  state and head of government
Political Parties: United Democratic
  Front; Malawi Congress Party;
  Alliance for Democracy; Malawi
  Democratic Party
Suffrage: universal at 18

MILITARY

Military Expenditures (% of GDP): 1.3%
Current Disputes: boundary dispute with
  Tanzania

ECONOMY

Currency ($ U.S. Equivalent): 135.9
  kwachas = $1
Per Capita Income/GDP: $600/$8.3
  billion
GDP Growth Rate: 8.5%
Inflation Rate: 14%
Labor Force by Occupation: 86%
  agriculture

Population Below Poverty Line: more
  than half
Natural Resources: limestone; uranium;
  coal; bauxite; arable land; hydropower
Agriculture: tobacco; tea; sugarcane;
  cotton; potatoes; cassava; sorghum;
  pulses; livestock
Industry: tobacco; sugar; tea; sawmill
  products; cement; consumer goods
Exports: $560.3 million (primary
  partners South Africa, United States,
  Germany)
Imports: $832 million (primary partners
  South Africa, United Kingdom,
  Zimbabwe)

SUGGESTED WEB SITES

http://www.maform.malawi.net
https://cia.gov/library/publications/the-
  world-factbook/geos/mi.html
http://www.africa.upenn.edu/Country
  _Specific/Malawi.html
http://www.state.gov/p/af/ci/mi/
http://allafrica.com/malawi/

Malawi Country Report

In 2003, Malawi was facing its worst famine in more than 50 years. In a land where most of the population engages in farming, the government was struggling to feed the people after the lack of rains in 2001–2002. The harvest in 2002 was 25 percent below that of the last five years. Some 6 million Malawians live below the poverty line, of whom an estimated 70 percent are at serious risk of starvation unless help is found quickly. The situation has been aggravated by Malawi's sale of strategic grain reserves, allegedly on the advice of IMF/World Bank experts. Very little of the money has been collected from the sales. As $40 million worth of maize grain (the staple food) went missing and unpaid for, apparently to local speculators as well as international buyers, people have began asking questions. The scandal could not have come at a worse time for President Bakili Muluzi, who was trying to get Parliament to approve a bill that would allow him to serve a third term in office instead of the normal two terms (which he has already completed). In his drive to remain in power, there have been increasing reports of systematic intimidation directed against Muluzi's opponents.

Parliament, however, refused to accept an amendment to the constitution that would allow president Muluzi to stand for a third term. Thus, Binguwa Mutharika was chosen as the candidate of the ruling

United Democratic Front. Viewed as a relative outsider, his nomination surprised many UDF members and led to several party heavyweight defections including Vice President Justin Malewezi, who subsequently contested the presidential election as an independent candidate.

DEVELOPMENT

As in other parts of Africa, there is increasing recognition in Malawi that rural development must be addressed from a perspective that recognizes the key role of women, especially in arable agriculture. Securing property rights for women has become an important development as well as human-rights issue.

However, the run-up to the poll was overshadowed by opposition claims of irregularities in the voters' roll. The presidential and parliamentary elections, originally planned for May 18, 2004, were postponed by two days following a High Court appeal by the main opposition Mgwirizano (Unity) coalition. The voting was not delayed for long, though, and on May 24, 2004 candidate Binguwa Mutharika was sworn in as President. European Union and Commonwealth observers said although voting passed peacefully, they were concerned about "serious inadequacies" in the poll.

Malawi's current crisis stands in contrast to the optimism that was generated in 1994 when Muluzi and his United Democratic Front (UDF) ended 30 years of dictatorial rule under Malawi's first president, Dr. Hastings Banda. Muluzi's victory over the then–96-year-old Banda brought an end to what had been one of Africa's most repressive regimes. But since Banda's death in 1997, a degree of nostalgia has emerged regarding his era, perhaps reflecting the failure of political liberalization to bring improvement to the country's weak economy, which is largely dependent on tobacco production. The spread of the HIV/AIDS pandemic and a rising crime rate have also shaken public confidence. While the old political order has been swept aside, the new order has yet to deliver better conditions for most Malawians. In 2004 President Maluzi, after admitting there was a major problem occurring due to the rise of AIDS and that his brother had died of the disease, announced the government would provide anti-viral drugs to AIDS sufferers free of charge.

Since the early months of independence in 1964, when he purged his cabinet and ruling Malawi Congress Party (MCP) of most of the young politicians who had promoted him to leadership in the nationalist struggle, Banda ruthlessly used his secret police and MCP's militia, the Malawi Young Pioneers (MYP), to eliminate potential alternatives to his highly personalized dictatorship. Generations of Malawians, including those living abroad, grew up with the knowledge that voicing critical thoughts about the self-proclaimed "Life President," or *Ngwazi* ("Great Lion"), could prove fatal. Only senior army officers, Banda's long-time "official state hostess" Tamanda Kadzamira, and her uncle John Tembo, the powerful minister of state, survived Ngwazi's jealous exercise of power.

FREEDOM

Although greatly improved since the end of the Banda era, serious human-rights problems remain, including the abuse and death of detainees by police. Prison conditions are poor. Lengthy pretrial detention, an inefficient judicial system, and limited resources have called into question the ability of defendants to receive timely and fair trials. High levels of crime have prompted a rise in vigilante justice.

In 1992, Banda's grip began to weaken. Unprecedented antigovernment unrest gave rise to an internal opposition, spearheaded by clergy, underground trade unionists, and a new generation of dissident politicians. By 1993, this opposition had coalesced into two major movements: the southern-based UDF, and the northern-based Alliance for Democracy (AFORD). The detention of AFORD's leader, Chakufwa Chihana, and others failed to stem the tide of opposition. A referendum in June showed two-to-one support for a return to multiparty politics. In November, while Banda was hospitalized in South Africa, young army officers seized the initiative by launching a crackdown against the MYP while purging a number of senior officers from their own ranks. Thereafter, the army played a neutral role in assuring the success of the election.

HEALTH/WELFARE

Malawi's health service is considered exceptionally poor even for an impoverished country. Though improving, the country has one of the highest child mortality rates in the world, and more than half of its children under age 5 are stunted by malnutrition.

While the ruthless efficiency of its security apparatus contributed to past perceptions of Malawi's stability, Banda did not survive by mere repression. A few greatly benefited from the regime. Until 1979, the country enjoyed an economic growth rate averaging 6 percent per year. Almost all this growth came from increased agricultural production. The postindependence government favored large estates specializing in exported cash crops. While in the past the estates were almost exclusively the preserve of a few hundred white settlers, today many are controlled by either the state or local individuals.

ACHIEVEMENTS

Although it is the poorest, most overcrowded country in the region, Malawi's response to the influx of Mozambican refugees was described by the U.S. Committee for Refugees as "no less than heroic."

In the 1970s, the prosperity of the estates helped to fuel a boom in industries involved in agricultural processing. Malawi's limited economic success prior to the 1980s came at the expense of the vast majority of its citizens, who survive as small landholders growing food crops. By 1985, some 86 percent of rural households farmed on less than five acres. Overcrowding has contributed to serious soil depletion while marginalizing most farmers to the point where they can have little hope of generating a significant surplus. In addition to land shortage, peasant production has suffered from low official produce prices and lack of other inputs. The northern half of the country, which has almost no estate production, has been relatively neglected in terms of government expenditure on transport and other forms of infrastructure. Many Malawian peasants have for generations turned to migrant labor as a means of coping with their poverty, but there have been far fewer opportunities for them in South Africa and Zimbabwe in recent years.

Under pressure from the World Bank, the Malawian government has since 1981 modestly increased its incentives to the small landholders. Yet these reforms have been insufficient to overcome the continuing impoverishment of rural households,

which has been aggravated in recent decades by a decline in migrant-labor remittances. The maldistribution of land in many areas remains a major challenge. On a more positive note, peace in Mozambique has reopened landlocked Malawi's access to the Indian Ocean ports of Beira and Nacala while reducing the burden of dealing with what once numbered 600,000 refugees. Communications infrastructure to the ports, damaged by war, is now being repaired.

Timeline: PAST

1500s
Malawi trading kingdoms develop

1859
Explorer David Livingstone arrives along Lake Malawi; missionaries follow

1891
The British protectorate of Nyasaland (present-day Malawi) is declared

1915
Reverend John Chilembwe and followers rise against settlers and are suppressed

1944
The Nyasaland African Congress, the first nationalist movement, is formed

1964
Independence, under the leadership of Hastings Banda

1967
Diplomatic ties are established with South Africa

1971
"Ngwazi" Hastings Kamuzu Banda becomes president-for-life

1990s
Bakili Muluzi is elected president, ending Banda's 30-year dictatorship; Banda dies in 1997

PRESENT

2000s
Political liberalization fails to improve the economy

Famine threatens millions of Malawians

2002
Railway line linking central Malawi and the Mozambican Port of Nacala reopened after almost 20 years, giving the nation access to the Indian Ocean coast

2004
Mutharika elected president; initiates anti-corruption campaign

Mozambique (Republic of Mozambique)

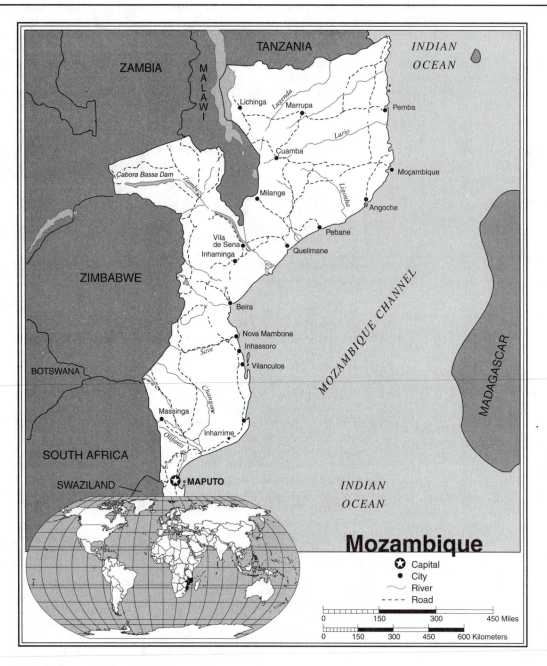

Mozambique Statistics

GEOGRAPHY

Area in Square Miles (Kilometers):
309,494 (801,590) (about twice the
size of California)

Capital (Population): Maputo
(1,134,000)

Environmental Concerns: civil war
and drought have had adverse
consequences on the environment;
water pollution; desertification

Geographical Features: mostly coastal
lowlands; uplands in center; high
plateaus in northwest; mountains in west

Climate: tropical to subtropical

PEOPLE

Population

Total: 20,905,585
Annual Growth Rate: 1.80%

Rural/Urban Population Ratio: 65/35
Major Languages: Portuguese; indigenous
dialects

Ethnic Makeup: nearly 100% indigenous
groups

Religions: 41% indigenous beliefs; 41%
Christian; 18% Muslim

Health

Life Expectancy at Birth: 41.4 years
(male); 40.4 years (female)

Infant Mortality: 138.5/1,000
live births
Physicians Available: 1/131,991 people
HIV/AIDS Rate in Adults:
12.6%–16.4%

Education

Adult Literacy Rate: 47.8%
Compulsory (Ages): 7–14

COMMUNICATION

Telephones: 67,000 main lines;
2,340,000 cellular/mobile
Daily Newspaper Circulation:
8/1,000 people
Televisions: 3.5/1,000 people
Internet Users: 178,000 (2005)

TRANSPORTATION

Highways in Miles (Kilometers): 17,886
(29,810)
Railroads in Miles (Kilometers): 1,913
(3,123)
Usable Airfields: 147
Motor Vehicles in Use: 89,000

GOVERNMENT

Type: republic
Independence Date: June 25, 1975
(from Portugal)
Head of State/Government: President
Armando Guebuza; Prime Minister
Luisa Diogo
Political Parties: Front for the
Liberation of Mozambique (Frelimo);
Mozambique National Resistance—
Electoral Union (Renamo)
Suffrage: universal at 18

MILITARY

Military Expenditures (% of GDP): 1%
Current Disputes: none; cease-fire since 1992

ECONOMY

Currency ($ U.S. Equivalent): 25.4
meticais = $1
Per Capita Income/GDP: $1,500/$29.7
billion
GDP Growth Rate: 7.9%
Inflation Rate: 13.2%
Unemployment Rate: 21%

Labor Force by Occupation: 81%
agriculture; 13% services; 6% industry
Population Below Poverty Line: 70%
Natural Resources: coal; titanium; natural
gas; hydropower
Agriculture: cotton; cassava; cashews;
sugarcane; tea; corn; rice; fruits;
livestock
Industry: processed foods; textiles;
beverages; chemicals; tobacco;
cement; glass; asbestos; petroleum
products
Exports: $2.4 billion (primary partners
South Africa, Zimbabwe, Spain)
Imports: $2.7 billion (primary partners
South Africa, Portugal, United
States)

SUGGESTED WEB SITES

http://poptel.org.uk/mozambique-news
https://www.cia.gov/library/publications/
the-world-factbook/geos/mz.html
http://news.bbc.co.uk/2/hi/africa/country_
profiles/1063120.stm
http://www.state.gov/r/pa/ei/bgn/
7035.htm

Mozambique Country Report

Mozambique has made steady economic and political progress over the past decade in the face of grinding poverty, natural disasters, and the immense burden of overcoming the legacy of a bitter civil war. Although many in the region note that the country has served as a kind of magnet for foreign investment, problems with human-rights issues remain with accusations of torture and harassment of any political opponent of the government. An example of this was seen in November of 2002 when two defendants, on trial for the murder of prominent journalist Carlos Cardoso, alleged that Nymphine Chissano, the son of President Chissano, was linked to the crime. Chissano denied any knowledge of the murder, and was not put on trial. In June 2002, the ruling Mozambique Liberation Front (Frelimo) party chose Armando Guebuza, an independence-struggle veteran, as its presidential candidate for the December 2004 presidential elections, after its long-serving incumbent, Joaquim Chissano, declined to run again.

In February 2000, the eyes of the world focused on devastating floods in Mozambique. In some places the country's two main rivers, the Limpopo and Save, expanded miles beyond their normal banks, engulfing hundreds of villages and destroying

DEVELOPMENT

 To maintain minimum services and to recover from wartime and flood destruction, Mozambique relies on the commitment of its citizens and international assistance. Western churches have sent relief supplies, food aid, and vehicles.

property and infrastructure. Many Mozambicans were left homeless. The disaster was a serious setback for the nation, which had been making steady economic progress after three decades of civil war. This was followed in 2002 by severe drought. Even before the floods and drought, Mozambique (which remains one of the world's poorest countries with much of the population living on an income of less than $1 a day) faced immense economic, political, and social challenges.

A 1992 cease-fire agreement, followed by the holding of multiparty elections in 1994 and 1999, has seemingly brought peace to the country. However, the opposition Mozambique National Resistance Movement (Renamo), which narrowly lost both polls, rejected the 1999 electoral outcome.

Since the 1994 elections Frelimo, which has governed the country since independence in 1975, has faced a large opposition bloc in Parliament from Renamo, its old civil-war adversary, which currently controls 117 out of 250 seats. A now-peaceful Renamo is, arguably, less of a challenge to the government than the dictates of international donors, upon whose funding it now depends. While the government must be concerned about improving the dismal living conditions endured by the majority of its people, the donors have insisted on fiscal austerity and a privatization program that has led to retrenchments as well as a loss of government influence.

FREEDOM

 While the status of political and civil liberties has improved, the government's overall human-rights record continues to be marred by security-force abuses (including extra-judicial killings, excessive use of force, torture, and arbitrary detention) and an ineffective and only nominally independent judicial system.

Frelimo originally came to power as a result of a liberation war. Between 1964 and 1974, it struggled against Portuguese

The drain on natural resources resulting from civil war, the displacement of approximately one fifth of the population, persistent drought, and, most recently, devastating floods, have led to the need for Mozambique to import food to stave off famine.

colonial rule. At a cost of some 30,000 lives, Mozambique gained its independence in 1975 under Frelimo's leadership. Although the new nation was one of the least-developed countries in the world, many were optimistic that the lessons learned in the struggle could be applied to the task of building a dynamic new society based on Marxist-Leninist principles.

HEALTH/WELFARE

Civil strife, widespread Renamo attacks on health units, and food shortages drastically curtailed health-care goals and led to Mozambique's astronomical infant mortality rate.

Unfortunately, hopes for any sort of postindependence progress were quickly dashed by Renamo, which was originally established as a counterrevolutionary fifth column by Rhodesia's (Zimbabwe) Central Intelligence Organization. More than 1 million people died due to the rebellion, a large proportion murdered in cold blood by Renamo forces. It is further estimated that, out of a total population of 17 million, some 5 million people were internally displaced, and about 2 million others fled to neighboring states. No African nation paid a higher price in its resistance to white supremacy.

Although some parts of Mozambique were occupied by the Portuguese for more than 400 years, most of the country came under colonial control only in the early twentieth century. The territory was developed as a dependency of neighboring colonial economies rather than that of Portugal itself. Mozambican ports were linked by rail to South Africa and the interior colonies of British Central Africa—that is, modern Malawi, Zambia, and Zimbabwe. In the southern provinces, most men, and many women, spent time as migrant laborers in South Africa. The majority of the males worked in the gold mines.

Most of northern Mozambique was granted to three predominantly British concessions companies, whose abusive policies led many to flee the colony. For decades, the colonial state and many local enterprises also relied on forced labor. After World War II, new demands were put on Mozambicans by a growing influx of Portuguese settlers, whose numbers swelled during the 1960s, from 90,000 to more than 200,000. Meanwhile, even by the dismal standards of European colonialism in Africa, there continued to be a notable lack of concern for human development. At independence, 93 percent of the African population in Mozambique were illiterate. Furthermore, most of those who had acquired literacy or other skills had done so despite the Portuguese presence.

ACHIEVEMENTS

Between 1975 and 1980, the illiteracy rate in Mozambique declined from 93% to 72% while classroom attendance more than doubled. Progress slowed during the 1980s due to civil war. Today, the overall literacy rate stands at about 40%.

Although a welcome event in itself, the sudden nature of the Portuguese empire's collapse contributed to the destabilization of postindependence Mozambique. Because Frelimo had succeeded in establishing itself as a unified nationalist front, Mozambique was spared an immediate descent into civil conflict, such as that which engulfed Angola, Portugal's other major African possession. However, the economy was already bankrupt due to the Portuguese policy of running Mozambique on a nonconvertible local currency.

The rapid transition to independence compounded this problem by encouraging the sudden exodus of almost all the Portuguese settlers.

Perhaps even more costly to Mozambique in the long term was the polarization between Frelimo and African supporters of the former regime, who included about 100,000 who had been active in its security forces. The rapid Portuguese withdrawal was not conducive to the difficult task of reconciliation. While Frelimo did not subject the "compromised ones" to bloody reprisals, their rights were circumscribed, and many were sent, along with prostitutes and other "antisocial" elements, to "reeducation camps." While the historically pro-Portuguese stance of the local Catholic hierarchy would have complicated its relations with the new state under any circumstance, Frelimo's Marxist rejection of religion initially alienated it from broader numbers of believers.

A TROUBLED INDEPENDENCE

Frelimo assumed power without the benefit or burden of a strong sense of administrative continuity. While it had begun to create alternative social structures in its "liberated zones" during the anticolonial struggle, these areas had encompassed only a small percentage of Mozambique's population and infrastructure. But Frelimo was initially able to fill the vacuum and launch aggressive development efforts. Health care and education were expanded, worker committees successfully ran many of the enterprises abandoned by the settlers, and communal villages coordinated rural development. However, efforts to promote agricultural collectivization as the foundation of a command economy generally led to peasant resistance and economic failure. Frelimo's ability to adapt and implement many of its programs under trying conditions was due largely to its disciplined mass base (the party's 1990 membership stood at about 200,000).

No sooner had Mozambique begun to stabilize itself from the immediate dislocations of its decolonization process than it became embroiled in the Rhodesian conflict. Mozambique was the only neighboring state to impose fully the "mandatory" United Nations economic sanctions against Rhodesia (present-day Zimbabwe). Between 1976 and 1980, this decision led to the direct loss of half a billion dollars in rail and port revenues. Furthermore, Frelimo's decision to provide bases for the fighters of the Patriotic Front led to a state of undeclared war with Rhodesia as well as its Renamo proxies.

Unfortunately, the fall of Rhodesia did not bring an end to externally sponsored destabilization. Renamo had the support of South Africa. By continuing Renamo's campaign of destabilization, the South African regime gained leverage over its hostile neighbors, for the continued closure of Mozambique's ports meant that most of their traffic had to pass through South Africa. In 1984, Mozambique signed a nonaggression pact with South Africa, which should have put an end to the latter's support of Renamo. However, captured documents and other evidence indicate that official South African support for Renamo continued at least until 1989, while South African supplies were still reaching the rebels under mysterious circumstances. In response, Zimbabwe, and to a lesser extent Malawi and Tanzania, contributed troops to assist in the defense of Mozambique.

In its 1989 Congress, Frelimo formally abandoned its commitment to the primacy of Marxist-Leninist ideology and opened the door to further political and economic reforms. Multipartyism was formally embraced in 1991. With the help of the Catholic Church and international mediators, the government opened talks with Renamo. In October 1992, Renamo's leader, Alfonso Dlakama, signed a peace accord that called for UN–supervised elections. The cease-fire finally came into actual effect in the early months of 1993, by which time the UN personnel on the ground

reported that some 3 million Mozambicans were suffering from famine.

Besides their mutual distrust, reconciliation between Renamo and Frelimo was troubled by their leaderships' inability to control their armed supporters. With neither movement able to pay its troops, apolitical banditry by former fighters for both sides increased. International financial and military support, mobilized through the United Nations, was inadequate to meet this challenge. In June and July 1994, a number of UN personnel, along with foreign-aid workers, were seized as hostages. The near-complete collapse of the country, however, has so far encouraged Mozambique's political leaders to sustain the peace drive.

Timeline: PAST

1497
Portuguese explorers land in Mozambique

1820s
The Northern Nguni of Shosagaane invade southern Mozambique, establishing the Gaza kingdom

1962
The Frelimo liberation movement is officially launched

1975
The liberation struggle is successful

1980s
Increased Renamo attacks on civilian and military targets; President Samora Machel is killed in a mysterious airplane crash; Joaquim Chissano becomes president

1990s
Renamo agrees to end fighting, participate in multiparty elections

PRESENT

2000s
Floods lead to enormous losses in life, property, and infrastructure in 2000
Drought in 2002

Namibia (Republic of Namibia)

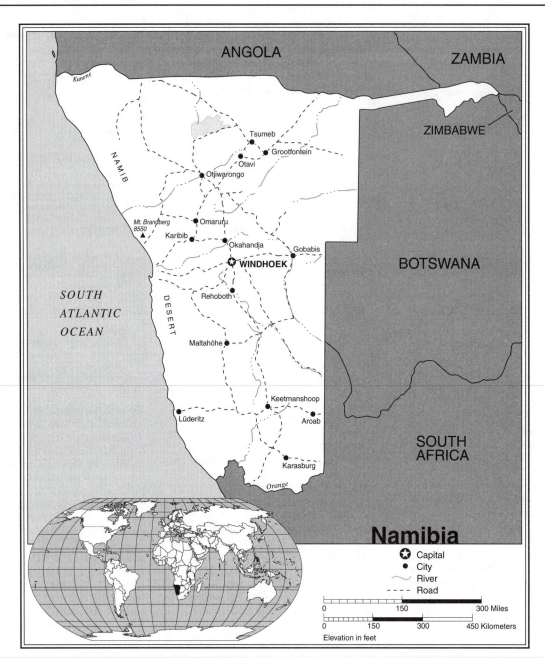

Namibia Statistics

GEOGRAPHY

Area in Square Miles (Kilometers):
318,261 (824,292) (about half the size of Alaska)

Capital (Population): Windhoek (216,000)

Environmental Concerns: very limited natural freshwater resources; desertification

Geographical Features: mostly high plateau; desert along coast and in east

Climate: desert

PEOPLE

Population

Total: 2,055,080
Annual Growth Rate: 0.48%
Rural/Urban Population Ratio: 70/30
Major Languages: English; Ovambo; Kavango; Nama/Damara; Herero; Khoisan; German; Afrikaans

Ethnic Makeup: 50% Ovambo; 9% Kavango; 7% Herero; 7% Damara; 27% others
Religions: 80%–90% Christian; 10%–20% indigenous beliefs

Health

Life Expectancy at Birth: 53 years (male); 50 years (female)
Infant Mortality: 55/1,000 live births
Physicians Available: 1/4,594 people
HIV/AIDS Rate in Adults: 21.3%

Education

Adult Literacy Rate: 85%
Compulsory (Ages): 6–16

COMMUNICATION

Telephones: 138,900 main lines; 495,000 cellular/mobile
Daily Newspaper Circulation: 27/1,000 people
Televisions: 28/1,000 people
Internet Users: 80,600

TRANSPORTATION

Highways in Miles (Kilometers): 39,220 (63,258)
Railroads in Miles (Kilometers): 1,429 (2,382)
Usable Airfields: 137
Motor Vehicles in Use: 129,000

GOVERNMENT

Type: republic
Independence Date: March 21, 1990 (from South African mandate)

Head of State/Government: President Hifikepunye Pohamba; Prime Minister Nahas Angula
Political Parties: South West Africa People's Organization; Democratic Turnhalle Alliance of Namibia; United Democratic Front; Monitor Action Group; others
Suffrage: universal at 18

MILITARY

Military Expenditures (% of GDP): 2.6%
Current Disputes: Plans for a dam along the Angola-Namibian border at Popa Falls were halted due to concerns over population displacements and harmful ecological impacts in the Okavango Delta region

ECONOMY

Currency ($ U.S. equivalent): 6.76 dollars = $1
Per Capita Income/GDP: $7,500/$15.27 billion
GDP Growth Rate: 2.9%
Inflation Rate: 5.3%

Unemployment Rate: 30%–40%
Labor Force by Occupation: 47% agriculture; 33% services; 20% industry
Natural Resources: diamonds; gold; tin; copper; lead; zinc; uranium; salt; cadmium; lithium; natural gas; possible oil, coal reserves; fish; vanadium; hydropower
Agriculture: millet; sorghum; peanuts; livestock; fish
Industry: meat packing; dairy products; fish processing; mining
Exports: $2.7 billion (primary partners United Kingdom, South Africa, Spain)
Imports: $2.6 billion (primary partners South Africa, United States, Germany)

SUGGESTED WEB SITES

http://www.govnet.gov.na/
http://www.sas.upenn.edu/African_Studies/Country_Specific/Namibia.html
https://www.cia.gov/library/publications/the-world-factbook/geos/wa.html

Namibia Country Report

The collapse of the UNITA rebel movement in neighboring Angola has brought to a close what had been a perennial source of insecurity along Namibia's northern border. In August 1999, Namibians were shocked when a small group of self-proclaimed separatists launched an armed attack on the town of Katima Mulilo. (Ultimately defeated, the separatists sought refuge in Botswana; most were involuntarily repatriated back to Namibia in 2001–2002.) Subsequent attacks along the border with war-torn Angola and the involvement of Namibian forces in the war in the Democratic Republic of the Congo (Congo-Kinshasa, or D.R.C.) further shook the country's peaceful international image. The incidents, however, did not fundamentally disturb Namibia's steady progress since its liberation from South African rule in 1990.

With the country now fully at peace for the first time in 30 years, the Namibian government is free to concentrate on domestic development. The material resources that went into the war effort can now be put toward peaceful use.

One area earmarked for urgent attention is land reform. Local observers were little surprised in September 2002 when President Samuel Nujoma voiced his support for the Zimbabwean government's seizure of white-held farms. In fact, Nujomo's own ruling

DEVELOPMENT

The Nujoma government has instituted English as the medium of instruction in all schools. (Before independence, English was discouraged for African schoolchildren, a means of controlling their access to skills necessary to compete in the modern world.) This effort requires new curricula and textbooks for the entire country.

party, the South West Africa People's Organization (SWAPO), has committed itself to redistributing to the African farmers half of the land currently owned by white absentee landlords. It is unlikely, however, that land reform in Namibia will be accompanied by the lawless violence that has marred recent developments in Zimbabwe.

Yet in a country where arable land is premium, land reform remains an issue. In August 2002 Prime Minister Theo-Ben Gurirab stated that the government viewed land reform as a priority. President Nujoma concurred with his Prime Minister, telling white farmers that they must embrace the reform program. This is not so remarkable except for the fact that the issue of land in Namibia is being worked out on the basis of willing seller willing buyer, with the government acting as the purchaser of the majority

population. Prompt government action has had its immediate results. During November 2003 the Union representing black farmworkers called off plans to invade 15 white-owned farms after reaching agreement with white farmers' group. The government says illegal land occupations will not be allowed.

FREEDOM

In line with Namibia's liberal Constitution, human rights are generally respected. There are some problem areas: Demonstrations that do not have prior police approval are banned. The president and other high officials have repeatedly attacked the independent press. There has not been a full accounting of missing detainees who were in SWAPO camps before independence. Security forces have admitted to cases of extra-judicial killing along the Angolan border.

Namibia became independent in 1990, after a long liberation struggle. Its transition from the continent's last colony to a developing nation-state marked the end of a century of often brutal colonization, first by Germany and later South Africa. The German colonial period (1884–1917) was marked by the annihilation of more than 60 percent of the African population in the

(United Nations photo 157251 by J. Isaac)

Developing agricultural production in Namibia is key to the country's economic future. The international economic sanctions that applied before independence have been lifted, and Namibia is now free to enter the potentially profitable markets of Europe and North America. This man working in a cornfield near Grootfontein is part of Namibia's crucial agricultural economy.

southern two thirds of the country, during the uprising of 1904–1907. The South African period (1917–1990) saw the imposition of apartheid as well as a bitter 26-year war for independence between the South African Army (SADF) and SWAPO. During that war, countless civilians, especially in the northern areas of the country, were harassed, detained, and abused by South African–created death squads, such as the *Koevoet* (the Afrikaans word for "crowbar").

Namibia's final liberation was the result of South African military misadventures and U.S.–Soviet cooperation in reducing tensions in the region. In 1987, as it had done many times before, South Africa invaded Angola to assist Jonas Savimbi's UNITA movement. Its objective was Cuito Cuanavale, a small town in southeastern Angola where the Luanda government had set up an air-defense installation to keep South African aircraft from supplying UNITA troops. The SADF met with fierce resistance from the Angolan Army and eventually committed thousands of its own troops to the battle. In addition, black Namibian soldiers were recruited and given UNITA uniforms to

fight on the side of the SADF. Many of these proxy UNITA troops later mutinied because of their poor treatment at the hands of white South African soldiers.

HEALTH/WELFARE

The social-service delivery system of Namibia must be rebuilt to eliminate the structural inequities of apartheid. Health care for the black majority, especially those in remote rural areas, will require significant improvements. Public-health programs for blacks, nonexistent prior to independence, must be created.

South Africa failed to capture Cuito Cuanavale, and its forces were eventually surrounded. Faced with military disaster, the Pretoria government bowed to decades of international pressure and agreed to withdraw from its illegal occupation of Namibia. In return, Angola and its ally Cuba agreed to send home troops sent by Havana in 1974 after South Africa invaded Angola for the first time. Key brokers of the cease-fire,

negotiations, and implementation of this agreement were the United States and the Soviet Union. This was the first instance of their post–Cold War cooperation.

A plebiscite was held in Namibia in 1989. Under United Nations supervision, more than 97 percent of eligible voters cast their ballots—a remarkable achievement given the vast distances that many had to travel to reach polling stations. SWAPO emerged as the clear winner, with 57 percent of the votes cast. The party's share of the vote increased to 73 percent in the subsequent 1995 elections; support for its main political rival, the Democratic Turnhalle Alliance, dropped to 15 percent.

CHALLENGES AND PROSPECTS

Namibia is a sparsely populated land. More than half of its more than 1.8 million residents live in the northern region known as Ovamboland. Rich in minerals, Namibia is a major producer of diamonds, uranium, copper, silver, tin, and lithium. A large gold mine recently began production, and the end of hostilities has opened up northern parts of the country to further mineral explorations.

Much of Namibia is arid. Until recently, pastoral farming was the primary agricultural activity, with beef, mutton, and goat meat the main products. Independence brought an end to international sanctions applied when South Africa ruled the country, giving Namibian agricultural goods access to the world market. Although some new investment has been attracted to the relatively well-watered but historically neglected northern border regions, most of Namibia's rural majority are barely able to eke out a living, even in nondrought years.

ACHIEVEMENTS

The government of President Sam Nujoma has received high praise for its efforts at racial and political reconciliation after a bitter 26-year war for independence. Nujoma has led these efforts and has impressed many observers with his exceptional political and consensus-building skills.

Despite the economic promise, the fledgling government of Namibia faces severe problems. It inherits an economy structurally perverted by apartheid to favor the tiny white minority. With a glaring division between fabulously wealthy whites and the oppressively poor black majority, the government is faced with the daunting problem of promoting economic development while encouraging the redistribution of wealth. Apartheid ensured that managerial positions were filled by whites, leaving a dearth of qualified and experienced nonwhite executives in the country. This past pattern of discrimination has contributed to high levels of black unemployment today.

The demobilization of 53,000 former SWAPO and South African combatants and the return of 44,000 exiles aggravated this problem. A few former soldiers—notably the Botsotsos, made up of former Koevoet members—turned to organized crime. Having already inherited a civil service bloated by too many white sinecures, the SWAPO administration resisted the temptation of trying to hire its way out of the problem. In 1991–1992, several thousand ex-combatants received vocational training in Development Brigades, modeled after similar initiatives in Botswana and Zimbabwe, but inadequate funding and preparation limited the program's success.

Another major problem lies in Namibia's economic dependence on South Africa. Before independence, Namibia had been developed as a captive market for South African goods, while its resources had been depleted by overexploitation on the part of South African firms. In 1990, all rail and most road links between Namibia and the rest of the world ran through South Africa. But South Africa's March 1, 1994, return of Walvis Bay, Namibia's only port, has greatly reduced this dependence. The port has now been declared a free-trade area. Namibia has also been linked to South Africa through a Common Monetary Area. In 1994, a new Namibian dollar was introduced, replacing the South African rand. But, at least for the time being, the currency's value remains tied to the rand.

The Nujoma government has taken a hard look at these and other economic problems and embarked on programs to solve them. SWAPO surprised everyone during the election campaign by modifying its previously strident socialist rhetoric and calling for a market-oriented economy. Since taking power, it has joined the International Monetary Fund and proposed a code for foreign investors that includes protection against undue nationalizations. Since independence, the Ministry of Finance has pursued conservative policies, which have calmed the country's largely white business community but have been criticized as insufficient to transform the economy for the greater benefit of the impoverished masses. In 2005 the government stepped up its efforts at land reform, beginning the expropriation of white-owned farms for the purpose of resettling the country's landless population.

The government recognizes the need to attract significant foreign investment to overcome the colonial legacy of underdevelopment. In 1993, a generous package of manufacturing incentives was introduced by the Ministry of Trade and Industry. In the same year, the Namibia National Development Corporation was established to channel public investment into the economy. It is too early to assess the success of these initiatives.

NAMIBIA'S FISHING INDUSTRY

Namibia's fishing sector has made an impressive recovery after years of decline. The country's coastal waters had long supported exceptionally high concentrations of sea life due to the upwelling of nutrients by the cold offshore current. But in the years before independence, overfishing, mostly by foreign vessels, nearly wiped out many species. Since then, the government has established a 200-nautical-mile Exclusive Economic Zone along Namibia's coast and passed a Sea Fisheries Act designed to promote the conservation and controlled exploitation of the country's marine resources. These measures have been backed up by effective monitoring on the part of the new Ministry of Fisheries and Marine Resources and the creation of a National Fisheries Research and Information Centre. A rapid recovery in fish stocks has led to an annual growth of 35 percent in the sector's value.

THE ROAD AHEAD

Since 2000, Namibia has shown that regional peace has the capacity to bring about major increases in development. Germany offered a formal apology for the colonial-era killings of tens of thousands of ethnic Hereros, but ruled out compensation for victims' descendants. In November 2004, Hifikepunye Pohamba, President Nujoma's nominee, won the presidential elections as the candidate from the South West African People's Organization (SWAPO). The elections were viewed as free and fair and nonviolent.

Timeline: PAST

1884–1885
Germany is given rights to colonize Namibia at the Conference of Berlin

1904–1907
Herero, Nama, and Damara rebellions against German rule

1966
The UN General Assembly revokes a 1920 South African mandate; SWAPO begins war for independence

1968
Bantustans, or "homelands," are created by South Africa

1971
A massive strike paralyzes the economy

1978
An internal government is formed by South Africa

1980s
Defeat at Cuito Cuanavale leads to a South African agreement to withdraw from Namibia; SWAPO wins UN-supervised elections; a new Constitution is approved

1990s
More than 1,000 refugees flee to Botswana from Namibia's Caprivi regions

PRESENT

2000s
The International Court of Justice awards the disputed Kasikili/Sedudu Island to Botswana

Namibian involvement in the Congo-Kinshasa war

Increased efforts at land reform

A bridge across the Zambezi river opens, giving hopes for a boost to regional trade

South Africa (Republic of South Africa)

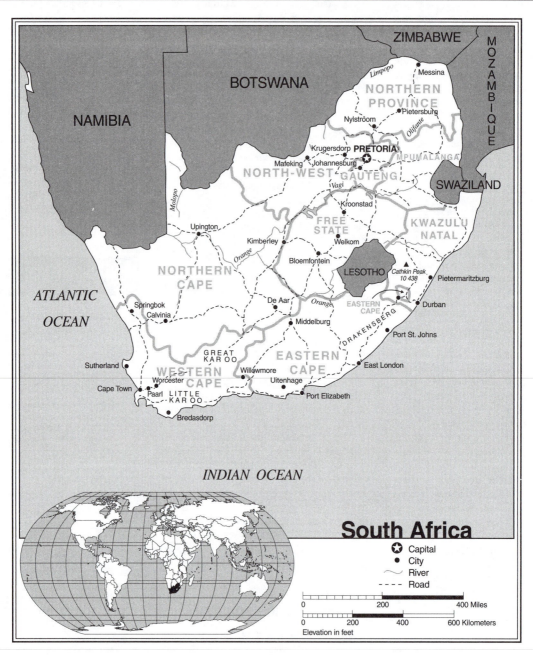

South Africa
- ⭐ Capital
- ● City
- ～ River
- --- Road

0 200 400 Miles
0 200 400 600 Kilometers
Elevation in feet

South Africa Statistics*

GEOGRAPHY

Area in Square Miles (Kilometers):
437,872 (1,222,480) (about twice the size of Texas)

Capital (Population): Pretoria (administrative) (1,590,000); Cape Town (legislative) (2,993,000); Bloemfontein (judicial) (364,000)

Environmental Concerns: water and air pollution; acid rain; soil erosion; desertification; lack of fresh water

Geographical Features: vast interior plateau rimmed by rugged hills and a narrow coastal plain

Climate: mostly semiarid; subtropical along the east coast

PEOPLE
Population

Total: 43,997,828
Annual Growth Rate: –0.46 %
Annual Birth Rate: 17.94 births/1,000 population

Annual Death Rate: 22.45 deaths/1,000 population

Rural/Urban Population Ratio: 50/50

Major Languages: Afrikaans; English; Ndebele; Pedi; Sotho; Swati; Tsonga; Tswana; Venda; Xhosa; Zulu

Ethnic Makeup: 79% black; 9.5% white; 9% Colored; 2.5% Indian

Religions: 68% Christian; 28.5% indigenous beliefs and animist; 2% Muslim; 1.5% Hindu

Health

Life Expectancy at Birth: 43.2 years
　(male); 42.5 years (female)
Infant Mortality: 61.7/1,000 live births
Physicians Available: 1/1,529 people
HIV/AIDS Rate in Adults: 21.5%

Education

Adult Literacy Rate: 86.4%
Compulsory (Ages): 7–16

COMMUNICATION

Telephones: 4,730,000 main lines;
　33,960,000 cellular/mobile
Daily Newspaper Circulation: 29/1,000
　people
Televisions: 128/1,000 people
Internet Users: 5,100,000

TRANSPORTATION

Highways in Miles (Kilometers): 215,157
　(358,596)
Railroads in Miles (Kilometers): 12,784
　(20,872)
Usable Airfields: 728
Motor Vehicles in Use: 6,000,000

GOVERNMENT

Type: republic
Independence Date: May 31, 1910 (from
　the United Kingdom)
Head of State/Government: President
　Thabo Mbeki is both head of state and
　head of government
Political Parties: African National
　Congress; New National Party; Inkatha
　Freedom Party; African Christian
　Democratic Party; Freedom Front;
　Pan-Africanist Congress; others
Suffrage: universal at 18

MILITARY

Military Expenditures (% of GDP): 1.7%
Current Disputes: civil unrest; territorial
　issues with Swaziland

ECONOMY

Currency ($ U.S. Equivalent): 6.76
　rands = $1
Per Capita Income/GDP: $13,300/$587.5
　billion
GDP Growth Rate: 5.7%
Inflation Rate: 4.6%

Unemployment Rate: 25.5%
Labor Force by Occupation: 45% services;
　30% agriculture; 25% industry
Population Below Poverty Line: 50%
Natural Resources: gold; chromium; coal;
　antimony; iron ore; manganese; nickel;
　phosphates; tin; diamonds; others
Agriculture: corn; wheat; sugarcane;
　fruits; vegetables; livestock products
Industry: mining; automobile assembly;
　metalworking; machinery; textiles;
　iron and steel; chemicals; fertilizer;
　foodstuffs
Exports: $63.8 billion (primary partners
　Europe, United States, Japan)
Imports: $69.9 billion (primary partners
　Europe, United States, Saudi Arabia)

SUGGESTED WEB SITES

http://www.gov.za
http://www.southafrica.co.za
https://www.cia.gov/library/publications/
　the-world-factbook/geos/sf.html

_____

*Note: When separated, figures for blacks and
whites vary greatly.

South Africa Country Report

Since taking over the South African presidency from Nelson Mandela in 1999, Thabo Mbeki has faced a series of major domestic and international challenges. Rising crime, the burgeoning HIV/AIDS pandemic, and the falling value of the country's currency (the rand) against the euro and the U.S. dollar have complicated the immense task of post-apartheid transformation. The economy remains healthy, with the tourist industry doing particularly well despite the international fallout from the 9/11 terrorist attacks in the United States. However, despite the growth of the black middle class, the distribution of wealth in South Africa remains highly skewed, largely reflecting the racial divisions of the old apartheid order. The Mbeki government's basic commitment to market-driven growth, coupled with affirmative-action policies for the previously disadvantaged, has been challenged from both the left and the right. The labor movement, led by the Congress of South African Trade Unions (COSATU), held a general strike against the government's privatization and general economic policies during 2002, notwithstanding COSATU's alliance with Mbeki's political party, the African National Congress (ANC).

DEVELOPMENT

The Government of National Unity's major priority was the implementation of the comprehensive Reconstruction and Development Plan. A major aspect of the plan was a government commitment to build 1 million low-cost houses each year for 5 years.

In April 2004, President Thabo Mbeki was elected by parliament to a second five-year term following the landslide (70% of the votes cast) general election victory of his ruling African National Congress (ANC) party. The election served to verify the popularity of the ANC throughout South Africa, and highlighted the woeful inadequacies of the opposition parties. Mongosuthu Buthelezi, the leader of the Inkatha Freedom Party, who had served as Minister of Home Affairs in the previous government, was dropped from President Mbeki's cabinet. However, even though the ANC won the election by a large margin, the structural conditions of massive poverty and low wages for working class people throughout South African society still plague the nation. Hence, in September 2004 hundreds of thousands of public

sector workers went on strike over pay. The government and the unions subsequently came to an agreement, but the threat of the private sector employees taking up the strike banner to increase their pay packages remains.

Moreover the possibilities of violence from white wing forces of the former racist apartheid regime still exist. Bomb explosions in Soweto and a blast near Pretoria during 2002 are thought to be the work of right-wing extremists and, police charged 17 right-wingers with plotting against the state.

In December 2000 local-government elections, the ANC took most of the 237 local councils (59 percent), but the Democratic Alliance—created five months previously from a merger of the Democratic Party (DP), the new National Party (NP), and the Federal Alliance—captured nearly a quarter of the votes. The Inkatha Freedom Party (IFP) won 9 percent. By 2002, however, many of the members from the NP had abandoned the Democratic Alliance in favor of an alliance with the ANC. The ANC also benefited in 2002 from the government being cleared of allegations of official corruption surrounding a large 1999 arms deal.

In the area of HIV/AIDS, Mbeki, along with many of his key associates, courted controversy by expressing skepticism about commonly accepted scientific beliefs about the causal link between the HIV virus and full-blown AIDS, as well as the value of antiretroviral therapies. In December 2001, the country's High Court ruled that pregnant women must be given antiretroviral drugs to help prevent transmission of HIV to their babies. In July 2002, the Constitutional Court ordered the government to provide key anti-AIDS drugs at all public hospitals. The government had argued that such drugs were too costly; but earlier, in April 2001, a group of 39 multinational pharmaceutical companies had withdrawn its legal battle to stop South Africa from importing generic (cheaper) AIDS drugs. The decision to drop the landmark court case was hailed as a major victory for the world's poorest countries.

In hosting the inaugural meeting of the African Union and the World Summit of Sustainable Development in 2002, after the 2001 United Nations Race Conference, South Africa enhanced its diplomatic standing while proving to be an ideal setting for such gatherings. Mbeki's leading efforts to build a "New Economic Partnership for African Development" (NEPAD) were, however, undermined by a lack of consensus with other key African leaders on its blueprint, as well as European and American unease at his inability or unwillingness to take a strong stand against the ruinous policies of Robert Mugabe in neighboring Zimbabwe.

FREEDOM

The government is committed to upholding human rights, which are generally respected. Members of the security forces have committed abuses, however, including torture and excessive use of force. Action has been taken to punish some of those involved. The Truth and Reconciliation Commission, created to investigate apartheid-era human-rights abuses, completed its investigations in 1998. It made recommendations for reparations for victims and granted amnesty for full disclosure of politically motivated crimes.

Mbeki's predecessor, Mandela, remains as a unifying father figure to most South Africans. His retirement ended an extraordinary period in which South Africa struggled to come to terms with its new status as a nonracial democracy, after a long history of white-minority rule.

In April 1994, millions of South Africans turned out to vote in their country's first nonracial elections. Most waited patiently for hours to cast their ballots for the first time. The result was a landslide victory for the African National Congress, which, under the new interim Constitution, would nonetheless cooperate with two of its long-standing rivals, the National Party and the Inkatha Freedom Party, in a "Government of National Unity" (GNU). On May 10, 1994, the ANC's leader was sworn in as South Africa's first black president. Despite the history of often violent animosity between its components, the GNU survived for two years, facilitating national reconciliation. In July 1996, the NP pulled out of the GNU, giving the ANC a freer hand to pursue its ambitious but largely unrealized program of "Reconstruction and Development."

South Africa has decisively turned away from its long, tragic history of racism. For nearly 3 1/2 centuries, the territory's white minority expanded and entrenched its racial hegemony over the nonwhite majority. After 1948, successive NP governments consolidated white supremacy into a governing system known as *apartheid* ("separatehood"). But in a dramatic political about-face, the NP government, under the new leadership of F. W. de Klerk, committed itself in 1990 to a negotiated end to apartheid. Political restrictions inside the country were relaxed through the unbanning of anti-apartheid resistance organizations, most notably the ANC, the Pan-Africanist Congress (PAC), and the South African Communist Party (SACP). Thereafter, three years of on-again, off-again negotiations, incorporating virtually all sections of public opinion, resulted in a 1993 consensus in favor of a five-year, nonracial, interim Constitution.

Notwithstanding its remarkable political progress in recent years, South Africa remains a deeply divided country. In general, whites continue to enjoy relatively affluent, comfortable lives, while the vast majority of nonwhites survive in a state of impoverished deprivation. The boundary between these two worlds remains deep. Under the pre-1990 apartheid system, nonwhites were legally divided as members of three officially subordinate race classifications: "Bantu" (black Africans), "Coloureds" (people of mixed race), or "Asians." (*Note:* Many members of these three groups prefer the common label of "black," which the government now commonly uses in place of Bantu as an exclusive term for black Africans, hereafter referred to in this text as *blacks.*)

THE ROOTS OF APARTHEID

White supremacy in South Africa began with the Dutch settlement at Cape Town in 1652. For 1 1/2 centuries, the domestic economy of the Dutch Cape Colony, which gradually expanded to include the southern third of modern South Africa, rested on a foundation of slavery and servitude. Much like the American South before the Civil War, Cape Colonial society was racially divided between free white settlers and nonwhite slaves and servants. Most of the slaves were Africans imported from outside the local region, although a minority were taken from Asia. The local blacks, who spoke various Khiosan languages, were not enslaved. However, they were robbed by the Europeans of their land and herds. Many were also killed either by European bullets or diseases. As a result, most of the Cape's Khiosan were reduced to a status of servitude. Gradually, the servant and slave populations, with a considerable admixture of European blood, merged to form the core of the so-called Coloured group.

HEALTH/WELFARE

Public-health and educational facilities are being desegregated. In its first 100 days, the new government introduced free child health-care and AIDS-prevention programs. A 10-year program of schooling is to be free to all children. Students have returned to school in large numbers. Crime remains a major problem, with a recent study concluding that South Africa is the most murderous country in the world. HIV/AIDS has reached pandemic proportions in South Africa.

At the beginning of the nineteenth century, the Cape Colony reverted to British control. In the 1830s, the British abolished slavery and extended legal rights to servants. But, as with the American South, emancipation did not end racial barriers to the political and economic advancement of nonwhites. Nonetheless, even the limited reforms that were introduced upset many of the white "Cape Dutch" (or "Boers"), whose society was evolving its own "Afrikaner" identity. (Today, some 60 percent of the whites and 90 percent of the Coloureds in South Africa speak the Dutch-derived Afrikaans language.) In the mid-nineteenth century, thousands of Afrikaners, accompanied by their Coloured clients, escaped British rule by migrating into the interior. They established two independent republics, the Transvaal and the Orange Free State, whose Constitutions recognized only whites as having any civil rights.

The Afrikaners, and the British who followed them, did not settle an empty land. Then, as now, most of the people living in the area beyond the borders of the old

(United Nations photo 1515685)

Resistance groups gained international recognition in their struggle against the South African apartheid regime.

they lacked a properly registered job, they were subject to deportation to one of the 10 "homelands."

ACHIEVEMENTS

With the end of international cultural and sporting boycotts, South African artists and athletes have become increasingly prominent. In 1993, Nelson Mandela and F. W. de Klerk were awarded the Nobel Peace Prize, following in the footsteps of their countrymen Albert Luthuli and Desmond Tutu.

Dutch Cape Colony were blacks who spoke languages linguistically classified as Bantu. While there are nine officially recognized Bantu languages in South Africa, all but two (Tsonga and Venda) belong to either the Sotho-Tswana (Pedi, Sotho, Tswana) or Nguni (Ndebele, Swati, Xhosa, and Zulu) subgroupings of mutually intelligible dialects.

Throughout the 1700s and 1800s, the indigenous populations of the interior and the eastern coast offered strong resistance to the white invaders. Unlike the Khiosan of the Cape, these communities were able to preserve their ethnolinguistic identities. However, the settlers eventually robbed them of most of their land as well as their independence. Black subjugation served the economic interests of white farmers, and later industrialists, who were able to coerce the conquered communities into providing cheap and forced labor. After 1860, many Asians, mostly from what was then British-ruled India, were also brought into South Africa to work for next to nothing on sugar plantations. As with the blacks and Coloureds, the Asians were denied civil rights.

The lines of racial stratification were already well entrenched at the turn of the twentieth century, when the British waged a war of conquest against the Afrikaner republics. During this South African, or Boer, War, tens of thousands of Afrikaners, blacks, and Coloureds died while interned

in British concentration camps. The camps helped to defeat the Afrikaner resistance but left bitter divisions between the resistance and pro-British English-speaking whites. However, it was the nonwhites who were the war's greatest losers. A compromise peace between the Afrikaners and the British Empire paved the way for the emergence, in 1910, of a self-governing "Union of South Africa," made up of the former British colonies and Afrikaner republics. In this new state, political power remained in the hands of the white minority.

"GRAND APARTHEID"

In 1948, the Afrikaner-dominated Nationalist Party was voted into office by the white electorate on a platform promising apartheid. Under this system, existing patterns of segregation were reinforced by a vast array of new laws. "Pass laws," which had long limited the movement of blacks in many areas, were extended to apply throughout the country. Black men and women were required to carry "passbooks" at all times to prove their right to be residing in a particular area. Under the Group Areas Act, more than 80 percent of South Africa was reserved for whites (who now make up no more than 14 percent of the population). In this area, blacks were confined to townships or white-owned farms, where, until recently, they were considered to be temporary residents. If

Under apartheid, the homelands—poor, noncontiguous rural territories that together account for less than 13 percent of South Africa's land—were the designated "nations" of South Africa's blacks, who made up more than 70 percent of the population. Each black was assigned membership in a particular homeland, in accordance with ethnolinguistic criteria invented by the white government. Thus, in apartheid theory, there was no majority in South Africa but, rather, a single white nation—which in reality remained divided among speakers of Afrikaans, English, and other languages, and 10 separate black nations. The Coloureds and the Asians were consigned a never clearly defined intermediate position as powerless communities associated with, but segregated from, white South Africa. The apartheid "ideal" was that each black homeland would eventually become "independent," leaving white South Africa without the "burden" of a black majority. Of course, black "immigrants" could still work for the "white economy," which would remain reliant on black labor. To assure that racial stratification was maintained at the workplace, a system of job classification was created that reserved the best positions for whites, certain middle-level jobs for Asians and Coloureds, and unskilled labor for blacks.

Before 1990, the NP ruthlessly pursued its ultimate goal of legislating away South Africa's black majority. Four homelands—Bophutatswana, Ciskei, Transkei, and Venda—were declared independent. The 9 million blacks who were assigned as citizens of these pseudostates (which were not recognized by any outside country) did not appear in the 1989 South African Census, even though most lived outside of the homelands. Indeed, despite generations of forced removals and influx control, today there is not a single magistrate's district (the equivalent of a U.S. county) that has a white majority.

While for whites apartheid was an ideology of mass delusion, for blacks it meant continuous suffering. In the 1970s alone, some 3.5 million blacks were forcibly relocated because they were living in "black spots" within white areas. Many more at some point in their lives fell victim to the pass laws. Within the townships and squatter camps that ringed the white cities, families survived from day to day not knowing when the police might burst into their homes to discover that their passbooks were not in order.

Under apartheid, blacks were as much divided by their residential status as by their assigned ethnicity. In a relative sense, the most privileged were those who had established their right to reside legally within a township like Soweto. Township dwellers had the advantage of being able to live with their families and seek work in a nearby white urban center. Many of their coworkers lived much farther away, in the peri-urban areas of the homelands. Some in this less fortunate category spent as much as one third of their lives on Putco buses, traveling to and from their places of employment. Still, the peri-urban homeland workers were in many ways better off than their colleagues who were confined to crowded worker hostels for months at a time while their families remained in distant rural homelands. There were also millions of female domestic workers who generally earned next to nothing while living away from their families in the servant quarters of white households. Many of these conditions still persist in South Africa.

Further down the black social ladder were those living in the illegal squatter camps that existed outside the urban areas. Without secure homes or steady jobs, the squatters were frequent victims of nighttime police raids. When caught, they were generally transported back to their homelands, from whence they would usually try once more to escape. The relaxation of influx-control regulations eased the tribulations of many squatters, but their lives remained insecure.

Yet even the violent destruction of squatter settlements by the state did not stem their explosive growth. For many blacks, living without permanent employment in a cardboard house was preferable to the hardships of the rural homelands. Nearly half of all blacks live in these areas today. Unemployment there tops 80 percent, and agricultural production is limited by marginal, overcrowded environments.

Economic changes in the 1970s and 1980s tended further to accentuate the importance of these residential patterns. Although their wages on average were only a fraction of those enjoyed by whites, many township dwellers saw their wages rise over several decades, partially due to their own success in organizing strong labor federations. At the same time, however, life in the homelands became more desperate as their populations mushroomed.

Apartheid was a totalitarian system. Before 1994, an array of security legislation gave the state vast powers over individual citizens, even in the absence of a state of emergency, such as existed throughout much of the country between 1985 and 1990. Control was more subtly exercised through the schools and other public institutions. An important element of apartheid was "Bantu Education." Beyond being segregated and unequal, black educational curricula were specifically designed to assure underachievement, by preparing most students for only semiskilled and unskilled occupations. The schools were also divided by language and ethnicity. A student who was classified as Zulu was taught in the Zulu language to be loyal to the Zulu nation, while his or her playmates might be receiving similar instruction in Tsonga or Sotho. Ethnic divisions were also often encouraged at the workplace.

LIMITED REFORMS

In 1982 and 1983, there was much official publicity about reforming apartheid. Yet the Nationalist Party's moves to liberalize the system were limited and were accompanied by increased repression. Some changes were simply semantic. In official publications, the term "apartheid" was replaced by "separate development," which was subsequently dropped in favor of "plural democracy."

A bill passed in the white Parliament in 1983 brought Asian and Coloured representatives into the South African government—but only in their own separate chambers, which remained completely subordinate to the white chamber. The bill also concentrated power in the office of the presidency, which eroded the oversight prerogatives of white parliamentarians. Significantly, the new dispensation completely excluded blacks. Seeing the new Constitution as another transparent attempt at divide-and-rule while offering them nothing in the way of genuine empowerment, most Asians and Coloureds refused to participate in the new political order. Instead, many joined together with blacks and a handful of progressive whites in creating a new organization, the United Democratic Front (UDF), which opposed the Constitution.

In other moves, the NP gradually did away with many examples of "petty" apartheid. In many areas, signs announcing separate facilities were removed from public places; but very often, new, more subtle signs were put up to assure continued segregation. Many gas stations in the Transvaal, for example, marked their bathroom facilities with blue and white figures to assure that everyone continued to know his or her place. Another example of purely cosmetic reform was the legalization of interracial marriage—although it was no longer a crime for a man and a woman belonging to different racial classifications to be wed, until 1992 it remained an offense for such a couple to live in the same house. In 1986, the hated passbooks were replaced with new "identity cards." Unions were legalized in the 1980s, but in the Orwellian world of apartheid, their leaders were regularly arrested. The UDF was not banned but, rather, was forbidden from holding meetings. Although such reforms were meaningless to most nonwhites living within South Africa, some outsiders, including the Reagan administration, were impressed by the "progress."

BLACK RESISTANCE

Resistance to white domination dates back to 1659, when the Khiosan first attempted to counter Dutch encroachments on their pastures. In the first half of the twentieth century, the African National Congress (founded in 1912 to unify what until then had been regionally based black associations) and other political and labor organizations attempted to wage a peaceful civil-rights struggle. An early leader within the Asian community was Mohandas (the Mahatma) Gandhi, who pioneered his strategy of passive resistance in South Africa while resisting the pass laws. In the 1950s, the ANC and associated organizations adopted Gandhian tactics on a massive scale, in a vain attempt to block the enactment of apartheid legislation. Although ANC president Albert Luthuli was awarded the Nobel Peace Prize, the NP regime remained unmoved.

The year 1960 was a turning point. Police massacred more than 60 persons when they fired on a passbook-burning demonstration at Sharpeville. Thereafter, the government assumed emergency powers, banning the ANC and the more recently formed Pan-Africanist Congress. As underground movements, both turned to armed struggle. The ANC's guerrilla organization, *Umkonto we Sizwe* ("Spear of the Nation"), attempted to avoid taking human lives in its attacks. *Poqo* ("Ourselves Alone"), the PAC's armed wing, was less constrained in its choice of targets but proved less able to sustain its struggle. By the mid-1960s, with the capture of such figures as Umkonto leader Nelson Mandela, active resistance had been all but fully suppressed.

A new generation of resistance emerged in the 1970s. Many nonwhite youths were attracted to the teachings of the Black Consciousness Movement (BMC), led by Steve Biko. The BMC and like-minded organizations rejected the racial and ethnic classifications of apartheid by insisting on the fundamental unity of all oppressed black peoples (that is, all nonwhites) against the white power structure. Black consciousness also rejected all forms of collaboration with the apartheid state, which brought the movement into direct opposition with homeland leaders like Gatsha Buthelezi, whom they looked upon as sellouts. In the aftermath of student demonstrations in Soweto, which sparked months of unrest across the country, the government suppressed the BMC. Biko was subsequently murdered while in detention. During the crackdown, thousands of young people fled South Africa. Many joined the exiled ANC, helping to reinvigorate its ranks.

Despite the government's heavy-handed repression, internal resistance to apartheid continued to grow. Hundreds of new and revitalized organizations—community groups, labor unions, and religious bodies—emerged to contribute to the struggle. Many became affiliated through coordinating bodies such as the UDF, the Congress of South African Trade Unions (COSATU), and the South African Council of Churches (SACC). SACC leader Archbishop Desmond Tutu became the second black South African to be awarded the Nobel Peace Prize for his nonviolent efforts to bring about change. But in the face of continued oppression, black youths, in particular, became increasingly willing to use whatever means necessary to overthrow the oppressors.

The year 1985 was another turning point. Arrests and bannings of black leaders led to calls to make the townships "ungovernable." A state of emergency was proclaimed by the government in July, which allowed for the increased use of detention without trial. By March 1990, some 53,000 people, including an estimated 10,000 children, had been arrested. Many detainees were tortured while in custody. Stone-throwing youths nonetheless continued to challenge the heavily armed security forces sent into the townships to restore order. By 1993, more than 10,000 people had died during the unrest.

TOWARD A NEW SOUTH AFRICA

Despite the Nationalist Party's ability to marshall the resources of a sophisticated military–industrial complex to maintain its totalitarian control, it was forced to abandon apartheid along with its four-decade-long monopoly of power. Throughout the 1980s, South Africa's advanced economy was in a state of crisis due to the effects of unrest and, to a lesser extent, of sanctions and other forms of international pressure. Under President P.W. Botha, the NP regime stubbornly refused to offer any openings to genuine reform. However, Botha's replacement in 1989 by F. W. de Klerk opened up new possibilities. The unbanning of the ANC, PAC, and SACP was accompanied by the release of many political prisoners. As many had anticipated, after gaining his freedom in March 1990, ANC leader Nelson Mandela emerged as the leading advocate for change. More surprising was the de Klerk government's willingness to engage in serious negotiations with Mandela and others. By August 1990, the ANC felt that the progress being made justified the formal suspension of its armed struggle.

Many obstacles blocked the transition to a postapartheid state. The NP initially advocated a form of power sharing that fell short of the concept of one person, one vote in a unified state. The ANC, UDF (disbanded in 1991), COSATU, and SACP, which were associated as the Mass Democratic Movement (MDM), however, remained steadfast in their loyalty to the nonracial principles of the 1955 Freedom Charter. Many members of the PAC and other radical critics of the ANC initially feared that the apartheid regime was not prepared to agree to its dismantlement and that the ongoing talks could only serve to weaken black resistance. On the opposite side of the spectrum were still-powerful elements of the white community who remained openly committed to continued white supremacy. In addition to the Conservative Party, the principal opposition in the old white Parliament, there were a number of militant racist organizations, which resorted to terrorism in an attempt to block reforms. Some within the South African security establishment also sought to sabotage the prospects of peace. In March 1992, these far-right elements suffered a setback when nearly 70 percent of white voters approved continued negotiation for democratic reform.

Timeline: PAST

1000–1500
Migration of Bantu-speakers into Southern Africa

1652
The first settlement of Dutch people in the Cape of Good Hope area

1659
The first Khiosan attempt to resist white encroachment

1815
The British gain possession of the Cape Colony

1820s
Shaka develops the Zulu nation and sets in motion the wars and migrations known as the Mfecane

1899–1902
The Boer War: the British fight the Afrikaners (Boers)

1910
The Union of South Africa gives rights of self-government to whites

1912
The African National Congress is founded

1948
The Nationalist Party comes to power on an apartheid platform

1960
The Sharpeville Massacre: police fire on demonstration; more than 60 deaths result

1976
Soweto riots are sparked off by student protests

1980s
Unrest in the black townships leads to the declaration of a state of emergency; thousands are detained while violence escalates; F. W. de Klerk replaces P. W. Botha as president; anti-apartheid movements are unbanned; political prisoners are released

1990s
Negotiations begin for a nonracial interim Constitution; nonracial elections in May 1994 result in an ANC-led Government of National Unity; Nelson Mandela becomes president

PRESENT

2000s
Thabo Mbeki is inaugurated as president

Mbeki's responses to the HIV/AIDS pandemic draw intense criticism

South African government approved a major program to tackle HIV and AIDS

Another troublesome factor was Buthelezi's Inkatha Freedom Party and other, smaller black groups that had aligned themselves in the past with the South African state. Prior to the elections, thousands were killed in clashes between Inkatha and ANC/MDM supporters, especially in the Natal/Kwazulu region. As the positions of the ANC and NP began to converge in 1993, the IFP delegation walked out of the negotiations and formed a "Freedom Alliance" with white conservatives and the leaders of the Bophutatswana and Ciskei homelands. It collapsed in March 1994, following the violent overthrow of the Bophutatswana regime and the defeat of groups of armed white right-wingers that rallied to its defense. Following this debacle, the IFP and more moderate white conservatives—the "Freedom Front"—agreed to participate in national elections. Attempts by more extreme right-wingers to disrupt the elections through a terrorist bombing campaign were crushed in a belated security crackdown.

The elections and the subsequent installation of the GNU were remarkably peaceful, despite organizational difficulties and instances of voting irregularities. In the end, all major parties accepted the result in which the ANC (incorporating MDM) attracted 63 percent of the vote, the NP 20 percent, IFP 10 percent, the Freedom Front 2.2 percent, and the PAC a disappointing 1.2 percent.

THE ROAD AHEAD

The near future for South Africa is uncertain. On the positive side, international tourism to South Africa is booming; South African artists, musicians, and film-makers are increasingly prominent on the world stage; and the country will be the center of world attention when it hosts the football (soccer) World Cup in 2010.

At the same time, South African society and the political leadership of Thabo Mbeki, in particular, face enormous challenges. These include the widespread prevalence of HIV/AIDS, large numbers of refugees entering the country from adjacent Zimbabwe, and the persistence of poverty and unemployment in large segments of the population. This, in turn, has been exacerbated by regional droughts in recent years. Government initiatives to provide adequate housing and rural electrification have been unable to keep up with demand. Perhaps most importantly, land reform remains an ongoing issue. Most farmland is still white-owned, and the government's efforts to acquire land for redistribution to black farmers have to date been mostly voluntary; in the future, however, forced large-scale expropriations seem likely. The current goal is to transfer 30 percent of the country's farmland to black South Africans by 2014.

Swaziland (Kingdom of Swaziland)

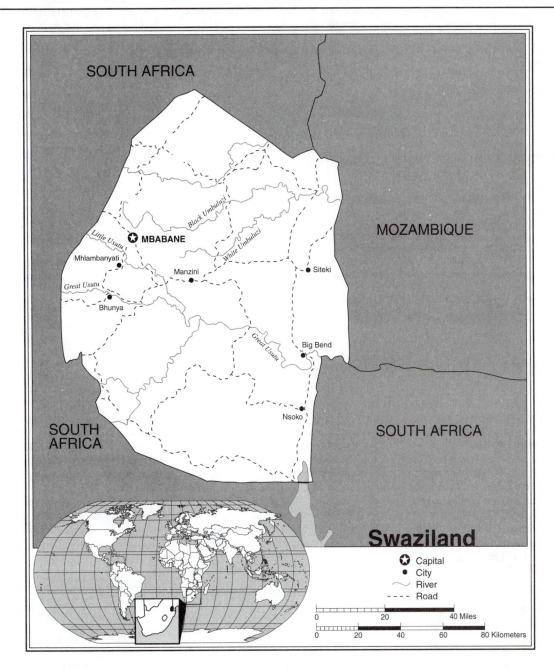

Swaziland Statistics

GEOGRAPHY

Area in Square Miles (Kilometers):
6,704 (17,366) (about the size of New Jersey)

Capital (Population): Mbabane (administrative) (80,000); Lobamba (legislative) (na)

Environmental Concerns: depletion of wildlife populations; overgrazing; soil degradation; soil erosion; limited potable water

Geographical Features: mostly mountains and hills; some sloping plains; landlocked

Climate: from tropical to temperate

PEOPLE

Population

Total: 1,133,066
Annual Growth Rate: −0.37%
Annual Birth Rate: 26.98 births/1,000 population

Annual Death Rate: 30.35 deaths/1,000 population

Rural/Urban Population Ratio: 74/26

Major Languages: English; SiSwati

Ethnic Makeup: 97% African; 3% European

Religions: 60% Christian; 40% indigenous beliefs

Health

Life Expectancy at Birth: 31.8 years (male); 32.6 years (female)

191

GLOBAL STUDIES

Infant Mortality: 109/1,000 live births
Physicians Available: 1/9,265 people
HIV/AIDS Rate in Adults: 38.8%

Education

Adult Literacy Rate: 82%

COMMUNICATION

Telephones: 4,400 main lines; 250,000 cellular/mobile
Televisions: 96/1,000 people
Internet Users: 27,000 (2003)

TRANSPORTATION

Highways in Miles (Kilometers): 1,769 (2,853)
Railroads in Miles (Kilometers): 186 (301)
Usable Airfields: 18
Motor Vehicles in Use: 37,000

GOVERNMENT

Type: monarchy; independent member of the British Commonwealth

Independence Date: September 6, 1968
Head of State/Government: King Mswati III; Prime Minister Absolom Themba Dlamini
Political Parties: Political parties formerly banned, but status now unclear under new (2006) constitution
Suffrage: universal at 18 yrs.

MILITARY

Military Expenditures (% of GDP): 4.7%
Current Disputes: territorial issues with South Africa

ECONOMY

Currency ($ U.S. Equivalent): 6.85 emalangeni = $1
Per Capita Income/GDP: $5,300/$6.0 billion
GDP Growth Rate: 2.1%
Inflation Rate: 5.7%

Unemployment Rate: 40%
Natural Resources: iron ore; asbestos; coal; clay; hydropower; forests; gold; diamonds; quarry stone; talc
Agriculture: corn; livestock; sugarcane; fruits; cotton; rice; sorghum; tobacco; peanuts
Industry: sugar processing; mining; wood pulp; beverages
Exports: $2.1 billion (primary partners South Africa, Europe, Mozambique)
Imports: $2.2 billion (primary partners South Africa, Europe, Japan)

SUGGESTED WEB SITES

http://www.swazi.com/government
http://www.sas.upenn.edu/African_ Studies/Country_Specific/Swaziland. html
https://www.cia.gov/library/ publications/the-world-factbook/ geos/wz.html

Swaziland Country Report

The alleged abduction of a female high school student in October 2002 focused international attention on the struggle between modernist and royal traditionalist forces in Swaziland. The young woman had been removed from her school to be considered for the honor of becoming the 11th wife of King Mswati III. In an unprecedented move, the potential bride's mother accused two of the Swazi king's close associates with kidnapping.

DEVELOPMENT

Much of Swaziland's economy is managed by the Tibiyo TakaNgwana, a royally controlled institution established in 1968 by Sobuza. It is responsible for the financial assets of the communal lands (upon which most Swazis farm) and mining operations.

A small, landlocked kingdom sandwiched between the much larger states of Mozambique and South Africa, casual observers have tended to look upon Swaziland as a peaceful island of traditional Africa that has been immune to the continent's contemporary conflicts. This image, now being increasingly challenged from within is a product of the country's status as the only precolonial monarchy in sub-

Saharan Africa to have survived into the modern era. Swazi sociopolitical organization is ostensibly governed in accordance with age-old structures and norms. But below this veneer of timelessness lies a dynamic society that has been subject to internal and external pressures. The holding of restricted, nonparty elections in 1993 and 1998 has not quelled the debate over the country's political future between defenders of the status quo and those who advocate a restoration of multiparty democracy.

FREEDOM

The current political order restricts many forms of opposition, although its defenders claim that local councils, *Tikhudlas*, allow for popular participation in decision making. The leading opposition group is the People's United Democratic Movement.

During the 1993 elections, a "stay-away" campaign in favor of reform, accompanied by quiet diplomacy by neighboring states, helped push the Swazi government toward dialogue on the issue. In 1996, King Mswati announced the appointment of a committee to draw up a new constitution. But progress has since been stalled. The offically

banned People's United Democratic Movement (PU-DEMO) and other civil-society groups have long called for a repeal of the 1973 royal decree that abolished constitutional rule, including the guarantee of basic freedoms.

From 1903 until the restoration of independence in 1968, the country remained a British colonial protectorate, despite sustained pressure for its incorporation into

HEALTH/WELFARE

Swaziland's low life expectancy and high infant mortality rates have resulted in greater public-health budget allocations. A greater emphasis has also been placed on preventive medicine. However, the extremely high rate of HIV/AIDS poses severe and long-term threats to the nation.

South Africa. Throughout the colonial period, the ruling Dlamini dynasty, which was led by the energetic Sobuza II after 1921, served successfully as a rallying point for national self-assertion on the key issues of regaining control of alienated land and opposing union with South Africa. Sobuza's personal leadership in both struggles contributed to the overwhelming popularity of his royalist Imbokodvo Party in the elections of 1964, 1967, and 1972. In 1973, faced with a modest but articulate opposition party, the Ngwane National Liberatory Congress, Sobuza dissolved Parliament and repealed the Westminster-style Constitution, characterizing it as "un-Swazi." In 1979, a new, nonpartisan Parliament was chosen; but authority remained with the king, assisted by his advisory council, the Liqoqo.

Sobuza's death in 1982 left many wondering if Swaziland's unique monarchist institutions would survive. A prolonged power struggle increased tensions within the ruling order. Members of the Liqoqo seized effective power and appointed a new "Queen Regent," Ntombi. However, palace intrigue continued until Prince Makhosetive, Ntombi's teenage son, was installed as King Mswati III in 1986, at age 18. The new king approved the demotion of the Liqoqo back to its advisory status and has ruled through his appointed prime minister and cabinet.

ACHIEVEMENTS

The University of Swaziland was established in the 1970s and now offers a full range of degree and diploma programs.

One of the major challenges facing any Swazi government is its relationship with South Africa. Under Sobuza, Swaziland managed to maintain its political autonomy while accepting its economic dependence on its powerful neighbor. The king also maintained a delicate balance between the apartheid state and the forces opposing it. In the 1980s, this balance became tilted, with a greater degree of cooperation between the two countries' security forces in curbing suspected African National Congress (ANC) activists. In an abrupt reversal of fortunes, Swaziland's prodemocracy activists now look to the new ANC–led government in South Africa for support.

Swaziland's economy, like its politics, is the product of both internal and external initiatives. Since independence, the nation has enjoyed a high rate of economic growth, led by the expansion and diversification of its agriculture. Success in agriculture has promoted the development of secondary industries, such as a sugar refinery and a paper mill. There has also been increased exploitation of coal and asbestos. Another important source of revenue is tourism, which depends on weekend traffic from South Africa.

Swazi development has relied on capital-intensive, rather than labor-intensive, projects. As a result, disparities in local wealth and dependence on South African investment have increased. Only 16 percent of the Swazi population, including migrant workers in South Africa, were in formal-sector employment by 1989. Until recently the economy was boosted by international investors looking for a politically preferable window to the South African market. An example is Coca Cola's decision to move its regional headquarters and concentrate plant from South Africa to Swaziland; the plant employs only about 100 workers but accounts for 20 percent of all foreign-exchange earnings. The current reform process in South Africa, however, is reducing Swaziland's attraction as a center for corporate relocation and sanctions-busting. It has also increased pressure for greater democracy.

A new constitution was signed by the king in 2005 for full implementation in 2006, but critics say the document still leaves ultimate power in the hands of the king. Royalists argue that democracy creates division, and that a king is a strong unifying force.

Timeline: PAST

1800s
Zulu and South African whites encroach on Swazi territory

1900
A protectorate is established by the British

1903
Britain assumes control over Swaziland

1968
Independence is restored

1973
Parliament is dissolved and political parties are banned

1982
King Sobuza dies

1986
King Mswati III is crowned, ending the regency period marked by political instability

1990s
Swaziland's relationship with South Africa shifts; pressures mount for increased democracy

PRESENT

2000s
AIDS is recognized as a formidable threat to the Swazi people

Pressure continues for multipartyism

An alleged kidnapping case draws international attention

New constitution signed by King Mswati III in 2005

Zambia (Republic of Zambia)

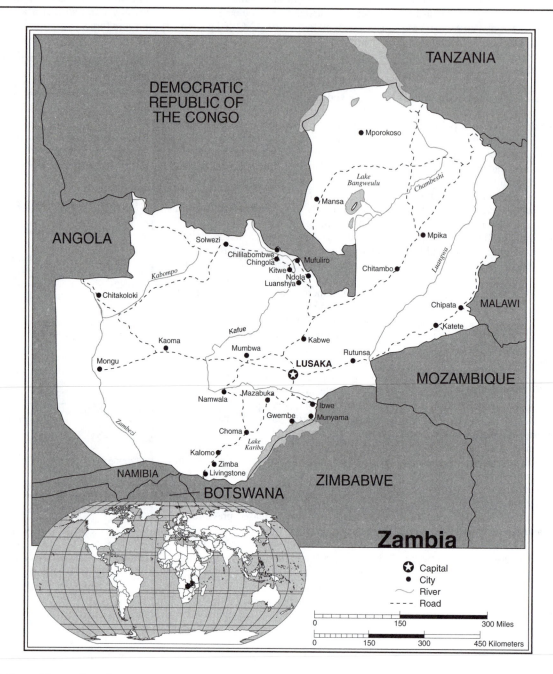

Zambia Statistics

GEOGRAPHY

Area in Square Miles (Kilometers):
290,724 (752,972) (about the size of Texas)

Capital (Population): Lusaka (1,718,000)

Environmental Concerns: air pollution; acid rain; poaching; deforestation; soil erosion; desertification; lack of adequate water treatment

Geographical Features: mostly high plateau with some hills and mountains; landlocked

Climate: tropical; modified by altitude

PEOPLE

Population

Total: 11,477,447
Annual Growth Rate: 1.6%

Rural/Urban Population Ratio: 60/40
Major Languages: English; Bemba; Nyanja; Ila-Tonga; Lozi; others

Ethnic Makeup: 99% African
Religions: 50% Christian; 48% indigenous beliefs; 2% others

Health

Life Expectancy at Birth: 38.3 years (male); 38.5 years (female)

Infant Mortality: 89.3/1,000 live births
Physicians Available:
   1/10,917 people
HIV/AIDS Rate in Adults: 16.5%

Education

Adult Literacy Rate: 81%
Compulsory (Ages): 7–14

COMMUNICATION

Telephones: 94,700 main lines;
   949,600 cellular/mobile
Daily Newspaper Circulation:
   13/1,000 people
Televisions: 32/1,000 people
Internet Users: 178,000

TRANSPORTATION

Highways in Miles (Kilometers):
   41,404 (66,781)
Railroads in Miles (Kilometers):
   1,327 (2157)
Usable Airfields: 107
Motor Vehicles in Use: 215,000

GOVERNMENT

Type: republic
Independence Date: October 24, 1964
   (from the United Kingdom)
Head of State/Government: President
   Levy Mwanawasa is both head of state
   and head of government
Political Parties: Movement for
   Multiparty Democracy; United
   National Independence Party; others
Suffrage: universal at 18

MILITARY

Military Expenditures (% of GDP): 1.8%
Current Disputes: none

ECONOMY

Currency ($ U.S. Equivalent): 3,602
   kwachas = $1
Per Capita Income/GDP: $1,000/$11.6
   billion
GDP Growth Rate: 5.8%
Inflation Rate: 9.0%
Unemployment Rate: 50%

Population Below Poverty Line: 86%
Labor Force by Occupation: 85%
   agriculture; 9% services; 6% industry
Natural Resources: copper; zinc; lead;
   cobalt; coal; emeralds; gold; silver;
   uranium; hydropower
Agriculture: corn; sorghum; rice; tobacco;
   cotton; seeds; cassava; peanuts;
   sugarcane
Industry: livestock; mining; foodstuffs;
   beverages; chemicals; textiles;
   fertilizer
Exports: $2.4 billion (primary partners
   United Kingdom, South Africa,
   Switzerland)
Imports: $2.6 billion (primary partners
   South Africa, United Kingdom,
   Zimbabwe)

SUGGESTED WEB SITES

http://www.zambia.co.zm
http://www.zamnet.zm
https://www.cia.gov/library/
   publications/the-world-factbook/
   geos/za.html

Zambia Country Report

After nearly four decades of independence, some three quarters of Zambia's population continue to live below the poverty line, earning less than $1 a day. Up to one in six has also been afflicted by the HIV virus, while many people continue to be struck down by malaria. Floods and drought since 2001 have aggravated Zambia's already poor agricultural output, placing some 2 million people at risk from starvation. The end of the civil war in Angola has, however, brought a welcome relief from border incursions.

DEVELOPMENT

Higher producer prices for agriculture, technical assistance, and rural-resettlement schemes are part of government efforts to raise Zambia's agricultural production. The agricultural sector has shown growth.

The man leading the country in the face of the above challenges is Zambia's third president, Levy Mwanawasa. In January 2002, he was sworn in, replacing his mentor, Frederick Chiluba. Chiluba had tried to alter the Constitution to allow him to run for a third term in office, but members of his own party in Parliament defeated the move. After obtaining the presidency,

Mwanawasa stunned the nation by dismissing most of Chiluba's appointees and calling upon Parliament to nullify Chiluba's immunity from prosecution, declaring that the former president was implicated in a series of corruption cases. In July, Parliament voted unanimously to lift the immunity. Although members of the opposition concurred with the ruling party, they further called for a commission of inquiry to also investigate Mwanawasa, who they alleged was implicated in Chiluba-era misdeeds. During September 2004 most of the charges of corruption against former president Frederick Chiluba were dropped, but within hours he was re-arrested on six new charges.

FREEDOM

Under the MMD, police have continued to commit extra-judicial killings and other abuses. The government has continued to try to limit press freedom, while failing to honor its 1991 promise to privatize the public media.

For many, Chiluba's presidency was a disappointment. They had hoped that his election in 1991 as the leader of the Movement for Multiparty Democracy (MMD)

was the beginning of a new era of democracy and development, after decades of decline under the one-party rule of his predecessor Kenneth Kaunda. But the Chiluba government largely failed to overcome the effects of high inflation and a shrinking gross domestic product, as well as the mounting challenge of the HIV/AIDS pandemic. Many educated Zambians have left their country in search of opportunities elsewhere.

Zambian politics and society became polarized following the controversial elections of 1996. In that poll, Chiluba and the MMD were reelected amid a boycott by opposition groups, including the former ruling party, the United National Independence Party (UNIP). There were reports of voter-registration irregularities and the enactment of a law barring UNIP's leader, Kaunda, and others from running on account of their being "foreigners." (Kaunda's father had been born before colonial boundaries in what is today Malawi.) The fairness of the elections was also compromised by MMD's use of state resources, especially the public media, in its campaign, and by the charging of Kaunda and nine other UNIP members with treason following a brief bombing campaign by an otherwise still shadowy group calling itself the Black Mambas (after an especially poisonous snake).

HEALTH/WELFARE

Life expectancy rates have increased in Zambia since independence, as a result of improved health-care facilities. However, AIDS increasingly looms as a critical problem in Zambia.

ACHIEVEMENTS

Zambia has long played a major role in the fight against white supremacy in Southern Africa. From 1964 until 1980, it was a major base for Zimbabwe nationalists.

In 1997, a Zambian Army captain took control of the national radio station and announced a coup. The plot had little support and was quickly crushed. In its aftermath, however, Parliament approved a 90-day state of emergency, during which time prominent critics of the government were detained on allegations of involvement in the coup. Domestic and international human-rights groups reported serious abuses throughout the period.

The deeper roots of Zambia's woes lie in Kenneth Kaunda's 27-year rule. During much of that period, the nation's economy steadily declined. Kaunda consistently blamed his country's setbacks on external forces rather than on his government's failings. There was some justification for his position. The high rate of return on exported copper made the nation one of the most prosperous in Africa until 1975. Since then, fluctuating, but generally depressed, prices for the metal—and the disruption of land-locked Zambia's traditional sea outlets as a result of strife in neighboring states—have had disastrous economic consequences.

Nonetheless, internal factors have also contributed to Zambia's decay. From the early years of Zambia's independence, Kaunda and UNIP showed little tolerance for political opposition. In 1972, the country was legally transformed into a one-party state in which power was concentrated in the hands of Kaunda and his fellow members of UNIP's Central Committee. After 1976, the government ruled with emergency powers. Although Zambia was never as repressive as such neighboring states as Malawi and Zaire/Democratic Republic of the Congo, torture and political detention without trial were common.

Timeline: PAST

A.D. 1889
Rhodes' South African Company is chartered by the British government

1924–1934
Development of the Copperbelt

1953–1963
Federation of Northern Rhodesia, Southern Rhodesia, and Nyasaland is formed; still part of British Empire

1964
Zambia gains independence

1972
Zambia becomes a one-party state under Kenneth Kaunda's United National Independence Party

1980s
South African military raids on Zambia

1990s
Kaunda is defeated in multiparty elections; Frederick Chiluba becomes the nation's second president; a coup attempt is thwarted; the government imposes a state of emergency

PRESENT

2000s
The country grapples with the HIV/AIDS pandemic

Levy Mwanawasa gains the presidency

In its rule, UNIP was supposedly guided by the philosophy of "humanism," a term that became synonymous with the "thoughts of Kaunda." The party also claimed adherence to socialism. But though it was once a mass party that spearheaded Zambia's struggle for majority rule and independence, UNIP came to stand for little other than the perpetuation of its own power.

An underlying economic problem has remained the decline of rural production, despite Zambia's considerable agricultural potential. The underdevelopment of agriculture is rooted in the colonial policies that favored mining to the exclusion of other sectors. Since independence, the rural areas have continued to be neglected in terms of infrastructural investment. Until recently Zambian farmers were paid little for their produce, with government subsidization of imported food. The result has been a continuous influx of individuals into urban areas, despite a lack of jobs for them, and falling food production.

Zambia's rural decline has severely constrained the government's ability to meet the challenge imposed by depressed export earnings from tourism, copper, and other industries. This has led to severe shortages of foreign exchange and chronic indebtedness. After years of relative inertia, the government, during the 1980s, devoted greater attention to rural development. Agricultural production rose modestly in response to increased incentives. But the size and desperate condition of the urban population discouraged the government from decontrolling prices altogether; rising maize prices in 1986 set off riots that left at least 30 people dead. The new MMD government ended the subsidies, but there has since been insufficient investment to revive the collapsed rural economy. More recently, however, limited economic improvements have begun to appear. The government has worked with the International Monetary Fund and the World Bank to reduce the country's foreign debt from $7.2 billion to $0.5 billion, and an anti-graft campaign by President Mwanawasa has made Zambia more attractive to foreign investment. Nonetheless, since 2002, the government has been adamant in its opposition to the importation of genetically modified grains as food aid, supposedly to protect domestic crops from contamination. Meanwhile, food shortages still threaten millions of Zambians.

Zimbabwe (Republic of Zimbabwe)

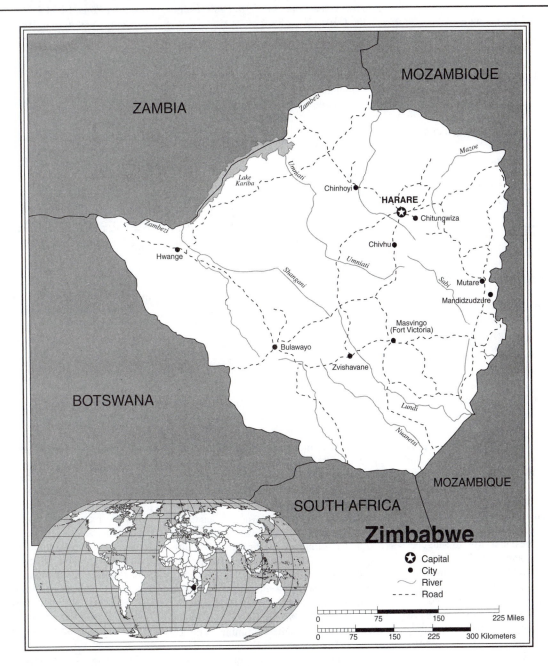

Zimbabwe Statistics

GEOGRAPHY

Area in Square Miles (Kilometers):
150,873 (390,759) (about the size of Montana)
Capital (Population): Harare (1,868,000)
Environmental Concerns: deforestation; soil erosion; land degradation; air and water pollution; poaching

Geographical Features: high plateau with higher central plateau (high veld); mountains in the east; landlocked
Climate: tropical; moderated by altitude

PEOPLE

Population

Total: 12,311,143
Annual Growth Rate: 0.6%
Rural/Urban Population Ratio: 65/35

Major Languages: English; Shona; Ndebele; Sidebele
Ethnic Makeup: 82% Shona; 14% Ndebele; 2% other African; 2% others
Religions: 50% syncretic (part Christian, part indigenous beliefs); 25% Christian; 24% indigenous beliefs; 1% Muslim

Health

Life Expectancy at Birth: 40.6 years (male); 38.4 years (female)

GLOBAL STUDIES

Infant Mortality: 51.1/1,000
live births
Physicians Available: 1/6,
909 people
HIV/AIDS Rate in Adults: 24.6%

Education

Adult Literacy Rate: 91%
Compulsory (Ages): 6–13

COMMUNICATION

Telephones: 331,700 main lines; 832,500
cellular/mobile
Daily Newspaper Circulation: 17/1,000
people
Televisions: 12/1,000 people
Internet Users: 1,220,000

TRANSPORTATION

Highways in Miles (Kilometers): 11,369
(18,338)
Railroads in Miles (Kilometers): 1,885
(3,077)
Usable Airfields: 322
Motor Vehicles in Use: 358,000

GOVERNMENT

Type: parliamentary democracy
Independence Date: April 18, 1980 (from
the United Kingdom)
Head of State/Government: Executive
President Robert Mugabe is both head
of state and head of government
Political Parties: Zimbabwe African
National Union–Patriotic Front;
Zimbabwe African National Union–
Ndonga; Movement for Democratic
Change; others
Suffrage: universal at 18

MILITARY

Military Expenditures (% of GDP): 3.8%
Current Disputes: Botswana and South
Africa have taken actions along border
to check flow of refugees out of
Zimbabwe

ECONOMY

Currency ($ U.S. Equivalent): 162.1
dollars = $1

Per Capita Income/GDP:
$2,100/$25.6 billion
GDP Growth Rate: ⊠4.1%
Inflation Rate: 1,034%
Unemployment Rate: 70%
Labor Force by Occupation: 66%
agriculture; 24% services; 10%
industry
Natural Resources: coal; minerals
and metals
Agriculture: coffee; tobacco; corn;
sugarcane; peanuts; wheat; cotton;
livestock
Industry: mining; steel; textiles
Exports: $1.7 billion (primary partners
South Africa, United Kingdom, Japan)
Imports: $2.1 billion (primary partners
South Africa, United Kingdom, United
States)

SUGGESTED WEB SITES

http://www.zimembassy-usa.org
http://www.zimbabwesituation.com/
http://www.zimweb.com/Dzimbabwe
.html
https://www.cia.gov/library/
publications/the-world-factbook/
geos/zi.html

Zimbabwe Country Report

Zimbabwe has been in the international spotlight in recent years. The emergence of a strong opposition party, the Movement for Democratic Change (MDC), appears to have been the spark that ignited a series of major initiatives aimed at winning the support of the masses of the people by the country's aging president, Robert Mugabe. In 2000, Mugabe gave his blessing to the occupation of white-owned commercial farms by supposed veterans of Zimbabwe's liberation war, which had ended two decades earlier. The takeover of the farms, and its accompanying campaign of intimidation, played a role in a narrow, disputed victory by Mugabe's Zimbabwean African National Union–Patriotic Front (ZANU–PF) party over the MDC in June 2000 parliamentary elections.

In order to increase popular support for his administration, Mugabe began expropriating white owned land throughout Zimbabwe. The farmers, who did not receive compensation, protested as wave after wave of veterans from the civil war invaded their farms. Some of the states within the international community, particularly Britain, responded by providing aid to MDC, and, in 2002 after highly contested elections which were riddled with inconsistencies and fraud, Zimbabwe was suspended from the Commonwealth. In December 2003, after a decision by the Commonwealth to extend the suspension of Zimbabwe indefinitely, Zimbabwe pulled out of the organization completely.

At the end of November 2002 Agriculture Minister Joseph Made stated that the land-grab was over and the government had seized 35 million acres of land from white farmers. Yet tremendous damage was done to the economy, with inflation raging at a rate of more than 400% a year. The opposition leader Morgan Tsvangirai was subsequently arrested twice and jailed for treason. He was acquitted in 2004 after a lengthy trial.

At the same time, there were growing reports of violence and intimidation directed against suspected MDC supporters, especially in rural areas, as well as attacks on independent journalists. During the presidential campaign, President Mugabe and his supporters blamed western countries, particularly Britain, for being behind a campaign to "recolonize" Zimbabwe. Mugabe described British prime minister Tony Blair as a liar, a scoundrel, and a thief. In the face of credible allegations of massive vote rigging, Mugabe was proclaimed the victor in the elections. Among the international election observers present (a number of European observers were barred) there was a division of opinion as to whether the outcome sufficiently reflected the will of the people. The British Commonwealth ultimately opted to suspend Zimbabwe's membership, while the European Union imposed travel and economic sanctions against Mugabe and his close associates.

DEVELOPMENT

The political turmoil under Mugabe's leadership in recent years has devastated the economy; the economic successes Zimbabwe enjoyed in the years immediately following independence have long disappeared. Large numbers of Zimbabweans have fled to neighboring South Africa and Botswana for economic survival.

FREEDOM

Since the 1990 lifting of the state of emergency that had been in effect since the days of the Federation, Zimbabwe's human-rights record has generally improved. Some government institutions, however, especially the Central Intelligence Organization, are still accused of extra-judicial abuses.

The chaos of the last few years has been accompanied by severe economic deprivation for the masses of Zimbabweans. Those relocated on former white-owned farms have suffered along with others due to the lack of such essential inputs as fertilizers, fuel, and water. To make matters worse, the country has been hit by severe drought. An estimated 1 million people now face the prospect of hunger and starvation in Zimbabwe, and the currency has lost a great deal of its value. Zimbabwe has moved from one of Southern Africa's "breadbaskets" to a dependent regional basket case. Most observers agree that things are going to worsen in the immediate future.

The Mugabe-led ZANU-PF party has dominated Zimbabwe's politics since the country's independence from Britain in 1980. The emergence in 2000 of MDC, led by the former trade unionist Morgan Tsangarai, has posed a formidable foe to ZANU. As a coalition movement, the MDS's primary program has been to replace Mugabe. Having initially failed in this effort, cleavages between various factions of the movement may become more noticeable. In many rural areas, MDC supporters have been driven underground by official repression, but MDC remains strong in the western Matebeleland region as well as major urban areas.

Ideologically, Mugabe belongs to the African liberationist tradition of the 1960s—strong and ruthless leadership, anti-Western, suspicious of capitalism, and deeply intolerant of dissent and opposition. With more than a third of the total land and up to 80 percent of the most productive farming areas in the hands of a few thousand whites before the recent seizure, land redistribution has been a key issue for Zimbabweans. Offering land to landless African farmers is seen by many as an attractive option. In this sense, Robert Mugabe does not stand alone. By adopting mob tactics toward the emotive issue of land—where there was already a widely accepted need for redistribution reform—Mugabe may have bought his regime some additional time.

Mugabe's policies in recent years increasingly have been undertaken for purposes of political expediency, and their consequences for the economy have been severe. Infrastructure has deteriorated, the country's exports, industrial production, and GDP has declined, and the inflation rate stands at over 1,000% annually. More than two out of every three Zimbabweans are unemployed. Many have chosen to leave the country, usually illegally, to seek some sort of economic livelihood in Botswana or South Africa. Zimbabwe's economic reputation lies in tatters.

Zimbabwe achieved its formal independence in April 1980, after a 14-year armed struggle by its disenfranchised black African majority. Before 1980, the country was called Southern Rhodesia—a name that honored Cecil Rhodes, the British imperialist who had masterminded the colonial occupation of the territory in the late nineteenth century. For its black African majority, Rhodesia's name was thus an expression of their subordination to a small minority of privileged white settlers whose racial hegemony was the product of Rhodes's conquest. The new name of Zimbabwe was symbolic of the greatness of the nation's precolonial roots.

THE PRECOLONIAL PAST

By the fifteenth century, Zimbabwe had become the center of a series of states that prospered through their trade in gold and other goods with Indian Ocean merchants. These civilizations left as their architectural legacy the remains of stone settlements known as *zimbabwes*. The largest of these, the so-called Great Zimbabwe, lies near the modern town of Masvingo. Within its massive walls are dozens of stella, topped with distinctive carved birds whose likeness has become a symbol of the modern state. Unfortunately, early European fortune-seekers and archaeologists destroyed much of the archaeological evidence of this site, but what survives confirms that the state had trading contacts as far afield as China.

From the sixteenth century, the Zimbabwean civilizations seem to have declined, possibly as a result of the disruption of the East African trading networks by the Portuguese. Nevertheless, the states themselves survived until the nineteenth century. And their cultural legacy is very much alive today, especially among the 71 percent of Zimbabwe's population who speak Shona. Zimbabwe's other major ethnolinguistic community are the Ndebele-speakers, who today account for about 16 percent of the population. This group traces its local origin to the mid-nineteenth-century conquest of much of modern Zimbabwe by invaders from the south under the leadership of Umzilagazi, who established a militarily strong Ndebele kingdom, which subsequently was ruled by his son.

HEALTH/WELFARE

Public expenditure on health and education has risen dramatically since independence. Most Zimbabweans now enjoy access to medical facilities, while primary-school enrollment has quadrupled. Higher education has also been greatly expanded. But the advances are threatened by downturns in the economy, and school fees have been reintroduced.

WHITE RULE

Zimbabwe's colonial history is unique in that it was never under the direct rule of a European power. In 1890, the lands of the Ndebele and Shona were invaded by agents of Cecil Rhodes's British South Africa Company (BSACO). In the 1890s, both groups put up stiff resistance to the encroachments of the BSACO settlers, but eventually they succumbed to the invaders. In 1924, the BSACO administration was dissolved and Southern Rhodesia became a self-governing British Crown colony. "Self-government" was, in fact, confined to the white-settler community, which grew rapidly but never numbered more than 5 percent of the population.

In 1953, Southern Rhodesia was federated with the British colonial territories of Northern Rhodesia (Zambia) and Nyasaland (Malawi). This Central African Federation was supposed to evolve into a "multiracial" dominion; but from the beginning, it was perceived by the black majority in all three territories as a vehicle for continued white domination. As the federation's first prime minister put it, the partnership of blacks and whites in building the new state would be analogous to a horse and its rider—no one had any illusions as to which race group would continue to be the beast of burden.

In 1963, the federation collapsed as a result of local resistance. Black nationalists established the independent "nonracial" states of Malawi and Zambia. For a while, it appeared that majority rule would also come to Southern Rhodesia. The local black community was increasingly well organized and militant in demanding full citizenship rights. However, in 1962, the white electorate responded to this challenge by voting into office the Rhodesia Front (RF), a party determined to uphold white supremacy at any cost. Using already-existing emergency powers, the new government moved to suppress the two major black nationalist movements: the Zimbabwe African People's Union (ZAPU) and the Zimbabwe African National Union (ZANU).

RHODESIA DECLARES INDEPENDENCE

In a bid to consolidate white power along the lines of the neighboring apartheid regime of South Africa, the RF, now led by Ian Smith, made its 1965 Unilateral Declaration of Independence (UDI) of any ties to the British Crown. Great Britain, along with the United Nations, refused to recognize this move. In 1967, the United Nations imposed mandatory economic sanctions against the "illegal" RF regime. But the sanctions were not fully effective, largely due to the fact that they were flouted by South Africa and the Portuguese authorities who controlled most of Mozambique until 1974. The United States continued openly to purchase Rhodesian chrome for a number of years, while many states and individuals engaged in more covert forms of sanctions-busting. The Rhodesian economy initially benefited from the porous blockade, which encouraged the development of a wide range of import-substitution industries.

With the sanctions having only a limited effect and Britain and the rest of the international community unwilling to engage in more active measures, it soon became clear that the burden of overthrowing the RF regime would be borne by the local population. ZANU and ZAPU, as underground movements, began to engage in armed struggle beginning in 1966. The success of their attacks initially was limited; but from 1972, the Rhodesian Security Forces were increasingly besieged by the nationalists' guerrilla campaign. The 1974 liberation of Mozambique from the Portuguese greatly increased the effectiveness of the ZANU forces, who were allowed to infiltrate into Rhodesia from Mozambican territory. Meanwhile, their ZAPU comrades launched attacks from bases in Zambia. In 1976, the two groups became loosely affiliated as the Patriotic Front.

ACHIEVEMENTS

Zimbabwe's capital city of Harare has become an arts and communications center for Southern Africa. Many regional as well as local filmmakers, musicians, and writers based in the city enjoy international reputations. And the distinctive malachite carvings of Zimbabwean sculptors are highly valued in the international art market.

Unable to stop the military advance of the Patriotic Front, which was resulting in a massive white exodus, the RF attempted to forge a power-sharing arrangement that preserved major elements of settler privilege. Although rejected by ZANU or ZAPU, this "internal settlement" was implemented in 1978–1979. A predominantly black government took office, but real power remained in white hands, and the fighting only intensified. Finally, in 1979, all the belligerent parties, meeting at Lancaster House in London, agreed to a compromise peace, which opened the door to majority rule while containing a number of constitutional provisions designed to reassure the white minority. In the subsequent elections, held in 1980, ZANU captured 57 and

ZAPU 20 out of the 80 seats elected by the "common roll." Another 20 seats, which were reserved for whites for seven years as a result of the Lancaster House agreement, were captured by the Conservative Alliance (the new name for the RF). ZANU leader Robert Mugabe became independent Zimbabwe's first prime minister.

THE RHODESIAN LEGACY

The political, economic, and social problems inherited by the Mugabe government were formidable. Rhodesia had essentially been divided into two "nations": one black, the other white. Segregation prevailed in virtually all areas of life, with those facilities open to blacks being vastly inferior to those open to whites. The better half of the national territory had also been reserved for white ownership. Large commercial farms prospered in this white area, growing maize and tobacco for export as well as a diversified mix of crops for domestic consumption. In contrast, the black areas, formally known as Tribal Trust Lands, suffered from inferior soil and rainfall, overcrowding, and poor infrastructure. Most black adults had little choice but to obtain seasonal work in the white areas. Black unskilled workers on white plantations, like the large number of domestic servants, were particularly impoverished. But until the 1970s, there were also few opportunities for blacks with higher skills as a result of a de facto "color bar," which reserved the best jobs for whites.

Despite its stated commitment to revolutionary socialist objectives, since 1980, the Mugabe government has taken an evolutionary approach in dismantling the socioeconomic structures of old Rhodesia. This cautious policy is, in part, based on an appreciation that these same structures support what, by regional standards, is a relatively prosperous and self-sufficient economy. Until 1990, the government's hands were also partially tied by the Lancaster House accords, wherein private property, including the large settler estates, could not be confiscated without compensation. In its first years, the government nevertheless made impressive progress in improving the livelihoods of the Zimbabwean majority by redistributing some of the surplus of the still white-dominated private sector. With the lifting of sanctions, mineral, maize, and tobacco exports expanded and import restrictions eased. Workers' incomes rose, and a minimum wage, which notably covered farm employees, was introduced. Rising consumer purchasing power initially benefited local manufacturers. Health and educational facilities were expanded, while a growing

number of blacks began to occupy management positions in the civil service and, to a lesser extent, in businesses.

Zimbabwe had hoped that foreign investment and aid would pay for an ambitious scheme to buy out many white farmers and to settle black peasants on their land. However, funding shortfalls resulted in only modest resettlement. Approximately 4,000 white farmers owned more than one third of the land. In 1992, the government passed a bill that allowed for the involuntary purchase of up to 50 percent of this land at an officially set price. While enjoying overwhelming domestic support, this land-redistribution measure came under considerable external criticism for violating the private-property and judicial rights of the large-scale farmers. Others pointed out that, besides producing large surpluses of food in nondrought years, many jobs were tied to the commercial estates. Revelations in 1993–1994 that some confiscated properties had been turned over to leading ZANU politicians gave rise to further controversy.

While gradually abandoning its professed desire to build a socialist society, the Zimbabwean government has continued to face a classic dilemma of all industrializing societies: whether to continue to use tight import controls to protect its existing manufacturing base or to open up its economy in the hopes of enjoying a takeoff based on export-oriented growth. While many Zimbabwean manufacturers would be vulnerable to greater foreign competition, there is now a widespread consensus that limits of the local market have contributed to stagnating output and physical depreciation of local industry in recent years.

POLITICAL DEVELOPMENT

The Mugabe government has promoted reconciliation across the racial divide. Although the reserved seats for whites were abolished in 1987, the white minority (whites now make up less than 2 percent of the population) is well represented within government as well as business. Mugabe's ZANU administration has shown less tolerance of its political opponents, especially ZAPU. ZANU was originally a breakaway faction of ZAPU. At the time of this split, in 1963, the differences between the two movements had largely been over tactics. But elections in 1980 and 1985 confirmed that the followings of both movements have become ethnically based, with most Shona supporting ZANU and Ndebele supporting ZAPU.

Initially, ZANU agreed to share power with ZAPU. However, in 1982, the alleged discoveries of secret arms caches, which

ZANU claimed ZAPU was stockpiling for a coup, led to the dismissal of the ZAPU ministers. Some leading ZAPU figures were also detained. The confrontation led to violence that very nearly degenerated into a full-scale civil war. From 1982 to 1984, the Zimbabwean Army, dominated by former ZANU and Rhodesian units, carried out a brutal counterinsurgency campaign against supposed ZAPU dissidents in the largely Ndebele areas of western Zimbabwe. Thousands of civilians were killed—especially by the notorious Fifth Brigade, which operated outside the normal military command structure. Many more fled to Botswana, including, for a period, the ZAPU leader, Joshua Nkomo.

Until 1991, Mugabe's stated intention was to create a one-party state in Zimbabwe. With his other black and white opponents compromised by their past association with the RF and its internal settlement, this largely meant coercing ZAPU into dissolving itself into ZANU. However, the increased support for ZAPU in its core Ndebele constituencies during the 1985 elections led to a renewed emphasis on the carrot over the stick in bringing about the union. In 1987, ZAPU formally merged into ZANU, but their shotgun wedding made for an uneasy marriage.

With the demise of ZAPU, new forces have emerged in opposition to Mugabe and the drive for a one-party state. Principal among these is the Zimbabwe Unity Movement (ZUM), led by former ZANU member Edger Tekere. In the 1990 elections, ZUM received about 20 percent of the vote, in a poll that saw a sharp drop in voter participation. The elections were also marred by serious restrictions on opposition activity and blatant voter intimidation. The deaths of ZUM supporters in the period before the elections reinforced the message of the government-controlled media that a vote for the opposition was an act of suicide. A senior member of the Central Intelligence Organization and a ZANU activist were subsequently convicted of the murder of ZUM organizing secretary Patrick Kombayi. However, they were pardoned by Mugabe.

Mugabe initially claimed that his 1990 victory was a mandate to establish a one-party state. But in 1991, the changing international climate, the continuing strength of the opposition, and growing opposition within ZANU itself caused him to shelve the project. Under 1992 election law, however, ZANU alone was made eligible for state funding.

The survival of political pluralism in Zimbabwe reflects the emergence of a civil society that is increasingly resistant to the concentration of power. Independent nongovernmental organizations have successfully taken up many social human-rights issues. Less successful have been attempts to promote an independent press, which has remained almost entirely in government/ZANU hands.

In 1992, the Forum Party, a new opposition movement, was launched, under the leadership of former chief justice Enoch Dumbutshena. But it failed to break the mold of Zimbabwean politics due to its own internal splits and failure to unite with other groups. As a result, Mugabe was easily reelected in March 1996 in a poll with low voter turnout (it was ultimately boycotted by the entire opposition).

Notwithstanding its continuing electoral success, public confidence in the ZANU government has been greatly eroded by its relative failure in handling the 1992 drought crisis. Despite warning signs of the impending catastrophe, little attempt was made to stockpile food. This failure resulted in widespread hunger and dependence on expensive food imports. Long-neglected waterworks, especially those serving Bulawayo, the country's second-largest city, proved to be inadequate. The government also lost support due to its seeming insensitivity to the plight of ordinary Zimbabweans suffering from high rates of unemployment and inflation. With inflation at 22 percent, a civil servants strike was sparked in August 1996 by an across-the-board 6 percent raise for ordinary workers as compared to a 130 percent raise for members of Parliament.

While the welfare of ordinary Zimbabweans may have improved since 1980, popular frustration with the status quo is increasing. In 1998, resentment against the government, resulting from continued economic decline, was aggravated in some quarters by Mugabe's decision to dispatch nearly 3,000 troops to the Democratic Republic of the Congo (D.R.C., the former Zaire) to defend the embattled regime of Laurent Kabila. With formal-sector unemployment in the range of 70 percent and inflation over 1,000 percent, it was a foreign adventure that the country could ill afford.

Over the past several years, Mugabe's hold on power in Zimbabwe has become increasingly autocratic. The ZANU party used fraud and intimidation to win the 2005 elections, giving it the two-thirds majority needed to amend the constitution at will. Shortly thereafter, the government began a slum demolition drive in Harare, ostensibly to promote law and order and development, but actually, according to most outside observers, to destroy the homes and livelihood of the political opposition; as many as 700,000 people were uprooted. Recently, the parliament announced Mugabe's term as president would be arbitrarily extended until 2010.

Timeline: PAST

1400s–1500s
Heyday of the gold trade and Great Zimbabwe

1840s
The Ndebele state emerges in Zimbabwe

1890
The Pioneer Column: arrival of the white settlers

1895–1897
Chimurenga: rising against the white intruders, ending in repression by whites

1924
Local government in Southern Rhodesia is placed in the hands of white settlers

1965
Unilateral Declaration of Independence

1966
Armed struggle begins

1980
ZANU leader Robert Mugabe becomes Zimbabwe's first prime minister

1990s
ZANU and ZAPU merge and win the 1990 elections; elections in 1995 result in a landslide victory for the ruling ZANU-PF

PRESENT

2000s
Mugabe pushes redistribution of white-owned commercial farms; economy deteriorates

2005
TANU-PF elected in controversial election

West Africa

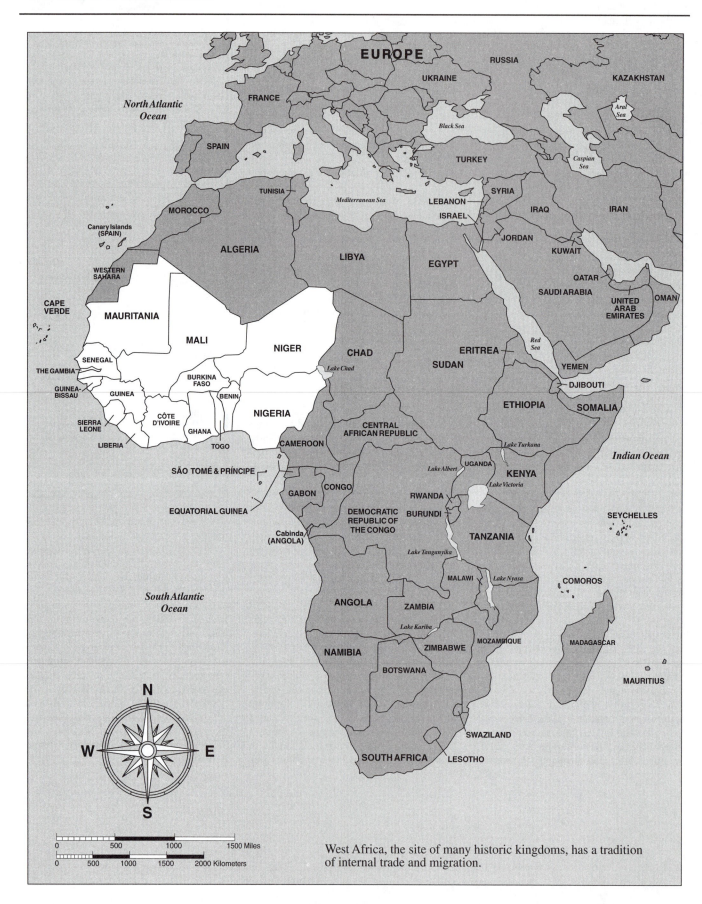

West Africa, the site of many historic kingdoms, has a tradition of internal trade and migration.

West Africa   Seeking Unity in Diversity

Anyone looking at a map of Africa can identify West Africa as the great bulge on the western coast of the continent. It is a region bound by the Sahara Desert to the north, the Atlantic Ocean to the south and west, and, in part, by the Cameroonian Mountains to the east. Each of these boundaries has historically been a bridge rather than a barrier, in that the region has long been linked through trade to the rest of the world.

At first glance, what is more striking is West Africa's great variety, rather than any of its unifying features. It contains the environmental extremes of desert and rain forest. While most of its people rely on agriculture, every type of occupation can be found, from herders to factory workers. Hundreds of languages are spoken; some are as different from one another as English is from Arabic or Japanese. Local cultural traditions and the societies that practice them are also myriad.

Yet the more closely one examines West Africa, the more one is impressed with the features that give the nations of the region a degree of coherence and unity. Some of the common characteristics and features of West Africa as a whole include the vegetation belts that stretch across the region from west to east, creating a similar environmental mix among the region's polities; the constant movement of peoples across local and national boundaries; and efforts being made by West African governments toward greater integration in the region, primarily through economic organizations. West Africans also share elements of a common history.

With the exception of Liberia, all the contemporary states of West Africa were the creations of competing European colonial powers—France, Germany, Great Britain, and Portugal—that divided most of the area during the late 1800s. Before this partition, however, much of the region was linked by the spread of Islam and patterns of trade, including the legacy of intensive involvement between the sixteenth and nineteenth centuries in the trans-Atlantic slave trade. From ancient times, great kingdoms expanded and contracted across the West African savanna and forest, giving rise to sophisticated civilizations.

WEST AFRICAN VEGETATION AND CLIMATE ZONES

Traveling north from the coastlines of such states as Nigeria, Ghana, and Côte d'Ivoire, one encounters tropical rain forests, which give way first to woodland savanna and then to more arid, more open plains. In Mali, Niger, and other landlocked areas to the north, the savanna gives way to the still drier Sahel environment, and finally to the Sahara Desert itself.

Whatever their ethnicity or nationality, the peoples living within each of these vegetation zones generally share the benefits and problems of similar livelihoods. For instance, cocoa, coffee, yams, and cassava are among the cash and food crops planted in the cleared forest and woodland zones, which stretch from Guinea to Nigeria. Groundnuts, sorghum, and millet are commonly harvested in the savanna belt that runs from Senegal to northern Nigeria. Herders in the Sahel, who historically could not go too far south with their cattle because of the presence of the deadly tsetse fly in the forest, continue to cross state boundaries in search of pasture.

People throughout West Africa have periodically suffered from drought. The effects of drought have often been aggravated in recent years by population pressures on the land. These factors have contributed to environmental changes and degradation. The condition of the Sahel in particular has deteriorated through a process of desertification, leading to large-scale relocations among many of its inhabitants. The eight Sahelian countries—Cape Verde, The Gambia, Burkina Faso, Mali, Senegal, Niger, Chad (in Central Africa), and Mauritania— have consequently formed the Committee for Struggle Against Drought in the Sahel (CILSS).

Farther to the south, large areas of woodland savanna have turned into grasslands as their forests have been cut down by land-hungry farmers. Drought has also periodically resulted in widespread brushfires in Ghana, Côte d'Ivoire, Togo, and Benin, fires that have transformed forests into savannas and savannas into deserts. Due to the depletion of forest, the Harmattan (a dry wind that blows in from the Sahara during January and February) now reaches many parts of the coast that in the recent past did not feel its breath. Its dust and haze have become a sign of the new year—and of new agricultural problems—throughout much of West Africa.

The great rivers of West Africa, such as The Gambia, Niger, Senegal, and Volta, along with their tributaries, have become increasingly important both as avenues of travel and trade and for the water they provide. Countries have joined together in large-scale projects designed to harness their waters for irrigation and hydroelectric power through regional organizations, like the Mano River grouping of Guinea, Liberia, and Sierra Leone and the Organization for the Development of the Senegal River, composed of Mali, Mauritania, and Senegal.

THE LINKS OF HISTORY AND TRADE

The peoples of West Africa have never been united as members of a single political unit. Yet some of the precolonial kingdoms that expanded across the region have great symbolic importance for those seeking to enhance interstate cooperation. The Mali empire of the thirteenth to fifteenth centuries, the Songhai empire of the sixteenth century, and the nineteenth-century Fulani caliphate of Sokoto, all based in the savanna, are widely remembered as examples of past supranational glory. The kingdoms of the southern forests, such as the Asante Confederation, the Dahomey kingdom, and the Yoruba city-states, were smaller than the great savanna empires to their north. Although generally later in origin and different in character from the northern states, the forest kingdoms are, nonetheless, sources of greater regional identity.

The precolonial states of West Africa gave rise to great urban centers, interlinked through extensive trade networks. This development was probably the result of the area's agricultural productivity, which supported a relatively high population

(Photo by Wayne Edge)

As this teenage girl in her uniform indicates, education remains a prominent theme for African youth.

density from early times. Many modern settlements have long histories. Present-day Timbuctu and Gao, in Mali, were important centers of learning and commerce in medieval times. Some other examples include Ouagadougou, Ibadan, Benin, and Kumasi, all in the forest zone. These southern centers prospered in the past by sending gold, kola, leather goods, cloth—and slaves—to the northern savanna and southern coast.

The cities of the savannas linked West Africa to North Africa. Beginning in the eleventh century, the ruling groups of the savanna increasingly turned to the universal vision of Islam. While Islam also spread to the forests, the southernmost areas were ultimately more strongly influenced by Christianity, which was introduced by Europeans, who became active along the West African coast in the fifteenth century. For centuries, the major commercial link among Europe, the Americas, and West Africa was the trans-Atlantic slave trade; during the 1800s, however, legitimate commerce in palm oil and other tropical products replaced it. New centers such as Dakar, Accra, and Freetown emerged—resulting either from the slave trade or from its suppression.

THE MOVEMENT OF PEOPLES

Despite the (incorrect) view of many who see Africa as being a continent made up of isolated groups, one constant characteristic of West Africa has been the transregional migration of its people. Herders have moved east and west across the savanna and south into the forests. Since colonial times, many professionals as well as laborers have sought employment outside their home areas.

Some of the peoples of West Africa, such as the Malinke, Fulani, Hausa, and Mossi, have developed especially well-established heritages of mobility. In the past, the Malinke journeyed from Mali to the coastal areas in Guinea, Senegal, and The Gambia. Other Malinke traders made their way to Burkina Faso, Liberia, and Sierra Leone, where they came to be known as Mandingoes.

The Fulani have developed their own patterns of seasonal movement. They herd their cattle south across the savanna during the dry season and return to the north during the rainy season. Urbanized Fulani groups have historically journeyed from west to east, often serving as agents of Islamization as well as promoters of trade. More recently, many Fulani have been forced to move southward as a result of the deterioration of their grazing lands. The Hausa, who live mostly in northern Nigeria and Niger, are found throughout much of West Africa. Indeed, their trading presence is so widespread that some have suggested that the Hausa language be promoted as a lingua franca, or common language, for West Africa.

Millions of migrant laborers are regularly attracted to Côte d'Ivoire and Ghana from the poorer inland states of Burkina Faso, Mali, and Niger, thus promoting continuing economic interdependence among these states. Similar large-scale migrations also occur elsewhere. The drastic expulsion of aliens by the Nigerian government in 1983 was startling to the outside world, in part because few had realized that so many Ghanaians, Nigeriens, Togolese, Beninois, and Cameroonians had taken up residence in Nigeria. Such immigration is not new, though its scale into Nigeria was greatly increased by that country's oil boom. Peoples such as the Yoruba, Ewe, and Vai, who were divided by colonialism, have often ignored modern state boundaries in order to maintain their ethnic ties. Other migrations also have roots in the colonial past. Sierra Leonians worked as clerks and craftspeople throughout the coastal areas of British West Africa, while Igbo were recruited to serve in northern Nigeria. Similarly, Beninois became the assistants of French administrators in other parts of French West Africa, while Cape Verdians occupied intermediate positions in Portugal's mainland colonies.

WEST AFRICAN INTEGRATION

Many West Africans recognize the weaknesses inherent in the region's national divisions. The peoples of the region would benefit from greater multilateral political cooperation and economic integration. Yet there are many obstacles blocking the growth of pan-regional development. National identity is probably even stronger today than it was in the days when Kwame Nkrumah, the charismatic Ghanaian leader, pushed for African unity but was frustrated by parochial interests. The larger and more prosperous states, such as Nigeria and Côte d'Ivoire, are reluctant to share their relative wealth with smaller countries, which, in turn, fear being swallowed.

One-party rule and more overt forms of dictatorship have recently been abandoned throughout West Africa. However, for the moment, the region is still politically divided between those states that have made the transition to multiparty constitutional systems of government and those that are still under effective military control. Overlapping ethnicity is also sometimes more a source of suspicion rather than a source of unity between states. Because the countries were under the rule of different colonial powers, French, English, and Portuguese serve today as official languages of the different nations, which also inherited different administrative traditions. Moreover, during colonial times, independent infrastructures were developed in each country; these continue to orient economic activities toward the coast and Europe rather than encouraging links among West African countries.

Political changes also affect regional cooperation and domestic development. Senegambia, the now defunct confederation of Senegal and The Gambia, was dominated by Senegal and resented by many Gambians. Cross-border tensions, such as those between Senegal and Mauritania, pose barriers in regional cooperation. In addition, internal conflicts, such as the decade-long civil wars in Liberia and Sierra Leone, present major challenges for neighboring countries such as Guinea and Côte d'Ivoire. The Liberian Civil War has also led to division between the supporters and opponents of a multinational peacekeeping force.

Despite the many roadblocks to unity, a number of multinational organizations have developed in West Africa, stimulated in large part by the severity of the common problems that the countries face. The West African countries have a good record of cooperating to avoid armed conflict and to settle their occasional border disputes. In addition to the multilateral agencies that are coordinating the struggle against drought and the development of various river basins, there are also various regional commodity cartels, such as the five-member Groundnut Council. The West African Examinations Council standardizes secondary-school examinations in most of the countries where English is an official language, and most of the Francophonic states have the same currency.

The most ambitious and broad organization in the region is the Economic Organization of West African States (ECOWAS), which includes all the states incorporated in the West African section of this text. Established in 1975 by the Treaty of Lagos, ECOWAS aims to promote trade, cooperation, and self-reliance. The progress of the organization in these areas has thus far been limited. But ECOWAS can point to some significant achievements. Several joint ventures have been developed; steps toward tariff reduction are being taken; and ECOWAS members have agreed in principle to eventually establish a common currency.

The ECOWAS states have shown an increasing willingness and capacity to play a leading role in collectively resolving their regional conflicts. Over the past decade, through its multinational peacekeeping force, ECOMOG, members of ECOWAS have jointly intervened to assist in the settlement of internal conflicts in Liberia and Sierra Leone. More recently, ECOWAS has also acted as a mediator in the ongoing civil conflict in Côte d'Ivoire. The modest success of these initiatives points to the pivotal role that must be played by Nigeria in any move toward greater regional cooperation. With about half of West Africa's population and economic output, a revitalized Nigeria has already demonstrated its potential for regional leadership. But Nigeria's own progress, as well as that of the region as a whole, is dependent on its making further progress toward overcoming its own internal political and economic weaknesses.

Benin (Republic of Benin)

Benin Statistics

GEOGRAPHY

Area in Square Miles (Kilometers):
43,483 (112,620) (about the size of
Pennsylvania)
Capital (Population): official:
Porto-Novo (225,000); de facto:
Cotonou (750,000)
Environmental Concerns: drought;
insufficient potable water;
poaching; deforestation;
desertification

Geographical Features: mostly flat to
undulating plain; some hills and low
mountains
Climate: tropical to semiarid

PEOPLE

Population

Total: 8,078,314
Annual Growth Rate: 2.91%
Rural/Urban Population Ratio: 58/42

Major Languages: French; Fon; Yoruba; others
Ethnic Makeup: 99% African (most
important groupings Fon, Adja,
Yoruba, and Bariba); 1% European
Religions: 43% Christian; 24% Muslim;
17% Vodoun; 16% other

Health

Life Expectancy at Birth: 52 years (male);
55 years (female)
Infant Mortality: 77.9/1,000 live
births

Physicians Available: 1/14,216 people
HIV/AIDS Rate in Adults: 1.9%

Education

Adult Literacy Rate: 35%
Compulsory (Ages): 6–12; free

COMMUNICATION

Telephones: 76,300 main lines; 750,000 cellular/mobile
Daily Newspaper Circulation: 2/1,000 people
Televisions: 4/1,000 people
Internet Users: 700,000

TRANSPORTATION

Highways in Miles (Kilometers): 4,208 (6,787)
Railroads in Miles (Kilometers): 464 (758)
Usable Airports: 5
Motor Vehicles in Use: 55,000

GOVERNMENT

Type: republic
Independence Date: August 1, 1960 (from France)
Head of State/Government: President Thomas Boni Yayi is both head of state and head of government
Political Parties: Alliance for Democracy and Progress; Front for Renewal and Development; African Movement for Democracy and Progress; many others
Suffrage: universal at 18

MILITARY

Military Expenditures (% of GDP): 1.7%
Current Disputes: territorial disputes with Burkina Faso, Niger, and Nigeria

ECONOMY

Currency ($ U.S. Equivalent): 522 CFA francs = $1

Per Capita Income/GDP: $1,100/$8.9 billion
GDP Growth Rate: 4%
Inflation Rate: 3.8%
Population Below Poverty Line: 33%
Natural Resources: small offshore oil deposits; limestone; marble; timber
Agriculture: palm products; cotton; corn; rice; yams; cassava; beans; sorghum; livestock
Industry: textiles; construction materials; food production; chemical production
Exports: $60.5 million (primary partners Brazil, France, Indonesia)
Imports: $839 million (primary partners France, China, United States)

SUGGESTED WEB SITES

http://www.benindaily.com
https://www.cia.gov/library/publications/the-world-factbook/geos/bn.html

Benin Country Report

Over the past decade, Benin has emerged as one of one of Africa's most stable and democratic states. This has coincided with improved economic growth, though the country remains among the world's poorest in terms of both per capita income and human development. Since gaining its independence from France in 1960, Benin has experienced a series of shifts in political and economic policy that have so far failed to lift most Beninois out of chronic poverty. In this respect, the country's on-going struggle for development can be seen as a microcosm of the challenges facing much of the African continent.

DEVELOPMENT

Palm-oil plantations were established in Benin by Africans in the mid-nineteenth century. They have continued to be African-owned and capitalist-oriented. Today, there are some 30 million trees in Benin, and palm-oil products are a major export used for cooking, lighting, soap, margarine, and lubricants.

Politically, Benin has been in the forefront of those nations on the continent making the transition away from an authoritarian centralized state toward greater democracy and market reforms. This process has not as yet been accompanied by a decisive shift toward a new generation of leadership. In March 1996, former president Mathieu Kérékou returned to power with 52 percent of the vote, defeating incumbent Nicephore Soglo in Benin's second ballot since the 1990 restoration of multiparty democracy. Five years earlier, Soglo had defeated Kérékou, who had ruled the country as a virtual dictator for 17 years before agreeing to a democratic transition. In the past, Kérékou styled himself as a Marxist Leninist and presided over a one-party state. Today, he presents himself as a "Christian Democrat," affirming that there can be no turning back to the old order. In Parliament, his Popular Revolutionary Party of Benin (PRPB) shares power with other groupings whose existence is primarily a reflection of ethnoregional rather than ideological divisions.

Kérékou's restoration did not result in any significant moves away from his predecessor's economic reforms, which had resulted in a modest rise in gross domestic product, increased investment, reduced inflation, and an easing of the country's debt burden. He is under pressure, however, to raise the living standards of Benin's impoverished masses.

THE OLD ORDER FALLS

Kérékou's first reign began to unravel in late 1989. Unable to pay its bills, his government found itself increasingly vulnerable to mounting internal opposition and, to a lesser extent, to external pressure to institute sweeping political and economic reforms.

FREEDOM

Since 1990, political restrictions have been lifted and prisoners of conscience freed. More recently, however, a number of citizens have been arrested for supposedly inciting people against the government and encouraging them not to pay taxes.

A wave of strikes and mass demonstrations swept through Cotonou, the country's largest city, in December 1989. This upsurge in prodemocracy agitation was partially inspired by the overthrow of Central/Eastern Europe's Marxist-Leninist regimes; ironically, the Stalinist underground Communist Party of Dahomey (PCD) also played a role in organizing much of the unrest. Attempts to quell the demonstrations with force only increased public anger toward the authorities.

In an attempt to defuse the crisis, the PRPB's state structures were forced to give up their monopoly of power by allowing a representative gathering to convene with the task of drawing up a new constitution. For 10 days in February 1990,

(United Nations photo)

Benin is one of the least-developed countries in the world. Beninois must often fend for themselves in innovative ways. The peddler pictured above moves among the lake dwellings of a fishing village, selling cigarettes, spices, rice, and other commodities.

the Beninois gathered around their television sets and radios to listen to live broadcasts of the "National Conference of Active Forces of the Nation." The conference quickly turned into a public trial of Kérékou and his PRPB. With the eyes and ears of the nation tuned in, critics of the regime, who had until recently been exiled, were able to pressure Kérékou into handing over effective power to a transitional government. The major task of this new, civilian administration was to prepare Benin for multiparty elections while trying to stabilize the deteriorating economy. Kérékou was subsequently returned to power through elections in 1996 and 2001, but a constitutional age limit prevented him from running again in 2006. He was succeeded in 2006 by a political outsider, Thomas Boni Yayi.

The political success of Benin's movement from dictatorship to democratically elected government placed the nation in the forefront of the democratization process then sweeping Africa. But liberating a nation from poverty is a much more difficult process.

A COUNTRY OF MIGRANTS

Benin is one of the least-developed countries in the world. Having for decades experienced only limited economic growth, in recent years the nation's real gross domestic product has actually declined.

HEALTH/WELFARE

One third of the national budget of Benin goes to education, and the percentage of students receiving primary education has risen to 50% of the school-age population. College graduates serve as temporary teachers through the National Service System, but more teachers and higher salaries are needed.

Emigration has become a way of life for many. The migration of Beninois in search of opportunities in neighboring states is not a new phenomenon. Before 1960, educated people from the then-French colony of Dahomey (as Benin was called until

1975) were prominent in junior administrative positions throughout other parts of French West Africa. But as the region's newly independent states began to localize their civil-service staffs, most of the Beninois expatriates lost their jobs. Their return increased bureaucratic competition within Benin, which, in turn, led to heightened political rivalry among ethnic and regional groups. Such local antagonisms contributed to a series of military coups between 1963 and 1972. These culminated in Kérékou's seizure of power.

While Beninois professionals can be found in many parts of West Africa, the destination of most recent emigrants has been Nigeria. The movement from Benin to Nigeria is facilitated by the close links that exist among the large Yoruba-speaking communities on both sides of the border. After Nigeria, the most popular destination has been Côte d'Ivoire. This may change, however, as economic recession in both of those states has led to heightened hostility against the migrants.

Recently the movement of migrants has been in the other direction as, since

2005, Benin has been forced to deal with a flood of Togolese refugees fleeing political unrest in their own country. The Benin government has appealed to the international community for aid in dealing with this influx.

THE ECONOMY

Nigeria's urban areas have also been major markets for food exports. This has encouraged Beninois farmers to switch from cash crops (such as cotton, palm oil, cocoa beans, and coffee) to food crops (such as yams and cassava), which are smuggled across the border to Nigeria. The emergence of this parallel export economy has been encouraged by the former regime's practice of paying its farmers among the lowest official produce prices in the region. Given that agriculture, in terms of both employment and income generation, forms the largest sector of the Beninois economy, the rise in smuggling activities has inevitably contributed to a growth of graft and corruption.

ACHIEVEMENTS

Fon appliquéd cloths have been described as "one of the gayest and liveliest of the contemporary African art forms." Formerly these cloths were used by Dahomeyan kings. Now they are sold to tourists, but they still portray the motifs and symbols of past rulers and the society they ruled.

Benin's small industrial sector is primarily geared toward processing primary products, such as palm oil and cotton, for export. It has thus been adversely affected by the shift away from producing these cash crops for the local market. Small-scale manufacturing has centered around the production of basic consumer goods and construction materials. The biggest enterprises are state-owned cement plants. One source of hope is that with privatization and new exploration, the country's small oil industry will undergo expansion.

Transport and trade are other important activities. Many Beninois find legal as well as illegal employment carrying goods. Due to the relative absence of rain forest (an impediment to travel), Benin's territory has historically served as a trade corridor between the coastal and inland savanna regions of West Africa. Today the nation's roads are comparatively well developed, and the railroad carries goods from the port at Cotonou to northern areas of the country. An extension of the railroad will eventually reach Niamey, the capital of Niger. The government has also tried, with little success, to attract tourists in recent years, through such gambits as selling itself as the "home of Voodoo."

POLITICS AND RELIGION

Kérékou's narrow victory margin in 1996 amid charges and countercharges of electoral fraud underscored the continuing north–south division of Beninois politics and society. Although he is now a self-proclaimed Christian, Kérékou's political base remains the mainly Muslim north, while Soglo enjoyed majority support in the more Christianized south. Religious allegiance in Benin is complicated, however, by the prominence of the indigenous belief system known as Voodoo. Having originated in Benin, belief in Voodoo spirits has taken root in the Americas, especially Haiti, as well as elsewhere in West Africa.

During his first presidency, Kérékou sought to suppress Voodoo, which he branded as "witchcraft." Soglo, on the other hand, publicly embraced Voodoo, which was credited with helping him recover from a serious illness in 1992. On the eve of the 1996 election, Soglo recognized Voodoo as an official religion, proclaiming January 10 as "Voodoo National Day."

Timeline: PAST

1625
The kingdom of Dahomey is established

1892
The French conquer Dahomey and declare it a French protectorate

1960
Dahomey becomes independent

1972
Mathieu Kérékou comes to power in the sixth attempted military coup since independence

1975
The name of Dahomey is changed to Benin

1990s
Kérékou announces the abandonment of Marxism-Leninism as Benin's guiding ideology; multiparty elections are held; Kérékou loses power to Nicephore Soglo; Kérékou is reelected 5 years later

PRESENT

2000s
Benin marks its 40th year of independence

Thomas Boni Yayi elected president

Togolese refugees cross into Benin

Poverty remains an overwhelming problem

Burkina Faso

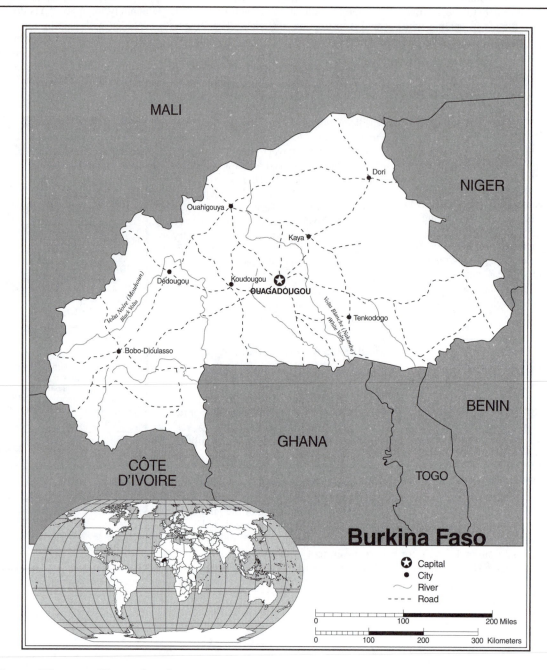

Burkina Faso Statistics

GEOGRAPHY

Area in Square Miles (Kilometers):
106,000 (274,500) (about the size of Colorado)
Capital (Population): Ouagadougou (862,000)
Environmental Concerns: drought; desertification; overgrazing; soil erosion; deforestation
Geographical Features: mostly flat to dissected, undulating plains; hills in west and southeast; landlocked
Climate: tropical; semiarid

PEOPLE

Population

Total: 14,326,203
Annual Growth Rate: 3.0%
Rural/Urban Population Ratio: 82/18
Major Languages: French; Mossi; Senufo; Fula; Bobo; Mande; Gurunsi; Lobi
Ethnic Makeup: about 40% Mossi; Gurunsi; Senufo; Lobi; Bobo; Mande; Fulani
Religions: 50% Muslim; 40% indigenous beliefs; 10% Christian

Health

Life Expectancy at Birth: 49 years (male); 48 years (female)

Infant Mortality: 89.8/1,000 live births
Physicians Available: 1/27,158 people
HIV/AIDS Rate in Adults: 4.2%

Education

Adult Literacy Rate: 22%
Compulsory (Ages): 7–14; free

COMMUNICATION

Telephones: 65,400 main lines; 1,017,000 cellular/mobile
Televisions: 4.4/1,000 people
Internet Users: 80,000

TRANSPORTATION

Highways in Miles (Kilometers): 7,504 (12,506)
Railroads in Miles (Kilometers): 385 (622)
Usable Airfields: 33
Motor Vehicles in Use: 55,000

GOVERNMENT

Type: parliamentary
Independence Date: August 5, 1960 (from France)

Head of State/Government: President Blaise Compaoré; Prime Minister Ernest Paramanga Yonli
Political Parties: Congress for Democracy and Progress; African Democratic Rally—Alliance for Democracy and Federation; others
Suffrage: universal

MILITARY

Military Expenditures (% of GDP): 1.2%
Current Disputes: territorial dispute with Benin and poorly defined border with Niger; accused by Côte d'Ivoire of backing rebels in that country's north

ECONOMY

Currency ($ U.S. Equivalent): 522 CFA francs = $1
Per Capita Income/GDP: $1,400/ $18.4 billion
GDP Growth Rate: 6.4%
Inflation Rate: 2.3%
Labor Force by Occupation: 90% agriculture

Population Below Poverty Line: 45%
Natural Resources: manganese; limestone; marble; gold; antimony; copper; bauxite; nickel; lead; phosphates; zinc; silver
Agriculture: peanuts; shea nuts; cotton; sesame; millet; sorghum; corn; rice; livestock
Industry: cotton lint; beverages; agricultural processing; soap; cigarettes; textiles; gold
Exports: $606 million (primary partners Venezuela, Benelux, Italy)
Imports: $1.2 billion (primary partners Côte d'Ivoire, Venezuela, France)

SUGGESTED WEB SITES

http://burkinaembassy-usa.org
http://www.sas.upenn.edu/ African_ Studies/Country_Specific/Burkina .html
https://www.cia.gov/library/ publications/the-world-factbook/ geos/uv.html

Burkina Faso Country Report

Notwithstanding some notable achievements, especially in the utilization of the Volta River and in the promotion of indigenous culture, Burkina Faso (formerly called Upper Volta) remains an impoverished country searching for a governing consensus. Recently its government has faced both domestic and external criticism over the state of the economy, human rights, and allegations that it has been involved in the smuggling of arms for diamonds ("blood diamonds") to the now-defeated rebel movements in Sierra Leone and Angola. In response to the latter allegation, in 2001 a UN–supervised body was set up to monitor the country's trade in weapons. Since falling gold prices forced the closure of its biggest gold mine, Burkina Faso has had little in the way of legitimate exports, leaving the landlocked, semiarid country with few economic prospects, and causing many of its citizens to seek opportunities elsewhere.

Much of Burkina Faso's four decades of independence has been characterized by chronic political instability, with civilian rule being interrupted by the military on seven different occasions. The restoration of multiparty democracy in 1991 under the firm guidance of former military leader Blaise Compaoré seemed to usher in an era

of greater political stability. Compaoré's reelection in November 1998 was accepted as legitimate by international observers. But the assassination a month later of independent journalist Robert Zongo touched off a wave of violent strikes and protests. Since then, there have been sustained calls for more fundamental political and social reform from an emerging generation of activists within civil society, including the traditionally powerful trade unions. An umbrella body known as the Collective of Democratic Organizations for the Masses and Political Parties has been formed to challenge the status quo.

DEVELOPMENT

Despite political turbulence, Burkina Faso's economy has recorded positive, albeit modest, annual growth rates for more than a decade. Most of the growth has been in agriculture. New hydroelectric projects have significantly reduced the country's dependence on imported energy.

But power has remained in the hands of Compaoré's hands. Along with his party, the Popular Democratic Organization–Worker's Movement (ODP–MT), he won elections

against fragmented opposition in 1991 and 1995, as well as 1998.

Before adopting the mantle of democracy, Compaoré rose to power through a series of coups, the last of which resulted in the overthrow and assassination of the charismatic and controversial Thomas Sankara. A man of immense populist appeal for many Burkinabé, Sankara remains as a martyr to their unfulfilled hopes. By the time of its overthrow, his radical regime had become the focus of a great deal of external as well as internal opposition.

Of the three men directly responsible for Sankara's toppling, two—Boukari Lingani and Henri Zongo—were executed following a power struggle with the third—Compaoré. It is in this context of sanguinary political competition that the assassination of a prominent media critic has once more called into question the government's commitment to political pluralism.

DEBILITATING DROUGHTS

At the time of its independence from France, in 1960, the landlocked country then named the Republic of Upper Volta inherited little in the way of colonial infrastructure. Since independence, progress has been hampered

(United Nations photo 154792 by John Isaac)

Since Burkina Faso gained its independence from France, its progress has been hampered by prolonged periods of drought. Local cooperatives have been responsible for small-scale improvements, such as the construction of the water barrage or barricade pictured above.

by prolonged periods of severe drought. Much of the country has been forced at times to depend on international food aid. To counteract some of the negative effects of this circumstance, efforts have been made to integrate relief donations into local development schemes. Of particular note have been projects instituted by the traditional rural cooperatives known as *naam,* which have been responsible for such small-scale but often invaluable local improvements as new wells and pumps, better grinding mills, and distribution of tools and medical supplies.

FREEDOM

There has been a surprisingly strong tradition of pluralism in Burkina Faso despite the circumscribed nature of human rights under successive military regimes. Freedoms of speech and association are still curtailed, and political detentions are common. The Burkinabé Movement for Human Rights has challenged the government.

Despite such community action, the effects of drought have been devastating.

Particularly hard-hit has been pastoral production, long a mainstay of the local economy, especially in the north. It is estimated that a recent drought destroyed about 90 percent of the livestock in Burkina Faso.

To counteract the effects of drought while promoting greater development, the Burkinabé government has developed two major hydroelectric and agricultural projects over the past decade. The Bagre and Kompienga Dams, located east of Ouagadougou, have significantly reduced the country's dependence on imported energy, while also supplying water for large-scale irrigation projects. This has already greatly reduced the need for imported food.

Most Burkinabé continue to survive as agriculturalists and herders, but many people are dependent on wage labor. In the urban centers, there exists a significant working-class population that supports the nation's politically powerful trade-union movement. The division between this urban community and rural population is not absolute, for it is common for individuals to combine wage labor with farming activities. Another population

category—whose numbers exceed those of the local wage-labor force—are individuals who seek employment outside of the country. At least 1 million Burkinabé work as migrant laborers in other parts of West Africa. This is part of a pattern that dates back to the early 1900s. Approximately 700,000 of these Burkinabé regularly migrate to Côte d'Ivoire. Returning workers have infused the rural areas with consumer goods and a working-class consciousness. Political unrest in Côte d-Ivoire and neighboring Ghana, however, has recently hindered the continuing ability of workers to find employment in these countries.

HEALTH/WELFARE

The inadequacy of the country's public health measures is reflected in the low Burkinabé life expectancy. Mass immunization campaigns have been successfully carried out, but in an era of structural economic adjustment, the prospects for a dramatic improvement in health appear bleak.

UNIONS FORCE CHANGE

As is the case in much of Africa, it is the salaried urban population (at least, next to the army) who have exercised the greatest influence over successive Burkinabé regimes. Trade-union leaders representing these workers have been instrumental in forcing changes in government. They have spoken out vigorously against government efforts to ban strikes and restrain unions. They have also demanded that they be shielded from downturns in the local economy. Although many unionists have championed various shades of Marxist-Leninist ideology, they, along with their natural allies in the civil service, arguably constitute a conservative element within the local society. During the mid-1980s, they became increasingly concerned about the dynamic Sankara's efforts to promote a nationwide network of grassroots Committees for the Defense of the Revolution (CDRs) as vehicles for empowering the nation's largely rural masses.

ACHIEVEMENTS

In 1997, a record total of 19 feature films competed for the Etalon du Yennenga award, the highest distinction of the biannual Pan-African Film Festival, hosted in Ouagadougou. Over the past 3 decades, this festival has contributed significantly to the development of the film industry in Africa. Burkina Faso has nationalized its movie houses, and the government has encouraged the showing of films by African filmmakers.

To many unionists, the mobilization and arming of the CDRs was perceived as a direct challenge to their own status. This threat seemed all the more apparent when Sankara began to cut urban salaries, in the name of a more equitable flow of revenue to the rural areas. When several union leaders challenged this move, they were arrested on charges of sedition. Sankara's subsequent overthrow thus had strong backing from within organized labor and the civil service. These groups, along with the military, remain the principal supporters of Compaoré's ODP–MT and its policy of "national rectification." Yet despite this support base, the government has moved to restructure the until recently all-encompassing public sector of the economy by reducing its wage bill. This effort has impressed international creditors.

Beyond its core of support, the ODP–MT government has generally been met with sentiments ranging from hostility to indifference. While Compaoré claimed—with some justification—that Sankara's rule had become too arbitrary and that he had resisted forming a party with a set of rules, many people mourned the fallen leader's death. In the aftermath of the coup, the widespread use of a new cloth pattern, known locally as "homage to Sankara," became an informal barometer of popular dissatisfaction. Compaoré has also been challenged by the high regard that has been accorded Sankara outside Burkina Faso, as a symbol of a new generation of African radicalism.

Compaoré, like Sankara, has sometimes resorted to sharp anti-imperialist rhetoric. However, his government has generally sought to cultivate good relations with France (the former colonial power) and other members of the Organization for Economic Cooperation and Development, as well as the major international financial institutions. But he has alienated himself from some of his West African neighbors, as well as the Euro–North American diplomatic consensus, through his close ties to Libya and past military support for Charles Taylor's National Patriotic Front in Liberia. Along with Taylor, Compaoré has more recently been accused of, but denies, providing support for the Revolutionary United Front rebels in Sierra Leone. To many outsiders, as well as the Burkinabé people themselves, the course of Compaoré's government remains ambiguous.

Since October 2002 the Ivory Coast has continually accused Burkina Faso of sheltering dissident Ivorian soldiers, many of whom are descendents of individuals who first arrived from Burkina Faso. In turn Burkina Faso raised concerns about attacks on Burkinabes in the Ivory Coast after the September 2002 Ivorian military uprising.

Timeline: PAST

1313
The first Mossi kingdom is founded

1896
The French overcome Mossi resistance and claim Upper Volta

1932
Upper Volta is divided among adjoining French colonies

1947
Upper Volta is reconstituted as a colony

1960
Independence under President Maurice Yameogo

1980s
Captain Thomas Sankara seizes power and changes the country's name to *Burkina* (Mossi for "land of honest men") *Faso* (Dioula for "democratic republic"); Sankara is assassinated in a coup; Blaise Compaoré succeeds as head of state

1990s
Compaoré introduces multipartyism, but his critics are skeptical

PRESENT

2000s
The country marks 4 decades of independence

Burkina Faso is believed to be involved in the "blood diamonds" trade

Cape Verde (Republic of Cape Verde)

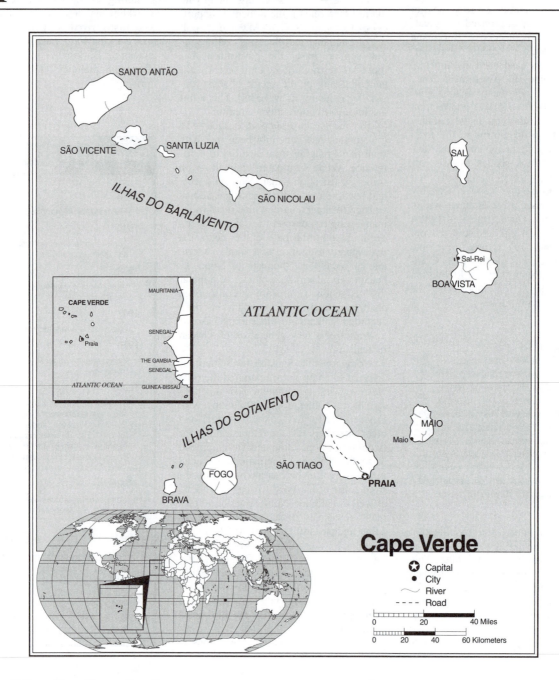

Cape Verde Statistics

GEOGRAPHY

Area in Square Miles (Kilometers): 1,557 (4,033) (about the size of Rhode Island)
Capital (Population): Praia (82,000)
Environmental Concerns: soil erosion; overgrazing; deforestation; desertification; threats to wildlife populations; overfishing
Geographical Features: steep; rugged; rocky; volcanic

Climate: temperate; precipitation meager and very erratic

PEOPLE

Population

Total: 423,613
Annual Growth Rate: 0.61%
Rural/Urban Population Ratio: 39/61
Major Languages: Portuguese; Kriolu

Ethnic Makeup: 71% Creole (mixed); 28% African; 1% European
Religions: Roman Catholicism fused with indigenous beliefs

Health

Life Expectancy at Birth: 68 years (male); 74 years (female)
Infant Mortality: 45.3/1,000 live births
Physicians Available: 1/4,208 people
HIV/AIDS Rate in Adults: 0.04%

Education

Adult Literacy Rate: 77%
Compulsory (Ages): 7–11

COMMUNICATION

Telephones: 71,600 main lines; 108,900
   cellular/mobile
Televisions: 2.6/1,000 people
Internet Users: 29,000

TRANSPORTATION

Highways in Miles (Kilometers): 686
   (1,100)
Railroads in Miles (Kilometers): none
Usable Airfields: 8
Motor Vehicles in Use: 18,000

GOVERNMENT

Type: republic
Independence Date: July 5, 1975 (from
   Portugal)

Head of State/Government: President
   Pedro Pires; Prime Minister José Maria
   Neves
Political Parties: Movement for
   Democracy; African Party for
   Independence of Cape Verde; Party
   for Democratic Convergence; Party of
   Work and Solidarity; others
Suffrage: universal at 18

MILITARY

Military Expenditures (% of GDP):
   0.7%
Current Disputes: none

ECONOMY

Currency ($ U.S. Equivalent): 88.0
   escudos = $1
Per Capita Income/GDP: $6,000/
   $3.13 billion
GDP Growth Rate: 5.5%
Inflation Rate: 5.4%

Unemployment Rate: 21%
Population Below Poverty Line: 30%
Natural Resources: salt; basalt rock;
   pozzuolana; limestone; kaolin; fish
Agriculture: bananas; corn; beans;
   sweet potatoes; sugarcane; coffee; fish
Industry: fish processing; salt mining;
   shoes and garments; ship repair; food
   and beverages
Exports: $88 million (primary
   partners Portugal, United Kingdom,
   Germany)
Imports: $561 million (primary partners
   Portugal, Germany, France)

SUGGESTED WEB SITES

http://www.sas.upenn.edu/African_
   Studies/Country_Specific/C_Verde
   .html
http://virtualcapeverde.net
https://www.cia.gov/library/
   publications/the-world-factbook/geos/
   cv.html

Cape Verde Country Report

On July 5, 2000, Cape Verdeans proudly celebrated a quarter-century of economic, political, and social progress since independence from Portugal. Despite a late start and unfavorable environmental conditions, the country has emerged as one of postcolonial Africa's tangible success stories.

Over the past decade this has been accompanied by a change in political direction. In 1992, Cape Verde adopted a new flag and Constitution, reflecting the country's transition to political pluralism. After 15 years of single-party rule by the African Party for the Independence of Cape Verde (PAICV), rising agitation led to the legalization of opposition groups in 1990. In January 1991, a quickly assembled antigovernment coalition, the Movement for Democracy (MPD), stunned the political establishment by gaining 68 percent of the votes and 56 out of 79 National Assembly seats. A month later, the MPD candidate, Antonio Mascarenhas Monteiro, defeated the long-serving incumbent, Aristides Pereira, in the presidential elections. It is a credit to both the outgoing administration and its opponents that this dramatic political transformation occurred without significant violence or rancor.

Parliamentary elections in December 1995 resulted in the MPD retaining power, albeit with a reduced majority. In 2001, the political pendulum swung back to PAICV in both the legislative and presidential elections, with Pedro Pires becoming the country's new leader.

The Republic of Cape Verde is an archipelago located about 400 miles west of the Senegalese Cape Verde, or "Green Cape," after which it is named. Unfortunately, green is a color that is often absent in the lives of the islands' citizens. Throughout its history, Cape Verde has suffered from periods of prolonged drought, which before the twentieth century were often accompanied by extremely high mortality rates (up to 50 percent). The last severe drought lasted from 1968 to 1984. Even in normal years, though, rainfall is often inadequate.

DEVELOPMENT

In a move designed to attract greater investment from overseas, especially from Cape Verdean Americans, the country has joined the International Finance Corporation. Efforts are under way to promote the islands as an offshore banking center for the West African (ECOWAS) region.

When the country gained independence, in 1975, there was little in the way of nonagricultural production. As a result, the new nation had to rely for its survival on foreign aid and the remittances of Cape Verdeans working abroad, but the postindependence period has been marked by a genuine improvement in the lives of most Cape Verdeans. In recent years, international tourism has become an important component of the local economy.

Cape Verde was ruled by Portugal for nearly 500 years. Most of the islanders are the descendants of Portuguese colonists, many of whom arrived as convicts, and African slaves who began to settle on the islands shortly after their discovery by Portuguese mariners in 1456. The merging of these two groups gave rise to the distinct Cape Verdean Kriolu language (which is also spoken in Guinea-Bissau). Under Portuguese rule, Cape Verdeans were generally treated as second-class citizens, although a few rose to positions of prominence in other parts of the Portuguese colonial empire. Economic stagnation, exacerbated by cycles of severe drought, caused many islanders to emigrate elsewhere in Africa, Western Europe, and the Americas.

FREEDOM

The new Constitution should entrench the country's recent political liberalization. Opposition publications have emerged to complement the state- and Catholic Church-sponsored media

In 1956, the African Party for the Independence of Guinea-Bissau and Cape Verde (PAIGC) was formed under the dynamic leadership of Amilcar Cabral, a Cape Verdean revolutionary who hoped to see the two Portuguese colonies form a united nation. Between 1963 and 1974, PAIGC waged a successful war of liberation in Guinea-Bissau that led to the independence of both territories. Although Cabral was assassinated by the Portuguese in 1973, his vision was preserved during the late 1970s by his successors, who, while ruling the two countries separately, maintained the unity of the PAIGC. This arrangement, however, began to break down in the aftermath of a 1980 coup in Guinea-Bissau and resulted in the party's division along national lines. In 1981, the Cape Verdean PAIGC formally renounced its Guinean links, becoming the PAICV.

HEALTH/WELFARE

Greater access to health facilities has resulted in a sharp drop in infant mortality and a rise in life expectancy. Clinics have begun to encourage family planning. Since independence, great progress has taken place in social services. Nutrition levels have been raised, and basic health care is now provided to the entire population.

After independence, the PAIGC/CV government was challenged by the colonial legacy of economic underdevelopment, exacerbated by drought. Massive famine was warded off through a reliance on imported foodstuffs, mostly received as aid. The government attempted to strengthen local food production and assist the 70 percent of the local population engaged in subsistence agriculture. Its efforts took the forms of drilling for underground water, terracing, irrigating, and building a water-desalinization plant with U.S. assistance. Major efforts were also devoted to tree-planting schemes as a way to cut back on soil erosion and eventually make the country self-sufficient in wood fuel.

ACHIEVEMENTS

Cape Verdean Kriolu culture has a rich literary and musical tradition. With emigrant support, Cape Verde bands have acquired modest followings in Western Europe, Lusophone Africa, Brazil, and the United States. Local drama, poetry, and music are showcased on the national television service.

With no more than 15 percent of the islands' territory potentially suitable for cultivation, the prospect of Cape Verde developing self-sufficiency in food appears remote. The few factories that exist on Cape Verde are small-scale operations catering to local needs. Only textiles have enjoyed modest success as an export. Another promising area is fishing.

Timeline: PAST

1462
Cape Verdean settlement begins

1869
Slavery is abolished

1940s
Thousands of Cape Verdeans die of starvation during World War II

1956
The PAIGC is founded

1973
Warfare begins in Guinea-Bissau; Amilcar Cabral is assassinated

1974
A coup in Lisbon initiates the Portuguese decolonization process

1975
Independence

1990s
The PAICV is defeated by the MPD in the country's first multiparty elections; Cape Verde adopts a new Constitution

PRESENT

2000s
Cape Verdeans celebrate 25 years of independence

Power shifts back to PAICV, with Pedro Pires becoming president

Côte d'Ivoire (Republic of Côte d'Ivoire)

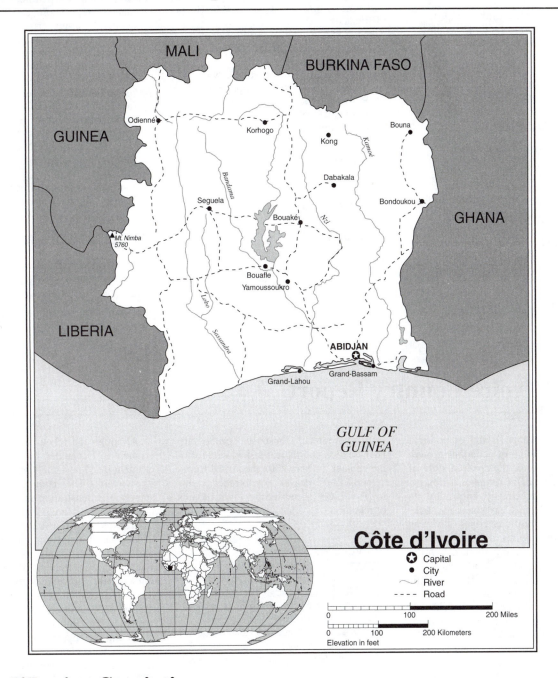

Côte d'Ivoire Statistics

GEOGRAPHY

Area in Square Miles (Kilometers):
124,503 (323,750) (about the size of New Mexico)
Capital (Population): Abidjan (administrative) (3,956,000); Yamoussoukro (political) (120,000)
Environmental Concerns: water pollution; deforestation

Geographical Features: mostly flat to undulating plains; mountains in the northwest
Climate: tropical to semiarid

PEOPLE

Population

Total: 18,013,409
Annual Growth Rate: 1.99%

Rural/Urban Population Ratio: 54/46
Major Languages: French; Dioula; many indigenous dialects
Ethnic Makeup: 42% Akan; 18% Voltaics or Gur; 11% Krous; 16% Northern Mandes; 10% Southern Mandes; 3% others
Religions: 60% Muslim; 22% Christian; 18% indigenous

GLOBAL STUDIES

Health

Life Expectancy at Birth: 46 years (male);
52 years (female)
Infant Mortality: 87.4/1,000 live births
Physicians Available: 1/11,745 people
HIV/AIDS Rate in Adults: 7.0%

Education

Adult Literacy Rate: 50.9%
Compulsory (Ages): 7–13; free

COMMUNICATION

Telephones: 260,900 main lines;
4,065,000 cellular/mobile
Televisions: 57/1,000 people
Internet Users: 300,000

TRANSPORTATION

Highways in Miles (Kilometers): 30,240
(50,400)
Railroads in Miles (Kilometers): 408
(660)
Usable Airfields: 4
Motor Vehicles in Use: 255,000

GOVERNMENT

Type: republic
Independence Date: August 7, 1960 (from
France)
Head of State/Government: President
Laurent Gbagbo; Prime Minister
Guillaume Soro
Political Parties: Democratic Party of
Côte d'Ivoire; Ivoirian Popular Front;
Rally of the Republicans; Ivoirian
Workers' Party; others
Suffrage: universal at 18

MILITARY

Military Expenditures (% of GDP):
1.6%
Current Disputes: civil war

ECONOMY

Currency ($ U.S. Equivalent): 581 CFA
francs = $1
Per Capita Income/GDP: $1,600/$29
billion
GDP Growth Rate: 1.2%

Inflation Rate: 2.4%
Unemployment Rate: 13%
Natural Resources: petroleum; diamonds;
manganese; iron ore; cobalt; bauxite;
copper; hydropower
Agriculture: coffee; cocoa beans;
bananas; palm kernels; corn; rice;
manioc; sweet potatoes; sugar; cotton;
rubber; timber
Industry: foodstuffs; beverages; oil
refining; wood products; textiles;
automobile assembly; fertilizer;
construction materials; electricity
Exports: $8.2 billion (primary partners
France, the Netherlands, United
States)
Imports: $5.1 billion (primary partners
France, Nigeria, China)

SUGGESTED WEB SITES

http://www.sas.upenn.edu/African_
Studies/Country_Specific/Cote.html
https://www.cia.gov/library/publications/
the-world-factbook/geos/iv.html

Côte d'Ivoire Country Report

Once considered an island of political stability and a model of economic growth in West Africa, since the death in 1993 of its first president Félix Houphouët-Boigny, Côte d'Ivoire (previously known by its English name, Ivory Coast) has been shaken by a series of military crises as well as sustained economic decline. In September 2002, a military mutiny sparked fighting that has left the country divided along regional and sectarian lines. The predominantly Muslim northern half of the country has come under the control of rebel soldiers, while the mainly Christian southern half has remained under the rule of the embattled government of Laurent Ghagbo. Although a partial truce between the two sides, upheld by French troops, was negotiated in October, intensive mediation efforts by neighboring states failed to reconcile the two sides. By the end of 2002, the opportunity for a quick end to the crisis appeared to be fading.

In fact the October ceasefire collapsed in November 2002 as armed groups clashed with government forces in a battle for the key cocoa-industry town of Daloa. Moving desperately towards reconciliation in January 2003, President Gbagbo accepted a peace deal at talks in Paris which proposed a power-sharing government. By March 2003 political parties and the rebels agreed on a new government to include nine members

from rebel ranks. "Consensus" prime minister, Seydou Diarra, was tasked with forming cabinet. In May 2003 the armed forces signed a "full" ceasefire with rebel groups in May 2003 to end almost eight months of rebellion.

DEVELOPMENT

It has been said that Côte d'Ivoire is "power hungry." The Soubre Dam, being developed on the Sassandra River, is the sixth and largest hydroelectric project in Côte d'Ivoire. It will serve the eastern area of the country. Another dam is planned for the Cavalla River, between Côte d'Ivoire and Liberia.

There are three rebel groups: the New Forces Movement (formerly the Ivory Coast Patriotic Movement (MPCI)), the Movement for Justice and Peace (MJP), and the Ivoirian Popular Movement of the Far West (MPIGO). In July 2003 at a ceremony held in the presidential palace, the military chiefs and rebels declared that the war was over. The rebels pulled out of the unity government in September 2003, after accusing President Gbagbo of failing to honor the peace agreement. During December 2003 the rebels attacked the state run and owned TV station.

Although the rebels rejoined the government in December, by March the government faced new challenges from within its own ranks. The major opposition parties staged a demonstration in the capital city of Abidjan in March 2004. Government troops tried to disperse the demonstration and began shooting indiscriminately into the crowd. The former ruling party—the Ivory Coast Democratic Party (PDCI)—immediately pulled out of the government, accusing President Gbagbo of "destabilising the peace process." A damning report written by the United Nations in May 2004 noted that the opposition rally was used as a pretext for a planned operation by security forces. The report says that more than 120 people were killed and alleges summary executions and torture. Attempting to halt the violence the UN deplored a contingent of peacekeepers into the country in May 2004. After a six-month period of initial success in curtailing the violence, the civil war was re-ignited in November 2004 when the Ivorian Air Force attacked the rebels. France was drawn into the conflict after nine of their soldiers were killed in an air strike. In retaliation for the attack against their troops, the French staged a counter attack on the Ivorian Air Force, destroying all of their planes and killing an undetermined number of Ivorian government soldiers. Violent anti-French protests ensued in Abidjan. The UN imposed an arms embargo against all the combatants in the Ivory Coast in November 2004.

POLITICAL POLARIZATION

Religious and ethnic divisions among Ivoirians in recent years have been aggravated by growing xenophobia against immigrants, who make up at least one third of the country's total population. Under Houphouët-Boigny, people from other African states were allowed to settle and even vote in Côte d'Ivoire. For more than a half-century, Ivoirians and non-Ivoirians alike lived under the certainty of Houphouët-Boigny's leadership. Known by friend and foe alike in his latter years as *Le Vieux* ("The Old Man"), he was a dominant figure not only in Côte d'Ivoire but also throughout Francophone Africa. A pioneering Pan-Africanist, he had served for three years as a French cabinet minister before leading his country to independence in 1960. During his subsequent 33-year rule, the Côte d'Ivoire was seemingly conspicuous for its social harmony as well as economic growth. But his paternalistic autocracy, exercised through the Democratic Party of Côte d'Ivoire (PDCI), had begun to break down before his death.

FREEDOM

Former president Konan Bédié showed little tolerance for dissent, within either the PDCI or society as a whole. Journalists by the score were jailed for such "offenses" as writing "insulting" articles. Six Ivoirian gendarmes were charged in connection with a mass grave discovered near Abidjan in 2000.

Political life entered a new phase in 1990. Months of mounting prodemocracy protests and labor unrest had led to the legalization of opposition parties, previously banned under the country's single-party government; and to the emergence within the PDCI itself, of a reformist wing seemingly committed to the liberalization process. Although the first multiparty presidential and legislative elections in October–November 1990 were widely regarded as having been less than free and fair by outside observers as well as the opposition, many believed that the path was open for further reform. But as Le Vieux's health declined, the reform process was increasingly held hostage by tensions within the PDCI as well as between it and opposition movements, of which the most prominent was Laurent Gbagbo's Ivoirian Popular Front (FPI). Gbagbo and others were briefly jailed in 1992 on charges of inciting violence after mass demonstrations turned to rioting.

Houphouët-Boigny was succeeded by Konan Bédié, a Christian southerner who came out ahead in a power struggle with Allassane Ouatarra, a northern technocrat who had occupied the post of prime minister. Once in power, Bédié stirred up ethnic discord and xenophobia against Muslim northerners. In 1995, he retained the presidency in elections boycotted by supporters of Ouatarra, who was banned from running for office due to a new law mandating that both parents of any presidential candidate must have been born in Côte d'Ivoire. The boycott enjoyed widespread support in the north. For the first time, immigrants were also banned from voting. Violent protests prior to the poll were met with repression.

Bédié's increasingly unpopular rule came to an abrupt end on December 24, 1999, when General Robert Guei assumed power following the country's first coup d'état. Initial international condemnation of the end of 39 years of uninterrupted civilian rule was muted by the obvious jubilation with which many greeted Bédié's overthrow. There was hope that the divisions of the Bédié era might be laid to rest. Guei reached out to Ouatarra and his supporters as well as other opposition and PDCI members. A new Constitution was drafted and accepted in a referendum. But political goodwill evaporated when, in a move designed to assure his own election, Guei excluded Ouatarra from running for president by reintroducing the provision that both parents of candidates must be Ivoirian. An attempted second coup by northern officers was then crushed, further increasing tensions.

With Bédié and others barred, Gbagbo was the only serious contender allowed to run against Guei in the October 2000 elections. Having lost the ballot, Guei's further attempts to rig the election results were frustrated by a popular uprising that led to Gbagbo's assumption of power. Many of Ouattara's supporters were killed following the rejection of their leader's call for new elections. Opposition boycotts of the December 2000 legislative elections resulted in Gbagbo's Ivoirian Popular Front emerging as the biggest single party in Parliament, with a turnout of only 33 percent. This was followed by another failed coup attempt in January 2001 and subsequent security clapdowns. Nevertheless, there were further calls for fresh presidential and legislative elections in March after Ouattara's party gained a majority at local polls.

In a move toward reconciliation, Gbagbo set up a "National Reconciliation Forum" in October 2001. This resulted in Outtara's return from a year-long exile and a subsequent, January 2002, meeting between the country's "big four"—President Gbagbo, Ouatarra, Guei, and Bédié. But the goodwill

created by the talks has since collapsed in the wake of fighting, which in its first days resulted in Guei's death, in disputed circumstances. Although Gbagbo was elected president with a five-year mandate in 2000, he received a seventh successive year in office in late 2006 under a UN resolution proposed as part of an ongoing peace plan.

ECONOMIC DOWNTURN

The on-going cycle of reform, repression, and increasingly violent political conflict has been taking place against the backdrop of a prolonged deterioration in Côte d'Ivoire's once-vibrant economy. The primary explanation for this downturn is the decline in revenue from cocoa and coffee, which have long been the country's principal export earners. This has led to mounting state debt, which in turn has pressured the government to adopt unpopular austerity measures.

The economy's current problems and prospects are best understood in the context of its past performance. During its first two decades of independence, Côte d'Ivoire enjoyed one of the highest economic growth rates in the world. This growth was all the more notable in that, in contrast to many other developing-world "success stories" during the same period, it had been fueled by the expansion of commercial agriculture. The nation had become the world's leading producer of cocoa and third-largest coffee producer.

HEALTH/WELFARE

Côte d'Ivoire has one of the lowest soldier-to teacher ratios in Africa. Education absorbs about 40% of the national budget. The National Commission to Combat AIDS has reported significant success in its campaign to promote condom use, by targeting especially vulnerable groups.

Although prosperity gave way to recession during the 1980s, the average per capita income of the country remained one of Africa's highest. Statistics also indicated that, on average, Ivoirians lived longer and better than people in many neighboring states. But the creation of a productive, market-oriented economy did not eliminate the reality of widespread poverty, leading some to question whether the majority of Ivoirians have derived reasonable benefit from their nation's wealth.

To the further dismay of many young Ivoirians struggling to enter the country's tight job market, much of the political and economic life of Côte d'Ivoire is controlled by its large and growing expatriate population, largely comprised of French and Lebanese. The size of these communities has multiplied since independence. Many foreigners are now quasi-permanent residents who have thrived while managing plantations, factories, and commercial enterprises. Others can be found in senior civil-service positions.

Another group who have until recently prospered are the commercial farmers, who include millions of medium- and small-scale producers. About two thirds of the workforce are employed in agriculture, with coffee alone being the principal source of income for some 2.5 million people. In addition to coffee, Ivoirian planters grow cocoa, bananas, pineapples, sugar, cotton, palm oil, and other cash crops for export. While some of these farmers are quite wealthy, most have only modest incomes.

ACHIEVEMENTS

Ivoirian textiles are varied and prized. Block printing and dyeing produce brilliant designs; woven cloths made strip by strip and sewn together include the white Korhogo tapestries, covered with Ivoirian figures, birds, and symbols drawn in black. The Ivoirian singer Alpha Blondy has become an international superstar as the leading exponent of West African reggae.

In recent years, the circumstance of Ivoirian coffee and cocoa planters has become much more precarious, due to fluctuations in commodities prices. In this respect, the growers, along with their colleagues elsewhere, are to some extent victims of their own success. Their productivity, in response to international demand, has been a factor in depressing prices through increased supply. In 1988, Houphouët-Boigny held cocoa in storage in an attempt to force a price rise, but the effort failed, aggravating the nation's economic downturn. The civil war in the country seriously disrupted the exportation of the cocoa crop in 2004, and threatened the supply of chocolates to western consumers during the Christmas season. As a result, the government has taken a new approach, scrapping plans for future expansion in cocoa production in favor of promoting food crops such as yams, corn, and plantains, for which there is a regional as well as a domestic market.

Until recently, Ivoirian planters continued to hire low-paid laborers from other West African countries. At any given time, there have been about 2 million migrant laborers in Côte d'Ivoire, employed throughout the economy. Their presence is not a new phenomenon but goes back to colonial times. Many laborers come from Burkina Faso, which was once a part of Côte d'Ivoire. A good road system and the Ivoirian railroad (which extends to the Burkinabé capital of Ouagadougou)

facilitated the travel of migrant workers to rural as well as urban areas.

DEBT AND DISCONTENT

Other factors may determine how much an Ivoirian benefits from the country's development. Residents of Abidjan, the capital, and its environs near the coast receive more services than do citizens of interior areas. Professionals in the cities make better salaries than do laborers on farms or in small industries. Yet persistent inflation and recession have made daily life difficult for the middle class as well as poorer peasants and workers.

The nonagricultural sectors of the national economy have also been experiencing difficulties. Many state industries are unable to make a profit due to their heavy indebtedness. Serious brush fires, mismanagement, and the clearing of forests for cash-crop plantations have put the nation's once-sizable timber industry in jeopardy. Out of a former total of 12 million hectares of forest, 10 1/2 million have been lost. Plans for expansion of offshore oil production have not been implemented due to an inability to raise investment capital.

Difficulty in raising capital for oil development is a reflection of the debt crisis that has plagued the country since the collapse of its cocoa and coffee earnings. Finding itself in the desperate situation of being forced to borrow to pay interest on its previous loans, the government suspended most debt repayments in 1987. Subsequent rescheduling of negotiations with international creditors resulted in a Structural Adjustment Plan (SAP). This plan has resulted in a reduction in the prices paid to farmers and a drastic curtailment in public spending, leading to severe salary cuts for public and parastatal workers. Recent pressure on the part of the international lending agencies for the Ivoirian government to cut back further on its commitment to cash crops is particularly ironic, given the praise that they bestowed on the same policies in the not-too-distant past. Many also see the imposition of such conditions as hypocritical given the heavy rate of agricultural subsidies within the European Union and United States. Those subsidies have further disadvantaged Ivoirian, along with other African, commercial farmers. With the country now on the brink of full-scale civil war, for most Ivoirians the harsh economic conditions are likely to continue to get worse before they get better.

THE SEARCH FOR STABILITY

The ability of various Côte d'Ivoire governments to gain acceptance for austerity measures has been compromised by

corruption and extravagance at the top. A notorious example of the latter was the basilica that was constructed at Yamoussoukro, the home village of Houphouët-Boigny (which also at great cost was made the nation's new capital city before his death). The air-conditioned basilica, patterned after the papal seat of St. Peter's in Rome, is the largest Christian church building in the world. Supposedly a personal gift of Houphouët-Boigny to the Vatican—a most reluctant recipient—its three-year construction is believed to have cost hundreds of millions of U.S. dollars.

The course of domestic conflict in Côte d'Ivoire is being watched elsewhere. For decades Houphouët-Boigny was the doyen of the more conservative, pro-Western leaders in Africa. Hostile to Libya and receptive to both Israel and to "dialogue" with South Africa, Côte d'Ivoire has remained especially close to France, which continues to maintain a military presence in the country. During the recent fighting, U.S. marines also intervened to evacuate foreign nationals.

Timeline: PAST

1700s
Agni and Baoulé peoples migrate to the Ivory Coast from the East

1893
The Ivory Coast officially becomes a French colony

1898
Samori Touré, a Malinke Muslim leader and an empire builder, is defeated by the French

1915
The final French pacification of the country takes place

1960
Côte d'Ivoire becomes independent under Félix Houphouët-Boigny's leadership

1980s
The PDCI approves a plan to move the capital from Abidjan to Houphouët-Boigny's home village of Yamoussoukro

1990s
Prodemocracy demonstrations lead to multiparty elections; Houphouët-Boigny dies

PRESENT

2000s
Côte d'Ivoire adjusts after the startling coup in late 1999

Laurent Gbagbo becomes president

A mass grave of 57 bullet-ridden bodies is discovered near Abidjan

French and UN peacekeepers continue to maintain a buffer zone between north and south

The Gambia (Republic of The Gambia)

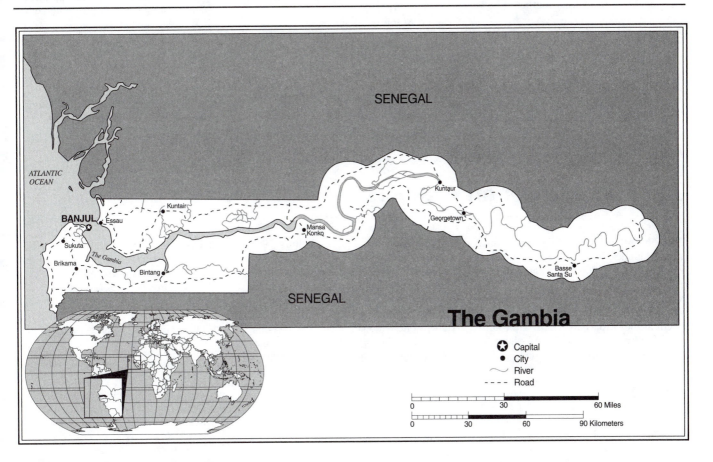

The Gambia Statistics

GEOGRAPHY

Area in Square Miles (Kilometers):
(4,361) (11,295) (about twice the size of Delaware)
Capital (Population): Banjul (418,000)
Environmental Concerns:
deforestation; desertification; water-borne diseases
Geographical Features: floodplain of The Gambia River flanked by some low hills
Climate: tropical; hot rainy season, cooler dry season

PEOPLE

Population

Total: 1,688,359
Annual Growth Rate: 2.78%
Rural/Urban Population Ratio: 68/32
Major Languages: English; Mandinka; Wolof; Fula; Sarakola; Diula; others

Ethnic Makeup: 42% Mandinka; 18% Fula; 16% Wolof; 24% others (99% African; 1% non-Gambian)
Religions: 90% Muslim; 9% Christian; 1% indigenous beliefs

Health

Life Expectancy at Birth: 53 years (male); 57 years (female)
Infant Mortality: 70.4/1,000 live births
Physicians Available: 1/14,536 people
HIV/AIDS Rate in Adults: 1.2%

Education

Adult Literacy Rate: 40.1%
Compulsory (Ages): 7–13; free

COMMUNICATION

Telephones: 52, 900 main lines; 404,300 cellular/mobile
Internet Users: 58,000

TRANSPORTATION

Highways in Miles (Kilometers): 1,584 (2,640)
Railroads in Miles (Kilometers): none
Usable Airfield: 1
Motor Vehicles in Use: 9,000

GOVERNMENT

Type: republic
Independence Date: February 18, 1965 (from the United Kingdom)
Head of State/Government: President Yahya Jammeh is both head of state and head of government
Political Parties: Alliance for Patriotic Reorientation and Construction; National Reconciliation Party; People's Democratic Organization for Independence and Socialism; others
Suffrage: universal at 18

MILITARY

Military Expenditures (% of GDP): 0.5%
Current Disputes: internal conflicts

ECONOMY

Currency ($ U.S. Equivalent): 28.3
    dalasis = $1
Per Capita Income/GDP: $2000/
    $3.3 billion
GDP Growth Rate: 6.5%

Inflation Rate: 1.5%
Labor Force by Occupation: 75%
    agriculture; 19% industry and services;
    6% government
Natural Resources: fish
Agriculture: peanuts; millet; sorghum;
    rice; corn, cassava; livestock; fish and
    forest resources
Industry: processing peanuts, fish, and
    hides; tourism; beverages; agricultural
    machinery assembly; wood- and
    metalworking; clothing

Exports: $135 million (primary partners
    Benelux, Japan, United Kingdom)
Imports: $249 million (primary partners
    China, Hong Kong, United Kingdom,
    the Netherlands)

SUGGESTED WEB SITES

http://www.gambianews.com
https://www.cia.gov/library/publications/
    the-world-factbook/geos/ga.html

The Gambia Country Report

Since his seizure of power in a 1994 coup, Yahya Jammeh has dominated politics in The Gambia. In 2001, he was reelected president in what international election monitors generally viewed as a free and fair poll. The government called for the elections, however, only shortly after Jammeh lifted a ban on politicians whom he had ousted from power.

DEVELOPMENT

Since independence, The Gambia has developed a tourist industry. Whereas in 1966 only 300 individuals were recorded as having visited the country, the figure for 1988–1989 was over 112,000. Tourism is now the second-biggest sector of the economy. Still, tourism has declined since 2000. After the February 2004 announcement of the discovery of large oil reserves, there is expected to be a major upturn in economic activity.

Subsequent parliamentary elections, in January 2002, were boycotted by most of the opposition, allowing Jammeh's Alliance for Patriotic Reorientation and Construction to win by a landslide. The Gambian opposition has otherwise been weakened by its internal divisions, all attempts to bring about a united front having failed. Opposition to Jammeh's rule has become more open.

In April 2000, Gambians were shocked when student protests in the capital city, Banjul, resulted in the killing of 14 people and the wounding of many more by government security forces. Many interpreted the violence as an ominous official response to the re-emergence of independent voices within the media and civil society, which have been pushing for greater openness and accountability in government.

Jammeh came to power in July 1994, after The Gambia's armed forces overthrew the government of Sir Dawda Jawara, bringing to an abrupt end what had been postcolonial West Africa's only example of uninterrupted multiparty democracy. Under international pressure, elections were held in September 1996 and January 1997, resulting in victories for Jammeh and the Alliance for Patriotic Reorientation and Construction. But the process was marred by the regime's continuing intolerance of genuine opposition. Since the failure of an alleged coup attempt in January 1995, critical voices have been largely silenced by an increasingly powerful National Intelligence Agency. Meanwhile, The Gambia's already weak economy has suffered from reduced revenues from tourism and foreign donors.

FREEDOM

Despite the imposition of martial law in the aftermath of the 1981 coup attempt, The Gambia has had a strong record of respect for individual liberty and human rights. Under its current regime, The Gambia has forfeited its model record of respect for freedoms of speech and association.

The Gambia is Africa's smallest noninsular nation. Except for a small seacoast, it is entirely surrounded by its much larger neighbor, Senegal. The two nations' separate existence is rooted in the activities of British slave traders who, in 1618, established a fort at the mouth of The Gambia River, from which they gradually spread their commercial and, later, political dominance upstream. Gambians have much in common with Senegalese. The Gambia's three major ethnolinguistic groups—the Mandinka, Wolof, and Fula (or Peul)—are found on both sides of the border. The Wolof

language serves as a lingua franca in both the Gambian capital of Banjul and the urban areas of Senegal. Islam is the major religion of both countries, while each also has a substantial Christian minority. The economies of the two countries are also similar, with each being heavily reliant on the cultivation of ground nuts (peanuts) as a cash crop.

Timeline: PAST

1618
The British build Fort James at the current site of Banjul, on the Gambia River

1807
The Gambia is ruled by the United Kingdom through Sierra Leone

1965
Independence

1970
Dawda Jawara comes to power

1980s
An attempted coup against President Dawda Jawara; the rise and fall of the Senegambia Confederation

1990s
Jawara is overthrown by a military coup; Yahya Jammeh becomes head of state

PRESENT

2000s
Government security forces kill 14 people during student protests

Jammeh is reelected president, but the opposition gains in parliamentary elections

Discovery of large oil reserves

In 1981, the Senegalese and Gambian governments were drawn closer together

(Photo by Wayne Edge)

Small general stores provide innumerable materials for everyday life including cloth, tools, and utensils.

by an attempted coup in Banjul. While Jawara was in London, dissident elements within his Paramilitary Field Force joined in a coup attempt with members of two small, self-styled revolutionary parties. Based on a 1965 mutual-defense agreement, Jawara received assistance from Senegal in putting down the rebels. Constitutional rule was restored, but the killing of 400 to 500 people during the uprising and the subsequent mass arrest of suspected accomplices left Gambians bitter and divided.

HEALTH/WELFARE

Forty percent of Gambian children remain outside the primary-school setup. Economic Recovery Program austerity has made it harder for the government to achieve its goal of education for all.

In the immediate aftermath of the coup, The Gambia agreed to join Senegal in a loose confederation, which some hoped would lead to a full political union. But from the beginning, the Senegambia Confederation was marred by the circumstances of its formation. The continued presence of Senegalese soldiers in their country led Gambians to speak of a "shotgun wedding." Beyond fears of losing their local identity, many believed that proposals for closer economic integration, through a proposed monetary and customs union, would be to The Gambia's disadvantage. Underlying this concern was the role played by Gambian traders in providing imports to Senegal's market. Other squabbles, such as a long-standing dispute over the financing of a bridge across The Gambia River, finally led to the Confederation's formal demise in 1989. But the two countries still recognize a need to develop alternative forms of cooperation.

ACHIEVEMENTS

Gambian *griots*—hereditary bards and musicians such as Banna and Dembo Kanute—have maintained a traditional art. Formerly, griots were attached to ruling families; now, they perform over Radio Gambia and are popular throughout West Africa.

The Gambia was modestly successful in rebuilding its politics in the aftermath of the 1981 coup attempt. Whereas the 1982 elections were arguably compromised by the detention of the main opposition leader, Sherif Mustapha Dibba, on (later dismissed) charges of complicity in the revolt, the 1987 and 1992 polls restored most people's confidence in Gambian democracy. In both elections, opposition parties significantly increased their share

223

of the vote, while Jawara's People's Progressive Party retained majority support.

Instances of official corruption had compromised the Jawara government's ability to use its electoral mandate to implement an Economic Recovery Program (ERP), which included austerity measures. The Gambia has always been a poor country. During the 1980s, conditions worsened as a result of bad harvests and falling prices for groundnuts, which usually account for half of the nation's export earnings. The tourist industry was also disrupted by the 1981 coup attempt. Faced with mounting debt, the government submitted to International Monetary Fund pressure by cutting back its civil service and drastically devaluing the local currency. The latter step initially led to high inflation, but prices have become more stable in recent years, and the economy as a whole has begun to enjoy a gross domestic product growth rate of up to 5 percent per year. As elsewhere, the negative impact of Structural Adjustment has proved especially burdensome to urban dwellers. Tourism, primarily to locations along the coast, has grown rapidly in recent years and is now a major contributor to economic growth. The discovery in 2004 of significant petroleum reserves offshore is also likely to reshape the economy, although it is expected to be several years before oil begins to flow.

Ghana (Republic of Ghana)

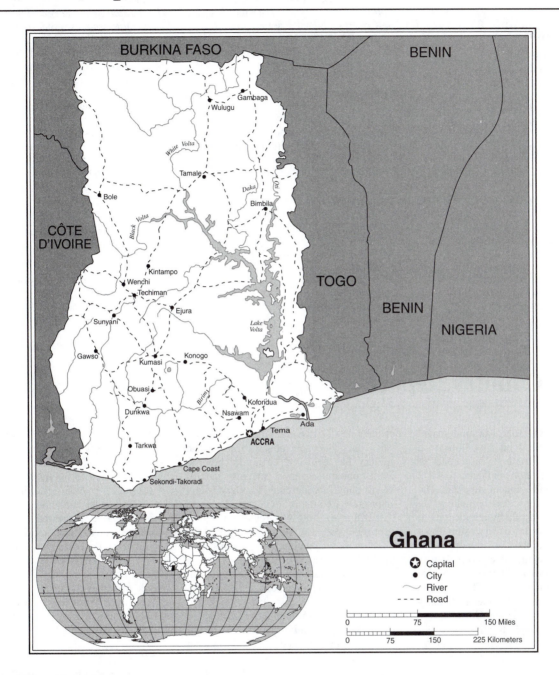

Ghana Statistics

GEOGRAPHY

Area in Square Miles (Kilometers):
92,100 (238,536) (about the size of Oregon)
Capital (Population): Accra (1,925,000)
Environmental Concerns: drought; deforestation; overgrazing; soil erosion; threatened wildlife populations; water pollution; insufficient potable water

Geographical Features: low plains with dissected plateau
Climate: tropical

PEOPLE

Population

Total: 22,931,299
Annual Growth Rate: 1.97%
Rural/Urban Population Ratio: 62/38

Major Languages: English; Akan; Ewe; Ga
Ethnic Makeup: nearly 100% African
Religions: 69% Christian; 15% indigenous beliefs; 16% Muslim

Health

Life Expectancy at Birth: 58 years (male); 60 years (female)
Infant Mortality: 53.6/1,000 live births
Physicians Available: 1/22,452 people
HIV/AIDS Rate in Adults: 3.1%

Education

Adult Literacy Rate: 64.5%
Compulsory (Ages): 6–16

COMMUNICATION

Telephones: 356,400 main lines;
  5,207,000 cellular/mobile
Daily Newspaper Circulation: 64/1,000
  people
Televisions: 15/1,000 people
Internet Users: 609,800

TRANSPORTATION

Highways in Miles (Kilometers): 24,428
  (39,400)
Railroads in Miles (Kilometers): 592 (953)
Usable Airfields: 12
Motor Vehicles in Use: 135,000

GOVERNMENT

Type: constitutional democracy
Independence Date: March 6, 1957 (from
  the United Kingdom)

Head of State/Government: President
  John Agyekum Kufuor is both head of
  state and head of government
Political Parties: National Democratic
  Congress; New Patriotic Party;
  People's Convention Party; Every
  Ghanaian Living Everywhere; others
Suffrage: universal at 18

MILITARY

Military Expenditures (% of GDP): 0.8%
Current Disputes: minor internal conflicts;
  issues associated with returning cocoa
  workers fleeing conflict in Côte
  d'Ivoire

ECONOMY

Currency ($ U.S. Equivalent): 9,175
  cedis = $1
Per Capita Income/GDP: $2,700/$60
  billion
GDP Growth Rate: 6.0%
Inflation Rate: 10.9%
Unemployment Rate: 20%

Labor Force by Occupation: 39%
  services; 36% agriculture; 25%
  industry
Population Below Poverty Line: 31.4%
Natural Resources: gold; timber;
  industrial diamonds; bauxite;
  manganese; fish; rubber; hydropower
Agriculture: cocoa beans; rice; coffee;
  cassava; peanuts; corn; shea nuts;
  bananas; timber; fish
Industry: mining; lumbering; light
  manufacturing; aluminum smelting;
  food processing
Exports: $3.8 billion (primary partners
  Togo, United Kingdom, Italy)
Imports: $6.6 billion (primary partners
  United Kingdom, Nigeria, United
  States)

SUGGESTED WEB SITES

http://www.ghana.gov.gh
http://www.ghana.com
http://www.ghana-embassy.org/
https://www.cia.gov/library/publications/
  the-world-factbook/geos/gh.html

Ghana Country Report

In December 2000, John Kufuor defeated then–vice-president John Atta Mills in a ballot that marked the first real transfer of power through elections in Ghana in 4 1/2 decades as an independent republic. The presidential elections also brought to an end two decades of rule by the incumbent Jerry Rawlings, who agreed to step down in accordance with the Constitution. President Kufuor inaugurated a reconciliation commission to look into human-rights violations during military rule. The commission began hearing testimonies in January 2003. Known as the "Gentle Giant," President Kufuor has sought to promote reconciliation without recrimination in a nation with a violent history of political division.

DEVELOPMENT

In the 1960s, Ghana invested heavily in schooling, resulting in perhaps the best-educated population in Africa. Today, hundreds of thousands of professionals who began their schooling under Nkrumah work overseas, annually remitting an estimated $1 billion to the Ghanaian economy. The discovery of off-shore oil reserves was announced in early 2007.

In the 1990s, Ghana made gradual but steady progress in rebuilding its economy as well as its political culture, after decades of decline. For many Ghanaians, these gains have been of modest benefit. The country has achieved economic growth, while implementing a socially painful World Bank/International Monetary Fund–sponsored Economic Recovery Program (ERP) that in 2001 was rewarded with a debt-relief package. Yet when adjusted for inflation, per capita income remains below the level that existed in 1957, when Ghana became the first colony in sub-Saharan Africa to obtain independence.

The country is also overcoming the legacy of political instability brought about by revolving-door military coups. In March 1992, Rawlings marked the country's 35th anniversary of independence by announcing an accelerated return to multiparty rule. Eight months later, he was elected by a large majority as the president of what has been hailed as Ghana's "Fourth Republic." Although the election received the qualified endorsement of international monitors, its result was rejected by the main opposition, the New Patriotic Party (NPP). The NPP subsequently boycotted parliamentary elections, allowing an easy victory for Rawlings's National Democratic Congress (NDC), which captured 189 out of 200 seats, with a voter turnout of just under 30 percent. After months of bitter standoff, the political climate has eased since December 1993, when the NPP agreed to enter into a dialogue

with the government about its basic demand that the interests of the ruling party be more clearly separated from those of the state.

Ghana's political transformation was a triumph for Rawlings, who ruled since 1981, when he and other junior military officers seized power as the Provisional National Defense Council (PNDC). In the name of ending corruption, they overthrew Ghana's previous freely elected government after it had been in office for less than two years. Rawlings was dismissive of elections at that time: "What does it mean to stuff bits of paper into boxes?" But political success seems to have altered his opinion.

FREEDOM

Ghana has a high degree of media freedom. Its press has been described by international observers as "one of the most unfettered on the continent." In addition, Ghana has played a prominent peacekeeping role throughout the region, sending forces to Côte d'Ivoire, Sierra Leone, Liberia, and the Democratic Republic of the Congo.

At its independence, Ghana assumed a leadership role in the struggle against colonial rule elsewhere on the continent. Both its citizens and many outside observers were optimistic about the country's future. As compared to many other former colonies, the country seemed to have a sound infrastructure for future progress. Unfortunately, economic development and political democracy have proven to be elusive goals.

The "First Republic," led by the charismatic Kwame Nkrumah, degenerated into a bankrupt and an increasingly authoritarian one-party state. Nkrumah had pinned his hopes on an ambitious policy of industrial development. When substantial overseas investment failed to materialize, he turned to socialism. His efforts led to a modest rise in local manufacturing, but the sector's productivity was compromised by inefficient planning, limited resources, expensive inputs, and mounting government corruption. The new state enterprises ended up being financed largely from the export earnings of cocoa, which had emerged as Ghana's principal cash crop during the colonial period. Following colonial precedent, Nkrumah resorted to paying local cocoa farmers well below the world market price for their output in an attempt to expand state revenues.

Nkrumah was overthrown by the military in 1966. Despite his regime's shortcomings, he is still revered by many as the leading pan-African nationalist of his generation. His warnings about the dangers of neo-imperialism have proved prophetic.

Since Nkrumah's fall, the army has been Ghana's dominant political institution, although there were brief returns to civilian control in 1969–1972 and again in 1979–1981. Both the military and the civilian governments abandoned much of Nkrumah's socialist commitment, but for years they continued his policy of squeezing the cocoa farmers, with the long-term result of encouraging planters both to cut back on their production and to attempt to circumvent the official prices through smuggling. This situation, coupled with falling cocoa

prices on the world market and rising import costs, helped to push Ghana into a state of severe economic depression during the 1970s. During that period, real wages fell by some 80 percent. Ghana's crisis was then aggravated by an unwillingness on the part of successive governments to devalue the country's currency, the cedi, which encouraged black-market trading.

RAWLINGS'S RENEWAL

By 1981, many Ghanaians welcomed the PNDC, seeing in Rawlings's populist rhetoric the promise of change after years of corruption and stagnation. The PNDC initially tried to rule through People's Defense Committees, which were formed throughout the country to act as both official watchdogs and instruments of mass mobilization. Motivated by a combination of idealism and frustration with the status quo, the vigilantism of these institutions threatened the country with anarchy until, in 1983, they were reined in. Also in 1983, the country faced a new crisis, when the Nigerian government suddenly expelled nearly 1 million Ghanaian expatriates, who had to be resettled quickly.

Faced with an increasingly desperate situation, the PNDC, in a move that surprised many, given its leftist leanings, began to implement the Economic Recovery Program. Some 100,000 public and parastatal employees were retrenched, the cedi was progressively devalued, and wages and prices began to reflect more nearly their market value. These steps have led to some economic growth, while annually attracting $500 million in foreign aid and soft loans and perhaps double that amount in cash remittances from the more than 1 million Ghanaians living abroad.

The human costs of ERP have been a source of criticism. Many ordinary Ghanaians, especially urban salary-earners, have suffered from falling wages coupled with rising inflation. Unemployment has also increased in many areas (today it is estimated at about 20 percent). Yet a recent survey found surprisingly strong support among "urban lower income groups" for ERP and the government in general. In the countryside, farmers have benefited from higher crop prices and investments in rural infrastructure, while there has been a countrywide boom in legitimate retailing.

ERP continues to have its critics, but it gained substantial support from politicians aligned with Ghana's three principal political tendencies: the Nkrumahists, loyal to the first president's pan-African socialist vision; the Danquah-Busia grouping, named after two past statesmen who struggled against Nkrumah for more liberal economic and political policies; and those loyal to the PNDC. In the November 1992

presidential elections, the NPP emerged as the main voice of the Danquah-Busia camp, while Rawlings's NDC attracted substantial support from Nkrumahists as well as those sympathetic to his own legacy. There was also a body of opinion that was critical of all three historic tendencies, characterizing the NPP and NDC as fronts for power-hungry men fighting yesterday's battles. During the April 1992 referendum to approve the new Constitution, more than half the registered voters (many Ghanaians complained that they were denied registration) failed to participate, despite the government and opposition's joint call for a large "yes" vote. Many also boycotted the November presidential elections. In December 1996, in a poll widely judged to have been fair, Rawlings was reelected. He narrowly defeated his former vice-president, John Kufuor, who enjoyed the backing of both the New Patriotic Party and the Convention People's Party—the same man who eventually would come to succeed him as president.

Guinea (Republic of Guinea)

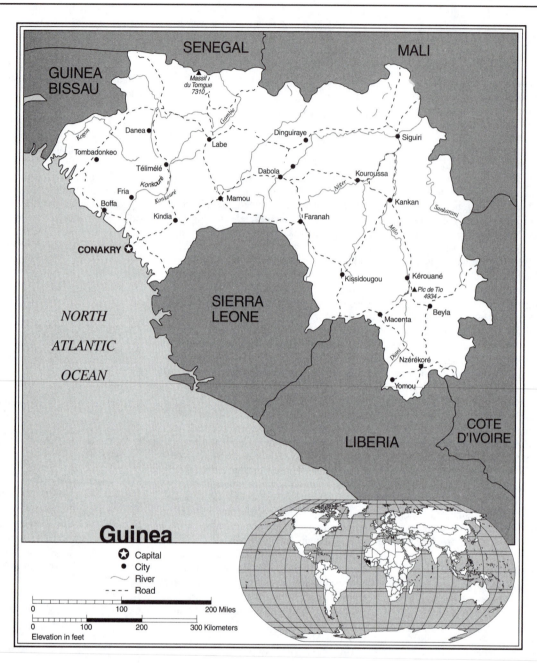

Guinea

- ⭐ Capital
- ● City
- 〰 River
- - - - Road

0   100   200 Miles

0   100   200   300 Kilometers

Elevation in feet

Guinea

GEOGRAPHY

Area in Square Miles (Kilometers): 95,000 (246,048) (about the size of Oregon)
Capital (Population): Conakry (1,272,000)
Environmental Concerns: deforestation; insufficient potable water; desertification; soil erosion and contamination; overfishing; overpopulation

Geographical Features: mostly flat coastal plain; hilly to mountainous interior
Climate: tropical

PEOPLE

Population

Total: 9,947,814
Annual Growth Rate: 2.62%
Rural/Urban Population Ratio: 68/32

Major Languages: French; many tribal languages
Ethnic Makeup: 40% Peuhl; 30% Malinke; 20% Soussou; 10% other African groups
Religions: 85% Muslim; 8% Christian; 7% indigenous beliefs

Health

Life Expectancy at Birth: 49 years (male); 51 years (female)

Infant Mortality: 88.6/1,000 live births
Physicians Available: 1/9,732 people
HIV/AIDS Rate in Adults: 3.2%

Education

Adult Literacy Rate: 30%
Compulsory (Ages): 7–13; free

COMMUNICATION

Telephones: 26,300 main lines; 189,000
 cellular/mobile
Televisions: 10/1,000 people
Internet Users: 50,000

TRANSPORTATION

Highways in Miles (Kilometers): 18,060
 (30,100)
Railroads in Miles (Kilometers): 509 (837)
Usable Airfields: 16
Motor Vehicles in Use: 33,000

GOVERNMENT

Type: republic
Independence Date: October 2, 1958
 (from France)

Head of State/Government: President
 (General) Lansana Conté; Prime
 Minister Francois Lonseny Fall
Political Parties: Party for Unity and
 Progress; Union for the New Republic;
 Rally for the Guinean People; many
 others
Suffrage: universal at 18

MILITARY

Military Expenditures (% of GDP): 1.7%
Current Disputes: cross-border
 instability from conflicts in Sierra
 Leone and Liberia fueled by refugee
 crisis; border dispute with Sierra
 Leone

ECONOMY

Currency ($ U.S. Equivalent): 5,350
 Guinean francs = $1
Per Capita Income/GDP: $2,100/$19.9
 billion
GDP Growth Rate: 2.2%
Inflation Rate: 30%

Labor Force by Occupation: 80%
 agriculture; 20% industry and
 services
Population Below Poverty Line: 40%
Natural Resources: bauxite; iron ore;
 diamonds; gold; uranium; hydropower;
 fish
Agriculture: rice; cassava; millet; sweet
 potatoes; coffee; bananas; palm
 products; pineapples; livestock
Industry: bauxite; gold; diamonds;
 alumina refining; light manufacturing
 and agricultural processing
Exports: $956 million (primary
 partners Belgium, United States,
 Ireland)
Imports: $704 million (primary partners
 France, United States, Belgium)

SUGGESTED WEB SITES

http://www.sas.upenn.edu/African_
 Studies/Country_Specific/Guinea.html
https://www.cia.gov/library/publications/
 the-world-factbook/geos/gv.html

Guinea Country Report

In recent years, Guinea has managed to maintain internal peace in the face of armed conflict along its borders. But renewed fighting in neighboring Sierra Leone, Liberia, and Côte d'Ivoire has revived fears that the country is being dragged into a wider regional conflict.

DEVELOPMENT

A measure of economic growth in Guinea was reflected in the rising traffic in Conakry harbor, whose volume rose 415% over a 4-year period. Plans are being made to improve the port's infrastructure, but regional conflicts threaten further development.

Since the end of 2000, incursions by rebels along Guinea's border regions with Liberia and Sierra Leone have claimed more than 1,000 lives and caused massive population displacement. The government has accused the governments of Liberia and Burkina Faso, the (now-disarmed) Revolutionary United Front (RUF) of Sierra Leone, and former Guinean Army mutineers of working together to destabilize Guinea. With tensions rising, Alpha Conde, leader of the opposition Guinean People's Rally (RPG), was sentenced in September 2000 to five years in prison, charged with

endangering state security and recruiting foreign mercenaries. By February 2001, the government began deploying attack helicopters to the front line to fight with rebels. Meanwhile, the United Nations high commissioner for refugees, Ruud Lubbers, warned that the country's refugee crisis, mostly the result of the conflicts in Sierra Leone and Liberia, was in danger of getting out of control. The country shelters more than half a million (estimates vary widely) cross-border refugees.

FREEDOM

Human rights continue to be restricted in Guinea, with the government's security forces being linked to disappearances, abuse of prisoners and detainees, torture by military personnel, and inhumane prison conditions.

At home, the harassment of journalists and opposition leaders has underscored the government's continued insecurity despite the 1992 transition to multiparty politics. In a constitutional referendum that took place in November 2001, voters endorsed President Lansana Conté's proposal to extend the presidential term from five to seven years. But the opposition boycotted

the poll, accusing Conté of trying to stay in office for life. During November 2003 opposition leader Jean-Marie Dore was detained for saying that President Conté was too ill to contest December's presidential election. After being released from jail Mr. Dore and his party boycotted the election in December 2003. With the main opposition parties boycotting the election President Conté won a third term in office.

Since coming to power in 1984, Conté has proven adept at surviving challenges to his authority. In April 1992, he announced that a new Constitution guaranteeing freedom of association would take immediate effect. Within a month, more than 30 political parties had formed. This initiative was a political second chance for a nation whose potential had been mismanaged for decades, under the dictatorial rule of its first president, Sekou Touré.

HEALTH/WELFARE

The life expectancy of Guineans is among the lowest in the world, reflecting the stagnation of the nation's health service during the Sekou Touré years.

From his early years as a radical trade-union activist in the late 1940s until his death in office in 1984, Sekou Touré was Guinea's dominant personality. A descendent of the nineteenth-century Malinke hero Samori Touré, who fiercely resisted the imposition of French rule, Sekou Touré was a charismatic but repressive leader. In 1958, he inspired Guineans to vote for immediate independence from France. At the time, Guinea was the only territory to opt out of Charles de Gaulle's newly established French Community. The French reacted spitefully, withdrawing all aid, personnel, and equipment from the new nation, an event that heavily influenced Guinea's postindependence path. The ability of Touré's Democratic Party of Guinea (PDG) to step into the administrative vacuum was the basis for Guinea's quick transformation into the African continent's first one-party socialist state, a process that was encouraged by the Soviet bloc.

ACHIEVEMENTS

More than 80% of the programming broadcast by Guinea's television service is locally produced. This output has included more than 3,000 movies. A network of rural radio stations is currently being installed.

Touré's rule was characterized by economic mismanagement and the widespread abuse of human rights. It is estimated that 2 million people—at the time about one out of every four Guineans—fled the country during his rule. At least 2,900 individuals disappeared under detention by the government.

By the late 1970s, Touré, pressured by rising discontent and his own apparent realization of his country's poor economic performance, began to modify both his domestic and foreign policies. This shift led to better relations with Western countries but little improvement in the lives of his people. In 1982, Amnesty International publicized the Touré regime's dismal record

of political killings, detentions, and torture, but the world remained largely indifferent.

On April 3, 1984, a week after Touré's death, the army stepped in, claiming that it wished to end all vestiges of the late president's dictatorial regime. The bloodless coup was well received by Guineans. Hundreds of political prisoners were released; and the once-powerful Democratic Party of Guinea, which during the Touré years had been reduced from a mass party into a hollow shell, was disbanded. A new government was formed, under the leadership of then-colonel Conté; and a 10-point program for national recovery was set forth, including the restoration of human rights and the renovation of the economy.

Faced with an empty treasury, the new government committed itself to a severe Structural Adjustment Program (SAP). This has led to a dismantling of many of the socialist structures that had been established by the previous government. While international financiers have generally praised it, the government has had to weather periodic unrest and coup attempts. In spite of these challenges, however, it has remained committed to SAP.

Guinea is blessed with mineral resources, which could lead to a more prosperous future. The country is rich in bauxite and has substantial reserves of iron and diamonds. New mining agreements, leading to a flow of foreign investment, have already led to a modest boom in bauxite and diamond exports. Small-scale gold mining is also being developed. These initiatives, however, are being threatened by the conflicts in neighboring states.

Guinea's greatest economic failing has been the poor performance of its agricultural sector. Unlike many of its neighbors, the country enjoys a favorable climate and soils. But, although some 80 percent of Guineans are engaged in subsistence farming, only 3 percent of the land is cultivated, and foodstuffs remain a major import. Blame for this situation can be placed, in large part, on the inefficient state-controlled marketing system that is a legacy of the Touré regime. These economic problems,

moreover, are contributing to growing political unrest; in 2006, massive strikes took place in urban areas across the country over corruption and deteriorating economic conditions. This only compounds the existing political uncertainty caused by instability among Guinea's neighbors and the lack of a clear political successor to an aging president in poor health.

Timeline: PAST

1700s

A major Islamic kingdom is established in the Futa Djalon

1898

Samori Touré is defeated by the French

1958

Led by Sekou Touré, Guineans reject continued membership in the French Community; an independent republic is formed

1978

French president Giscard d'Estaing visits Guinea: the beginning of a reconciliation between France and Guinea

1980s

Sekou Touré's death is followed by a military coup; the introduction of SAP leads to urban unrest

1990s

President Lansana Conté begins to establish a multiparty democracy; multiparty elections are held for the presidency; Conté claims victory

PRESENT

2000s

Guinea stays the course of Structural Adjustment despite severe hardships

Fears intensify regarding a regional conflict

Guinea, Sierra Leone, and Liberia agree on measures to secure mutual borders and to tackle insurgency

Prime Minister Lounseny resigns from office

Guinea-Bissau (Republic of Guinea-Bissau)

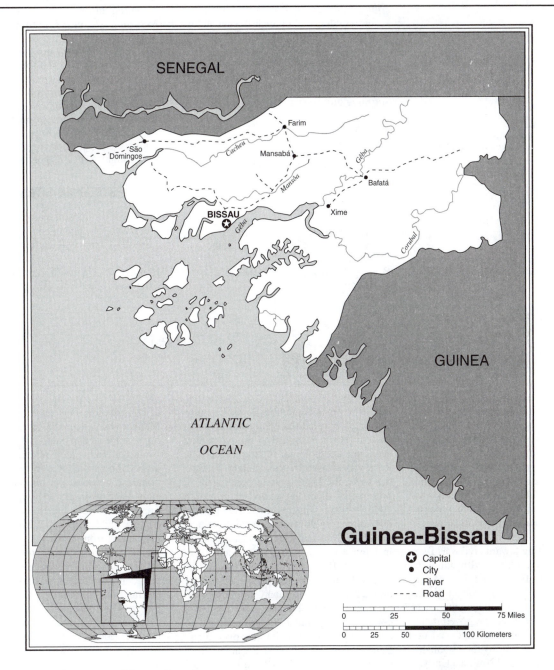

Guinea-Bissau Statistics

GEOGRAPHY

Area in Square Miles (Kilometers):
13,948 (36,125) (about 3 times the size of Connecticut)
Capital (Population): Bissau (292,000)
Environmental Concerns: soil erosion; deforestation; overgrazing; overfishing
Geographical Features: mostly low coastal plain, rising to savanna in the east
Climate: tropical

PEOPLE
Population

Total: 1,472,780
Annual Growth Rate: 2.1%
Rural/Urban Population Ratio: 77/23
Major Languages: Portuguese; Kriolo; various African languages
Ethnic Makeup: 30% Balanta; 20% Fula; 14% Manjaca; 13% Mandinka;

23% others (99% African; 1% others)
Religions: 50% indigenous beliefs; 45% Muslim; 5% Christian

Health

Life Expectancy at Birth: 45.4 years (male); 49 years (female)
Infant Mortality: 104/1,000 live births
Physicians Available: 1/9,477 people
HIV/AIDS Rate in Adults: 10%

Education

Adult Literacy Rate: 42.4%
Compulsory (Ages): 7–13

COMMUNICATION

Telephones: 10, 200 main lines; 95,000 cellular/mobile
Internet Users: 37,000

TRANSPORTATION

Highways in Miles (Kilometers): 2,610 (4,350)
Railroads in Miles (Kilometers): none
Usable Airfields: 24
Motor Vehicles in Use: 6,000

GOVERNMENT

Type: republic
Independence Date: September 10, 1974 (from Portugal)

Head of State/Government: President João Bernardo "Nino" Vieira; Prime Minister Martinho N'Dafa Cabi
Political Parties: African Party for the Independence of Guinea-Bissau and Cape Verde; Front for the Liberation and Independence of Guinea; United Social Democratic Party; Social Renovation Party; Democratic Convergence; others
Suffrage: universal at 18

MILITARY

Military Expenditures (% of GDP): 3.1%
Current Disputes: trouble along the border with Senegal

ECONOMY

Currency ($ U.S. Equivalent): 523 Communaute Financiere Africaine francs (XOF) = $1
Per Capita Income/GDP: $900/$1.2 billion
GDP Growth Rate: –7%
Inflation Rate: 4%
Labor Force by Occupation: 82% agriculture
Natural Resources: fish; timber; phosphates; bauxite; petroleum
Agriculture: corn; beans; cassava; cashew nuts; cotton; fish and forest products; peanuts; rice; palm kernels
Industry: agricultural-products processing; beverages
Exports: $116 million (primary partners India, Italy, South Korea)
Imports: $176 million (primary partners Portugal, Senegal, Thailand)

SUGGESTED WEB SITES

http://www.guineabissau.com
http://www.sas.upenn.edu/African_Studies/Country_Specific/G_Bissau.html
https://www.cia.gov/library/publications/the-world-factbook/geos/pu.html

Guinea-Bissau Country Report

In February 2000, Kumba Yala of the Social Renovation Party (PRS) took 72 percent of the vote in the second round of presidential elections, defeating the candidate of the former ruling African Party for the Independence of Guinea-Bissau and Cape Verde (PAIGC). Yala's election was the culmination of an 18-month process that brought a measure of political peace to the country, which in 1998 had appeared to be heading toward civil war. Two months of fighting, which had resulted in the displacement of up to one third of the country's population, was brought to an end in August 1998 with the signing of a cease-fire accord between the government and rebel soldiers. This was followed up in November of that year by the establishment of a "Government of National Unity," which presided over a transition to genuine multiparty politics.

DEVELOPMENT

With help from the UN Development Program, Guinea-Bissau has improved the tourism infrastructure of the 40-island Bijagos Archipelago in the hopes of bringing in much-needed revenues.

Yala's reign came to an end when he was ousted from the presidency in a bloodless military coup in September 2003. The military chief who led the coup said the move was, in part, a response to the worsening economic and political situation. Henrique Rosa was chosen by the military authorities to be the head of state pending fresh presidential elections, expected in March 2005. A businessman whose only previous involvement in politics had been his chairing of the National Elections Commission in Guinea-Bissau's first free elections in 1994, Mr. Rosa was at first reluctant to accept the post. He was persuaded to take on the role by the Roman Catholic Bishop of Bissau, Jose Camnate, who headed a committee appointed by the military to help set up a caretaker civilian government. Before taking up his post President Rosa said that he hoped to be a "guarantor of justice, freedom, and peace" for the people of Guinea-Bissau.

The Yala government faced the unenviable challenge of promoting economic development. Since independence, the country has consistently been listed as one of the world's 10 poorest countries. Unfortunately, the period since Yala's installation has been marred by continued political instability. Prior to the 2003 coup, there had been three other attempted coups, hundreds of lives lost in war and political violence, and the pulling out of the ruling coalition by one of the major partners due to lack of consultation. Former president General Mane was killed in 2000 after allegedly trying to stage a coup. Secretary-General Kofi Annan of the United Nations intervened to urge political dialogue in order to defuse domestic tensions. An International Monetary Fund team praised improvements in financial controls, but this came after the country had lost tens of millions of dollars in revenue from corrupt practices of government officials. Two prime ministers and the foreign minister were dismissed by the president for various failings. Meanwhile, the head of the Supreme Court and three judges were dismissed by Yala for allegedly overturning the presidents' decision to expel leaders of a Muslim sect from the country.

FREEDOM

The police have engaged in arbitrary arrests and torture. The fighting between government and rebel troops resulted in some 13,000 civilian casualties during the 1990s.

To many outsiders, the nation has been better known for its prolonged liberation war, from 1962 to 1974, against Portuguese colonial rule. Mobilized by the PAIGC, the freedom struggle in Guinea-Bissau played a major role in the overthrow of the Fascist dictatorship in Portugal itself and the liberation of its other African colonies.

The origins of Portuguese rule in Guinea-Bissau go back to the late 1400s. The area was raided for centuries as a source of slaves, who were shipped to Portugal and its colonies of Cape Verde and Brazil. With the nineteenth-century abolition of slave trading, the Portuguese began to impose forced labor within Guinea-Bissau itself.

In 1956, six *assimilados*—educated Africans who were officially judged to have assimilated Portuguese culture—led by Amilcar Cabral, founded the PAIGC as a vehicle for the liberation of Cape Verde as well as Guinea-Bissau. From the beginning, many Cape Verdeans, such as Cabral, played a prominent role within the PAIGC. But the group's largest following and main center of activity were in Guinea-Bissau. In 1963, the PAIGC turned to armed resistance and began organizing itself as an alternative government. By the end of the decade, the movement was in control of two thirds of the country. In those areas, the PAIGC was notably successful in establishing its own marketing, judicial, and educational as well as political institutions. Widespread participation throughout Guinea-Bissau in the 1973 election of a National Assembly encouraged a number of countries to formally recognize the PAIGC declaration of state sovereignty.

HEALTH/WELFARE

Guinea-Bissau's health statistics remain appalling: an overall 48-year life expectancy, 12% infant mortality, and more than 90% of the population infected with malaria.

INDEPENDENCE

Since 1974, the leaders of Guinea-Bissau have tried to confront the problems of independence while maintaining the idealism of their liberation struggle. The nation's weak economy has limited their success. Guinea-Bissau has little in the way of mining or manufacturing, although explorations have revealed potentially exploitable reserves of oil, bauxite, and phosphates. More than 80 percent of the people are engaged in agriculture, but urban populations depend on imported foodstuffs. This situation has been generally attributed to the poor infrastructure and a lack of

incentives for farmers to grow surpluses. Efforts to improve the rural economy during the early years of independence were hindered by severe drought. Only 8 percent of the small country's land is cultivated.

Under financial pressure, the government adopted a Structural Adjustment Program (SAP) in 1987. The peso was devalued, civil servants were dismissed, and various subsidies were reduced. The painful effects of these SAP reforms on urban workers were cushioned somewhat by external aid. Nonetheless, the country remains burdened by heavy foreign debt and relies heavily on international aid.

ACHIEVEMENTS

With Portuguese assistance, a new fiber-optic digital telephone system is being established in Guinea-Bissau.

In 1988, in a desperate move, the government signed an agreement with Intercontract Company, allowing the firm to use its territory for five years as a major dump site for toxic waste from Britain, Switzerland, and the United States. In return, the government was to earn up to $800 million. But the deal was revoked after it was exposed by members of the country's exiled opposition; a major environmental catastrophe would have resulted had it gone through.

POLITICAL DEVELOPMENT

Following the assassination of Amilcar Cabral, in 1973, his brother, Luis Cabral, succeeded him as the leader of the PAICG, thereafter becoming Guinea-Bissau's first president. Before 1980, both Guinea-Bissau and Cape Verde were separately governed by a united PAIGC, which had as its ultimate goal the forging of a political union between the two territories. But in 1980, Luis Cabral was overthrown by the military, which accused him of governing through a "Cape Verdean clique." João Vieira, a popular commander during the liberation war who had also served as prime minister, was appointed as the new head of state. As a result, relations between Cape Verde and Guinea-Bissau deteriorated, leading to a breakup in the political links between the two nations.

The PAIGC under Vieira continued to rule Guinea-Bissau as a one-party state

for 10 years. The system's grassroots democracy, which had been fostered in its liberated zones during the war, gave way to a centralization of power around Vieira and other members of his military-dominated Council of State. Several coup attempts resulted in increased authoritarianism.

But the government reversed course, and in 1991, the country formally adopted multipartyism. Progress has been slow. An alleged coup attempt in 1993 led to the detention and subsequent trial of a leading opposition figure, João da Costa, on charges of plotting the government's overthrow. Elections finally occurred in July 1994. The vote resulted in a narrow second-round victory for Vieira against a very divided opposition. In October 2005 Vieira was again elected president, succeeding Henrique Rosa.

Timeline: PAST

1446
Portuguese ships arrive; claimed as Portuguese Guinea; slave trading develops

1915
Portugal gains effective control over most of the region

1956
The African Party for the Independence of Guinea-Bissau and Cape Verde is formed

1963–1973
Liberation struggle in Guinea-Bissau under the PAIGC and Amilcar Cabral

1973
Amilcar Cabral is assassinated; the PAIGC declares Guinea-Bissau independent

1974
Revolution in Portugal leads to recognition of Guinea-Bissau's independence

1980
João Vieira comes to power through a military coup, ousting Luis Cabral

1990s
The country moves toward multipartyism; "Government of National Unity"

PRESENT

2000s
Kumba Yala of the Social Renovation (or Renewal) Party is elected president

Vieira re-elected president

Liberia (Republic of Liberia)

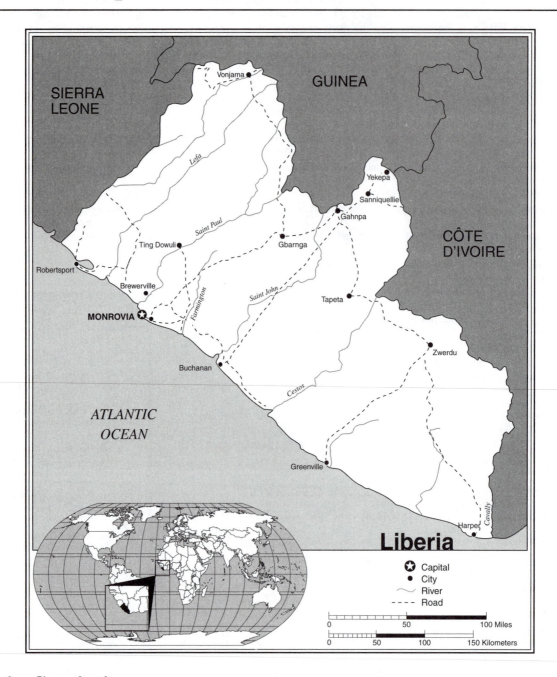

Liberia Statistics

GEOGRAPHY

Area in Square Miles (Kilometers): 43,000
(111,370) (about the size of Tennessee)
Capital (Population): Monrovia (491,000)
Environmental Concerns: soil erosion;
deforestation; loss of biodiversity;
water pollution
Geographical Features: mostly flat to rolling
coastal plains, rising to rolling plateau and
low mountains in the northeast
Climate: tropical

PEOPLE
Population

Total: 3,195,931
Annual Growth Rate: 4.8%
Rural/Urban Population Ratio: 56/44
Major Languages: English; Kpelle; Grio;
Kru; Krahn; others
Ethnic Makeup: 95% indigenous groups;
5% Americo-Liberian
Religions: 40% indigenous beliefs; 40%
Christian; 20% Muslim

Health

Life Expectancy at Birth: 38.9 years
(male); 41.9 years (female)
Infant Mortality: 149.7/1,000 live
births
Physicians Available: 1/8,333 people
HIV/AIDS Rate in Adults: 5.9%

Education

Adult Literacy Rate: 57.5%
Compulsory (Ages): 7–16; free

COMMUNICATION

Telephones: 6,900 main lines; 160,000 cellular/mobile
Daily Newspaper Circulation: 15/1,000 people
Televisions: 20/1,000 people
Internet Users: 1,000 (2002)

TRANSPORTATION

Highways in Miles (Kilometers): 6,180 (10,300)
Railroads in Miles (Kilometers): 306 (490)
Usable Airfields: 53
Motor Vehicles in Use: 28,000

GOVERNMENT

Type: republic
Independence Date: July 26, 1847
Head of State/Government: President Ellen Johnson-Sirleaf; Vice president Joseph Nyuma Boakai

Political Parties: National Patriotic Party; National Democratic Party of Liberia; Liberian Action Party; Liberian People's Party; United People's Party; others
Suffrage: universal at 18

MILITARY

Military Expenditures (% of GDP): 1.3%
Current Disputes: cross-border and regional refugee issues with Guinea, Sierra Leone, Côte d'Ivoire, and Ghana

ECONOMY

Currency ($ U.S. Equivalent): 59.4 Liberian dollar = $1 U.S.
Per Capita Income/GDP: $900/$2.8 billion
GDP Growth Rate: 7.8%
Inflation Rate: 15%
Unemployment Rate: 85%
Labor Force by Occupation: 70% agriculture; 22% services; 8% industry

Population Below Poverty Line: 80%
Natural Resources: iron ore; timber; diamonds; gold; hydropower
Agriculture: rubber; rice; palm oil; cassava; coffee; cocoa beans; sugarcane; bananas; sheep; goats; timber
Industry: rubber processing; food processing; diamonds
Exports: $910 million (primary partners Belgium, Germany, Italy)
Imports: $4.8 billion (primary partners France, South Korea, Japan)

SUGGESTED WEB SITES

http://www.fol.org
http://www.blackworld.com/country/liberia.htm
http://www.cia.gov/cia/publications/factbook/geos/li.html
https://www.cia.gov/library/publications/the-world-factbook/geos/li.html

Liberia Country Report

In August 2000, Liberian president Charles Taylor declared a state of emergency as fighting intensified in the north of the country. Since then, rebels calling themselves Liberians United for Reconciliation and Democracy (LURD) have made major advances against government forces. The excesses of President Taylor's troops, who are accused of pillaging the rural countryside, may have strengthened the rebels' hand. There has also been unrest in the urban areas, with Amnesty International accusing government security forces of brutally suppressing civilian protesters. In May 2001, the United Nations Security Council re-imposed an arms embargo on Liberia to punish Taylor for trading weapons for diamonds ("blood diamonds") from rebels in Sierra Leone.

DEVELOPMENT

Liberia's economic and social infrastructure was devastated by the war. Today people are surviving primarily through informal-sector bartering and trading.

Citing a reduced threat from rebels, the state of emergency was lifted in Liberia in September 2002. The rebels initiated a major offensive in March 2003, which ultimately led to the end of the Taylor administration. The rebels launched battles simultaneously on numerous fronts and moved to within 10 kilometers of the capital Monrovia. Throwing fuel upon the fire in the middle of Liberian peace negotiations taking place in Ghana, the high court in Sierra Leone issued an indictment accusing President Taylor of war crimes over his alleged backing of rebels in Sierra Leone (which had also earned Liberia two years of UN-imposed sanctions). In July, as fighting intensified around the capital, the West African regional group ECOWAS agreed to provide peacekeepers, arriving in August 2003 led by the Nigerians. Surprisingly, once the Nigerians were in the capital, Charles Taylor left the country for good. A transitional government—composed of rebel, government, and civil society groups—assumed control in October 2003. Chariman Gyunde Bryane was sworn in as head of the interim government. In 2005 Ellen Johnson-Sirleaf, a former finance minister who has worked for the UN and the World Bank, was formally elected president.

In December 2003 the UN launched a major peacekeeping mission, deploying thousands of troops in rebel-held territory, stating that their aim was to disarm former combatants. During February 2004 international donors pledged more than $500m in reconstruction aid, and the UN Security Council voted to freeze the assets of Charles Taylor. He is scheduled to be tried for war crimes at The Hague in 2008.

FREEDOM

The Taylor government has tried to reestablish the rule of law. The various government security forces continue to be linked to abuses. In 1998, Taylor accused rivals of plotting a coup and jeopardizing continued efforts to build postwar reconciliation in the country. In 2000, he declared a state of emergency when civil fighting intensified in the north of the country.

The LURD forces, who are said to be composed of veterans of past civil strife in Sierra Leone as well as Liberia, have also been accused of human-rights abuses. Their provisioning from among the general population certainly contributed to a rise in hunger in rebel-controlled areas, in northeastern Liberia.

The renewed violence in Liberia between 2000 and 2003 dashed the hopes of those who had believed that the country had achieved peace following the extreme horrors of the previous conflict. Between 1989 and 1996, some 200,000 people were killed. Among the survivors, approximately 750,000 fled the country as refugees, while another 1.2 million were internally displaced, out of a total population of only 2.6 million people. The war ended in July 1997 with Taylor and his National Patriotic Front of Liberia (NPFL) receiving about three quarters of

(United Nations photo 11233 by N. van Praag)

The Liberian Civil War of 1989–1996 left the country destitute. Political anarchy destroyed much of the infrastructure, economy, and culture. Nearly a tenth of the population were killed, many more displaced from their homes.

the vote in internationally supervised elections. These elections were the culmination of a year-long process to restore peace to the country. Taylor's subsequent inauguration brought stability to the country—but it is now under renewed threat.

The restoration of peace in Liberia after July 1997 was overseen by a West African regional military force (ECOMOG) of just over 10,000. The force was deployed throughout the country to provide the security, facilitate the disarmament and demobilization of local combatants, and protect returning refugees. Its relative success in carrying out these functions came about only after years of frustration. When the force finally withdrew in 1998, it left behind 10,000 to 25,000 locally fathered children. ECOMOG's security role was taken over by the reconstituted Armed Forces of Liberia, an uneasy mix of former civil-war rivals.

At present, the security situation in Liberia remains uncertain, and stability is maintained in large part due to the continuing presence of 15,000 UN peacekeeping troops. Efforts to repair the economy and infrastructure have, so far, been sluggish. Both of these create major challenges for current President Ellen Johnson-Sirleaf. Her election as the first democratically elected female president in Africa, however, is seen by many Liberians as an attempt to put the devastation of the civil war behind them. Johnson-Sirleaf has stated that rebuilding and reconciliation are the two primary goals of her administration.

AFRICAN-AMERICAN-AFRICANS

Among the African states, Liberia shares with Ethiopia the distinction of having avoided European rule. Between 1847 and 1980, Liberia was governed by an elite made up primarily of descendants of African-Americans who had begun settling along its coastline two decades earlier. These "Americo-Liberians" make up only 5 percent of the population. But they dominated politics for decades through their control of the governing True Whig Party (TWP). Although the republic's Constitution was ostensibly democratic, the TWP rigged the electoral process.

HEALTH/WELFARE

Outside aid and local self-help efforts were mobilized against famine in Liberia in 1990–1991. But the long and brutal Civil War of the 1990s took a dreadful toll on Liberians' health and well-being.

Most Liberians belong to indigenous ethnolinguistic groups, such as the Kpelle, Bassa, Grio, Kru, Krahn, and Vai, who were conquered by the Americo-Liberians during the 1800s and early 1900s. Some individuals from these subjugated communities accepted Americo-Liberian norms. Yet book learning, Christianity, and an ability to speak English helped an indigenous person to advance within the state only if he or she accepted its social hierarchy

by becoming a "client" of an Americo-Liberian "patron." In a special category were the important interior "chiefs," who were able to maintain their local authority as long as they remained loyal to the republic.

During the twentieth century, Liberia's economy was transformed by vast Firestone rubber plantations, iron-ore mining, and urbanization. President William Tubman (1944–1971) proclaimed a "Unification Policy," to promote national integration, and an "Open-Door Policy," to encourage outside investment in Liberia. However, most of the profits that resulted from the modest external investment that did occur left the country, while the wealth that remained was concentrated in the hands of the TWP elite.

During the administration of Tubman's successor, William Tolbert (1971–1980), Liberians became more conscious of the inability of the TWP to address the inequities of the status quo. Educated youths from all ethnic backgrounds began to join dissident associations rather than the regime's patronage system.

As economic conditions worsened, the top 4 percent of the population came to control 60 percent of the wealth. Rural stagnation drove many to the capital city of Monrovia (named after U.S. president James Monroe), where they suffered from high unemployment and inflation. The inevitable explosion occurred in 1979, when the government announced a 50 percent price increase for rice, the national food staple. Police fired on demonstrators, killing and wounding hundreds. Rioting, which resulted in great property damage, led the government to appeal to neighboring Guinea for troops. It was clear that the TWP was losing its grip. Thus Sergeant Samuel Doe enjoyed widespread support when, in 1980, he led a successful coup.

ACHIEVEMENTS

Through a shrewd policy of diplomacy, Liberia managed to maintain its independence when Great Britain and France conquered neighboring areas during the late nineteenth century. It espoused African causes during the colonial period; for instance, Liberia brought the case of Namibia to the World Court in the 1950s.

DOE DOESN'T DO

Doe came to power as Liberia's first indigenous president, a symbolically important event that many believed would herald substantive changes. Some institutions of the old order, such as the TWP and the

Masonic Temple (looked upon as Liberia's secret government) were disbanded. The House of Representatives and Senate were suspended. Offices changed hands, but the old administrative system persisted. Many of those who came to power were members of Doe's own ethnic group, the Krahn, who had long been prominent in the lower ranks of the army.

Doe declared a narrow victory for himself in the October 1985 elections, but there was widespread evidence of ballot tampering. A month later, exiled general Thomas Quiwonkpa led an abortive coup attempt. During and after the uprising, thousands of people were killed, mostly civilians belonging to Quiwonkpa's Grio group who were slaughtered by loyalist (largely Krahn) troops. Doe was inaugurated, but opposition-party members refused to take their seats in the National Assembly. Some, fearing for their lives, went into exile.

During the late 1980s, Doe became increasingly dictatorial. Many called on the U.S. government, in particular, to withhold aid until detainees were freed and new elections held. The U.S. Congress criticized the regime but authorized more than $500 million in financial and military support. Meanwhile, Liberia suffered from a shrinking economy and a growing foreign debt, which by 1987 had reached $1.6 billion.

Doe's government was not entirely to blame for Liberia's dire financial condition. When Doe came to power, the Liberian treasury was already empty, in large part due to the vast expenditures incurred by the previous administration in hosting the 1979 Organization of African Unity Conference. The rising cost of oil and decline in world prices for natural rubber, iron ore, and sugar had further crippled the economy. But government corruption and instability under Doe made the bad situation worse.

DOE'S DOWNFALL

Liberia's descent into violent anarchy began on December 24, 1989, when a small group of insurgents, led by Charles Taylor, who had earlier fled the country amid corruption charges, began a campaign to overthrow Doe. As Taylor's NPFL rebels gained ground, the war developed into an increasingly vicious interethnic struggle among groups who had been either victimized by or associated with the regime. Thousands of civilians were thus massacred by ill-disciplined gunmen on both sides; hundreds of thousands began to flee for their lives. By June 1990, with the rump of Doe's forces besieged in Monrovia, a small but efficient breakaway armed faction of the NPFL, under the ruthless leadership of a former soldier named Prince Johnson, had emerged as a deadly third force.

By August, with the United States unwilling to do more than evacuate foreign nationals from Monrovia (the troops of Doe, Johnson, and Taylor had begun kidnapping expatriates and violating diplomatic immunity), members of the Economic Community of West African States decided to establish a framework for peace by installing an interim government, with the support of the regional peacekeeping force known as ECOMOG: the ECOWAS Monitoring Group. The predominantly Nigerian force, which also included contingents from Ghana, Guinea, Sierra Leone, The Gambia, and, later, Senegal, landed in Monrovia in late August. This coincided with the nomination, by a broad-based but NPFL–boy-cotted National Conference, of Amos Sawyer, a respected academic, as the head of the proposed interim administration.

Initial hopes that ECOMOG's presence would end the fighting proved to be naïve. On September 9, 1990, Johnson captured Doe by shooting his way into ECOMOG headquarters. The following day, Doe's gruesome torture and execution were videotaped by his captors. This "outrage for an outrage" did not end the suffering. Protected by a reinforced ECOMOG, Sawyer was able to establish his interim authority over most of Monrovia, but the rest of the country remained in the hands of the NPFL or of local thugs.

Repeated attempts to get Johnson and Taylor to cooperate with Sawyer in establishing an environment conducive to holding elections proved fruitless. While most neighboring states have supported ECOMOG's mediation efforts, some have provided support (and, in the case of Burkina Faso, troops) to the NPFL, which has encouraged Taylor in his on-again, off-again approach toward national reconciliation.

In September 1991, a new, fiercely anti-NPFL force, the United Liberation Movement of Liberia (ULIMO), emerged from bases in Sierra Leone. The group is identified with former Doe supporters. Subsequent clashes between ULIMO and NPFL on both sides of the Liberian–Sierra Leonean border contributed to the April 1992 overthrow of the Sierra Leonean government as well as the failure of an October 1991 peace accord brokered by the Côte d'Ivoire's then-president, Felix Houphouët-Boigny.

In October 1992, ECOWAS agreed to impose sanctions on the NPFL for blocking Monrovia. ECOMOG then joined ULIMO and remnants of the Armed Forces of Liberia (AFL) in a counteroffensive. In 1993, yet another armed faction, the Liberia Peace Council (LPC), emerged to challenge Taylor for control of southeastern Liberia. In March 1994, an all-party interim State Council, agreed to in principle eight months earlier, was finally sworn in. But it quickly collapsed, while a violent split in ULIMO contributed to further anarchy. In July 2002, UN secretary-general Kofi Annan warned that the Liberian conflict threatens the United Nations' peacekeeping work in neighboring countries.

Timeline: PAST

1500s
The Vai move onto the Liberian coast from the interior

1822
The first African-American settlers arrive from the United States

1871
The first coup exchanges one Americo-Liberian government for another

1931
The League of Nations investigates forced-labor charges

1944
President William Tubman comes to office

1971
William Tolbert becomes president

1980s
Tolbert is assassinated; a military coup brings Samuel Doe to power

1990s
Civil war leads to the execution of Doe, anarchy, and foreign intervention; Charles Taylor and the NPFL win power in internationally supervised elections; the Civil War ends

PRESENT

2000s
President Taylor declares a state of emergency

Civil war resumes

President Taylor steps down and is indicted for war crimes

Ellen Johnson-Sirleaf elected president

Mali (Republic of Mali)

Mali Statistics

GEOGRAPHY

Area in Square Miles (Kilometers):
478,819 (1,240,142) (about twice the size of Texas)

Capital (Population): Bamako (1,161,000)

Environmental Concerns: soil erosion; deforestation; desertification; insufficient potable water; poaching

Geographical Features: mostly flat to rolling northern plains covered by sand; savanna in the south; rugged hills in the northeast

Climate: subtropical to arid

PEOPLE

Population

Total: 11,995,402
Annual Growth Rate: 2.68%
Rural/Urban Population Ratio: 71/29
Major Languages: French; Bambara; numerous African languages

Ethnic Makeup: 50% Mande; 17% Peul; 12% Voltaic; 6% Songhai; 10% Tuareg and Maur (Moor); 5% others

Religions: 90% Muslim; 9% indigenous beliefs; 1% Christian

Health

Life Expectancy at Birth: 47.6 years (male); 51.5 years (female)
Infant Mortality: 105.7/1,000 live births
Physicians Available: 1/18,376 people
HIV/AIDS Rate in Adults: 1.9%

Education

Adult Literacy Rate: 46.4%
Compulsory (Ages): 7–16; free

COMMUNICATION

Telephones: 75,000 main lines; 869,600 cellular/mobile
Televisions: 12/1,000 people
Internet Users: 70,000

TRANSPORTATION

Highways in Miles (Kilometers): 9,362 (15,100)
Railroads in Miles (Kilometers): 452 (729)
Usable Airfields: 27
Motor Vehicles in Use: 41,000

GOVERNMENT

Type: republic
Independence Date: September 22, 1960 (from France)

Head of State/Government: President Amadou Toumani Touré; Prime Minister Modibo Sidibe
Political Parties: Alliance for Democracy; National Congress for Democratic Initiative; Sudanese Union/African Democratic Rally; others
Suffrage: universal at 18

MILITARY

Military Expenditures (% of GDP): 1.9%
Current Disputes: none

ECONOMY

Currency ($ U.S. Equivalent): 523 CFA francs = $1
Per Capita Income/GDP: $1,300/$14.8 billion
GDP Growth Rate: 5.1%
Inflation Rate: 4.5%
Unemployment Rate: 14.6% in urban areas

Labor Force by Occupation: 80% agriculture and fishing
Population Below Poverty Line: 64%
Natural Resources: hydropower; bauxite; iron ore; manganese; tin; phosphates; kaolin; salt; limestone; gold; uranium; copper
Agriculture: millet; sorghum; corn; rice; sugar; cotton; peanuts; livestock
Industry: food processing; construction; phosphate and gold mining; consumer-goods production
Exports: $323 million (primary partners Brazil, South Korea, Italy)
Imports: $1.85 billion (primary partners Côte d'Ivoire, France, Senegal)

SUGGESTED WEB SITES

http://www.maliembassy-usa.org
https://www.cia.gov/library/publications/the-world-factbook/geos/ml.html

Mali Country Report

Amadou Toumani Touré, the army general credited with rescuing Mali from military dictatorship and handing it back to its people, won the presidential elections of May 2002. He entered office on a program of anticorruption, peace, and development aimed at alleviation of poverty. This program resonated strongly with the population because corruption was viewed as rampant. In July 2000, an anticorruption commission published a report highlighting embezzlement and mismanagement within a number of state-owned companies and other public bodies.

DEVELOPMENT

In 1989, the government received international funding to overhaul its energy infrastructure. The opening of new gold mines has provided the economy with a boost.

Touré will be building on the legacy of his immediate predecessor, Dr. Alpha Konare, who stepped down from power after two terms in office that moved Mali away from its authoritarian past. The current democratic order was inaugurated a year after a coup led by Touré ended the dictatorial regime of Moussa Traoré. Like his predecessor, Modibo Keita (the first president of Mali), Traoré had governed Mali as a single-party state. True to their word, the coup leaders who seized power in 1991 following bloody antigovernment riots presided over a quick transition to civilian rule.

FREEDOM

The human-rights situation in Mali has improved in recent years, though international attention was drawn to the suppression of opposition demonstrations in the run-up to the 1997 elections.

Konare ruled as an activist scholar who, like many Malians, found political inspiration in his country's rich heritage. But his efforts to rebuild Mali were hampered by a weak economy, aggravated by the 1994 collapse in value of the CFA franc. In 1994 and 1995, violence occurred between security forces and university students protesting against economic hardship. The plight of Malian economic refugees in France gained international attention in 1996, when a number sought sanctuary in a Parisian church and went on a hunger strike in protest against attempts to deport them. The government has enjoyed greater success in reaching a

(still fragile) settlement with Tuareg rebels in the country's far north.

AN IMPERIAL PAST

The published epic of Sundiata Keita, the thirteenth-century A.D. founder of the great Mali Empire, is recognized throughout the world as a masterpiece of classical African literature. In Mali itself, Sundiata remains a source of national pride and unity.

HEALTH/WELFARE

About a third of Mali's budget is devoted to education. A special literacy program in Mali teaches rural people how to read and write, by using booklets that concern fertilizers, measles, and measuring fields.

Sundiata's state was one of three great West African empires whose centers lay in modern Mali. Between the fourth and thirteenth centuries, the area was the site of the prosperous, ancient Ghana. The Mali Empire was superseded by that of Songhai, which was conquered by the Moroccans at the end of the sixteenth century. All these empires were in fact confederations. Although they encompassed vast areas united under a single supreme ruler, local communities generally enjoyed a great deal of autonomy.

ACHIEVEMENTS

For centuries, the ancient Malian city of Timbuctu was a leading center of Islamic learning and culture. Chronicles published by its scholars of the Middle Ages still enrich local culture.

From the 1890s until 1960, another form of imperial unity was imposed over Mali (then called French Sudan) and the adjacent territories of French West Africa. The legacy of broader colonial and precolonial unity as well as its landlocked position have inspired Mali's postcolonial leaders to seek closer ties with neighboring countries.

Mali formed a brief confederation with Senegal during the transition period to independence. This initial union broke down after only a few months, but since then the two countries have cooperated in the Organization for the Development of the Senegal River and other regional groupings. The Senegalese port of Dakar, which is linked by rail to Mali's capital city, Bamako, remains the major outlet for Malian exports. Mali has also sought to strengthen its ties with nearby Guinea. In 1983, the two countries signed an agreement to harmonize policies and structures.

ENVIRONMENTAL CHALLENGES

Mali is one of the poorest countries in the world. About 80 percent of the people are employed in (mostly subsistence) agriculture and fishing, but the government usually has to rely on international aid to make up for local food deficits. Most of the country lies within either the expanding Sahara Desert or the semiarid region known as the Sahel, which has become drier as a result of recurrent drought. Much of the best land lies along the Senegal and Niger Rivers, which support most of the nation's agropastoral production. In earlier centuries, the Niger was able to sustain great trading cities such as Timbuctu and Djenne, but today, most of its banks do not even support crops. Efforts to increase cultivation have so far been met with limited overall success.

Mali's frequent inability to feed itself has been largely blamed on locust infestation, drought, and desertification. The inefficient state-run marketing and distribution systems, however, have also had a negative impact. Low official produce prices have encouraged farmers either to engage in subsistence agriculture or to sell their crops on the black market. Thus, while some regions of the country remain dependent on international food donations, crops continue to be smuggled across Mali's borders. Recent policy commitments to liberalize agricultural trading, as part of an International Monetary Funding–approved Structural Adjustment Program (SAP), have yet to take hold.

In contrast to agriculture, Mali's mining sector has experienced promising growth. The nation exports modest amounts of gold, phosphates, marble, and uranium. Potentially exploitable deposits of bauxite, manganese, iron, tin, and diamonds exist. The Manantali Dam in southwestern Mali opened in December 2001. It is expected to provide electricity and jobs for thousands of Malians.

For decades, Mali was officially committed to state socialism. Its first president, Keita, a descendant of Sundiata, established a command economy and one-party state during the 1960s. His attempt to go it alone outside the CFA Franc Zone proved to be a major failure. Under Traoré, socialist structures were modified but not abandoned. Agreements with the IMF ended some government monopolies, and the country adopted the CFA franc as its currency. But the lack of a significant class of private entrepreneurs and the role of otherwise unprofitable public enterprises in providing employment discouraged radical privatization.

MALI, MUSIC, AND THE WORLD

In recent years, Malian musicians have dominated African music on the world stage. The country has produced more internationally known pop musicians than any other African country. Performers include artists such as Salief Keita, Hebib Kaite, Nanou Cool, and Amadou and Miriam. Their styles are a mixture of both contemporary and traditional sounds that transcend traditional ethnic boundaries. Each January, Mali annually hosts the "Festival in the Desert" music festival at the Essakane Oasis.

Timeline: PAST

1250–1400s
The Mali Empire extends over much of the upper regions of West Africa

late 1400s–late 1500s
The Songhai Empire controls the region

1890
The French establish control over Mali

1960
The Mali Confederation

1968
Moussa Traoré and the Military Committee for National Liberation grab power

1979
Traoré's Democratic Union of the Malian People is the single ruling party

1979–1980
School strikes and demonstrations; teachers and students are detained

1990s
The country's first multiparty elections are held; economic problems stir civic unrest

PRESENT

2000s
The Touré government explores ways to strengthen the economy

Ousmane Issoufi Maiga appointed Prime Minister

Mauritania (Islamic Republic of Mauritania)

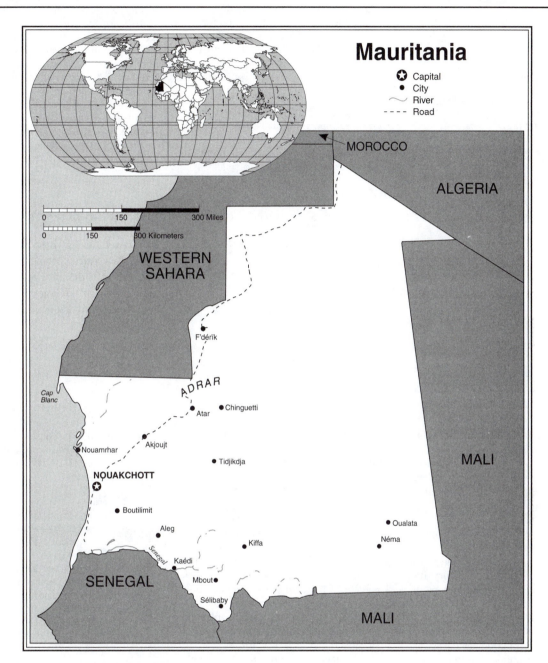

Mauritania Statistics

GEOGRAPHY

Area in Square Miles (Kilometers):
398,000 (1,030,700) (about 3 times the size of New Mexico)
Capital (Population): Nouakchott (626,000)
Environmental Concerns: overgrazing; deforestation; soil erosion; desertification; very limited natural freshwater resources; overfishing

Geographical Features: mostly barren, flat plains of the Sahara; some central hills
Climate: desert

PEOPLE

Population

Total: 3,270,065
Annual Growth Rate: 2.87%

Rural/Urban Population Ratio: 44/56
Major Languages: Hasanixa; Soninke; Arabic; Pular; Wolof
Ethnic Makeup: 40% mixed Maur/black; perhaps 30% Maur; 30% black
Religion: 100% Muslim

Health

Life Expectancy at Birth: 51 years (male); 56 years (female)

Infant Mortality: 68.1/1,000 live births
Physicians Available: 1/11,085 people
HIV/AIDS Rate in Adults: 0.6%

Education

Adult Literacy Rate: 51.2%
Compulsory (Ages): 6–12

COMMUNICATION

Telephones: 34,900 main lines; 1,060,000 cellular/mobile
Internet Users: 100,000

TRANSPORTATION

Highways in Miles (Kilometers): 4,560 (7,600)
Railroads in Miles (Kilometers): 439 (717)
Usable Airfields: 25
Motor Vehicles in Use: 26,500

GOVERNMENT

Type: republic
Independence Date: November 28, 1960 (from France)

Head of State/Government: President Sidi Ould Cheikh Abdallahi; Prime Minister Zeine Ould Zeidane
Political Parties: Democratic and Social Republican Party; Union for Democracy and Progress; Popular Social and Democratic Union; others
Suffrage: universal at 18

MILITARY

Military Expenditures (% of GDP): 5.5%
Current Disputes: internal ethnic tensions; friction with Senegal over use of the Senegal River; inactive claim to Western Sahara

ECONOMY

Currency ($ U.S. equivalent): 271 ouguiyas = $1
Per Capita Income/GDP: $2,600/$8.1 billion
GDP Growth Rate: 14.1%
Inflation Rate: 7%
Unemployment Rate: 20%
Labor Force by Occupation:

50% agriculture; 40% services; 10% industry
Population Below Poverty Line: 50%
Natural Resources: iron ore; gypsum; fish; copper; phosphates
Agriculture: millet; sorghum; dates; root crops; cattle and sheep; fish products
Industry: iron-ore and gypsum mining; fish processing
Exports: $784 million (primary partners France, Japan, Italy)
Imports: $1.12 billion (primary partners France, United States, Spain)

SUGGESTED WEB SITE

http://www.state.gov/r/pa/ei/bgn/5467.htm
http://www.africa.upenn.edu/Country_ Specific/Mauritania.html
https://www.cia.gov/library/publications/ the-world-factbook/geos/mr.html

Mauritania Country Report

Since the adoption of its current Constitution in 1991, Mauritania has legally been a multiparty democracy. But in practice, power remains in the hand of President Ould Taya's Republican Social Democratic Party (PRDS). The ruling party won large majorities in the 1992 and 1997 elections, which were boycotted by the leading opposition groupings. Participation in the 2001 elections resulted in some opposition gains but yet another controversial victory for the PRDS. Action for Change, a new party claiming to represent the Haratine (or Harratin), Mauritania's Arab-oriented black underclass of ex-slaves, won four seats. But in the beginning of 2002, the party was banned. Multiparty politics has thus so far failed to assure either social harmony or a respect for human rights. Neither has it resolved the country's severe social and economic problems.

DEVELOPMENT

Mauritania's coastal waters are among the richest in the world. During the 1980s, the local fishing industry grew at an average annual rate of more than 10%. Many now believe that the annual catch has reached the upper levels of its sustainable potential.

Amidst allegations of fraud President Taya won the elections of November 2003 with more than 67% of the votes during the first round. There were attempted coups during June 2003 and August and September 2004. Although each of the three coups failed, there is always the possibility that a future coup might succeed.

For decades, Mauritania has grown progressively drier. Today, about 75 percent of the country is covered by sand. Less than 1 percent of the land is suitable for cultivation, 10 percent for grazing. To make matters worse, the surviving arable and pastoral areas have been plagued by grasshoppers and locusts.

In the face of natural disaster, people have moved. Since the mid-1960s, the percentage of urban dwellers has swelled, from less than 10 percent to 53 percent, while the nomadic population during the same period has dropped, from more than 80 percent to perhaps 20 percent. In Nouakchott, the capital city, vast shanty-towns now house nearly a quarter of the population. As the capital has grown, from a few thousand to 626,000 in a single generation, its poverty—and that of the nation as a whole—has become more obvious. People seek new ways to make a living away from the land, but there are few jobs. The best hope for lifting up the economy may lie

in offshore oil exploration. A prospecting report in 2002 has attracted the interest of major international oil companies.

FREEDOM

The Mauritanian government is especially sensitive to continuing allegations of the existence of chattel slavery in the country. While slavery is outlawed, there is credible evidence of its continued existence. In 1998, five members of a local advocacy group SOS–Esclaves (Slaves) were sentenced to 13 months' imprisonment for "activities within a non-authorized organization."

Mauritania's heretofore faltering economy has coincided with an increase in racial and ethnic tensions. Since independence, the government has been dominated by the Maurs (or Moors), who speak Hasaniya Arabic. This community has historically been divided between the aristocrats and commoners, of Arab and Berber origin, and the Haratine, who were black African slaves who had assimilated Maurish culture but remain socially segregated. Including the Haratine, the Maurs account for perhaps 60 percent of the citizenry (the government has refused to release comprehensive data from the last two censuses).

The other half of Mauritania's population is composed of the "blacks," who mostly speak Pulaar, Soninke, or Wolof. Like the Maurs, all these groups are Muslim. Thus Mauritania's rulers have stressed Islam as a source of national unity. The country proclaimed itself an Islamic republic at independence, and since 1980 the Shari'a—the Islamic penal code—has been the law of the land.

Muslim brotherhood has not been able to overcome the divisions between the northern Maurs and southern blacks. One major source of friction has been official Arabization efforts, which are opposed by most southerners. In recent years, the country's desertification has created new sources of tension. As their pastures turned to sand, many of the Maurish nomads who did not find refuge in the urban areas moved southward. There, with state support, they began in the 1980s to deprive southerners of their land.

HEALTH/WELFARE

There have been some modest improvements in the areas of health and education since the country's independence, but conditions remain poor. Mauritania has received low marks regarding its commitment to human development.

Oppression of blacks has been met with resistance from the underground Front for the Liberation of Africans in Mauritania (FLAM). Black grievances were also linked to an unsuccessful coup attempt in 1987. In 1989, interethnic hostility exploded when a border dispute with Senegal led to race riots

that left several hundred "Senegalese" dead in Nouakchott. In response, the "Moorish" trading community in Senegal became the target of reprisals. Mauritania claimed that 10,000 Maurs were killed, but other sources put the number at about 70. Following this bloodshed, more than 100,000 refugees were repatriated across both sides of the border. Mass deportations of "Mauritanians of Senegalese origin" have fueled charges that the Nouakchott regime is trying to eliminate its non-Maurish population.

ACHIEVEMENTS

There is a current project to restore ancient Mauritanian cities, such as Chinguette, which are located on traditional routes from North Africa to Sudan. These centers of trade and Islamic learning were points of origin for the pilgrimage to Mecca and were well known in the Middle East.

Tensions between Mauritania and Senegal were eased in June 2000 by the newly elected Senegalese president Abdoulaye Wade. This helped to reduce cross-border raids by deported Mauritanians. Genuine peace, however, will require greater reform within Mauritania itself and provision for the return of refugees.

A bloodless coup deposed the long-ruling President Taya in 2005, replacing him with a military council that stated its intention was to prepare the country for a democratically elected government in two years' time. Accordingly, elections were held in 2007, and Sidi Ould Cheikh Abdallahi became Mauritania's first democratically elected president (in what were considered

fair elections) since the country gained independence from France in 1960.

Timeline: PAST

1035–1055
The Almoravids spread Islam in the Western Sahara areas through conquest

1920
The Mauritanian area becomes a French colony

1960
Mauritania becomes independent under President Moktar Ould Daddah

1978
A military coup brings Khouma Ould Haidalla and the Military Committee for National Recovery to power

1979
The Algiers Agreement: Mauritania makes peace with Polisario and abandons claims to Western Sahara

1980
Slavery is formally abolished

1990s
Multiparty elections are boycotted by the opposition; tensions continue between Mauritania and Senegal

PRESENT

2000s
Desertification takes its toll on the environment and the economy

It is estimated that 90,000 Mauritanians still live in servitude, despite the legal abolishment of slavery

Senegal and Mauritania seek better relations

Sidi Ould Cheikh Abdallahi is elected president

Niger (Republic of Niger)

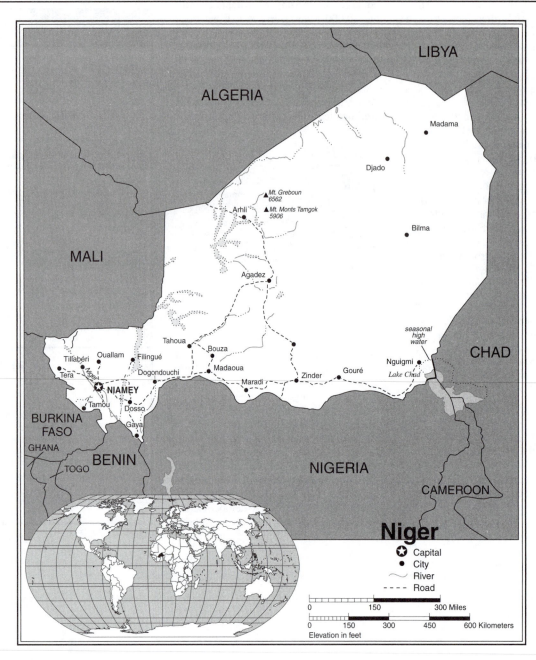

Niger Statistics

GEOGRAPHY

Area in Square Miles (Kilometers):
489,191 (1,267,000) (about twice the size of Texas)
Capital (Population): Niamey (821,000)
Environmental Concerns: overgrazing; deforestation; soil erosion; desertification; poaching and habitat destruction
Geographical Features: mainly desert plains and sand dunes; flat to rolling plains in the south; hills in the north; landlocked
Climate: desert; tropical in the extreme south

PEOPLE

Population

Total: 12,894,865
Annual Growth Rate: 2.90%
Rural/Urban Population Ratio: 80/20
Major Languages: French; Hausa; Djerma
Ethnic Makeup: 56% Hausa; 22% Djerma; 8% Fula; 8% Tuareg; 6% others
Religions: 80% Muslim; 20% indigenous beliefs and Christian

Health

Life Expectancy at Birth: 44 years (male); 44 years (female)
Infant Mortality: 122/1,000 live births

Physicians Available: 1/35,141 people
HIV/AIDS Rate in Adults: 1.2%

Education

Adult Literacy Rate: 28.7%
Compulsory (Ages): 7–15, free

COMMUNICATION

Telephones: 34,900 main lines; 1,060,000 cellular/mobile
Televisions: 2.8 per 1,000 people
Internet Users: 40,000 (2006)

TRANSPORTATION

Highways in Miles (Kilometers): 6,262 (10,100)
Railroads in Miles (Kilometers): none
Usable Airfields: 28
Motor Vehicles in Use: 51,500

GOVERNMENT

Type: republic
Independence Date: August 3, 1960 (from France)

Head of State/Government: President Mamadou Tandja is both head of state and head of government
Political Parties: National Movement for a Developing Society–Nassara; Democratic and Social Convention–Rahama; Nigerien Party for Democracy and Socialism–Tarayya; Nigerien Alliance for Democracy and Social Progress–Zaman-lahia; others
Suffrage: universal at 18

MILITARY

Military Expenditures (% of GDP): 1.3%
Current Disputes: territorial dispute with Libya; boundary disputes over Lake Chad; poorly defined boundary with Benin

ECONOMY

Currency ($ U.S. Equivalent): 581 CFA francs = $1
Per Capita Income/GDP: $1,000/$12.4 billion

GDP Growth Rate: 3.5%
Inflation Rate: 0.2%
Labor Force by Occupation: 90% agriculture; 6% industry and commerce; 4% government
Population Below Poverty Line: 63%
Natural Resources: uranium; coal; iron ore; tin; phosphates; gold; petroleum
Agriculture: millet; sorghum; peanuts; cotton; cowpeas; cassava; livestock
Industry: cement; brick; textiles; chemicals; agricultural products; food processing; uranium mining
Exports: $222 million (primary partners France, Nigeria, Spain)
Imports: $588 million (primary partners France, Côte d'Ivoire, United States)

SUGGESTED WEB SITES

http://www.friendsofniger.org
http://www.cia.gov/library/publications/the-world-factbook/geos/ng.html

Niger Country Report

Niger is ranked by the United Nations as the world's second-poorest country, after war-ravaged Sierra Leone. This circumstance can in part be blamed on poor governance. For most of the past four decades, since it gained independence from France in 1960, Niger has been governed by a succession of military regimes that have left it bankrupt. This has led to chronic instability, as the government has regularly failed to pay its salaries, resulting in strikes by civil servants and mutinies by soldiers. In November 1999, the current president, Mamadou Tandja, was elected under a new Constitution. But ultimate power remains in the hands of the military, which, in January 1996, overthrew Niger's last elected government. In July 1996, the leader of the coup, Colonel Ibrahim Bare Mainassara, claimed victory in elections that were widely condemned as fraudulent. Mainassara's subsequent assassination in April 1999 opened the door to a return to civilian rule, but at this writing, a military committee under strongman Major Daouda Mallam-Wanke continues to wield influence over the government.

DROUGHT AND DESERTIFICATION

Most Nigeriens subsist through small-scale crop production and herding. Yet farming is especially difficult in Niger. Less than 10 percent of the nation's vast territory is suitable for cultivation even during the best of times. Most of the cultivable land lies along the banks of the Niger River. Unfortunately, much of the past four decades has been the worst of times. During this period, Nigeriens have been constantly challenged by recurrent drought and an ongoing process of desertification.

DEVELOPMENT

Nigerien village cooperatives, especially marketing cooperatives, predate independence and have grown in size and importance in recent years. They have successfully competed with well-to-do private traders for control of the grain market. In September 2004 the Nigerien government granted gold mining permits to a number of European nations in an effort to increase gold mining and production.

Drought had an especially catastrophic effect during the 1970s. Most Nigeriens were reduced to dependency on foreign food aid, while about 60 percent of their livestock perished. Some people believe that the ecological disaster that afflicted Africa's Sahel region (which includes southern Niger) during that period was of such severity as to disrupt the delicate long-term balance between desert and savanna. Others, however, have concluded that the intensified desertification of recent years is primarily rooted in human, rather than natural, causes, which can be reversed. In particular, many attribute environmental degradation to the introduction of inappropriate forms of cultivation, overgrazing, deforestation, and new patterns of human settlement.

FREEDOM

Nigeriens have been effectively disenfranchised by the 1996 coup and subsequent fraudulent presidential election. Security forces are known to beat and intimidate opposition political figures. The private media are a target of repression, with a number of journalists having been detained. Opposition meetings and demonstrations are often banned.

Ironically, much of the debate on people's negative impact on the Sahel environment has been focused on some of the agricultural-development schemes that once were perceived as the region's salvation. In their attempts to boost local food production, international aid agencies often promoted so-called Green Revolution programs. These were designed to increase per-acre yields, typically through the intensive planting of new seeds and reliance on imported fertilizers and pesticides. Such projects often led to higher initial local outputs that proved unsustainable, largely due to expensive overhead. In addition, many experts promoting the new agricultural techniques failed to appreciate the value of traditional technologies and forms of social organization in limiting desertification while allowing people to cope with drought. It is now appreciated that patterns of cultivation long championed by Nigerien farmers allowed for soil conservation and reduced the risks associated with pests and poor climate.

HEALTH/WELFARE

A national conference on educational reform stimulated a program to use Nigerien languages in primary education and integrated the adult literacy program into the rural development efforts. The National Training Center for Literacy Agents is crucial to literacy efforts.

The government's recent emphasis has been on helping Niger's farmers to help themselves through the extension of credit, better guaranteed minimum prices, and improved communications. Vigorous efforts have been made in certain regions to halt the spread of desert sands by supporting village tree-planting campaigns. Given the local inevitability of drought, the government has also increased its commitment to the stockpiling of food in granaries. But for social and political as much as economic reasons, government policy has continued to discourage the flexible, nomadic pattern of life that has long characterized many Nigerien communities.

The Nigerien government's emphasis on agriculture has, in part, been motivated by the realization that the nation could not rely on its immense uranium deposits for future development. The opening of uranium mines in the 1970s resulted in the country becoming the world's fifth-largest producer. By the end of that decade, uranium exports accounted for some 90 percent of Niger's foreign-exchange earnings. Depressed international demand throughout the 1980s, however, resulted in substantially reduced prices and output. Although uranium still accounts for 75 percent of foreign-exchange earnings, its revenue contribution in recent years is only about a third of what it was prior to the slump.

The uranium production has in recent years led to some controversy. In January 2003 U.S. President George W. Bush claimed

that Iraq tried to acquire uranium from Niger for its nuclear program. This claim was also made in the United Kingdom in a September 2002 dossier on Iraq. Both the United States and the United Kingdom's claims, however, were proven to be unfounded. In March 2003 the Nuclear Regulatory Agency informed the UN that documents relating to the Iraq-Niger uranium claim were forged.

MILITARY RULE

For nearly half of its existence after its independence, Niger was governed by a civilian administration, under President Hamani Diori. In 1974, during the height of drought, Lieutenant Colonel Seyni Kountché took power in a bloodless coup. Kountché ruled as the leader of a "Supreme Military Council," which met behind closed doors. Ministerial portfolios, appointed by the president, were filled by civilians as well as military personnel. In 1987, Kountché died of natural causes and was succeeded by Colonel Ali Saibou.

ACHIEVEMENTS

Niger has consistently demonstrated a strong commitment to the preservation and development of its national cultures through its media and educational institutions, the National Museum, and events such as the annual youth festival at Agades.

The National Movement for the Development of Society (MNSD) was established in 1989 as the country's sole political party, after a constitutional referendum in which less than 4 percent of the electorate participated. But, as was the case in many other countries in Africa, the year 1990 saw a groundswell of local support for a return to multipartyism. In Niger, this prodemocracy agitation was spearheaded by the nation's labor confederation, which organized a widely observed 48-hour general strike. Having earlier rejected the strikers "as a handful of demagogues," in 1991, President Saibou agreed to the formation of a National Conference to prepare a new constitution.

The conference ended its deliberations with the appointment of an interim government, headed by Amadou Cheffou, which led the country to multiparty elections in February–March 1993. After two rounds of voting, the presidential contest was won by Mahamane Ousmane. Ousmane's Alliance of Forces for Change (AFC) opposition captured 50 seats in the new 83-seat National Assembly, while the MNSD became the major opposition party, with 29 seats.

Ousmane's government made a promising start by reaching peace agreements with two rebel movements, the Tuareg Front for

the Liberation of Air and Azaouad and the Organization of Army Resistance. But the nation's economic crisis deepened with the 1994 devaluation of the CFA franc. Naturally, Ousmane's political status was weakened. In February 1995, the opposition coalition, led by Hama Amadou, gained control of the National Assembly, resulting in an uneasy government of "cohabitation." Serious student unrest was followed by the military coup in January 1996 that resulted in the installation of Colonel Ibrahim Bare Mainassara as president. The current president is former military man Mamadou Tandja, elected in 1999 and then re-elected in 2004 under a new constitution. Although democratically elected, his ties to the military remain strong.

In 2007, a Tuareg insurgency began in northern Niger under the leadership of the MNJ (Niger Movement for Justice). The insurgency represents a flare-up of the dispute that was never fully resolved a decade earlier. Although a peace agreement was reached at the time, current rebels maintain the terms of the deal were never fully implemented.

Timeline: PAST

1200s–1400s
The Mali Empire includes territories and peoples of current Niger areas

1400s
Hausa states develop in the south of present-day Niger

1800s
The area is influenced by the Fulani Empire, centered at Sokoto, now in Nigeria

1906
France consolidates rule over Niger

1960
Niger becomes independent

1974
A military coup brings Colonel Seyni Kountché and a Supreme Military Council to power

1987
President Kountché dies and is replaced by Ali Saibou

1990s
The Nigerien National Conference adopts multipartyism; President Ibrahim Bare Mainassara is assassinated

PRESENT

2000s
President Mamadou Tandja holds power under the new Constitution

The military retains significant influence

Tuareg insurgency in north in 2007

Nigeria (Federal Republic of Nigeria)

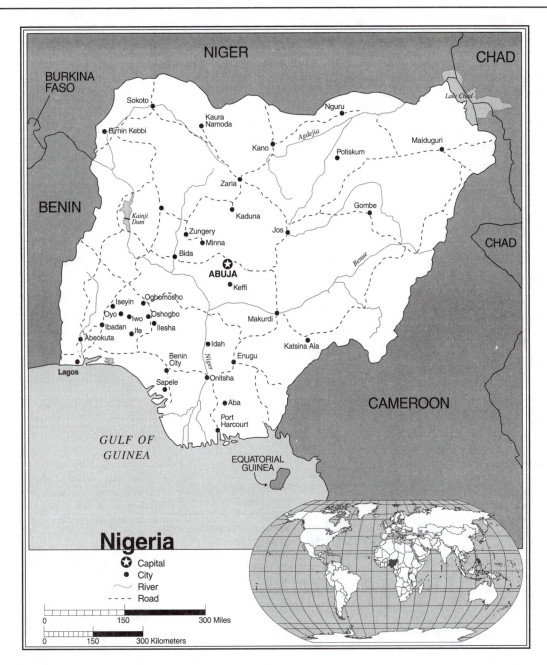

Nigeria Statistics

GEOGRAPHY

Area in Square Miles (Kilometers): 356,669 (923,768) (twice the size of California)

Capital (Population): Abuja (420,000)

Environmental Concerns: soil degradation; deforestation; desertification; drought

Geographical Features: southern lowlands merge into central hills and plateaus; mountains in southeast; plains in north

Climate: varies from equatorial to arid

PEOPLE

Population

Total: 135,031,164

Annual Growth Rate: 2.38%

Rural/Urban Population Ratio: 57/43

Major Languages: English; Hausa; Yoruba; Ibo; Fulani

Ethnic Makeup: about 21% Hausa; 21% Yoruba; 18% Ibo; 9% Fulani; 31% others

Religions: 50% Muslim; 40% Christian; 10% indigenous beliefs

Health

Life Expectancy at Birth: 46.8 years (male); 48.1 years (female)

Infant Mortality: 95.5/1,000 live births

Physicians Available: 1/4,496 people
HIV/AIDS Rate in Adults: 5.4%

Education

Adult Literacy Rate: 68%
Compulsory (Ages): 6–15; free

COMMUNICATION

Telephones: 1,688,000 main lines;
32,322,000 cellular/mobile
Daily Newspaper Circulation: 18 per
1,000 people
Televisions: 38 per 1,000 people
Internet Users: 8,000,000

TRANSPORTATION

Highways in Miles (Kilometers): 120,524
(194,394); but much of the road system
is barely usable
Railroads in Miles (Kilometers): 2,147, (3,505)
Usable Airfields: 70
Motor Vehicles in Use: 954,000

GOVERNMENT

Type: republic in transition from military rule
Independence Date: October 1, 1960
(from the United Kingdom)

Head of State/Government: President
Umaru Yar'Adua is both head of state
and head of government
Political Parties: People's Democratic
Party; Alliance for Democracy; All
People's Party
Suffrage: universal at 18

MILITARY

Military Expenditures (% of GDP): 1.5%
Current Disputes: civil strife; various
border disputes

ECONOMY

Currency ($ U.S. Equivalent): 127.4
nairas = $1
Per Capita Income/GDP: $1,500/$191
billion
GDP Growth Rate: 5.3%
Inflation Rate: 8.2%
Unemployment Rate: 5.8%
Labor Force by Occupation: 70%
agriculture; 20% services; 10%
industry
Population Below Poverty Line: 60%

Natural Resources: petroleum; tin;
columbite; iron ore; coal; limestone;
lead; zinc; natural gas; hydropower
Agriculture: cocoa; peanuts; rubber;
yams; cassava; sorghum; palm oil;
millet; corn; rice; livestock; timber;
fish
Industry: mining; petroleum; food
processing; textiles; cement; building
materials; chemicals; agriculture
products; printing; steel
Exports: $57.5 billion (primary partners
United States, Spain, India)
Imports: $26.9 billion (primary partners
United Kingdom, United States,
France)

SUGGESTED WEB SITES

http://www.nigeria.com

http://www.nigeriatoday.com

http://www.nigeriadaily.com

http://nigeriaworld.com

https://www.cia.gov/library/publications/
the-world-factbook/geos/ni.html

Nigeria Country Report

Nigeria, the "sleeping giant of Africa," is showing signs of waking up. The country has been a driving force behind the New Partnership for African Development (NEPAD), which commits African states to good governance, respect for human rights, and efforts to end regional conflicts. In return, the continent is seeking more aid and foreign investment, and a lifting of trade barriers that impede African exports. The Nigerian government has also been playing a leading role in attempts to bring peace to West Africa, where it is generally considered an honest broker. Nigeria's military has been active in the settlement of regional disputes in Liberia, Côte d'Ivoire, and Sierra Leone. But the country's regional diplomatic standing was compromised in October 2002, when it reneged on a previous agreement to abide by the judgment of the International Court of Justice in a long-running border dispute with Cameroon.

Recent general elections were held in April 2007, at which time Umaru Yar'Adua was elected president. Although the elections were severely criticized by both domestic and foreign observers with accusations of widespread vote-rigging, they were nonetheless a milestone for the country, marking the first civilian-to-civilian transfer of power in the country's history.

DEVELOPMENT

Nigeria hopes to mobilize its substantial human and natural resources to encourage labor-intensive production and self-sufficient agriculture. Recent bans on food imports will increase local production, and restrictions on imported raw materials should encourage research and local input for industry.

With a vast population of nearly 130 million, Nigeria's human resources are yet to be fully tapped in the interest of the country. Poverty and inequality between the rich and the poor remain extreme. Nigeria's industrious people hope that the restoration of democracy will allow them to make renewed progress in the face of these challenges. But ethnic/religious tension and corruption have continued to plague Nigeria. Transparency International has ranked the country as the second most corrupt in the world. In January 2002, a blast at a munitions dump in the principal city, Lagos, left more than 1,000 people dead, sparking renewed calls for public accountability.

Since early 2000, attempts to introduce Shari'a (Islamic law) in northern areas

of the country have touched off severe violence between Muslim and Christian communities, as well as international condemnation for stoning sentences against single mothers convicted of adultery. The most serious violence occurred in 2001, when some 40,000 people were reportedly displaced following ethnic fighting between the Tiv people and several smaller ethnic groups in the central Nasarawa state. In February 2002, some 100 people were killed and thousands more left temporarily homeless in Lagos, as a result of further ethnic strife, which the city's governor suggested was orchestrated by retired army officers seeking to restore military rule.

Despite such incidents, there are signs that Nigeria's civil society is being rebuilt after almost two decades of military rule. Nigeria's transition to civilian rule in 2003 followed the unexpected deaths of its last dictator, General Sani Abacha, and his most famous political prisoner, Chief Mashood Abiola. (The latter was considered by many to have won annulled 1993 presidential elections.) In the wake of the deaths, a caretaker administration under General Abdulsalem Abubakar, in cooperation with previously repressed sections of civil society, promised to restore democracy.

The Nigerian government's credibility at home and abroad was enhanced by the freeing of political prisoners and Abubakar's personal paying of respects to the late Abiola. Besides the jailing of such figures as Abiola, the Abacha regime had reduced Nigeria to the status of a pariah state through its execution of dozens of political opponents, including the internationally prominent writer, ecologist, and human-rights activist Ken Saro Wiwa.

FREEDOM

Under Abacha, Nigeria had one of the world's worst human-rights records. In 1998, the Nigerian Advocacy Group for Human Rights joined other international groups in issuing a statement insisting that nothing essentially changed after Abubakar succeeded Abacha. With the transition to civilian rule the situation should improve.

Since Nigeria's independence, in 1960, its citizens have been through an emotional, political, and material rollercoaster ride. It has been a period marred by inter-ethnic violence, economic downturns, and mostly military rule. But there have also been impressive levels of economic growth, cultural achievement, and human development. To some people, this land of great extremes typifies both the hopes and frustrations of its continent.

Nigeria's hard-working population is responsible for one of Africa's largest economies. But per capita income is still only $840 per year, which is about average for the globe's most impoverished continent but down from Nigeria's estimated 1980 per capita income of $1,500.

A decade ago, it was common to equate Nigeria's wealth with its status as Africa's leading oil producer, but oil earnings have since plummeted. Although hydrocarbons still account for about 90 percent of the country's export earnings and 75 percent of its government revenue, the sector's current contribution to total gross domestic product is a more modest 20 percent.

NIGERIA'S ROOTS

For centuries, the River Niger, which cuts across much of Nigeria, has facilitated long-distance communication among various communities of West Africa's forest and savanna regions. This fact helps to account for the rich variety of cultures that have emerged within the territory of Nigeria over the past millennium. Archaeologists and historians have illuminated the rise and fall of many states whose cultural legacies continue to define the nation.

Precolonial Nigeria produced a wide range of craft goods, including leather, glass, and metalware. The cultivation of cotton and indigo supported the growth of a local textiles industry. During the mid-nineteenth century, southern Nigeria prospered through palm-oil exports, which lubricated the wheels of Europe's Industrial Revolution. Earlier, much of the country was disrupted through its participation in the slave trade. Most African-Americans have Nigerian roots.

Today, more than 250 languages are spoken in Nigeria. Pidgin, which combines an English-based vocabulary with local grammar, is widely used as a lingua franca in the cities and towns. Roughly two thirds of Nigerians speak either Hausa, Yoruba, or Igbo as a home language. During and after the colonial era, the leaders of these three major ethnolinguistic groups clashed politically from their separate regional bases.

HEALTH/WELFARE

Nigeria's infant mortality rate is now believed to have dropped to about 95 per 1,000 live births. (Some estimate it to be as high as 150 per 1,000.) While social services grew rapidly during the 1970s, Nigeria's strained economy since then has led to cutbacks in health and education.

The British, who conquered Nigeria in the late nineteenth and early twentieth centuries, administered the country through a policy of divide-and-rule. In the predominantly Muslim, Hausa-speaking north, they co-opted the old ruling class while virtually excluding Christian missionaries. But in the south, the missionaries, along with their schools, were encouraged, and Christianity and formal education spread rapidly. Many Yoruba farmers of the southwest profited through their cultivation of cocoa. Although most remained as farmers, many of the Igbo of the southeast became prominent in nonagricultural pursuits, such as state employees, artisans, wage workers, and traders. As a result, the Igbo tended to migrate in relatively large numbers to other parts of the colony.

REGIONAL CONFLICTS

At independence, the Federal Republic of Nigeria was composed of three states: the Northern Region, dominated by Hausa speakers; the Western Region, of the Yoruba; and the predominantly Igbo Eastern Region. National politics quickly deteriorated into conflict among these three regions. At one time or another, politicians

in each of the areas threatened to secede from the federation. In 1966, this strained situation turned into a crisis following the overthrow by the military of the first civilian government.

In the coup's aftermath, the army itself was divided along ethnic lines; its ranks soon became embroiled in an increasingly violent power struggle. The unleashed tensions culminated in the massacre of up to 30,000 Igbo living in the north. In response, the Eastern Region declared its independence, as the Republic of Biafra. The ensuing civil war between Biafran partisans and federal forces lasted for three years, claiming an estimated 2 million lives. During this time, much of the outside world's attention became focused on the conflict through visual images of the mass starvation that was occurring in rebel-controlled areas under federal blockade. Despite the extent of the war's tragedy, the collapse of Biafran resistance was followed by a largely successful process of national reconciliation. The military government of Yakubu Gowon (1966–1975) succeeded in diffusing ethnic politics, through a restructured federal system based on the creation of new states. The oil boom, which began soon after the conflict, helped the nation-building process by concentrating vast resources in the hands of the federal government in Lagos.

ACHIEVEMENTS

When many of their leading writers, artists, and intellectuals were exiled and the once-lively press was suppressed, Nigerians found some solace in the success of their world-class soccer team and other athletes. In 2003, Nigeria's first satellite, NigeriaSat-1, was launched by Russian Rocket.

CIVILIAN POLITICS

Thirteen years of military rule ended in 1979. A new Constitution was implemented, which abandoned the British parliamentary model and instead adopted a modified version of the U.S balance-of-powers system. In order to encourage a national outlook, Nigerian presidential candidates needed to win a plurality that included at least one-fourth of the vote in two-thirds of the states.

Five political parties competed in the 1979 elections. They all had similar platforms, promising social welfare for the masses, support for Nigerian business, and a foreign policy based on nonalignment and anti-imperialism. Ideological differences tended to exist within the parties as much as among them, although the People's Redemption Party (PRP) of Aminu Kano became the political home for many Socialists. The most successful party was the somewhat right-of-center National Party of Nigeria (NPN), whose candidate, Shehu Shagari, won the presidency.

New national elections took place in August and September 1983, in which Shagari received more than 12 million of 25.5 million votes. However, the reelected government did not survive long. On December 31, 1983, there was a military coup, led by Major General Muhammad Buhari. The 1979 Constitution was suspended, Shagari and others were arrested, and a federal military government was reestablished. Although no referendum was ever taken on the matter, it is clear that many Nigerians welcomed the coup: this initial response was a reflection of widespread disillusionment with the Second (civilian) Republic.

The political picture seemed very bright in the early 1980s. A commitment to national unity was well established. Although marred by incidents of political violence, two elections had successfully taken place. Due process of law, judicial independence, and press freedom—never entirely eliminated under previous military rulers—had been extended and were seemingly entrenched. But the state was increasingly seen as an instrument of the privileged that offered little to the impoverished masses, with an electoral system that, while balancing the interests of the elite in different sections of the country, failed to empower ordinary citizens. A major reason for this failing was pervasive corruption. People lost confidence as certain officials and their cronies became millionaires overnight. Transparent abuses of power had also occurred under the previous military regime. Conspicuous kleptocracy (rule by thieves) had been tolerated during the oil-boom years of the 1970s, but it became the focus of popular anger as Nigeria's economy contracted during the 1980s.

OIL BOOM—AND BUST

Nigeria, as a leading member of the Organization of Petroleum Exporting Countries (OPEC), experienced a period of rapid social and economic change during the 1970s. The recovery of oil production after the Civil War and the subsequent hike in its prices led to a massive increase in government revenue. This allowed for the expansion of certain types of social services. Universal primary education was introduced, and the number of universities increased from five (in 1970) to 21

(in 1983). A few Nigerians became very wealthy, while a growing middle class was able to afford what previously had been luxuries.

Oil revenues had already begun to fall off when the NPN government embarked upon a dream list of new prestige projects, most notably the construction of a new federal capital at Abuja, in the center of the country. While such expenditures provided lucrative opportunities for many businesspeople and politicians, they did little to promote local production.

Agriculture, burdened by inflationary costs and low prices, entered a period of crisis, leaving the rapidly growing cities dependent on foreign food. Nonpetroleum exports, once the mainstay of the economy, either virtually disappeared or declined drastically.

Although the oil industry is responsible for the vast majority of Nigeria's foreign exchange earnings, corruption has meant few Nigerians have benefitted from the wealth. This, in turn, has fueled problems throughout the country. In July 2003 a nationwide strike took place for nine days in a successful attempt to get government to reduce the price of fuel. During September 2004 deadly battles between gangs in the oil city of Port Harcourt prompted a strong crackdown by troops. The human-rights group Amnesty International cited the death toll at 500, after the government authorities claimed that only 20 people died. A very successful four-day general strike over fuel prices took place in October 2004, stoking fears about the country's oil exports and driving up the price of oil worldwide.

While gross indicators appeared to report impressive industrial growth in Nigeria, most of the new industry depended heavily on foreign inputs and was geared toward direct consumption rather than the production of machines or spare parts. Selective import bans led merely to the growth of smuggling.

The golden years of the 1970s were also banner years for inappropriate expenditures, corruption, and waste. For a while, given the scale of incoming revenues, it looked as if these were manageable problems. But GDP fell drastically in the 1980s with the collapse of oil prices. As the economy worsened, populist resentment grew.

In 1980, an Islamic movement condemning corruption, wealth, and private property defied authorities in the northern metropolis of Kano. The army was called in, killing nearly 4,000. Similar riots subsequently occurred in the cities of Maiduguri, Yola, and Gombe. Attempts by the government to control organized labor by

reorganizing the union movement into one centralized federation sparked unofficial strikes (including a general strike in 1981). In an attempt to placate the growing number of unemployed Nigerians, more than 1 million expatriate West Africans, mostly Ghanaians, were suddenly expelled, a domestically popular but essentially futile gesture.

REFORM OR RETRIBUTION?

Buhari justified the military's return to power on the basis of the need to take drastic steps to rescue the economy, whose poor performance he blamed almost exclusively on official corruption. A "War Against Indiscipline" was declared, which initially resulted in the trial of a number of political leaders, some of whose economic crimes were indeed staggering. The discovery of large private caches of naira (the Nigerian currency) and foreign exchange fueled public outrage. Tribunals sentenced former politicians to long jail terms. In its zeal, the government looked for more and more culprits, while jailing journalists and others who questioned aspects of its program. In 1985, Major General Ibrahim Babanguida led a successful military coup, charging Buhari with human-rights abuses, autocracy, and economic mismanagement.

Babanguida released political detainees. In a clever strategy, he also encouraged all Nigerians to participate in national forums on the benefits of an International Monetary Fund loan and Structural Adjustment Program (SAP). The government turned down the loan but used the consultations to legitimize the implementation of "home-grown" austerity measures consistent with IMF and World Bank prescriptions.

The 1986 budget signaled the beginning of SAP. The naira was devalued, budgets were restricted, and the privatization of many state-run industries was planned. Because salaries remained the same while prices rose, the cost of basic goods rose dramatically, with painful consequences for middle- and working-class Nigerians as well as for the poor.

Although the international price of oil improved somewhat in the late 1980s, there was no immediate return to prosperity. Continued budgetary excesses on the part of the government (which heaped perks on its officer corps and created more state governments to soak up public coffers), coupled with instability, undermined SAP sacrifices. In 1988, the government attempted a moderate reduction in local fuel subsidies. But when, as a result, some transport owners raised fares by 50 to 100 percent, students and workers protested, and bank staff and other workers went on strike. Police killed demonstrators in Jos. Domestic fuel prices have since remained among the lowest in the world, encouraging a massive smuggling of petroleum to neighboring states. This has recently led to the ironic situation of a severe local petroleum shortage. The same corruption and mismanagement has also undercut the potential benefits the country could expect to derive for the current oil price boom.

The government faced additional internal challenges while seeking to project an image of stability to foreign investors. Coup attempts were foiled in 1985 and 1991, while chronic student unrest led to the repeated closure of university campuses. Religious riots between Christians and Muslims became endemic in many areas, leading to hundreds, if not thousands, of deaths.

A series of national elections were held in 1992 between the two officially sponsored parties. But public indifference and/or fear of intimidation, institutionalized by the replacement of the (ideally, secret) ballot with a procedure of publicly lining up for one's candidate, compromised the results. Allegations of gross irregularities led to the voiding of first-round presidential primary elections and the banning of all the candidates. After additional delays, accompanied by a serious antigovernment rioting in Lagos and other urban areas, escalating intercommunal violence, and further clampdowns on dissent, a presidential poll was finally held in June 1993 between two government-approved candidates: Mashood Abiola and Bashir Tofa. The result was a convincing 58 percent victory for the SDP's Abiola, though an estimated 70 percent of the electorate refused to participate in the charade.

The government annulled the results before they had been officially counted (the final results were released by local officials in defiance of Babanguida's regime). Instead, in August 1992, he resigned and installed an interim government led by an ineffectual businessman, Ernest Shonekan. Growing unrest—aggravated by an overnight 600 percent increase in domestic fuel prices and a dramatic airline hijacking by a group calling itself the Movement for the Advancement of Democracy (MAD)—led to the interim regime's rapid collapse. In November, the defense minister, General Sani Abacha, reimposed full military rule.

Resistance to military rule steadily increased throughout 1994. Abiola was arrested in June after proclaiming himself president. His detention touched off nationwide strikes, which shut down the oil industry and other key sectors of the economy. The return to civilian rule eventually occurred in 2003.

CULTURAL PROMINENCE

Nigeria is renowned for its arts. Contemporary giants include Wole Solyinka, who received the Nobel Prize for Literature for his work—plays such as "The Trials of Brother Jero" and "The Road," novels such as *The Interpreters,* and poems and nonfiction works. Two other literary giants are Chinua Achebe, author of *Things Fall Apart, A Man of the People,* and *Anthills of the Savannah;* and the feminist writer Buchi Emecheta, whose works include *The Joy of Motherhood.* The legendary Fela Anikulado Kuti's "Afro-Beat" sound and critical lyrics have made him a local hero and international music megastar. Also prominent is "King" Sunny Ade, who has brought Nigeria's distinctive Juju music to international audiences.

Timeline: PAST

1100–1400
Ancient life flourishes

1851
The first British protectorate is established at Lagos

1960
Nigeria becomes independent as a unified federal state

1966–1970
Military seizure of power; proclamation of Biafra; civil war

1979
Elections restore civilian government

1980s
Muhammed Buhari's military coup ends the Second Republic; later, Buhari is toppled by Ibrahim Babanguida; lean times

1990s
Babanguida resigns; Sani Abacha takes the reins; civil unrest and violence intensify; military strongman Abdulsalam Abubakar takes power; elections bring civilian Olusegun Obasanjo to power

PRESENT

2000s
Ethnic and religious conflict intensifies

Hopes for democratic pluralism in Nigeria revive

First civilian transfer of power in Nigeria's history

Senegal (Republic of Senegal)

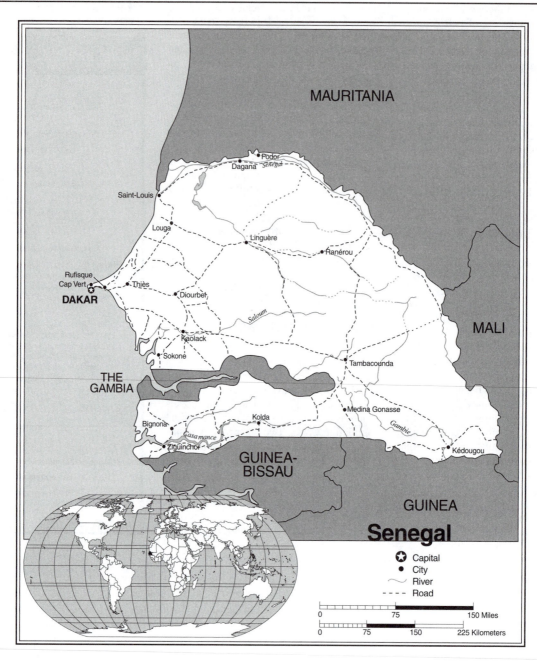

Senegal

★ Capital
● City
～ River
--- Road

0   75   150 Miles
0   75   150   225 Kilometers

Senegal Statistics

GEOGRAPHY

Area in Square Miles (Kilometers):
76,000 (196,840) (about the size of South Dakota)
Capital (Population): Dakar (2,160,000)
Environmental Concerns: poaching; deforestation; overgrazing; soil erosion; desertification; overfishing
Geographical Features: low, rolling plains, foothills in the southeast; Gambia is almost an enclave of Senegal
Climate: tropical

PEOPLE

Population

Total: 12,521,851
Annual Growth Rate: 2.65%
Rural/Urban Population Ratio: 53/47

Major Languages: French; Wolof; Pulaar; Diola; Mandinka
Ethnic Makeup: 43% Wolof; 24% Pular; 15% Serer; 18% others
Religions: 94% Muslim; 5% Christian; 1% indigenous beliefs

Health

Life Expectancy at Birth: 55 years (male); 58 years (female)

Infant Mortality: 60.2/1,000 live births
Physicians Available: 1/14,825 people
HIV/AIDS Rate in Adults: 0.8%

Education

Adult Literacy Rate: 39%
Compulsory (Ages): 7–13

COMMUNICATION

Telephones: 282,600 main lines;
  2,983,000 cellular/mobile
Televisions: 6.9/1,000 people
Internet Users: 650,000

TRANSPORTATION

Highways in Miles (Kilometers): 8,746
  (14,576)
Railroads in Miles (Kilometers): 565 (905)
Usable Airfields: 20
Motor Vehicles in Use: 160,000

GOVERNMENT

Type: republic
Independence Date: April 4, 1960 (from
  France)

Head of State/Government:
  President Abdoulaye Wade;
  Prime Minister Cheikh Hadjbou
  Saumare
Political Parties: Socialist Party;
  Senegalese Democratic Party;
  Democratic League–Labor Party
  Movement; Independence and Labor
  Party; others
Suffrage: universal at 18

MILITARY

Military Expenditures (% of GDP):
  1.4%
Current Disputes: civil unrest; issue with
  The Gambia; tensions with Mauritania
  and Guinea-Bissau

ECONOMY

Currency ($ U.S. equivalent): 523 CFA
  francs = $1
Per Capita Income/GDP: $1,800/$21.5
  billion
GDP Growth Rate: 2.0%
Inflation Rate: 2.1%
Unemployment Rate: 48%

Labor Force by Occupation: 70%
  agriculture
Population Below Poverty Line: 54%
Natural Resources: fish; phosphates; iron
  ore
Agriculture: peanuts; millet; sorghum;
  corn; rice; cotton; vegetables;
  livestock; fish
Industry: agricultural and fish processing;
  phosphate mining; fertilizer
  production; petroleum refining;
  construction materials
Exports: $1.4 billion (primary partners
  France, Italy, Spain)
Imports: $3.0 billion (primary
  partners France, Nigeria,
  Germany)

SUGGESTED WEB SITES

http://www.senegal-online.com/anglais/
  index.html
http://www.sas.upenn.edu/African_
  Studies/Country_Specific/Senegal.html
https://www.cia.gov/library/publications/
  the-world-factbook/geos/sg.html

Senegal Country Report

The year 2002 was marked by both triumph and tragedy for the people of Senegal. At the World Cup, the national soccer team beat world champions France in the opening game before going to qualify for the quarterfinals. But the nation was subsequently thrown into grief when hundreds of lives were lost in a ferryboat disaster. Both incidents took attention away from the country's broader struggle to pull itself out of chronic poverty.

DEVELOPMENT

The recently built Diama and Manantali Dams will allow for the irrigation of many thousands of acres for domestic rice production. At the moment, large amounts of rice are imported to Senegal, mostly to feed the urban population.

In March 2000, Senegalese politics entered a new era with the electoral victory of veteran opposition politician Abdoulaye Wade over incumbent Abdou Diouf. Wade became the country's third president. Like his predecessors, Wade faces daunting challenges. Much of Senegal's youthful, relatively well-educated population

remains unemployed. Widespread corruption and a long-running separatist rebellion in the southern region of Casamance will also test the new regime. Taking a step-by-step approach, Wade has been able to bring about a reduction in the separatist rebellion, and corruption is on the decline. But, also like his predecessors, Wade should be able to draw upon the underlying strength of Senegal's culturally rich multiethnic society, which has maintained its cohesion through decades of adversity.

FREEDOM

Senegal's generally favorable human-rights record is marred by persistent violence in its southern region of Casamance, where rebels are continuing to fight for independence. A 2-year cease-fire broke down in 1995 after an army offensive was launched against the rebel Movement of Democratic Forces of Casamance.

To his great credit President Wade can claim to have reduced tensions, and an end is in sight to the long simmering, low intensity separatist war, going on since independence in the southern Casamance region.

Since the start of the war hundreds of people have been killed and thousands have fled to Guinea-Bissau. Rebel fighters remain active, although the leader of the Movement of Democratic Forces of Casamance declared in 2003 that the war was over.

THE IMPACT OF ISLAM

The vast majority of Senegalese are Muslim. Islam was introduced into the region by the eleventh century A.D. and was spread through trade, evangelism, and the establishment of a series of theocratic Islamic states from the 1600s to the 1800s.

Today, most Muslims are associated with one or another of the Islamic Brotherhoods. The leaders of these Brotherhoods, known as marabouts, often act as rural spokespeople as well as the spiritual directors of their followers. The Brotherhoods also play an important economic role. For example, the members of the Mouride Brotherhood, who number about 700,000, cooperate in the growing of the nation's cash crops.

FRENCH INFLUENCE

In the 1600s, French merchants established coastal bases to facilitate their trade in slaves and gum. As a result, the coastal communities have been influenced by French culture for generations. More territory in the interior gradually fell under French political control.

Although Wolof is used by many as a lingua franca, French continues to be the common language of the country, and the educational system maintains a French character. Many Senegalese migrate to France, usually to work as low-paid laborers. The French maintain a military force near the capital, Dakar, and are major investors in the Senegalese economy. Senegal's judiciary and bureaucracy are modeled after those of France.

HEALTH/WELFARE

Like other Sahel countries, Senegal has a high infant mortality rate and a low life expectancy rate. Health facilities are considered to be below average, even for a country of Senegal's modest income, but recent child-immunization campaigns have been fairly successful.

POLITICS

Under Diouf, Senegal strengthened its commitment to multipartyism. After succeeding Leopold Senghor, the nation's scholarly first president, Diouf liberalized the political process by allowing an increased number of opposition parties effectively to compete against his own ruling Socialist Party (PS). He also restructured his administration in ways that were credited with making it less corrupt and more efficient. Some say that these moves did not go far enough, but Diouf, who inclined toward reform, had to struggle against reactionary elements within his own party.

In national elections in 1988, Diouf won 77 percent of the vote, while the Socialists took 103 out of 120 seats. Outside observers believed that the elections had been plagued by fewer irregularities than in the past. However, opposition protests against alleged fraud touched off serious rioting in Dakar. As a result, the city was placed under a three-month state of emergency. Diouf's principal opponent, Abdoulaye Wade of the Democratic Party (PD), was among those arrested and tried for incitement. But subsequent meetings between Diouf and Wade resulted in an easing of tensions. Indeed, in 1991, Wade shocked many by accepting the post of minister

of state in Diouf's cabinet. In 2000, Wade himself was elected president.

In March 1995, a new, multiparty "Government of National Unity" was formed, which survived despite the defection of one of its members, the Independent Labor Party, in September 1996. But interparty tension grew in the face of Diouf's failure to appoint an independent elections commission in preparation for elections in November 1996.

THE ECONOMY

Many believe that the *Sopi* (Wolof for "change") riots of 1988 were primarily motivated by popular frustration with Senegal's weak economy, especially among its youth (about half of the Senegalese are under age 21), who face an uncertain future. Senegal's relatively large (47 percent) urban population has suffered from rising rates of unemployment and inflation, which have been aggravated by the country's attempt to implement an International Monetary Fund–approved Structural Adjustment Program (SAP). In recent years, the economy has grown modestly but has so far failed to attract the investment needed to meet ambitious privatization goals. Among rural dwellers, drought and locusts have also made life difficult. Fluctuating world market prices and disease as well as drought have undermined groundnut exports.

ACHIEVEMENTS

Dakar, sometimes described as the "Paris of West Africa," has long been a major cultural center for the region. Senegalese writers such as former president Leopold Senghor were founders of the Francophonic African tradition of Negritude.

Senegal has also been beset by difficulties in its relations with neighboring states. The Senegambia Confederation, which many hoped would lead to greater cooperation with The Gambia, was dissolved in September 1989. Relations with Guinea-Bissau are strained as a result of that nation's failure to recognize the result of international arbitration over disputed, potentially oil-rich waters. Senegalese further suspect that individuals in Guinea-Bissau may be linked to the separatist unrest in Senegal's Casamance region. There some 1,000 people died in an insurgency campaign between the Senegalese

Army and the guerrillas of the Movement of Democratic Forces of Casamance. In July 1993, the rebels agreed to a cease-fire, but the cease-fire collapsed in 1995. In August 2000, the rebels agreed to reopen talks with Wade's new administration.

But the major source of cross-border tension has been Mauritania. In 1989, long-standing border disputes between the two countries led to a massacre of Senegalese in Mauritania, setting off widespread revenge attacks against Mauritanians in Senegal. More than 200,000 Senegalese and Mauritanians were repatriated. Relations between the two countries have remained tense, in large part due to the persecution of Mauritania's "black" communities by its Maur-dominated military government. Many Mauritanians belonging to the persecuted groups have been pushed into Senegal, leading to calls for war, but in 1992, the two countries agreed to restore diplomatic, air, and postal links.

Timeline: PAST

1659
The French occupy present-day St. Louis and, later, Gorée Island

1700s
The Jolof kingdom controls much of the region

1848
All Africans in four towns of the coast vote for a representative to the French Parliament

1889
Interior areas are added to the French colonial territory

1960
Senegal becomes independent as part of the Mali Confederation; shortly afterward, it breaks from the Confederation

1980s
President Leopold Senghor retires and is replaced by Abdou Diouf; Senegalese political leaders unite in the face of threats from Mauritania

1990s
Serious rioting breaks out in Dakar protesting the devaluation of the CFA franc

PRESENT

2000s
Tensions remain with Guinea-Bissau and Mauritania

Abdoulaye Wade wins the presidency

Sierra Leone (Republic of Sierra Leone)

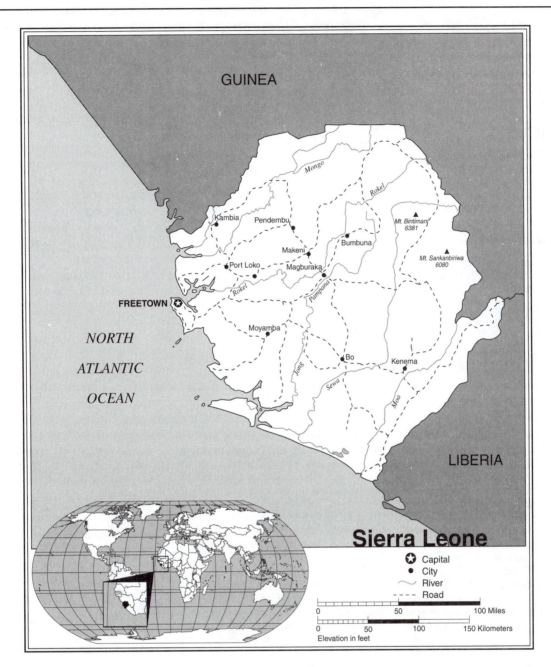

Sierra Leone Statistics

GEOGRAPHY

Area in Square Miles (Kilometers):
27,925 (72,325) (about the size of
South Carolina)
Capital (Population): Freetown (837,000)
Environmental Concerns: soil exhaustion;
deforestation; overfishing; population
pressures
Geographical Features: a coastal
belt of mangroves; wooded, hilly

country; upland plateau;
mountainous east
Climate: tropical; hot, humid

PEOPLE

Population

Total: 6,144,562
Annual Growth Rate: 2.3%
Rural/Urban Population Ratio: 64/36

Major Languages: English, Krio,
Temne, Mende
Ethnic Makeup: 30% Temne; 30%
Mende; 30% other African; 10% others
Religions: 60% Muslim; 30% indigenous
beliefs; 10% Christian

Health

Life Expectancy at Birth: 38 years (male);
43 years (female)
Infant Mortality: 158.3/1,000 live births

GLOBAL STUDIES

Physicians Available: 1/10,832 people
HIV/AIDS Rate in Adults: 7.0%

Education

Adult Literacy Rate: 35.1%

COMMUNICATION

Telephones: 24,000 main lines; 113,200 cellular/mobile
Internet Users: 10,000

TRANSPORTATION

Highways in Miles (Kilometers): 7,020 (11,700)
Railroads in Miles (Kilometers): 52 (84)
Usable Airfields: 10
Motor Vehicles in Use: 44,000

GOVERNMENT

Type: constitutional democracy
Independence Date: April 27, 1961 (from the United Kingdom)

Head of State/Government: President Ernest Bai Koroma is both head of state and head of government
Political Parties: Sierra Leone People's Party; National Unity Party; others
Suffrage: universal at 18

MILITARY

Military Expenditures (% of GDP): 2.3%
Current Disputes: hopes for a lasting peace after a decade of civil war

ECONOMY

Currency ($ U.S. Equivalent): 2,962 leones = $1
Per Capita Income/GDP: $900/$5.5 billion
GDP Growth Rate: 7.1%
Inflation Rate: 1.0%
Population Below Poverty Line: 68%
Natural Resources: diamonds; titanium ore; bauxite; gold; iron ore; chromite

Agriculture: coffee; cocoa; palm kernels; rice; palm oil; peanuts; livestock; fish
Industry: mining; petroleum refining; small-scale manufacturing
Exports: $185 million (primary partners New Zealand, Belgium, United States)
Imports: $531 million (primary partners Czech Republic, United Kingdom, United States)

SUGGESTED WEB SITES

http://www.sierra-leone.org
http://www.sierraleonenews.com
http://www.fosalone.org
http://www.africanews.org/west/sierraleone/
http://www.sas.upenn.edu/African_Studies/ Country_Specific/ S_Leone.html
https://www.cia.gov/library/publications/the-world-factbook/geos/sl.html

Sierra Leone Country Report

In 2002, Sierra Leone emerged from a decade of civil war with the help of Britain (its former colonial power), a large United Nations peacekeeping mission, and other international elements. More than 17,000 UN troops disarmed tens of thousands of rebels and militia fighters. It was the biggest UN peacekeeping success in Africa for many years, following debacles in the 1990s in Angola, Rwanda, and Somalia. Currently the country is rebuilding its infrastructure and civil society. President Ahmed Tejan Kabbah won a landslide victory in May elections, in which his Sierra Leone People's Party also secured a majority in Parliament. In July 2002, a "Truth and Reconciliation Commission" was established to help the people of Sierra Leone overcome the trauma of the war, which was characterized by widespread atrocities.

In July 2003 rebel leader Foday Sankoh died in prison of natural causes while waiting to be tried for war crimes. In August 2003 President Kabbah testified to the Truth and Reconciliation commission that he had no say over operations of pre-government militias during the civil war. The much awaited disarmament and rehabilitation of more than 70,000 civil war combatants was officially completed in February 2004. In March 2004 the UN backed War Crimes Tribunal opened a courthouse to try senior militia leaders from both sides of civil war—the trials themselves began in June.

Sierra Leone's period of political instability began in April 1992, when army Captain Valentine Strasser announced the overthrow of the long-governing All People's Congress (APC). The coup was initially welcomed, as the APC governments of the deposed president Joseph Momoh and is similarly deposed predecessor Siaka Stevens had been renowned for their institutionalized corruption and economic incompetence. But disillusionment grew as the Strasser-led National Provisional Ruling Council postponed holding multiparty elections, while sinking into its own pattern of corruption. The emergence of the RUF insurgency brought further misery, with both the rebels and army being accused of abuses.

Hopes that the (in many quarters unexpected) successful holding of democratic elections in February–March 1996 would lead to peace and reconciliation were dashed in May 1997, when dissident junior officers overthrew the elected government of President Kabbah. An Armed Forces Revolutionary Council (AFRC), led by Major Johnny Paul Koroma (who had been awaiting trial on charges stemming from an earlier coup attempt) banned political parties and all public demonstrations and meetings and announced that all legislation would be made by military decree. The AFRC soon revealed itself to be a vehicle of the rebel Revolutionary United Front (RUF) as well as of elements within the military unwilling to accept a return to civilian control.

DEVELOPMENT

The recently relaunched Bumbuna hydroelectric project should reduce Sierra Leone's dependence on foreign oil, which has accounted for nearly a third of its imports. In response to threats of boycotting, the country's Lungi International Airport was upgraded. Persistent inflation and unemployment have taken a severe toll on the country's people.

FREEDOM

The deposed AFRC/RUF regime unleashed a terror campaign, including extra-judicial killings, torture, mutilation, rape, beatings, arbitrary arrest, and the detention of unarmed civilians. Junta forces killed and/or amputated the arms of detainees. Prior to the coup, RUF was infamous for its murderous attacks on civilians during raids in which children were commonly abducted and forced to commit atrocities against their relatives as a form of psychological conditioning.

The AFRC/RUF regime attracted overwhelming regional condemnation, with the international community sanctioning efforts by the Economic Community of West African States (ECOWAS) to restore Kabbah to power. This was finally achieved in February 1998, when military units of ECOMOG, the Nigerian-led ECOWAS peace-monitoring force, attacked and routed the junta's forces in the capital city, Freetown, after Koroma abandoned his agreement to step down peacefully.

In January 1999, rebels backing the RUF seized parts of the capital city, Freetown, from ECOMOG. After weeks of bitter fighting they were driven out, but 5,000 people had been killed, and the city was devastated. A cease-fire was declared that May, following a further ECOMOG offensive against the RUF. In July, after six weeks of talks in Lomé, Togo, a new peace agreement was signed under which the rebels were to receive posts in government and assurances that they would not be prosecuted for war crimes. In accordance with the agreement, the RUF leader, Foday Sankoh, was brought into a transitional government pledged to restoring democracy, law, and order, with UN peacekeeper assistance.

HEALTH/WELFARE

Life expectancy for both males and females in Sierra Leone is only in the 40s, while the infant mortality rate, 144.3 per 1,000 live births, remains appalling. In 1990, hundreds, possibly thousands, of Sierra Leone children were reported to have been exported to Lebanon on what amounted to slave contracts. The UNEP Human Development Index rates Sierra Leone last, out ot 174 countries.

In November–December 1999, UN forces arrived to police the agreement, but ECOMOG troops continued to be attacked outside Freetown. In April–May 2000, as rebel troops attacked the capital, UN forces came under attack in the eastern part of the country, but far worse was in store when first 50, then several hundred UN troops were abducted. To protect and evacuate British citizens, 800 British paratroopers were sent to Freetown. Working alongside the UN, these troops helped to recapture hostages and secure the airport, while Sankoh was captured. In January 2001, presidential and parliamentary elections were postponed due to continuing strife. But by March the rebel army had begun to surrender, allowing for its forces' disarmament and participation in the elections.

Sierra Leone is the product of a unique colonial history. Freetown was founded by waves of black settlers who were brought there by the British. The first to arrive were

ACHIEVEMENTS

The Sande Society, a women's organization that trains young Mende women for adult responsibilities, has contributed positively to life in Sierra Leone. Beautifully carved wooden helmet masks are worn by women leaders in the society's rituals. Ninety-five percent of Mende women join the Society.

the so-called "Black Poor," a group of 400 people sent from England in 1787. Shortly thereafter, former slaves from Jamaica and Nova Scotia arrived; they had gained their freedom by fighting with the British, against their American masters, in the U.S. War of Independence. About 40,000 Africans who were liberated by the British and others from slave ships captured along the West African coast were also settled in Freetown and the surrounding areas in the first half of the nineteenth century.

The descendants of Sierra Leone's various black settlers blended African and British ways into a distinctive *Krio*, or Creole, culture. Besides speaking English, they developed their own Krio language, which has become the nation's lingua franca. Today, the Krio make up only about 5 percent of Sierra Leone's multiethnic population.

As more people were given the vote in the 1950s, the indigenous communities ended Krio domination in local politics. The first party to win broad national support was the Sierra Leone People's Party (SLPP), under Sir Milton Margai, which led the country to independence in 1961. During the 1967 national elections, the SLPP was narrowly defeated by Stevens' APC. From 1968 to 1985, Stevens presided over a steady erosion of Sierra Leone's economy and civil society. The APC's increasingly authoritarian control coincided with the country's economic decline. Although rich in its human as well as natural resources at independence, today Sierra Leone is ranked as one of the world's poorest countries.

Revenues from diamonds (which formed the basis for prosperity during the 1950s) and gold have steadily fallen due to the depletion of old diggings and massive smuggling. The two thirds of Sierra Leone's labor force employed in agriculture have suffered the most from the nation's faltering economy. Poor producer prices, coupled with an international slump in demand for cocoa and robusta coffee, have cut into rural incomes. The promise by Stevens' successor, Momoh, to improve producer prices as part of a "Green Revolution" program went unfulfilled. Like its minerals, much of Sierra Leone's agricultural production has been smuggled out of the country. In 1989, the cost of servicing Sierra Leone's foreign

debt was estimated to be 130 percent of the total value of its exports. This grim figure led to the introduction of an International Monetary Fund–supported Structural Adjustment Program (SAP), whose austerity measures made life even more difficult for urban dwellers.

At this point in time, the Sierra Leone government is slowly re-establishing its authority after more than a decade of civil war in which at least 50,000 people are thought to have died and two million people (almost a third of the population) displaced. The last UN peacekeeping forces withdrew in 2005. In some ways the situation in Sierra Leone provides lessons for Africa. Disciplined armies can be forces of stability, just as undisciplined armies can give rise to chaos. The final phase of the conflict also demonstrated the potential of obtaining peace through concerted efforts of the regional states accompanied by external powers. Perhaps another lesson was the usefulness of targeted economic sanctions. In the case of Sierra Leone, the RUF survived for many years through profits gained through diamond smuggling. The relative success in separating such "blood diamonds" from legitimate exports has given rise to greater international control over the marketing of the gems, which may prove to be a model for similar situations in the future.

Timeline: PAST

1400–1750
Early inhabitants arrive from Africa's interior

1787
Settlement by people from the New World and recaptured slave ships

1801
Sierra Leone is a Crown colony

1898
Mende peoples unsuccessfully resist the British in the Hut Tax War

1961
Independence

1978
The new Constitution makes Sierra Leone a one-party state

1985
President Siaka Stevens steps down; Joseph Momoh, the sole candidate, is elected

1990s
Debt-servicing cost mounts; SAP; Liberian rebels destabilize Sierra Leone; Momoh is overthrown

PRESENT

2000s
Civil war ends, rebuilding begins

Togo (Togolese Republic)

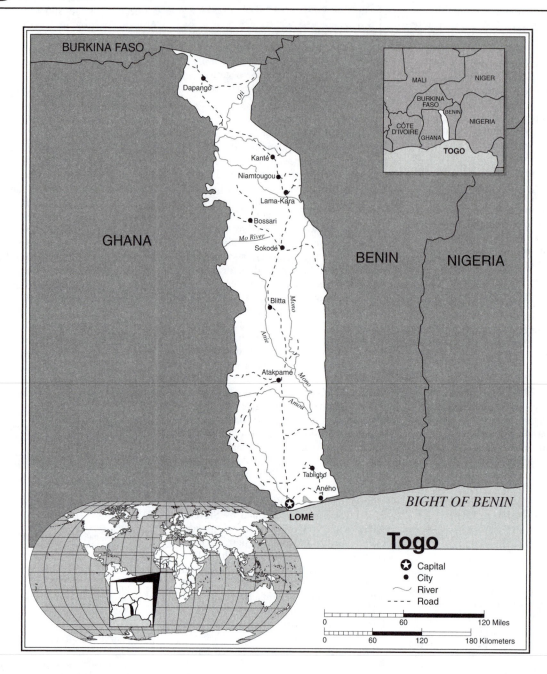

Togo Statistics

GEOGRAPHY

Area in Square Miles (Kilometers):
21,853 (56,600) (about the size of West Virginia)

Capital (Population): Lomé (732,000)

Environmental Concerns: drought; deforestation

Geographical Features: gently rolling savanna in north; central hills; southern plateau; low coastal plain with extensive lagoons and marshes

Climate: tropical to semiarid

PEOPLE

Population

Total: 5,701,579

Annual Growth Rate: 2.72%

Rural/Urban Population Ratio: 67/33

Major Languages: French; Ewe; Mina; Dagomba; Kabye; Dasomsa

Ethnic Makeup: 99% African—Ewe; Mina; Kabye; many others

Religions: 70% indigenous beliefs; 20% Christian; 10% Muslim

Health

Life Expectancy at Birth: 56 years (male); 60 years (female)

Infant Mortality: 59.2/1,000 live births
Physicians Available: 1/11,270 people
HIV/AIDS Rate in Adults: 4.1%

Education

Adult Literacy Rate: 61%
Compulsory (Ages): 6–12

COMMUNICATION

Telephones: 82,100 main lines; 708,000
cellular/mobile
Televisions: 36/1,000 people
Internet Users: 320,000

TRANSPORTATION

Highways in Miles (Kilometers): 4,512
(7,520)
Railroads in Miles (Kilometers): 376
(568)
Usable Airfields: 9
Motor Vehicles in Use: 109,000

GOVERNMENT

Type: republic under transition to
multiparty democratic rule

Independence Date: April 27, 1960
(from French-administered UN
trusteeship)
Head of State/Government: President
Faure Gnassingbe; Prime Minister
Yawovi Agboyibo
Political Parties: Assembly of the
Togolese People; Coordination des
Forces Nouvelles; Action Committee
for Renewal; Patriotic Pan-African
Convergence; Union of Forces for
Change; others
Suffrage: universal for adults

MILITARY

Military Expenditures (% of GDP):
1.8%
Current Disputes: civil unrest; tensions
with Benin

ECONOMY

Currency ($ U.S. Equivalent): 581 CFA
francs = $1
Per Capita Income/GDP: $1,500/$7.6
billion
GDP Growth Rate: 3.3%

Inflation Rate: –1%
Labor Force by Occupation: 65%
agriculture; 30% services; 5%
industry
Population Below Poverty Level: 32%
Natural Resources: phosphates;
limestone; marble; arable land
Agriculture: coffee; cocoa; yams;
cassava; millet; sorghum; rice;
livestock; fish
Industry: phosphates mining; textiles;
handicrafts; agricultural processing;
cement; beverages
Exports: $612 million (primary partners
Benin, Nigeria, Ghana)
Imports: $1.0 billion (primary
partners Ghana, France, Côte
d'Ivoire)

SUGGESTED WEB SITES

http://www.republicoftogo.com/
http://www.sas.upenn.edu/ African_
Studies/Country_Specific/Togo.html
https://www.cia.gov/library/publications/
the-world-factbook/geos/to.html

Togo Country Report

In recent years, Togo has become a prime example of the difficulty of achieving democratic reform in the face of determined resistance by a ruling clique that enjoys military backing and a strong ethnic support base. For the past four decades, the country has been politically dominated by supporters of its long-serving president, Gnassingbé Eyadéma. Their grip on power was evident once more in October 2002, when Eyadéma's Assembly (or Rally) of the Togolese People (RPT) party won another landslide victory in legislative elections, even in the face of continuing allegations of vote rigging and human-rights abuses. The true political contest may have occurred earlier in the year, when an apparent power struggle resulted in Eyadéma's sacking his prime minister and longtime ally, Agbeyome Kodjo. The outcome reconfirmed Eyadéma's status as one of Africa's true political survivors.

Emerging from the ranks of the military, Eyadéma first seized power in 1967. This followed a period of instability in the wake of the assassination of the country's first president, Sylvanius Olympio, by the Togolese military. In 1969, Eyadéma institutionalized his increasingly dictatorial regime as a one-party state. All Togolese have been required

to belong to the RPT. But in 1991, faced with mass prodemocracy demonstrations in Lomé, the capital city, Eyadéma acquiesced to opposition calls for a "National Conference" that would end the RPT's monopoly of power. Since then, Eyadéma has survived Togo's turbulent return to multiparty politics with characteristic ruthlessness, skillfully taking advantage of the weakness of his divided opponents.

DEVELOPMENT

Much hope for the future of Togo is riding on the recently created Free Trade Zone at Lomé. Firms within the zone are promised a 10-year tax holiday if they export at least three quarters of their output. The project is backed by the U.S. Overseas Private Investment Corporation.

In December 2002, the Parliament altered the constitution by removing a clause which would have barred President Eyadéma from seeking a third presidential term. In June 2003 Eyadéma was re-elected president of the country. With his election victory in hand President Eyadéma reinstated the previous Prime Minister Koffi Sama and his

government, then began talks on a national unity government in July 2003. A new unity government was announced, but the main opposition parties were not included.

DEMOCRACY VS. DICTATORSHIP

Meeting in July–August 1991, the National Conference turned into a public trial of the abuses of the ruling regime. Resisting the president's attempts to dissolve it, the Conference appointed Kokou Koffigoh as the head of an interim government, charged with preparing the country for multiparty elections. The RPT was to be disbanded, and Eyadéma himself was barred from standing for reelection.

FREEDOM

Togo continues to have a poor human-rights record. Its progovernment security forces have been responsible for extra-judicial killings, beatings, arbitrary detentions, and interference with citizens' rights to movement and privacy. Freedoms of speech and of the press are restricted. Interethnic killings have led to major population displacements.

(United Nations photo 117,584 by Anthony Fisher)

Potable water is not universally available in Togo. While food production in Togo is officially said to be adequate, outside observers contend that the drought-prone north is uncomfortably reliant on the more agriculturally productive southern areas.

presidential poll. Thereafter, Eyadéma gave ground, agreeing to internationally supervised legislative elections in February 1994. After two rounds of voting, amid escalating violence, Eyadéma's RPT and the main opposition—Action Committee for Renewal (CAR), led by Yaovi Agboyibor—each controlled about 35 seats in the 75-seat Assembly. (The situation was clouded by judicial reviews of the results in five constituencies.) The balance of power rested with former Organization of African Unity secretary-general Edem Kodjo's Togo Union for Democracy (UTD), which had entered the election allied with CAR. But in May, Kodjo became prime minister, with Eyadéma's backing. The failure of the moderate opposition to capitalize on its apparent victory in undoubtedly flawed elections strengthened the determination of the militants to carry on by other means.

In early 2005 upon Eyadéma's death, his son, Faure Gnassingbe, succeeded him to the presidency in an election that many claimed was rigged. Street violence ensued, in which hundreds of people were reported killed and as many as 40,000 fled to neighboring countries. Gnassingbe eventually yielded and permitted new elections to occur. The second set of elections subsequently confirmed his presidency. In 2006 the major political parties agreed to a national unity government, with parliamentary elections scheduled for sometime in 2007. The political situation currently remains unsettled.

STRUCTURAL ADJUSTMENT

Togo's political crisis has taken place against a backdrop of economic restructuring. In 1979, Togo adopted an economic-recovery strategy that many consider to have been a forerunner of other Structural Adjustment Programs (SAPs) introduced throughout most of the rest of Africa. Faced with mounting debts as a result of falling export revenue, the government began to loosen the state's grip over the local economy. Since 1982 a more rigorous International Monetary Fund/World Bank–supported program of privatization and other market-oriented reforms has been pursued. Given this chronology,

In November–December 1991, however, soldiers loyal to Eyadéma launched a bloody attack on Koffigoh's residence. The French, whose troops had intervened in the past to keep Eyadéma in power, refused Koffigoh's plea for help. Instead, the coup attempt ended with the now-almost-irrelevant Koffigoh and Eyadéma agreeing to maintain their uneasy cohabitation. Elections were henceforth to include the RPT. Despite the "compromise," there was an upsurge in political violence in 1992, which included the May shooting of Gilchrist Olympio (the son of Sylvanus) and other Eyadéma opponents. In September, "rebel" soldiers once more held the government hostage.

A January 1993 massacre of the prodemocracy demonstrators pushed the country

even further to the brink. Some 300,000 southern Togolese, mostly Ewe-speakers, fled the country, fearing "ethnic cleansing" by the largely northern, Kabye-speaking army. In 1993–1994, exiled anti-Eyadéma militants—many of whom coalesced as the Front of the National Committee for the Liberation of the Togolese People (FNCL)— began to fight back. The army chief of staff was among those killed during a daring raid on the main military headquarters in Lomé, in which grenades were also thrown into Eyadéma's bedroom.

In July 1993, Eyadéma and his more moderate opponents signed a peace accord in Burkina Faso, pledging renewed movement toward election. A month later, however, the opposition boycotted a snap

Togo's economic prospects have become a focus of attention for those looking for lessons about the possible effects of SAP. Both proponents and opponents of SAP have grounds for debate.

ACHIEVEMENTS

The name of Togo's capital, Lomé, is well known in international circles for its association with the Lomé Convention, a periodically renegotiated accord through which products from various African, Caribbean, and Pacific countries are given favorable access to European markets.

Supporters of Togo's SAP point out that since 1985, the country has enjoyed an average growth in gross domestic product of 3.3 percent per year. While this statistic is an improvement over the 1.7 percent rate recorded between 1973 and 1980, however, it is well below the 7.2 percent growth that prevailed from 1965 to 1972. (The GDP growth rate in 2002 was estimated at 2.2 percent.) During the 1980s, there was a rise in private consumption, 7.6 percent per year, and a drop in inflation, from about 13 percent in 1980 to an estimated 2 percent in 1989. A rate of 2.3 percent was estimated for 2002.

The livelihoods of certain segments of the Togolese population have materially improved during the past decade. Beneficiaries include some of the two thirds of the workforce employed in agriculture. Encouraged by increased official purchase prices, cash-crop farmers have expanded their outputs of cotton and coffee. This is especially true in the case of cotton production, which tripled between 1983 and 1989. Nearly half the nation's small farmers now grow the crop.

Balanced against the growth of cotton has been a decline in cocoa, which emerged as the country's principal cash crop under colonialism. Despite better producer prices during the mid-1980s, output fell as a result of past decisions not to plant new trees. Given the continuing uncertainty of cocoa prices, this earlier shift may prove to have

been opportune. The long-term prospects of coffee are also in doubt, due to a growing global preference for the arabica beans of Latin America over the robusta beans that thrive throughout much of West Africa. As a result, the government had to reverse course in 1988, drastically reducing its prices for both coffee and cocoa, a move that it hopes will prove to be only temporary.

Eyadéma's regime claimed great success in food production, but its critics have long countered official reports of food self-sufficiency by citing the importation of large quantities of rice, a decline in food production in the cotton-growing regions, and widespread childhood malnutrition. The country's food situation is complicated by an imbalance between the drought-prone northern areas and the more productive south. In 1992, famine threatened 250,000 Togolese, mostly northerners.

There have been improvements in transport and telecommunications. The national highway system, largely built by the European Development Fund, has allowed the port of Lomé to develop as a transshipment center for exports from neighboring states as well as Togo's interior. At the same time, there has been modest progress in cutting the budget deficit. But it is in precisely this area that the cost of Togo's SAP is most apparent. Public expenditures in health and education declined by about 50 percent between 1982 and 1985. Whereas school enrollment rose from 40 percent to more than 70 percent during the 1970s, it has slipped back below 60 percent in recent years.

The ultimate justification for Togo's SAP has been to attract overseas capital investment. In addition to sweeping privatization, a Free Trade Zone has been established. But overseas investment in Togo has always been modest. There have also been complaints that many foreign investors have simply bought former state industries on the cheap rather than starting up new enterprises. Furthermore, privatization and austerity measures are blamed for unemployment and wage cuts among urban workers. One third of the state-divested enterprises have been liquidated.

Whatever the long-term merits of Togo's SAP, it is clear that it has so far resulted in neither a pattern of sustainable growth nor an improved standard of living for most Togolese. For the foreseeable future, the health of Togo's economy will continue to be tied to export earnings derived from three commodities—phosphates, coffee, and cocoa—whose price fluctuations have been responsible for the nation's previous cycles of boom and bust.

Timeline: PAST

1884
Germany occupies Togo

1919
Togo is mandated to Britain and France by the League of Nations following Germany's defeat in World War I

1956–1957
UN plebiscites result in the independence of French Togo and incorporation of British Togo into Ghana

1960
Independence is achieved

1963
Murder of President Sylvanus Olympio; a new civilian government is organized after the coup

1967
The coup of Colonel Etienne Eyadéma, now President Gnassingbé Eyadéma

1969
The Coalition of the Togolese People becomes the only legal party in Togo

1990s
Prodemocracy demonstrations lead to interim government and the promise of multiparty elections; Eyadéma survives escalating violence and controversial elections

PRESENT

2000s
Eyadéma retains power
Eyadéma is named chairman of the OAU

Articles from the World Press

Selected by William G. Moseley

Angola: Plenty of Oil, a Forgotten War and New Hope, That's Cabinda

The tiny Cabinda enclave accounts for close to 65 per cent of Angola's oil, amounting to more than 80 per cent of the country's revenues. But the province, which has fought for three decades to secede, remains one of the poorest in Angola. An agreement signed this week could determine its destiny.

PETER KAGWANJA

Without Cabinda, Angola would have no oil to talk about, but thanks to the tiny enclave, the country is sub-Saharan Africa's second biggest oil producer after Nigeria. So it can be understood why Cabinda secessionists have fought government forces for autonomy for three decades.

It does not matter that Cabinda, which is only 7,300 sq km, is separated from the rest of Angola by some 60 km wide strip along the lower Congo river and wedged between Congo Brazzaville and the Democratic Republic of Congo, that's where Angola's oil wells are located.

It was therefore a great relief when finally a peace deal was signed on Tuesday this week between the government and separatists to end a conflict that's often dubbed "Angola's forgotten war," one that began soon after Angola's independence from Portugal in 1975 and has forced about 400,000 of Cabinda's estimated 600,000 population to seek refuge in neighbouring countries. Cabinda was formerly a Portuguese protectorate that was incorporated into Angola when the Portuguese withdrew from both territories in 1975.

The deal preserves Angola's territorial unity while granting a "special status" to the oil-rich northern province. The special status gives the Cabinda provincial government additional powers, including greater control over the region's economy and other functions normally reserved for central government.

The agreement follows the Angolan parliament's passing of an amnesty law covering the Cabinda conflict, and is a formal version of a ceasefire negotiated under the auspices of the African Union and signed on July 15 in Brazzaville, the capital of the Republic of Congo, whose president, Denis Sassou Nguesso, the current AU chairman, is an ally of Luanda's.

"Today we turn the page on a sad chapter in our history. The peace deal we have just signed is irreversible," General Antonio Bento Bembe, who signed for an umbrella group of rebel movements, said at a colourful ceremony in the southern coastal town of Namibe, 700 km south of the capital Luanda.

Bembe is the secretary-general of the Front for the Liberation of the Enclave of Cabinda (FLEC) and head of the Cabindan Forum for Dialogue, which has been negotiating for the separatists at talks brokered by the Republic of Congo, which is on Cabinda's northern border. The Forum also brings together civil society, church and political parties.

Angola's Territorial Administration Minister Virgilio Ferreira de Fontes Pereira signed for the government. "Cabinda will be granted a special status which respects Angola's territorial integrity, because Cabinda Province is an integral part of Angola," Pereira said at the ceremony.

Forget their Tragic Past

National Assembly President Roberto de Almeida, representing Angolan President Jose Eduardo dos Santos, welcomed Tuesday's signing as a new start for the country, urging Angolans to forget their tragic pasts and work for unity.

But there are fears that the peace deal could collapse due to lack of broad-based support in the enclave and the fractured nature of the separatist movement, with some leaders questioning Bembe's authority.

Talks over Cabinda's destiny have been on-and-off since the early 1980s—including mediations by Gabon and Congo Brazzaville in 1986 and 1989. But these talks have been no more than a dialogue of the deaf as the government insisted on territorial unity and the Cabinda secessionists demanded autonomy.

Recent talks started with an exploratory round in Libreville, Gabon, from June 8 to 10 with follow-up meetings from June 17 to 24, which set the stage for the final round in Massabi, northern Cabinda, where the agreement was clinched on July 1, and officially announced by President Eduardo dos Santos.

The agreement has a distinct military hue just like the Luena Ceasefire Accord of April 4, 2002, which ended hostilities between the Movement for the Popular Liberation of Angola (MPLA) government and the National Union of the Total Liberation of Angola (UNITA).

In a Nutshell, the Agreement:

- Recognises Cabinda's unique history and some sort of special designation within the Angolan state, but no autonomy to the enclave;
- Condemns "every act of political rebellion and terrorism, practiced by anyone, against law and order" and commits the two sides to uphold the rule of law and democratic institutions, as well as peace and national reconciliation for Cabinda;
- It provides for the stationing of FLEC units in designated areas of Cabinda and calls on the Angolan Armed Forces to provide logistical support to FLEC units;
- Offers amnesty for independence fighters who surrender and turn over their weapons.

The government has every reason to embrace the peace deal, which General Sachipengo Nunda, the deputy chief of staff of Angolan Armed Forces (FAA), had last month praised as "an important step in the beginning of the ceasefire."

Embers of Secessionism

But even as Bembe hailed the accord when it was clinched in early July as "the first step in the journey to Cabinda's pacification," he had a difficult task selling it at home.

Disenchantment with the top-down Marxist-style of the MPLA elite, a strong quest for a Cabindan identity and a deep sense of being left out of power and the economy have concertedly stoked the embers of secessionism.

In addition to producing cash-crops like coffee, rubber and palm oil, Cabinda accounts for close to 65 per cent of Angola's oil production—estimated at about 900,000 barrels a day, amounting to more than 80 per cent of Angola's revenues. Oil exports from the enclave are reportedly worth the equivalent of US$100,000 per annum for every Cabindan. But the province remains one of the poorest in Angola despite a trifling 10 per cent of Cabinda's taxes from oil revenues that the central government has been remitting to the enclave in line with a 1996 agreement.

FLEC, founded in 1963, has steadily fought Luanda. Even then, Cabinda remained on the fringes of Angola's 27-year-old civil war between the MPLA government and UNITA rebels.

Predictably, after the February 2002 battlefield death of UNITA leader Jonas Savimbi, the Cabinda insurgents were left out of the Luena Ceasefire Agreement of April 4, 2002 that returned peace to Angola.

Analysts like Jean-Michel Mabeko-Tali highlight Cabinda's suspension in a limbo between "no peace" and "no war." But the government's military strategy of pacifying the enclave after 2002 amounted to a one-sided war.

In October 2002, the government deployed some 30,000 of its battle-hardened Forças Armadas Angola (FAA) troops to finish off FLEC's ragtag army, estimated at 2,000 strong.

The counter-insurgency campaign came at a high price, especially to the government, which soon realised that it was winning in the battlefield but losing the moral war.

For instance, a damning report, Terror in Cabinda, released by local human rights groups in December 2002 drew world attention to its soldiers targeting civilians instead of the insurgents, including such abuses as summary executions, murders, disappearances, arbitrary detention, torture, rape and looting.

These reports wiped out any iota of local support for the government, further tilting opinion in favour of independence. Luanda made a significant climb down from its military offensive to counter a real possibility of the Cabinda conflict being internationalised, allowing the founder of FLEC, Ranque Franque, to visit Luanda in July 2003.

A face-off with civil society over the civic association, Mpalabanda, fostered an atmosphere of distrust of the government's intentions. And even though Mpalabanda was eventually launched under the auspices of the Catholic Church in Cabinda in March 2004, the government lost potential allies in Cabinda's civic sphere.

The imperative to settle the Cabinda question ahead of the country's general elections, recently postponed from September 2006 to 2007, is behind the government's recent push for a peace deal with the separatists.

But while relative calmness and reduced military confrontation made Cabinda ripe for a peace settlement, persisting distrust diminishes the odds of a peaceful solution securing the requisite support at the grassroots.

Divided Leadership

On its part, Cabinda's leadership is badly divided on strategy, personality and power, making it difficult to speak with one voice and giving the government reason to stick to its military path.

Pressure from ordinary Cabindans, civil society and the church, which preferred negotiations with the government under a single banner, forced rival elite factions to unite under FLEC and to create the Cabindan Dialogue Forum in August 2004. However, power wrangles linger on, hampering the emergence of a united front.

Unresolved issues of authority within FLEC and the Forum could torpedo the agreement. Indeed, analysts say Cabinda risks balkanising into warring blocs aligned to party secretary-general Bembe and president N'Zita Henrique Tiago.

Last month, there was disarray over the negotiations with Tiago denying knowledge of any agreement between FLEC and Luanda or contact with President dos Santos.

Mpalabanda's spokesman, Raul Danda, backed the Tiago bloc, charging that Bembe had no power to speak for Cabindans or for the armed rebels and claiming that he is on the government's payroll. Bembe rejected this criticism as "irresponsible and unpatriotic."

The international community has been typically mute on the agreement. "Internationally, the Cabinda conflict is not seen as a big issue," a diplomat said. However, this week the US described the peace deal as "an important milestone toward peace and reconciliation."

Success in brokering the Luena agreement in April 2002—in contrast to earlier futile efforts by the UN and Angola's neighbours like South Africa—bolstered the government's confidence in its own ability to pacify Cabinda. This is also partly responsible for Cabinda's invisibility in the international radar.

For the peace deal to hold, international actors like the UN, the EU and the US, as well as African institutions like Sadc, need to encourage the government to drop its military approach and urge Cabinda forces to unite so that Cabindans can participate in the crucial general elections slated for 2007—a critical threshold in Angola's transition to lasting peace and democracy.

DR. PETER KAGWANJA is Research Associate, Centre for International Political Studies (CIPS), University of Pretoria. With reporting by Reuters.

Africa Insight is an initiative of the Nation Media Group's Africa Media Network

Post-Apartheid Vineyards

Land redistribution begins to transform South Africa's wine country.

WILLIAM G. MOSELEY

As I walked through the rows of grape vines with a representative of one of South Africa's few worker co-owned vineyards, I could tell that he was proud of what his group had accomplished. Nearly all of the 60 members of the Bouwland partnership trust are coloured or black farm workers. They own a controlling share of the Bouwland vineyard and wine label, producing 17,000 bottles of wine per year, with exports to Europe and Canada. By all accounts, this is an amazing achievement for an effort that is only three years old. But the group is also nervous. They are still heavily dependent on the expertise and equipment of their white partners, and they must repay a substantial commercial bank loan. This project and others like it represent a small but growing number of worker-owned vineyards in post-Apartheid South Africa. These efforts embody the hopes, dreams, and challenges of those who aspire to make the new South Africa a reality for the working poor.

In 1994, the African National Congress (ANC) took power in South Africa under the leadership of Nelson Mandela, formally ending decades of state-sponsored discrimination. Among a wide range of exclusionary policies during the Apartheid era were restrictions on the ownership of farmland by non-whites outside of the homelands or Bantustans—a policy that left only 13% of the country's land for the entire majority black population. This led to complete white domination of commercial agriculture, particularly in the Western Cape Province, an area often thought of as the historical hearth of white farming. Of all of South Africa's provinces, agriculture in the Western Cape is the most commercialized and export-oriented. Wine exports in particular have skyrocketed since Apartheid ended and the international community lifted sanctions. While South African wines were once unheard of in North American and European supermarkets, they now compete with wines from their southern hemisphere counterparts, mainly Chile and Australia, for a share of the "good value" wine market (i.e., reasonable-quality wines of low to moderate price). In fact. South Africa's wine production nearly quadrupled between 1994 and 2004, and the country is now the eighth or ninth largest wine producer in the world. But what has this growth meant for South Africa's historically disadvantaged groups, particularly the farm workers who comprise one of the poorest segments of the country's

population? What is the ANC government doing, if anything, to ensure that the wealth from growing wine exports trickles down to the poorest workers?

While many North Americans are familiar with the struggle against Apartheid and the subsequent political opening in the 1990s, fewer may be aware of efforts to transform South Africa's economy. The ANC has promised to redress the legacy of discriminatory land ownership policies in the farming sector through a land reform program that facilitates the transfer of land from whites to blacks (a generic term in South Africa that encompasses people of African, mixed race and Indian origin). In fact, the government has pledged to redistribute 30% of the country's agricultural land by 2014. Land reform is part of a broader transformation strategy for South Africa's agricultural sector aimed at increasing black participation in decision-making. The wine industry in the Western Cape is one instance where the effects of that strategy are visible, and this is significant given its economic importance to the province, its growing export potential, and the history of white dominance.

The Coloured Farm Worker Population and the South African Wine Industry

Wine production in South Africa's Western Cape Province dates back to the 17th century, when the Dutch established an outpost at Cape Town to provision ships sailing from Europe to the Far East. Because the area's local Khoisan population was sparse and unaccustomed to agricultural labor, the Dutch brought slaves from East Africa, Madagascar, and the East Indies to work their farms. The farm laborer population evolved into a mixed race or mulatto group, locally referred to as coloureds, who now comprise 60% of the Western Cape's population.

Even though slavery was abolished in 1834, conditions on farms remained difficult and wages were low. The historic relationship between white farmers and farm workers has often been described in terms of paternalism and dependency. Permanent farm workers (as opposed to seasonal laborers) lived on the farms, often for multiple generations. In addition to meager

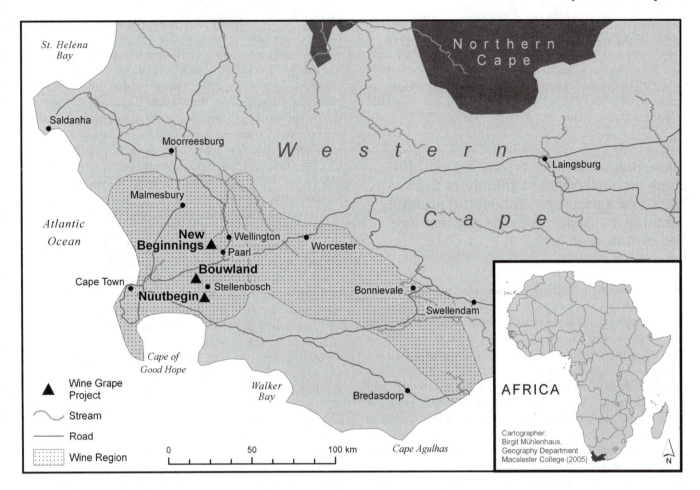

wages, permanent workers typically received housing, food, and wine. Many farm workers bought goods on credit at the company stores their bosses owned and fell into the classic debt-bondage cycle. The provision of cheap wine to workers as a component of compensation, known as the "tot or dop" system, was used to attract and retain workers in a low-wage industry (and the poorest white farmers were often the greatest abusers of this practice). While this practice has been illegal since the 1960s, and more strictly monitored in the post-Apartheid era, alcoholism continues to be a major problem among farm workers.

Raising grapes required a tremendous amount of labor, so those farms with larger areas in grape production often employed 30 to 60 permanent workers who lived on the farm with their families. Spouses and children would then join the workforce at key moments in the agricultural season. Until the end of Apartheid, wine production remained limited because international sanctions blocked exports. Furthermore, other than the dreg wine reserved for the coloured farm workers in the Western Cape, wine consumption was reserved largely for whites—blacks in other parts of the country were encouraged to drink beer.

Post-Apartheid Agriculture

Since the end of Apartheid, shifts in the international political economy, as well as a number of policies and programs at the national level, have had a profound impact on commercial agriculture and on the wine industry in particular. At the international level, the biggest change was the end of sanctions on products that were clearly South African. This change had little impact on exports whose origin was ambiguous, such as table fruit, whose sate continued unabated in Europe during the Apartheid era. But as origin and label are extremely important for all but the cheapest wines, the end of sanctions represented a huge opening of markets for the South African wine industry. As a result, South African wine production went from 38.9 million liters in 1994 to 153.4 million liters in 2004. Today, there are some 4,400 farming units that produce wine grapes in South Africa. Almost all are in the Western Cape because the Mediterranean climate in this region favors their production (see map). The livelihoods of over 108,000 South Africans depend on the wine industry.

Once Apartheid ended, international financial institutions such as the World Bank and the IMF pressed South Africa to adopt neoliberal economic policies that encouraged export orientation and free trade. Key donors, including the United States, pushed the ANC government to focus narrowly on establishing a procedural democracy, rather than pursuing a broader vision of democracy involving economic justice. The ANC would also come under pressure from the World Bank to adopt a policy of negotiated land reform based on the principle of willing seller/ willing buyer, rather than a more radical alternative.

Within this international context, the formerly Marxist ANC: government developed five sets of policies that would affect wine farming: 1) liberalizing agricultural trade and deregulating the marketing of agricultural products; 2) abolishing certain tax concessions and reducing direct subsidies to farmers; 3) introducing a minimum wage and other protections for farm workers; 4) implementing land reform policies and programs; and 5) setting broad goals for black empowerment and transformation in the agricultural sector.

> **There has been more private support for black empowerment in viticulture than any other agricultural subsector, probably because the opportunity for new markets and profits is so high.**

In order to ensure food self-sufficiency at the national level, and to cater to an important constituency of the conservative National Party, Apartheid-era governments provided white commercial farms with a range of subsidies and tariff protections. The ANC government subsequently moved toward a dramatic liberalization of South African agricultural policy. This shift was motivated not only by external pressures, but also by the need to redirect resources away from agricultural subsidy programs to other areas, and by little sympathy in the new government for the situation of white commercial farmers. The increasingly competitive commercial agriculture sector has led to the loss of smaller and more marginal farms. With farms going out of business—and with commercial farmers seeking to avoid offering newly required legal protections to workers—the number of permanent farm laborer positions has dropped.

Land Redistribution and Transformation in the Agricultural Sector

Since the late 1990s, land redistribution programs have provided government grants to help blacks and coloureds acquire land when they are not in a position to benefit from land restitution. This program provides approximately $3,080 per eligible individual for the purchase of farmland (or more if the beneficiary contributes additional capital). In the Western Cape, the majority of land redistribution beneficiaries are current or former farm workers. Because farmland is relatively expensive in the province (especially vineyard appropriate land), large groups of beneficiaries, often 50 to 100 people, must pool their grants in order to buy a farm, in some instances, farms are purchased outright at market prices from willing sellers and then run independently by the land redistribution beneficiaries. In other instances, people use their grants to buy a portion of an existing farm, going into partnership with a white farmer. This second approach, known as a share equity scheme, is the only approach used to date with vineyards.

The reasons why vineyards have not been purchased outright number at least two: the purchase price of most vineyards is so high that it would take a vast number of grantees to purchase one; and there are certain advantages to going into partnership with an established wine grape farmer who presumably already has the know-how and contacts needed to run a successful vineyard. As of early 2005, there were 101 government land redistribution projects in the Western Cape, and of these nine were share equity schemes producing wine grapes. To put this in perspective, there are 7,185 commercial farms in the Western Cape, of which roughly 2,372 produce 100 tons or more of grapes annually. As such, land redistribution projects only constitute 1.4% of all farms in the Western Cape, and projects focused on the production of wine grapes make up less than half of one percent of all farms in this category. However, in addition to the nine government supported share equity schemes, there are also a number of worker co-owned vineyards that have been privately financed by progressive commercial farmers, international donors, foundations, and local wine industry groups.

South Africa's land redistribution program has been criticized from both right and left. Many conservative white South Africans believe that black or coloured farmers are incapable of effectively managing commercial farms. They see land redistribution as a waste of the government's money at best and, at worst, a program that could lead to collapse of the agricultural sector. Current problems with neighboring Zimbabwe's land reform process, including a series of disputed farm occupations by black war veterans, have only further fueled these fears.

Critics of the program from the political left, and even center, have focused on several issues. First, the pace at which the program is redistributing land has been exceptionally slow. By mid-2005, a little less than 3% of the formerly white-owned land had been redistributed to black or coloured South Africans, a long way from the 30% targeted for redistribution by 2014. Second, critics are questioning the "willing seller/willing buyer" principle that relies on the voluntary sale of commercial farms at market value, as the government does not have anything close to the level of resources needed to purchase 30% of white-owned farmland at market prices by 2014. Third, whether the large-scale, commercial orientation of the land redistribution program is appropriate has come into question at a time when so many commercial farms are going under. Finally, there are some specific concerns about share equity schemes because this mechanism may be manipulated by white farmers to obtain capital without actually relinquishing control. Furthermore, some have questioned how realistic it is to go into partnership with someone who may previously have been the autocratic "boss."

In addition to land redistribution, the South African government has a broader plan for transformation in the agricultural sector. This includes setting targets to increase the representation of blacks in management positions, to increase black ownership of agro-enterprises, and to increase the supply of produce to supermarkets by black-owned farms. Increasing black participation in the management of farms is key because farm workers have been excluded for years from the business and management side of farming. While farm workers are highly skilled in certain tasks, such as the pruning of grape vines, under Apartheid few blacks and coloureds were able to develop the managerial and business skills needed to run commercial farms.

Moving farm workers into management positions will develop a cadre of black people who could go on to run successful commercial farms of their own.

While encouraging ownership of wineries and wine labels by black business interests is important for economic equality in South Africa, this is not the same as ownership by farm workers. Farm ownership by the emerging black upper class of business entrepreneurs does not automatically help the poor; worker-owned wineries and vineyards have a better chance of doing so.

Three Worker Co-Owned Vineyards

The Bouwland partnership trust, the Nelson's Creek New Beginnings project and the Nuutbegin trust represent three different models of worker co-owned vineyards (see map). The Bouwland partnership trust came into being in 2003, when 60 land redistribution beneficiaries (of whom 55 are farm workers from the nearby Beyerskloof and Kanonkop vineyards) bought a 76% share of the 56-hectare Bouwland vineyard from Beyerskloof outside of Stellenbosch (of which 40 hectares is planted in Pinotage, Cabernet Sauvignon, and Merlot grapes). The trust's membership is roughly half male and half female, a split that is not only required by the government to receive grants, but that reflects the significant presence of women as farm workers in the South African wine industry. The group went into partnership with the winemaker for Beyerskloof and Kanonkop and with the owner of a London-based wine distribution firm. Using land redistribution grants from the government, and a commercial bank loan, they purchased both a majority share of the vineyard and a stake in the established Bouwland wine label.

The Bouwland trust operates with a somewhat complicated labor arrangement. Rather than working on their land during off hours, the trust shares the cost of a team of workers with Beyerskloof (which includes many trust members) that spends 40% of its time on the Bouwland land. The Bouwland property has no infrastructure, but rather relies on Beyerskloof for the use of its equipment and tasting room. With the exception of one full time employee who is involved in marketing and management, nearly of all of the group's shareholders have kept their day jobs as farm laborers on the nearby Beyerskloof and Kanonkop vineyards. The group currently produces and sells 17,000 cases of wine annually but is just breaking even, largely because they are paying off a loan. Their wine is sold in local supermarkets and exported to the UK, the Netherlands, Belgium, Denmark, Germany, and Canada. They currently are working with their Canadian distributor to expand exports to the United States. This is a solid project with a bright future, but the group is wrestling with the fact that it has yet to turn a profit, as well as some concerns about its dependence on Beyerskloof.

The Nelson's Creek New Beginnings Project is the oldest and most celebrated worker-owned vineyard in South Africa. This project began in 1997 when the owner of Nelson's Creek winery and vineyard gave 9.5 hectares of land to 18 of his workers as an

---

A Sampling of South Africa's Worker Co-Owned Vineyards and Wineries

Bouwland

Description: Formed in 2003, this farm outside of Stellenbosch is 74% owned by farm workers.

Contact Information: Tel: +27 21 865-2135; Fax: +27 21 865-2683; Email: bouwland@.co M ; Website: wwww,bouwland.co.za. Address: P.O. Box 62, Koelenhof 7605 South Africa

Wines: Chenin Blanc, Cabernet-Sauvignon-Merlot

Export destinations: U.K., the Netherlands, Belgium, Denmark, Germany and Canada. They are working with their Canadian distributor to expand exports to the United States.

New Beginnings

Description: The oldest and most celebrated worker co-owned vineyard in South Africa, this project began in 1997 when the owner of Nelson's Creek winery and vineyard gave 9.5 hectares of land to 18 of his workers as an expression of thanks for their efforts on his farm.

Contact Information: Tel: +27 21 869-8453; Fax: +27 21 869-8424; Email: newbeginnings@nelsonscreek.co.za. Website: www.nelsonscreek.co.za/new_beginnings/ new_beginnings.htm. Address; P.O. Box 2009, Windmeul, 7630 Paarl, South Africa

Wines: Chardonnay, Cabernet Sauvignon, Pinotage

Export Destinations: Germany and the Netherlands. Export opportunities to the United States are being explored.

Thandi

Description: This is the label under which Nuutbegin and three other worker co-owned vineyards sell their wine. Thandi became the first wine brand in the world to achieve fair trade status.

Contact information: Tel: +27 21 886 6458; Fax: +27 21 886 6589; Email: rydal@thandi.com; Website: www. thandi.com/. Address: R310, Lynedoch, P.O. Box 465, Stellenbosch 7613, South Africa

Wines: Pinot Noir, Cabernet Sauvignon, Chardonnay, Sauvignon Blanc-Semillon, Merlot-Cabernet

Export Destinations: U.K., the Netherlands, Belgium, Germany, and Japan. The label will be introduced to the United States, Canada and Scandinavia shortly.

---

expression of thanks for their efforts on his farm. The vineyard has subsequently grown to 13.5 hectares (the additional land was purchased from Nelson's Creek), producing Chardonnay, Cabernet Sauvignon and Merlot grapes. The group has its own wine label, New Beginnings, and sells wines to local supermarkets, along with exports to Germany and the Netherlands. Export opportunities to the United States are being explored.

The group is reliant on Nelson's Creek for equipment, management, and winemaking expertise. The New Beginnings project is turning a profit and its members are using the money to buy food and consumer goods and pay their children's school fees.

The Nuutbegin trust began in 2000 when 99 farm workers from the Waterskloof and Fransmanskloof vineyards obtained land redistribution grants to purchase a 50% share of a long-term lease from the municipality for 25 hectares of prime vineyard land. The other two partners, the owners of the Waterskloof and Fransmanskioof vineyards, each have a 25% stake in the project. The group produces Merlot, Shiraz, and Cabernet Sauvignon grapes which are sold to the Thandi winery, in which the Nuutbegin trust has a 7% stake. Thandi produces a variety of wines, sourcing its grapes from four different worker co-owned vineyards in the area. Significantly, this is the first wine label to be fair-trade accredited in the world. While this accreditation should allow Thandi to fetch a small premium on the global market, Nuutbegin's 7% share in the label means that its returns from this end of the business are more limited. All of the shareholders have maintained their day jobs as farm workers, and they coordinate with the owners of Waterskloof and Fransmanskloof to schedule time to work the vines at Nuutbegin. Like Bouwland, this group has yet to turn a profit, and they are somewhat concerned about their continuing dependence on their white partners.

The Way Forward

As these case studies make clear, land redistribution and black empowerment in the wine industry are extremely challenging. High land prices and capital costs, not to mention the need for sophisticated business and wine-making expertise, mean that worker co-owned vineyards and wine labels are few in number, slow to start, and often dependent on the good graces of white employers and partners. It is important to note that the real money to be made in viticulture is in the selling of wine, not in the production of grapes. So vineyards with their own labels, such as the Bouwland and New Beginnings projects, have an advantage. Furthermore, because land, investment, and capital costs are so high, new projects must take on significant debt obligations that severely limit profits in the early years. Unlike

Bouwland and Nuutbegin, New Beginnings did not incur significant debt; thus it can generate dividends for its membership more quickly and so benefit from a higher level of worker interest in the project.

The role of government land redistribution initiatives in the viticulture sector may always be minimal because the costs are so high. Interestingly, there has been more private support for black empowerment in viticulture than any other agricultural subsector, probably because the opportunity for new markets and profits is so high. This presents both an opportunity and a danger. On the positive side, private money means additional support for projects such as New Beginnings. But there is also a danger that private backers may see black empowerment and fair trade solely as means to earning greater profits rather than as paths toward economic justice. The key to lasting change will be having policy makers, academics, and consumers who are attuned to the difference between vineyards and wine labels that are truly co-owned by workers and those that are co-owned by black business interests with no or nominal participation of the workers.

Alas, what should North American and European wine consumers with a conscience do? I say seek out, and demand that your local wine market order, those South African labels that are co-owned and produced by farm workers (see "A Sampling of South Africa's Worker Co-Owned Vineyards and Wineries"). Yes, the South African land redistribution program is not perfect, but a growing market for worker-friendly wines will make existing ventures more profitable and encourage more white wine-makers to go into partnership with their workers. This is more than just fair trade—it is about creating a marketplace that rewards those working for change and economic justice, a world where workers really benefit from the fruits of their labor.

WILLIAM MOSELEY is an assistant professor of geography and former coordinator of the African Studies program at Macalester College in Saint Paul, Minn. His books include *Taking Sides: Clashing Views on Controversial African Issues* and *African Environment and Development: Rhetoric, Programs, Realities.*

Acknowledgement—I wish to thank my research assistant, Elizabeth Kruger, for her invaluable help in the field. I am also grateful to the farm workers who so graciously shared their time with me.

From *Dollars & Sense*, January/February 2006, pp. 16–21. Reprinted by permission of Dollars & Sense, a progressive economics magazine. www.dollarsandsense.org

ABCs of AIDS Prevention

Uganda has been widely recognized for its successes in stemming the AIDS crisis, but its policies fail to address the inequalities that make women vulnerable to the disease.

Jessica Weisberg

Uganda is one of a handful of countries to have dramatically reduced its overall HIV infection rate in the past 10 years. It's widely viewed as a global leader in AIDS policy and is seen as a model for other countries in Africa and the global South. Its approach, known as "ABC," stands for "Abstinence, Be faithful, and Condoms"—but critics refer to it as "A-B-and sometimes-C" because of policymakers' emphasis on the first two over the third.

Despite Uganda's notable successes in stemming the AIDS epidemic, ABC has serious limitations. The policy primarily targets male behavior and fails to protect a particularly vulnerable population: married women. It offers little to girls forced by poverty to exchange one of their only assets—their bodies—for basic necessities or school fees. And by focusing on prevention, the policy fails to expand affordable and available treatments to those who've already contracted the disease—or address the core economic and social inequalities that make women susceptible to infection.

Nevertheless, President Bush has routinely cited Uganda's emphasis on abstinence and fidelity in defending its own abstinence-oriented global initiatives. In fact, the United States has adopted the ABC model as the centerpiece of its international AIDS policy.

In his 2004 State of the Union address, Bush declared optimistically, "AIDS can be prevented." Prevented? AIDS can be treated; with anti-retroviral therapies, widely available since early 1996, the otherwise fatal illness takes on a chronic character. By prevention, the president was referring not to a vaccine but to abstinence. He's been known to say it "works every time."

A few months after the address, in May 2004, Congress passed the President's Emergency Plan for AIDS Relief (PEPFAR). It allocated $15 billion dollars for AIDS programs worldwide over five years, with a focus on 15 "target countries" which are home to more than 50% of all people with HIV: Botswana, Côte d'Ivoire, Ethiopia, Kenya, Mozambique, Namibia, Nigeria, Rwanda, South Africa, Tanzania, Uganda, Zambia, Vietnam, Guyana, and Haiti.

Twenty percent of PEPFAR funding will go to prevention programs. (The balance goes to support services and treatment.) By law, at least one-third of those prevention funds must be used to promote abstinence. The first allocation of $100 million in PEPFAR grants for abstinence programs was announced in October. Nine of the 11 organizations that won the grants were faith-based organizations. Under PEPFAR, such groups are allowed to exclude information about contraception from their educational programs. Ambassador Randall Tobias, head of the State Department's Office of Global AIDS, has cited Uganda's accomplishments when PEPFAR's abstinence program has faced questions.

Uganda's Way

Since Ugandan President Yoweri Museveni initiated the ABC program in the mid-1990s, the country has undergone enormous reductions in HIV prevalence (the percentage of individuals living with HIV/AIDS). The percent of infected individuals in Uganda has declined from around 30% in the early 1990s to 6% in 2004, according to the United Nations and the Ugandan government. Although some scientists question the validity of those specific figures, arguing that survey methodology is flawed and that the reduction in prevalence rates may in part reflect the deaths of those who had HIV in the 1990s, most agree that Uganda has secured the most dramatic turnaround in AIDS of any country to date. Museveni brought this about by aggressively raising AIDS awareness, by using radio and other modes of mass communication, involving churches and nongovernmental organizations, and by crafting messages that resonated with Ugandan culture; for example, he introduced the slogan "zero grazing" to encourage monogamy in the cattle-oriented society.

The effectiveness of Uganda's AIDS prevention and treatment policies has varied, though, with respect to gender. Far more women than men have become infected with HIV since ABC was implemented. According to the Uganda AIDS Commission, there were 99,031 new HIV cases in the country in

2001. Of these, females were three to six times more likely to become infected by HIV than males in the 15 to 19 age bracket, according to the Uganda Women's Network. In the 20 to 24 age bracket, the HIV infection rate among women remains twice as high as that of men.

There are several reasons for this disparity. Most importantly, research indicates that marriage actually increases the chance of HIV infection. In fact, the most dramatic increase in prevalence rates in recent years has occurred among monogamous married women; even as the overall percentage of people with HIV has fallen, the percentage of married women with HIV has increased. One study found that in rural Uganda, 88% of HIV-infected women age 15 to 19 are married.

For the majority of married couples in Uganda, the woman is at least six years younger than her husband. Paul Zeitz of the advocacy group Global AIDS Alliance points out that abstinence programs could "in effect be encouraging women to marry earlier," placing them at risk of infection by older husbands. "What use is abstinence, what use is fidelity if he is already infected and brings it into the marriage?" Stephen Lewis asked the Agence France Presse. Zeitz goes so far as to argue: "Abstinence [promotion] could be leading to a public health crisis."

Take Suzan, a 17-year-old mother from Ndeeba, a Kampala suburb, whose 62-year-old husband recently died of AIDS. She was infected by her late husband, and is unable to afford treatment.

With such large age differences between wives and husbands, Ugandan women like Suzan often outlive their husbands. When a man dies, his family typically repossesses his assets, robbing the woman of all her property and making her remaining years all the more difficult. In Suzan's case, her husband's family has taken away both their land and her child.

Another Ugandan woman, Juliet, is a 27-year-old widow with four children. Her in-laws also took away her home and land upon her husband's death. She is now hospitalized with an advanced case of AIDS, and her children are struggling to support themselves.

Women like Suzan and Juliet are overlooked by the ABC program's emphasis on abstinence and fidelity. Both women were abstinent before marriage and then faithful, but neither their own behavior nor the ABC program did anything to protect them from contracting the disease or to treat them once they were infected.

Condoms too are of little use to married women in a culture where extramarital polygamy is common but wives are unaware of their husbands' affairs. Even if women have suspicions, many adhere to patriarchal mores against vocally questioning their husbands' behavior. Those same mores also deter women from telling their husbands to wear condoms.

Harriet Abwoli, interviewed in 2003 for the Human Rights Watch report "Just Die Quietly," described her experience: "He used to force me to have sex with him. He would beat me and slap me when I refused. I never used a condom with him. . . . When I got pregnant I went for a medical check-up. When I gave birth, and the child had passed away, they told me I was HIV-positive. I cried. The doctor told me, 'Wipe your tears, the whole world is sick.'"

"Women do not have negotiation power," says researcher Sarah Kalloch, who has done considerable fieldwork in Uganda. "Women do not have control over their own bodies." Kalloch describes instances of wife-swapping, wife inheritance, and widespread marital rape. Rape and domestic violence are "virtually impossible to prosecute" due to legal discrimination. "ABC is not enough for women in Uganda. They need legal rights that give them control over their bodies, their relationships, and who they marry," Kalloch says.

They also need basic economic security. Uganda's abstinence program has attempted to reach "high risk" populations such as soldiers and truck drivers, but has sent mixed messages by disparaging female HIV victims for indulgent or "promiscuous" behavior. So long as extreme economic deprivation continues to force young girls to barter for food and basic economic needs with sex, this sort of message will do little to save those who lack access to income and resources.

In the poverty-stricken northern region of Uganda, it's common for parents to force their teen and pre-teen daughters into sex work. "The mother will simply say to her daughters, 'come back with food,'" said Paul Zeitz of Global AIDS Alliance. Zeitz refers to this practice as "survival sex," since selling sex is not a profession for most of these girls, but a measure driven by dire economic necessity. Most customers are truck drivers and traveling soldiers, who prefer young girls, believing that they are free of HIV. Truck drivers synchronize their routes with school tuition deadlines (which vary by region), when girls are most likely to be waiting at truck stops for customers, according to a study conducted by the group.

When asked if abstinence programs fail women, Randall Tobias said, "One of the best ways to protect vulnerable women from HIV is to instill the 'ABC' message in men. . . . " To Tobias, "the ABC model is a simple conceptualization of the major tenets of what happened in Uganda and can be implemented elsewhere with some local adaptation."

But as Lynn Amowitz, a Harvard medical school professor who has researched women's health and human rights in Afghanistan, observes: "The forms discrimination and stigma take differ from country to country. In some places, it's widow inheritance, in others it's that women are considered minors." Extending abstinence programs to these countries, with their distinct social dynamics, is unlikely to slow the feminization of HIV and AIDS. Without specific prevention programs that take such practices into account, the burden of HIV/AIDS will continue to disproportionately affect women.

The most dramatic increase in HIV prevalence rates has occurred among monogamous married women.

Already, 58% of the 25 million people living with AIDS in sub-Saharan Africa are women. Adult women are up to 1.3 times more likely to be infected with HIV than their male counterparts, and women and girls now make up three-quarters of the 6.2 million young people (age 15 to 24) with AIDS. Because women serve as the primary caregivers for their own children and work in disproportionate numbers in schools, as nurses, and in social services, the feminization of AIDS ravages the socioeconomic fabric of their communities. Furthermore, the epidemic will be passed on to future generations, as the likelihood of mother-to-child transmission is estimated at 30%.

Treatment Possibilities

The situation is not hopeless. Life-extending drugs such as nevaripine and anti-retroviral therapies do exist. The World Health Organization (WHO) has engineered generic anti-retrovirals that will reduce the cost of therapy to $148 dollars a year, compared to an average $548 a year for namebrand drugs.

But the Bush administration has put the breaks on treatment. Under PEPFAR, all drugs sold abroad must be approved by the FDA. Even generic drugs that have already undergone the WHO's meticulous prequalification standards must be reexamined by the FDA before they are distributed abroad through the program. This rule will indefinitely delay the availability of affordable medication.

What's more, PEPFAR allocates no funds for distributing nevaripine, which at a cost of $4 per person can reduce the likelihood of mother-to-child transmission by almost 90%. Likewise, it does not fund the development of microbicides, topical products that women could use, undetected, to prevent sexual transmission of HIV. Protesters at the International AIDS Conference in Bangkok last July condemned Ambassador Tobias and President Bush for prioritizing pharmaceutical patent rights over public health needs and ideology over efficacy.

Women's economic marginalization is a global problem, and severe in the 15 countries that PEPFAR will target. President Bush's vague declaration that "AIDS can be prevented" is, in fact, correct. Prevention programs can provide a cost-effective means of gradually reducing HIV prevalence, but only if such programs address specific economic inequities that underlie patterns of transmission, dismantle barriers to economic independence for women, empower married women, and deliver messages in a culturally accessible manner. Just as important, they cannot ignore the necessity of investing in treatment for women and their daughters, who are already infected. Otherwise, women's social and economic powerlessness will continue to render them disproportionately vulnerable to the HIV epidemic. For women, the solution to the AIDS crisis is a lot more complicated than A-B-C.

Resources

"The ABC Debate Heats Up," *Africa News,* July 13, 2004; Garbus, Lisa and Elliot Marseille, *Country AIDS Analysis Project: HIV/AIDS in Uganda,* San Francisco: AIDS Policy Research Center, University of California San Francisco, 2003; "Health: Women Demand Stepped-Up AIDS Treatment, Prevention," Inter Press Service, 2002; Ingham, Richard, "U.N. Envoy Blasts U.S. for "Ideological Agenda" on Abstinence to Combat AIDS," Agence France Presse, Bangkok, July 15, 2004; "Just Die Quietly," Human Rights Watch, 2003; Klein, Alonso Luiza, "Women's Social Representation of Sex, Sexuality, and AIDS in Brazil," *Women's Experiences with HIV/AIDS: An International Perspective.* New York: Columbia University Press, 1996; Ntabade, Catherine, "Abolish Polygamy," The Uganda Women's Network; Otterman, Sharon, "AIDS: The U.S. Anti-AIDS Program," Council of Foreign Relations," November 28, 2003; <www.siecus.org/policy/PUpdates/pdate0073.html>; "Uganda Puts Morality Before Condoms," Global News Wire, July 15, 2004.

Jessica Weisberg is a former *Dollars & Sense* intern and a student at Brown University.

From *Dollars & Sense,* Issue 257, January/February 2005, pp. 10–13, 18. Reprinted by permission of Dollars & Sense, a progressive economics magazine. www.dollarsandsense.org

The Fight to Save Congo's Forests

Christian Parenti

At the heart of central Africa's great rainforests lies Kisangani, a small city in the Democratic Republic of Congo (DRC) some 1,300 miles from the mouth of the Congo River. The town began as a Belgian trading post, Stanleyville, and was Conrad's model for Kurtz's inner station in *Heart of Darkness*. No roads connect Kisangani to the rest of the world; over the past two decades they have all collapsed and been retaken by the jungle. Even river navigation is blocked beyond here, as a massive course of falls stretches for sixty miles upstream.

If the vast and isolated forests of the Congo Basin—the second-largest tropical woodlands on the planet—had a capital, it would be this sleepy city of crumbling colonial-era Art Deco buildings and empty boulevards. Down by the river women sell caterpillars to eat, but no one buys them. The sky is low and gray, but it never seems to rain. In the government buildings, yellow-eyed malarial old men sit in empty offices next to moldering stacks of handwritten files. There are no computers, electricity or, in many offices, even glass in the dark wooden window frames.

In a strange twist, this general dilapidation—the result of Congo's traumatic history—has inadvertently preserved Congo's massive tropical forests. First, Mobutu Sese Seko's thirty-two-year kleptocracy destroyed what infrastructure the Belgians had built. Then years of civil war and invasion by Uganda and Rwanda took an estimated 4 million lives, through violence and the attendant ravages of disease. All this chaos warded off the great timber interests. As a result the Congo Basin's massive forests—most of which lie within the DRC—are the world's healthiest and most intact.

An estimated 40 million people depend on these woodlands, surviving on traditional livelihoods. At a global level, Congo's forests act as the planet's second lung, counterpart to the rapidly dwindling Amazon. They are a huge "carbon sink," trapping carbon that could otherwise become carbon dioxide, the main cause of global warming. The Congo Basin holds roughly 8 percent of the world's forest-based carbon. These jungles also affect rainfall across the North Atlantic. In other words, these distant forests are crucial to the future of climate stability, a bulwark against runaway climate change.

But the isolation of the DRC's woodlands is ending. Since 2003 a massive United Nations mission has helped create relative stability, though several vicious and overlapping wars continue to gnaw at the country's eastern regions. Now most of the DRC is safe for logging. Over the past four years timber firms have set upon the forest in search of high-priced hardwoods. They control about one-quarter of Congo's forests, an area the size of California.

Blessed by the World Bank as catalysts of development, the companies operate largely unsupervised because the DRC lacks a functioning system of forest control. The government has written a new forestry code that requires companies to invest in local development and follow a supposedly sustainable, twenty-five-year cycle of rotational logging. But many companies ignore these stipulations; some have used intimidation and bribery; others log in blatantly illegal ways with no regard for the long-term damage they are causing.

And now the massive mahogany, afromosia, teak and wenge trees of Congo are making their way downriver, past the lower falls and over the sea to re-emerge as parquet flooring and lawn furniture in the homes of French, Italian and Chinese yuppies.

If these woodlands are deforested, the carbon they trap will be released into the atmosphere. Environmentalists say that if deforestation continues unabated, by 2050 the DRC could release as much carbon dioxide as Britain has in the past sixty years. On the ground, this would likely mean desertification, mass migration, hunger, banditry and war.

But an effort is afoot to halt Congo's plunder. "This is a make or break period," says Filip Verbelen, a forest campaigner with Greenpeace. "Logging is not helping the DRC's economy, and it is destroying the environment. The damage has to be contained now before it is too late."

Among the major timber firms in the DRC is an American company called Safbois, owned by a secretive family firm called the Blattner Group. The Blattners' other Congo-based businesses include construction, road building, telecommunications, aviation, trucking, port services and agriculture. The managing director, Daniel Blattner, splits his time between a Philadelphia suburb and the DRC, where his family has run businesses since just after independence.

The Blattners have operated in Congo for forty-six years. They purchased some of their best assets after the despotic Mobutu seized them from their Belgian owners. Environmentalists charge that Safbois is logging in violation of local agreements and national laws and with no regard for the well-being of people or the environment.

To investigate all this, I set out to visit Safbois's main timber concession, a 667,000-acre expanse of public land the firm gets to log. It lies near the town of Isangi, where the Lomami River meets the Congo. It is an area of tremendous biodiversity, home to 32,000 people, mostly subsistence farmers.

The first leg of the trip is a flight to Kisangani. I am carrying five forms of official documentation, yet the authorities insist I need more. The underpaid civil servants here toy officiously with the components of a defunct colonial police state, not for the sake of law and order but to demand survival-level bribes. When the authorization is finally ready, it is hand-written on old brown paper, but stamped and signed. On the verso is a typed document concerning veterinary medicine. It reads: "Congo Belge, District de Stanleyville, Secrétariat . . . 7 février 1957."

To reach the Safbois concession, a local guide and I ride motorcycles west from Kisangani along the Congo on trails that only twenty years earlier had been blacktop roads. The bridges are mostly washed away or blown up, so we cross each tributary by loading our motorcycles into dugout canoes. A continual string of villages unfolds, each composed of thatched-roof mud huts. At times the path is filled with a sweet floral fragrance and clouded with white and purple butterflies. Forests give way to patches of grassland, then clumps of bamboo and then more forest.

After a day of riding, a modern multistory brick building emerges from the wall of jungle greenery: we have arrived at the Institut Facultaire des Sciences Agronomiques de Yangambi. Built in the late 1960s with Belgian aid, the old forestry university at Yangambi is now closed; only a skeleton crew maintains the buildings. But the university still houses a huge biological archive: stuffed birds, pressed leaves, wood samples, 150,000 species in all. There's a dusty old lab, abandoned offices and, according to the watchman, "a cave where King Leopold liked to hide." But the Belgian King Leopold, who owned Congo as a personal fiefdom between 1885 and 1909, never actually set foot in Congo. The university starts to feel like a Surrealist's jungle amusement park, or a monument designed to mock Congo's pathetic lack of a real forest policy. It is the embodiment of everything that should be, but is not.

'This company came here just to cut trees, and from the beginning it has been nothing but lies, lies, lies.'

—village chief Frédéric Makofi

The next day we cross the Congo and ride deep into the Safbois concession to Baluolambila village. Along a flat stretch of road we stop to talk with a village chief. "This company came here just to cut trees, and from the beginning it has been nothing but lies, lies, lies," says the chief, Frédéric Makofi, as several men gathered around nod their approval. Chief Makofi wants clinics and schools and building materials and transportation. He says much of this was promised but not delivered.

The new Congolese forest code requires that logging companies draw up social responsibility contracts with the communities in their concessions—essentially the law asks the firms to set up company towns. Greenpeace, among others, has attacked this corporate-centered model because it undermines the state's responsibility to create a functioning system of social services. But in the Isangi concession, people say the Blattners won't even create a company town. They claim Safbois used intimidation to force through an agreement and then failed to deliver the promised schools and clinics.

"According to Section 89 of the forestry code, the company must build schools and clinics while they cut the trees. But they are only cutting," says Chief Makofi. He says the company gave the people some gifts and started construction on one school. "At first the people were happy that the company had arrived because they thought logging would equal development." But, Makofi says, it hasn't.

"We don't have any norms or restrictions to impose on the company. This is our first time dealing with anything like this. There are places that are sacred and the company has gone in to those places and cut trees there. Those trees they are cutting were helping us," explains Chief Makofi. "We want development in exchange." Like many people, Makofi thinks that a well-managed forestry policy could ensure that trees are replanted and allowed to grow while still providing enough timber and income to help raise the standard of living here—balancing environmental protection and development.

His complaints are echoed throughout the Safbois concession. In another village, a mile or two away, we meet a farmer named François Likungo. "There is nothing for our benefit," says Likungo. "And the forest has changed—all the animals have gone. We used to catch antelope and porcupine and possums in snares. But now the animals flee the noise of the machines. Before Safbois came we ate meat five times a month. But now it is just vegetables and cassava."

First come the roads, and companies take a few hardwoods; then come poachers, settlers and agro firms, and deforestation picks up speed.

Two women standing nearby explain that childbirth is risky because the closest clinic has no medicine. School and medicine cost money, but this is an almost cashless society. Among the mob of kids clustered around are several with ringworm sores on their scalps and faces.

We ride farther in and soon the jungle opens onto huge smoldering clearings. Here another Blattner company, Busira Lomami, is clearing land for palm oil groves. It's a dramatic example of the chain of exploitation created by logging: first come the roads, and the companies take a few hardwoods; then on those roads come poachers, settlers and agricultural companies, and the deforestation starts to pick up speed.

At the Safbois compound—a cluster of trailers and mud huts surrounded by a stockade wall—I meet Kanzi, the company's chief engineer. Several months ago, when a Safbois official tried to sink a boat full of activists, a Greenpeace researcher and an Italian journalist were on board and filmed the event. The company came off looking thuggish, so now Safbois is on its best behavior. Kanzi stiffly but politely explains the situation from the company's point of view.

He says that there have been big misunderstandings. The company stopped building the one school after conflicts emerged between villages. The company is waiting for agreement from all the people in the concession before beginning to build schools and clinics in earnest. And he says that far from being exploiters, the company is harassed by environmentalists, who force it to tiptoe around the elephants, okapi and other exotic forest-dwelling animals.

According to Kanzi, tax collectors besiege the company. He offers a rather unimpressive example. "We had to pay $10 just to bring in 20,000 liters of gasoline here at our port. That is very expensive." He says, "The local people are happy to see us. But their friends and brothers, who have gone off to be educated, the intellectuals, they come back and excite the people to do bad things. They stir up trouble." When I ask how much they have logged, Kanzi snaps that it is none of my business.

After our interview I tour the logging camp with another foreman. A stoned police officer with a pet monkey on his shoulder wanders around, and in the distance one can hear chain saws. A harsh sun breaks through the clouds. The foreman explains that the workers are all from distant parts of the country. At the Safbois camp they and their families live in dirt-floored huts. The foreman tells me (and my little video camera) that the Blattners have not paid the eighty or so loggers here since April—five months ago.

To understand the local government's strange relationship of dependence on Safbois, I interview Crispin Kakwaka, the Administrateur de Territoire, at his office back in Isangi. Kakwaka describes the local government's appalling lack of resources. "We have nothing for forest control," he says. "The company gave us a few motorcycles for transportation, that is all. But we can't even inspect the amount of timber the company is sending downriver. We have to rely on whatever statistics they supply."

Coordinating opposition to Safbois is a small NGO called CAPDH. It survives on little grants, mostly from the Belgian government and UN civic education contracts it received during recent elections. Not quite a social movement or a social service organization, CAPDH is a network of about two dozen local intellectuals—part-time teachers, clerks, literate river pilots. Most, though not all, are men, and many of them studied for a few years at the provincial university in Kisangani.

"They [the police and provincial officials] forced the chiefs to sign the social agreement," says Delphin Ningo Likula, CAPDH's leader. "They surrounded the meeting and sent police after the chiefs who would not come to the meeting." Another CAPDH activist, Emmanuel Bofia, tells me, "The company hides logs in the forest, so the true amount they are cutting is not known. They cut trees in graveyards, trees in village meeting areas. They take the caterpillar trees. They are even cutting in the nature preserves deep in the jungle."

How does Safbois respond to these charges? Reached on his cellphone in Philadelphia, owner Daniel Blattner is irate. He denies that his firm is running amok in Isangi and explains away the villagers' frustration as follows: "We have a twenty-five-year concession, and we are building infrastructure as we go. We cannot—it is impossible—to build it all at once! We gave out plenty of support—over sixty bicycles, farming implements. They want 450 kilometers of road. By the time we leave, they'll have 1,000!"

About ten days after I left the Safbois concession, villagers, angry about broken promises and environmental damage, marched on the Safbois compound, pelting it with rocks. Police were called in and fired their guns into the air. Two protesters were reported injured. Days later, a survey party from a different timber firm was attacked near Isangi. The situation in the forest is tense. But to understand the forces driving these events, one must venture beyond the realm of villages, loggers, rough-edged timber camp managers and even comfortable Philadelphia-based capitalists like Daniel Blattner.

The real power behind the throne in Congo is the World Bank. It is the single largest lender to this hugely indebted government—$4 billion so far. In 2002 the government of Joseph Kabila signed a moratorium on new timber contracts. But the edict was contradicted by other new laws. Now the Bank is funding a complicated, painfully slow process of timber contract review. The government of the DRC will determine the legality and environmental impact of all 156 industrial timber concessions; tax cheats and despoilers will (in theory) have their contracts revoked. But so far the process is badly behind schedule. Meanwhile, the logging goes on.

In Kinshasa, I meet Kankonde Mukadi, the Bank's forest specialist. Why doesn't the Bank move forcefully to save Congo's forests? His response is high-minded flimflam: "This is a sovereign country. We can only make recommendations based on research."

Environmentalists laugh at this. Lionel Diss of Rainforest Foundation, Norway, was in Congo on a research trip and summed up the Bank's power thus: "If the Bank cut off funds to the DRC government and started imposing green criteria on new loans, and two or three of the most powerful embassies placed phone calls of concern to ministers, and European governments were ready with forest-conservation subsidies, things could be very different."

The real power behind the throne in Congo is the World Bank, the single largest lender to this hugely indebted government.

But in Congo, the Bank's hypocrisy knows no bounds: Despite its stated concern for the rule of law and sustainable forestry, its International Finance Corporation (IFC) is directly invested in some of the worst Congolese logging.

In mid-August the environment minister in Bandundu province impounded two barges of timber belonging to Olam, a $5 billion-a-year Singapore-based transnational corporation that the DRC accused of lying about the amount of timber it shipped, underpaying its taxes and using special "individual concessions" intended for small Congolese operators. The local government forced Olam to pay $34,000 in back taxes, plus some fines. Then in late August, Olam—still under pressure for what DRC officials say were numerous forms of environmentally destructive fraud—abruptly relinquished its two main timber concessions.

The World Bank, it turns out, had invested $15 million in Olam stock and in August still owned $11 million worth. IFC's spokesperson, Corrie Shanahan, was remarkably unfazed by the scandal. "Olam is a client of ours in several countries. We consider them to be a responsible company," said Shanahan. Asked if the DRC's legal actions against Olam were not grounds to reconsider the IFC's investment, Shanahan said, "We believe that Olam has good intentions, and I can't comment on the opinions of the DRC government."

To follow up on all these matters, I meet the DRC's minister of environment, Didace Pembe Bokiaga, in his mahogany-lined office. Behind his desk is a mounted water buffalo head and rising from the floor, two massive ivory elephant tusks. It's not the greenest image, but Pembe says the right things. "President Kabila is working very hard to root out corruption. . . . We have already recuperated 18 million hectares [of forest] for the state." This last is true, but most of it was land deemed unworthy of logging by timber firms.

"If these are the lungs of the planet, then the donor countries should subsidize us not to log most of it. But we need employment and we will have a sustainable forestry," says Pembe.

My faith in the minister is later shaken when an important timber executive tells how Pembe doubled the "area tax" on logging concessions, only to offer to undo the increase for a contribution of $300,000. The minister denies this charge.

Whatever the truth in this instance, Congo is still a kleptocracy; its massive civil service preys on every productive aspect of the economy. Transparency International rates it as one of the eight most corrupt nations on earth.

Corruption is a common complaint from the companies operating in the DRC, which also excoriate the government for its incompetence. The former general director of Safbois, Françoise Van de Ven, is secretary general of the DRC's main timber syndicate, the Fédération des Industriels du Bois. In her taut Flemish-accented English, she tells the familiar story of an industry under siege.

"This country is totally broken down. So we have to do everything. We build our own roads, run our own port facilities. You can't even get the normal large ships in the port at Matadi because the government has left it in ruins, undredged, no proper cranes. Everything is on the companies. And it is very expensive. At least 20 percent of operating costs goes to taxes.

And what do we get? Nothing. And if we build the schools, which we do, will the government send teachers?" She pauses to take a drag on her cigarette and sip her latte.

Congo's culture of corruption extends even to many village chiefs. In one notorious case, a logging company called Safo provided cement, tin roofing, machetes, nets and other basic wares as part of its social contract. The materials went to village chiefs, but instead of hauling the goods to their communities, a merchant offered the chiefs cash for the supplies and resold the goods in nearby towns. Infuriated, the villagers blockaded roads, made threats of black magic against officials and clashed with police; several activists were detained, and one was beaten to death by cops.

The most cogent critic I met in Congo was Arthur Kepel. Born in Kinshasa, he was recruited into Mobutu's secret police, was later the chief of intelligence for the UN mission here and is now with the International Crisis Group. His summation of the Congolese political class—a group he knows well—is painfully blunt: "They worship money. You should ask them, What are they doing for Congo? You can't blame it all on the Belgians. What are these Congolese doing for their country now?" Not that Kepel spares the Belgians. "They owe a moral debt to this country. They plundered it."

When I ask him about the international community, he again counters with a question. "What international community? Do the Americans and French coordinate against corruption here? Or does each ambassador try to get the best position for their own national interest, build relations that help the companies from their country get better deals? What do you think?"

Are there any politicians in Parliament who are genuinely trying to protect the environment and create development? Kepel pauses, scrolls through his phone, gives me a number. "But I warn you. He doesn't shake hands."

The next day I meet the man in question, Ne Muanda Nsemi, Member of Parliament and spiritual leader of a sect called Bund dia Kongo. Last May 134 of his followers were massacred by Kabila's troops as they protested against dirty dealing in local elections. Nsemi wears yellow and white vestments and receives me at his simple compound in a hillside neighborhood of Kinshasa. He explains that around a distant star circles a planet called Kongo and that the inhabitants of the old Bakongo kingdom, which once ruled parts of western Congo, were descended from extraterrestrials and Ethiopians. The whole story involves a tsunami, sunken continents, migration from Australia and many other surprising details.

I wonder if this is Kepel's idea of a joke. Then I get in a question about forest policy. Suddenly the millenarian discourse gives way to nuts-and-bolts politics. "The international community should pay for conferences that can be broadcast to educate people about the value of the forest and about the law. In Parliament we need to cooperate across party lines." He says the DRC needs sustainable forest industries, scientific management of the resources and subsidies from industrialized economies to preserve the forest for the sake of climate stability. "This planet is getting warmer—everyone needs these forests."

The main Congolese environmental organization working to save the forests is a small NGO called OCEAN, which serves as the link between international outfits like Greenpeace and local community groups in the concessions. This nascent green movement is calling for an immediate halt to illegal logging, by which they mean most logging in the DRC. But they also say that the DRC needs to develop the rule of law if a logging moratorium is to work—a long-term project, to say the least.

If the forests are to be saved, there will have to be north-to-south subsidies—call them conservation concessions or climate reparations. Paying the DRC not to log is hardly without problems, such as the boundless corruption of local officialdom—but even despite this, subsidies could help to keep chain saws and bulldozers out of the forests.

The communities desperately trying to leverage funds from logging firms will need something else in order to survive. And if massive subsidies are good enough for the tidy gingerbread farmsteads of Germany, the pretty backdrops of France and for US agribusiness, then surely the richest economies can spend to save the wilds of Congo, upon which we all depend. If Congo is deforested, the impact will be grim—and global.

CHRISTIAN PARENTI is a frequent contributor to *The Nation*. Research support was provided by the Investigative Fund of The Nation Institute.

The Long Journey of a Young Democracy

Africa's richest country, not yet free of demons, is facing a year of decision.

The township of Soweto, Johannesburg's largest, was once a byword for violence and black deprivation. Look at it now. In the Diepkloof neighbourhood, shiny new cars are parked next to elegant houses protected by security systems. Shopping malls are planned, banks have opened and tourists are coming. New bars and restaurants stay open all night, drawing in the rich blacks who now live, during the week, in quiet suburbs of Johannesburg that used to be all-white.

Even the poorest corners of South Africa now look better. Roads are being paved. People who were left in the dark and cold by the apartheid regime, which ended in 1994, now have lights, a roof over their heads and access to fresh water. Flush toilets are replacing buckets. Black South Africans are pushing up property prices and propelling the economy in general; black economic empowerment, brought in to redress the injustices of apartheid, has spurred the creation of a small but wealthy black business elite.

The economy is now growing steadily, at almost 5% last year; inflation has been tamed; investment is looking up; trade has been liberalised; and public debt has been cut by half since 1999. In his budget last week Trevor Manuel, the finance minister, announced a surplus for the first time in history. Another is expected in the coming year. A whopping 2 trillion rand ($285 billion) will be spent in the next three years, mainly on social services and infrastructure, and a social security system will be set up, all being well, by 2010.

South Africa now has an efficient constitutional court, a free press and active watchdogs—from a vocal (if small) political opposition to a crowd of think-tanks, campaigning groups and civic organisations. Flushed with virtue, the country that used to be an international pariah has become a mediator of conflicts in such cockpits as Burundi and Congo. President Thabo Mbeki was a driving force behind the creation of the African Union and the New Partnership for Africa's Development, which (if only it were brave enough to challenge Robert Mugabe in Zimbabwe) is meant to foster an African renaissance.

The country's influence extends beyond politics. Large South African companies, once corralled by international sanctions, have turned into proper multinationals. South Africa, which has 6% of sub-Saharan Africa's people but accounts for more than a third of its GDP, has a diversified economy and first-world financial services. Nigeria's economy, the next-largest in sub-Saharan Africa, is three times smaller.

The reaction to Mr Mbeki's state-of-the-nation address last month, however, was not as upbeat as all that. This is a young, vulnerable democracy, and democratic ways still need to grow much deeper roots. The next general election is in 2009, but much of the country's future will be decided this year: the ruling African National Congress (ANC) will thrash out policies in June and almost certainly choose its next leader in December.

A good economic performance has failed to make much difference to the lives of millions of South Africans. Although half a million jobs are being created every year, unemployment remains stubbornly high at 25%—or, on a broader definition, close to 40%. Almost half the population are poor; around a quarter get government handouts. The Congress of South African Trade Unions (Cosatu) and the Communist Party, the ANC's allies, argue that the government's economic policy has been far too business-friendly.

The government has also come under fire both at home and abroad for its catastrophic handling of HIV/AIDS. The virus now infects 5.5m people, affects many millions more and kills close to 1,000 people every day. Failure to see disaster coming in the mid-1990s was later compounded by Mr Mbeki's blinkered views of the disease—and he still cannot bring himself to say that HIV causes AIDS. The health minister, Manto Tshabalala-Msimang—a fan of beetroot, garlic and traditional medicine—was temporarily replaced this week as a strange lung infection confined her once again to hospital. She too has been attacked for giving muddled advice about anti-retroviral drugs.

Under much pressure, the government has now made anti-retrovirals available to around 250,000 people. Although campaigners argue that this roll-out is far too slow, two people—the dynamic deputy president, Phumzile Mlambo-Ngcuka, and the straight-talking deputy health minister, Nozizwe Madlala-Routledge, are breathing new life into the official response. Activists and the government talk to each other these days, though new AIDS infections show little sign of abating.

Crime also remains a serious worry. In Soweto recently Thato Radebe, a 14-year-old schoolgirl, was raped, stabbed and stoned to death near her home. Her body was found in the veld with condoms, bottles and sticks around it; the whole community was shocked. Ever more government money is being thrown at crime fighting, to little effect. Though official numbers, now almost a year old, show a slow improvement in most crime rates, violent crime remains among the worst in the world, with more than 50 people killed every day and a serious assault every two minutes. Armed robberies have spiked dramatically over the past year.

The government's generally respectable policies, backed by a plump budget, are often defeated by weaknesses in the civil service. It inherited a fragmented administration whose main purpose was to deliver superior public services to the white minority, while keeping other South Africans under the apartheid boot. The democratic government tried to create a unified, efficient bureaucracy that would reflect the new political dispensation. In the process, many experienced white civil servants left or were pushed out.

This has changed the face of the administration, but severely hurt its ability to deliver at every level. Ministries, hospitals and schools are struggling to hire enough skilled people; many prefer the better salaries and working conditions of the private sector, or are going abroad. Municipalities, half of which are in serious trouble, are finding it harder to deliver basic services, let alone to expand provision of water, sanitation and electricity.

Angry demonstrations last year made it clear that the poor are frustrated. The left wants a change of economic direction and more government intervention, and to some extent this is occurring. A plan to accelerate economic growth and share wealth was announced last year. The government and various state-owned enterprises have embarked on a programme to spruce up infrastructure, not least in time for the football World Cup in 2010 for which South Africa, to its delight, is host nation. The final will be played in Soccer City on the outskirts of Soweto, where the country's biggest stadium is being rebuilt and roofed to take the crowds.

The real ticket out of poverty, however, is education. One of the worst legacies of apartheid has been inferior schooling for South Africa's black majority. Plenty of government money has been pumped in, but with slim results. Although enrollment is up, the schools fall far short of what is needed. One international survey ranked South Africa last of 45 countries in science scores, behind Ghana and Botswana.

Power Tends to Corrupt

The government's frustration is evident in the way it handles criticism. Critics are often denounced as racists or "coconuts"—black on the outside but white on the inside. People who "whinge" about crime are told that they should leave the country; those who do leave are called traitors. Debate feels more stifled than a decade ago.

The increasing centralisation of power is also disturbing. The president—who leads both the country and the ANC—now chooses not only his own ministers, but also provincial premiers and mayors of large cities where the ANC has won a majority of the votes. That used to be the job of the local party. Parliament

needs to put on some muscle to become a better check on the executive. As it is, state institutions risk becoming extensions of the ruling party. Political pressures on the South African Broadcasting Corporation are undermining its independence.

Fighting within the ANC may also be weakening institutions. The National Intelligence Agency has been racked by a scandal involving unauthorised surveillance and allegedly fake e-mails suggesting a political conspiracy to prevent Jacob Zuma, the former deputy president, from getting the top job. The agency's head has lost his job but is fighting back; the whole mess smells of political dirty tricks.

Reports of conflicts of interest or outright corruption surface regularly. This shows that the country's watchdogs are alive and barking, but also that public office is too often seen as a way to get rich. Some politicians and government officials move into business with worrying speed. Black economic empowerment (BEE), which, among other things, encourages companies to hive off a slice of equity to blacks, has been accused of mainly helping a lucky, well-connected few, rather than nurturing entrepreneurs and creating jobs. Revised rules, which should spread the benefits more broadly through procurement, employment and social programmes, are at least some improvement on how things have been done in the past.

Mr Mbeki deplores what he sees as the relentless pursuit of personal enrichment. The ANC is making new rules to clarify the fuzzy line between party and government jobs on the one hand and business interests on the other. The sacking in 2005 of Mr Zuma when his financial adviser, Schabir Shaik, was convicted of fraud and corruption was generally applauded. Yet many South Africans feel that the fight against wrongdoing is not even-handed.

The main opposition party, the Democratic Alliance (DA), has largely failed to capitalise on these shortcomings. It has built its base by appealing to the white and Coloured minorities. So far, only one-tenth of its electorate is black. Until it reaches black voters, who make up 80% of South Africa's 47m people, the DA—which is to choose a new leader this year—has no prospect of coming to power.

The main opposition comes from the left-wing ranks of the ruling alliance itself. (No doubt the ANC's leaders think with horror of Zimbabwe or Zambia, where the opposition to liberation movements ultimately emerged from trade-union ranks.) The Communist Party has been making noises about running its own election campaigns. The ANC's trade-union allies have criticised the government's handling of Zimbabwe, HIV/AIDS and BEE. Both complain that they have been sidelined by Mr Mbeki's centralising rule. But for all their posturing, and despite lively rumours, neither group is likely to part company with the ANC for some time yet.

Unless the lot of the poor improves faster, pressure from the left will become ever harder to resist. Calls for a more pro-poor, pro-labour stance strike a strong chord with the party's rank and file. The battle should come to a head in June, when the ANC debates a policy platform ahead of the party elections in December. Since the party dominates South African politics—with 70% of the vote at the last general election—its next boss is more or less guaranteed to become president in 2009.

The Coming Leader

Disagreements over economic policy and leadership style have now crystallised around the political succession—and Mr Zuma, who remains the ANC's number two. He was cleared of rape last year, and charges of financial shenanigans were kicked out of court in September. Mr Zuma's most ardent supporters, mainly within the left-leaning ranks of the ruling alliance, maintain that these trials were political devices to prevent him from becoming South Africa's next president.

Mr Zuma's chances rest on three things: a court case, support within the ANC, and the alternatives. The National Prosecuting Authority has not ruled out reviving the corruption charges. This would kill his chances only if he is found guilty; otherwise, perceptions of victimisation would probably boost his popularity.

His standing within the party is hard to gauge. ANC leaders in KwaZulu Natal, his home province, have said he is their presidential candidate. So has the ANC Youth League. Elsewhere, it is a toss-up. Party branches—and, after them, the party's regional and provincial outfits—nominate candidates for the top ANC jobs, including the president, and also choose delegates to the party conference that elects them. As many of these branches are revived for the campaign, trench warfare is likely to erupt over the succession.

The support of the party bigwigs is also vital. Traditionally only one candidate is left by the time the presidential vote takes place at the party conference. Potential candidates are not even supposed to say they are up for the job. Recent allegations that Tokyo Sexwale, a prominent businessman and a former provincial premier, has been canvassing for support were slapped down by party leaders. Even Mr Zuma, known for his loud singing, has been rather quiet lately.

He is charismatic, charming, and can stir up a crowd—especially a Zulu crowd—like no one else. Yet many people, both inside and outside the ANC, are aghast at the thought that he might be president. The cloud of suspicion related to the fraud and corruption charges has not yet faded, and he has shown serious lapses of judgment (including believing that a quick shower could protect him from HIV infection). A pragmatist to the core—or perhaps shameless populist would be closer to it—Mr Zuma seems much cleverer at saying whatever people want to hear than at formulating a policy and sticking to it. This makes him a skilled negotiator and peacemaker, as he showed when he intervened in the early 1990s in KwaZulu Natal, then on the brink of civil war. But according to Raenette Taljaard of the Helen Suzman Foundation, a local think-tank, he would be "a malleable, pliable president"—and one who might be too inclined to endorse the interventionism the left is pleading for.

Other names are also mentioned. The party's secretary-general, Kgalema Motlanthe, is considered a potential compromise candidate, but his name has been linked—rightly or wrongly—to the trouble at the National Intelligence Agency. Cyril Ramaphosa, a former trade unionist turned businessman and a key negotiator in the democratic transition, could make a political comeback, but may not please the left. The deputy president, Ms Mlambo-Ngcuka, is mentioned; but she owes her political fortunes to Mr Mbeki, and probably does not have enough standing of her own within the party.

Lastly, not impossibly, the shrewd and technocratic Mr Mbeki might stay. The ANC leadership in the Eastern Cape has called for him to seek a third term as party leader. Mr Mbeki, who has to step down as president after two terms, may be tempted to remain in the party post, which has no time limit.

Nurturing the Rainbow

Whoever he or she turns out to be, the next president will have to rebuild bridges not only within the party, but also within the country. The warm and generous feelings of Nelson Mandela's time have receded, and Mr Mbeki has failed to paint a vision to inspire South Africans of every creed and colour. Both the government and the opposition have played the race card when it suits them. Pieter Mulder, the leader of an opposition group called Freedom Front Plus, recently remarked: "We do not know each other and do not debate with each other."

South Africa's democracy is young, and its institutions still need to be nurtured, protected and shaped. The space for debate needs to be broadened, and race relations handled with care. Racial fractures did not disappear with apartheid, and the followers of political parties can still largely be divided into black and white. Fewer Indians and Coloureds have been showing up to vote, indicating that many have not found a political home.

The astounding success of a recent song about Koos de la Rey, a famous Boer general during the war against the British, is raising many eyebrows. Some fear that the old-fashioned nationalism of the Afrikaners (whites of European descent) is raising its head again. But Tim du Plessis, the editor of an Afrikaans newspaper, argues that Afrikaners are merely migrating to a new space, between dead-end radicalism and ANC co-option. He points to a young, post-apartheid generation of Afrikaners reclaiming and reinventing their identity, unburdened by their parents' guilt.

In his candid speech last month, Mr Mbeki appealed to South Africans to help eradicate "all that is ugly and repulsive in human society". He regretted that South Africa's ability to unite in pursuit of a "commonly defined national agenda" was still in question. But solving the problems of crime, AIDS and unemployment requires just such unity, as well as a fresh approach, and the government needs to get better at bringing everyone on board. It is with this daunting task in mind that the ANC must choose its next president.

Underwriting Liberian Rebirth
Political Reform and Economic Progress

ELLEN JOHNSON-SIRLEAF

The 3.5 million people of my small West African nation of Liberia ended a most auspicious year on November 8, 2006. That day marked the first anniversary of an historic vote by the people of a nation founded almost 160 years ago, when freed American and later Caribbean slaves joined indigenous Africans of varying ethnic groups to become Africa's first independent state. On that day in 2005, our people decisively chose a new government to direct their affairs for the subsequent six years. Liberians made the historic decision of democratically electing their own, and indeed Africa's, first female head of state. In a real sense, that act signaled our people's firm commitment to breaking with the past 25 years of debilitating instability, which included a devastating civil war for more than half of that time. When that process of political change was formally consummated with the swearing-in of my inclusive and human rights sensitive administration on January 16, 2006, Liberia laid the political infrastructure for a new dawn. A long awaited national renaissance was underway. It was a sweet victory for a people that had endured so much for far too long.

Within a mere 10 months in office, my administration has already taken the first vital steps on the long road to national economic recovery, all of which are taken in pursuit of the hitherto elusive goals of shared growth and development. But our nation is fully aware that we cannot confront the enormous challenges ahead on our own. We will need to draw strength and support once again, as in our past crises, from our partners and friends—regionally and internationally. Such strategic partnerships for development are imperative. Given the unequivocal commitment of my new administration to conducting our business differently from how it was done in the past and the resilience and determination of our people, however, I am fully confident that as a nation, we will surmount the enormous challenges that lie ahead in our reconstruction endeavors.

From Relative Prosperity to Absolute Poverty

In less than three decades, Liberia underwent a tragic collapse from experiencing post-war growth and relative success to being one of the poorest nations on earth. The seeds for this dramatic collapse were sown many years prior to the 1980 military coup that triggered the decline. For many decades, political and eco-

nomic power in Liberia had become increasingly concentrated in the hands of a few. Together with a closed political system that over time had bred corruption, this restricted access to the decision-making process limited the space for civil society participation in the governance process. These limitations fueled ethnic and class animosities and rivalries. Political agitation and tension in response to years of monopolization of power and privilege added to the problem. This resulted in the 1980 *coup d'etat* led by Master Sergeant Samuel Doe, which toppled then-president William Tolbert. The military coup was followed by periods of severe instability, which culminated in a deadly 14 year civil war that began in 1989.

That instability, which was exacerbated by the actions of the Charles Taylor administration and a series of earlier interim regimes, also resulted in continued sharp declines in our national fortunes. By the time an internationally brokered cessation of hostilities took effect in August 2003, Liberia had qualified as a failed state for many years. The economy had completed a free fall that had lasted two decades, with national incomes plummeting almost nine-fold from twenty years earlier, to annual per capita levels of well under US$200. Our national budget dwindled to as low as US$80 million in 2005, in stark contrast to some US$900 million in 1980. We were by then externally indebted to the tune of some US$3.5 billion (now about US$3.7 billion). Poverty, both income and non-income based, had implanted itself among our people in an alarming manner. Some three quarters of Liberians were living on less than US$1 per day. The entire nation had been virtually deprived of basic services and infrastructure such as roads, clean water, electric power, and solid waste disposal. By some estimates, well over three quarters of our formal sector employment had been lost, resulting in severe hardship for most households. Rampant corruption had become a way of life, and our social institutions and social capital had been destroyed. In virtually every sector, managerial and technical capacity was fragile across the nation. Clearly, we could no longer attain any of our Millennium Development Goals by 2015.

Responding to Poverty

Poverty, corruption, and destroyed social capital broadly formed the distressing national social and economic architecture that my government faced upon assuming office in January

2006. Virtually everything needed to be done, while our own resources were too negligible to make even a minimal impact. Securing quick, substantive, and sustained external support and assistance was therefore an urgent priority.

Some of that necessary assistance had fortunately already come, and it was quickly expanded. Official donor assistance since the cessation of hostilities in 2003 has averaged some US$500 million per year, a significant portion of which has gone toward the massive cost of maintaining some 15,000 United Nations Mission in Liberia peacekeeping forces—one of the largest ever assembled in the world. Vital support of a humanitarian and developmental nature has also come principally from the rest of the UN system, the United States, the United Kingdom, the People's Republic of China, the World Bank, the European Union, the African Development Bank, the International Monetary Fund (IMF), and a number of regional African governments including Nigeria and Ghana. This timely and welcome support has undoubtedly permitted my new government to plunge headlong into the arduous task of rebuilding our severely broken country.

In our reconstruction efforts, we have taken several political, economic, and military measures. First, our country is now at peace. In concrete terms, we have completed the deactivation of the former Armed Forces of Liberia (AFL) soldiers. We are far along in rebuilding a smaller and more professional army than the AFL, and we are vetting the first class of recruits for training. We have deactivated the ineligible members of our Special Security Forces and are in the process of restructuring our National Police Force. Our partners have helped us to facilitate the return and rehabilitation of approximately 80,400 refugees, 61,000 ex-combatants, and some 321,000 internally displaced persons, many of whom have received modest packages of agricultural tools and equipment in time for the current farming season.

Second, we have taken the first critical steps on the long road to rebuilding our institutions and strengthening the rule of law. We have completed a new anti-corruption policy, and its implementation strategy is almost concluded. Our Governance Reform Commission continues to spearhead important reforms. One of these reforms is the finalization of a Code of Conduct for our civil servants; it is built on the public declaration of assets that each government leader had to make just after inauguration. Our Civil Service Commission is well advanced in the process of restructuring our civil service; it operates with a goal of introducing a merit system of proper compensation, performance indicators, and retirement plans. Additionally, a Truth & Reconciliation Commission is now operational.

Third, the revitalization of our economy is underway. Revenue performance has been strong for the just concluded fiscal year and is already well above targets for this fiscal year. Implementation of the IMF Staff-Monitored Program is near completion, and we are discussing a successor program that will further deepen the reforms and ultimately allow us to write off our enormous external debt. We have cancelled all forestry concessions, many of which were rushed through by the Interim Government under questionable circumstances in a process that began in 2003. We are also in the process of reviewing all other contracts and concessions of the recent past to ensure that the national interest is protected. We expect to conclude this review and complete renegotiation of the larger and more strategic concessions, including ones for iron ore and rubber, by December 31, 2006. We are working closely with our development partners under the Governance Economic Management Assistance Program to ensure better public resource management. International sanctions on our forestry sector have been lifted, and I have signed into law new forestry legislation that will bring benefits to concerned communities and protect the environment for future generations. Moreover, we have made progress in meeting the requirements for lifting international sanctions on diamonds, and we hope this will be achieved early in 2007.

"We are fully conscious as a nation that we cannot singularly confront the enormous challenges ahead."

Finally, after years of seeing our infrastructure and basic services destroyed, we are now making tangible progress in the rehabilitation of our roads, schools, and health facilities, as well as in the limited restoration of some electricity and water to the capital, Monrovia. We are steadily expanding and rehabilitating these vital services to our people.

Our Vision for the Renaissance

In short, we did not accomplish everything we aimed for during the first 10 months of our administration, but we have nonetheless made significant progress. We have a long way to go, but we are clear on where we are going, where we want to be, and what we hope to accomplish for our people over the next several years. We are presently in the final stages of preparation for our first Interim Poverty Reduction Strategy (IPRS) covering the period from January 2007 through the end of June 2008, which will be followed by a full Poverty Reduction Strategy (PRS) through 2011. Our IPRS sets a broad policy direction that will emphasize three issues: (a) consolidating and maintaining the national peace and a secure environment; (b) investing in our human resources, especially in education and health; and (c) determining how to quickly revitalize our economy and rebuild our badly damaged physical and social infrastructure, while at the same time facilitating export-led job creation, especially in the areas of agriculture and trade.

On that basis, by the end of the full PRS timeframe in 2011, which coincides with the end of my tenure, I will have made a difference in establishing a secure, peaceful, and stable Liberian nation that has neither civil conflict nor warlords. The new Liberian security and police forces will ensure the protection of our nation. The economy will have strongly rebounded with robust job growth. This will be driven by a recovery in the private sector, especially with regard to agriculture, mining, minerals, forestry (including rubber), stronger urban services, renewed investment, and increased trade with competitive Liberian firms once again exporting to the region and beyond. The budget will be balanced with much stronger revenue performance, and the World Bank's Heavily Indebted Poor Country debt relief process will have been completed. The civil service will be much smaller, better paid, and more professional than it is currently. Systematic corruption will have been greatly reduced, and land reform will have been completed. Local governments and communities will be more empowered as a result of decentralization. Schools will have re-opened throughout the country, and most children will be in school. Basic health services will have been revitalized so most Liberians will have access to them, and the country will be making progress on reducing child mortality and fighting major diseases such as malaria and HIV/AIDS. Electricity and water will have been restored to most of the nation, and the road network will have been largely rebuilt.

The realization of our national vision is not without challenges. A continuation of the political impasse in the Cote d'Ivoire with the possibility of a return to conflict would undermine our fragile peace and put undue pressure on our economy. Anything less than a peaceful transition in Guinea will have a similar effect.

On the national front, failure to address the vulnerability of the war-affected youth through educational programs and gainful employment runs the risk of threatening the nation's stability, as these youth could be recruited once again by non-state actors. This could divert scarce resources from the security sector, thereby undermining the rehabilitation of social and economic infrastructure. We face similar threats from the many domestic and external groups who have claims against the nation for salary and trade arrears. These are claims that ironically are being reactivated after being ignored by the previous repressive governments that had originally incurred such outstanding, and sometimes bogus, debts.

A final challenge lies in the impact that a land reform program will have on the important agricultural sector, because it seeks to replace the traditional land tenure systems and redistribute land to the landless urban poor and indigenous communities.

Opportunities for Partnership

Ambitious as all this seems, it is not unrealistic, especially given the will of the Liberian people, to tackle and overcome these challenges once the government becomes more stable. Liberia is not poor, but for many years it has been poorly managed. Indeed, we are blessed with almost year-round rainfall and abundant sunshine. We possess sizeable mineral reserves, including high-grade iron, diamonds, gold, and bauxite, with good prospects for offshore oil reserves. We have some 40 percent of the sub-region's natural forests. We are rich in marine life, both inland and offshore. Water is abundant with enormous energy potential. We are Africa's largest producer of rubber, which accounts for a sizeable proportion of our exports. We have a few well-located ports and harbors, with the real potential for serving as a gateway and transshipment point for the entire West Africa region. And for many years now, we have managed one of the largest "flags of convenience" shipping registries in the world.

But while the potential for our economic and social renaissance is enormous, sizeable quantities of private capital investment will doubtlessly be required. Strong, smart partnerships and alliances to effect the desired transformation of our economy will be imperative. The IMF, for instance, estimates that even if we had private sector-led growth at over 10 percent per annum for the next decade or more, we would still not be able to regain the levels of development we had attained as late as 1988, just prior to the civil war. Such is the enormity of the current national deficit.

Creating Space for Private Capital

A principal task for us, as a consequence, is the creation of the best possible space for attracting global capital in the face of intense competition over such resources. In carrying out this task, however, we must confront an environment for private sector-led development that is still far from propitious. Our energy costs are still far too high, and supplies of electricity, though improving, are far too unreliable. Access to finance for our domestic private sector is still very difficult; our approval processes for business licenses, work permits, and visas are still too lengthy. At 35 percent, our corporate income tax is far steeper than those of our neighbors. Land ownership and tenure remain far too complicated. Our investment incentive regimes and framework are dated, and our administrative and regulatory environment is much too cumbersome.

For these reasons, my government has already embarked on a serious remodeling of our business environment. With assistance from the World Bank Group, especially the Foreign Investment and Advisory Services and the International Finance Corporation, as well as the IMF, we are already firmly committed to upgrading the environment for private sector development. The key elements include: (a) reviewing and revising any existing legislation that formally discriminates against foreign investors and ensuring that our employment laws and regulations are revised to reflect international standards; (b) converting our National Investment Commission (NIC) into a "One Stop Shop" while also reviewing and revising our dated Investment Incentives Code; (c) reducing the bureaucratic hassles on private businesses by taking actions such as lessening excessive inspections of their operations; (d) comprehensively overhauling customs arrangements by enacting changes that include defining appropriate levels of tariffs and prioritizing the implementation of a fully integrated automated system; (e) holistically reviewing existing taxation arrangements, including discretionary practices for taxpayers and granting incentives only on the basis of a published set of rules open to any qualified investors; and (f) establishing a solid mechanism for public-private dialogue through a transparent and institutionalized process while strengthening lines of communication to our private sector.

Much of this work has already begun and is occupying center stage in our current to medium term development and poverty reduction agendas. These strongly emphasize growth led by the private sector, particularly by the agricultural, mining, forestry, urban service, and smaller manufacturing sectors.

Confronting Implementation Challenges

But as we embark on this new private sector-driven course for our nation, we are not unmindful of other, more general post-conflict challenges and resulting possible risks which may await us. These include occasional tensions between the three arms of our young government as each one confronts the steep learning curve of democracy; a multiparty legislature in which the administration has a minority presence; a still somewhat suspicious civil society with whom we must increasingly closely work; a donor community that is on occasion unduly wary of the past and the future; and the somewhat fragile political realities in parts of Liberia. Those factors, together with the constant challenges of a large pool of underemployed youth and the citizens' understandably high expectations of quick wins and changes to their livelihood, present a complex mosaic of issues toward which our new government must be constantly responsive and vigilant. None of these challenges will be solved by quick fixes. All will require strong partnerships.

The above notwithstanding, there are two additional major challenges with which we, as a nation, will have to seriously grapple in the immediate coming years. They are formidable in their own right, but they are equally a source of some skepticism for both our well-wishers and critics. The challenges revolve around two questions: the first regards the veritable commitment and capability of my government to seriously root out the endemic and systemic corruption that has haunted our way of life and our institutions for so long, while the second concerns doubts as to our resolve to facilitate the private sector-led activities that will underpin durable economic growth and recovery.

I will begin by addressing the question of corruption in our society. I have every confidence that we will win this fight. One simple reason is that this is not a cause to which merely my own administration is committed. I am convinced that the Liberian nation as a whole is fully prepared to face the challenges of breaking with our odious past. As outlined above, our new government has focused much of its attention on institutional reforms in this area. With growing assistance from our partners, we are also fully committed in our efforts to enhance our system of compensation for our public service workers, who are among the most poorly remunerated in the world. These efforts should reduce the pressure on both our public officials and private sector participants, who were in the past typically the objects of harassment in the conduct of their businesses.

"A principal task for us . . . Is to create the best possible space for attracting global capital in the face of intense competition over such resources."

Of keen importance in this fight against corruption are our traditional institutions. Our families, aided by our reenergized churches, are already regaining confidence, providing better sup-port for each other, and positively reverting to often forgotten social values and norms. In discharging our mandate for more open, transparent authority, my own government is taken to task almost weekly by our press of over a half dozen free newspapers and over a dozen radio stations for perceived failures. And in recent months, our trade unions have increasingly started to challenge their perceived injustices in the employment system.

Most importantly, if we take the long view, we cannot succeed in the fight against corruption if we do not quickly re-educate our people, especially the young. Our education system has already become involved once again in the routine teaching of better values and ethical standards to our children, which were so ably imparted to my generation and those preceding it through our parents. For that reason, we are committing to increasing levels of budgetary resources (some 10 percent this fiscal year) to education at all levels.

The fight against corruption is my administration's principal fight. And we dare not fail. But it is equally, and no less importantly, a fight of our people as a whole. This imbues me with significant confidence for its long term success.

In the second major challenge regarding my administration's commitment to private sector development, I am particularly conscious that my ongoing review of some 160-odd contracts and concessions (half of which include domestic lease agreements for our government offices signed under the previous government), may incite a measure of skepticism. Largely because of the previous poor recordkeeping, there have been delays in the arrival of crucial partner-funded technical support at the Public Procurement and Concessions Commission (PPCC) office, which is the statutory body in charge of reviewing these documents. In addition, such review has been hindered by the administration's steep learning curve in understanding the laws behind the PPCC and major weaknesses in the capacity of our judicial and legal systems. As a result, we are behind on the previously-agreed timeline for completing these reviews. It is a massive task, but it is still a very necessary one, particularly at this juncture.

My administration recognizes that much is at stake in reviewing these agreements. We need to be completely sure that every signed contract or concession to which our government is committed brings us maximum financial value, both now and in the nature. Successful completion of the reviews is equally important in assuring our investing friends that in their welcomed desire to invest in our new Liberia, their ownership and other legal rights are fully protected by law—with appropriate recourses for their violations.

Additionally, any necessary government oversight will be guided by more transparent and open regulations and procedures. Our partners must equally be assured that when we decide on a public tender for an operation that they are co-funding, we have followed both the letter and spirit of existing laws and regulations, especially our Public Procurement Act that has been effective since January 2006. On this basis, instead of sending a signal of weak commitment to private investments, we are utilizing our ongoing reviews to lay a firm foundation for more sustained rights and guarantees for our future investing partners.

Rejoining the Comity of Nations

All told, then, Liberia is back, and it is worthy of resuming its place in the comity of nations. Join us in strategic development partnerships and in helping to underwrite our bright future. We have begun to set the stage for our speedy and meaningful reinsertion into the global economy. After only 10 months of our new government, we are moving swiftly in a direction that will create a nation with which the rest of the world can engage and with which investors can do business. As a nation, we must continue to approach the future with confidence and ensure that our renaissance emerges, even in the face of enormous challenges.

ELLEN JOHNSON-SIRLEAF *is the current president of Liberia and Africa's first elected female head of state.*

Toppling a Tyrant

All Zimbabweans have reason to be rid of Robert Mugabe.

Just how much more misery and brutality can Zimbabweans take? Quite a lot, calculates Robert Mugabe, the country's thuggish 83-year-old president. He has just declared himself ready to stand in next year's election for another six-year term. The appalling beating inflicted this week on the main leader of the opposition, Morgan Tsvangirai, and other members of his Movement for Democratic Change (MDC) while they were in police custody shows how far Mr Mugabe and his henchmen will go to cling to power. Sadly, Zimbabwe's best hope is that the country's immiseration has gone so far that support for Mr Mugabe's misrule is now eroding even in his own ruling ZANU-PF party. Mr Mugabe has outfoxed opponents for 27 years, and may do so again. But the outside world can help by making clear how a post-Mugabe government could end the country's isolation.

The latest violence came on March 11th when riot police prevented political, civic and church groups from holding a rally in support of political change. One activist was shot dead and Mr Tsvangirai and 50 others were arrested. Although divided, the opposition showed courage in bringing the resistance to Mr Mugabe's autocratic rule back onto the streets. But all Zimbabweans are now feeling the effects of the catastrophe that has overtaken the country.

Once the bread-basket of southern Africa and one of the continent's wealthiest countries, Zimbabwe is now a basket-case and suffers a severe shortage of food. It is also the world's fastest-shrinking peacetime economy, with unemployment now standing at 80%. Its inflation rate is the world's highest: currently 1,730%, although the IMF thinks that figure could rise to over 4,000% by year's end. From infant mortality to life below the poverty line, the country's unhappiest trendlines run remorselessly upwards. To stifle dissent and quash opposition, Zimbabwe has been turned into a police state where elections are routinely rigged.

The effect on ordinary Zimbabweans has been dreadful. Some 3m of them (out of a population of 13m) have fled the poverty and chaos of home, many to neighbouring South Africa. Despite all this, until now Mr Mugabe has been able to count on support from his rural heartlands. Yet even his backers there are being hurt by the scale of the economic collapse. And therein lies the hope.

There are reports of threatened rebellions in the army, the police and the civil service over derisory and irregular pay. Bigwigs in ZANU-PF with extensive business interests have seen their own fortunes hit by the rampant inflation. Economic embargoes imposed on Zimbabwe by America, Britain and others in response to Mr Mugabe's tyranny are taking their toll too. As a result, some factions within the ruling party want Mr Mugabe to go in 2008, when his current presidential term ends. They then presumably hope to re-connect Zimbabwe with the foreign donors and financial institutions that could rescue it from decline.

The damage Mr Mugabe is doing to Zimbabwe is on such a scale that almost any opposition needs to be encouraged. But nudging him out will not be easy. He cares not a fig for what "neo-colonialists" in Britain and America might think of him, his methods or his ruinous economic policies. What his opponents need most of all, therefore, whether they are in the MDC or in ZANU-PF, is the backing and encouragement of their fellow Africans.

Devising the Rescue

That has been conspicuously lacking. And it may be again. South Africa's response to the latest violence has been inaudible. The African Union, supposedly the continent's guardian of good governance, has likewise kept mum. Yet condemnation of what is happening in Zimbabwe by Mr Mugabe's peers would not only help loosen his grip on power, it would also set standards to which ordinary Zimbabweans could hope to hold a post-Mugabe government.

For there is a difficulty. Many erstwhile supporters who might see their own interests best served now by nudging the president aside have themselves done some of the plundering that has brought Zimbabwe to ruin. It is not enough therefore for outsiders simply to accept a "more moderate" successor from within the ruling party and let the regime return to tyranny as usual. Clear conditions need to be set for Mr Mugabe's successors to claim the aid and diplomatic support that could put Zimbabwe back on its feet. The first should be demonstrably free and fair elections as quickly as possible.

Taking Care of Business

**Creating a better business environment
is crucial for bolstering growth in Africa.**

MICHAEL KLEIN

I n mid-2006 the World Economic Forum held an Africa regional meeting in Cape Town. The opening panel featured three presidents: Thabo Mbeki of South Africa, Armando Guebuza of Mozambique, and Jakaya Kikwete of Tanzania. A little over a decade ago, the presidents of these countries might have discussed apartheid, civil war, and alternatives to the market economy. This time around they discussed policies to promote economic growth and support the private sector as the engine of growth. Pointed questions from young Africans in the audience—unencumbered by any apprehension about African "big men"—were about term limits for heads of state.

The debate in and about Africa has changed, and so has the reality on the ground. Although performance varies from country to country, and there are still plenty of laggards, macroeconomic policy has much improved, fiscal deficits are under better control, inflation has come down dramatically, debt levels are substantially reduced, and the share of international trade in the economies has risen. Coupled with these improvements, the number of conflicts across the continent has dwindled—down to about half a dozen from about 20 reported by the International Peace Research Institute as recently as 1999 (Gleditsch and others, 2002).

About that time, Paul Collier, Oxford's eminent observer of African economic development, surmised that peace and macroeconomic stability would give African economies positive per capita income growth. In fact, 3 percent per capita growth would not be too hard to achieve if economies also started opening up and allowed businesses to flourish (World Bank, 2000). But Collier was too cautious. Peace, macroeconomic stability, and a small dose of business-friendly policies have brought annual per capita growth of 3–5 percent to more than a dozen African countries, home to more than one-fourth of Africa's population. Moreover, there has been an acceleration of growth across the continent, with Africa growing faster than Latin America for several years in a row. This is quite a turnaround from the last three decades of the 20th century, when per capita income, on average, shrank slightly.

Of course, the same growth slowdown occurred in Asia in the decades preceding the 1950s, before it took off with spectacular growth. Can Africa now effect a similar takeoff? Given the scope for catching up with more advanced economies, analysts believe that African economies technically have a good chance to achieve growth rates approaching 10 percent (assuming population growth of a hit over 2 percent annually). Thus, it is conceivable that Africa could, on average, reach the income level of recent entrants to the European Union by 2050. Were this to happen, today's children in Africa would leapfrog all of history's stages of development in a lifetime. To make it happen, however, Africa desperately needs major improvements in its business climate—long seen as deterring mainstream investment—combined with long-term policies to strengthen education and develop infrastructure. At the same time, it will need to maintain well-founded macroeconomic policies.

Sources of Growth

One of Africa's biggest problems is that, in general, growth is not being driven by expansion of the formal sector. To some degree, the current upturn has been triggered by strong commodity prices, coupled with resource transfers from remittances and aid. Ghana is a case in point. Remittances equivalent to 10 percent of GDP, aid flows of about 5 percent of GDP, and a boom in cocoa prices and other commodities have stimulated domestic demand. People from rural areas are moving to urban areas, where demand is strong. In their new, mostly informal urban occupations, productivity tends to be double or more that in rural occupations, thereby improving overall growth (World Bank, 2006).

While informal sector expansion is useful, sustained growth eventually requires larger firms operating in the formal economy that can get access to credit and trade with more and more partners, benefit from contract enforcement, and hire larger workforces. In a few countries, some signs of activity are emerging beyond basic informal urban activities and outside the commodity sector.

In recent years, the cut-flower business out of Kenya and Uganda has blossomed; fish products from Uganda have found new markets. Most recently the Nigerian film industry, "Nollywood," has overtaken both Hollywood and the Indian

Hollywood industries in the number of films produced annually. Nollywood, now the second largest source of jobs in Nigeria after agriculture, provides jobs for a million people.

So there is dynamism, and all the successes emerged without specific government support. The question is how this dynamism can be unleashed further. Clearly the immediate focus needs to be on creating a better investment climate, in which firms can be formally established and can flourish. Encouraging private investment is critical for sustaining growth in the economy. In the successful East Asian economies, private investment was five times that of public investment. In contrast, in Africa in recent decades public investment has been double that of private investment.

Creating a Better Business Environment

For longer-term development, governments and outside observers typically worry about levels of education and the state of physical infrastructure. These are clearly deficient. But plenty of things can be done to improve the business climate more quickly—for example, streamlining the myriad rules and regulations that make life hard for businesses and that drive people in to the informal sector. These rules govern the registration of new businesses and the ability of companies to hire workers and get credit, trade and enforce contracts, and reinvest.

Some observers feel that rules and regulations do not matter much in Africa because enforcement is weak and most people operate in the informal economy. But that approach gets things backward. People are in the informal economy because rules are overly restrictive in the formal sector, whereas enforcement is by bureaucratic discretion rather than by the hook. The Doing Business project of the World Bank Group has shown that rules for business are more cumbersome in Africa than anywhere in the world. Nowhere is it harder to form a business, nowhere is it harder for banks to get comfortable with the credit history of prospective borrowers, and nowhere is it more cumbersome to trade. Even labor regulation is often prohibitive. Sierra Leone leads the world in the required number of remunerated vacation days for formally employed workers—38 a year. The result: the informal sector blossoms. The regulations that ostensibly protect citizens leave them exposed and reduce opportunities for more productive and better-paid work.

Cutting red tape also applies on the trade front. Africa obviously suffers tremendously from bad roads, unreliable or nonexistent electricity supply, inefficient ports, and the like. But the biggest holdup for goods is not the time spent in transit: it is the paperwork, inspections, and customs procedures, according to the Doing Business data.

Similarly, short-term gains can be made by improving the management of existing companies. Even if workers' educational standards are relatively low, what matters is how rudimentary skills are put to use. African textile and garment firms are almost as productive as Chinese ones on the factory floor. The biggest productivity differences recorded in the World Bank's enterprise surveys are 2 to 1. But, overall, Chinese firms are much more productive. When taking into account the purchasing, selling, and other activities of a firm (total factor productivity), the productivity differences can be as high as 10 to 1. In other words, African workers with decent management can be very productive. We do not have to wait for children to go to school and come back in eight years or so before growth can start to take off.

Starting to Change

Just three years back, when the World Bank Group's Doing Business series appeared for the first time, African ministers were upset that, yet again, the World Bank was chiding them for insufficient progress rather than recognizing the significant advances made on the macroeconomic front. Today, governments throughout the continent have started to embrace the microeconomic reform agenda. According to the 2006 Doing Business report, Africa was in the middle of the pack of reformers in 2005. The latest report shows that two African countries—Ghana and Tanzania—were among the top reformers in 2006 (World Bank and International Finance Corporation, 2006a, b). The most popular reform in Africa is simplification of business registration. Property titling and registration has also gained momentum. Africa is thus tackling the basic issues highlighted and popularized by the Peruvian economist Hernando de Soto (see "Hearing the Dogs Bark" in F&D, December 2003).

Creating a more business-friendly environment may seem difficult, but African countries are edging in the right direction. Even if we take out the front-runners with the best business environment in sub-Saharan Africa—Botswana, Mauritius, Namibia, and South Africa—several other countries have made advances in different areas. Thus, if we took the best regulations currently in place in these other countries and combined them into a hypothetical "reformed country," the country would look like Sweden on the indicators of the Doing Business report—hypothetically among the top 20 countries in the world.

When it comes to substantive reforms, it is useful to ask businesses for feedback. Some form of formal public-private dialogue is critical. Encouragingly, more and more African governments are establishing some type of investor council that opens up communication between the private sector and the highest levels of government.

Much remains to be done, but it is obviously possible to advance greatly with only partial reforms. India is a case in point. Small reforms of the domestic business environment in the mid-1980s opened up opportunities for businesses and signaled that the government was abandoning ideas of central planning (Rodrik and Subramanian, 2004).

The reforms to consider in the poorest countries will typically include business registration, contract enforcement, property titling and registration, trade facilitation, credit bureaus, and tax reform. In Africa, taxes are very high for businesses. Those collected from formal businesses exceed the levels in all other parts of the world. No wonder firms remain informal. Ghana, one of the top reformers in Africa, was very successful in raising revenues to plug its fiscal deficit. Revenue generation rose by 7 percentage points of GDP in just five years from

2000 onward—good for the government budget, but a massive burden on the private sector. In Africa as a whole, government expenditure net of transfer payments is higher than in most parts of the world and close to industrial country levels.

Advancing the Agenda

African leaders have not begun to embrace change just because the World Bank said so. Upon reflection, governments in Africa and elsewhere have come to realize that a better business environment is actually good politics. It helps create jobs and reduce the informal sector, where people are unprotected and often employed in low-paid work. It helps integrate young people and women in the workforce. All in all, the agenda is about success on the basis of rules, and not on the basis of whom one knows.

Governments all over the world have learned that stable macroeconomic policy is good for a country, and the poor in particular, not least because the poor cannot take their money out of the country or otherwise hedge against inflation. At the same time, there has been a backlash, mostly in Latin America, against privatization of state assets in the natural resource sector and in infrastructure. Many governments are reluctant to let go of what they believe to be control of the commanding heights of the economy. But the very same governments that resist high-profile privatizations are embracing reforms of the business environment, not least in Africa.

It is hoped that collaborative efforts among governments, the private sector, and donor nations will help advance the agenda. Under the stewardship of the New Partnership for Africa's Development, the Investment Climate Facility for Africa was launched in June 2006 at the World Economic Forum meeting in Cape Town. With more than $100 million committed by donors so far, the facility has the potential to facilitate and support reform efforts in the business environment all over Africa during its planned seven-year life.

Critical to success will be the message that governments send out. If reforms are just on paper to satisfy some outside party, but governments do not seem to embrace the reform spirit, they will not work. Equally, if firms become convinced that governments will, step by step, move ahead with reforms, they will invest even when initial reforms are modest. After all, investors make the biggest returns when they invest in a weak business environment that subsequently improves.

> **"If firms become convinced that governments will, step by step, move ahead with reforms, they will invest even when initial reforms are modest"**

Trite as it sounds, the leaders of Africa are the ultimate key to success. What heads of state like Thabo Mbeki, Armando Guebuza, and Jakaya Kikwete say at meetings like that of the World Economic Forum actually matters. They set the tone. When the tone is right and action follows, even if it is only step by step, private investors at home and abroad will take heart and take risks. When the history of the 21st century will be written, it may become clear that Africa today is where East Asia was in the late 1950s—just about to surprise the world.

References

Eifert, Benn, Alan Gelb, and Vijaya Ramachandran, 2005. "Business Environment and Comparative Advantage in Africa: Evidence from the Investment Climate Data," Working Paper No. 56 (Washington; Center for Global Development).

Gleditsch, Nils Petter, Peter Wallensteen, Mikael Eriksson, Margareta Sollenberg, and Havard Strand, 2002. "Armed Conflict 1946–2001: A New Dataset," *Journal of Peace Research,* No. 39 (September), pp. 615–37; data available at http://www. prio.no/cscw/armedconflict, version 03–2005.

Maddison, Angus, 2001. The World Economy: A Millennial Perspective (Paris: Organization for Economic Cooperation and Development).

Rodrik, Dani, and Arvind Subramanian, 2004, "From 'Hindu Growth' to Productivity Surge: The Mystery of the Indian Growth Transition," IMF Working Paper No. 04/77 (Washington: International Monetary Fund).

World Bank, 2000. *Can Africa Claim the 21st Century?* (Washington).

_____, 2006. "Investment Climate Assessment: Ghana" (unpublished; Washington).

World Bank and International Finance Corporation, 2006a. *Doing Business in 2006;* Creating Jobs (Washington).

_____, 2006b. *Doing Business in 2007: How to Reform* (Washington).

Michael Klein is the Chief Economist of the International Finance Corporation.

On the Brink

Containing a potential HIV explosion in the strife-torn Niger delta is a tough job—but circumstances are forcing the oil and gas industries to confront it.

COLIN MACILWAIN

Bonny Island's strategic location, at the mouth of the Niger River in west Africa, has always been a blessing and a curse. An important trading post for at least seven centuries, the island shipped hundreds of thousands of slaves from inland tribes to the Americas. Its Ibani people have retained good relations with foreign businesses ever since, even as the island's main export changed from people to oil and gas.

The traditional rulers of Bonny Island have helped to maintain a relative stability here in this oil-rich but desperately poor region. That is one reason why Bonny Island hosts the largest-ever industrial investment in Africa: a US$15-billion gas-liquefaction plant that compresses and exports millions of tonnes of natural gas—enough to feed half the gas needs of France.

The plant, run by a consortium of oil and gas companies known as Nigerian Liquefied Natural Gas (NLNG), expanded spectacularly after Nigeria's government decided that the gas that had previously been flared off should be compressed and exported. The plant now draws thousands of skilled workers from all over the world, as well as impoverished workers from the surrounding regions. Although accurate figures are hard to come by, the island's population has grown from perhaps 30,000 a decade ago to 100,000 or more today.

That influx has set the stage for a new menace. A combination of migration, fast money and rampant prostitution may be placing the island on the brink of an AIDS explosion. And so NLNG, with help from its sister oil companies, has chosen Bonny Island for an experiment that could change the face of public health in the entire Niger Delta: a partnership between the local community, government agencies and oil and gas companies that strives to study, test for and eventually control AIDS on the island.

The project is unusual in that it seeks to pull together industry and government money to support an initiative that will be built from the ground up, within the community of Bonny Island. It places great emphasis on self-help groups and other mechanisms that will involve all of the relevant groups in the community, from schoolteachers to sex workers, in the nitty-gritty of AIDS education and prevention.

"We are in Bonny Island because it is isolated and relatively secure," says Donald de Korte, a veteran AIDS physician and consultant to the US drug giant Merck who is overseeing the project. Relatively is a key word here; in late December, the oil company Shell evacuated family members of expatriate staff from Bonny Island after car bombings and armed attacks elsewhere in the delta.

Money for Nothing

The project, called Ibani-se after the local people and their word for 'energy,' is the first of its kind in Nigeria. The country has an HIV prevalence of about 4%—much lower than that in southern or eastern Africa, perhaps because of western Africa's retained tradition of male circumcision. Still, an estimated 3 million adults in Nigeria are HIV-positive—more than anywhere else except South Africa and India.

With the exception of a few big city hospitals, little counselling and treatment are available; only about 5% of Nigerians who need antiretroviral treatment are getting it, says de Korte. Nigeria is awash with oil and cash, but not much of that makes it into basic health services for the country. Oil money has helped the Nigerian government to clear its $32 billion debt since 2004. But the economic activity generated by the production of oil and gas has inflated prices in the Niger Delta, fuelling social division.

The Ibani-se initiative is being supported initially by industry sponsors including NLNG, Shell and ExxonMobil, who have done other outreach programmes on the island. There is a discernable dichotomy here. On the one hand, the initiative hopes to achieve a sustainable partnership that is anchored in the community. But others have a more jaundiced view—grounded in past experience in the region—that nothing will function on Bonny Island unless NLNG does it, and pays for it.

Still, the project has a determined leader in de Korte, a Dutch physician who used to run Merck's business in Africa and then, from 2000 to 2004, led one of the continent's largest and most comprehensive AIDS treatment programmes, in Botswana. De Korte was tapped by officials from Shell and NLNG to chair the panel overseeing the initiative, after they heard him talk about his views on how AIDS should be fought. Since then de Korte has been working to constitute Ibani-se as a non-governmental organization (NGO), which would make it eligible for financial support from international bodies such as the Global Fund to fight AIDS, Tuberculosis and Malaria, or the US President's Emergency Plan For AIDS Relief (PEPFAR).

The key to the project is not to pour in drugs, money or equipment, which would in all likelihood be stolen, but rather to build something that is sustainable. To that end, de Korte and his team have painstakingly consulted a wide range of people on the island, including businessmen, sex workers, fishermen, the Navy, drivers, market traders, churches and mosques, and the twelve 'houses' of the Ibani people.

Reaching High

The initial goals of Ibani-se are, at first glance, quite modest. The project plans to have 50 patients on antiretroviral treatment by the end of the year, for example, and to have 800 patients—a third of those who could benefit—on treatment by the end of 2009. But given current conditions—with minimal public-health infrastructure, few people being tested or counselled, and practically no one getting drugs—these goals are much more ambitious than they initially appear.

"We need to rise up against the stigma and discrimination that surrounds AIDS."
—King Edward XI

The medical focal point of the initiative will be Bonny Island's dilapidated, 60-bed general hospital, where a team of 26 medical staff deal with 450 patients a week. The hospital is supposed to be being renovated; last month, the patients were crowded into just one of the four wards while they waited for the other wards to be fixed. "A lot needs be done" to upgrade the hospital, admits Douglas Pepple, the senior physician at the hospital, "but you have to start somewhere."

At present, the only people who can get AIDS drugs on Bonny Island are pregnant women, who are entitled to treatment until their baby is born. Everyone else has to go to a hospital in Port Harcourt—the sprawling capital of the delta, 50 kilometres up the pirate-ridden river. No one knows anyone on the island who has managed to complete the trip.

Ibani-se may help to change that situation. It was launched on 1 December 2006—the last World AIDS Day. The day has a high, if ambiguous, profile in Nigeria. In the morning, local radio stations discuss the issue of AIDS, and O Network, MTV's popular African affiliate, broadcasts a question-and-answer session in which South African schoolchildren interrogate ex-US president Bill Clinton about AIDS. It also shows videos of ditties such as *Put You On the Game,* in which Los Angeles rapper The Game threatens women with a life of prostitution.

Then, King Edward XI of Bonny Island and Peter Odili, the governor of Rivers State, arrive in the town of Akiama to officially launch Ibani-se. After a slow start the ceremony soon gathers steam, as about 500 schoolchildren and other islanders crowd into the community hall.

The king—who lives for most of the year in Nigeria's capital Abuja, where he chairs a confederation of Nigeria's traditional rulers—tells the crowd about an initial baseline study for the project. The survey, based on a representative sample of Bonny Island's adult population, found that an estimated 9,600 people on the island are now HIV-positive. "There's an urgent need to commence an HIV treatment programme," the king says. "We need to rise up against the stigma and discrimination that surrounds AIDS."

"The community is yet to come to terms with the fact that AIDS is a big issue here."
—Samson Sunday

Empty Gestures

For the event, Shell had shipped in a $40,000 machine to test CD4 counts—a measure of immune function—and dropped it, incongruously, on the floor of the hall. The gesture does not exactly thrill Ibani-se's organisers; nobody on the island knows how to use the machine. Thanking Shell for the gift, the king takes an adroit swipe at the donor: "$20,000 [sic] is nothing compared with what we will have to do in the future to mount a project that must be sustainable," he tells the community.

The budget of the programme has been modest so far, with about $600,000 donated by NLNG last year and $1.4 million set to be forthcoming in 2007. Merck has contributed the time of de Korte and other outside consultants, and plans to eventually supply drugs to the programme at a reduced rate.

The initiative's small group of permanent staff are Nigerian healthcare workers, hired mainly from other NGOs. "The community is yet to come to terms with the fact that AIDS is a big issue here," says one of the team, Samson Sunday. "They know it exists, but they see it as a blight from the outside that only affects a small number of people. The first promising sign is that community leaders are accepting that they are sitting on a time bomb if they don't do something soon."

The project's start-up has been much tougher than anticipated. Ibani-se still hasn't attained the legal status that it seeks as an NGO, despite trying for the past year and a half. Basic logistics are immensely problematic. Project managers didn't want new vehicles at first, as ostentatious transportation is the first thing that tends to divide community projects in Africa from the communities they purport to serve. But as a result, the project has become too dependent on NLNG for logistical support. Ibani-se's staff have found, to their frustration, that while they wait for transport and phone lines, staff at the gas company have other priorities.

The headquarters of the project is also still located on NLNG's fortified residential compound, whose manicured lawns and smart buildings look more like a retirement complex in Florida than the 'real' island outside the gates. Ibani-se is planning to move to one of the only concrete buildings in Bonny Town, the island's largest village. The building was constructed 20 years ago by Shell as a community library, but it has never been used and has stood derelict ever since.

It is palpable that local participants in the project are expecting some material gain. "There is hardly any volunteerism on the island," says de Korte, who wants as many people as possible on Bonny Island to devote some of their own time to the project. But so far, "community engagement has only scratched the surface". The whole exercise has been much more difficult than expected, he admits. "I underestimated the Nigerian environment."

Platforms for Success

On the other hand, de Korte is proud of the baseline survey done last summer by a Nigerian NGO, the Society for Family Health. The survey forms the basis for the project's action plan and provides the first detailed examination of sexual practices and HIV prevalence on Bonny Island. It shows that the prevalence of HIV is now 7.8%—double what it was five years ago. The study is not yet complete or cleared for release, but it is already identifying areas that Ibani-se could focus on, such as the sexual behaviour of the local sex workers and the 17,000 staff and contractors at the NLNG plant.

Not everyone on the island was surveyed, however. An extension to the liquefied gas plant, being built by an international consortium led by the US corporation Halliburton, employs another 1,700 workers. The consortium declined to participate in the survey, citing security concerns. Unlike the gas liquefaction plant itself—which is increasingly staffed by Nigerians—almost all the workers in the extension are white expatriates.

Brian Buckley, general manager for production at NLNG, says that the Ibani-se project is just one component of the gas company's plan to tackle social issues on the island. He says that he is hopeful that Halliburton workers will participate in the project later on. NLNG staff have already done so, he points out, although not many of the expatriates volunteered for testing. From the company's point of view, Buckley says, the Ibani-se programme is vital to the long-term future of the plant. "We don't want to end up with our workforce depleted, like the mines in South Africa," he says. "The kids growing up on this island are the future of this community."

World AIDS Day may have provided a glimpse of that future. Before and after the king's ceremony, long lines of people queued patiently to be counselled individually in a small interview cubicle, then give blood and be tested for AIDS. The four Ibani-se counsellors worked for hours and tested 100 people, but eventually ran out of time. They took down details of 121 more people for subsequent testing—taking the project some way towards its initial goal of testing 3,000 people by the end of the year.

If Ibani-se takes off as planned, its cost will rise significantly: thousands of islanders could end up on antiretroviral drugs priced at perhaps $60 per month. De Korte is confident that the Global Fund and other sources will help to foot the bill. But a spokesman for the fund, Jon Liden, says that public–private partnerships are "not as easy in practice as we had thought". Efforts to fight AIDS in Nigeria, he says, have varied tremendously in quality; on several occasions, the fund has not renewed grants to Nigeria, "due to poor performance".

Addressing the Stigma

World AIDS Day saw the project off to an auspicious start though, and the king's words provided some assurance that the initiative has buy-in at the right levels. "We are pleased that the king has given his support," says Ibiba Chidi, a project manager for Ibani-se.

For now, one of the project's focal points will be education. Stigma continues to surround AIDS on Bonny Island: health workers have uncovered very few people who admit to being HIV-positive. At the ceremony, a woman who was billed as speaking for people who are HIV-positive said she was, in fact, speaking out for a friend who is.

The other focal point, again reflecting data from the baseline survey, will be the activities of sex workers on the island. Project officials estimate that some 500 prostitutes work in Monkey village, on the main drag between the NLNG residential compound and the gas plant, where men gather at night to meet girls.

25-year old Joy Odudu runs a makeshift wooden bar in the ramshackle village. "I came to the island to work, but was looking for a job for a year and none was coming," she says. She claims that site managers wanted a bribe of 40,000 naira (more than US$300) from women seeking employment there.

Odudu, whose arm was shot by river bandits, says that about half the men who frequent her bar after dark are expatriates, and that some of them will pay girls extra not to use condoms. She says she doesn't know how often this happens—"we can't follow them into their rooms"—but that arguments between clients and girls, and between girls, have exposed the practice. One Australian worker, she asserts, was paying girls $300 or $400 for nights of unprotected sex.

> "We don't want to end up with our workforce depleted, like the mines in South Africa."
>
> —Brian Buckley

A nightly curfew, introduced after three oil workers were kidnapped on Bonny Island last August, is hurting business, Odudu says. But the expatriates are still coming, curfew or no curfew, says Peters Kunamon, headman of a section of Monkey village, Odudu's protector and a member of Ibani-se's community interface committee.

Asked about the project itself, both Odudu and Kunamon say it will win their support if it provides them with some material benefit. "It is supposed to be voluntary—but we need to eat," says Kunamon, who also runs a pharmacy store in the village that will sell condoms. "The project is good if it gives us something." Kunamon mentions something else that others are not keen to point out: women with day jobs on the site, he alleges, are also 'working' there at night.

Lucy, a girl at the bar, is just as direct. As she realizes that visitors are here for a chat, not for sex, her mood swings between charm and irritation. "You want jiggy-jiggy? Condoms or no condoms—what does it matter?" she asks sarcastically, voice rising. "We have to pay 100 naira here for water, to wash in the morning. We need to eat! We have nothing!"

Setting the Scene

Back inside the compound at the close of World AIDS Day, the Sun goes down soon after six, as it does all year round so near the equator. Soon after, as the curfew takes effect, engineers converge on the open-air cocktail bar, where local musicians provide some outdoor entertainment. It's an attractive setting, with elegant log cabins and decks and an outdoor pool whose racing section is 49 metres long. If it were an olympian 50 metres, apparently, the law would require NLNG to open it to the public; in this intensely fortified zone, that wouldn't do at all.

Buckley is there, on what happens to be his last day as production manager. Next week, he is off to run an even larger (and more peaceable) liquefied-gas facility in Oman. He relaxes with a beer and a group of friends, most of whom sport polo shirts and chinos, the international uniform of the professional man at rest.

But all around the outer reaches of the extensive bar pavilion, smartly dressed Nigerian girls who don't look at all like petrochemical engineers are hanging out. Their teeth and eyes sparkle in the evening light, they have the great posture you only get from learning to balance ten litres of water on your head at the age of four, and they're keen to strike up conversation with strangers. "Five thousand naira," one of them whispers, by way of introduction. "All night long!"

COLIN MACILWAIN writes for Nature from Edinburgh.

Glossary of Terms and Abbreviations

Acquired Immune Deficiency Syndrome (AIDS) A disease of immune system dysfunction widely believed to be caused by the human immunodeficiency virus (HIV), which allows opportunistic infections to take over the body.

African Development Bank Founded in 1963 under the auspices of the United Nations Economic Commission on Africa, the bank, located in Côte d'Ivoire, makes loans to African countries, although other nations can apply.

African National Congress (ANC) Founded in 1912, the group's goal is to achieve equal rights for blacks in South Africa through nonviolent action. "Spear of the Nation," the ANC wing dedicated to armed struggle, was organized after the Sharpeville massacre in 1960.

African Party for the Independence of Guinea-Bissau and Cape Verde (PAIGC) An independence movement that fought during the 1960s and 1970s for the liberation of present-day Guinea-Bissau and Cape Verde from Portuguese rule. The two territories were ruled separately by a united PAIGC until a 1981 coup in Guinea-Bissau caused the party to split along national lines. In 1981 the Cape Verdean PAIGC formally renounced its Guinea links and became the PAICV.

African Socialism A term applied to a variety of ideas (including those of Nkrumah and Senghor) about communal and shared production in Africa's past and present. The concept of African socialism was especially popular in the early 1960s. Adherence to it has not meant governments' exclusion of private-capitalist ventures.

African Union (AU) Founded in 2001 as a successor to the *Organization of African Unity (OAU)* (founded 1963), its membership consists of fifty-three of the fifty-four independent of Africa (Morocco is not a member). Like the OAU before it, its goal is to promote peace and security as well as social and economic development.

Afrikaners South Africans of European descent who speak Afrikaans and are often referred to as *Boers* (Afrikaans for "farmers").

Algiers Agreement The 1979 peace agreement when Mauritania made peace with the Polisario and abandoned claims to Western Sahara.

Aouzou Strip A barren strip of land between Libya and Chad contested by both countries.

Apartheid Literally, "separatehood," a South African policy that segregated the races socially, legally, and politically.

Arusha Declaration A document issued in 1967 by Tanzanian President Julius Nyerere, committing the country to socialism based on peasant farming, democracy under one party, and self-reliance.

Assimilado The Portuguese term for Africans who became "assimilated" to Western ways. Assimilados enjoyed equal rights under Portuguese law.

Azanian People's Organization (AZAPO) Founded in 1978 at the time of the Black Consciousness Movement and revitalized in the 1980s, the movement works to develop chapters and bring together black organizations in a national forum.

Bantu A major linguistic classification for many Central, Southern, and East African languages.

Bantustans Areas, or "homelands," to which black South Africans were assigned "citizenship" as part of the policy of apartheid.

Basarawa Peoples of Botswana who have historically been hunters and gatherers.

Berber The collective term for the indigenous languages and peoples of North Africa.

Black Consciousness Movement A South African student movement founded by Steve Biko and others in the 1970s to promote pride and empowerment of blacks.

Boers See *Afrikaners.*

Brotherhoods Islamic organizations based on specific religious beliefs and practices. In many areas, brotherhood leaders and their spiritual followers gain political influence.

Cabinda A small, oil-rich portion of Angola separated from the main body of that country by a coastal strip of the Democratic Republic of the Congo.

Caliphate The office or dominion of a caliph, the spiritual head of Islam.

Cassava A tropical plant with a fleshy, edible rootstock; one of the staples of the African diet. Also known as manioc.

Chimurenga A Shona term meaning "fighting in which everyone joins," used to refer to Zimbabwe's fight for independence.

Committee for the Struggle against Drought in the Sahel (CILSS) A grouping of eight West African countries, formed to fight the effects of drought in the region.

Commonwealth of Nations An association of nations and dependencies loosely joined by the common tie of having been part of the British Empire.

Copperbelt A section of Zambia with a high concentration of copper-mining concessions.

Creole A person or language of mixed African and European descent.

Dergue From the Amheric word for "committee," the ruling body of Ethiopia following the Revolution in 1974 to the 1991 Revolution (it was overthrown by the Ethiopian People's Revolutionary Democratic Front).

East African Community (EAC) Established in 1967, this organization grew out of the East African Common Services Organization begun under British rule. The EAC included Kenya, Tanzania, and Uganda in a customs union and involved common currency and development of infrastructure. It was disbanded in 1977, and the final division of assets was completed in 1983.

Economic Commission for Africa (ECA) Founded in 1958 by the Economic and Social Committee of the United Nations to aid African development through regional centers, field agents, and the encouragement of regional efforts, food self-sufficiency, transport, and communications development.

Economic Community of Central African States (CEEAC, also known as ECCA) An organization of all of the Central African

Glossary of Terms and Abbreviations

states, as well as Rwanda and Burundi, whose goal is to promote economic and social cooperation among its members.

Economic Community of West Africa (CEAO) An economic organization of former French colonies that was formed to promote trade and regional economic cooperation.

Economic Organization of West African States (ECOWAS) Established in 1975 by the Treaty of Lagos, the organization includes all of the West African states except Western Sahara. The organization's goals are to promote trade, cooperation, and self-reliance among its members.

Enclave Industry An industry run by a foreign company that uses imported technology and machinery and exports the product to industrialized countries; often described as a "state within a state."

Eritrean People's Liberation Front (EPLF) The major group fighting the Ethiopian government for the independence of Eritrea.

European Community See *European Union.*

European Union (EU) Known as the European Community until 1994, this is the collective designation of three organizations with common membership—the European Economic Community, the European Coal and Steel Community, and the European Atomic Energy Community. Sometimes also referred to as the Common Market.

Evolués A term used in colonial Zaire (the Democratic Republic of the Congo) to refer to Western-educated Congolese.

Fokonolas Indigenous village management bodies.

Food and Agricultural Organization of the United Nations (FAO) Established in 1945 to oversee good nutrition and agricultural development. **Franc Zone** (Commonly known as the CFA [*le franc des Colonies Françaises d'Afrique*] franc zone.) This organization includes members of the West African Monetary Union and the monetary organizations of Central Africa that have currencies linked to the French franc. Reserves are managed by the French treasury and guaranteed by the French franc.

Freedom Charter Established in 1955, this charter proclaimed equal rights for all South Africans and has been a foundation for almost all groups in the resistance against apartheid.

Frelimo See *Mozambique Liberation Front.*

French Equatorial Africa (FEA) The French colonial federation that included present-day Democratic Republic of the Congo, Central African Republic, Chad, and Gabon.

French West Africa The administrative division of the former French colonial empire that included the current independent countries of Senegal, Côte d'Ivoire, Guinea, Mali, Niger, Burkina Faso, Benin, and Mauritania.

Frontline States A caucus supported by the Organization of African Unity (consisting of Tanzania, Zambia, Mozambique, Botswana, Zimbabwe, and Angola) whose goal was to achieve black majority rule in all of Southern Africa.

Green Revolution Use of Western technology and agricultural practices to increase food production and agricultural yields.

Griots Professional bards of West Africa, some of whom tell history and are accompanied by the playing of the kora or harp-lute.

Gross Domestic Product (GDP) The value of production attributable to the factors of production in a given country regardless of their ownership. GDP equals GNP minus the product of a country's residents originating in the rest of the world.

Gross National Product (GNP) The sum of the values of all goods and services produced by a country's residents at home and abroad in any given year, less income earned by foreign residents and remitted abroad.

Guerrilla A member of a small force of irregular soldiers. Generally, guerrilla forces are made up of volunteers who make surprise raids against the incumbent military or political force.

Harmattan In West Africa, the dry wind that blows in from the Sahara Desert during January and February, which now reaches many parts of the West African coast. Its dust and haze are a sign of the new year and of new agricultural problems.

Homelands See *Bantustans.*

Horn of Africa A section of northeastern Africa including the countries of Djibouti, Ethiopia, Somalia, and the Sudan.

Hut Tax Instituted by the colonial governments in Africa, this measure required families to pay taxes on each building in the village.

International Monetary Fund (IMF) Established in 1945 to promote international monetary cooperation.

Irredentism An effort to unite certain people and territory in one state with another, on the grounds that they belong together.

Islam A religious faith started in Arabia during the seventh century A.D. by the Prophet Muhammad and spread in Africa through African Muslim leaders, migrations, and wars.

Janjawid (also "Janjaweed") Arabic-speaking militia groups responsible for attacks on rural populations in the Darfur region of western Sudan. They are widely believed to have the backing of the Sudanese government.

Jihad A struggle, or "holy war," waged as a religious duty on behalf of Islam to rid the world of disbelief and error.

Koran Writings accepted by Muslims as the word of God, as revealed to the Prophet Mohammed.

Krio The Sierra Leone term for *Creole,* it refers to both the urbanized Creole descendents of the country's original black settlers during the British colonial period and country's English-based Creole language.

Lagos Plan of Action Adopted by the Organization of African Unity in 1980, this agreement calls for self-reliance, regional economic cooperation, and the creation of a pan-African economic community and common market by the year 2000.

League of Nations Established at the Paris Peace Conference in 1919, this forerunner of the modern-day United Nations had 52 member nations at its peak (the United States never joined the organization) and mediated in international affairs. The league was dissolved in 1945 after the creation of the United Nations.

Least Developed Countries (LDCs) A term used to refer to the poorest countries of the world, including many African countries.

Lingua Franca A shared language used for communication between members of different language groups.

Maghrib An Arabic term, meaning "land of the setting sun," that is often used to refer to the former French colonies of Morocco, Algeria, and Tunisia.

Mahdi The expected messiah of Islamic tradition; or a Muslim leader who plays a messianic role.

Malinke (Mandinka, or Mandinga) One of the major groups of people speaking Mande languages. The original homeland of the Malinke was Mali, but the people are now found in Mali, Guinea-Bissau, The Gambia, and other areas, where they are sometimes called Mandingoes. Some trading groups are called Dyoula.

Marabout A dervish Muslim in Africa believed to have supernatural power.

Marxist-Leninism Sometimes called "scientific socialism," this doctrine derived from the ideas of Karl Marx as modified by Vladimir Lenin; it was the ideology of the Communist Party of the Soviet Union and has been modified in many ways by other persons and groups who still use the term. In Africa, some political parties or movements have claimed to be Marxist-Leninist but have often followed policies that conflict in practice with the ideology; these governments have usually not stressed Marx's philosophy of class struggle.

Mfecane The movement of people in the nineteenth century in the eastern areas of present-day South Africa to the west and north as the result of wars led by the Zulus.

Movement for the Liberation of Angola (MPLA) Beginning as an important independence movement in Angola's struggle for independence, the MPLA is now Angola's dominant political party, ruling the country continuously since independence in 1975.

Mozambique Liberation Front (Frelimo) Mozambique's single ruling party following a 10-year struggle against Portuguese colonial rule, which ended in 1974.

Mozambique National Resistance See *Renamo*.

Muslim A follower of the Islamic faith.

Naam A traditional work cooperative in Burkina Faso.

National Front for the Liberation of Angola (FNLA) One of the major Angolan liberation movements; its original focus was limited to the northern Kongo-speaking population.

National Union for the Total Independence of Angola (UNITA) One of three groups that fought the Portuguese during the colonial period in Angola, later backed by South Africa and the U.S. CIA in fighting the independent government of Angola.

National Youth Service Service to the state required of youth after completing education, a common practice in many African countries.

Nkomati Accords An agreement signed in 1984 between South Africa and Mozambique, pledging that both sides would no longer support opponents of the other.

Nonaligned Movement (NAM) A group of nations that chose not to be politically or militarily associated with either the West or the former communist bloc.

Nongovernmental Organizations (NGO) A private voluntary organization or agency working in relief and development programs.

Organization for the Development of the Senegal River (OMVS) A regional grouping of countries bordering the Senegal River that sponsors joint research and projects.

Organization of African Unity (OAU) See *African Union.*

Organization of Petroleum Exporting Countries (OPEC) Established in 1960, this association of some of the world's major oil-producing countries seeks to coordinate the petroleum policies of its members.

Pan Africanist Congress (PAC) A liberation organization of black South Africans that broke away from the ANC in the 1950s.

Parastatals Agencies for production or public service that are established by law and that are, in some measure, government organized and controlled. Private enterprise may be involved, and the management of the parastatal may be in private hands.

Pastoralist A person, usually a nomad, who raises livestock for a living.

Polisario Front Originally a liberation group in Western Sahara seeking independence from Spanish rule. Today, it is battling Morocco, which claims control over the Western Sahara. See Saharawi Arab Democratic Republic (SADR).

Popular Movement for the Liberation of Angola (MPLA) A Marxist liberation movement in Angola during the resistance to Portuguese rule; now the governing party in Angola.

Renamo A South African-backed rebel movement that attacked civilians in an attempt to overthrow the government of Mozambique.

Rinderpest A cattle disease that periodically decimates herds in savanna regions.

Saharawi Arab Democratic Republic (SADR) The Polisario Front name for Western Sahara, declared in 1976 in the struggle for independence from Morocco.

Sahel In West Africa, the borderlands between savanna and desert.

Sanctions Coercive measures, usually economic, adopted by nations acting together against a nation violating international law.

Savanna Tropical or subtropical grassland with scattered trees and undergrowth.

Shari'a The Islamic code of law.

Sharpeville Massacre The 1960 demonstration in South Africa in which 60 people were killed when police fired into the crowd; it became a rallying point for many antiapartheid forces.

Sorghum A tropical grain that is a traditional staple in the savanna regions.

Southern African Development Community (SADC) Originally formed by nine southern and east African states for the purpose of freeing themselves from economic dependence on apartheid South Africa, today it serves to coordinate economic and security programs among member states. Current membership includes: Angola, Botswana, Democratic Republic of Congo, Lesotho, Madagascar, Malawi, Mauritius, Mozambique, Namibia, South Africa, Tanzania, and Zimbabwe.

South-West Africa People's Organization (SWAPO) Angola-based freedom fighters who had been waging guerrilla warfare against the presence of South Africa in Namibia since the 1960s. The United Nations and the Organization of African Unity now recognize SWAPO as the only authentic representative of the Namibian people.

Glossary of Terms and Abbreviations

Structural Adjustment Program (SAP) Economic reforms encouraged by the International Monetary Fund, which include devaluation of currency, cutting government subsidies on commodities, and reducing government expenditures.

Swahili A trade and government Bantu language (see *lingua franca*) that covers much of East Africa and Congo region.

Tsetse Fly An insect that transmits sleeping sickness to cattle and humans. It is usually found in the scrub-tree and forest regions of Central Africa.

Ujaama In Swahili, "familyhood"; government-sponsored cooperative villages in Tanzania.

Unicameral A political structure with a single legislative branch.

Unilateral Declaration of Independence (UDI) A declaration of white minority settlers in Rhodesia, claiming independence from the United Kingdom in 1965.

United Democratic Front (UDF) A multiracial, black-led group in South Africa that gained prominence during the 1983 campaign to defeat the government's Constitution, which gave only limited political rights to Asians and Coloureds.

United Nations (UN) An international organization established on June 26, 1945, through official approval of the charter by delegates of 50 nations at a conference in San Francisco, California. The charter went into effect on October 24, 1945.

United Nations Development Program (UNDP) Established to create local organizations for increasing wealth through better use of human and natural resources.

United Nations Educational, Scientific, and Cultural Organization (UNESCO) Established on November 4, 1946, to promote international collaboration in education, science, and culture.

United Nations High Commission for Refugees (UNHCR) Established in 1951 to provide international protection for people with refugee status.

Villagization A policy whereby a government relocates rural dwellers to create newer, more concentrated communities.

West African Monetary Union (WAMU) A regional association of member countries in West Africa (Benin, Burkina Faso, Côte d'Ivoire, Mali, Niger, Senegal, and Togo) that have vested authority to conduct monetary policy in a common central bank.

World Bank A closely integrated group of international institutions providing financial and technical assistance to developing countries.

World Health Organization (WHO) Established by the United Nations in 1948, this organization promotes the highest possible state of health in countries throughout the world.

Bibliography

SOURCES FOR STATISTICAL REPORTS

U.S. State Department *Background Notes* (2007)
C.I.A. World *Factbook* (2007)
World Bank *World Development Reports* (2005/2006/2007)
UN *Population* and *Vital Statistics Reports* (2007)
Population Reference Bureau *World Population Data Sheet* (2007)
The New York Times Almanac 2007
BBC *Country Profiles* (2007)
The Economist Intelligence Unit (2007)

RESOURCE CENTERS

African Studies Centers provide special services for schools, libraries, and community groups. Contact the center nearest you for further information about resources available.

African Studies Center
  Boston University
  270 Bay State Road
  Boston, MA 02215

African Studies Program
  Indiana University
  Woodburn Hall 221
  Bloomington, IN 47405

African Studies Educational Resource Center
  100 International Center
  Michigan State University
  East Lansing, MI 49923

African Studies Program
  630 Dartmouth
  Northwestern University
  Evanston, IL 60201

Africa Project
  Lou Henry Hoover Room 223
  Stanford University
  Stanford, CA 94305

African Studies Center
  University of California
  Los Angeles, CA 90024

Center for African Studies
  470 Grinter Hall
  University of Florida
  Gainesville, FL 32611

African Studies Program
  University of Illinois
  1208 W. California, Room 101
  Urbana, IL 61801

African Studies Program
  1450 Van Hise Hall
  University of Wisconsin
  Madison, WI 53706

Council on African Studies
  Yale University
  New Haven, CT 06520

Foreign Area Studies
  The American University
  5010 Wisconsin Avenue, NW
  Washington, DC 20016

African Studies Program
  Center for Strategic and International Studies
  Georgetown University
  1800 K Street, NW
  Washington, DC 20006

REFERENCE WORKS, BIBLIOGRAPHIES, AND OTHER SOURCES

Africa Research Bulletin (Political Series), Africa Research Ltd., Exeter, Devon, England (monthly).

Africa South of the Sahara (updated yearly) (Detroit: Gale Research).

Africa Today: An Atlas of Reproductible Pages, rev. ed. (Wellesley: World Eagle, 1990).

Rosalid Baucham, *African-American Organizations: A Selective Bibliography* (Organizations and Institutional Groups) (New York: Garland, 1997).

Chris Cook and David Killingray, *African Political Facts Since 1945* (New York: Facts on File, 1990).

David E. Gardinier, *Africana Journal* notes, Volume xvii. A Bibliographic Library Guide and Review Forum (New York: Holmes & Meier, 1997).

Colin Legum, ed., *Africa Contemporary Record* (New York: Holmes & Meier) (annual).

MAGAZINES AND PERIODICALS

Africa News, P.O. Box 3851, Durham, NC 27702.
Africa Now, 212 Fifth Avenue, Suite 1409, New York, NY 10010.
Africa Recovery, DPI, Room S-1061, United Nations, New York, NY 10017.
Africa Today, 64 Washburn Avenue, Wellesley, MA 02181.
African Arts, University of California, Los Angeles, CA.
African Concord, 5–15 Cromer Street, London WCIH 8LS, England.
The Economist, 122 E. 42nd Street, 14th Floor, New York, NY 10168.
Newswatch, 62 Oregun Road, P.M.B. 21499, Ikeja, Nigeria.
The UNESCO Courier, 31, Rue François Bonvin, 75732, Paris CEDEX 15, France.
The Weekly Review, P.O. Box 42271, Nairobi, Kenya.
West Africa, Graybourne House, 52/54 Gray Inn Road, London WCIX 8LT, England.

NOVELS AND AUTOBIOGRAPHICAL WRITINGS

Chinua Achebe, *Things Fall Apart* (Portsmouth: Heinemann, 1965).
  This is the story of the life and values of residents of a traditional Igbo village in the nineteenth century and of its first contacts with the West.

Bibliography

_____, *No Longer at Ease* (Portsmouth: Heinemann, 1963).
The grandson of the major character of *Things Fall Apart* lives an entirely different life in the modern city of Lagos.

Ayi Kwei Armah, *The Beautiful Ones Are Not Yet Born* (London: Heinemann, 1992).

André Brink, *A Dry White Season* (New York: Penguin, 1989).

Syl Cheney-Choker, *The Last Harmattan of Alusine Dunba* (London: Heinemann, 1991).

Tsitsi Dangarembga, *Nervous Conditions* (Seal Press Feminist Publishing, 2002).

Buchi Emecheta, *The Joys of Motherhood* (New York: G. Braziller, 1979).
The story of a Nigerian woman who overcomes great obstacles to raise a large family and then finds that the meaning of motherhood has changed.

Nadine Gordimer, *Burgher's Daughter* (New York: Viking, 1980).

_____, *A Soldier's Embrace* (New York: Viking, 1982).
These short stories treat the effects of apartheid on people's relations with each other. Films made from some of these stories are available at the University of Illinois Film Library, Urbana-Champaign, IL and the Boston University Film Library, Boston, MA.

Harris, Eddy, *Native Stranger: A Black American's journey into the heart of Africa* (New York: Simon and Schuster, 1992).

Bessie Head, *Question of Power* (London: Heinemann, 1974).

Cheik Amadou Kane, *Ambiguous Adventure* (Portsmouth: Heinemann, 1972).
This autobiographical novel of a young man coming of age in Senegal, in a Muslim society, and, later, in a French school.

F. Kietseng, *Comrade Fish: Memoirs of a Motswana in the ANC Underground* (Pula Publishing, 1999).

Alex LaGuma, *Time of the Butcherbird* (Portsmouth: Heinemann, 1979).
The people of a long-standing black community in South Africa's countryside are to be removed to a Bantustan.

Camara Laye, *The Dark Child* (Farrar Straus and Giroux, 1954).
This autobiographical novel gives a loving and nostalgic picture of a Malinke family of Guinea.

Nelson Mandela, *Long Walk to Freedom: The Autobiography of Nelson Mandela* (New York: Little, Brown, 1995).

Mda, Zakes, *The Heart of Redness: A Novel* (New York: Farrar, Straus, Giroux, 2002).
A novel of post-apartheid South Africa that imaginatively links a contemporary village dispute with events from the 19th century.

Okot p'Bitek, *Song of Lawino* (Portsmouth: Heinemann, 1983).
A traditional Ugandan wife comments on the practices of her Western-educated husband and reveals her own life-style and values.

Alexander McCall Smith, *The No. 1 Ladies' Detective Agency* (New York: Anchor Books, 2003).
The first in a popular series of novels set in Botswana.

Wole Soyinka, *Ake: The Years of Childhood* (New York: Random House, 1983).
Soyinka's account of his first 11 years is full of the sights, tastes, smells, sounds, and personal encounters of a headmaster's home and a busy Yoruba town.

_____, *Death and the King's Horsemen* (New York: W. W. Norton, 2002).

Ngugi wa Thiong'o, *A Grain of Wheat* (Portsmouth: Heinemann, 1968).
A story of how the Mau-Mau movement and the coming of independence affected several individuals after independence as well as during the struggle that preceded it.

Amos Tutuola, *The Palm-Wine Drinkard* (Grove Press, 1994).

Yvonne Vera, *Butterfly Burning* (Baobab Books, 2000).

INTRODUCTORY BOOKS

Philip G. Altbach, *Muse of Modernity: Essays on Culture as Development in Africa* (Lawrenceville, NJ: Africa World, 1997).

Tony Binns, *People and Environment in Africa* (New York: Wiley, 1995).

Raymond Bonner, *At the Hand of Man: Peril and Hope for Africa's Wildlife* (New York: Random House, 1994).

Gwendolen Carter and Patrick O'Meara, eds., *African Independence: The First Twenty-Five Years* (Midland Books, 1986).
Collected essays surrounding issues such as political structures, military rule, and economics.

John Chiasson, *African Journey* (Upland, CT: Bradbury Press, 1987).
An examination into Africa's social life and customs.

Basil Davidson, *Africa in History* (New York: Macmillan, 1991).
A fine discussion of African history.

_____, *The African Genius* (Boston: Little, Brown, 1979). Also published as *The Africans*.
Davidson discusses the complex political, social, and economic systems of traditional African societies, translating scholarly works into a popular mode without distorting complex material.

_____, *The Black Man's Burden: Africa and the Curse of the Nation State* (New York: Random House, 1992).
A discussion on Africa's government and the status of the nation-state.

_____, *A History of Africa,* 2nd ed. (Unwin Hyman, 1989).
A comprehensive look at the historical evolution of Africa.

Christopher Ehret, *An African Classical Age: Eastern and Southern Africa in World History, 1000 B.C. to A.D. 400* (Charlottesville: University of Virginia Press, 2001).

Clementine M. Faik-Nzuji, *Tracing Memory: Glossary of Graphic Signs and Symbols in African Art & Culture* (Seattle, WA: University of Washington Press, 1997).

Timothy J. Keegan, *Colonial South Africa and the Origins of the Racial Order* (Charlottesville: University of Virginia Press, 1997).

Anthony Appiah Kwame, Henry Louis Gates Jr., eds., *Africana: The Encyclopedia of the African and African American Experience* (BasicCivitas Books, 1999).

Paul E. Lovejoy, *Transformations in Slavery: A History of Slavery in Africa* (Cambridge: Cambridge University Press, 2000).

Amina Mama, *Beyond the Mask: Race, Gender and Identity* (London: Routledge, 1995).

John Mbiti, *African Religions and Philosophy* (Portsmouth: Heinemann, 1982).
This work by a Ugandan scholar is the standard introduction to the rich variety of religious beliefs and rituals of African peoples.

Mosely, William G., ed., *Taking Sides: Clashing Views on African Issues* (Dubuque, Iowa: McGraw-Hill, 2007).
A good introduction to various arguments surrounding some of the key economic, social, political and environmental issues facing Africa today.

V. Y. Mudimbe, *The Invention of Africa* (Bloomington: Indiana University Press, 1988).

Joseph M. Murphy, *Working the Spirit: Ceremonies of the African Diaspora* (Boston: Beacon Press, 1994).

Newman, James, *The Peopling of Africa: A Geographical Interpretation* (New Haven: Yale University Press, 1995).

A sweeping overview of Africa's cultural history.

J. H. Kwabena Nketia, *The Music of Africa* (New York: Norton, 1974).

The author, a Ghanaian by birth, is Africa's best-known ethnomusicologist.

Gladson I. Nwanna, *Do's and Don'ts around the World: A Country Guide to Cultural and Social Taboos and Etiquette in Africa* (Baltimore: World Travel Institute, 1998).

Oliver, Roland, *The African Experience* (New York: HarperCollins Publishers, 1991).

Keith R. Richburg, *Out of Africa: A Black Man Confronts Africa* (New York: Basic Books, 1997).

Kevin Shillington, *History of Africa* (New York: Macmillan, 1995).

Bengt Sundkler and Christopher Steed, *A History of the Church in Africa* (Cambridge: Cambridge University Press, 2000).

John Thornton, *Africa and Africans in the Making of the Atlantic World, 1400–1800* (Cambridge: Cambridge University Press, 1998).

J. B. Webster, A. A. Boahen, and M. Tidy, *The Revolutionary Years: West Africa Since 1800* (London: Longman, 1980).

An interesting, enjoyable, and competent introduction.

Frank Willett, *African Art* (New York: Oxford University Press, 1971).

A work to read for both reference and pleasure.

COUNTRY AND REGIONAL STUDIES

Howard Adelman and John Sorenson, eds., *African Refugees* (Boulder: Westview, 1993).

Howard Adelman and Astri Suhrke, eds., *The Path of a Genocide: The Rwanda Crisis From Uganda to Zaire* (Transaction Publishing, 1999).

Allan R. Booth, *Swaziland: Tradition and Change in a Southern African Kingdom* (Boulder: Westview Press, 1984).

Thomas Borstelmann, *Apartheid, Colonialism, and the Cold War: The United States and Southern Africa* (New York: Oxford University Press, 1993).

Louis Brenner, ed., *Muslim Identity and Social Change in Sub-Saharan Africa* (Bloomington: Indiana University Press, 1993).

Marcia M. Burdette, *Zambia: Between Two Worlds* (Boulder: Westview Press, 1988).

Amilcar Cabral, *Unity and Struggle* (Monthly Review Press, 1981).

Joao M. Cabrit, *Mozambique: The Tortuous Road to Democracy* (Palgrave Macmillan, 2001).

Thomas Callaghy and John Ravenhill, eds., *Hemmed In: Global Responses to Africa's Economic Decline* (New York: Columbia University Press, 1994).

W. Joseph Campbell, *The Emergent Independent Press in Benin and Coté d'Ivoire: From Voice of the State to Advocate of Democracy* (New York: Praeger, 1998).

Robin Cohen and Harry Goulbourne, eds., *Democracy and Socialism in Africa* (Boulder: Westview Press, 1991).

Maureen Covell, *Madagascar: Politics, Economy, and Society* (London and New York: F. Pinter, 1987).

W. A. Edge and M. H. Lekorwe, *Botswana, Politics and Society* (J. L. van Schaik, 1998).

Norman Etherington, *The Great Treks: The Transformation of Southern Africa, 1815–1854* (London: Longman, 2001).

Robert Fatton, *The Making of a Liberal Democracy: Senegal's Passive Revolution, 1975–85* (Boulder: L. Rienner, 1987).

Foreign Area Studies (Washington, DC: Government Printing Office).

Pumla Gobodo-Madikizela, *A Human Being Died That Night: A South African Story of Forgiveness* (New York: Houghton-Mifflin, 2003).

April A. Gordon and Donald L. Gordon, *Understanding Contemporary Africa* (Boulder: L. Rienner Publishers, 1996).

Phillip Gourevitch, *We Wish to Inform You That Tomorrow We Will Be Killed With Our Families: Stories From Rwanda* (Picador, 1999).

Angelique Haugerud, *The Culture of Politics in Modern Kenya* (Cambridge: Cambridge University Press, 1997).

Adam Hochschild, *King Leopold's Ghost* (New York: Houghton-Mifflin, 1999).

A fascinating and wrenching account of how Belgium's King Leopold ravaged Congo.

Tony Hodges, *Western Sahara: The Roots of a Desert War* (Westport: Laurence Hill & Co., 1983).

Gaim Kibreab, *Refugees and Development in Africa: The Case of Eritrea* (Trenton: Red Sea Press, 1987).

Gerhard Kraus, *Human Development from an African Ancestry* (London: Karnak House, 1990).

David D. Laitin and Said S. Samatar, *Somalia: Nation in Search of a State* (Boulder: Westview Press, 1987).

Karl Maier, *Angola: Promises and Lies* (Independence Educational Publishers, 2002).

Mahmoud Mamdani, *Citizen and Subject* (Princeton: Princeton University Press, 1996).

Georges Nzongola-Ntalaja, *The Congo: From Leopold to Kabila: A People's History* (Zed Books, 2002).

Adebayo O. Olukoshi and Liisa Laakso, *Challenges to the Nation-State in Africa* (Uppsala: Nordiska Afrikainstitutet, in cooperation with Institute of Development Studies, University of Helsinki, 1996).

Eghosa E. Osaghae, *Crippled Giant: Nigeria Since Independence* (Bloomington: Indiana University Press, 1998).

Thomas O'Toole, *The Central African Republic: The Continent's Hidden Heart* (Boulder: Westview Press, 1986).

Richard Pankhurst, *The Ethiopians: A History* (London: Blackwell, 2001).

Deborah Pellow and Naomi Chazan, *Ghana: Coping With Uncertainty* (Boulder: Westview Press, 1986).

F. Jeffress Ramsay, Barry Morton, and Themba Mgadla, *Building a Nation: A History of Botswana* (Gaborone: Longman Botswana, 1996).

Richard Sandbrook, *The Politics of Africa's Economic Recovery* (Cambridge: Cambridge University Press, 1993).

Wisdom J. Tettey, ed., et al., *Critical Perspectives on Politics and Socio-Economic Development in Ghana* (African Social Studies Series, 6) (Brill Adademic Publishers, 2003).

Thompson, Leonard, *A History of South Africa* (New Haven: Yale University Press, 2001).

Teun Voeten, Roz Vatter-Buck, trans., *How de Body? One Man's Terrifying Journey Through an African War* (Thomas Dunne Books, 2002).

C. W. Wigwe, *Language, Culture, and Society in West Africa* (Elms Court, UK: Arthur H. Stockwell, 1990).

Gabriel Williams, *Liberia: The Heart of Darkness* (Trafford, 2002).

Edwin Wilmsen, *Land Filled With Flies, A Political Economy of the Kalahari* (Chicago: University of Chicago Press, 1989).

Index

A

African National Congress (ANC), 159, 160, 172, 185, 186, 188, 189, 190, 193

African Union, 29, 54, 57, 76, 186

Afrikaner, 186, 187

Ahidjo, Ahmadou, 18

Algeria, 107–116; black resistance, 188–189; Christians in, 113; corsairs, 109; debt and, 108; economy of, 113; foreign policy of, 113; formation of, 187; France and, 106, 108, 109–111, 113, 115; fundamentalists and, 113–114; geography, 106–107; history, 109–110; IMF and, 113; independence and, 110, 111–113; Kabyle movement and, 109, 110; Muslims in, 113; "National Contract" for, 114; Regency of Algiers and, 109; women in, 114, 115

Algerian socialism, 111–112, 113

Ali, Muhammad, 93, 119, 120

Almoravids, 140, 153, 243

Al-Qadhafi, Muammar, 25, 133–137

al-Sadat, Anwar, 122–123

Amin, Idi, 22, 50, 53, 101, 102

Amnesty International, 18, 33, 38, 86, 230, 235

Angola, Republic of, 162–165; Blood diamonds and, 163; civil war in, 163–165; colonial legacy of, 164–165; corruption and, 164; international interference in, 163; Popular Movement for the Liberation of Angola (MPLA), 163, 164, 165; Republic of Congo and, 28; UNITA and, 163, 164, 165

Aouzou Strip, 25, 136, 137

apartheid, 158, 160, 161, 164, 169, 182, 183, 185–189, 193, 199

Arusha Declaration, 96, 97

Asians: in Uganda, 101, 102; in Mauritius, 78; in East Africa, 47, 50

Axum Empire, 66

B

BaKongo, 13, 27, 28, 29, 157

Bamileke Rebellion, 18

"Bantu education," 188

Bantu language, 17, 18, 47, 101, 157, 186, 187

"Bantu line", 17

Bantu race, 186

Barre, Said, 89–90

Belgium: 29, 32, 33, 34, 35, 49, 52, 82, 83

Ben Bella, Ahmed, 111–112

Benin, Republic of, 206–209; corruption and, 209; debt and, 207; democratization in, 208; economy of, 209; emigration and, 208–209; France and, 207; Marxist-Leninist regime in, 207–208; Muslims in, 209

Berbers, 47,106; in Algeria,108, 109, 114, 115; in Libya, 130; in Mauritania, 242; in Morroco 140, 141, 142, 145; in Tunis, 148

Bioko, 39

Biya, Paul, 17, 19

Blood diamonds, 163, 211, 235, 257

Boer War, 187

Boganda, Bartholmy, 15, 21–22

Bokassa, Jean-Bedel, 22

Bongo, Omar, 41, 42

Botswana, Republic of, 166–169; British rule and, 168–169; Christians in, 168; corruption and, 167; drought and, 167, 169; economic success of, 167–169; HIV/AIDS and, 167, 169; South Africa and, 169; women and 169

Bourguiba, Habib, 149–152

Bouteflika, Abdulaziz, 113, 115, 116

Bozize, François, 21, 22

Brazzaville, 28, 29, 30

Buganda, 101

Burkina Faso, 210–213; Blood diamonds and, 211; drought and, 211–212; France and, 211, 213; political instability in, 211; trade unions and, 211, 212, 213

Burundi, Republic of, 5, 8, 15, 33, 35, 47, 48, 49, 50, 51–54; Christians in, 53, 54; France and, 50; Germany and, 53

Bushmen, 4, 158, 168

C

Cairo, 105, 109, 118, 119

Cameroon, 16–19; Christians in, 19; corruption and, 19; France and, 18; Muslims in, 18; Nigeria and, 17; post-colonial politics, 18–19; World Bank and, 19

Cape Verde, Republic of, 214–216; drought and, 215, 216; political pluralism and, 215; Portugal and, 215

Carthage, 105, 148, 149

cattle, social and economic importance, 47, 53, 71, 82, 89, 103, 169, 202, 203

Central Africa: China and, 22; geographic distinctiveness, 11–13; France and, 13–15; Islam in, 2, 4, 11, 17, 19, 24; region defined, 11; regional dynamics of, 15

Central African Franc (CFA) Zone, 11, 14

Central African Republic: 20–22; corruption and, 21, 22; debt and, 22; drought and, 22; food production and 22; foreign debt and, 22; France and, 15, 21, 22; human rights and, 21;

natural resources of, 21; World Bank and, 22

Chad, 23–26; Central African Republic and, 24; Christians in, 24, 25; complex ethnic and regional alliances of, 24–25; Darfur and, 24; drought and, 26; France and, 25; Frolinat and, 25; Movement for Democracy and Justice in Chad (MDJT), 24; Muslims in, 24

China, 8, 22, 41, 50, 53, 142, 157, 199

Comoros, Union of, 55–57; corruption and, 57; France and, 56, 57; Muslims in, 56

Congo, Democratic Republic of (Zaire), 31–36; Belgian rule and, 33; conflict in, 32–33; corruption and, 32, 34, 35; cultural attributes of, 33; debt and, 35; economic disaster in, 34–35; Egypt and, 121, 122, 123, 124, 126, 127; France and, 34, 35, 36; geography, 33; history, 33; independence movement in, 33–34; Libya and, 137; Morocco and, 143, 145; pre-colonial states in, 33; Soviet Union and, 34; women in, 33, 34

Congo, Republic of the (Brazzaville), 27–30; Angola and, 28; unrest in, 36; debt and, 28, 30; economy of, 30; France and, 29, 30; IMF and, 35; literacy in, 30; under Mobutu, 34–36; oil and, 30

Coptic Christians, 119, 66

corsairs, 109, 130, 131, 141, 149

Côte d'Ivoire, Republic of, 217–220; Christians in, 218; civil war in, 218–219; corruption and, 220; debt and, 219, 220; economy, 219–220; France and, 218, 220; Muslim/Christian division in, 218; Muslims in Cote d' Ivoire, 218, 219; repression in, 219

Customs and Economic Union of Central African States (UDEAC), 15

D

Dacko, David, 22

Darfur, 5, 24, 25, 26, 83, 94, 137

Debt, Africa and, 5, 6, 9. *See also* country listings

Déby, Idriss, 24, 25

DeGaulle, Charles, 111

Denard, Bob, 57

Dergue, 63, 65, 67, 68

Destourian Socialism, 150

Djibouti, Republic of, 58–60; France and, 59, 60

drought: in Africa, 4, 5, 7; in Central Africa, 13; in East Africa, 47, 48, 49; in Southern Africa, 160; in West Africa, 201, 203, 205. *See also* country listings

Index

E

East Africa: cattle herding societies and, 47; Christians in, 46, 47, 48; drought and, 49; Great Britain in, 48; Islamic influence in, 47, 49; Muslims in, 47; slave trade and, 47; Savannah zones, 47; South Asian laborers and, 47; southern states of, 49–50; subregions of, 48; Swahili culture and, 47; wars within, 49

East African Common Services Organization, 49–50

East African Community, 50, 102

Eboue, Felix, 14, 41. *Also* Emboue

ECOMOG, 205, 236, 237, 257

Economic Community of Central African States (ECCA), 15, 50

Economic Organization of the West African States (ECOWAS), 205, 215, 235, 237, 257

Egypt, 117–128; ancient history of, 118–119; Christians in, 119, 124; corruption and, 123; drought and, 126; economy of, 126–127; fundamentalism and, 124–126, 127; Great Britain and, 106, 121; Islam in, 119, 120; independence and, 120–121; Israel and 121, 122–124; Muslim Brotherhood in, 123, 124, 125, 126, 127; Soviet Union and, 121–122; women and, 123, 126; World Bank and, 122, 127

EPRDF, 63, 65, 66, 68

Equatorial Guinea, Republic of, 37–39; corruption and, 39; exiles from, 39; forced labor and, 38–39; France and, 39; oil in, 38; Soviet Union and, 63; 67; Spain and, 39

Eritrea, State of, 49, 61–63; drought and, 63; industrial infrastructure of, 62, 63; Ethiopia and, 62–63, 66; food aid dependency and, 63; Italy and 62; Muslims in, 5

Ethiopia, Federal Democratic Republic of, 5, 47, 48, 49, 50, 64–68; Christians in, 48, 66; drought and, 67, 68; Eritrea and, 62–63, 66; multi-ethnicity of, 67, 68; France and, 48; Muslims in, 9; Soviet Union and, 65, 67, 68, 90; turmoil in, 8, 66–68

European Union, 1, 104, 220; Botswana and, 169; Morocco and, 139, 143, 144; Tunisia and, 148, 151; Zimbabwe and, 220

F

Fang, 13, 39, 40

food, import dependence and: Angola, 165; Burkina Faso, 212; Comoros, 56; Congo (Democratic Republic), 35; Djibouti, 59; Eritrea, 62, 63; Lesotho, 171; Mozambique, 177; Nigeria, 245; Zambia, 196

forced labor, 14, 30, 33, 39, 41, 45, 178, 187, 233

France, 8, 11, 14. See country listings.

French Equatorial Africa, 13, 14, 15, 21, 30

G

Gabonese Republic (Gabon), 40–42; oil and, 41; France and, 41, 42

Gambia, The Republic of The, 221–224; Christians in, 218, 222; corruption and, 224; debt and, 224; IMF and, 224; Senegal and, 222–223; tourism in, 222

Ghana, Republic of, 225–227; corruption and, 226, 227; debt and, 226; World Bank's Economic Recovery Program and, 226, 227

"Ghost Town Campaign," 19

Great Man-Made River (GMR) project, 134–135

Green Book, The (Qadhafi), 133, 134

"Green March," 142, 143, 145, 153

Guinea, Republic of, 228–230; corruption and, 230; fear of regional conflict and, 229; France and, 230; Structural Adjustment Program and, 230

Guinea-Bissau, Republic of, 231–233; debt and, 233; drought and, 233; planned toxic dump site in, 233; Portuguese rule and, 232–233; Structural Adjustment Program, 233

H

Habyarimanaa, Juvenal, 82, 83

Hassan II, 133, 142, 143, 144, 145, 153, 154

HIV/AIDS pandemic, 2, 6–7; *See also* country statistical profiles

Houphouët-Boigny, Felix, 218, 219

Hutus, 49, 52–53, 54

Hutu-Tutsi animosity, roots of, 82

hydroelectric power in: Burkina Faso, 211, 212; Congo (Democratic Republic of), 32, 33; Côte d'Ivoire, 218; East Africa, 50; Rwanda, 81; Sierra Leone, 256; West Africa, 203

I

International Monetary Fund (IMF) and: Africa, 6, 8. See also country listings

Ismail. Mulay, 141, 145, 153

K

Kabila, Joseph, 32, 36

Kabila, Laurent, 32, 36

Kagame, Paul, 81, 82, 83, 100

Kaunda, Kenneth, 196

Kenya, Republic of, 5, 47–50, 69; cash crops and, 72; Christians in, 71; corruption and, 70, 72; drought and, 70; Great Britain and, 71; interethnic conflict and, 71; Mau Mau movement and, 71–72; pre-colonial period of, 71; tourism, 70–71; women and, 72

Kenyatta, Jomo, 71

khedives, 120

Khoisan, 157, 158, 168

Kingdom of the Kongo, 8, 25, 29, 32

Kolelas, Bernard, 28, 29

L

language, political implications of, 17, 18, 59, 62

Leopold, King of Belgium, Democratic Republic of Congo and, 29, 33, 35

Lesotho, Kingdom of, 170–172; British rule and 171–172; Christians in, 172; corruption and, 171; drought and, 171, 172; South Africa and, 171–172

Liberia, Republic of, 234–237; African Americans and, 236; Blood diamonds and, 235; corruption and, 237; debt and, 237; Doe, Samuel, and, 236–237; ECOMOG and, 237; Firestone and, 236; Structural Adjustment Program, 240; UN peacekeeping mission and, 235; World Bank and, 235; True Whig Party of, 236

Libya, 129–138; Arab and Berber heritage, 130; corsairs and, 130–131; British and U.S presence in, 133; Chad war and, 136; corruption and, 135; economy of, 134–135; foreign policy of, 136; France and, 131, 132, 136, 137; Great Man-Made River project and, 134–135; Islam and, 130, 131, 134; Italy and, 131–132; regions of, 130, 132–133; Sanusiya Movement, 131; social revolution and, 133–134; Soviet Union and, 134; World War II and, 132; women in, 133, 135, 137

Lissouba, Pascal, 28, 29

Lumumba, Patrice, 33–34, 35

M

M'ba, Leon, 41–42

Madagascar, Republic of, 73–76; Christians in, 74; corruption and, 76; debt and, 76; France and, 50, 74, 75; Malay influence, 74; World Bank and, 75

Malawi, Republic of, 173–175; famine in, 173; HIV/AIDS and, 174; women and, 174; World Bank and, 174, 175

Mali, Republic of, 238–240; corruption and, 239; drought and, 240

Mandela, Nelson, 35, 52, 53, 159, 160, 161, 185, 186, 187, 189

Marxism: in Central Africa, 8, 11, 29, 35, 45, 49; in Eastern Africa, 67, 68, 75

Mau Mau movement, 71–72

Mauritania, Islamic Republic of , 5, 241–243; ethnic groups of, 242–243; France and, 153; hydroelectric power and, 203; Islam and, 243; Muslim Brotherhood in, 243; natural disaster and, 242; Senegaland, 205, 253; Western Sahara and, 143, 154

Mauritius, Republic of, 77; economic development in, 79; France and, 50, 78; Great Britain and, 50, 78; South Asian population of, 78

Mbeki, Thabo, 185, 190

"Mfecane" period, 157

Mobutu, Joseph Desiré, 8, 32, 34; foreign assistance to, 35

Mogae, Festus, 6, 167

Moi, Daniel arap, 70, 71, 72
Morocco, 138–146; Arab settlement and, 140; debt and, 141, 144; drought and, 144 economy of, 144–145; emigration and, 139; France and, 141–142; independence and, 142; geography, 139–140; history of, 140–141; Muslims in,139; partitioning by Europeans, 141; politics in, 142–145; reform in, 145; Western Sahara and, 142–144; women in, 141, 142, 143, 145
Movement for the Social Evolution of Black Africa (MESAN), 21–22
Mozambique, Republic of, 176–179; drought and, 177, 178, 179; floods of 2000 and, 177; human rights and, 177; Portugal and, 178; independence of, 179; women and, 178
Mubarak, Hosni, 123–124
Mugabe, Robert, 7, 161, 186, 198, 199, 200, 201
Museveni, Yowerdi, 100–102

N
Namibia, Republic of, 180–183; apartheid in, 183; fishing industry in, 183; German colonization and, 181–182; land reform and, 181; South African colonization and, 182; UNITA and, 181
Nari Valley, 28
Nasser, Gamal Abdel, 118, 119, 121–122, 125, 126, 127
National Resistance Movement (Uganda), 50, 100–102
New Partnership for African Development (NEPAD), 186, 248
Nguema, Macias, 38, 39
Niger, Republic of, 244–246; drought, desertification and, 245, 246; France and, 245
Nigeria, Federal Republic of, 244–251; Christians in, 209, 248, 249; British rule and, 249; corruption in, 248, 250, 251; ethnic/religious tension in, 248, 249; IMF and, 250; languages in, 249; Muslims in, 248, 249; oil and, 249, 250, 251; regional conflicts within, 249; Structural Adjustment Program, 250–251; World Bank and, 250
Nilotic language, 47
Ninja rebels, 28, 29, 30
Nkrumah, Kwame, 205, 226, 207
nomads, 87,104–105, 140, 143, 153
North Aftrica: Arab-Islamic culture of, 104, 105, 106, 107; French language and, 106; oil and, 105; Muslims in, 105; Ottoman Empire and, 106; population growth of, 104; water and, 104–105
Nyerere, Julius, 50, 53, 97, 98, 99

O
Obiang Nguela Mbasogo, 38–39
Obote, Milton, 101–102

oil, 8, 19, 25, 26, 45, 41, 92, 93, 94; 134. *See also* country listings
Organization of African Unity, 8, 25, 29, 32, 67, 90, 154, 237, 260
Ottoman Empire: Algeria an, 109; Egypt and, 119, 121; Libya and, 130, 131; North Africa and, 106; Tunisia and, 149

P
Pan Africanist Congress (PAC), 159, 160, 172, 186, 188, 189, 190
Patassé, Ange-Félix, 21, 22
Polisario, 113, 144, 153, 154
"Preferential Trade Area," 50

Q
Qadhafi, M. *See* al-Qadhafi

R
Ratisraka, Didier, 75–76
Ravalomanana, Marc, 76
Regency of Algiers, 109
Renamo, 57, 159, 160, 177, 178, 179
Rhodesia. *See* Zimbabwe
Rio de Oro, 139, 153, 154
Rwanda, (Rwandese Republic), 5, 8, 15, 32, 33, 35, 36, 47, 48, 49, 50, 52, 53, 54, 80–83, 100

S
Sadat, Anwar. *See* al-Sadat
Sahel region, 7, 24, 148, 203; 240, 245
Sahrawis, 113, 144, 153, 154, 155
Sande Society, The, 34
São Tomé and Príncipe, Democratic Republic of, 43–45; corruption and, 45; debt and, 44; economic growth in, 45; France and, 44; politics in, 45
Sassou-Nguesso, Denis, 28, 29, 30
Selassie, Haile, 62, 65, 66, 67
Senegal, Republic of, 252–254; Christians in, 218; corruption and, 253; drought and, 254; French influence on, 253–254; Gambia and, 222, 223, impact of Islam on, 253; Structural Adjustment Program, 254; Sétif massacre, 110
Seychelles, Republic of, 84–86; France and, 50
Sierra Leone, Republic of, 255–257; Blood diamonds and, 257; civil war in, 256; corruption in, 256; debt and, 256; ECOWAS and, 257; Great Britain and, 256; settlement by freed blacks, 257; U.N. peacekeeping in, 256, 257
slave trade, 7, 33, 39, 45, 47, 50, 78, 79, 86, 149, 157, 164, 203, 204, 249. *See also* forced labor
Somalia, 8, 47, 48, 49, 59, 60,87–90; drought and, 88, 90; Ethiopia and, 67–68; Soviet Union and, 48, 90; U.S. involvement in, 88
South Africa, Republic of, 184–190; apartheid in, 186–189; economic

disparity in, 186; HIV/AIDS and 185, 186, 189, 190; military power of, 159; women and, 185
South West African People's Organization (SWAPO), 181, 182, 183
Southern Africa Development Community (SADC), 9, 50, 79, 153, 163, 166
Southern Africa Development Coordination Conference (SADCC), 159
Soviet Union, 34, 121–122, 63, 67, 48, 90, 65, 67, 68, 134
Spain: Equatorial Guinea and, 39; Morocco and, 106, 139, 140, 141, 143–144; Tunisia and, 148; Western Sahara and, 139, 140, 151, 152, 153
Spanish Sahara, 143, 153
Sudan, Republic of the, 91–94; Christians in, 92; corruption in, 94; debt and, 94; drought and, 93, 94; Muslims in, 92, 93; oil and, 92, 93, 94; women and, 94
Suez Canal, 120, 121, 122, 126
Swahili, culture and language, 33, 47, 71, 98
Swaziland, Kingdom of, 191–193; HIV/ AIDS and, 192

T
Tanzania, United Republic of, 5, 7, 33, 47, 48, 49, 50, 53, 95–98, 101, 102; debt and, 96
Taylor, Charles, 235–237
Togimi, Youssouf, 24
Togo (Togolese Republic), 258–261; drought and, 260–261; IMF/World Bank and, 260; women and, 260
Tombalbaye, Françoise, 25
tourism: in Kenya, 70; in Maruitius, 79; in Seychelles, 85, 86; in Tanzania, 98
toxic waste dumping, 39, 233
Trovoada, Miguel, 44
Tshisekedi, Etienne, 32–33
Tuareg, 108, 109, 239, 246
Tunisia, Republic of, 147–152; Christians in, 148, 149; economy of, 151; European Union and, 148, 151; France and 149; human rights and, 149–152; Islam and, 148, 150; Islamic fundamentalism and, 150–151, 152; women and, 150, 151; World Bank and, 151
Tutsis, 49, 52, 53, 54, 82
Twa, 53, 81, 82

U
U.N. peacekeeping, in: Angola, 163; Burundi, 54; Eritrea, 62; Liberia, 235, 236; Rwanda, 82; Sierra Leone, 256
Uganda, Republic of, 5, 7, 8, 9, 32, 36, 47, 49, 50, 82, 94, 96, 98, 99,–102; Christians in, 102; corruption and, 100; HIV/AIDS and, 101, 102; four kingdoms within, 101

Index

Uhuru, 2
UNISOM, 89, 90
UNITA, 19, 24, 28, 35, 159, 160, 161, 163, 164, 165, 181, 182
UNITAF, 89, 90
United Nations, 2006 Human Development Report, 3, 5
UPRONA, 53, 54

V

villagization, 54, 68, 90, 98

W

West Africa, 202–205; pre-colonial era of, 203–204; Islam and, 203, 204; barriers to political integration in, 205; population mobility of, 204–205; vegetation and climate zones of, 203
Western Sahara, 153–155; France and, 153; Mauritania and, 153; Morocco and, 153, Organization of African Unity and, 154; Rio de Oro of, 139, 153, 154; Spain and, 139, 140, 151, 152, 153; United Nations and, 153–155
women: African governments and, 7; agriculture and, 5, 9; HIV/AIDs and 6; politics and, 9; workforce and, 9. *See also* country listings
World Bank: 8, 19, 22, 75, 122, 127, 151, 174, 175, 196, 226, 235, 250, 260. *See also* country listings

Z

Zaire, 5, 8, 11, 12, 15, 28, 29, 32, 33, 34, 35, 50, 53, 54, 57. Under Mobutu, 34–35. *See also* Democratic Republic of the Congo
Zambia, Republic of, 194–196; debt and, 196; drought and, 195; HIV/AIDS and, 195; World Bank and, 196
Zenawiu, Meles, 65
Zimbabwe, Republic of, 197–201; drought and, 199, 201; collapse of, 198–201; expropriation of farms and, 198; British Commonwealth and, 198; pre-colonial past of, 199; segregation in, 200–201